Everyone's
Mark Twain

Compiled by
Caroline Thomas Harnsberger

South Brunswick and New York: A. S. Barnes and Company
London: Thomas Yoseloff Ltd

Library of Congress Catalogue Card Number: 70-107117

A. S. Barnes and Co., Inc.
Cranbury, New Jersey 08512

Thomas Yoseloff Ltd
108 New Bond Street
London W1Y OQX, England

ISBN: 0-498-07622-9
Printed in the United States of America

Dedicated
to my father,
James Oscar Thomas,
who built the fire;
and to my friend,
Clara Langdon Clemens,
who kindled it.

FOREWORD

Mrs. Harnsberger has created a method of easy reference to my father's writing which, in my opinion, is comprehensive and most practical. Every question likely to be posed by admirers of Mark Twain is answered in this collection of quotations. More than this, the author gives a clear-cut portrait of the man himself through the medium of his own pen. My father has said:

"What a wee little part of a person's life are his acts and his words! His real life is led in his head and is known to none but himself. All day long, and every day, the mill of his brain is grinding and his thoughts, not those other things, are his history. His acts and his words are merely the visible, thin crust of his world, with its scattered snow summits and its vacant wastes of water—and they are so trifling a part of his bulk; a mere skin enveloping it. The mass of him is hidden—it and its volcanic fires that toss and boil, and never rest, night nor day. . . . Biographies are but the clothes and buttons of the man; the biography of the man himself cannot be written."

In partial refutation of the last sentence, Mrs. Harnsberger has succeeded in gathering the self-expressed thoughts and convictions of Mark Twain in such a way as to present a true picture of his heart and mind drawn in his own frank words. They are a sincere reflection of his innermost self and they are convincing.

FOREWORD

To quote my father once more:

"What is a government without energy? And what is *a man* without energy? Nothing—nothing at all. What is the greatest thing in 'Paradise Lost'—the Arch-Fiend's terrible energy! What was the greatest feature in Napoleon's character? His unconquerable energy! Sum all the gifts that man is endowed with, and we give our greatest share of admiration to his energy. And today, if I were a heathen, I would rear a statue to Energy, and fall down and worship it!"

For this quality of intellectual or spiritual energy Mark Twain had special reverence, and I know that if he were alive today he would agree with me in hearty acclaim of Caroline Harnsberger's possession of it. Only a dynamic impulse and talent could have achieved such an exceptional product as this inclusive guide to the wisdom and humor of Mark Twain.

I hope and believe this distinguished reference book will be a fore-runner of similar forms of aid to information on other literary lights. And I cordially commend it, not only to the attention of the lovers of my father's writings, but to the reader who has not yet become acquainted with Mark Twain.

Clara Clemens

PREFACE

Mark Twain lived during the years 1835 to 1910. He was an interested witness of a time when man's methods of living were undergoing their greatest change; when such important innovations as the railroad, the telegraph, the telephone, the electric light, the typewriter, the type-setting machine (an invention in which he invested and lost $190,000), the sewing-machine, the phonograph, the automobile, the fountain-pen and the airplane were being introduced.

Mark Twain had something to say about all these. His reaction to them was probably typical of the average man of that day. When he made the observation that a telephone is "a time-saving, profanity-breeding, useful invention, and in America is to be found in all houses except parsonages," he passed to us an historical record of the early difficulties of modern invention.

When he said, "None of us can have as many virtues as the fountain-pen, or half its cussedness; but we can try," he reflected not only on a new device, but also on his favorite topic—the human race.

Mark Twain was widely divergent in his interests. There is hardly a subject about which he did not express an opinion. Once he said he had "a large cargo of the most interesting and important private opinions about every great matter under the sun, but that they are not for print." The opinions which *did* see print, however, are vast, and they furnish tempting material for a compilation of this kind.

It has been the attempt of this compiler to concentrate in abridged form the outstanding sections and phrases from the pen of Mark Twain which are most characteristic *of* him. *Everyone's Mark Twain* contains his typical wisdom and humor expressed in his own words without the dubious "benefit" of a compiler's comment.

With few exceptions, this book does not contain stories *about* Mark Twain aside from those told by himself, his official biographer, Albert Bigelow Paine, and his daughters. The hundreds of anecdotes told about him are seldom authoritative, and are therefore not included.

Here for the first time the comments of Mark Twain have been arranged and indexed according to subject matter so they may be rediscovered in a painless fashion. Even the devotees of Mark Twain—realizing that this prolific author habitually produced the unexpected, even in the placement of his subject matter—have found it necessary at one time or another to scamper endlessly through the twenty-five volumes of the Collected Works or the various other books by and about Mark Twain in order to find some appropriate but elusive quotation. It is found, for example, that an interesting description of Lake Tahoe on the California border is inserted in his European travel book, "The Innocents Abroad." The story of the bluejay as told by the Nevada miner, Jim Baker, is placed in another European setting, "A Tramp Abroad." A sketch about the afflictions produced by amateur musicians is written under the misleading title, "The Touching Story of George Washington's Boyhood." It is hoped that the confusion of where-to-find-what is hereby eliminated.

The page numbers have been placed at the end of each reference to emphasize the fact that specific and accurate information is given. The reader may then turn to these pages and, in most cases, secure Mark Twain's elaboration of the subject at hand.

Page numbers from the Collected Works, which are listed

individually in the bibliography, are from the uniform *Author's National Edition*, published by Harper and Brothers, New York. Since the writings of Mark Twain have been collected and published in various editions, the page numbers will vary, but a quotation may be found, nevertheless, through the volume number, chapter number, or the name of the sketch or excerpt supplied after each entry.

A number of quotations from original manuscripts are given their first printing in this volume. These, as well as parts of letters and newspaper articles which have been put into book form for the first time, are called to the reader's attention.

The compiler wishes to direct the thought of the reader once more to the year of Mark Twain's death—1910. This makes impressive the fact that although nearly a century has passed since his writing reached its prime, his remarks remain *timeless*.

As a direct consequence of the very inventions whose birth Mark Twain witnessed, the pace of our world has been so accelerated that we find greater diversion but less leisure. We have become surrounded by an aura of tension, stress and hurry. For this reason, few people find the opportunity to read the complete writings of Mark Twain to cull his benefits.

For the average hurried reader, then, here is the core and essence of Mark Twain!

For those speakers and writers caught in the hurry-scurry, here are suitable Mark Twain quotations for every purpose and occasion, so arranged that they may be found within a few seconds!

It is the compiler's hope that these pages have captured the mirror which Mark Twain holds for us to peer into and truly see ourselves. May we laugh at ourselves, as he intended, and may we thereby secure for ourselves the balance which enables us to live with greater ease in a world of *any* pace.

CAROLINE THOMAS HARNSBERGER

EVERYONE'S MARK TWAIN

A

ABROAD *See also* ASS, FORGETFULNESS, OPINION

To go abroad has something of the same sense that death brings. I am no longer of ye—what ye say of me is now of no consequence—but of how much consequence when I am with ye and of ye. I know you will refrain from saying harsh things *because* they can't hurt me, since I am out of reach and cannot hear them. This is why we say no harsh things of the dead.

Going abroad we let up on the weight and wear and responsibility of housekeeping—we go and board with somebody, who is suffering it but it troubles us not . . . to go abroad is the true rest—you cease wholly to keep house, then, both national and domestic.

Mark Twain's Notebook, p. 131

ACCENT *See* LANGUAGE

ACCIDENT *See also* DOG, INVENTION, MADNESS, PROVIDENCE

I am not able to conceive of such a thing as the thing which we call an *accident*—that is to say, an event without a cause. Each event has its own place in the eternal chain of circumstances, and whether it be big or little it will

15

infallibly cause the *next* event, whether the next event be the breaking of a child's toy or the destruction of a throne. . . . But I like that word "accident," although it is, in my belief, absolutely destitute of meaning. I like it because it is short and handy and because it answers so well and so conveniently, and so briefly, in designating happenings which we should otherwise have to describe as odd, curious, interesting, and so on . . .

Mark Twain in Eruption, p. 386

One million of us . . . die annually. Out of this million ten or twelve thousand are stabbed, shot, drowned, hanged, poisoned, or meet a similarly violent death in some other popular way . . . The Erie Railroad kills from 23 to 46; the other 845 railroads kill an average of one-third of a man each; and the rest of that million, amounting in the aggregate to the appalling figure of nine hundred and eighty-seven thousand six hundred and thirty-one corpses, die naturally in their beds!

You will excuse me from taking any more chances on those beds. The railroads are good enough for me.

"The Danger of Lying in Bed"
The $30,000 Bequest, Etc., p. 260

ACHIEVEMENT   *See also* CHARACTER

When we do not know a person—and also when we do— we have to judge his size by the size and nature of his achievements, as compared with the achievements of others in his special line of business—there is no other way.

Christian Science, Book II, Chapt. I, p. 102

ACQUIREMENT

There is some dignity about an acquirement, because it is a product of your own labor. It is wages earned, whereas to be able to do a thing merely by the grace of God, and not by your own effort, transfers the distinction to our heavenly home—where possibly it is a matter of pride and satisfaction, but it leaves you naked and bankrupt.

Mark Twain's Autobiography, Paine, II, p. 257

ADAM *See also* CAIN, COPYRIGHT, EDEN, GARDEN OF, FOR-
BID, NAME, TEMPERAMENT, TOMB

Adam and Eve had many advantages, but the principal
one was, that they escaped teething.
> "Pudd'nhead Wilson's Calendar"
> *Pudd'nhead Wilson*, Chapt. IV, p. 38

Adam went on naming his descendants until he ran out
of names, and then said gravely, "Let the rest be called
Smith."
> *Letter to the Alta Californian*, October 28, 1868,
> *The Twainian*, Mar.–April 1949, p. 5

It was not that Adam ate the apple for the apple's sake,
but because it was forbidden. It would have been better
for us—oh infinitely better for us—if the *serpent* had been
forbidden.
> *Mark Twain's Notebook*, p. 275

Whoever has lived long enough to find out what life is,
knows how deep a debt of gratitude we owe to Adam, the
first benefactor of our race. He brought death into the
world.
> "Pudd'nhead Wilson's Calendar,"
> *Pudd'nhead Wilson*, Chapt. III, p. 30

What a good thing Adam had—when he said a good
thing he knew nobody had said it before.
> *Mark Twain's Notebook*, p. 67

Let us be grateful to Adam our benefactor. He cut us out
of the "blessing" of idleness, and won for us the "curse"
of labor.
> "Pudd'nhead Wilson's New Calendar,"
> *Following the Equator*, I, Chapt. XXXIII, p. 320

ADMONITION *See* ADVICE

ADVERSARY *See* INSANITY

ADVERSITY

By trying we can easily learn to endure adversity. Another man's, I mean.

> "Pudd'nhead Wilson's New Calendar,"
> *Following the Equator*, II, Chapt. III, p. 35

ADVERTISING *See* THINGS

ADVICE *See also* CUSTOM, EGG, MARRIAGE, VANITY, WALL
STREET, YOUTH

[Letter, Hartford, Conn., Jan. 16, 1881]: How can I advise another man wisely, out of such a capital as a life filled with mistakes? Advise him how to avoid the like? No—for opportunities to make the same mistakes do not happen to any two men. Your own experience may possibly teach you, but another man's can't. I do not know anything for a person to do but just peg along, doing the things that offer, and regretting them the next day. It is my way and everybody's.

> *Mark Twain, His Life and Work*, Will Clemens, p. 12

[An admonition for the general betterment of the race's condition]: Diligently train your ideals *upward* and *still upward* toward a summit where you will find your chiefest pleasure in conduct which, while contenting you, will be sure to confer benefits upon your neighbor and the community.

> *What Is Man? and Other Essays*, Chapt. IV, p. 54

You mustn't volunteer advice to a slave-driver unless you want to damage the cause you are arguing for.

> *A Connecticut Yankee in King Arthur's Court*,
> Chapt. XXXV, p. 322

If you are of any account, stay at home and make your way by faithful diligence; but if you are "no account" go away from home, and then you will *have* to work, whether you want to or not. Thus you become a blessing to your friends by ceasing to be a nuisance to them—if the people you go among suffer by the operation.

> *Roughing It*, II, Chapt. XXXVIII, p. 339

Always obey your parents—when they are present.

Be respectful to your superiors, if you have any.
Get up with the lark.
Begin the practice of the art of lying, early.
Never handle firearms carelessly.
Read good books, "Innocents Abroad," etc.
Build your character thoughtfully and painstakingly upon these precepts, and by and by, when you have got it built, you will be surprised and gratified to see how nicely and sharply it resembles everybody else's.

"Advice to Youth,"
Mark Twain's Speeches [1923], p. 104

[Advice for a proper frame of mind for undergoing a surgical operation]: Console yourself with the reflection that you are giving the doctor pleasure, and that he is getting paid for it.

Mark Twain, Henderson, p. 115

AFFECTION   *See also* CAT, FRIEND, LETTERS, LOVE
Praise is well, compliment is well, but affection—that is the last and *final* and most precious reward that any man can win, whether by character or achievement. . .

"Books, Authors and Hats,"
Mark Twain's Speeches (1923), p. 343

AFRICA   *See* CLOCK

AGE   *See also* ASS, BIRTHDAY, DISAPPOINTMENT, DROWNING,
    DUTY, EARLY RISING, METHUSELAH, OPPORTUNITY, YOUTH
Neither a man nor a boy ever thinks the age he *has* is exactly the best one—he puts the *right* age a few years older or a few years younger than he is.

"Extract from Captain Stormfield's Visit to Heaven,"
The Mysterious Stranger, Etc., p. 246

Whatever a man's age may be, he can reduce it several years by putting a bright-colored flower in his buttonhole.

The American Claimant, Etc., Chapt. XX, p. 174

Age enlarges and enriches the powers of some musical

instruments—notably those of the violin—but it seems to set a piano's teeth on edge.

"Rambling Notes of an Idle Excursion,"
Tom Sawyer Abroad, Etc., p. 290

At that time I thought old age valuable, I do not know why. All young people think it, I believe, they being ignorant and full of superstitions.

Personal Recollections of Joan of Arc,
II, Book III, Chapt. XVI, p. 253

Age has taught me charity of speech.

Ibid., Book III, Chapt. XVI, p. 253

Seventy is old enough. After that there is too much risk.

Following the Equator, I, Chapt. XXIX, p. 295

We can't reach old age by another man's road. My habits protect my life but they would assassinate you.

"Seventieth Birthday,"
Mark Twain's Speeches (1910), p. 431

If you find you can't make seventy by any but an uncomfortable road, don't you go.

Ibid. (1923), p. 257

At the end of this year I shall be sixty-three—if alive—and about the same if dead.

Mark Twain's Autobiography, Paine, I, p. 171

The older we grow the greater becomes our wonder at how much ignorance one can contain without bursting one's clothes.

Mark Twain's Speeches (1910), p. 140

I was young and foolish then; now I am old and foolisher.

Mark Twain, a Biography, Paine, II, p. 1086

Lord save us all from old age and broken health and a hope tree that has lost the faculty of putting out blossoms.

Mark Twain's Letters, II, p. 546

I saw men whom thirty years had changed but slightly; but their wives had grown old. These were good women; it is very wearing to be good.

Life on the Mississippi, Chapt LV, p. 407

. . . age is not determined by years, but by trouble and

by infirmities of mind and body.
"Unconscious Plagiarism,"
Mark Twain's Speeches (1923), p. 79

Life would be infinitely happier if we could only be born at the age of 80 and gradually approach 18.
Autobiography with Letters, William L. Phelps, p. 965

But I am seventy; seventy, and would nestle in the chimney corner, and smoke my pipe, and read my book, and take my rest, wishing you well in all affection, and that when you in your turn shall arrive at pier No. 70 you may step aboard your waiting ship with a reconciled spirit, and lay your course toward the sinking sun with a contented heart.
"Seventieth Birthday,"
Ibid. (1923), p. 262

If I had been helping the Almighty when he created man, I would have had him begin at the other end, and start human beings with old age. How much better to start old and have all the bitterness and blindness of age in the beginning!
Mark Twain, a Biography, Paine, III, p. 1440

I am admonished in many ways that time is pushing me inexorably along; I am approaching the threshold of age; in 1977 I shall be 142.
Letter to Kansas Jubilee Committee,
Hartford Courant, July 24, 1901

AGREEMENT   *See* TALK

AILMENTS   *See also* DISEASE, DOCTORS, HEALTH, ILLNESS,
MEDICINE, RHEUMATISM

[In a dyspeptic moment in London, Twain wrote a friend to explain his inability to accept an invitation]:

Dear Lee—I can't. I am in a family way with three weeks undigested dinners in my system, and shall just roost here and diet and purge till I am delivered. Shall I name it after you? Yr. friend, Sam'l L. Clemens. (1907)
Ms. in New York City Public Library

ALARM

ALARM *See* BABY, FRIGHT

ALLEGORY *See* ANGER, ANIMALS

ALPHABET *See* SPELLING
I myself am a simplified speller. I belong to that unhappy guild that is patiently and hopefully trying to reform our drunken old alphabet by reducing his whiskey.

> "A Simplified Alphabet,"
> *What is Man? and Other Essays,* p. 262

ALPS *See* MOUNTAIN, GLACIER

AMAZEMENT
Well, sir, his head-lights were bugged out like tompions; and his mouth stood that wide open that you could have laid a ham in it without him noticing it.

> "Rambling Notes of an Idle Excursion,"
> *Tom Sawyer Abroad, Etc.,* p. 261

R. did not answer. Her faculties were caked, she had not yet found her voice.

> "Those Extraordinary Twins,"
> *Pudd'nhead Wilson,* p. 239

AMBITION *See* PEOPLE

AMERICA *See also* ARMY, ENGLAND, FOURTH OF JULY, GIRL, HOME, HUMOR, ICE-STORM, INVENTION, LAW, MANNERS, MONEY, MOTTO, POLITENESS, POLITICS, STOVE, VOTING, WASHINGTON, D.C.
[An Englishman is] a person who does things because they have been done before. [An American is] a person who does things because they haven't been done before.

> *Mark Twain's Notebook,* p. 169

Just in this one matter lies the main charm of life in Europe—comfort. In America, we hurry—which is well; but when the day's work is done, we go on thinking of losses and gains, we plan for the morrow, we even carry our busi-

ness cares to bed with us . . . we burn up our energies
with these excitements, and either die early or drop into a
lean and mean old age at a time of life which they call a
man's prime in Europe . . . What a robust people, what a
nation of thinkers we might be, if we would only lay ourselves on the shelf occasionally and renew our edges!

The Innocents Abroad, I, Chapt. XIX, p. 241

It is a toiling, thinking, determined nation, this of ours,
and little given to dreaming. It appreciates the fact that
the moment one thing is ended, it must be crossed out and
dropped, and something else begun. Our Alexanders do not
sit down and cry because there are no more worlds to con-
quer, but snatch off their coats and fall to shinning around
and raising corn and cotton, and improving sewing machines.

(June 30, 1867)

Travels With Mr. Brown, p. 163

. . . there is only one thing that can be called by the
wide name "American." That is the national devotion to
ice-water.

"What Paul Bourget Thinks of Us,"
Literary Essays, p. 154

AMUSEMENT *See* COVETOUSNESS, WORK

ANCESTORS *See also* CAIN, PRIDE, RELIGION, WAR

[In Heidelberg castle]: There are many aged portraits
. . . I bought a couple . . . I bought them to start a portrait gallery of my ancestors with. I paid a dollar and a half
for the duke and two and a half for the princess. One can
lay in ancestors at even cheaper rates than these, in Europe, if he will mouse among old picture shops and look
out for chances.

A Tramp Abroad, II, Appendix B, p. 283

"Well, General, I suppose life can never get entirely dull
to an American, because whenever he can't strike up any
other way to put in his time he can always get away with
a few years trying to find out who his grandfather was!"

. . . I was back at him as quick as a flash: "Right, Your Excellency! But I reckon a Frenchman's got *his* little stand-by for a dull time, too; because when all other interests fail he can turn in and see if he can't find out who his father was!"

"What Paul Bourget Thinks of Us," *Literary Essays,* p. 163

An autobiography is the most treacherous thing there is. It lets out every secret its author is trying to keep; it lets the truth shine unobstructed through every harmless little deception he tries to play; it pitilessly exposes him as a tin hero worshipping himself as Big Metal every time he tries to do the modest-unconsciousness act before the reader. This is not guessing; I am speaking from autobiographical personal experience; I was never able to refrain from mentioning, with a studied casualness that could deceive none but the most incautious reader, that an ancestor of mine was sent ambassador to Spain by Charles I., nor that in a remote branch of my family there exists a claimant to an earldom, nor that an uncle of mine used to own a dog that was descended from the dog that was in the Ark; and at the same time I was never able to persuade myself to call a gibbet by its right name when accounting for other ancestors of mine, but always spoke of it as the "platform"— puerilely intimating that they were out lecturing when it happened.

Christian Science, Book II, Chapt. I, p. 104

I would rather be a dog's ancestor than a lieutenant-governor's posterity.

Sam Clemens of Hannibal, p. 2

As concerneth length of line and multiplicity of ancestors—in that property I am as poor as Jesus: no grandfather.

Ibid., p. 6

I wanted to let out the fact that I had some ancestors, too; but I did not want to pull them out of their graves by the ears . . . Phelps was in the same difficulty. In fact, he looked distraught now and then—just as a person looks who wants to uncover an ancestor purely by accident and cannot think of a way that will seem accidental enough. But, at last, after dinner, he made a try. He took us about his drawing-room, showing us the pictures, and finally stopped before a rude and ancient engraving. It was the picture of the court that tried Charles I. There was the pyramid of judges in Puritan slouch hats, and below them three bare-headed secretaries seated at a table. Mr. Phelps put his finger upon one of the three and said, with exulting indifference:

"An ancestor of mine."

I put my finger on a judge, and retorted with scathing languidness:

"Ancestor of mine. But it is a small matter. I have others."

Mark Twain's Autobiography, Paine, I, p. 84

ANGEL *See also* FOOD, ILLNESS, LANGUAGE, TRAVEL

The walls were hung with pious pictures . . . pictures historically commemorative of curative miracles which had been achieved by the waters when nobody was looking. That is, nobody but angels; they are always on deck when there is a miracle to the fore—so as to get put in the picture, perhaps. Angels are as fond of that as a fire company; look at the old masters.

A Connecticut Yankee in King Arthur's Court,
Chapt. XXII, p. 185

ANGER *See also* LETTERS, PROFANITY, TEMPER

He began to swell, and went on swelling and swelling and swelling until he had reached the dimensions of a god of about the second or third degree. Then the fountains of his great deep were broken up, and for two or three minutes I couldn't see him for the rain. It was words, only words, but they fell so densely that they darkened the atmosphere.

Mark Twain In Eruption, p. 145

Sometimes he smiled . . . but when he straightened

himself up like a liberty-pole, and the lightning begun to
flicker out from under his eyebrows, you wanted to climb
a tree first, and find out what the matter was afterward.
The Adventures of Huckleberry Finn, Chapt. XVIII, p. 146

When angry, count four; when very angry, swear.
"Pudd'nhead Wilson's Calendar,"
Pudd'nhead Wilson, Chapt. X, p. 89

Her eyes blazed up, and she jumped for him like a wildcat, and when she was done with him she was rags and he
wasn't anything but an allegory.
"A Horse's Tale,"
The Mysterious Stranger, Etc., p. 167

ANIMAL *See also* BRUTALITY, CAMEL, CAT, CONGRESSMAN,
DOG, FLEA, FROG, HORSE, MAN, MONKEY, MULE

It is just like man's vanity and impertinence to call an
animal dumb because it is dumb to his dull perceptions.
What Is Man? and Other Essays, Chapt. VI, p. 84

No brute ever does a cruel thing—that is the monopoly
of those with the moral sense. When a brute inflicts pain
he does it innocently.
The Mysterious Stranger, Etc., Chapt. IV, p. 50

The coyote is a living, breathing allegory of Want. He is
always hungry. He is always poor, out of luck and friendless. The meanest creatures despise him, and even the fleas
would desert him for a velocipede. He is so spiritless and
cowardly that even while his exposed teeth are pretending
a threat, the rest of his face is apologizing for it.
Roughing It, I, p. 48

Two beautiful deer came sauntering across the grounds
and stopped and looked me over as impudently as if they
thought of buying me. Then they seemed to conclude that
they could do better for less money, and sauntered indo-
lently away.
S.L.C. to C.T., p. 18

ANNIVERSARIES *See also* BIRTHDAY

What ought to be done to the man who invented the

celebrating of anniversaries? Mere killing would be too light. Anniversaries are very well up to a certain point, while one's babies are in the process of growing up: they are joy-flags that make gay the road and prove progress; and one looks down the fluttering rank with pride. Then presently one notices that the flagstaffs are in process of a mysterious change of some sort—change of shape. Yes, they are turning into milestones. They are marking something lost now, not gained. From that time on it were best to suppress taking notice of anniversaries. [1896]

Mark Twain's Notebook, p. 300

ANSWER *See* CONVERSATION, KNOWLEDGE

ANT *See also* RELIGION, SLEEP

It seems to me that in the matter of intellect the ant must be a strangely overrated bird. During many summers, now, I have watched him, when I ought to have been in better business, and I have not yet come across a living ant that seemed to have any more sense than a dead one. I refer to the ordinary ant, of course; I have had no experience of those wonderful Swiss and African ones which vote, keep drilled armies, hold slaves, and dispute about religion. Those particular ants may be all that the naturalist paints them, but I am persuaded that the average ant is a sham. I admit his industry, of course; he is the hardest working creature in the world—when anybody is looking—but his leather-headedness is the point I make against him. He goes out foraging, he makes a capture, and then what does he do? Go home? No—he goes anywhere but home. He doesn't know where home is. His home may be only three feet away—no matter, he can't find it. He makes his capture, as I have said; it is generally something which can be of no sort of use to himself or anybody else; it is usually seven times bigger than it ought to be; he hunts out the awkward-est place to take hold of it; he lifts it bodily up in the air by main force, and starts; not toward home, but in the opposite direction; not calmly and wisely, but with a frantic haste which is wasteful of his strength; he fetches up against a pebble, and instead of going around it, he climbs over it backwards dragging his booty after him, tumbles down on the other side, jumps up in a passion, kicks the dust off his clothes, moistens his hands, grabs his property viciously, yanks it this way, then that, shoves it ahead of him a moment, turns tail and lugs it after him another moment, gets madder and madder, then presently hoists it into the air and goes tearing away in an entirely new direction; comes to a weed; it never occurs to him to go around it; no, he must climb it; and he does climb it, dragging his worthless property to the top—which is as bright a thing to do as it would be for me to carry a sack of flour from Heidelberg to Paris by way of Strasburg steeple; when he gets up there he finds that that is not the place; takes a cursory glance at the scenery and either climbs down again or tumbles down, and starts off once more—as usual, in a new direction. At the end of half an hour, he fetches up within six inches of the place he started from and lays his burden down; meantime he has been over all the ground for two yards around, and climbed all the weeds and pebbles he came across. Now he wipes the sweat from his brow, strokes his limbs, and then marches aimlessly off, in as violent a hurry as ever. He traverses a good deal of zigzag country, and by and by stumbles on his same booty again. He does not remember to have ever seen it before; he looks around to see which is not the way home, grabs his bundle and starts; he goes through the same adventures he had before; finally stops to rest, and a friend comes along. Evidently the friend remarks that a last year's grasshopper leg is a very noble acquisition, and inquires where he got it. Evidently the proprietor does not remember exactly where he did get it, but thinks he got it "around here somewhere." Evidently the friend contracts to help him freight it home. Then, with a judgment peculiarly antic (pun not intentional), they take hold of opposite ends of that grasshopper leg and begin to tug with all their might in opposite directions. Presently they take a rest and confer together. They decide that something is wrong, they can't make out what. Then they go at it again, just as before. Same result. Mutual recriminations follow. Evidently each accuses the other of being an obstructionist. They warm up, and the dispute ends in a fight. They lock themselves together and chew each other's jaws for a while; then they roll and tumble on the ground till one loses a horn or a leg and has to haul off for repairs. They make up and go to work again in the same old insane way, but the crippled ant is at a disadvantage; tug as he may, the other one drags off the booty and him at the end of it. Instead of giving up, he hangs on, and gets his shins bruised against every obstruction that comes in the way. By and by, when that grasshopper leg has been dragged all over the same old ground once more, it is finally dumped at about the spot where it originally lay, the two perspiring ants inspect it thoughtfully and decide that dried grasshopper legs are a poor sort of property after all, and then each starts off in a different direction to see if he can't find an old nail or something else that is heavy enough to afford entertainment and at the same time valueless enough to make an ant want to own it.

Science has recently discovered that the ant does not lay up anything for winter use. This will knock him out of literature, to some extent. He does not work, except when people are looking, and only then when the observer has a green, naturalistic look, and seems to be taking notes. This amounts to deception, and will injure him for the Sunday-schools. He has not judgment enough to know what is good to eat from what isn't. This amounts to ignorance, and will impair the world's respect for him. He cannot stroll around a stump and find his way home again. This amounts to idiocy, and once the damaging fact is established, thoughtful people will cease to look up to him, the sentimental will cease to fondle him. His vaunted industry is but a vanity and of no effect, since he never gets home with anything he starts with. This disposes of the last remnant of his reputation and wholly destroys his main usefulness as a moral agent, since it will make the sluggard hesitate to go to him any more. It is strange, beyond comprehension, that so manifest a humbug as the ant has been able to fool so many nations and keep it up so many ages without being found out.

A Tramp Abroad, I, Chapt. XXI, p. 217

ANVIL   *See* CONSCIENCE

APOLOGY   *See* BORE

APPLE   *See* TEMPERAMENT

APPROVAL   *See also* COMFORT, FATHER, SACRIFICE
We can secure other people's approval if we do right and try hard; but our own is worth a hundred of it, and no way has been found out of securing that.

"Pudd'nhead Wilson's New Calendar,"
Following the Equator, I, Chapt. XIV, p. 140

ARBITRATION   *See* ARMY

ARCHITECTURE   *See* ICE-STORM, NATURE

ARGUMENT   *See also* TALK, TEMPER, THEORY
Arguments have no chance against petrified training; they wear it as little as the waves wear a cliff.

A Connecticut Yankee in King Arthur's Court,
Chapt. XVII, p. 137

When you can't cure a disaster by argument, what is the use to argue?

Ibid., Chapt. XXVII, p. 342

There is nothing like instances to grow hair on a bald-headed argument.

From an unpublished manuscript, "British Copyright"

ARISTOCRACY   *See also* MONARCHY, MONEY
The only aristocracy worth mentioning is that of brains.

Harper's Weekly, Dec. 23, 1905, p. 1884

I have been an author for 20 years and an ass for 55.

Mark Twain's Letters, II, p. 543

. . . it is no harm to be an ass, if one is content to bray and not kick . . .

Personal Recollections of Joan of Arc,
I, Bk. II, Chapt. III, p. 126

Even the most gifted human being is merely an ass, and always an ass, when his forbears have furnished him an idol to worship.

Mark Twain—Macy

[The knights in armor]: What a pity . . . that men with such superb strength—strength enabling them to stand up cased in cruelly burdensome iron and drenched with perspiration, and hack and batter and bang each other for six hours on a stretch—should not have been born at a time when they could put it to some useful purpose. Take a jackass, for instance: a jackass has that kind of strength, and puts it to a useful purpose, and is valuable to the world because he *is* a jackass; but a nobleman is not valuable because he is a jackass. It is a mixture that is always ineffectual, and should never have been attempted in the first place.

A Connecticut Yankee in King Arthur's Court,
Chapt. XV, p. 119

At 50 a man can be an ass without being an optimist but not an optimist without being an ass.

More Maxims of Mark, p. 5

None but an ass pays a compliment and asks a favor at the same time. There are many asses.

Ibid., p. 11

ASSASSINATION *See also* CRIME

A peculiarly formidable . . . motive [to assassinate] . . . which society could not hope to deal with successfully—[was] *vanity* and a thirst for notoriety. [1845]

"A Scrap of Curious History,"
What is Man? and Other Essays, p. 190

It seems strange to me that the statesmen and lawmakers

of the world do not recognize . . . that new deterrents will have to be invented to meet the emergency. This ought to be easy to do, if, as I believe, the . . . mania has its origin in a vulgar vanity; for *vanity* cannot stand humiliation and ridicule. The man who will kill a chief magistrate for glory's sake will think twice before he will do it for humiliation's sake. He would not do it with genuine alacrity if he knew he would have to spend the rest of his life on exhibition in the Place de la Concorde clad in the short skirts and pink tights of a ballet girl, with a parasol in his hand and the passers-by privileged to pelt him with over-due eggs. The stocks were a valuable institution; their value lay in the fact that they inflicted humiliation. Something of their sort could be revived with profit, I think. The inflated anarchist seeking a gaudy martyrdom, with pictures of himself in the papers, would hardly apply there, I think. [June 25, 1894]

An unpublished letter, recipient unknown

It is the *noise* the attempt . . . to assassinate would make in the world that would breed . . . subsequent attempts, by unsettling the rickety minds of men who envy the criminal his vast notoriety . . .

Nothing will check the . . . ruler-murder but absolute silence—the absence of pow-wow about them. How are you going to manage that? By gagging every witness . . . by abolishing all newspapers. [1901]

Mark Twain's Letters, II, p. 713

It may take a shooting-case six months to breed another ruler-tragedy, but it will breed it. There is at least one mind somewhere which will brood, and wear, and decay itself to the killing-point and produce that tragedy. . . .

The wild talk you see in the papers! . . . And a District Attorney wants a law which shall punish with death *attempts* upon a President's life—this, mind you, as a deterrent. It would have no effect—or the opposite one . . .

It is the *noise* the attempt would make in the world that would breed the subsequent attempts, by unsettling the rickety minds of men who envy the criminal his vast notoriety . . .

Nothing will check the . . . ruler-murder but absolute silence—the absence of pow-wow about them. How are you going to manage that? By gagging every witness and jamming him into a dungeon . . . by abolishing all newspapers . . . [Sept. 1901]
Mark Twain's Letters, II, p. 715

ASTONISHMENT

He was astonished clear down to his corns.
A Connecticut Yankee in King Arthur's Court,
Chapt. XXIII, p. 199

ASTRONOMY *See also* TRAVEL

An occultation of Venus is not half so difficult as an eclipse of the sun, but because it comes seldom the world thinks it's a grand thing.
More Maxims of Mark, p. 11

ATOM *See* PREDESTINATION

AUDIENCE *See also* EXPERIENCE, LECTURING

An audience likes a speaker with the same weaknesses and the same virtues as they themselves have. If the lecturer's brow is too high and the brows of the audience are too low, look out. Or, if a high-brow audience sees a low-brow lecturer there's trouble.
Mark Twain and I, Opie Read, p. 53

Remember, the audience most surely and powerfully stirred is the *small* audience, when you've learned all the deep arts of your trade. They rise in their might when you let them see that theirs are welcome faces and that you are not ashamed of them for being a small house.
From an unpublished letter to Clara Clemens,
March 5, 1907

I never had the courage to talk across a long, narrow

room. I should be at the end of the room facing all the audience. If I attempt to talk across a room I find myself turning this way and that, and thus at alternate periods I have part of the audience behind me. You ought never to have any part of the audience behind you; you never can tell what they are going to do.

Mark Twain's Speeches (1923), p. 386

AUSTEN, JANE   *See* LIBRARY, LITERARY CRITICISM

AUSTRALIA   *See* FORGETFULNESS, KNOWLEDGE, MEASURE-MENT, TREE

AUSTRIA   *See* DUEL, ROYALTY

AUTHOR   *See also* ASS, EXPERIENCE
I never saw an author who was aware that there is any dimensional difference between a fact and a surmise.

My Father Mark Twain, Clara Clemens, p. 86

There are three infallible ways of pleasing an author, and the three form a rising scale of compliment: 1, To tell him you have read one of his books; 2, To tell him you have read all of his books; 3, To ask him to let you read the manuscript of his forthcoming book. No. 1 admits you to his respect; No. 2 admits you to his admiration; No. 3 carries you clear into his heart.

"Pudd'nhead Wilson's Calendar,"
Pudd'nhead Wilson, Chapt. XI, p. 96

AUTHORITY   *See also* STATESMANSHIP
He "showed off"—making a deal of the sputter and fuss that insect authority delights in.

The Adventures of Tom Sawyer, Chapt. IV, p. 42

AUTOBIOGRAPHY   *See also* ANCESTOR, LIFE, NARRATIVE, ROYALTY, WRITING
An Autobiography is the truest of all books; for while it inevitably consists mainly of extinctions of the truth, shirk-

ings of the truth, partial revealments of the truth, with hardly an instance of plain straight truth, the remorseless truth *is* there, between the lines, where the author-cat is raking dust upon it which hides from the disinterested spectator neither it nor its smell.

Mark Twain-Howells Letters, II, p. 782

Tomorrow I mean to dictate a chapter (in my Autobiography) which will get my heirs and assigns burnt alive if they venture to print it this side of 2006 A.D.

I dote on this book as Adam used to dote on a fresh new deformed child after he was 900 years old and wasn't expecting any more surprises.

Ibid., p. 810

An autobiography that leaves out little things and enumerates only big ones is no proper picture of the man's life at all; his life consists of his feeling and his interests, with here and there an incident apparently big or little to hang the feelings on.

Ibid., I, p. 288

AUTOGRAPH *See* WRITING

AX *See also* BEGGAR, HUMAN RACE

There is no man so poor but what at intervals some man comes to him with an ax to grind. By and by the ax's aspect becomes familiar to the proprietor of the grindstone. He perceives that it is the same old ax. If you are a governor you know that the stranger wants an office. The first time he arrives you are deceived; he pours out such noble praises of you and your political record that you are moved to tears; there's a lump in your throat and you are thankful that you have lived for this happiness. Then the stranger discloses his ax, and you are ashamed of yourself and your race. Six repetitions will cure you.

Mark Twain, a Biography, Paine, III, p. 1422

B

BABY *See also* CLERGYMAN, DISEASE, FATHER, GIRL, NURSE

The idea that a baby doesn't amount to anything! Why, *one* baby is just a house and a front yard full by itself. *One* baby can furnish more business than you and your whole Interior Department can attend to. He is enterprising, irrepressible, brimful of lawless activities. Do what you please, you can't make him stay on the reservation. Sufficient unto the day is one baby. As long as you are in your right mind don't you ever pray for twins. Twins amount to a permanent riot. And there ain't any real difference between triplets and an insurrection.

"The Babies,"
Mark Twain's Speeches (1923), p. 60

"Tom" was a bad baby from the very beginning of his usurpation. He would cry for nothing; he would burst into storms of devilish temper without notice, and let go scream after scream and squall after squall, then climax the thing with "holding his breath"—that frightful specialty of the teething nursling, in the throes of which the creature exhausts its lungs, then is convulsed with noiseless squirmings and twistings and kickings in the effort to get its breath, while the lips turn blue and the mouth stands wide and rigid, offering for inspection one wee tooth set in the lower rim of a hoop of red gums; and when the appalling stillness has endured until one is sure the lost breath will never return, a nurse comes flying, and dashes water in the child's face, and—presto! the lungs fill, and instantly discharge a shriek, or a yell, or a howl which bursts the listening ear and surprises the owner of it into saying words which would not go well with a halo if he had one.

Pudd'nhead Wilson, Chapt. IV, p. 38

The baby . . . kept me awake. This occurs every night and it embitters me, because I see how needless it was to put in the other burglar alarm, a costly and complicated contrivance, which cannot be depended upon, because it's always getting out of order; whereas, although the baby is always getting out of order, too, it can nevertheless be depended on.

Mark Twain, Will Clemens, p. 187

Howells had favorably reviewed *The Innocents Abroad*, and after the first moment of their introduction had passed Clemens said: "When I read that review of yours I felt like the woman who said that she was so glad that her baby had come white."

Mark Twain's Letters, I, p. 166

The girl who was rebuked for having borne an illegitimate child excused herself by saying, "But it is such a *little* one."

"To My Missionary Critics,"
Europe and Elsewhere, p. 285

BACHELOR *See* DISEASE, MARRIAGE

BACON *See* FOOD

BADNESS *See* BABY, CAIN, LANGUAGE, NATURE

BALLOON

Thing to make meteoric observations and commit suicide with.

More Maxims of Mark, p. 6

BAND *See* COMPLIMENT

BANQUET

A banquet is probably the most fatiguing thing in the world except ditchdigging. It is the insanest of all recreations. The inventor of it overlooked no detail that could furnish weariness, distress, harassment, and acute and long-sustained misery of mind and body.

Mark Twain in Eruption, p. 320

At the first banquet mentioned in history that other prodigal son who came back from his travels was invited to stand up and have his say. They were all there, his brethren, David and Goliath,—and if he had had such experience as I have had he would have waited until those other people got through talking. He got up and testified to all his failings. Now if he had waited before telling all about his riotous living until the others had spoken he might not have given himself away as he did. . .

"Lotus Club Dinner,"
Mark Twain's Speeches (1923), p. 162

BARBER

All things change except barbers, the ways of barbers, and the surroundings of barbers. These never change.

"About Barbers," *Sketches New and Old,* p. 344

A barber seldom rubs you like a Christian.

Ibid., p. 344

I always had a yearning to be a king. This may never be, I suppose, but, at any rate, it will always be a satisfaction to me to know that, if I am not a king, I am the next thing to it. I have been shaved by the king's barber.

Mark Twain's Letters, I, p. 111

BATH *See also* ENGLAND, FLEA, POETRY, RHEUMATISM

The doctor said I was a grand proof of what these baths could do; said I had come here as innocent of disease as a grindstone, and inside of three weeks these baths had sluiced out of me every important ailment known to medical science, along with considerable more that were entirely new and patentable.

"Aix, Paradise of Rheumatics,"
Europe and Elsewhere, p. 108

It is a mistake that there is no bath that will cure people's manners. But drowning would help."

"Marienbad—A Health Factory,"
Ibid., p. 126

What I have been through in these two weeks would free a person of pretty much everything in him that wasn't nailed there—any loose thing, any unattached fragment of bone, or meat or morals, or disease or propensities or accomplishments, or what not.

Ibid., p. 119

Here endeth my experience of the celebrated Turkish bath, and here also endeth my dream of the bliss the mortal revels in who passes through it. It is a malignant swindle. The man who enjoys it is qualified to enjoy anything that is repulsive to sight or sense . . .

The Innocents Abroad, II, Chapt. VII, p. 107

BEAUTY *See also* CHANGE, COLOR, ENGLAND, FLEA, GRANT, U. S., ICE-STORM, LAKE, NATURE, POETIC PROSE

[The beauty of Lake Tahoe]: In the early morning one watches the silent battle of dawn and darkness upon the waters of Tahoe with a placid interest; but when the shadows sulk away and one by one the hidden beauties of the shore unfold themselves in the full splendor of noon; when the still surface is belted like a rainbow with broad bars of blue and green and white, half the distance from circumference to center; when, in the lazy summer afternoon, he lies in a boat, far out to where the dead blue of the deep water begins, and smokes the pipe of peace and idly winks at the distant crags and patches of snow from under his cap-brim; when the boat drifts shoreward to the white water, and he lolls over the gunwhale and gazes by the hour down through the crystal depths and notes the colors of the pebbles and reviews the finny armies gliding in procession a hundred feet below; when at night he sees moon and stars, mountain ridges feathered with pines, jutting white capes, bold promontories, grand sweeps of rugged scenery topped with bald, glimmering peaks, all magnificently pictured in the polished mirror of the lake, in richest, softest detail, the tranquil interest that was born with the morning deepens and deepens, by sure degrees till it culminates at last in resistless fascination!

The Innocents Abroad, II, Chapt. XXI, p. 265

A soap bubble is the most beautiful thing, and the most exquisite, in nature; . . . . I wonder how much it would take to buy a soap bubble, if there was only one in the world?

Ibid., II, Chapt. XIII, p. 183

A thoroughly beautiful woman and a thoroughly homely woman are creations which I love to gaze upon, and which I cannot tire of gazing upon, for each is perfect in her own line, and it is *perfection,* I think, in many things, and perhaps most things, which is the quality that fascinates us.

Mark Twain's Autobiography, Paine, I, p. 323

[The ice-storm]: Here in London the other night I was talking with some Scotch and English friends, and I mentioned the ice-storm, using it as a figure—a figure which failed, for none of them had heard of the ice-storm. One gentleman, who was very familiar with American literature, said he had never seen it mentioned in any book. That is strange. And I, myself, was not able to say that I had seen it mentioned in a book; and yet the autumn foliage, with all other American scenery, has received full and competent attention.

The oversight is strange, for in America the ice-storm is an event. And it is not an event which one is careless about. When it comes, the news flies from room to room in the house, there are bangings on the doors, and shoutings, "The ice-storm! the ice-storm!" and even the laziest sleepers throw off the covers and join the rush for the windows. The ice-storm occurs in mid-winter, and usually its en-

chantments are wrought in the silence and the darkness
of the night. A fine drizzling rain falls hour after hour upon
the naked twigs and branches of the trees, and as it falls it
freezes. In time the trunk and every branch and twig are
incased in hard pure ice; so that the tree looks like a skele-
ton tree made all of glass—glass that is crystal-clear. All
along the under side of every branch and twig is a comb
of little icicles—the frozen drip. Sometimes these pendants
do not quite amount to icicles, but are round beads—frozen
tears.

The weather clears, toward dawn, and leaves a brisk,
pure atmosphere and a sky without a shred of cloud in it—
and everything is still, there is not a breath of wind. The
dawn breaks and spreads, the news of the storm goes about
the house, and the little and the big, in wraps and blankets,
flock to the window and press together there, and gaze
intently out upon the great white ghost in the grounds, and
nobody says a word, nobody stirs. All are waiting—waiting
for the miracle. The minutes drift on and on, with not a
sound but the ticking of the clock; at last the sun fires a
sudden sheaf of rays into the ghostly tree and turns it into
a white splendor of glittering diamonds. Everybody catches
his breath, and feels a swelling in his throat and a moisture
in his eyes—but waits again; for he knows what is coming:
there is more yet. The sun climbs higher, and still higher,
flooding the tree from its loftiest spread of branches to its
lowest, turning it to a glory of white fire; then in a moment,
without warning, comes the great miracle, the supreme
miracle, the miracle without its fellow in the earth; a gust
of wind sets every branch and twig to swaying, and in an
instant turns the whole white tree into a spouting and
spraying explosion of flashing gems of every conceivable
color; and there it stands and sways this way and that, flash!
flash! flash! a dancing and glancing world of rubies, emeralds, diamonds, sapphires, the most radiant spectacle, the
most blinding spectacle, the divinest, the most exquisite,
the most intoxicating vision of fire and color and intolerable

and unimaginable splendor that ever any eye has rested upon in this world, or will ever rest upon outside of the gates of heaven.

Following the Equator, II, Chapt. XXIII, p. 277

To me this serene and noiseless life out here (in Florence, Italy, 1893), with the unimaginable beauty of the view—which is never twice the same, for God persistently neglects the rest of His universe to play with the sun and get up "effects" and show off what He can do here—is heaven, and I want to stay in this one when I die, on account of doubts about being a pet in the other one, there's so many people gone there who know about me and will talk, of course.

Mark Twain to Mrs. Fairbanks, p. 269

BED *See also* ACCIDENT, EARLY

In the matter of beds all ships have been badly edited, ignorantly edited, from the beginning. The selection of beds is given to some hearty, strong-backed, self-made man, when it ought to be given to a frail woman . . . accustomed to backaches and insomnia . . . In Noah's Ark the beds were simply scandalous. Noah set the fashion, and it will endure in one degree of modification or another till the next flood.

Following the Equator, II, Chapt. XXVIII, p. 329

In bed the steam heat can't boil you into a fever, nor a dying furnace give you a chill. And no one interrupts you with remarks about the weather. Work in bed is a pretty good gospel, for a man at my time of life [70 yrs.], anyway, when the blood is easily frosted.

New York American, Dec. 1, 1905

I have made it a rule to go to bed when there wasn't anybody left to sit up with; get up when I had to. This has resulted in an unswerving regularity of irregularity.

Mark Twain's Speeches (1923), p. 257

BEES *See also* IDIOT

The drowsing murmur of the . . . studying scholars

soothed the soul like the spell that is in the murmur of bees.
The Adventures of Tom Sawyer, p. 72

BEGGAR

. . . the coat of arms of the human race ought to consist of a man with an ax on his shoulder proceeding toward a grindstone, or it ought to represent the several members of the human race holding out the hat to one another; for we are all beggars, each in his own way. One beggar is too proud to beg for pennies, but will beg for an introduction into society; another does not care for society, but he wants a postmastership; another will inveigle a lawyer into conversation and then sponge on him for free advice. The man who wouldn't do any of these things will beg for the Presidency. Each admires his own dignity and greatly guards it, but in his opinion the others haven't any. Mendicancy is a matter of taste and temperament, no doubt.

Mark Twain, a Biography, Paine, III, p. 1421

If the beggar instinct were left out of an Indian he would not "go" any more than a clock without a pendulum.
Roughing It, I, Chapt. XIX, p. 155

BEHAVIOR

Let us endeavor so to live that when we come to die even the undertaker will be sorry.

"Pudd'nhead Wilson's Calendar"

Pudd'nhead Wilson, Chapt. VI, p. 56

Few things are harder to put up with than the annoyance of a good example.

Ibid., Chapt. XIX, p. 182

BELIEF *See also* BRAVERY

Beliefs are *acquirements*, temperaments are *born*; beliefs are subject to change, nothing whatever can change temperament.

What is Man? and *Other Essays*, p. 107

If a man doesn't believe as we do, we say he is a crank, and that settles it. I mean it does nowadays, because now we can't burn him.

Following the Equator, II, p. 212

BELLS *See* CHURCH

BENEVOLENCE *See also* MISSIONARY
We do no benevolences whose *first* benefit is not for ourselves.

"Unpublished Chapters from the
Autobiography of Mark Twain,"
Harper's Magazine, Aug. 1922, p. 315

BERLIN, GERMANY *See* EARTHQUAKE, EYE, HOUSE, NEWS-
PAPER, POLICEMAN, TRAVEL

BERMUDA *See also* HAIR, HEAVEN, MUSIC, ROAD
You go to heaven if you want to—I'd druther stay here.
I could live here always and be contented.

The Twainian—Jan.–Feb. 1948, p. 1

BIBLE *See also* CHANGE, ENGLAND, HOUSE, LEARNING, LI-
BRARY, LITERARY CRITICISM, MIND, MIRACLE, MISSISSIPPI
RIVER, PUNISHMENT, STREET, WOMAN, WORDS
When one reads Bibles, one is less surprised at what the
Deity knows than at what he doesn't know.

Mark Twain's Notebook, p. 385
I was compelled to read an unexpurgated Bible through
before I was 15 years old. None can do that and ever draw
a clean, sweet breath again this side of the grave.

Mark Twain, a Biography, Paine, III, p. 1281
[Huck and Nigger Jim discuss Solomon]: . . . "Don't you
know about the harem? Solomon had one: he had about a
million wives!"

"Why, yes, dat's so; I—I'd done forgot it. A harem's a
bo'd'n-house, I reck'n. Mos' likely dey has rackety times in
de nussery. En I reck'n de wives quarrels considable; en
dat 'crease de racket. Yit dey say Sollermun de wises' man
dat ever live! I doan' take no stock in dat. Bekase why:

46

would a wise man want to live in de mids' er sich a blim-blammin' all de time? No—'deed he wouldn't. A wise man 'ud take en buil' a biler-factry; en den he could shet *down* de biler-factry when he want to res'."

"Well, but he *was* the wisest man, anyway; because the widow she told me so, her own self."

"I doan k'yer what de widder say, he *warn't* no wise man nuther. He had some er de dad-fetchedes' ways I ever see. Does you know 'bout dat chile he 'uz gwyne to chop in two?"

"Yes, the widow told me all about it."

"*Well*, den! Warn' dat de beatenes' notion in de worl'? You jes' take en look at it a minute. Dah's de stump, dah—dat's one er de women; heah's you—dat's de yuther one; I's Sollermun; en dish yer dollar bill's de chile. Bofe un you claims it. What does I do? Does I shin aroun' mongs' de neighbors en fine out which un you de bill *do* belong to, en han' it over to de right one, all safe en soun', de way dat anybody dat had any gumption would? No: I take en whack de bill in *two*, en give half un it to you en de yuther half to de yuther woman. Dat's de way Sollermun was gwyne to do wid de chile. Now I want to ask you; what's de use er dat half a bill?—can't buy nothin' wid it. En what use is a half a chile? I wouldn' give a dern for a million un um."

"But hang it, Jim, you've clean missed the point—blame it, you've missed it a thousand mile."

"Who? Me? Go 'long. Doan' talk to *me* 'bout yo' pints. I reckon I knows sense when I sees it; en dey ain' no sense in sich doin's as dat. De 'spute warn't 'bout a half a chile, de 'spute was 'bout a whole chile; en de man dat think he kin settle a 'spute 'bout a whole chile wid a half a chile doan' know enough to come in out'n de rain. Doan' talk to me 'bout Sollermun, Huck, I knows him by de back."

"But I tell you you don't get the point."

"Blame de pint! I reck'n I knows what I knows. En mine you, de *real* pint is down furder—it's down deeper. It lays in de way Sollermun was raised. You take a man dat's got on'y one or two chillen; is dat man gwyne to be wasteful o' chillen? No, he ain't; he can't 'ford it. *He* know how to value 'em. But you take a man dat's got 'bout five million chillen runnin' roun' de house, en it's diffunt. *He* as soon chop a chile in two as a cat. Dey's plenty mo'. A chile er two, mo' er less, warn't no consekens to Sollermun, dad fatch him!"

The Adventures of Huckleberry Finn, Chapt. XIV, p. 111

The Christian's Bible is a drug store. Its contents remain the same; but the medical practice changes . . . The world has corrected the Bible. The Church never corrects it; and also never fails to drop in at the tail of the procession—and take the credit of the correction . . . During many ages there were witches. The Bible said so. The Bible commanded that they should not be allowed to live. Therefore the Church, after eight hundred years, gathered up its halters, thumbscrews, and firebrands, and set about its holy work in earnest. She worked hard at it night and day during nine centuries and imprisoned, tortured, hanged, and burned whole hordes and armies of witches, and washed the Christian world clean with their foul blood.

Then it was discovered that there was no such thing as witches, and never had been. One does not know whether to laugh or to cry.

. . . There are no witches. The witch text remains; only the practice has changed. Hell fire is gone, but the text remains. Infant damnation is gone, but the text remains. More than two hundred death penalties are gone from the law books, but the texts that authorized them remain.

"Bible Teaching and Religious Practice"
Europe and Elsewhere, p. 387

BICYCLE *See also* DOG, GERMAN LANGUAGE

Jean and I go bicycling evenings. She runs beside the machine, and picks it up when I plunge off. I am progressing all the time. Yesterday I learned a new way to fall off.

Love Letters of Mark Twain, p. 259

BIGAMIST *See* OPTIMIST

BILLIARDS

Once in Nevada I dropped into a billiard-room casually, and picked up a cue and began to knock the balls around. The proprietor, who was a red-headed man, with such hair as I have never seen anywhere except on a torch, asked me if I would like to play. I said, "Yes." He said, "Knock the balls around a little and let me see how you can shoot." So I knocked them around and thought I was doing pretty well, when he said, "That's all right; I'll play you left-handed." It hurt my pride, but I played him. We banked for the shot and he won it. Then he commenced to play, and I commenced to chalk my cue to get ready to play, and he went on playing, and I went on chalking my cue; and he played and I chalked all through that game. When he had run his string out I said:

"That's wonderful! perfectly wonderful! If you can play that way left-handed what could you do right-handed?"

"Couldn't do anything," he said. "I'm a left-handed man."

Mark Twain, a Biography, Paine, III, p. 1306

[Mark Twain] had experimented, a great many years before, with what was in the nature of a trick on some unsuspecting player. It consisted in turning out twelve pool-balls on the table with one cue-ball, and asking his guest how many caroms he thought he could make with all those twelve balls to play on. He had learned that the average player would seldom make more than thirty-one counts, and usually, before this number was reached, he would miss through some careless play or get himself into a position where he couldn't play at all. The thing looked absurdly easy. It looked as if one could go on playing all day long, and the victim was usually eager to bet that he could make fifty or perhaps a hundred; but for more than an hour I tried it patiently, and seldom succeeded in scoring more than fifteen or twenty without missing. Long after the play itself ceased to be amusing to me, he insisted on my going on and trying it some more, and he would throw himself back and roar with laughter, the tears streaming down his cheeks, to see me work and fume and fail.

Ibid., p. 1366

BIOGRAPHY See also LIFE

What a wee little part of a person's life are his acts and his words! His real life is led in his head, and is known to none but himself . . . Biographies are but the clothes and buttons of the man—the biography of the man himself cannot be written.

Mark Twain's Autobiography, Paine, I, p. 2

Apparently no narrative that tells the facts of a man's life in the man's own words, can be uninteresting.

Love Letters of Mark Twain, p. 249

What is biography? Unadorned romance. What is romance? Unadorned biography. Adorn it less and it will be better than it is.

Mark Twain, a Biography, Paine, II, p. 871

BIRDS See also EARLY RISING

When I had stood ten minutes, thinking and imagining, and getting my spirit in tune with the place, and in the right mood to enjoy the supernatural, a raven suddenly uttered a hoarse croak over my head. It made me start; and then I was angry because I started. I looked up, and the creature was sitting on a limb right over me, looking down at me. I felt something of the same sense of humiliation and injury which one feels when he finds that a human stranger has been clandestinely inspecting him in his privacy and mentally commenting upon it. I eyed the raven, and the raven eyed me. Nothing was said during some seconds. Then the bird stepped a little way along his limb to get a better point of observation, lifted his wings, stuck his head far down below his shoulders toward me, and croaked again—a croak with a distinctly insulting expression about it. If he had spoken in English he could not have said any more plainly than he did say in raven, "Well, what do *you* want here?" I felt as foolish as if I had been caught in some mean act by a responsible being, and reproved for it. However, I made no reply; I would not bandy words with a raven. The adversary waited a while, with his shoulders still lifted, his head thrust down between them, and his keen bright eye fixed on me; then he threw out two or three more insults, which I could not understand, further than that I knew a portion of them consisted of language not used in church.

I still made no reply. Now the adversary raised his head and called. There was an answering croak from a little distance in the wood,—evidently a croak of inquiry. The adversary explained with enthusiasm, and the other raven dropped everything and came. The two sat side by side on the limb and discussed me as freely and offensively as two great naturalists might discuss a new kind of bug. The thing became more and more embarrassing. They called in another friend. This was too much. I saw that they had the advantage of me, and so I concluded to get out of the scrape by walking out of it. They enjoyed my defeat as much as any low white people could have done. They craned their necks and laughed at me (for a raven *can* laugh just like a man), they squalled insulting remarks after me as long as they could see me. They were nothing but ravens—I knew that,—what they thought about me could be a matter of no consequence,—and yet when even a raven shouts after you, "What a hat!" "Oh, pull down your vest!" and that sort of thing, it hurts you and humiliates you, and there is no getting around it with fine reasoning and pretty arguments.

A Tramp Aboard, I Chapt. II, p. 22

There's more *to* a bluejay than any other creature. He has got more moods, and more different kinds of feelings than other creatures; and, mind you, whatever a bluejay feels, he can put into language. And no mere commonplace language, either, but rattling, out-and-out book-talk—and bristling with metaphor, too—just bristling! And as for command of language—why *you* never see a bluejay get stuck for a word. No man ever did. They just boil out of him! And another thing: I've noticed a good deal, and there's no bird, or cow, or anything that uses as good grammar as a bluejay. You may say a cat uses good grammar. Well, a cat does—but you let a cat get excited once; you let a cat get to pulling fur with another cat on a shed, nights, and you'll hear grammar that will give you lockjaw . . . Now I've never heard a jay use bad grammar but very seldom; and when they do, they are as ashamed as a human; they shut right down and leave.

You may call a jay a bird. Well, so he is, in a measure—because he's got feathers on him, and don't belong to no church, perhaps; but otherwise he is just as much a human as you be. And I'll tell you why. A jay's gifts, and instincts, and feelings, and interests, cover the whole ground. A jay hasn't any more principle than a Congressman . . . A jay can cry, a jay can laugh, a jay can feel shame, a jay can reason and plan and discuss, a jay likes gossip and scandal, a jay has got a sense of humor, a jay knows when he is an ass just as well as you do—maybe better. If a jay ain't human, he better take in his sign.

Ibid., Chapt. II, p. 24

The song of the nightingale is the deadliest known to ornithology. That demoniacal shriek can kill at thirty yards. The note of the cue-owl is infinitely soft and sweet—soft and sweet as the whisper of a flute. But penetrating—oh, beyond belief; it can bore through boiler-iron. It is a lingering note, and comes in triplets, on the one unchanging key: *hoo-o-o, hoo-o-o, hoo-o-o;* then a silence of fifteen seconds, then the triplet again; and so on, all night. At first it is divine; then less so; then trying; then distressing; then excruciating; then agonizing, and at the end of two hours the listener is a maniac.

Following the Equator, II, Chapt. XX, p. 242

Jim Baker's Bluejay Yarn:

There stands in (a lonely corner of California) a log
cabin, with a plank roof—just one big room . . . nothing
between the rafters and the floor. Well, one Sunday morning I was sitting in front of my cabin . . . when a bluejay
lit on that house, with an acorn in his mouth, and says,
"Hello, I reckon I've struck something." When he spoke, the
acorn dropped out of his mouth and rolled down the roof
. . . but he didn't care; his mind was all on the thing he
had struck. It was a knot-hole in the roof. He cocked his
head to one side, shut one eye and put the other one to the
hole, like a 'possum looking down a jug; then he glanced
up with his bright eyes, gave a wink or two with his wings
. . . and his tail both, and says, . . . "If I ain't in luck!—why
it's a perfectly elegant hole!" So he flew down and got that
acorn, and fetched it up and dropped it in, and was just
tilting his head back, with the heavenliest smile on his
face, when all of a sudden he was paralyzed into a listening
attitude and that smile faded gradually out of his countenance like breath off'n a razor, and the queerest look of
surprise took its place. Then he says, "Why, I didn't hear
it fall!" He cocked his eye at the hole again, and took a long
look; raised up and shook his head; . . . walked round and
round the hole and spied into it from every point of the
compass. No use. Now he took a thinking attitude . . . and
scratched the back of his head with his right foot a minute,
and finally says, "Well, it's too many for *me* . . . must be a
mighty long hole; however, . . . no time to fool around here,
I got to tend to business; I reckon it's all right—chance it,
anyway."

So he flew off and fetched another acorn and dropped
it in, and tried to flirt his eye to the hole quick enough to
see what become of it, but he was too late. He held his
eye there as much as a minute; then he raised up and
sighed, and says, "Confound it, I don't seem to understand
this thing . . . however I'll tackle her again." He fetched
another acorn, and done his level best to see what become
of it, but he couldn't. He says, "Well, I never struck no

such a hole as this before." Then he begun to get mad. He held in for a spell, walking up and down the comb of the roof and shaking his head and muttering to himself; but his feelings got the upper hand of him, presently, and he broke loose and cussed himself . . . I never see a bird take on so about a little thing. When he got through he walks to the hole and looks in again for half a minute; then he says, "Well, you're a long hole . . . and a mighty singular hole . . . but I've started in to fill you, and I'm damned if I *don't* fill you, if it takes a hundred years."

And with that, away he went. You never see a bird work so since you was born. He laid into his work . . . and the way he hove acorns into that hole for about two hours and a half was one of the most exciting and astonishing spectacles I ever struck. He never stopped to take a look any more—he just hove 'em in and went for more. Well, at last he could hardly flop his wings, he was so tuckered out. He comes a-drooping down, once more, sweating like an ice-pitcher, drops his acorn in and says, "*Now* I guess I've got the bulge on you by this time!" So he bent down for a look. If you'll believe me, when his head come up again he was just pale with rage. He says, "I've shoveled acorns enough in there to keep the family thirty years, and if I can see a sign of one of 'em I wish I may land in a museum with a belly full of sawdust."

He just had strength enough to crawl up on to the comb and lean his back agin the chimbly, and then he . . . begun to free his mind. I see in a second that what I mistook for profanity in the mines was only just the rudiments, as you may say.

Another jay was going by, and heard him doing his devotions, and stops to inquire what was up. The sufferer told him the whole circumstance, and says, "Now yonder's the hole, and if you don't believe me, go and look for yourself." So this fellow went and looked . . . He couldn't seem to make it out, so he raised a yell, and three more jays come. They all examined the hole . . . made the sufferer tell it

54

over again . . . discussed it, and got off as many leather-headed opinions about it as an average crowd of humans could have done.

They called in more jays; then more and more, till pretty soon this whole region 'peared to have a blue flush about it. Such jawing and disputing and ripping and cussing, you never heard. Every jay in the whole lot put his eye to the hole and delivered a . . . chuckle-headed opinion about the mystery . . . They examined the house all over, too. The door was standing half open, and at last one old jay happened to go and light on it and look in. Of course, that knocked the mystery galley-west. . There lay the acorns, scattered all over the floor. He flopped his wings and raised a whoop. "Come here." he says . . . "Hang'd if this fool hasn't been trying to fill up a house with acorns!" They all came a-swooping down . . . and as each fellow lit on the door and took a glance, the whole absurdity of the contract the first jay had tackled hit him home and he fell over backwards suffocating with laughter . . .

Well, sir, they roosted around here on the housetop and the trees for an hour, and guffawed over that thing like human beings. It ain't any use to tell me a bluejay hasn't got a sense of humor, because I know better. And memory, too. They brought jays here from all over the United States to look down that hole, every summer for three years. Other birds, too. And they could all see the point, except an owl that come from Nova Scotia to visit the Yo Semite, and he took this thing in on his way back. He said he couldn't see anything funny in it. But then he was a good deal disappointed about Yo Semite, too.

A Tramp Abroad, I, Chapt. III, p. 27

BIRTHDAY

Why is it that we rejoice at a birth and grieve at a funeral? It is because we are not the person involved.

"Pudd'nhead Wilson's Calendar"

Pudd'nhead Wilson, Chapt. IX, p. 82

(BIRTHDAY)

[Part of a speech delivered by Mark Twain at a dinner given at Delmonico's, Dec. 5, 1905, to celebrate his seventieth birthday]:

The seventieth birthday! It is the time of life when you arrive at a new and awful dignity; when you may throw aside the decent reserves which have oppressed you for a generation and stand unafraid and unabashed upon your seven-terraced summit and look down and teach—unrebuked. You can tell the world how you got there. It is what they all do. You shall never get tired of telling by what delicate arts and deep moralities you climb up to that great place . . .

I have achieved my seventy years in the usual way: by sticking strictly to a scheme of life which would kill anybody else. It sounds like an exaggeration, but that is really the common rule for attaining old age. When we examine the programme of any of these garrulous old people we always find that the habits which have preserved them would have decayed us . . . I will offer here, as a sound maxim, this: That we can't reach old age by another man's road.

Threescore and ten!

It is the Scriptural statute of limitations. After that, you owe no active duties; for you the strenuous life is over. You are a time-expired man, to use Kipling's military phrase: You have served your term, well or less well, and you are mustered out. You are become an honorary member of the republic, you are emancipated, compulsions are not for you, nor any bugle call but "lights out." You pay the time-worn duty bills if you choose, or decline if you prefer—and without prejudice—for they are not legally collectible.

The previous-engagement plea, which in forty years has cost you so many twinges, you can lay aside forever; on this side of the grave you will never need it again. If you shrink at thought of night, and winter, and the late home-coming from the banquet and the lights and the laughter through the deserted streets—a desolation which would not remind you now, as for a generation it did, that your friends are

56

sleeping, and you must creep in a-tiptoe and not disturb
them, but would only remind you that you need not tiptoe,
you can never disturb them more—if you shrink at thought
of these things, you need only reply, "Your invitation honors
me, and pleases me because you still keep me in your
remembrance, but I am seventy; seventy, and would nestle
in the chimney corner, and smoke my pipe, and read my
book, and take my rest, wishing you well in all affection,
and that when you in turn shall arrive at pier No. 70 you
may step aboard your waiting ship with a reconciled spirit,
and lay your course toward the sinking sun with a contented heart."

"Seventieth Birthday"
Mark Twain's Speeches [1923], p. 254

BLASTING   *See* EXAGGERATION

BLINDNESS   *See also* GENIUS, KELLER, HELEN
Blindness is an exciting business . . . If you don't believe it, get up some dark night on the wrong side of your
bed when the house is on fire and try to find the door.
Midstream, Helen Keller, p. 48

BLOOD   *See* WAR

BLUE JAY   *See* BIRDS

BLUNDER   *See* PROVIDENCE

BLUSH   *See also* DRINK, HEAT
Man is the only animal that blushes. Or needs to.
"Pudd'nhead Wilson's New Calendar,"
Following the Equator, I, Chapt. XXVII, p. 264
When the missionaries first took up their residence in
Honolulu, the native women would pay their families fre-
quent visits, day by day, not even clothed with a blush.
Roughing It, II, Chapt. XXVI, p. 241

BOAT   *See also* HUMAN RACE, SEA, SHIP, SIMILES, SLOWNESS

Perhaps *most* of them were not always reverent during that Holy Land trip. It was a trying journey, and after fierce days of desert hills the reaction might not always spare even the holiest memories. Jack was particularly sinful. When they learned the price for a boat on Galilee, and the deacons who had traveled nearly half around the world to sail on that sacred water were confounded by the charge, Jack said:

"Well, Denny, do you wonder now that Christ walked?"

> *Mark Twain, a Biography*, Paine, I, p. 337

"Just about the close of that long, hard winter," said the Sunday-school superintendent, "as I was wending toward my duties one brilliant Sabbath morning, I glanced down toward the levee, and there lay the City of Hartford!—no mistake about it, there she was, puffing and panting, after her long pilgrimage through the ice. A glad sight? Well, I should say so! And then came a pang, right away, because I should have to instruct empty benches, sure; the youngsters would all be off welcoming the first steamboat of the season. You can imagine how surprised I was when I opened the door and saw half the benches full! My gratitude was free, large, and sincere. I resolved that they should not find me unappreciative. I said: 'Boys, you cannot think how proud it makes me to see you here, nor what renewed assurance it gives me of your affection. I confess that I said to myself, as I came along and saw that the City of Hartford was in—'

" '*No! But is she, though!*'

"And as quick as any flash of lightning I stood in the presence of empty benches! I had brought them the news myself."

> "Memoranda," *The Galaxy Magazine*,
> May 1870, p. 726

At eight o'clock, promptly, we backed out and . . . crossed the river . . . the whole thing was over and done with before a mate in the olden time could have got his

profanity-mill adjusted to begin the preparatory services.
> *Life on the Mississippi,* Chapt. XXIII, p. 189

I never saw a finer show than the passage of that boat was, through the fierce turmoil of water. Alternately she rose high and plunged deep, throwing up sheets of foaming spray and shaking them off like a mane. Several times she seemed to fairly bury herself, and I thought she was gone for good, but always she sprang high aloft the next moment, a gallant and stirring spectacle to see.
> "Down the Rhone,"
> *Europe and Elsewhere,* p. 164

BODY *See* MAN, SOUL

BOOK *See also* CLASSIC, COPYRIGHT, CRITIC, HUMOR, IDEAL, INTEREST, LIBRARY, READER, SCOTT, SUCCESS, WRITING

There was some books, too, piled up perfectly exact, on each corner of the table. One was a big family Bible full of pictures. One was *Pilgrim's Progress,* about a man that left his family, it didn't say why. I read considerable in it now and then. The statements was interesting, but tough.
> *The Adventures of Huckleberry Finn,*
> Chapt. XVII, p. 141

If all poetry and nonsense that have been discharged upon the "fountains" and bland scenery of this region [The Holy Land], were collected in a book, it would make a most valuable volume to burn.
> *The Innocents Abroad,* II, Chapt. XX, p. 249

My books are water: those of the great geniuses are wine. Everybody drinks water.
> *Mark Twain's Notebook,* p. 190

There ain't nothing more to write about, and I am rotten glad of it, because if I'd a knowed what a trouble it was to make a book, I wouldn't a tackled it, and ain't a-going to no more.
> *The Adventures of Huckleberry Finn,*
> Chapt. the Last, p. 374

BORE

That oyster-brained bore . . . I was satisfied he was of too small a calibre to know how to receive an apology with magnanimity.

Mark Twain's Letters, I, p. 221

BOUNTY

. . . the governments of the world [have] tried [the bounty system], and wept over it, and discarded it, every half century since man was created. . .

. . . the best way to increase wolves in America, rabbits in Australia, and snakes in India, is to pay a bounty on their scalps. Then every patriot goes to raising them.

"Chapters from My Autobiography"
The North American Review, May 3, 1907, p. 3

BOYHOOD See also DISAPPOINTMENT, FIGHT, SCHOOL, WEATHER, WRITING

It reminds me of the journal I opened with the New Year, once, when I was a boy and a confiding and a willing prey to those impossible schemes of reform which well-meaning old maids and grandmothers set for the feet of unwary youths at that season of the year—setting oversized tasks for them, which, necessarily failing, as infallibly weaken the boy's strength of will, diminish his confidence in himself, and injure his chances of success in life. Please accept of an extract:

"Monday—Got up, washed, went to bed.

"Tuesday—Got up, washed, went to bed.

"Wednesday—Got up, washed, went to bed.

"Thursday—Got up, washed, went to bed.

"Friday—Got up, washed, went to bed.

"Friday fortnight—Got up, washed, went to bed.

"Following month—Got up, washed, went to bed."

I stopped, then, discouraged. Startling events appeared to be too rare, in my career, to render a diary necessary. I still reflect with pride, however, that even at that early age I washed when I got up.

The Innocents Abroad, II, Chapt. XXXII, p. 427

It is a glorious thing to be a boy's idol, for it is the only worship one can swear to as genuine.

Mark Twain to Mrs. Fairbanks, p. 169

Schoolboy days are no happier than the days of after life, but we look back upon them regretfully because we have forgotten our punishments at school, and how we grieved when our marbles were lost and our kites destroyed —because we have forgotten all the sorrows and privations of that canonized epoch and remember only its orchard robberies, its wooden sword pageants, and its fishing holidays.

The Innocents Abroad, II, Chapt. XXVII, p. 362

BRAINS *See also* ARISTOCRACY, FISH, INTELLECT, LOVE, LUCK, MIND, PLAGIARISM

. . . the insanity plea was a rather far-fetched compliment to pay the prisoner, inasmuch as one must first have brains before he can go crazy, and there was surely nothing in the evidence to show that McFarland had enough of the raw material to justify him in attempting anything more imposing than a lively form of idiocy.

"Unburlesquable Things,"
Galaxy Magazine, July 1870, p. 137

No man's brains ever originated an idea. It is an astonishing thing that after all these ages the world goes on thinking the human brain machinery can originate a thought. It can't. It never has done it. In all cases, little and big, the thought is born of a suggestion; and in *all* cases the suggestions come to the brain from the outside. The brain never acts except from exterior impulse.

. . .

Man's mind is a clever machine, and can work up materials into ingenuous fancies and ideas, but it can't create the material; none but the gods can do that.

Mark Twain's Letters, II, p. 813

BRAVERY *See also* IDEA

When a person in Joan of Arc's position tells a man he is brave, he *believes* it; and *believing* it is enough; in fact, to believe yourself brave is to *be* brave; it is the one only essential thing.

Personal Recollections of Joan of Arc,
I, Bk. II, Chapt. XI, p. 208

BREEDING

. . . there isn't anything you can't stand if you are only born and bred to it.

A Connecticut Yankee in King Arthur's Court,
Chapt. VIII, p. 68

Good breeding consists in concealing how much we think of ourselves and how little we think of the other person.

Mark Twain's Notebook, p. 345

BRIBERY

You cannot deny we would have to go without the services of some of our ablest men, sir, if the country were opposed to—to—bribery.

The Gilded Age, II, Chapt. IV, p. 55

BRIC-A-BRAC *See also* FOOD

I am proud to know that I lose my reason as immediately in the presence of a rare jug with an illustrious mark on the bottom of it, as if I had just emptied that jug.

A Tramp Abroad, I, Chapt. XX, p. 191

BROKER

The place where stocks are daily bought and sold is called by interested parties the . . . Board of Brokers, but by the impartial and disinterested the Den of the Forty Thieves; the latter name is regarded as the most poetic, but the former is considered the most polite.

"Daniel In the Lion's Den—and Out Again,"
Sketches of the Sixties, p. 144

BROTHERHOOD *See also* DEMOCRACY, PEACE

The universal brotherhood of man is our most precious possession—what there is of it.

Mark Twain's Notebook, p. 347

BROWNING, ROBERT *See also* READER

One's glimpses and confusions, as one reads Browning, remind me of looking through a telescope (the small sort which you must move with your hand, not clock-work). You toil across dark spaces which are (to *your* lens) empty; but every now and then a splendor of stars and suns bursts upon you and fills the whole field with flame.

Mark Twain, a Biography, Paine, II, p. 847

BRUTALITY

I said it was a brutal thing.

[Satan]: "No, it was a human thing. You should not insult the brutes by such a misuse of that word; they have not deserved it . . . It is like your paltry race—always lying, always claiming virtues which it hasn't got, always denying them to the higher animals, which alone possess them. No brute ever does a cruel thing—that is the monopoly of those with the Moral Sense. When a brute inflicts pain he does it innocently; it is not wrong; for him there is no such thing as wrong. And he does not inflict pain for the pleasure of inflicting it—only man does that. Inspired by that mongrel Moral Sense of his! A sense whose function is to distinguish between right and wrong, with liberty to choose which of them he will do. Now what advantage can he get out of that? He is always choosing, and in nine cases out of ten he prefers the wrong. There shouldn't be any wrong; and without the Moral Sense there couldn't be any. And yet he is such an unreasoning creature that he is not able to perceive that the Moral Sense degrades him to the bottom layer of animated beings and is a shameful possession."

The Mysterious Stranger, Etc., Chapt. V, p. 50

BUBBLES *See* BEAUTY, LIFE

BUFFOON

The thing that gravels [my wife] is that I am so persistently glorified as a mere buffoon, as if that entirely covered my case—which she denies with venom.

Mark Twain's Letters, I, p. 264

BUGLE   *See* MUSIC, TRAVEL

BULL   *See* EDUCATION

BURGLAR   *See* FRIGHT, GUN

BURLESQUE

It is not possible to write a burlesque so broad that some innocent will not receive it in good faith as being a solemn statement of fact.

"Memoranda," *Galaxy* magazine,
Sept. 1870, p. 431

BUSINESS   *See* JEWS

BUSY   *See* SIMILES

C

CABBAGE *See* TRAINING

CAIN

. . . we have an insanity plea that would have saved Cain.

"Americans and the English,"
Mark Twain's Speeches (1923), p. 35

There are some natures which never grow large enough to speak out and say a bad act *is* a bad act, until they have inquired into the politics of the nationality of the man who did it. And they are not really scarce, either. Cain is branded a murderer so heartily and unanimously in America, only because he was neither a Democrat nor a Republican. The Feejee Islander's abuse of Cain ceased very suddenly when the white man mentioned casually that Cain was a Feejee Islander. The next remark of the savage, after an awkward pause, was:

"Well, what did Abel come fooling around there for?"

"Memoranda," *Galaxy Magazine*,
May 1870, p. 762

After Adam, my ancestor was Cain, who married his sister Mary Ann, and had by her a litter of sons and daughters who were also his nephews and nieces. It made a good deal of talk.

Marginal Note in *Views of Religion,* Noyes

CALAMITY   *See also* RAFTSMEN

The calamity that comes is never the one we had prepared ourselves for. [1896]

Love Letters of Mark Twain, p. 317

CALIFORNIA   *See also* FUNERAL, OPERA, SAN FRANCISCO, WIND

. . . all scenery in California requires *distance* to give it its highest charm. The mountains are imposing in their sublimity and their majesty of form and altitude, from any point of view—but one must have distance to soften their ruggedness and enrich their tintings; a Californian forest is best at a little distance, for there is a sad poverty of variety in species, the trees being chiefly of one monotonous family—redwood, pine, spruce, fir—and so, at a near view there is a wearisome sameness of attitude in their rigid arms, stretched downward and outward in one continued and reiterated appeal to all men to "Sh!—don't say a word! —You might disturb somebody!" Close at hand, too, there is a reliefless and relentless smell of pitch and turpentine; there is a ceaseless melancholy in their sighing and complaining foliage; one walks over a soundless carpet of beaten yellow bark and dead spines of the foliage till he feels like a wandering spirit bereft of a footfall . . .

Roughing It, II, Chapt. XV, p. 148

CALCULATION   *See* EUROPE

CALMNESS   *See* FRENCH PEOPLE

CAMEL   *See also* SHUDDER

In Syria, once, at the head-waters of the Jordan, a camel took charge of my overcoat while the tents were being pitched, and examined it with a critical eye, all over, with as much interest as if he had an idea of getting one made like it; and then, after he was done figuring on it as an article of apparel, he began to contemplate it as an article of diet. He put his foot on it, and lifted one of the sleeves out with his teeth, and chewed and chewed at it, gradually taking it in, and all the while opening and closing his eyes in a kind of religious ecstasy, as if he had never tasted anything as good as an overcoat before in his life. Then he smacked his lips once or twice, and reached after the other sleeve. Next he tried the velvet collar, and smiled a smile of such contentment that it was plain to see that he regarded that as the daintiest thing about an overcoat. The tails went next, along with some percussion caps and cough candy, and some fig-paste from Constantinople. And then my newspaper correspondence dropped out, and he took a chance in that—manuscript letters written for the home papers. But he was treading on dangerous ground, now. He began to come across solid wisdom in those documents that was rather weighty on his stomach; and occasionally he would take a joke that would shake him up till it loosened his teeth; it was getting to be perilous times with him, but he held his grip with good courage and hopefully, till at last he began to stumble on statements that not even a camel could swallow with impunity. He began to gag and gasp, and his eyes to stand out, and his forelegs to spread, and in about a quarter of a minute he fell over as stiff as a carpenter's work-bench, and died a death of indescribable agony. I went and pulled the manuscript out of his mouth, and found that the sensitive creature had choked to death on one of the mildest and gentlest statements of fact that I ever laid before a trusting public.

Roughing It, I, Chapt. III, p. 32

CAPACITY

To succeed in the other trades, capacity must be shown; in the law, concealment of it will do.

"Pudd'nhead Wilson's New Calendar,"
Following the Equator, II, Chapt. I, p. 11

CAPITAL *See* DOG

CARD GAMES *See* CONFIDENCE, GAMES, SHIP

CARE *See* FORGETFULNESS

CARNEGIE, ANDREW *See* HYMN-BOOK, IRISHMEN

CARPET *See* EXAGGERATION

CASTES
You see, in a country where they have ranks and castes, a man isn't ever a man, he is only part of a man, he can't ever get his full growth.
> *A Connecticut Yankee in King Arthur's Court,*
> Chapt. XXXIII, p. 294

. . . Caste does not exist and cannot exist except by common consent of the masses outside of its limits. I thought caste created itself and perpetuated itself; but it seems quite true that it only creates itself, and is perpetuated by the people whom it despises.
> *The American Claimant, Etc.,* Chapt. XI, p. 93

CAT *See also* DOG, EDUCATION, FABLE, GERMAN LANGUAGE, HOME, MOTHER, PUN, VALUE
One of the most striking differences between a cat and a lie is that a cat has only nine lives.
> "Pudd'nhead Wilson's Calendar,"
> *Pudd'nhead Wilson,* Chapt. VII, p. 63

We should be careful to get out of an experience only the wisdom that is in it—and stop there; lest we be like the cat that sits down on a hot stove-lid. She will never sit down on a hot stove-lid again—and that is well; but also she will never sit down on a cold one any more.
> "Pudd'nhead Wilson's New Calendar,"
> *Following the Equator,* I, Chapt. XI, p. 125

Of all God's creatures there is only one that cannot be made the slave of the lash. That one is the cat. If man could be crossed with the cat it would improve man, but it would deteriorate the cat.

Mark Twain's Notebook, p. 236

She had a disgraceful old yellow cat that she thought as much of as if he was twins.

Punch, Brothers, Punch, p. 71

CATACOMBS   *See also* TOMB

[In Rome]: I naturally pass to the picturesque horrors of the Capuchin Convent. . . . Here was a spectacle for sensitive nerves! Evidently the old masters had been at work in this place . . . decorations were in every instance formed of human bones! There were shapely arches, built wholly of thigh bones; there were startling pyramids, built wholly of grinning skulls; there were quaint architectural structures . . . built of shin bones and the bones of the arm; on the wall were elaborate frescoes, whose curving vines were made of knotted human vertebrae; whose delicate tendrils were made of sinews and tendons; whose flowers were formed of knee-caps and toe-nails . . . there was a careful finish about the work, and an attention to details that betrayed the artist's love of his labors as well as his schooled ability. . . .

"These are the bones of four thousand departed monks."

"Their different parts are well separated—skulls in one room, legs in another, ribs in another—there would be stirring times here for a while if the last trump should blow. Some of the brethren might get hold of the wrong leg, in the confusion, and the wrong skull, and find themselves limping, and looking through eyes that were wider apart or closer together than they were used to."

The Innocents Abroad, II, Chapt. I, p. 9

CATHEDRAL

I tried all the different ways I could think of to compel myself to understand how large St. Peter's was, but with small success. . . . It is estimated that the floor of the church affords standing room for—for a large number of people; I have forgotten the exact figures. But it is no matter—it is near enough.

Innocents Abroad, I, Chapt. XXVI, p. 347

(Cathedral of Milan): What a wonder it is! So grand, so solemn, so vast! . . . How sharply its pinnacled angles and its wilderness of spires were cut against the sky, and how richly their shadows fell upon its snowy roof! It was a vision!—a miracle!—an anthem sung in stone, a poem wrought in marble! . . . In the midst of . . . the rank on rank of carved and fretted spires . . . the central steeple towers proudly sweep up like the mainmast of some great Indiaman among a fleet of coasters.

Ibid., Chapt. XVIII, p. 226

CAULIFLOWER   *See* TRAINING

CAYOTE   *See* DOG, FLEA, SPEED, WANT

CEMETARY   *See* DOG

CENSURE   *See* COMPLIMENT

CERTAINTY   *See* REPUTATION

CHAMELEON   *See* CONGRESSMAN, PREJUDICE

CHANCE   *See* DENTISTRY, LIFE, NECESSITY

CHANGE   *See also* CONSISTENCY, TEETH

We leave for Boston tomorrow to give Livy a week's rest and change of aggravations—usually styled "change of scene."

Mark Twain, Business Man, p. 146

We change and *must* change constantly, and keep on changing as long as we live. What then is the true gospel of consistency? *Change.*

Mark Twain's Speeches (1923), p. 121

Change is the handmaiden Nature requires to do her miracles with. The land that has four well-defined seasons cannot lack beauty, or pall with monotony. Each season brings a world of enjoyment and interest in the watching of its unfolding, its gradual, harmonious development, its culminating graces—and just as one begins to tire of it, it passes away and a radical change comes, with new witcheries and new glories in its train. And I think that to one in sympathy with nature, each season, in its turn, seems the loveliest.

Roughing It, II, Chapt. XV, p. 150

How stunning are the changes which age makes in a man while he sleeps. When I finished Carlyle's *French Revolution* in 1871, I was a Girondin; every time I have read it since, I have read it differently—being influenced and changed, little by little, by life and environment (and Taine and St. Simon): and now I lay the book down once more, and recognize that I am a Sansculotte!—and not a pale, characterless Sansculotte, but a Marat. Carlyle teaches no such gospel: so the change is in *me*—in my vision of the evidences.

People pretend that the Bible means the same to them at 50 that it did at all former milestones in their journey. I wonder how they can lie so. It comes of practice, no doubt. They would not say that of Dickens' or Scott's books. *Nothing* remains the same. When a man goes back to look at the house of his childhood, it has always *shrunk*: there is no instance of such a house being as big as the picture in memory and imagination call for. Shrunk how? Why, to its correct dimensions: the house hasn't altered; this is the first time it has been in focus.

Well, that's loss. To have house and Bible shrink so, under the disillusioning corrected angle, is loss—for a moment. But there are compensations. You tilt the tube skyward and bring planets and comets and corona flames a hundred and fifty thousand miles high into the field.

Mark Twain's Letters, II, p. 490

71

CHARACTER *See also* MISSISSIPPI RIVER, MONOTONY, SUSPICION

One must keep up one's character. Earn a character first if you can, and if you can't, then assume one. From the code of morals I have been following and revising and revising for 72 years I remember one detail. All my life I have been honest—comparatively honest. I could never use money I had not made honestly—I could only lend it.

"General Miles and the Dog,"
Mark Twain's Speeches (1910), p. 394

There is no character, howsoever good and fine, but it can be destroyed by ridicule, howsoever poor and witless. Observe the ass, for instance: his character is about perfect, he is the choicest spirit among all the humbler animals, yet see what ridicule has brought him to. Instead of feeling complimented when we are called an ass, we are left in doubt.

"Pudd'nhead Wilson's Calendar,"
Pudd'nhead Wilson, p. vii

Character is the architect of achievements.

"A Defense of General Funston,"
North American Review, May 1902, p. 614

Earn a character if you can, and if you can't then assume one.

Mark Twain's Speeches (1910), p. 394

CHARITY *See also* AGE, REPENTANCE

I do seem to be extraordinarily interested in a whole lot of arts and things that I have got nothing to do with. It is a part of my generous, liberal nature; I can't help it. I feel the same sort of charity to everybody that was manifested by a gentleman who arrived at home at two o'clock in the morning from the club and was feeling so perfectly satisfied with life, so happy, and so comfortable, and there was his house weaving, weaving, weaving around. He watched his chance, and by and by when the steps got in his neighborhood he made a jump and climbed up and got on the portico.

And the house went on weaving and weaving and weaving, but he watched the door, and when it came around his way he plunged through it. He got to the stairs, and when he went up on all fours the house was so unsteady that he could hardly make his way, but at last he got to the top and raised his foot and put it on the top step. But only the toe hitched on the step, and he rolled down and fetched up on the bottom step, with his arm around the newel-post, and he said: "God pity the poor sailors out at sea on a night like this."

> "Copyright,"
> *Mark Twain's Speeches* (1910), p. 320

CHASTITY   *See* SPELLING, PRINTING

CHEATING

. . . one day St. Peter and the devil chanced to be thrown together, and found it pretty dull to pass the time. Finally they got to throwing dice for a lawyer. The devil threw sixes. Then St. Peter threw sixes. The devil threw sixes once more. Then St. Peter threw sevens, and the devil said: "Oh, come now, Your Honor, cheat fair. None of your playing miracles here."

> "O'Shah," *Europe and Elsewhere*, p. 72

CHEERFULNESS   *See also* DUTY, HOPE, WOMAN

A healthy and wholesome cheerfulness is not necessarily impossible to any occupation.

> "The Undertaker's Chat,"
> *Sketches New and Old*, p. 329

The best way to cheer yourself is to try to cheer somebody else up.

> *Mark Twain's Notebook*, p. 310

CHICAGO   *See also* PROFANITY, SATAN

Chicago changes so fast that, every time you visit it, it seems like going to a new city. They are erecting many fine buildings in St. Louis, but they are erecting many more and finer buildings in Chicago.

Chicago is a wonderful place. It numbers among its citizens more active, bold, thoroughly enterprising men than does any city in the Union, possibly save New York. It is the center, as you know, of a vast railway system which drains the country in every direction.

Other communities have what they consider their own legitimate country about them to back them up, and they regard their sovereignty over such regions as unimpeachable. Chicago recognizes no such sovereignties. She marches right into the enemy's country with her railroads, with an audacity which is delightful, and, in a very short time, she breaks down the "divine right" prejudices of that region and takes the trade.

It is a maxim in less feverish communities that, whenever a railroad to any place makes itself a necessity, it will be built—that is, whenever there shall be trade enough to warrant it. Chicago has changed all that. Wherever she finds a place to build a railroad to—she builds a railroad to that place. She creates trade thereafterward easily enough.

Three out of every five men you meet in Chicago have a live, shrewd, cosmopolitan look in their faces. These are the sort of people who have made the city what it is and will yet double its wealth, its population, and its importance. [1868]

Alta California, Nov. 15, 1868

CHICKEN   *See also* NOISE, PROVIDENCE

F. called upstairs to know what part of the chicken I wanted—told him to give me the port side for'rard of the wheel.

Mark Twain to Mrs. Fairbanks, p. 67

CHILD   *See also* BIBLE, FATHER, MEDICINE, MORALS, TEMPER, YOUTH

Yesterday a thunder-stroke fell upon me . . . I found that all their lives my children have been afraid of me . . . All the concentrated griefs of fifty years seemed colorless by the side of that pathetic revelation. [1886]

Mark Twain-Howells Letters, II, p. 575

[Re the baby, nearly 2 years old]: Every time she discontinues a mispronunciation, and enters upon the correct form of pronouncing that word, never to retreat from it again, and never again to charm our ears with the music that was in the old lame sound of it, we feel that something that was precious has gone from us to return no more; a subtle, elusive, but nevertheless *real* sense of loss—and when we analyze it we find that the meaning of it is, that we are losing our *baby*—she is becoming a little girl, to blend with the vast and arid wastes of unindividualized little girlhood and cease to be a centre of wondering admiration, a rich unfailing source of daily and hourly surprises. [1876]

Mark Twain to Mrs. Fairbanks, p. 193

The irritating thing about ungoverned children is that they often make as orderly and valuable men and women as do the other kind.

Mark Twain's Notebook, p. 266

Rev. Charles Stowe took his little seven-year old son with him to Chicago to attend a Convention of Congregational clergymen. During the trip he reminded the boy now and then that he must be on his best behavior there. He said: "We shall be the guests of a clergyman, there will be other guests—clergymen and their wives—and you must be careful to let those people see by your walk and conversation that you are of a godly household." The admonition bore fruit. At the first breakfast which they ate in the Chicago clergyman's house he heard his little son say in the meekest and most reverent way to the lady opposite him,

"Please, won't you, for Christ's sake, pass the butter?"

"Chapters from My Autobiography,"
North American Review, Dec. 7, 1906, p. 1095

The burnt child shuns the fire until the next day.

More Maxims of Mark, p. 6

The earned heartbreak of a little child must be high and honorable testimony for a parting spirit to carry before the throne.

Mark Twain to Mrs. Fairbanks, p. 193

. . . nothing pleases a child so much as to be a member of something or other. Your rightly constituted child don't care chucks what it is, either. I joined the Cadets of Temperance, once, when I was a boy. That was an awful take-in; no smoking or anything allowed—not even any bad language; but they had beautiful red scarfs. I stood it three months, and then sidled out. I liked the red scarfs well enough, but I could not stand the morality.

"Missionary Business,"
Mark Twain's Travels with Mr. Brown, p. 211

We are always too busy for our children; we never give them the time nor the interest they deserve. We lavish gifts upon them; but the most precious gift—our personal association, which means so much to them—we give grudgingly and throw it away on those who care for it so little. But we are repaid for it at last. There comes a time when we want their company and their interest. We want it more than anything in the world, and we are likely to be starved for it, just as they were starved so long ago. There is no appreciation of my books that is so precious to me as appreciation from my children. Theirs is the praise we want, and the praise we are least likely to get.

Mark Twain, a Biography, Paine, III, p. 1299

CHINA *See* MISSIONARY, MONEY

CHOIR *See* MUSIC, SINGING

CHRISTIAN SCIENCE *See also* HUMAN RACE, ILLNESS, MIND, UNCLE

[From a letter to J. Wylie Smith, Aug. 7, 1909]:

My view of the matter has not changed. To-wit, that

Christian Science is valuable; that it has just the same value now that it had when Mrs. Eddy stole it from Quimby; that its healing principle (its most valuable asset) possesses the same force now that it possessed a million years before Quimby was born; that Mrs. Eddy the fraud . . . *organized* that force and is *entitled to high credit for that.* Then with a splendid sagacity she hitched it to the shirt-tail of a religion—the surest of all ways to secure friends for it, and support.

Mark Twain's Letters, II, p. 833

Christian Science is humanity's boon.

Mark Twain, a Biography, Paine, III, p. 1271

CHRISTIANITY *See also* BOAT, CLIMATE, CONFIDENCE, KILLING, LOGIC, LUCK, MORALS, PATRIOTISM, PEACE, PRINCIPLE, PUNISHMENT, RELIGION, SURVIVAL, WEAKNESS

If Christ were here now there is one thing he would not be—a Christian.

Mark Twain's Notebook, p. 328

A man can be a Christian *or* a patriot, but he can't legally be a Christian *and* a patriot—except in the usual way: one of the two with the mouth, the other with the heart. The spirit of Christianity proclaims the brotherhood of the race and the meaning of that strong word has not been left to guesswork, but made tremendously definite—the Christian must forgive his brother man all crimes he can imagine and commit, and all insults he can conceive and utter—forgive these injuries how many times?—seventy times seven—another way of saying there shall be no limit to this forgiveness. That is the spirit and the law of Christianity. Well—patriotism has *its* law. And it also is a perfectly definite one, there are no vaguenesses about it. It commands that the brother over the border shall be sharply watched and brought to book every time he does us a hurt or offends us with an insult. Word it as softly as you please, the spirit of patriotism is the spirit of the dog and the wolf. The moment there is a misunderstanding about a boundary line or a hamper of fish or some other squalid matter, see patriotism rise, and hear him split the universe with his war-whoop. The spirit of patriotism being in its nature jealous and selfish, is just in man's line, it comes natural to him—he can live up to all its requirements to the letter; but the spirit of Christianity is not in its entirety possible to him.

The prayer concealed in what I have been saying is, not that patriotism should cease and not that the talk about universal brotherhood should cease, but that the incongruous firm be dissolved and each limb of it be required to transact business by itself, for the future.

Ibid., p. 332

All that is great and good in our particular civilization came straight from the hand of Jesus Christ.

Mark Twain, the Man and His Work,
Wagenknecht, p. 206

The so-called Christian nations are the most enlightened and progressive . . . but in spite of their religion, not because of it. The Church has opposed every innovation and discovery from the day of Galileo down to our own time, when the use of anesthetics in childbirth was regarded as a sin because it avoided the biblical curse pronounced against Eve. And every step in astronomy and geology ever taken has been opposed by bigotry and superstition. The Greeks surpassed us in artistic culture and in architecture five hundred years before the Christian religion was born.

Mark Twain, a Biography, Paine, III, p. 1534

All Christendom is a soldier-camp. The poor have been taxed in some nations to the starvation point to support the giant armaments which the Christian governments have built up, each to protect itself from the rest of the Christian brotherhood.

Ibid., p. 1467

CHRISTMAS *See* SANTA CLAUS, TELEPHONE

CHURCH *See also* CATHEDRAL, CONGREGATION, LECTURING, MISSIONARY, MORALS, NOSE, RELIGION, REPENTANCE, REVERENCE, SIMILES, SINGING

The church is always trying to get other people to reform; it might not be a bad idea to reform itself a little, by way of example. It is still clinging to one or two things which were useful once, but which are not useful now, neither are they ornamental. One is the bell ringing to remind a clock-caked town that it is church time, and another is the reading from the pulpit of a tedious list of "notices" which everybody who is interested has already read in the newspaper. The clergyman even reads the hymn through—a relic of an ancient time when hymn books were scarce and costly; but everybody has a hymn book, now, and so the public reading is no longer necessary. It is not merely unnecessary, it is generally painful; for the average clergyman could not fire into his congregation with a shotgun and hit a worse reader than himself, unless the weapon scattered shamefully. I am not meaning to be flippant and irreverent, I am only meaning to be truthful. The average clergyman, in all countries and of all denominations, is a very bad reader. One would think he would at least learn how to read the Lord's Prayer, by and by, but it is not so. He races through it as if he thought the quicker he got it in, the sooner it would be answered. A person who does not appreciate the exceeding value of pauses, and does not know how to measure their duration judiciously, cannot render the grand simplicity and dignity of a composition like that effectively.

A Tramp Abroad, II, Chapt. VII, p. 92

The altar cloth of one aeon is the doormat of the next.

Mark Twain's Notebook, p. 346

CHURCHILL, WINSTON

There was talk of that soaring and brilliant young statesman, Winston Churchill . . . I had met him at Sir Gilbert Parker's seven years before, when he was twenty-three years old, and had met him and introduced him to his lecture audience a year later in New York, when he had come over to tell of lively experiences he had had as a war correspondent in the South African war, and in one or two wars on the Himalayan frontier of India.

Sir Gilbert said, "Do you remember the dinner here seven years ago?"

"Yes," I said, "I remember it."

"Do you remember what Sir William Vernon Harcourt said about you?"

"No."

"Well, you didn't hear it. You and Churchill went to the top floor to have a smoke and a talk, and Harcourt wondered what the result would be. He said that whichever of you got the floor first would keep it to the end, without a break; he believed that you, being old and experienced, would get it and that Churchill's lungs would have a half-hour's rest for the first time in five years. When you two came down, by and by, Sir William asked Churchill if he had had a good time, and he answered eagerly, 'Yes.' Then he asked you if you had had a good time. You hesitated, then said without eagerness, 'I have had a smoke.'"

Mark Twain in Eruption, p. 330

CIRCUMSTANCE   *See also* INFLUENCE

Circumstances make man, not man circumstances.

Mark Twain's Notebook, p. 379

A man may *plan* as much as he wants to, but nothing of consequence is likely to come of it until the magician *circumstance* steps in and takes the matter off his hands.

"The Turning Point of My Life,"
What Is Man? and Other Essays, p. 133

Even the clearest and most perfect circumstantial evidence is likely to be at fault, after all, and therefore ought to be received with great caution. Take the case of any pencil, sharpened by any woman: if you have witnesses, you will find she did it with a knife; but if you take simply the aspect of the pencil, you will say she did it with her teeth.

"Pudd'nhead Wilson's Calendar,"
Pudd'nhead Wilson, Chapt. XX, p. 195

CITIZENSHIP *See also* COUNTRY, GOVERNMENT

A little of citizenship ought to be taught at the mother's knee and in the nursery. Citizenship is what makes a republic; monarchies can get along without it. What keeps a republic on its legs is good citizenship.

"Layman's Sermon,"
Mark Twain's Speeches (1923), p. 281

. . . every citizen of the republic ought to consider himself an unofficial policeman, and keep unsalaried watch and ward over the laws and their execution.

"Traveling With a Reformer,"
Literary Essays, p. 97

CIVILIZATION *See also* EXPERIENCE, HUMAN RACE

Civilization is a limitless multiplication of unnecessary necessaries.

More Maxims of Mark, p. 6

My idea of our civilization is that it is a shoddy, poor thing and full of cruelties, vanities, arrogances, meannesses and hypocrisies.

Mark Twain, a Biography, Paine, II, p. 1096

Would it not be prudent to get our Civilization tools together, and see how much stock is left on hand in the way of Glass Beads and Theology, and Maxim Guns and Hymn Books, and Trade Gin and Torches of Progress and Enlightenment (patent adjustable ones, good to fire villages with, upon occasion), and balance the books, and arrive at the profit and loss, so that we may intelligently decide whether to continue the business or sell out the property and start a new Civilization Scheme on the proceeds?

"To the Person Sitting in Darkness,"
Europe and Elsewhere, p. 255

We easily perceive that the peoples furthest from civilization are the ones where equality between man and woman are furthest apart—and we consider this one of the signs of savagery. But we are so stupid that we can't see that we thus plainly admit that no civilization can be perfect until exact equality between man and woman is included.

Mark Twain's Notebook, p. 256

. . . one of the worst things about civilization is, that anybody that gits a letter with trouble in it comes and tells you all about it and makes you feel bad, and the newspapers fetches you the troubles of everybody all over the world, and keeps you downhearted and dismal 'most all the time, and it's such a heavy load for a person.

Tom Sawyer Abroad, Etc., Chapt. VII, p. 67

What is "real" civilization? Nobody can answer that conundrum. Any system which has in it: human slavery, despotic government, inequality, numerous and brutal punishments for crime, superstition almost universal, ignorance almost universal—and dirt and poverty almost universal—is *not* a real civilization, and any system which has none of them is. . . .

How old is real civilization? A century ago it had not appeared anywhere in the world during a single instant since the world was made. Civilization must surely mean the humanizing of a people, not a class. There is to-day but one real civilization in the world. We . . . hoisted its flag when we disposed of slavery.

Mark Twain's Speeches (1923), p. 150

CLAM   *See also* OYSTER

Although I am debarred from making a speech by circumstances which I will presently explain, I yet claim the privilege of adding my voice to yours in deep and sincere welcome and homage to Edwin Booth; of adding my admiration of his long and illustrious career and blemishless character; and thereto my gratification in the consciousness that his great sun is not yet westering, but stands in full glory in the zenith.

I wish to ask your attention to a statement, in writing. It is not safe or wise to trust a serious matter to off-hand speech—especially when you are trying to explain a thing. Now, to make a clean breast, and expose the whole trouble right at the start, I have been entertaining a stranger; I have been at it two days and two nights, and am worn and jaded, and, in fact, defeated. He may be known to some of you. He is classified in natural history as the Long Clam, and in my opinion is the most disastrous fish that swims the sea. If you don't know him personally, let him alone; take him at hearsay, and meddle no further. He is a bivalve. When in his ulster, he is shaped like a weaver's shuttle, but there the resemblance ends: the weaver's shuttle travels, but the Long Clam abides; and you can digest a weaver's shuttle, if you wait, and pray. It is your idea, of course, to entertain yourself with the Long Clam; so you lay him on a bed of coals; he opens his mouth like a carpet-sack and smiles; this looks like mutual regard, and you think you are friends, but it is not so: that smile means, "it is your innings now—I'll see you later." You swallow the Long Clam—and history begins. It begins, but it begins so remotely, so clandestinely that you don't know it. You have several hours which you can't tell from repose. Then you go to bed. You close your eyes and think you are gliding off to sleep. It is at this point that the Long Clam rises up and goes to the bat. The window rattles; the Long Clam calls your attention to it. You whirl out of bed and wedge the sash—the wrong sash. You get nearly to sleep; the sash rattles again. The Long Clam reminds you. You whirl out and pound in some more wedges. You plunge into bed with emphasis; a sort of bogus unconsciousness begins to dull your brain; then some water begins to drip somewhere. Every drop that falls, hurts. You think you will try mind-cure on that drip and so neutralize its effects. This causes the Long Clam to smile. You chafe and fret for fifteen minutes, then you earthquake yourself out of bed and explore for that drip with a breaking heart, and language to match. But you never find it. When you go back to bed this time, you understand that your faculties are all up for the night, there is business on hand, and you have got to superintend. The procession begins to move. All the crimes you have ever committed, and which you supposed you had forgotten, file past—and every one of them carries a banner. The

(CLAM)

Long Clam is on hand to comment. All the dead and buried indignities you have ever suffered, follow; they bite like fangs, they burn like fire. The Long Clam is getting in his work, now. He has dug your conscience out and occupied the old stand; and you will find that for real business, one Long Clam is worth thirty consciences. The rest of that night is slow torture at the stake. There are lucid instants at intervals, occupied by dreams; dreams that stay only half a second, but they seem to expose the whole universe, and disembowel it before your eyes; other dreams that sweep away the solar system and leave the shoreless void occupied from one end to the other by just you and the Long Clam. Now you know what it is to sit up with a Long Clam. Now you know what it is to try to entertain a Long Clam. Now you know what it is to try to keep a Long Clam amused; to try to keep a Long Clam from feeling lonesome; to try to make a Long Clam satisfied and happy. As for me, I would rather go on an orgy with anybody in the world than a Long Clam: I would rather never have any fun at all than try to get it out of a Long Clam. A Long Clam doesn't know when to stop. After you've had all the fun you want, the Long Clam is just getting fairly started. In my opinion there is too much company about a Long Clam. A Long Clam is more sociable than necessary. I've got this one along yet. It's two days, now, and this is the third night, as far as I've got. In all that time I haven't had a wink of sleep that didn't have an earthquake in it, or a cyclone, or an instantaneous photograph of Sheol. And so all that is left of me is a dissolving rag or two of former humanity and a fading memory of happier days; the rest is Long Clam. That is the explanation. That is why I don't make a speech. I am perfectly willing to make speeches for myself, but I am not going to make speeches for any Long Clam that ever fluttered. Not after the way I've been treated. Not that I don't respect the Long Clam, for I do. I consider the Long Clam by long odds the capablest creature that swims the salt sea; I consider that Long Clam the Depew of the watery world, just as I consider Depew the

Long Clam of the great world of intellect and oratory. If any of you find life uneventful, lacking variety, not picturesque enough for you, go into partnership with a Long Clam.

An unpublished speech by Mark Twain, circa 1885

CLASS
The master minds of all nations, in all ages, have sprung in affluent multitude from the mass of the nation . . . not from its privileged classes.

A Connecticut Yankee in King Arthur's Court, p. 220

CLASSIC   *See also* READER
Classic: A book which people praise but don't read.

Following the Equator, I, Chapt. XXV, p. 245

CLEMENS, SAMUEL L.   *See also* DEBT, DESCRIPTION, FAMILY, MARK TWAIN'S, TWAIN, MARK
Mark Twain's real name was Samuel Langhorne Clemens. His wife was Olivia Langdon Clemens. His family consisted of: one son, Langdon, who died at the age of 1½ years (1872); three daughters—Susan Olivia, who died at the age of 24 (1896), Jean, who died at the age of 29 (1909), and Clara Langdon, died at 88, in California (1962).

CLERGYMAN   *See also* CHURCH, ENGLAND, MINISTER, PREACHER, READER, SUNDAY
I always travel with clergymen when I can. It is better for them, it is better for me. And any preacher who goes out with me in stormy weather and without a lightning rod is a good one.

"Speech in Aid of the Blind,"
Mark Twain's Speeches (1910), p. 328
Minister to ship captain who is complaining of deserting sailors: "Don't swear captain, that won't mend the matter."
Captain: "Brother Damon, it's all very well for you to say, don't swear, and it's all right too—I don't say anything

against it—but don't you know that if you should ship a crew of sailors for Heaven and were to stop at Hell 2½ hrs. for provisions, some damned son-of-a-gun would run away."

Mark Twain's Notebook, p. 24

There was a little clergyman who was prone to jump at conclusions sometimes. One day he was invited to officiate at a christening. He went. There sat the relatives—intelligent-looking relatives they were. The little clergyman's instinct came to him to make a great speech. He was given to flights of oratory that way—a very dangerous thing, for often the wings which take one into the clouds of oratorical enthusiasm are wax and melt up there, and down you come.

But the little clergyman couldn't resist. He took the child in his arms, and, holding it, looked at it a moment. It wasn't much of a child. It was a little like a sweet potato. Then the little clergyman waited impressively, and then: "I see in your countenances," he said, "disappointment of him. I see you are disappointed with this baby. Why? Because he is so little. My friends, if you had but the power of looking into the future you might see that great things may come of little things. There is the great ocean, holding the navies of the world, which come from little drops of water no larger than a woman's tears. There are the great constellations in the sky, made up of little bits of stars. Oh, if you could consider his future you might see that he might become the greatest poet of the universe, the greatest warrior the world has ever known, greater than Caesar, than Hannibal, than—er—er" (turning to the father) "what's his name?"

The father hesitated, then whispered back: "His name? Well, his name is Mary Ann."

"Education and Citizenship,"
Mark Twain's Speeches (1923), p. 380

Benefit of Clergy: Half rate on the railroad.

More Maxims of Mark, p. 6

CLEVELAND, GROVER *See also* MORALS

[From a letter to Miss Jean Clemens, June 19, 1908]:

Mr. Cleveland? Yes, he was a drinker in Buffalo, and loose morally. But *since* then? I have to doubt it. And of course I *want* to doubt it, for he has been a most noble public servant—and in that capacity he has been utterly without blemish. Of all our public men of today he stands first in my reverence and admiration, and the next one stands two-hundred-and-twenty-fifth. He is the only statesman we have now. We had two, but Senator Hoar is dead. Drinks? No, I hope it is a mistake. However, Cleveland *drunk* is a more valuable asset to this country than the whole batch of the rest of our public men *sober*. He is high-minded; all his impulses are great and pure and fine. I wish we had another of this sort.

From a hitherto unpublished letter

CLIMATE   *See also* COLD, FRANCE, VARIETY, WEATHER
It is your human environment that makes climate.
"Pudd'nhead Wilson's New Calendar,"
Following the Equator, I, Chapt. IX, p. 107
Fort Yuma is probably the hottest place on earth. The thermometer stands at 120 degrees in the shade there all the time—except when it varies and goes higher. The occupants get so used to the terrific heat that they suffer without it. There is a tradition . . . that a very, very wicked soldier died there, once, and of course, went straight to the hottest corner of perdition—and the next day he *telegraphed back for his blankets*.
Roughing It, II, Chapt. XV, p. 153
[In Nevada]: Sometimes we have the seasons in their regular order, and then again we have winter all the summer and summer all winter. Consequently, we have never yet come across an almanac that would just exactly fit this latitude. It is mighty regular about not raining, though . . . It will start in here in November and rain about four, and sometimes as much as seven days on a stretch; after that, you may loan out your umbrella for twelve months, with the serene confidence which a Christian feels in four aces. Sometimes the winter begins in November and winds up

in June, and sometimes there is a bare suspicion of winter in March and April, and summer all the balance of the year. But as a general thing??????

"Washoe, Information Wanted,"
The Washoe Giant in San Francisco, p. 62

CLOCK *See also* MOUSE, WATCH

For years my pet aversion had been the cuckoo clock; now here I was, at last, right in the creature's home (Switzerland); so wherever I went that distressing *"hoo'*hoo! *hoo'*hoo! *hoo'*hoo!" was always in my ears. For a nervous man, this was a fine state of things. Some sounds are hatefuller than others, but no sound is quite so inane, and silly, and aggravating as the *"hoo'*hoo" of a cuckoo clock, I think. I bought one, and am carrying it home to a certain person; for I have always said that if the opportunity ever happened, I would do that man an ill turn. What I meant was, that I would break one of his legs, or something of that sort; but in Lucerne I instantly saw that I could impair his mind. That would be more lasting, and more satisfactory every way. So I bought the cuckoo clock; and if I ever get home with it, he is "my meat," as they say in the mines. I thought of another candidate—a book reviewer whom I could name if I wanted to,—but after thinking it over, I didn't buy him the clock. I couldn't injure his mind.

A Tramp Abroad, I, Chapt. XXVI, p. 268

Woke up and heard the clock strike four. I said—I seem to have been asleep a long time. Wonder what time I did go to bed. And I got up and lit a candle and looked at my watch *to see.*

Mark Twain's Letters, II, p. 553

First cuckoo I ever heard outside of a clock. Was surprised how closely it imitated the clock—and yet of course it could never have heard a clock. The hatefulest thing in the world is a cuckoo clock.

Mark Twain's Notebook, p. 135

[At Colonel Sellers house]: There were no mantel ornaments, unless one might bring himself to regard as an ornament a clock which never came within fifteen strokes of striking the right time, and whose hands always hitched together at twenty-two minutes past anything and traveled in company the rest of the way home.

"Remarkable clock!" said Sellers, and got up and wound it. "I've been offered—well, I wouldn't expect you to believe what I've been offered for that clock . . . silence . . . she's begun to strike! You can't talk against her—you have to just be patient and hold up till she's said her say. Ah—well, as I was saying . . . she's beginning again! Nineteen, twenty, twenty-one . . . go it, old girl, don't mind me. . . . Isn't that a good, spirited tone. She can wake the dead. Sleep? Why you might as well try to sleep in a thunder-factory. Now just listen at that. She'll strike a hundred and fifty, now, without stopping—you'll see. There ain't another clock like that in Christendom."

The Gilded Age, I, Chapt. VII, p. 87

CLOTHES   *See also* DRESS, DIGNITY, MONARCHY, SOUL
. . . nobody can be very ungraceful in nicely-fitting beautiful clothes after he has grown a little used to them—especially if he is for the moment unconscious of them.

The Prince and the Pauper, Chapt. XVI, p. 152

. . . what would a man be—what would *any* man be—without his clothes? As soon as one stops and thinks over that proposition, one realizes that without his clothes a man would be nothing at all; that the clothes do not merely make the man, the clothes *are* the man; that without them he is a cipher, a vacancy, a nobody, a nothing.

Titles—another . . . artificiality—are a part of his clothing. They and the dry-goods conceal the wearer's inferiority and make him seem great and a wonder, when at bottom there is nothing remarkable about him. They can move a nation to fall on its knees and sincerely worship an Emperor who, without the clothes and the title, would drop to the rank of the cobbler and be swallowed up and lost sight of in the massed multitude of the inconsequentials . . .

A policeman in plain clothes is one man; in his uniform he is ten. Clothes and title are the most potent thing, the most formidable influence, in the earth. They move the human race to willing and spontaneous respect for the judge, the general, the admiral, the bishop, the ambassador, the frivolous earl, the idiot duke, the sultan, the king, the emperor. No great title is efficient without clothes to support it.

. . . Is the human race a joke? Was it devised and patched together in a dull time when there was nothing important to do? Has it no respect for itself? . . . I think my respect for it is drooping, sinking—and my respect for myself along with it. . . . There is but one restorative—*clothes!* respect-reviving, spirit-uplifting clothes! heaven's kindliest gift to man, his only protection against finding himself out: they deceive him, they confer dignity upon him; without them he has none. How charitable are clothes, how beneficent, how puissant, how inestimably precious! Mine are able to expand a human cipher into a globe-shadowing portent; they can command the respect of the whole world—including my own, which is fading. I will put them on.

"The Czar's Soliloquy,"
North American Review, March 1905, p. 321

[From a speech for The Savage Club dinner, London, July 6, 1907]:

Now I think I ought to apologize for my clothes. At home I venture things that I am not permitted by my family to venture in foreign parts. I was instructed before I left home and ordered to refrain from white clothes in England. I meant to keep that command fair and clean, and I would have done it if I had been in the habit of obeying instructions, but I can't invent a new process in life right away. I have not had white clothes on since I crossed the ocean until now.

In these three or four weeks I have grown so tired of gray and black that you have earned my gratitude in permitting me to come as I have. I wear white clothes in the depth of winter in my home, but I don't go out in the streets in them. I don't go out to attract too much attention. I like to attract some, and always I would like to be dressed so that I may be more conspicuous than anybody else.

If I had been an ancient Briton, I would not have contented myself with blue paint, but I would have bankrupted the rainbow. I so enjoy gay clothes in which women clothe themselves that it always grieves me when I go to the opera to see that, while women look like a flower-bed, the men are a few gray stumps among them in their black evening dress. These are two or three reasons why I wish to wear white clothes. When I find myself in assemblies like this, with everybody in black clothes, I know I possess something that is superior to everybody else's. Clothes are never clean. You don't know whether they are clean or not, because you can't see.

Here or anywhere you must scour your head every two or three days or it is full of grit. Your clothes must collect just as much dirt as your hair. If you wear white clothes you are clean, and your cleaning bills get so heavy that you have to take care. I am proud to say that I can wear a white suit of clothes without a blemish for three days. If you need any further instruction in the matter of clothes I shall be glad to give it to you. I hope I have convinced some of you that it is just as well to wear white clothes as any other kind. I do not want to boast. I only want to make you understand that you are not clean.

"The Savage Club Dinner"
Mark Twain's Speeches (1923), p. 354

Clothes make the man. Naked people have little or no influence in society.

More Maxims of Mark, p. 6

At a public function in a European court all foreign representatives except ours wear clothes which in some way distinguish them from the unofficial throng, and mark them as standing for their *countries.* But our representative appears in a plain black swallow-tail, which stands for neither country nor people. It has no nationality. It is found in all countries; it is as international as a night-shirt. It has no particular meaning: but our Government tries to give it one; it tries to make it stand for Republican Simplicity, modesty and unpretentiousness. Tries, and without doubt fails, for it is not conceivable that this loud ostentation of simplicity deceives any one. The statue that advertises its modesty with a fig-leaf really brings its modesty under suspicion. Worn officially, our nonconforming swallow-tail is a declaration of ungracious independence in the matter of manners, and is uncourteous.

> "Diplomatic Pay and Clothes"
> *The Man That Corrupted Hadleyburg, Etc.*, p. 217

I talked in a snow-white fulldress, swallow-tail and all, and dined in the same. It's a delightful impudence. I think I will call it my dontcareadam suit. But in the case of the private dinner I will always ask permission to wear it first, saying:

"Dear Madam, may I come in my dontcareadams?"

> *My Father Mark Twain*, Clara Clemens, p. 153

A girl . . . came along the great thorough-fare dressed like Eve before the fall.

> *The Innocents Abroad*, II, Chapt. XXXI, p. 405

COFFEE

Vienna coffee! It was the first thing I thought of—that unapproachable luxury—that sumptuous coffee-house coffee, compared with which all other European coffee and all American hotel coffee is mere fluid poverty.

> "At the Appetite Cure,"
> *Literary Essays*, p. 299

. . . moved to a new hotel, just opened—good fare and coffee that a Christian may drink without jeopardizing his eternal soul.

> *Mark Twain's Notebook*, p. 7

[In Europe]: You can get what the European hotel-keeper thinks is coffee, but it resembles the real thing as hypocrisy resembles holiness. It is a feeble, characterless, uninspiring sort of stuff, and almost as undrinkable as if it had been made in an American hotel. The milk used for it is what the French call "Christian" milk—milk which has been baptized.

A Tramp Abroad, II, Chapt. XX, p. 259

[Recipe for German coffee]: Take a barrel of water and bring it to a boil; rub a chicory berry against a coffee berry, then convey the former into water. Continue the boiling and evaporation until the intensity of the flavor and aroma of the coffee and chicory has been diminished to a proper degree; then set aside to cool. Now unharness the remains of a once cow from the plow, insert them in a hydraulic press, and when you shall have acquired a teaspoonful of that pale blue juice which a German superstition regards as milk, modify the malignity of its strength in a bucket of tepid water and ring up the breakfast. Mix the beverage in a cold cup, partake with moderation, and keep a wet rag around your head to guard against over-excitement.

Ibid., p. 265

COFFIN   See FIRE

COLD   See also MOUNTAIN, WEATHER

The captain has been telling how, in one of his Arctic voyages, it was so cold that the mate's shadow froze fast to the deck and had to be ripped loose by main strength. And even then he got only about two-thirds of it back.

Following the Equator, II, Chapt. XXVI, p. 311

I met [an old man] out in Iowa who had come up from Arkansas. I asked him whether he had experienced much cold during the preceding winter, and he exclaimed, "Cold! If the thermometer had been an inch longer we'd all have frozen to death!"

Mark Twain and I, Opie Read, p. 44

There are only two seasons in the region round about Mono Lake—and these are, the breaking up of one winter and the beginning of the next. . . . Under favorable circumstances it snows at least once in every single month in the year, in the little town of Mono. So uncertain is the climate in summer that a lady who goes out visiting cannot hope to be prepared for all emergencies unless she takes her fan under one arm and her snow shoes under the other. When they have a Fourth of July procession it generally snows on them, and they do say that as a general thing when a man calls for a brandy-toddy there, the barkeeper chops it off with a hatchet and wraps it up in a paper, like maple sugar. And it is further reported that the old soakers haven't any teeth—wore them out eating gin cocktails and brandy punches. I do not endorse that statement—I simply give it for what it is worth—and it is worth—well, I should say, millions, to any man who can believe it without straining himself. But I do endorse the snow on the Fourth of July— because I know that to be true.

Roughing It, I, Chapt. XXXVIII, p. 298

[To Katy]: Close the door. It isn't that the open door lets the cold *in,* but it lets the coziness *out.*

Lifetime with Mark Twain, p. 167

COLLECTION PLATE *See* MISSIONARY, REPENTANCE

COLLECTOR

A true collector attaches no value to a collection that is not complete. His great heart breaks, he sells his hoard, he turns his mind to some field that seems unoccupied.

"The Canvasser's Tale"
Tom Sawyer Abroad, p. 364

COLLEGE

A few months ago I was told that the Johns Hopkins University had given me a degree. I naturally supposed this constituted me a Member of the Faculty, and so I started in to help what I could there. I told them I believed they were perfectly competent to run a college as far as the higher branches of education are concerned, but what they needed was a little help here and there from a practical commercial man. I said the public is sensitive to little things and they wouldn't have full confidence in a college that didn't know how to spell John.

Mark Twain's Notebook, p. 206

COLLEGE DEGREES

Mark Twain had conferred upon him the following honorary degrees:

Master of Arts—Yale College—June, 1888
Doctor of Laws—Yale College—Oct., 1901
Doctor of Letters—University of Missouri—June, 1902
Doctor of Literature—Oxford University—June, 1907

COLOR

. . . presently you come to the main object of your trip—Lake Annecy. It is a revelation; it is a miracle. It brings the tears to a body's eyes, it affects you just as all things that you instantly recognize as perfect affect you—perfect music, perfect eloquence, perfect art, perfect joy, perfect grief. It stretches itself out there in a caressing sunlight, and away toward its border of majestic mountains, a crisped and radiant plain of water of the divinest blue that can be imagined. All the blues are there, from the faintest shoal-water suggestion of the color, detectable only in the shadow of some overhanging object, all the way through, a little blue and a little bluer still, and again a shade bluer, till you strike the deep, rich Mediterranean splendor which breaks the heart in your bosom, it is so beautiful.

"Aix, the Paradise of Rheumatics,"
Europe and Elsewhere, p. 110

COLUMBUS, CHRISTOPHER   *See also* SHIP

October 12, the Discovery. It was wonderful to find America, but it would have been more wonderful to miss it.

"Pudd'nhead Wilson's Calendar,"
Pudd'nhead Wilson, p. 223

In a museum in Havana there are two skulls of Christopher Columbus, "one when he was a boy and one when he was a man."

The Adventures of Thomas Jefferson Snodgrass, p. x

(COLUMBUS, CHRISTOPHER)

Columbus' ship being small and very old, we know that we may draw from these two facts several facts, several absolute certainties in the way of minor details which history has left unrecorded. For instance: being small, we know that she rolled and pitched and tumbled in any ordinary sea, and stood on her head or her tail or lay down with her ear in the water, when storm seas ran high; also, that she was used to having billows plunge aboard and wash her decks from stem to stern; also, that the storm racks were on the table all the way over, and that nevertheless a man's soup was oftener in his lap than in his stomach . . . there was only one stateroom, the size of a grave, with a tier of two or three berths in it of the dimensions and comfortableness of coffins, and that when the light was out the darkness in there was so thick and real that you could bite into it and chew it like gum; also, that the only promenade was on the lofty poop-deck astern . . .

From these absolutely sure data we can competently picture the daily life of the great discoverer. In the early morning he paid his devotions at the shrine of the Virgin. At eight bells he appeared on the poop-deck promenade . . .

He walked the promenade thoughtfully, he noted the aspects of the sky and the course of the wind; he kept an eye out for drifting vegetation and other signs of land; he jawed the man at the wheel for pastime; he got out an imitation egg and kept himself in practice on his old trick of making it stand on its end; now and then he hove a life-line below and fished up a sailor who was drowning on the quarter deck; the rest of his watch he gaped and yawned and stretched, and said he wouldn't make the trip again to discover six Americas. For that was the kind of natural human person Columbus was when not posing for posterity.

At noon he took the sun and ascertained that the good ship had made three hundred yards in twenty-four hours, and this enabled him to win the pool. Anybody can win the pool when nobody but himself has the privilege of straightening the ship's run and getting it right . . .

When he returned, the King of Spain, marveling, said—
as history records:

"This ship seems to be leaky. Did she leak badly?"

"You shall judge for yourself, sire. I pumped the Atlantic
Ocean through her sixteen times on the passage."

This is General Horace Porter's account. Other authorities say fifteen.

"About All Kinds of Ships,"
The American Claimant, Etc., p. 474

COMEDY   *See also* HUMOR, MOOD
Comedy keeps the heart sweet; but we all know that
there is wholesome refreshment for both mind and heart in
an occasional climb among the pomps of the intellectual
snow-summits built by Shakespeare and those others. Do
I seem to be preaching? It is out of my line: I only do it
because the rest of the clergy seem to be on vacation.

"About Play-Acting,"
The Man That Corrupted Hadleyburg, Etc., p. 215

It improves a comic paper to put in a joke once-in-a-
while.

Original Notes of Mark Twain

. . . [he possesses] the first virtue of a comedian, which
is to do humorous things with grave decorum and without
seeming to know that they are funny.

"In the Metropolis,"
The Washoe Giant in San Francisco, p. 76

COMET   *See* HALLEY'S COMET

COMFORT   *See also* AMERICA
A man will do *anything,* no matter what it is, *to secure
his spiritual comfort* . . . A man cannot be comfortable
without *his own* approval.

What is Man? and Other Essays, Chapt. II, p. 17

COMMUNISM
Now that we are fixed [financially] at last, of course the

communists and the asinine government will go to work and smash it all. [1878]

Mark Twain-Howells Letters, I, p. 237

Communism is idiocy. They want to divide up the property. Suppose they did it. It requires brains to keep money as well as to make it. In a precious little while the money would be back in the former owner's hands and the communist would be poor again. The division would have to be remade every three years or it would do the communist no good.

Mark Twain, a Biography, Paine, II, p. 644

COMPENSATION

. . . it was the great law of compensation—the great law that regulates Nature's heedless agents, and sees that when they make a mistake, they shall at the self-same moment prevent that mistake from working evil consequences. Behold, the same gust of wind that blows a lady's dress aside, and exposes her ankle, fills your eyes so full of sand that you can't see it. Marvellous are the works of Nature!

"Concerning that Conundrum,"
Sketches of the Sixties, p. 127

COMPLAINT *See also* FAULT, LIFE, MONOTONY, NEW ORLEANS, TELEPHONE

I think a compliment ought always to precede a complaint, where one is possible, because it softens resentment and insures for the complaint a courteous and gentle reception.

Mark Twain's Letters, II, p. 723

[A letter to the Hartford Gas Company, Feb. 12, 1891]:
Dear Sirs:
Some day you will move me almost to the verge of irritation by your chuckle-headed Goddamned fashion of shutting your Goddamned gas off without giving any notice to your Goddamned parishioners. Several times you have come within an ace of smothering half of this household in their beds and blowing up the other half by this idiotic, not to

say criminal, custom of yours. And it has happened again today. Haven't you a telephone?

Ys,

S L Clemens

Mark Twain's Notebook, p. 212

COMPLIMENT *See also* ASS, COMPLAINT, CONVICTION, DOG, PLAGIARISM

Do not offer a compliment and ask a favor at the same time. A compliment that is charged for is not valuable.

Mark Twain's Notebook, p. 380

A dozen direct censures are easier to bear than one morganatic compliment.

"Pudd'nhead Wilson's New Calendar,"

Following the Equator, I, Chapt. IV, p. 59

An occasional compliment is necessary, to keep up one's self-respect. The plan of the newspaper is good and wise; when you cannot get a compliment in any other way pay yourself one.

Mark Twain's Notebook, p. 237

Compliments always embarrass a man. You do not know anything to say. It does not inspire you with words. There is nothing you can say in answer to a compliment. I have been complimented myself a great many times, and they always embarrass me—I always feel that they have not said enough.

"Fulton Day, Jamestown,"

Mark Twain's Speeches, (1923), p. 362

To say a compliment well is a high art and few possess it.

Mark Twain's Letters, II, p. 685

You must not pay a person a compliment and then straightway follow it with a criticism.

Mark Twain's Notebook, p. 379

There are three infallible ways of pleasing an author, and the three form a rising scale of compliment: 1, to tell him you have read one of his books; 2, to tell him you have read all of his books; 3, to ask him to let you read the manuscript of his forthcoming book. No. 1 admits you to his respect;

99

No. 2 admits you to his admiration; No. 3 carries you clear into his heart.

"Pudd'nhead Wilson's Calendar,"
Pudd'nhead Wilson, Chapt. XI, p. 96

Now here's the compliment of a little Montana girl which came to me indirectly. She was in a room in which there was a large photograph of me. After gazing at it steadily for a time, she said: "We've got a John the Baptist like that." She also said: "Only ours has more trimmings." I suppose she meant the halo.

"The Last Lotus Club Speech,"
Mark Twain's Speeches (1923), p. 370

The compliment that helps us on our way is not the one that is shut up in the mind, but the one that is spoken out.

Mark Twain, a Biography, Paine, II, p. 902

. . . her effort is entitled to the praise which the country journalist conferred upon the Essex band after he had praised the whole Fourth of July celebration in detail, and had exhausted his stock of compliments. But he was obliged to lay something in the nature of a complimentary egg, and with a final heroic effort he brought forth this, "The Essex band done the best they could."

Mark Twain's Autobiography, Paine, II, p. 341

CONCEIT *See also* EQUATOR, GLACIER

If there is one thing in the world that will make a man peculiarly and insufferably self-conceited, it is to have his stomach behave itself, the first day at sea, when nearly all his comrades are seasick.

The Innocents Abroad, I, Chapt. III, p. 62

CONDUCT *See also* ADVICE, UNDERTAKER

All gods are better than their conduct.

Mark Twain's Notebook, p. 379

CONFIDENCE *See also* COLLEGE, KNOWLEDGE, RELIGION, SUCCESS

He had the serene confidence which a Christian feels in four aces.

"Washoe, Information Wanted,"
The Washoe Giant in San Francisco, p. 62

To the 1902 Hannibal High School class: I have never distributed diplomas before, therefore I can do it with greater confidence. There is nothing that saps one's confidence as the knowing how to do a thing.

Hannibal Morning Journal, Apr. 23, 1910

CONGREGATION

It was a wooden-faced congregation—just the sort to see no incongruity in the Majesty of Heaven, stooping to beg and plead and sentimentalize over such and see in their salvation an important matter.

Mark Twain's Notebook, p. 155

CONGRESSMAN *See also* BIRD, CRITIC, FLEA, GOD, ISCARIOT, LIGHTNING, LIQUOR

Reader, suppose you were an idiot. And suppose you were a member of Congress. But I repeat myself.

Mark Twain, a Biography, Paine, II, p. 724

In Congress, drawn out dullness is more effective than paragraphic humor. A speaker on the floor should always know what to say, and then not say it.

Mark Twain and I, Opie Read, p. 47

It could probably be shown by facts and figures that there is no distinctly native criminal class except Congress.

"Pudd'nhead Wilson's New Calendar,"
Following the Equator, I, Chapt. VIII, p. 98

[The Washoe tarantulas]: Proud? . . . Indeed, they would take up a straw and pick their teeth like a member of Congress.

Roughing It, I, Chapt. XXI, p. 176

[A description of a chameleon in the court-yard of a South African hotel]:

. . . A couple of skinny cones project from the sides of

his head, with a wee shiny bead of an eye set in the apex of each; and these cones turn bodily like pivot-guns and point every-which-way, and they are independent of each other; each has its own exclusive machinery. When I am behind him and C. in front of him, he whirls one eye rearwards and the other forwards—which gives him a most Congressional expression (one eye on the constituency and one on the swag); and then if something happens above and below him he shoots out one eye upward like a telescope and the other downward—and this changes his expression, but does not improve it.

Following the Equator, II, Chapt. XXIX, p. 342

A moral coward and a Congressman seem to be synonymous terms when there's an Irishman in the fence.

Mark Twain to Mrs. Fairbanks, p. 237

CONNECTICUT *See* GENTLEMAN, HARTFORD, SCENERY

CONSCIENCE *See also* FOOD, IDEAL, MONEY, PAIN, POLITICS, REMORSE, SERENITY, SMELL

If I had the remaking of man, he wouldn't have any conscience. It is one of the most disagreeable things connected with a person; and although it certainly does a great deal of good, it cannot be said to pay, in the long run; it would be much better to have less good and more comfort. Still, this is only my opinion, and I am only one man; others, with less experience, may think differently. They have a right to their view. I only stand to this: I have noticed my conscience for many years, and I know it is more trouble and bother to me than anything else I started with. I suppose that in the beginning I prized it, because we prize anything that is ours; and yet how foolish it was to think so. If we look at it in another way, we see how absurd it is: if I had an anvil in me would I prize it? Of course not. And yet when you come to think, there is no real difference between a conscience and an anvil—I mean for comfort. I have noticed it a thousand times. And you could dissolve an anvil with acids, when you couldn't stand it any longer;

but there isn't any way that you can work off a conscience
—at least so it will stay worked off; not that I know of,
anyway.

> *A Connecticut Yankee in King Arthur's Court,*
> Chapt. XVIII, p. 146

His conscience leaked out through one of his pores when
he was little . . .

> "In Defense of General Funston,"
> *The North American Review,* May, 1902, p. 621

It seems to me that a man should secure the *well done,
faithful servant,* of his own conscience *first* and foremost,
and let all other loyalties go.

> "Consistency,"
> *Mark Twain's Speeches* (1923), p. 123

All the consciences I have ever heard of were nagging,
badgering, fault-finding, execrable savages! Yes; and always in a sweat about some poor little insignificant trifle
or other—destruction catch the lot of them, I say! I would
trade mine for the small-pox and seven kinds of consumption, and be glad of the chance.

> "The Facts Concerning the Recent
> Carnival of Crime in Connecticut,"
> *Tom Sawyer Abroad, Etc.,* p. 315

Conscience, man's moral medicine chest.

> *Mark Twain's Autobiography,* Paine, II, p. 8

Conscience . . . is that mysterious autocrat, lodged in a
man, which compels the man to content its desires. It may
be called the Master Passion—the hunger for Self-Approval.

> *What Is Man? and Other Essays,* Chapt. VI, p. 98

[In Hawaii]: Nearby is an interesting ruin—the meager
remains of an ancient temple—a place where human sacrifices were offered up in those old bygone days when the
simple child of nature, yielding momentarily to sin when
sorely tempted, acknowledged his error when calm reflection had shown it to him, and came forward with noble
frankness and offered up his grandmother as an atoning
sacrifice—in those old days when the luckless sinner could
keep on cleansing his conscience and achieving periodical

happiness as long as his relations held out; . . .

Letters from the Sandwich Islands p. 40

I hadn't done nothing. But that's always the way; it don't make no difference whether you do right or wrong, a person's conscience ain't got no sense, and just goes for him *anyway*. If I had a yaller dog that didn't know no more than a person's conscience does I would pison him. It takes up more room than all the rest of a person's insides, and yet ain't no good, nohow. Tom Sawyer he says the same.

The Adventures of Huckleberry Finn,
Chapt. XXXIII, p. 300

An uneasy conscience is a hair in the mouth.

Mark Twain's Notebook, p. 392

CONSERVATIVE *See* RADICAL

CONSISTENCY *See also* CHANGE, LOYALTY, RESPECT, RIGHT

What . . . is the true gospel of consistency? *Change.* Who is the *really* consistent man? The man who changes. Since change is the law of his *being*, he cannot *be* consistent if he sticks in a rut. . . . Which is the real and right consistency? To be consistent to a sham and an empty name, or consistent to the law of one's *being*, which is *change*, [that] requires him to move forward and keep abreast of his best mental and moral progress, his highest convictions of the right and the true?

Mark Twain's Speeches (1923), p. 121

CONSPICUOUSNESS *See* POWER, RIGHT

CONSTITUTION *See* LAW

CONTROVERSY *See* TALK

CONUNDRUM

A religious conundrum: If a congress of Presbyterians is

a presbytery, what is a congress of dissenters?

Answer: A dysentery. Joe, you can sell the above to some religious paper or get it off on Dean Sage as original.

> To Rev. Joseph H. Twichell, Dec. 30, 1875
> *Original ms. in Yale Collection*

CONVERSATION *See also* POSSESSION, TALK

The circumstances and the atmosphere always have so much to do in directing a conversation, especially a German conversation, which is only a kind of an insurrection, anyway.

> "Meisterschaft,"
> *The American Claimant*, p. 318

. . . his answers were so final and exact that he did not leave a doubt to hang conversation on.

> "Rambling Notes of an Idle Excursion,"
> *Punch, Brothers, Punch*, p. 81

He had a good memory, and a tongue hung in the middle. This is a combination which gives immortality to conversation.

> *Roughing It*, I, Chapt. XXXV, p. 273

. . . the great foundation-rule and basic principle governing conversation between a shouter and a deaf person is irrelevancy and persistent desertion of the topic in hand.

> "A Little Note to M. Paul Bourget,"
> *Literary Essays*, p. 168

CONVICTION

The longer I live, the clearer I perceive how unmatchable . . . a compliment one pays when he says of a man, "he has the courage of his convictions."

> *Mark Twain-Howells Letters*, II, p. 586

Whatever you say, say it with conviction.

> *My Father • Mark Twain*, Clara Clemens, p. 134

What God lacks is convictions—stability of character. He ought to be a Presbyterian or a Catholic or *something*—not try to be everything.

> *Mark Twain's Notebook*, p. 344

. . . when a man is known to have no settled convictions of his own he can't convince other people.

Mark Twain's Letters, I, p. 357

CONVINCING   *See also* LIGHTNING

The old saw says—"let a sleeping dog lie." Experience knows better; experience says, If you want to *convince* do it yourself.

Written in Clara Clemens' copy of *The Gilded Age*

COPYRIGHT   *See also* LAW, PIRACY

Whenever a copyright law is to be made or altered, then the idiots assemble.

Mark Twain's Notebook, p. 382

Only one thing is impossible for God: to find any sense in any copyright law on the planet.

Ibid., p. 381

Adam was the author of sin, and I wish he had taken out an international copyright on it. For international copyright could have won, then. But when there came to be two men, it was too late, because there was one to oppose it, and experience shows that that fellow would have had the most influence.

Ibid., p. 128

There is a great deal of nonsense talked about international copyright. The proper way to treat a copyright is to make it exactly like real-estate in every way. It will settle itself under these conditions. If Congress were to bring in a law that a man's life was not to extend over 160 years, somebody would laugh. That law wouldn't concern anybody. The man would be out of the jurisdiction of the court. A term of years in copyright comes to exactly the same thing. No law can make a book live or cause it to die before the appointed time.

. . . The book that will live forever can't be artificially kept up at inflated prices. There will always be very expensive editions of it and cheap ones issuing side by side.

From Sea to Sea, Kipling, p. 171

CORPSE *See* SMOKING

COUNTENANCE *See* FACE, JOKE, SIMILES

COUNTRY *See also* FREEDOM, GOVERNMENT, PATENT, POLITICS, WAR

It is not *parties* that make or save countries or that build them to greatness—it is clean men, clean ordinary citizens, rank and file, the masses. Clean masses are not made by individuals standing back till the rest become clean . . . I think a man's first duty is to his own honor; not to his country and not to his party.

Mark Twain's Letters, II, p. 445

I asked Tom if countries always apologized when they had done wrong, and he says: "Yes; the little ones does."

Tom Sawyer Abroad, Etc., Chapt. XII, p. 121

You see my kind of loyalty was loyalty to one's country, not to its institutions or its office-holders. The country is the real thing, the substantial thing, the eternal thing; it is the thing to watch over, and care for, and be loyal to; institutions are extraneous, they are its mere clothing, and clothing can wear out, become ragged, cease to be comfortable, cease to protect the body from winter, disease, and death. To be loyal to rags, to shout for rags, to worship rags, to die for rags—that is a loyalty of unreason, it is pure animal; it belongs to monarchy, was invented by monarchy; let monarchy keep it.

A Connecticut Yankee in King Arthur's Court,
Chapt. XIII, p. 104

COURAGE

Courage observes; reflects; calculates; surveys the whole situation; counts the cost, estimates the odds, makes up its mind; then goes at the enterprise resolute to win or perish . . . Recklessness does not reflect, it plunges fearlessly in with a hurrah, and takes the risks, whatever they may be, regardless of expense.

Christian Science, Book II, Chapt. VI, p. 154

(COURAGE)

Courage is resistance to fear, mastery of fear—not absence of fear. Except a creature be part coward it is not a compliment to say it is brave; it is merely a loose misapplication of the word. Consider the flea! Incomparably the bravest of all the creatures of God, if ignorance of fear were courage. Whether you are asleep or awake he will attack you, caring nothing for the fact that in bulk and strength you are to him as are the massed armies of the earth to a sucking child; he lives both day and night and all days and nights in the very lap of peril and the immediate presence of death, and yet is no more afraid than is the man who walks the streets of a city that was threatened by an earthquake ten centuries before. When we speak of Clive, Nelson and Putnam as men who "didn't know what fear was," we ought to add the flea—and put him at the head of the procession.

"Pudd'nhead Wilson's Calendar,"
Pudd'nhead Wilson, Chapt. XII, p. 115

It is curious . . . that physical courage should be so common in the world, and moral courage so rare.

Mark Twain in Eruption, p. 69

In the matter of courage we all have our limits.

Mark Twain's Speeches (1923), p. 386

COURTEOUSNESS   *See* GENTLEMEN, POLITENESS

COURT OF JUSTICE   *See* INSANITY, IRISHMEN

COVETOUSNESS

There is no such thing as *material* covetousness. All covetousness is spiritual . . . Any so-called material thing that you want is merely a symbol: you want it not for *itself,* but because it will content your spirit for the moment . . . Money has no *material* value; if you remove its spiritual value nothing is left but dross. It is so with all things, little or big, majestic or trivial—there are no exceptions. Crowns, scepters, pennies, paste jewels, village notoriety, world-wide fame—they are all the same, they have no *material* value: while they content the *spirit* they are precious, when this

fails they are worthless.
>*What Is Man? and Other Essays,* Chapt. VI, p. 93

Tom said to himself that it was not such a hollow world, after all. He had discovered a great law of human action, without knowing it—namely, that in order to make a man or a boy covet a thing, it is only necessary to make the thing difficult to attain. If he had been a great and wise philosopher, like the writer of this book, he would now have comprehended that Work consists of whatever a body is *obliged* to do, and that Play consists of whatever a body is not obliged to do. And this would help him to understand why constructing artificial flowers or performing on a tread-mill is work, while rolling ten-pins or climbing Mont Blanc is only amusement.
>*The Adventures of Tom Sawyer,* Chapt. II, p. 20

COWARDICE   *See* CONGRESSMAN, HUMAN RACE, PRINCIPLE, REVOLUTION

. . . Have read and lectured a good many times at matinees where of course ladies were largely in the majority.

In such places failure may be counted upon. In fact, hardly anything can prevent it but a carefully organized *claque* . . .

For several reasons. To begin with, ladies are cowards about expressing their feelings before folk; men *become* cowards in the presence of ladies.
>*Mark Twain's Notebook,* p. 200

You are a coward when you even *seem* to have backed down from a thing you openly set out to do.
>*Ibid.,* p. 126

There are several good protections against temptations but the surest is cowardice.
>"Pudd'nhead Wilson's New Calendar,"
>*Following the Equator,* I, Chapt. XXXVI, p. 339

COYOTE   *See* DOG, FLEA, SPEED, WANT

COZINESS   *See* WEATHER

CREATION

On this up trip [up the Mississippi] I saw a little towhead (infant island) half a mile long, which had been formed during the past nineteen years. Since there was so much time to spare that nineteen years of it could be devoted to the construction of a mere towhead, where was the use, originally, in rushing this whole globe through in six days? It is likely that if more time had been taken, in the first place, the world would have been made right, and this ceaseless improving and repairing would not be necessary now. But if you hurry a world or a house, you are nearly sure to find out by and by that you have left out a towhead, or a broom-closet, or some other little convenience, here and there, which has got to be supplied, no matter how much expense or vexation it may cost.

Life on the Mississippi, Chapt. LI, p. 375

CREEDS *See* DOCTRINE, MONEY, SOCIETY

CREMATION

As for me, I hope to be cremated. I made that remark to my pastor once, who said, with what he seemed to think was an impressive manner: "I wouldn't worry about that, if I had your chances."

Much he knew about it—the family all so opposed to it.

Life on the Mississippi, Chapt. XLIII, p. 327

CRIME *See also* ASSASSINATION, CONGRESSMAN, LAW, PUNISHMENT, REFLECTION

Nothing incites to money-crimes like great poverty or great wealth.

More Maxims of Mark, p. 10

The lunatic's (assassin's) mind space is all occupied with the matter in hand; there is no room in it for reflections upon what may happen to *him*. That comes after the crime.

Mark Twain's Letters, II, p. 715

CRITIC *See also* GRAMMAR, LITERARY CRITICISM, SCOTT, Walter

I like criticism, but it must be my way.

Mark Twain's Autobiography, Paine, II, p. 247

We hate the critic and think him brutally and maliciously unjust, but he could retort with overwhelming truth: "You will feel just as I do about your book if you will take it up and read it ten years hence."

Mark Twain's Notebook, p. 219

The critic's symbol should be the tumble-bug; he deposits his egg in somebody else's dung, otherwise he could not hatch it.

Ibid., p. 392

Experience has not taught me very much, still it has taught me that it is not wise to criticize a piece of literature, except to an *enemy* of the person who wrote it; then if you praise it that enemy admires you for your honest manliness, and if you dispraise it he admires you for your sound judgment.

Mark Twain, a Biography, Paine, I, p. 506

The critic assumes every time that if a book doesn't meet the cultivated-class standard it isn't valuable . . . The critic has actually imposed upon the world the superstition that a painting by Raphael is more valuable to the civilizations of the earth than is a chromo; and the august opera more than the hurdy-gurdy and the villagers' singing society; and the Latin classics than Kipling's far-reaching bugle-note; and Jonathan Edwards than the Salvation Army . . . If a critic should start a religion it would not have any object but to convert angels, and they wouldn't need it. It is not that little minority who are already saved that are best worth lifting up, I should think, but the mighty mass of the uncultivated who are underneath. That mass will never see the old masters—that sight is for the few; but the chromo-maker can lift them all one step upward toward appreciation of art; they cannot have the opera, but the hurdy-gurdy and the singing-class lift them a little way toward that far height; they will never know Homer, but the passing rhymester of their day leaves them higher than he found them; they may never even hear of the Latin classics, but they will strike step with Kipling's drum-beat and they will march; for all Jonathan Edwards' help they would die in their slums, but the Salvation Army will beguile some of them to a purer air and a cleaner life.

. . . I have never tried, in even one single little instance, to help cultivate the cultivated classes. I was not equipped for it either by native gifts or training. And I never had any ambition in that direction, but always hunted for bigger game—the masses. I have seldom deliberately tried to instruct them, but I have done my best to entertain them, for they can get instruction elsewhere.

Ibid., Paine, II, p. 894

I believe that the trade of critic, in literature, music, and the drama, is the most degraded of all trades, and that it has no real value—certainly no large value . . . However, let it go. It is the will of God that we must have critics, and missionaries, and congressmen, and humorists, and we must bear the burden.

Mark Twain's Autobiography, Paine, II, p. 69

As a rule, the grammar was leaky and the construction more or less lame; but I did not much mind these things. They are common defects of my own, and one mustn't criticize other people on grounds where he can't stand perpendicular himself.

A Connecticut Yankee in King Arthur's Court,
Chapt. XXVI, p. 240

CROOK *See* WORM

CROWD *See also* HUMAN RACE, LUCK

They swarmed up towards Sherburn's house, a-whooping and raging like Injuns, and everything had to clear the way or get run over and tromped to mush, and it was awful to see. . . . They swarmed in front of Sherburn's palings as thick as they could jam together, and you couldn't hear yourself think for the noise. . . . Then there was a racket of ripping and tearing and smashing, and down goes [the fence], and the front wall of the crowd begins to roll in like a wave.

Just then Sherburn steps out on to the roof of his little front porch, with a double-barrel gun in his hand, and takes his stand, perfectly ca'm and deliberate, not saying a word. The racket stopped, and the wave sucked back. . . . The stillness was awful creepy and uncomfortable. . . . "Now *leave* . . ." tossing his gun up across his left arm and cocking it when he says this.

The crowd washed back sudden, and then broke all apart, and went tearing off every which way . . . I could a stayed if I wanted to, but I didn't want to.

The Adventures of Huckleberry Finn,
Chapt. XXII, p. 195

The moment the bells stopped, those banked masses broke and poured over the line like a vast black wave, and for as much as a half hour it continued to flow, and then it solidified itself, and you could have walked upon a pavement of human heads to—well, miles.

A Connecticut Yankee in King Arthur's Court,
Chapt. XXIII, p. 198

CUCKOO *See* CLOCK

CURE *See* BATH, ILLNESS, MIND, WATER

CURIOSITY *See* RUMOR

CUSTOM *See also* LAW, REMARK, SHIP

Customs are not enacted, they grow gradually up, imperceptibly and unconsciously, like an oak from its seed. Customs do not concern themselves with right or wrong or reason. But they have to be obeyed. . . . Laws are sand, customs are rock. Laws can be evaded and punishment escaped, but an openly transgressed custom brings sure punishment.

Letters from the Earth, p. 156

A country's laws are written upon paper . . . its customs are engraved upon brass. One may play with the one, but not with the other. It is less risky for a stranger to dance upon our Constitution in the public square than to affront one of our solidified customs. The one is merely eminently respectable, the other is sacred.

S.L.C. to C.T., p. 11

Laws can be evaded and punishment escaped, but an openly transgressed custom brings sure punishment. The penalty may be unfair, unrighteous, illogical, and a cruelty; no matter, it will be inflicted just the same . . . Custom is custom; it is built of brass, boiler-iron, granite; facts, reasonings, arguments have no more effect upon it than the idle winds have upon Gibraltar.

Mark Twain, a Biography, Paine, III, p. 1285

Often, the less there is to justify a traditional custom, the harder it is to get rid of it.

The Adventures of Tom Sawyer, Chapt. V, p. 49

Custom is a petrifaction; nothing but dynamite can dislodge it for a century.

"Diplomatic Pay and Clothes,"
The Man That Corrupted Hadleyburg, Etc., p. 219

Have a place for everything and keep the thing somewhere else. This is not advice, it is merely custom.

Mark Twain's Notebook, p. 347

D

DAMNATION *See* HUMAN RACE

DARKNESS *See also* SIMILES
There has never been darkness any thicker than that. It just lay in cakes.

> "In Aid of the Blind,"
> *Mark Twain's Speeches* (1923), p. 312

The darkness . . . was so thick and real that you could bite into it and chew it like gum.

> "About Ships,"
> *The American Claimant,* p. 474

DAYS *See* TIME

DEATH *See also* ABROAD, ACCIDENT, ADAM, BIRTHDAY, CREMATION, DIGNITY, FREEDOM, HURRY, LIFE, MARRIAGE, MISSISSIPPI RIVER, SLOWNESS, UNDERTAKER
The Impartial Friend: Death—the only immortal who treats us all alike, whose pity and whose peace and whose refuge are for all—the soiled and the pure—the rich and the poor—the loved and the unloved.

> *Moments with Mark Twain,* Paine, p. 299

I was sorry to have my name mentioned as one of the

great authors, because they have a sad habit of dying off. Chaucer is dead, Spencer is dead, so is Milton, so is Shakespeare, and I am not feeling very well myself.

> "Statistics,"
> *Mark Twain's Speeches* (1910), p. 278

[I am] not sorry for anybody who is granted the privilege of prying behind the curtain to see if there is any contrivance that is half so shabby and poor and foolish as the invention of mortal life.

> *Mark Twain to Mrs. Fairbanks,* p. 274

Pity is for the living, envy is for the dead.

> "Pudd'nhead Wilson's New Calendar,"
> *Following the Equator,* I, Chapt. XIX, p. 189

Jean has been enriched with the most precious of all gifts—the gift which makes all other gifts mean and poor—death.

> "The Death of Jean,"
> *What is Man? and Other Essays,* p. 118

I think we never become really and genuinely our entire and honest selves until we are dead—and not then until we have been dead years and years. People ought to start dead, and then they would be honest so much earlier.

> *Mark Twain in Eruption,* p. 203

In London, a cousin of Mark Twain, Dr. Jim Clemens, fell ill, and the newspapers had it presently that Mark Twain was lying at the point of death. A reporter ferreted him out and [showed him the cabled] instructions from his paper . . . His orders read:

"If Mark Twain very ill, five hundred words. If dead, send one thousand."

[Mark Twain] smiled grimly as he handed back the cable.

"You don't need as much as that," he said. "Just say the report of my death has been grossly exaggerated."

> *Mark Twain, a Biography,* Paine, II, p. 1039

DEBT

Due to a combination of circumstances: the panic of

1893; the failure of the Paige Typesetter, into which Twain had poured $3000–4000 a month; losses due to the disastrous failure of his last publication, THE LIFE OF POPE LEO XIII; investment in models of a small bust of General Grant, sculptured by Gerhardt, which Twain duplicated in great numbers, to his loss; the embezzlement of $25,000 in 1887, from Charles L. Webster & Co. by Scott, an employee—led to the closing of the Webster Company on April 18, 1894, at a loss of $96,000, and resulted in a total indebtedness of $160,000 for Mark Twain.

By going on a world lecture tour and collecting royalties from his books, Twain was able to pay off his creditors in full by Jan. 1896, with $13,000 capital to spare.

Mark Twain, Business Man, p. 394,
and *Mark Twain-Howells Letters*, II, p. 669

DECENCY

Each race determines for itself what indecencies are. Nature knows no indecencies; man invents them.

Mark Twain's Notebook, p. 288

DECISION

How to Reach a Decision when in Doubt: Arrive at a decision. This will settle your mind, then you will do the other thing.

S.L.C. to C.T., p. 14

DEED

The good and evil results that flow from *any* act, even the smallest, breed on and on, century after century, forever and ever and ever, creeping by inches around the globe, affecting all its coming and going populations until the end of time, until the final cataclysm.

"The Dervish and the Offensive Stranger,"
Europe and Elsewhere, p. 311

I recognized that I had scored *one* good deed for sure on my halo account.

Mark Twain, a Biography, Paine, III, p. 1241

DEGREES *See* COLLEGE

DELICACY *See* INDELICACY

DELIGHT *See* PLEASURE

DEMOCRACY *See also* GOVERNMENT, MONARCHY, NATURE
The aim of democracy is harmony, its goal is Brotherhood.

> *Letterhead of Mark Twain Society of New York*

We adore titles and heredities in our hearts, and ridicule them with our mouths. This is our Democratic privilege.

> *Mark Twain's Autobiography,* Paine, III, p. 350

DENTISTRY

Some people who can skirt precipices without a tremor have a strong dread of the dentist's chair, whereas I was born without any prejudices against the dentist's chair; when in it I am interested, am not in a hurry, and do not greatly mind the pain. Taken by and large, my style of make has advantages over the other, I think. Few of us are obliged to circumnavigate precipices, but we all have to take a chance at the dental chair.

People who early learn the right way to choose a dentist have their reward. Professional superiority is not everything; it is only part. All dentists talk while they work. They have inherited this from their professional ancestors, the barbers. The dentist who talks well—other things being equal—is the one to choose. He tells anecdotes all the while and keeps his man so interested and entertained that he hardly notices the flight of time. For he not only tells anecdotes that are good in themselves, but he adds nice shadings to them with his instruments as he goes along, and now and then brings out effects which could not be produced with any other kind of tools at all. All the time that such a dentist as this is plowing down into a cavity with that spinning gouge . . . it is observable that he has found out where he has uncovered a nerve down in there, and that he only visits it at intervals, according to the needs of his anecdote, touching it lightly, very lightly and swiftly, now and then, to brighten up some happy conceit in his tale and call a delicate electric attention to it; and all the while he is working gradually and steadily up toward his climax with veiled and consummate art—then at last the spindle stops whirling and thundering in the cavity, and you know that the grand surprise is imminent, now—is hanging in the very air. You can hear your heart beat as the dentist bends over you with his grip on the spindle and his voice diminished to a murmur. The suspense grows bigger—bigger—bigger—your breath stops—then your heart. Then with lightning suddenness the "nub" is sprung and the spindle drives into the raw nerve! The most brilliant surprises of the stage are pale and artificial compared with this.

It is believed by people generally, or at least by many— that the exquisitely sharp sensation which results from plunging the steel point into the raw nerve is pain, but I think that this is doubtful. It is so vivid and sudden that one has no time to examine properly into its character. It is probably impossible, with our human limitations, to determine with certainty whether a sensation of so high and perfect an order as that is pain or whether it is pleasure. Its location brings it under the disadvantage of a common prejudice; and so men mistake it for pain when they might perceive that it is the opposite of that if it were anywhere but in a tooth. I may be in error, but I have experimented with it a great deal and I am satisfied in my own mind that it is not pain. It is true that it always feels like pain, but that proves nothing—ice against a naked back always passes for fire. I have every confidence that I can eventually prove to everyone's satisfaction that a nerve-stab produces pleasure; and not only that, but the most exquisite pleasure, the most perfect felicity which we are capable of feeling. I would not ask more than to be remembered hereafter as the man who conferred this priceless benefaction upon his race.

"Down the Rhone,"
Europe and Elsewhere, p. 161

The German [grammar has a] kind of parenthesis [made] by splitting a verb in two and putting half of it at the beginning of an exciting chapter and the *other half* at the end of it . . .

It reminds a person of those dentists who secure your instant and breathless interest in a tooth by taking a grip on it with the forceps, and then stand there and drawl through a tedious anecdote before they give the dreaded jerk. Parentheses in literature and dentistry are in bad taste.

"The Awful German Language,"
A Tramp Abroad, II, Appendix D, p. 293

DESCRIPTION *See also* VOCABULARY

[Translation of part of a German letter to Bayard Taylor asking for a passport, May 7, 1878]:

My description is as follows: Born 1835; 5 ft. 8½ inches tall; weight about 145 pounds, sometimes a bit under, sometimes a bit over; dark brown hair and red moustache, full face with very high ears and light gray beautiful beaming eyes and a damned good moral character.

"New Letters of Mark Twain,"
American Literature, March, 1936, p. 48

A description of Judge Griswold of Hannibal: His long black hair lay close to his head, and was kept to the rear by his ears as one keeps curtains back by brackets.

Sam Clemens of Hannibal, p. 66

DESERT *See also* ENGLAND

Tom Sawyer and Jim discussing the Sahara Desert:

"This desert is about the shape of the United States, and if you was to lay it down on top of the United States, it would cover the land of the free out of sight like a blanket. . . . If you laid the Great Sahara down with her edge on the Pacific, she would cover the United States and stick out past New York six hundred miles into the Atlantic Ocean. . . ."

Jim says: "I reckon dis Desert wa'nt made at all. . . . *I b'lieve it uz jes like when you's buildin' a house; dey's allays a lot o' truck en rubbish lef' over. What does you do wid it? Doan' you take en k'yart it off en dump it into a ole vacant back lot? 'Course. Now, den, it's my opinion hit was jes like dat—dat de Great Sahara warn't made at all, she jes happen.*"

Tom Sawyer Abroad, Chapt. IX, p. 88

DESERVING *See* HONORS

DESPOTISM *See also* GOVERNMENT

An earthly despotism would be the absolutely perfect earthly government if . . . the despot were the perfectest individual of the human race, and his lease of life perpetual. But as a perishable, perfect man must die, and leave his despotism in the hands of an imperfect successor, an earthly despotism is not merely a bad form of government, it is the worst form possible.

A Connecticut Yankee in King Arthur's Court,
Chapt. X, p. 79

DESTINY *See* PROVIDENCE

DEVIL *See* CHEATING

DIARY *See* BOYHOOD, JOURNAL

DICTIONARY *See also* PREACHER

. . . try to keep your feelings where you can reach them with the dictionary.

"Political Economy,"
Sketches New and Old, p. 20

We sailed for America, and there made certain preparations. . . . Two members of my family elected to go with me. Also a carbuncle. The dictionary says a carbuncle is a kind of jewel. Humor is out of place in a dictionary.

Following the Equator, I, Chapt. I, p. 15

When we reached the station on the farther verge of the desert, we were glad, for the first time, that the dictionary was along, because we never could have found language to tell how glad we were, in any sort of dictionary but an unabridged one with pictures in it.

Roughing It, I, Chapt. XVIII, p. 152

DIET   *See also* FOOD

In the matter of diet—I have been persistently strict in sticking to the things which didn't agree with me until one or the other of us got the best of it.

"Seventieth Birthday,"
Mark Twain's Speeches (1923), p. 257

DIGNITY

. . . what sorry shows and shadows we are. Without our clothes and our pedestals we are poor things and much of a size; our dignities are not real, our pomps are shams. At our best and stateliest we are not suns, as we pretended, and teach, and believe, but only candles; and any bummer can blow us out.

"The Memorable Assassination,"
What Is Man? and Other Essays, p. 170

It does us all good to unbend sometimes.

The Prince and the Pauper, Chapt. XIX, p. 188

He had arrived at the dignity of Death—the only earthly dignity that is not artificial—the only safe one. The others are traps that can beguile to humiliation.

Mark Twain's Notebook, p. 398

DILIGENCE   *See* ADVICE

DIPLOMACY

DIPLOMAT   *See also* LAW, PRINCIPLE, WORDS

They want to send me abroad, as a Consul or a Minister.

I said I didn't want any of the pie. God knows I am mean enough and lazy enough, now, without being a foreign consul.

Mark Twain's Letters, I, p. 149

DIRECTIONS

Somewhere or other among these myriads [of islands] Samoa is concealed, and not discoverable on the map. Still if you wish to go there, you will have no trouble about finding it if you follow the directions given by Robert Louis Stevenson to Dr. Conan Doyle and to Mr. J. M. Barrie. "You go to America, cross the continent to San Francisco, and then it's the second turning to the left." To get the full flavor of the joke one must take a glance at the map.

Following the Equator, I, Chapt. VII, p. 89

"The *castle*, you understand; where is the castle?"

"Oh, as to that, it is great, and strong, and well beseen, and lieth in a far country. Yes, it is many leagues."

"*How* many?"

"Ah, fair sir, it were woundily hard to tell, they are so many, and do so lap the one upon the other, and being made all in the same image and tincted with the same color, one may not know the one league from its fellow, nor how to count them except they be taken apart, and ye wit well it were God's work to do that, being not within man's capacity; for ye will note—"

"Hold on, hold on, never mind about the distance; *whereabouts* does the castle lie? What's the direction from here?"

"Ah, please you sir, it hath no direction from here; by reason that the road lieth not straight, but turneth evermore; wherefore the direction of its place abideth not, but is some time under the one sky and anon under another, whereso if ye be minded that it is in the east, and wend thitherward, ye shall observe that the way of the road doth yet again turn upon itself by the space of half a circle, and this marvel happing again and yet again and still again, it will grieve you that you had thought by vanities of the

mind to thwart and bring to naught the will of Him that
giveth not a castle a direction from a place except it pleas-
eth Him, and if it please Him not, will the rather that even
all castles and all directions thereunto vanish out of the
earth, leaving the places wherein they tarried desolate and
vacant, so warning His creatures that where He will He
will, and where He will not He—"

"Oh, that's all right, that's all right, give us a rest; never
mind about the direction, *hang* the direction—"

A Connecticut Yankee in King Arthur's Court,
Chapt. XI, p. 85

DIRT   *See also* LAND

This Civita Vecchia is the finest nest of dirt, vermin, and
ignorance we have found yet, except that African perdition
they call Tangier, which is just like it. The people here live
in alleys two yards wide, which have a smell about them
which is peculiar, but not entertaining. It is well the alleys
are not wider, because they hold as much smell now as a
person can stand, and, of course, if they were wider they
would hold more, and then the people would die. . . They
are indolent, as a general thing, and yet have few pastimes.
They work two or three hours at a time, but not hard, and
then they knock off and catch flies. This does not require
any talent, because they only have to grab—if they do not
get the one they are after, they get another. It is all the
same to them. They have no partialities. Whichever one
they get is the one they want.

They have other kinds of insects, but it does not make
them arrogant. They are very quiet, unpretending people.
They have more of these kind of things than other communities, but they do not boast.

They are very uncleanly—these people—in face, in person and in dress. When they see anybody with a clean
shirt on, it arouses their scorn. The women wash clothes,
half the day, at the public tanks in the streets, but they are
probably somebody else's. Or maybe they keep one set to

wear and another to wash; because they never put on any that have ever been washed. . .

The Innocents Abroad, I, Chapt. XXV, p. 334

(*Munich, 1878*): It is the greatest country for Art and dirt in the world; they have all kinds of Art and all kinds of dirt; there is more dirt than Art, of course, because the dirt has had the longer start and more people have devoted themselves to learning how to make it and make it right; but Art is coming, Art is progressing here all the time; this very year there is to be a prodigious international Art Exhibition here which will astonish the world—and if they will follow it up with a dirt exhibition their fortune is made.

Samuel Langhorne Clemens, p. 10

(*Gretchen, the young maid, in Munich; 1878*):

Gretchen was baptised when she was a little baby, and it was her last wash. . . . We could have had her washed, but we didn't want to. She wouldn't be *our* Gretchen any more. . . . We wanted her just as she was. . . . She was *our* Gretchen . . . *our* love, *our* friend, . . . *our* personal property, *our* real estate, and we wouldn't allow a single . . . layer of it to be planed off.

Mark Twain-Howells Letters, I, p. 243

There is but one thing we took solid and healing comfort in, and that was our gentle young colored girl who waits on our table. But, alas, day before yesterday she fell in the cistern and the color all came off. We require her to fall in every day now. We have clean table linen, now.

Samuel Langhorne Clemens, p. 9

DISAGREEABLE *See* PEOPLE

DISAPPOINTMENT *See also* MONEY

The dreams of my boyhood? No, they have not been realized. For all who are old, there is something infinitely pathetic about the subject . . . for in no gray-head's case can it suggest any but one thing—disappointment. Disappointment is its own reason for its pain: the quality or dignity of the hope that failed is a matter aside. The dream's valuation of a thing lost—not another man's—is the only standard to measure it by, and his grief for it makes it large and great and fine, and is worthy of our reverence in all cases.

Has *any* boyhood dream ever been fulfilled? I must doubt it.

"My Boyhood Dreams,"
The Man That Corrupted Hadleyburg, Etc., p. 246

DISASTER

It would be so natural . . . so like the traps set for men from the beginning of time—for Disaster to sneak along in my tracks for seven years, disguised as Good Fortune; and then drop his handsome mask and grin at me out of his skinless skull, and insult me with riches when they had lost their value for me. [Dec. 26, 1902]

Mark Twain-Howells Letters, II, p. 757

DISCOVERY *See also* COLUMBUS, CHRISTOPHER, PLEASURE

Unquestionably the discovery of the Mississippi is a datable fact which considerably mellows and modifies the shiny newness of our country, and gives her a most respectable outside aspect of rustiness and antiquity.

De Soto merely glimpsed the river, then died and was buried in it by priests and soldiers. One would expect the priests and the soldiers to multiply the river's dimensions by ten—the Spanish custom of the day—and thus move other adventurers to go at once and explore it. On the contrary, their narratives, when they reached home, did not excite that amount of curiosity. The Mississippi was left unvisited by whites during a term of years which seems incredible in our energetic days. One may "sense" the interval to his mind, after a fashion, by dividing it up this way: after De Soto glimpsed the river, a fraction short of a quarter of a century elapsed, and then Shakespeare was born; lived a trifle more than half a century, then died; and when he had been in his grave considerably more than half a century, the *second* white man saw the Mississippi.

In our day we don't allow a hundred and thirty years to elapse between glimpses of a marvel. If somebody should discover a creek in the county next to the one that the North Pole is in, Europe and America would start fifteen costly expeditions thither; one to explore the creek, and the other fourteen to hunt for each other.

Life on the Mississippi, Chapt. I, p. 20

DISEASE *See also* BATH, DICTIONARY, EDUCATION, HABIT, HEALTH, ILLNESS, OPINION, RIVER, WATER

Man is a museum of diseases, a home of impurities . . . if he was made for any purpose at all, it must have been for the support and entertainment of microbes.

Mark Twain, the Man and His Work, p. 139

The baby was seized with scarlet fever . . . We gave early warning, and of course nobody has entered the house in all this time but one or two reckless old bachelors—and they probably wanted to carry the disease to the children of former flames of theirs. [1882]

Mark Twain's Letters, I, p. 422

DISPOSITION *See also* FAULT

[His] disposition was *born* in him, he did not create It; It was the architect of his character; his character was the architect of his achievements.

"In Defense of General Funston,"
The North American Review, May 1902, p. 614

It is a dear and lovely disposition, and a most valuable one, that can brush away indignities and discourtesies and seek and find the pleasanter features of an experience.

Mark Twain's Autobiography, Paine, II, p. 171

DISTANCE *See also* CALIFORNIA, FLEA

We have plowed a long way over the sea, and there's twenty-two hundred miles of restless water between us, now, besides the railway stretch. And yet you are so present with us, so close to us that a span and a whisper would

bridge the distance. [To Dr. John Brown, 1873]
> *Mark Twain's Letters,* I, p. 209

DOCTOR *See also* ADVICE, MEDICINE, OSTEOPATHY, WRITING
Rev. Hobson and Dr. Robinson was down to the end of town a-hunting together—that is, I mean the doctor was shipping a sick man to t'other world, and the preacher was pinting him right.
> *The Adventures of Huckleberry Finn,*
> Chapt. XXV, p. 219

He has been a doctor a year now, and has had two patients—no, three, I think; yes, it *was* three. I attended their funerals.
> *The Gilded Age,* I, Chapt. X, p. 122

The physician's is the highest and worthiest of all occupations, or would be if human nature did not make superstitions and priests necessary.
> *Mark Twain's Notebook,* p. 166

He had had much experience of physicians, and said "the only way to keep your health is to eat what you don't want, drink what you don't like, and do what you'd druther not."
> "Pudd'nhead Wilson's New Calendar,"
> *Following the Equator,* II, Chapt. XIII, p. 151

A half-educated physician is not valuable. He thinks he can cure everything.
> *Mark Twain's Notebook,* p. 219

I have been practicing now for seven months. When I settled on my farm in Connecticut in June I found the community very thinly settled—and since I have been engaged in practice it has become more thinly settled still. This gratifies me, as indicating that I am making an impression on my community. . .

. . .

Of course, the practice of medicine and surgery in a remote country-district has its disadvantages, but in my case I am happy in a division of responsibility. I practice in conjunction with a horse-doctor, a sexton, and an undertaker.

The combination is air-tight, and once a man is stricken in our district escape is impossible to him.

. . .

Not long ago a fellow came along with a rolling gait and a distressed face. We asked him what was the matter. We always hold consultations on every case, as there isn't business enough for four. He said he didn't know, but that he was a sailor, and perhaps that might help us to give a diagnosis. We treated him for that, and I never saw a man die more peacefully.

"Dr. Mark Twain, Farmeopath,"
Mark Twain's Speeches (1910), p. 334

In all these decades he has never had anything really the matter with him but doctor-sickness . . . strictly select, strictly aristocratic, confined to the rich and renowned, is doctor-sickness; and for steady lastingness can give points to immortality.

Letters from the Earth, p. 106

He wrote a doctor's hand—the hand which from the beginning of time has been so disastrous to the apothecary and so profitable to the undertaker.

"Those Extraordinary Twains,"
Pudd'nhead Wilson, p. 306

DOCTRINE

Creeds mathematically precise, and hair-splitting niceties of doctrine, are absolutely necessary for the salvation of some kinds of souls, but surely the charity, the purity, the unselfishness that are in the hearts of men like these would save their souls though they were bankrupt in the true religion—which is ours.

The Innocents Abroad, I, Chapt. XXV, p. 333

DOG   *See* CONSCIENCE, CONVINCE, HAPPINESS, LIE, MONEY, NEWSPAPER, TEMPER, WATER

In the train, during a part of the return journey from Baroda, we had the company of a gentleman who had with him a remarkable looking dog. I had not seen one of its

kind before, as far as I could remember; though of course
I might have seen one and not noticed it, for I am not acquainted with dogs but only with cats. This dog's coat was
smooth and shiny and black, and I think it had tan trimmings around the edges of the dog, and perhaps underneath. It was a long, low dog, with very short, strange legs,
legs that curved inboard, something like parentheses turned
the wrong way)(. Indeed, it was made on the plan of a
bench for length and lowness. It seemed to be satisfied, but
I thought the plan poor, and structurally weak, on account
of the distance between the forward supports and those
abaft. With age the dog's back was likely to sag; and it
seemed to me that it would have been a stronger and more
practicable dog if it had some more legs. It had not begun
to sag yet, but the shape of the legs showed that the undue
weight imposed upon them was beginning to tell. It had
a long nose, and floppy ears that hung down, and a resigned
expression of countenance. I did not ask what kind of a
dog it was, or how it came to be deformed, for it was plain
that the gentleman was very fond of it, and naturally he
could be sensitive about it. From delicacy I thought it best
not to seem to notice it too much. No doubt a man with a
dog like that feels just as a person does who has a child
that is out of true. The gentleman was not merely fond of
the dog, he was also proud of it—just the same, again, as a
mother feels about her child when it is an idiot. I could
see that he was proud of it, notwithstanding it was such a
long dog and looked so resigned and pious. . . It had won
prizes in dog shows, both in India and in England—I saw
them. He said its pedigree was on record in the Kennel
Club, and that it was a well-known dog. He said a great
many people in London could recognize it the moment they
saw it. I did not say anything, but I did not think it anything strange; I should know that dog again, myself, yet
I am not careful about noticing dogs. He said that when
he walked along in London, people often stopped and
looked at the dog. Of course I did not say anything for I
did not want to hurt his feelings, but I could have explained

to him that if you take a great long low dog like that and waddle it along the street anywhere in the world and not charge anything, people will stop and look. He was gratified because the dog took prizes. But that was nothing; if I were built like that I could take prizes myself.

Following the Equator, II, Chapt. IX, p. 99

He arrives with the early morning and the market people, and there is a dog that arrives at about the same time and barks steadily at nothing till he dies, and they fetch another dog just like him. The bark of this breed is the twin of the whip volley, and stabs like a knife.

"Aix, the Paradise of Rheumatics"
Europe and Elsewhere, p. 101

If you pick up a starving dog and make him prosperous, he will not bite you. This is the principal difference between a dog and a man.

"Pudd'nhead Wilson's Calendar"
Pudd'nhead Wilson, Chapt. XVI, p. 158

Spending one's capital is feeding a dog on his own tail.
Mark Twain's Notebook, p. 345

[The speed of a cayote]: But if you start a swift-footed dog after him, you will enjoy it ever so much—especially if it is a dog that has a good opinion of himself, and has been brought up to think he knows something about speed. The cayote will go swinging gently off on that deceitful trot of his, and every little while he will smile a fraudful smile over his shoulder that will fill that dog entirely full of encouragement and worldly ambition, and make him lay his head still lower to the ground, and stretch his neck further to the front, and pant more fiercely, and stick his tail out straighter behind, and move his furious legs with a yet wilder frenzy, and leave a broader, and higher and denser cloud of desert sand smoking behind, and marking his long wake across the level plain! And all this time the dog is only a short twenty feet behind the cayote, and to save the soul of him he cannot understand why it is that he cannot get perceptibly closer; and he begins to get aggravated, and it makes him madder and madder to see how gently the cayote glides along and never pants or sweats or ceases to smile; and he grows still more and more incensed to see how shamefully he has been taken in by an entire stranger, and what an ignoble swindle that long, calm, soft-footed trot is; and next he notices that he is getting fagged, and that the cayote actually has to slacken speed a little to keep from running away from him—and *then* that town-dog is mad in earnest, and he begins to strain and weep and swear, and paw the sand higher than ever, and reach for the cayote with concentrated and desperate energy. This "spurt" finds him six feet behind the gliding enemy, and two miles from his friends. And then, in the instant that a wild new hope is lighting up his face, the cayote turns and smiles blandly upon him once more, and with a something about it which seems to say: "Well, I shall have to tear myself away from you, bub—business is business, and it will not do for me to be fooling along this way all day"—and forthwith there is a rushing sound, and the sudden splitting of a long crack through the atmosphere, and behold that dog is solitary and alone in the midst of a vast solitude!

It makes his head swim. He stops, and looks all around; climbs the nearest sand-mound, and gazes into the distance; shakes his head reflectively, and then, without a word, he turns and jogs along back to his train, and takes up a humble position under the hindmost wagon, and feels unspeakably mean, and looks ashamed, and hangs his tail at half-mast for a week. And for as much as a year after that, whenever there is a great hue and cry after a cayote, that dog will merely glance in that direction without emotion, and apparently observe to himself, "I believe I do not wish any of the pie."

Roughing It, I, Chapt. V, p. 49

We four always spread our common stock of blankets together on the frozen ground, and slept side by side; and finding that our foolish, long-legged hound pup had a deal of animal heat in him, Oliphant got to admitting him to the bed, between himself and Mr. Ballou, hugging the dog's warm back to his breast and finding great comfort in it. But in the night the pup would get stretchy and brace his feet against the old man's back and shove, grunting complacently the while; and now and then, being warm and snug, grateful and happy, he would paw the old man's back simply in excess of comfort; and at yet other times he would dream of the chase and in his sleep tug at the old man's back hair and bark in his ear. The old gentleman complained mildly about these familiarities, at last, and when he got through with his statement he said that such a dog as that was not a proper animal to admit to bed with tired men, because he was "so meretricious in his movements and so organic in his emotions." We turned the dog out.

Ibid., I, Chapt. XXVII, p. 219

There ain't no such a thing as an accident. When my Uncle Lem was leaning up agin a scaffolding once, sick, or drunk, or suthin', an Irishman with a hod full of bricks fell on him out of the third story and broke the old man's back in two places. People said it was an accident. Much accident there was about that. He didn't know what he was there for, but he was there for a good object. If he hadn't been there the Irishman would have been killed. Nobody can ever make me believe anything different from that. Uncle Lem's dog was there. Why didn't the Irishman fall on the dog? Becuz the dog would a seen him a coming and stood from under. That's the reason the dog warn't appinted. A dog can't be depended on to carry out a special providence.

Ibid., II, Chapt. XII, p. 125

Fifteen or twenty years ago, Decoration Day happened to be more like the Fourth of July for temperature than like the 30th of May. Twichell was orator of the day. He pelted his great crowd of old Civil War soldiers for an hour in the biggest church in Hartford, while they mourned and sweltered. Then they marched forth and joined the procession of other old soldiers and tramped through clouds of dust to the cemetery and began to distribute the flags and the flowers—a tiny flag and a small basket of flowers to each military grave. This industry went on and on and on, everybody breathing dust—for there was nothing else to breathe; everybody streaming with perspiration; everybody tired and wishing it was over. At last there was but one basket of flowers left, only one grave still undecorated. A fiery little major, whose patience was all gone, was shouting:

"Corporal Henry Jones, Company C, Fourteenth Connecticut Infantry—"

No response. Nobody seemed to know where that corporal was buried.

The major raised his note a degree or two higher:

"Corporal Henry Jones, Company C, Fourteenth Connecticut Infantry. Does anybody know where that man is buried?"

No response. Once, twice, three times, he shrieked again, with his temper ever rising higher and higher:

"Corporal Henry Jones, Company C, Fourteenth Connecticut Infantry. Doesn't anybody know where that man is buried?" No response. Then he slammed the basket of flowers on the ground, and said to Twichell, "Proceed with the finish."

The crowd massed themselves together around Twichell with uncovered heads, the silence and solemnity interrupted only by subdued sneezings, for these people were buried in the dim cloud of dust. After a pause Twichell began an impressive prayer, making it brief to meet the exigencies of the occasion. In the middle of it he made a pause. The drummer thought he was through, and let fly a rub-a-dub-dub—and the little major stormed out, "*Stop* that drum!" Twichell tried again. He got almost to the last word safely, when somebody trod on a dog and the dog let out a howl of anguish that could be heard beyond the frontier. The major said, "God damn that dog!"—and Twichell said, "Amen."

Mark Twain's Autobiography, Paine, II, p. 210

We are unanimous in the pride we take in good and genuine compliments paid us, in distinctions conferred

upon us, in attentions shown us. There is not one of us, from
the emperor down, but is made like that. Do I mean attentions shown us by the great? No, I mean simply flattering attentions, let them come whence they may. We despise
no source that can pay us a pleasing attention—there is no
source that is humble enough for that. You have heard a
dear little girl say of a frowzy and disreputable dog: "He
came right to me and let me pat him on the head, and he
wouldn't let the others touch him!" and you have seen her
eyes dance with pride in that high distinction. You have
often seen that. If the child were a princess, would that
random dog be able to confer the like glory upon her with
his pretty compliment? Yes; and even in her mature life and
seated upon a throne, she would still remember it, still
recall it, still speak of it with frank satisfaction.

"Does the Race of Man Love a Lord?"
The $30,000 Bequest, Etc., p. 274

[Learning to ride a bicycle]: . . . Within the next five
days I achieved so much progress that the boy couldn't
keep up with me. He had to go back to his gate-post, and
content himself with watching me fall at long range.

There was a row of low stepping-stones across one end
of the street, a measured yard apart. Even after I got so I
could steer pretty fairly I was so afraid of those stones that
I always hit them. They gave me the worst falls I ever got
in that street, except those which I got from dogs. I have
seen it stated that no expert is quick enough to run over a
dog; that a dog is always able to skip out of his way. I
think that that may be true; but I think that the reason he
couldn't run over the dog was because he was trying to.
I did not try to run over any dog. But I ran over every dog
that came along. I think it makes a great deal of difference.
If you try to run over the dog he knows how to calculate,
but if you are trying to miss him he does not know how to
calculate, and is liable to jump the wrong way every time.
It was always so in my experience. Even when I could not
hit a wagon I could hit a dog that came to see me practice.
They all liked to see me practice, and they all came, for

there was very little going on in our neighborhood to entertain a dog. It took time to learn to miss a dog, but I achieved even that.

. . .

Get a bicycle. You will not regret it, if you live.

"Taming the Bicycle,"
What is Man? and Other Essays, p. 295

By what right has the dog come to be regarded as a "noble" animal? The more brutal and cruel and unjust you are to him the more your fawning and adoring slave he becomes; whereas, if you shamefully misuse a cat once she will always maintain a dignified reserve toward you afterward—you can never get her full confidence again.

Mark Twain, a Biography, Paine, II, p. 685

Shall we ever laugh again? If I could only see a dog that I knew in the old times! and put my arms around his neck and tell him all, everything, and ease my heart!

[June 12, 1904]
Mark Twain-Howells Letters, II, p. 759

Several dogs came bounding over the fence, with great riot and noise, and each of them took a soldier by the slack of his trousers and began to back away with him. We could not shoot the dogs without endangering the persons they were attached to; so we had to look on helpless, at what was perhaps the most mortifying spectacle of the Civil War. . . . The old man and his son came and undid the dogs without difficulty, all but Bowers's; but they couldn't undo his dog, they didn't know his combination; he was of the bull kind, and seemed to be set with a Yale time-lock . . .

"The Private History of a Campaign that Failed,"
The American Claimant, p. 246

DOUBT   *See also* KILLING

. . . when all is said and done, the one sole condition that makes spiritual happiness and preserves it is the absence of doubt.

Mark Twain in Eruption, p. 339

When in doubt, tell the truth.

> *Mark Twain's Speeches* (1923), p. 184

When Mark Twain was introduced as the man who had said, "When in doubt, tell the truth," he replied that he had invented that maxim for others, but that when in doubt himself, he used more sagacity.

> *Mark Twain, a Biography*, Paine, III, p. 1280

DREAM   *See also* DISAPPOINTMENT

. . . everything in a dream is more deep and strong and sharp and real than is ever its pale imitation in the unreal life which is ours when we go about awake and clothed with our artificial selves in this vague and dull-tinted artificial world. When we die we shall slough off this cheap intellect, perhaps, and go abroad into Dreamland clothed in our real selves, and aggrandized and enriched by the command over the mysterious mental magician who is here not our slave, but only our guest.

> "My Platonic Sweetheart,"
> *The Mysterious Stranger, Etc.*, p. 304

Old Age . . . [the] belated fag-end of a foolish dream, a dream that was so ingeniously dreamed that it seemed real all the time. . . .

> *Mark Twain, a Biography*, Paine, III, p. 1256

Nothing exists; all is a dream. God—man—the world—the sun, the moon, the wilderness of stars—a dream, all a dream; they have no existence. *Nothing exists save empty space—and you!* . . . And you are but a *thought*—a vagrant thought, a useless thought, a homeless thought, wandering forlorn among the empty eternities!

> *The Mysterious Stranger, Etc.*, Chapt. XI, p. 138

DRESS   *See also* CLOTHES, MUSIC, SOUL

I have found that when a man reaches the advanced age of seventy-one years, as I have, the continual sight of dark clothing is likely to have a depressing effect upon him. Light-colored clothing is more pleasing to the eye and enlivens the spirit. Now, of course, I cannot compel everyone to wear such clothing just for my especial benefit, so I do the next best thing and wear it myself . . .

I am decidedly for pleasing color combinations in dress. I like to see the women's clothes, say, at the opera. What can be more depressing than the sombre black which custom requires men to wear upon state occasions? A group of men in evening clothes looks like a flock of crows, and is just about as inspiring.

"Dress Reform and Copyright,"
Mark Twain's Speeches (1910), p. 86

DRINK *See also* CHARITY, LIQUOR, OCCUPATION, PROHIBITION

Doctor Rice's friend . . . came home drunk and explained it to his wife, and his wife said to him, "John, when you have drunk all the whiskey you want, you ought to ask for sarsaparilla." He said, "Yes, but when I have drunk all the whiskey I want I can't say sarsaparilla."

"Sixty-seventh Birthday,"
Mark Twain's Speeches (1923), p. 245

[A] modest man, tolerably far gone with beer and other matters, enters a saloon (twenty-five cents is the price for anything and everything . . .) and lays down a half dollar; calls for whiskey and drinks it; the barkeeper makes change and lays the quarter in a wet place on the counter; the modest man fumbles at it with nerveless fingers, but it slips and the water holds it; he contemplates it, and tries again; same result; observes that people are interested in what he is at, blushes; fumbles at the quarter again—blushes—puts his forefinger carefully, slowly down, to make sure of his aim—pushes the coin toward the barkeeper, and says with a sigh:

"('ic!) Gimme a cigar!"

Roughing It, II, Chapt. XIV, p. 143

Bemis took care of himself during this part of the evening, and did not make an overpowering success of it, either, for he came into our room in the hotel about eleven o'clock, full of cheerfulness, and talking loosely, disjointedly, and indiscriminately, and every now and then tugging out a ragged word by the roots that had more hiccups than syllables in it . . .

Ibid., I, Chapt. XIII, p. 112

How I do hate those enemies of the human race who go around enslaving God's free people with *pledges*—to quit drinking instead of to quit wanting to drink.

Mark Twain's Letters, II, p. 459

DROWNING   *See also* ARK, MOTHER, RIVER, SIMILES

I should like to call back Will Bowen, and John Garth and the others, and live the life, and be as we were, and make holiday until fifteen, then all drown together.

Letters to Will Bowen, p. 9

DUELING

I think I could wipe out a dishonor by crippling the other man, but I don't see how I could do it by letting him cripple me.

Mark Twain, a Biography, Paine, III, p. 1514

Much as the modern French duel is ridiculed by certain smart people, it is in reality one of the most dangerous institutions of our day. Since it is always fought in the open air the combatants are nearly sure to catch cold. M. Paul de Cassagnac, the most inveterate of the French duelists, has suffered so often in this way that he is at last a confirmed invalid; and the best physician in Paris has expressed the opinion that if he goes on dueling for fifteen or twenty years more—unless he forms the habit of fighting in a comfortable room where damps and draughts cannot intrude— he will eventually endanger his life. This ought to moderate the talk of those people who are so stubborn in maintaining that the French duel is the most health-giving of recreations because of the open-air exercise it affords. And it ought also to moderate that foolish talk about French duelists and socialist-hated monarchs being the only people who are immortal.

A Tramp Abroad, I, Chapt. VIII, p. 60

(DUELING)

1898. As concerns dueling. This pastime is as common in Austria today as it is in France. But with this difference, that here in the Austrian States the duel is dangerous, while in France it is not. Here it is tragedy, in France it is comedy; here it is a solemnity, there it is monkey-shines; here the duellist risks his life, there he does not even risk his shirt. Here he fights with pistol or sabre, in France with a hairpin—a blunt one. Here the desperately wounded man tries to walk to the hospital; there they paint the scratch so that they can find it again, lay the sufferer on a stretcher, and conduct him off the field with a band of music.

At the end of a French duel the pair hug and kiss and cry, and praise each other's valor; then the surgeons make an examination and pick out the scratched one, and the other one helps him on to the litter and pays his fare; and in return the scratched one treats to champagne and oysters in the evening, and then "the incident is closed," as the French say. It is all polite, and gracious, and pretty, and impressive. At the end of an Austrian duel the antagonist that is alive gravely offers his hand to the other man, utters some phrases of courteous regret, then bids him good-by and goes his way, and that incident also is closed. The French duellist is painstakingly protected from danger, by the rules of the game. His antagonist's weapon cannot reach so far as his body; if he gets a scratch it will not be above his elbow. But in Austria, the rules of the game do not provide against danger, they carefully provide *for* it, usually. Commonly the combat must be kept up until one of the men is disabled; a non-disabling slash or stab does not retire him.

"Chapters from My Autobiography,"
The North American Review, Sept. 1907, p. 13

DUTY *See* ARK, COUNTRY, MAN, POLITICS

. . . when a man stands on the verge of seventy-two you know perfectly well that he never reached that place without knowing what this life is—heartbreaking bereavement. And so our reverence is for our dead. We do not forget them; but our duty is toward the living; and if we can be cheerful, cheerful in spirit, cheerful in speech and in hope, that is a benefit to those who are around us.

"Books, Authors and Hats,"
Mark Twain's Speeches (1923), p. 341

Duties are not performed for duty's *sake*, but because their *neglect* would make the man *uncomfortable*. A man performs but *one* duty—the duty of contenting his spirit, the duty of making himself agreeable to himself.

What Is Man? and *Other Essays,* Chapt. II, p. 20

Make it a point to do something every day that you don't want to do. This is the golden rule for acquiring the habit of doing your duty without pain.

"Pudd'nhead Wilson's New Calendar,"
Following the Equator, II, Chapt. XXII, p. 250

Do your duty today and repent tomorrow.

More Maxims of Mark, p. 6

E

EARLY RISING

Well enough for old folks to rise early, because they have done so many mean things all their lives they can't sleep anyhow.

Mark Twain's Notebook, p. 21

Go to bed early, get up early—this is wise. Some authorities say get up with the sun; some others say get up with one thing, some with another. But a lark is really the best thing to get up with. It gives you a splendid reputation with everybody to know that you get up with the lark; and if you get the right kind of lark, and work at him right, you can easily train him to get up at half past nine, every time— it is no trick at all.

"Advice to Youth,"
Mark Twain's Speeches (1923), p. 105

Rise early. It is the early bird that catches the worm. Don't be fooled by this absurd saw; I once knew a man who tried it. He got up at sunrise and a horse bit him.

Mark Twain's Notebook, p. 12

How is a man to grow healthier, and wealthier, and wiser by going to bed early and getting up early, when he fails to accomplish these things when he does not go to bed at all?

And as far as becoming wiser is concerned, you might put all the wisdom I acquired in these experiments in your eye, without obstructing your vision any to speak of.

"Early Rising,"
The Washoe Giant in San Francisco, p. 84

The reason we get up at six . . . is because we want to see what time it is. Partly this, and partly because we have heard that early rising is beneficial. We then go back to bed.
Love Letters of Mark Twain, p. 146

EARTH

Captain Stormfield tries to explain to the head clerk at the gate of heaven, which planet he came from:

The clerk got a balloon and sailed up and up . . . in front of a map that was as big as Rhode Island. He went on up till he was out of sight, and by and by he came down and got something to eat and went up again. . . . He kept on doing this for a day or two, and finally he came down and said he thought he had found that solar system, but it might be fly-specks. So he got a microscope and went back. It turned out better than he feared. He had rousted out our system, sure enough. He got me to describe our planet and its distance from the sun, and then he says to his chief—

"Oh, I know the one he means, now, sir. It is on the map. It is called the Wart."
Captain Stormfield's Visit to Heaven, p. 23

EARTHQUAKE

If there were an earthquake in Berlin the police would take charge of it and conduct it in that sort of orderly way that would make you think it was a prayer-meeting. That is what an earthquake generally ends in, but this one would be different from those others; it would be kind of soft and self-contained, like a republican praying for a mugwump.

"The German Chicago,"
The American Claimant, Etc., p. 509

. . . they gave him a teaspoonful of liquid quinine and it set his vitals on fire. He made several grimaces which gave

me a better idea of the Lisbon earthquake than any I have
ever got of it from paintings and descriptions.

Following the Equator, II, Chapt. XXIV, p. 290

An earthquake of sudden joy shook him from dome to
cellar.

Mark Twain in Eruption, p. 92

ECCENTRICITY *See* VIRTUE, WALL STREET

ECHO

You could utter a word and it would talk back at you for
fifteen minutes.

"The Canvasser's Tale,"
Tom Sawyer Abroad, Etc., p. 366

We are nothing but echoes. We have no thoughts of our
own, no opinions of our own, we are but a compost heap
made up of the decayed heredities, moral and physical.

Mark Twain's Notebook, p. 312

ECSTASY

It was an ecstasy; and an ecstasy is a thing that will not
go into words; it feels like music, and one cannot tell about
music so that another person can get the feeling of it.

The Mysterious Stranger, Etc., Chapt. III, p. 25

EDDY, MARY BAKER *See* CHRISTIAN SCIENCE, HUMAN
RACE, UNCLE

EDEN, GARDEN OF

But there is a defect—only one, but it is a defect which
almost entitles it to be spelled with a capital D. This is the
defect of loneliness. We have not a single neighbor who is
a neighbor . . .

I feel for Adam and Eve now, for I know how it was
with them . . . The Garden of Eden I now know was an
unendurable solitude. I know that the advent of the serpent
was a welcome change—anything for society.

Mark Twain, a Biography, Paine, III, p. 1315

EDITOR   *See also* PRINTING

I am not an editor of a newspaper, and shall always try to do right and be good, so that God will not make me one . . .

The Galaxy Magazine, Dec. 1870, p. 881

EDUCATION   *See also* TRAINING, EXPERIENCE, SCHOOLING

It is best to prove things by experiment; then you *know;* whereas if you depend on guessing and supposing and conjecturing, you will never get educated.

Eve's Diary [1906], p. 85

Well, I ain't denying that a thing's a lesson if it's a thing that can happen twice just the same way. There's lots of such things, and *they* educate a person, that's what Uncle Abner always said; but there are forty *million* lots of the other kind—the kind that don't happen the same way twice —and they ain't no real use, they ain't no more instructive than the small-pox. When you've got it, it ain't no good to git vaccinated afterward, because the small-pox don't come but once. But, on the other hand, Uncle Abner said that the person that had took a bull by the tail once had learnt sixty or seventy times as much as a person that hadn't, and said a person that started in to carry a cat home by the tail was gitting knowledge that was always going to be useful to him, and warn't ever going to grow dim or doubtful.

Tom Sawyer Abroad, Etc., Chapt. X, p. 96

Education consists mainly in what we have unlearned.

Mark Twain's Notebook, p. 346

The self-taught man seldom knows anything accurately, and he does not know a tenth as much as he could have known if he had worked under teachers; and besides, he brags, and is the means of fooling other thoughtless people into going and doing as he himself has done. There are those who imagine that the unlucky accidents of life— life's "experiences"—are in some way useful to us. I wish I could find out how. I never knew one of them to happen twice. They always change off and swap around and catch you on your inexperienced side. If personal experience can be worth anything as an education, it wouldn't seem likely that you could trip Methuselah; and yet if that old person could come back here it is more than likely that one of the first things he would do would be to take hold of one of these electric wires and tie himself all up in a knot. Now . . . the wiser thing would be for him to ask somebody whether it was a good thing to take hold of. But that would not suit him; he would be one of the self-taught kind that go by experience; he would want to examine for himself. And he would find, for his instruction, that the coiled patriarch shuns the electric wire; and it would be useful to him, too, and would leave his education in quite a complete and rounded-out condition, till he should come again, some day, and go to bouncing a dynamite-can around to find what was in it.

"Taming the Bicycle,"
What Is Man? and Other Essays, p. 290

EGG   *See also* SCENERY
Behold, the fool saith, "Put not all thine eggs in the one basket"—which is but a manner of saying, "Scatter your money and your attention"; but the wise man saith, "Put all your eggs in the one basket and—WATCH THAT BASKET."

"Pudd'nhead Wilson's Calendar,"
Pudd'nhead Wilson, Chapt. XV, p. 145

EGYPT   *See* RAILROAD, SPHINX

ELECTRICITY   *See* WORDS

ELEVATOR
What has made these skyscrapers possible is the elevator. The cigar box which the European calls a "lift" needs but to be compared with our elevators to be appreciated. The lift stops to reflect between floors. That is all right in a hearse, but not in elevators. The American elevator acts like the man's patent purge—it worked. As the inventor

said, "This purge doesn't waste any time fooling around; it attends strictly to business."

"Municipal Government,"
Mark Twain's Speeches (1923), p. 215

In Europe an elevator is even to this day a rarity and a curiosity. Especially a curiosity. As a rule it seats but three or four persons—often only two—and it travels so slowly and cautiously and timorously and piously and solemnly that it makes a person feel creepy and crawly and scary and dismal and repentant.

"Some National Stupidities,"
Europe and Elsewhere, p. 180

ELOQUENCE   *See also* TALK, WORDS

How moving is the eloquence of the untaught when it is the heart that is speaking!
Love Letters of Mark Twain, p. 350

EMBARRASSMENT   *See also* BLUSH, DRINK, GIRL, INDE-
PENDENCE

The little book [Swedenborg] is charmingly written, and it interested me. But it flies too high for me. Its concretest things are filmy abstractions to me, and when I lay my grip on one of them and open my hand, I feel as embarrassed as I used to feel when I thought I had caught a fly.
Mark Twain's Letters, II, p. 545

I had to sneak out . . . I went up to where there was a board fence and practiced climbing backwards and forwards through a knothole for as much as an hour.
The Twainian, Jan.–Feb. 1949, p. 6

EMOTION   *See also* BEAUTY, DOG, FEAR, FEELING, FLAG,
FRIGHT, HAPPINESS, LAUGHTER, MUSIC, NATURE, PERFEC-
TION, PLEASURE, PROFANITY

. . . all full of tears and flapdoodle . . .
The Adventures of Huckleberry Finn,
Chapt. XXV, p. 218

EMPTY *See* HOUSE

ENDEAVOR *See* UNDERTAKER

ENEMY

It takes your enemy and your friend, working together, to hurt you to the heart; the one to slander you and the other to get the news to you.

> "Pudd'nhead Wilson's New Calendar,"
> *Following the Equator*, II, Chapt. IX, p. 96

. . . he lacks the common wisdom to keep still that deadly enemy of a man, his own tongue.

> *Letters from the Sandwich Islands*, p. 116

This is just the way in this world; an enemy can partly ruin a man, but it takes a good-natured injudicious friend to complete the thing and make it perfect.

> *Pudd'nhead Wilson*, Chapt. V, p. 52

Experience has not taught me very much, still it has taught me that it is not wise to criticize a piece of literature, except to an *enemy* of the person who wrote it; then if you praise it the enemy admires you for your honest manliness, and if you dispraise it he admires you for your sound judgment.

> *Mark Twain, a Biography*, Paine, I, p. 506

ENERGY *See also* AMERICA

What is government without energy? And what is a *man* without energy? Nothing—nothing at all. What is the grandest thing in Paradise Lost—the Arch-Fiend's terrible energy! What was the greatest feature in Napoleon's character? His unconquerable energy! Sum all the gifts that man is endowed with, and we give our greatest share of admiration to his energy. And today, if I were a heathen, I would rear a statue to Energy, and fall down and worship it!

> *Mark Twain, a Biography*, Paine, I, p. 146

ENGLAND *See also* AMERICA, CHURCHILL, WINSTON, GAME, HOTEL, HUMAN RACE, HUMOR, LIE

It has taken nearly a hundred years to bring the English and Americans into kindly and mutually appreciative relations, but I believe it has been accomplished at last. It was a great step when the two last misunderstandings were settled by arbitration instead of cannon. It is another great step when England adopts our sewing machines without claiming the invention—as usual. It was another when they imported one of our sleeping cars the other day. And it warmed my heart more than I can tell, yesterday, when I witnessed the spectacle of an Englishman ordering an American sherry cobbler of his own free will and accord— and not only that, but with a great brain and a level head reminding the barkeeper not to forget the strawberries. With a common origin, a common language, a common literature, a common religion, and—common drinks, what is longer needful to the cementing of the two nations together in a permanent bond of brotherhood?

> "Americans and the English,"
> *Mark Twain's Speeches* (1923), p. 34

English afternoon tea is an affront to luncheon and an insult to dinner.

> *Source Undetermined*

. . . in the matter of certain physical patent rights there is only one England. Now that I have sampled the globe, I am not in doubt. There is a beauty of Switzerland, and it is repeated in the glaciers and snowy ranges of many parts of the earth; there is a beauty of the fiord, and it is repeated in New Zealand and Alaska; there is a beauty of Hawaii, and it is repeated in ten thousand islands of the Southern seas; there is a beauty of the prairie and the plain, and it is repeated here and there in the earth; each of these is worshipful, each is perfect in its way, yet holds no monopoly of its beauty; but that beauty which is England is alone—it has no duplicate. It is made up of very simple details—just grass, and trees, and shrubs, and roads, and hedges, and gardens, and houses, and vines, and churches, and castles, and here and there a ruin—and over it all a mellow dream-haze of history. But its beauty is incomparable, and all its own.

> *Following the Equator,* I, Chapt. XXIX, p. 292

It is indeed a mighty estate, and I perceive now that the English are mentioned in the Bible: "Blessed are the meek, for they shall inherit the earth."

> "Queen Victoria's Jubilee,"
> *Europe and Elsewhere,* p. 205

So we got back to talking about the size of the Desert again, and the more we compared it with this and that and t'other thing, the more nobler and bigger and grander it got to look right along. And so, hunting among the figgers, Tom found, by and by, that it was just the same size as the Empire of China. Then he showed us the spread the Empire of China made on the map, and the room she took up in the world. Well, it was wonderful to think of, and I says:

"Why, I've heard talk about this Desert plenty of times, but *I* never knowed before how important she was."

Then Tom says:

"Important! Sahara important! That's just the way with some people. If a thing's big, it's important. That's all the sense they've got. All they can see is *size*. Why, look at England. It's the most important country in the world; and yet you could put it in China's vest-pocket; and not only that, but you'd have the dicken's own time to find it again the next time you wanted it. And look at Russia. It spreads all around and everywhere, and yet ain't no more important in this world than Rhode Island is, and hasn't got half as much in it that's worth saving."

> *Tom Sawyer Abroad, Etc.,* Chapt. IX, p. 90

As soon as the Jubilee was fairly over we broke up housekeeping and went for a few days to what is called in England "an hotel." If we could have afforded an horse and an hackney cab we could have had an heavenly good time flitting around on our preparation errands, and could have finished them up briskly; but the buses are slow and they wasted many precious hours for us. A bus is a sort of great cage on four wheels, and is six times as strong and eleven times as heavy as the service required of it demands —but that is the English of it. The bus aptly symbolizes the national character. The Englishman requires that everything about him shall be stable, strong, and permanent, except the house which he builds to rent. His own private house is as strong as a fort. The rod which holds up the lace curtains could hold up an hippopotamus. The three-foot flagstaff on his bus, which supports a Union Jack the size of a handkerchief, would still support it if it were one of the gates of Gaza. Everything he constructs is a deal heavier and stronger than it needs to be. He built ten miles of terraced benches to view the Jubilee procession from, and put timber enough in them to make them a permanent contribution to the solidities of the world—yet they were intended for only two days' service.

When they were being removed an American said, "Don't do it—save them for the Resurrection." If anything gets in the way of the Englishman's bus it must get out of it or be bowled down—and that is English. It is the serene self-sufficient spirit which has carried his flag so far. He ought to put his aggressive bus in his coat of arms, and take the gentle unicorn out.

"Letters to Satan,"
Europe and Elsewhere, p. 213

There, hand to hand, we fought like wild beasts, for there was no give-up to those English—there was no way to convince one of those people but to kill him, and even then he doubted.

Personal Recollections of Joan of Arc,
I, Book II, Chapt. XXII, p. 300

The war has brought England and America close together—and to my mind that is the biggest dividend that any war in this world has ever paid. If this feeling is ever to grow cold again I do not wish to live to see it.

Mark Twain, a Biography, Paine, II, p. 1064

How curiously unanecdotical the colonials and the ship-going English are—I believe I haven't told an anecdote or

151

heard one since I left America, but Americans when grouped drop into anecdotes as soon as they get a little acquainted.

Ibid., Paine, II, p. 1015

[*Address at a Savage Club dinner, Sept. 28, 1872*]:

The Library at the British Museum I find particularly astounding. I have read there hours together, and hardly made an impression on it. I revere that library. It is the author's friend. I don't care how mean a book is, it always takes one copy. (A copy of every book printed in Great Britain must by law be sent to the British Museum, a law much complained of by publishers.) And then every day that author goes there to gaze at that book, and is encouraged to go on in the good work. And what a touching sight it is of a Saturday afternoon to see the poor, careworn clergymen gathered together in that vast reading-room cabbaging sermons for Sunday! You will pardon my referring to these things. Everything in this monster city interests me, and I cannot keep from talking, even at the risk of being instructive. People here seem always to express distances by parables. To a stranger it is just a little confusing to be so parabolic—so to speak. I collar a citizen, and I think I am going to get some valuable information out of him. I ask him how far it is to Birmingham, and he says it is twenty-one shillings and sixpence. Now we know that doesn't help a man who is trying to learn. I find myself down-town somewhere, and I want to get some idea where I am—being usually lost when alone—and I stop a citizen and say, "How far is it to Charing Cross?" "Shilling fare in a cab," and off he goes. I suppose if I were to ask a Londoner how far it is from the sublime to the ridiculous he would try to express it in a coin.

Ibid., Paine, III, p. 1632

[Said during the Boer War in 1900]: England must not fall; it would mean an inundation of Russian and German political degradations which would envelop the globe and steep it in a sort of Middle-Age night and slavery which would last till Christ comes again. Even wrong—and she is

152

wrong—England must be upheld. He is an enemy of the human race who shall speak against her now.

Mark Twain's Letters, II, p. 693

The human being is a curious and interesting invention. It takes a Cromwell and some thousands of preaching and praying soldiers and parsons ten years to raise the standards of English official and commercial morals to a respectworthy altitude, but it takes only one Charles II a couple of years to pull them down into the mud again.

Mark Twain in Eruption, p. 81

ENGLISH LANGUAGE   *See also* GRAMMAR, GUIDE, LANGUAGE

The outlook is that the English-speaking race will dominate the earth a hundred years from now, if the sections do not get to fighting each other.

Following the Equator, I, Chapt. XIV, p. 168

No one can write perfect English and keep it up through a stretch of ten chapters. It has never been done. It was approached in the "well of English undefiled" . . . ; it has been approached in several English grammars. I have even approached it myself; but none of us has made port.

Christian Science, Book I, Chapt. IX, p. 88

ENJOYMENT   *See* LAUGHTER

ENVIRONMENT   *See also* CLIMATE, RELIGION

Environment is the chief thing to be considered when one is proposing to predict the future of Christian Science. It is not the ability to reason that makes the Presbyterian, or the Baptist, or the Methodist, or the Catholic, or the Mohammedan, or the Buddhist, or the Mormon; it is *environment.*

Christian Science, Book I, Chapt. IX, p. 93

ENVY   *See also* DEATH

Man will do many things to get himself loved, he will do

all things to get himself envied.

> "Pudd'nhead Wilson's New Calendar,"
> *Following the Equator,* I, Chapt. XXI, p. 207

I never greatly envied anybody but the dead. I always envy the dead.

> "Mark Twain's Life,"
> *The Mark Twain Omnibus,* p. xxii

EPITAPH *See also* EXAGGERATION

One night a Negro woman was burned to death in a house next door to us, and Riley said that our landlady would be oppressively emotional at breakfast, because she generally made use of such opportunities as offered, being of a morbidly sentimental turn, and so we should find it best to let her talk along and say nothing back—it was the only way to keep her tears out of the gravy. Riley said there never was a funeral in the neighborhood but that the gravy was watery for a week.

And, sure enough, at breakfast the landlady was down in the very sloughs of woe—entirely brokenhearted. Everything she looked at reminded her of that poor old negro woman, and so the buckwheat cakes made her sob, the coffee forced a groan, and when the beefsteak came on she fetched a wail that made our hair rise. Then she got to talking about the deceased, and kept up a steady drizzle till both of us were soaked through and through. Presently she took a fresh breath and said, with a world of sobs:

"Ah, to think of it, only to think of it!—the poor old creature. For she was so faithful. Would you believe it, she had been a servant in that self-same house and that self-same family for twenty-seven years come Christmas, and never a cross word and never a lick! And, oh, to think she should meet such a death at last!—a-sitting over the red-hot stove at three o'clock in the morning and went to sleep and fell on it and was actually roasted! Not just frizzled up a but, but literally roasted to a crisp! Poor faithful creature, how she was cooked! I am but a poor woman, but even if I have to scrimp to do it, I will put up a tombstone over that lone sufferer's grave—and Mr. Riley if you would have the goodness to think up a little epitaph to put on it which would sort of describe the awful way in which she met her—"

"Put it, 'Well done, good and faithful servant,'" said Riley, and never smiled.

"Riley—Newspaper Correspondent,"
Sketches New and Old, p. 203

EQUALITY

Equality ought to make men noble-minded.
The American Claimant, Chapt. XII, p. 100

EQUATOR

There isn't a Parallel of Latitude but thinks it would have been the Equator if it had had its rights.

"Pudd'nhead Wilson's New Calendar,"
Following the Equator, II, Chapt. XXXIII, p. 392

The equator was wisely put where it is, because if it had been run through Europe all the kings would have tried to grab it.

Mark Twain, a Biography, Paine, II, p. 1009

Sept. 5. Closing in on the equator this noon. A sailor explained to a young girl that the ship's speed is poor because we are climbing up the bulge toward the center of the globe; but that when we should once get over, at the equator, and start down-hill, we should fly. When she asked him the other day what the foreyard was, he said it was the front yard, the open area in the front end of the ship. That man has a good deal of learning stored up, and the girl is likely to get it all.

Afternoon. Crossed the equator. In the distance it looked like a blue ribbon stretched across the ocean. Several passengers kodak'd it.

Following the Equator, I, Chapt. IV, p. 60

ERROR   *See also* MIND

The wise change their minds when they perceive that

they have been in error.

Joan of Arc, I, Book II, Chapt. I, p. 108

ETERNITY

People in trying to justify Eternity say we can put it in learning all the knowledge acquired by the inhabitants of the myriads of stars. We shan't need that. We could use up two Eternities in learning all that is to be learned about our own world and the thousands of nations that have arisen and flourished and vanished from it. Mathematics alone would occupy me eight million years.

Mark Twain's Notebook, p. 170

ETIQUETTE *See* HUMAN RACE

EUROPE *See also* AMERICA, CLOTHES, COFFEE, COLOR,
  ELEVATOR, FIRE, GUIDE, HOME, IGNORANCE, TRAVEL

We leave for Europe in a few days [1891], to remain there until we shall get tired—a point which I shall reach in 30 days, Jean in 60, Clara in 90, Susie in a hundred, and Livy in six months. 30 and 60 are 90, and 90 are 180, and a hundred are 280. So that it is 280 days and six months that we are to be away . . . I am dismayed at the result of this calculation, and I wish I hadn't made it.

Mark Twain to Mrs. Fairbanks, p. 267

EVE *See* EDEN, GARDEN OF

I was greatly interested in the incident of Eve and the serpent, and thought Eve's calmness was perfectly noble. I asked Mr. B. if he had ever heard of another woman who, being approached by a serpent, would not excuse herself and break for the nearest timber.

Is Shakespeare Dead? Chapt. II, p. 20

The first historical apple that fell revealed to Eve the attractions of dress, and the second historical apple that fell revealed to Newton the attraction of gravitation. No charge.

A Mark Twain Bibliography—Merle Johnson, p. 185

The true Southern watermelon is a boon apart, and not

to be mentioned with commoner things. It is chief of this world's luxuries, king by the grace of God over all the fruits of the earth. When one has tasted it, he knows what the angels eat. It was not a Southern watermelon that Eve took: we know it because she repented.

"Pudd'nhead Wilson's Calendar,"
Pudd'nhead Wilson, Chapt. XIV, p. 132

EVIDENCE *See also* CIRCUMSTANCE

It was not my opinion; I think there is no sense in forming an opinion when there is no evidence to form it on. If you build a person without any bones in him he may look fair enough to the eye, but he will be limber and cannot stand up; and I consider that *evidence* is the bones of an opinion.

Personal Recollections of Joan of Arc,
I, Book I, Chapt. II, p. 24

EVIL *See* MONEY

EVOLUTION *See* UNIVERSE, WALLACE, Alfred Russell

EXAGGERATION *See also* DEATH, EPITAPH, LIE, RAFTS-
MEN, RIVER, SLOWNESS, TRAVEL, UNCLE

Age has taught me wisdom. If a spectacle is going to be particularly imposing I prefer to see it through somebody else's eyes, because that man will always exaggerate. Then I can exaggerate his exaggeration, and my account of the thing will be the most impressive.

"O'Shah,"
Europe and Elsewhere, p. 53

I've always reckoned that looking at the new moon over your left shoulder is one of the carelessest and foolishest things a body can do. Old Hank Bunker done it once, and bragged about it; and in less than two years he got drunk and fell off of the shot-tower, and spread himself out so that he was just a kind of a layer, as you may say; and they slid him edgeways between two barn doors for a coffin, and buried him so, so they say, but I didn't see it.

The Adventures of Huckleberry Finn, Chapt. X, p. 82

"Well, one day Wheeler was a-meditating and dreaming around in the carpet factory and the machinery made a snatch at him and first you know he was a-meandering all over that factory, from the garret to the cellar, and everywhere, at such another gait as—why, you couldn't even see him; you could only hear him whiz when he went by. Well, you know a person can't go through an experience like that and arrive back home the way he was when he went. No, Wheeler got wove up into thirty-nine yards of best three-ply carpeting. The widder was sorry, she was uncommon sorry, and loved him and done the best she could fur him in the circumstances, which was unusual. She took the whole piece—thirty-nine yards—and she wanted to give him proper and honorable burial, but she couldn't bear to roll him up; she took and spread him out full length, and said she wouldn't have it any other way. She wanted to buy a tunnel for him but there wasn't any tunnel for sale, so she boxed him in a beautiful box and stood it on the hill on a pedestal twenty-one feet high, and so it was monument and grave together, and economical—sixty foot high—you could see it from everywhere—and she painted on it, 'To the loving memory of thirty-nine yards best three-ply carpeting containing the mortal remainders of Millington G. Wheeler go thou and do likewise.' "

Mark Twain in Eruption, p. 222

John James Godfrey was hired by the Hayblossom Mining Company in California to do some blasting for them—the "Incorporated Company of Mean Men," the boys used to call it. Well, one day he drilled a hole about four feet deep and put in an awful blast of powder, and was standing over it ramming it down with an iron crowbar about nine foot long, when the cussed thing struck a spark and fired the powder, and scat! away John Godfrey whizzed like a sky-rocket, him and his crowbar! Well, sir, he kept on going up in the air higher and higher, till he didn't look any bigger than a boy—and he kept going on up higher and higher, till he didn't look any bigger than a doll—and he kept on going up higher and higher, till he didn't look any bigger than a little small bee—and then he went out of sight! Presently he came in sight again, looking like a little small bee—and he came along down further and further, till he looked as big as a doll again—and down further and further, till he was as big as a boy again—and further and further, till he was a full-sized man once more; and then him and his crowbar came a-whizzing down and lit right exactly in the same old tracks and went to r-ramming down, and r-ramming down, and r-ramming down again, just the same as if nothing had happened! Now, do you know, that poor cuss warn't gone only sixteen minutes, and yet that incorporated company of mean men *docked him for the lost time!*

Roughing It, II, Chapt. XXXVI, p. 321

There was a singular circumstance. The ship lay becalmed that entire fortnight in exactly the same spot. Then a handsome breeze came fanning over the sea, and we spread our white wings for flight. But the vessel did not budge. The sails bellied out, the gale strained at the ropes, but the vessel moved not a hair's breadth from her place. The captain was surprised. It was some hours before we found out what the cause of the detention was. It was barnacles. They collect very fast in that part of the Pacific. They had fastened themselves to the ship's bottom; then others had fastened themselves to the first bunch; others to these, and so on, down and down and down, and the last bunch had glued the column hard and fast to the bottom of the sea which is five miles deep at that point. So the ship was simply become the handle of a walking cane five miles long—yes, and no more movable by wind and sail than a continent is. It was regarded by every one as remarkable.

"About All Kinds of Ships,"
The American Claimant, Etc., p. 481

With an unusually competent aim for him, he landed a

stone on the side of my head which raised a bump there
that felt like the Matterhorn.

> "Chapters from My Autobiography,"
> *The North American Review,* Nov. 2, 1906, p. 841

He was only waiting for a sure opportunity, Then he
landed a cobblestone on the side of my head which raised
a bump there so large that I had to wear two hats for a
time.

> *Mark Twain's Autobiography,* Paine, II, p. 284

People who always feel jolly, no matter where they are
or what happens to them—who have the organ of hope pre-
posterously developed—who are endowed with an uncon-
gealable sanguine temperament—who never feel concerned
about the price of corn—and who cannot, by any possibility, discover any but the *bright* side of a picture—are
very apt to go to extremes, and exaggerate with 40-horse
microscopic power.

> *Mark Twain's Letters,* I, p. 64

EXAMPLE

Few things are harder to put up with than the annoyance
of a good example.

> "Pudd'nhead Wilson's Calendar,"
> *Pudd'nhead Wilson,* Chapt. XIX, p. 182

EXCITEMENT *See also* FRENCH PEOPLE

A person who is excited never can throw straight.

> *Joan of Arc,* II, Book III, Chapt. XXI, p. 282

EXCURSION

The impressive solemnity of such a pleasure trip [to the
Cliff House] is only equalled by an excursion to Lone
Mountain in a hearse.

> *The Washoe Giant in San Francisco,* p. 83

EXERCISE *See also* HEALTH

I have never taken any exercise except sleeping and
resting, and I never intend to take any. Exercise is loath-

some. It cannot be any benefit when you are tired; and I was always tired.

Mark Twain's Speeches (1923), p. 259

I take my only exercise acting as pallbearer at the funerals of my friends who exercised regularly.

Source Undetermined

I am pushing sixty—that is enough exercise for me.

Source Undetermined

EXIT

It is easier to stay out than get out.

"Pudd'nhead Wilson's New Calendar,"
Following the Equator, I, Chapt. XVIII, p. 179

EXPECTANCE *See* THINGS

EXPEDITION *See also* DISCOVERY

As soon as Sir Sagramor got well, he notified me that there was a little account to settle between us, and he named a day three or four years in the future; place of settlement, the lists where the offense had been given. I said I would be ready when he got back. You see, he was going for the Holy Grail. The boys all took a flier at the Holy Grail now and then. It was a several years' cruise. They always put in the long absence snooping around, in the most conscientious way, though none of them had any idea where the Holy Grail really was, and I don't think any of them actually expected to find it, or would have known what to do with it if he *had* run across it. You see, it was just the Northwest Passage of that day, as you may say; that was all. Every year expeditions went out holy grailing, and next year relief expeditions went out to hunt for *them*. There was worlds of reputation in it, but no money.

A Connecticut Yankee in King Arthur's Court,
Chapt. IX, p. 75

EXPERIENCE *See also* ADVICE, CAT, CONVINCING, CRITIC, DISPOSITION, EDUCATION, ENEMY, LIE, TRAVEL, WISDOM

Civilization largely consists in hiding human nature. When the barbarian learns to hide it we account him enlightened. . . . It is experience . . . but so is rheumatism. I knew a fellow, an epileptic, that had more experience along the line of fits than any man in Pike County, but it never got him anywhere.

Mark Twain and I, Opie Read

The most permanent lessons in morals are those which come, not of booky teaching, but of experience.

A Tramp Abroad, II, Chapt. XVIII, p. 239

Captain Phillips takes a just pride in his driving and in the speed of his horse. . . The Captain's whip came down fast, and the blows started so much dust out of the horse's hide that during the last half of the journey we rode through an impenetrable fog, and ran by a pocket compass in the hands of Captain Fish, a whaler captain of twenty-six years' experience, who sat there through that perilous voyage as self-possessed as if he had been on the euchre-deck of his own ship.

Letters from Sandwich Islands, p. 34

. . . by some subtle law all tragic human experiences gain in pathos by the perspective of time. We realize this when in Naples we stand musing over the poor Pompeiian mother, lost in the historic storm of volcanic ashes eighteen centuries ago, who lies with her child gripped close to her breast, trying to save it, and whose despair and grief have been preserved for us by the fiery envelope which took her life but eternalized her form and features.

"My Debut as a Literary Person,"
The Man That Corrupted Hadleyburg, Etc., p. 120

Experience is an author's most valuable asset; experience is the thing that puts the muscle and the breath and the warm blood into the book he writes.

"Is Shakespeare Dead?"
What Is Man? and Other Essays, p. 318

I do that kind of speech (I mean an offhand speech), and do it well, and make no mistake, in such a way to deceive the audience completely and make that audience believe it is an impromptu speech—that is art.

I was frightened out of it at last by an experience of Doctor Hayes. He was a sort of Nansen of that day. He had been to the North Pole, and it made him celebrated. He had even seen the polar bear climb the pole.

He had made one of those magnificent voyages such as Nansen made, and in those days when a man did anything which greatly distinguished him for the moment he had to come on to the lecture platform and tell all about it.

Doctor Hayes was a great, magnificent creature like Nansen, superbly built. He was to appear in Boston. He wrote his lecture out, and it was his purpose to read it from manuscript; but in an evil hour he concluded that it would be a good thing to preface it with something rather handsome, poetical, and beautiful that he could get off by heart and deliver as if it were the thought of the moment.

He had not had my experience, and could not do that. He came on the platform, held his manuscript down, and began with a beautiful piece of oratory. He spoke something like this:

"When a lonely human being, a pigmy in the midst of the architecture of nature, stands solitary on those icy waters and looks abroad to the horizon and sees mighty castles and temples of eternal ice raising up their pinnacles tipped by the pencil of the departing sun—"

Here a man came across the platform and touched him on the shoulder, and said: "One minute." And then to the audience:

"Is Mrs. John Smith in the house? Her husband has slipped on the ice and broken his leg."

And you could see the Mrs. John Smiths get up everywhere and drift out of the house, and it made great gaps everywhere. Then Doctor Hayes began again: "When a lonely man, a pigmy in the architecture—" The janitor came in again and shouted: "It is not Mrs. John Smith! It is Mrs. John Jones!"

Then all the Mrs. Joneses got up and left. Once more the speaker started, and was in the midst of the sentence when he was interrupted again, and the result was that the lecture was not delivered. But the lecturer interviewed the janitor afterward in a private room, and of the fragments of that janitor they took "twelve basketsful."

"To the Whitefriars,"
Mark Twain's Speeches (1923), p. 182

. . . I have been an author for 20 years and an ass for 55.
Mark Twain, a Biography, Paine, II, p. 916

It is from experiences such as mine that we get our education of life. We string them into jewels or into tinware, as we may choose.   *Ibid.,* III, p. 1277

. . . war talk by men who have been in a war is always interesting; whereas, moon talk by a poet who has not been in the moon is likely to be dull.

Life on the Mississippi, Chapt. XLV, p. 338

Experience teaches us only one thing at a time—and hardly that, in my case.

From an unpublished letter to
Clara Clemens, Feb. 5, 1893

Moralizing, I observed, then, that "all that glitters is not gold."

Mr. Ballou said I could go further than that, and lay it up among my treasures of knowledge, that *nothing* that glitters is gold. So I learned then, once for all, that gold in its native state is but dull, unornamental stuff, and that only lowborn metals excite the admiration of the ignorant with an ostentatious glitter. However, like the rest of the world, I still go on underrating men of gold and glorifying men of mica. Commonplace human nature cannot rise above that.

Roughing It, I, Chapt. XXVIII, p. 228

EXPERIMENT *See* EDUCATION, PATIENCE

EXPERT *See* NOVEL

EXPRESS *See* SLOWNESS

EXPRESSION *See also* FACE
   They gave the drunk a teaspoonful of liquid quinine and it set his vitals on fire. He made several grimaces which gave me a better idea of the Lisbon earthquake than any I have ever got of it from paintings and descriptions.
   Following the Equator, II, Chapt. XXIV, p. 290
   . . . barring that natural expression of villainy which we all have, the man looked honest enough.
   "A Mysterious Visit,"
   Sketches New and Old, p. 418
   The bust [of Shakespeare] . . . there in the Stratford Church. The precious bust, the priceless bust, the calm bust, the serene bust, the emotional bust, with the dandy moustache, and the putty face, unseamed of care—that face which has looked passionlessly down upon the awed pilgrim for a hundred and fifty years . . . will still look down upon the awed pilgrim three hundred years more, with the deep, deep, deep, subtle . . . expression of a bladder.
   "Is Shakespeare Dead?"
   What Is Man? and Other Essays, p. 366

EXTREMES *See* COLD, EXAGGERATION, WEATHER

EYES
   [As nearsighted as] . . . the Western editor, who would rub out with his nose whatever he wrote with his pen.
   "From Author's Sketch Book, Nov. 1870"
   The Twainian, May 1940, p. 2
   He said the common eye sees only the outside of things, and judges by that, but the seeing eye pierces through and reads the heart and soul, finding there capacities which the outside didn't indicate or promise, and which the other eye couldn't detect.
   Personal Recollections of Joan of Arc,
   I, Book II, Chapt. XI, p. 206

(EYES)

[She] always eats till her eyes bug out like boltheads on a jail door.

"Scandal,"

Mark Twain's Travels with Mr. Brown, p. 26

The eye has a good memory.

Mark Twain, a Biography, Paine, II, p. 753

. . . when a person knows how to use his eyes, everything has got a meaning to it; but most people's eyes ain't any good to them.

Tom Sawyer Abroad, Etc., Chapt. VII, p. 69

I got not one smile; not one line in those offended faces relaxed; I thawed nothing of the winter that looked out of those frosty eyes.

"Playing Courier,"

The American Claimant, Etc., p. 487

Berlin is a rest to the eye.

"The German Chicago"
Ibid., p. 507

EYE GLASSES *See* SPECTACLES

FABLE

(*Animals looked in the mirror and saw only themselves*):
Moral; by the cat: you can find in a text whatever you bring if you will stand between it and the mirror of your imagination. You may not see your ears, but they will be there.

"A Fable"
The Mysterious Stranger, p. 284

FACE   *See also* EXPRESSION, JOKE, SIMILES, VANITY

[He was] a long, cadaverous creature, with lanky locks hanging down to his shoulders, and a weak stubble bristling from the hills and valleys of his face.

Mark Twain, His Life and Work, Will Clemens,
p. 210

A fearful convulsion of his countenance was suggestive of a wink being swallowed by an earthquake.

Roughing It, I, Chapt. II, p. 22

. . . When he is off his guard, he has exactly that look on his face which you always see on the face of a man who is saving up his daughter to marry her to a duke.

Following the Equator, II, Chapt. XIII, p. 158

A soldier at the great gate admitted us without further authority than my countenance, and I suppose he thought he was paying me a handsome compliment when he did so; and so did I until I reflected that the place was a penitentiary.

Letters from the Sandwich Islands, p. 57

Why do you sit there looking like an envelope without any address on it . . .?

The American Claimant, Etc., Chapt. XXV, p. 224

. . . the purity and probity in those girls' faces is as clearcut as the mint-stamp on gold coin. . . .

Mark Twain, Business Man, Webster, p. 363

FACT   *See also* INFORMATION, VOCABULARY

Get your facts first and then you can distort them as much as you please.

From Sea to Sea, Kipling, p. 180

Fact and presumption are, for business purposes, all the same to them. They know the difference, but they also know how to blink it. They know, too, that while in history-building a fact is better than a presumption, it doesn't take a presumption long to bloom into a fact when *they* have the handling of it. They know by old experience that when they get hold of a presumption-tadpole he is not going to *stay* tadpole in their history-tank; no, they know how to develop him into the giant four-legged bullfrog of *fact*, and make him sit up on his hams and puff on his chin, and look important and insolent and come-to-stay: and assert his genuine simon-pure authenticity with a thundering bellow that will convince everybody because it is so loud. The thug is aware that loudness convinces sixty persons where reasoning convinces but one.

"Is Shakespeare Dead?"
What Is Man? and Other Essays, p. 354

. . . we do not deal much in facts when we are contemplating ourselves.

"Does the Race of Man Love a Lord?"
The $30,000 Bequest, Etc., p. 284

I am not one of those who in expressing opinions confine themselves to facts. I don't know anything that mars good literature so completely as too much truth. Facts contain a deal of poetry, but you can't use too many of them without damaging your literature.

"The Savage Club Dinner,"
Mark Twain's Speeches (1910) p. 389

I never saw an author who was aware that there was any dimensional difference between a fact and a surmise.

My Father Mark Twain, Clara Clemens, p. 86

. . . if you are going to find out the facts of a thing, what's the sense in guessing out what ain't the facts and wasting ammunition? I didn't lose no sleep.

"Tom Sawyer, Detective"
Tom Sawyer Abroad, Etc., p. 146

How empty is theory in presence of fact!

A Connecticut Yankee in King Arthur's Court, Chapt.
A Connecticut Yankee in King Arthur's Court,
Chapt. XLIII, p. 396

It may be that this girl had a fact in her somewhere, but I don't believe you could have sluiced it out with a hydraulic; nor got it with the earlier forms of blasting, even; it was a case for dynamite.

Ibid., Chapt. XI, p. 87

. . . [His] vocabulary is too limited, and so, by consequence, descriptions suffer in the matter of variety. They run too much to level Saharas of fact, and not enough to picturesque detail. . . .

Ibid., XV, p. 117

The best way to manage—in fact, the only sensible way— is to disguise repetitiousness of fact under variety of form: skin your fact each time and lay on a new cuticle of words. It deceives the eye; you think it is a new fact. . . .

Ibid., XXVI, p. 239

. . . You get a leetle too much costumery onto your statements: always dress a fact in tights, never in an ulster. . . .

Life on the Mississippi, Chapt. XXXIV, p. 275

FAILURE   *See also* DEBT

It is not in the least likely that any life has ever been lived which was not a failure in the secret judgment of the person who lived it.

Mark Twain's Notebook, p. 385

FAITH   *See also* MIND

There are those who scoff at the schoolboy, calling him frivolous and shallow. Yet it was the schoolboy who said: "Faith is believing what you know ain't so."

"Pudd'nhead Wilson's New Calendar"
Following the Equator, I, Chapt. XII, p. 132

FAME

Fame is a vapor; popularity an accident; the only earthly certainty is oblivion.

Mark Twain's Notebook, p. 114

After browsing among the stately ruins of Rome, of Baiae, of Pompeii, and after glancing down the long marble ranks of battered and nameless imperial heads that stretch down the corridors of the Vatican, one thing strikes me with a force it never had before: the unsubstantial, unlasting character of fame. Men lived long lives in the olden times, and struggled feverishly through them, toiling like slaves, in oratory, in generalship, or in literature, and then laid them down and died, happy in the possession of an enduring history and a deathless name. Well, twenty little centuries flutter away, and what is left of these things? A crazy inscription on a block of stone, which stuffy antiquaries bother over and tangle up and make nothing out of but a bare name (which they spell wrong)—no history, no tradition, no poetry—nothing that can give it even a passing interest.

The Innocents Abroad, II, Chapt. IV, p. 53

When one receives a letter from a great man for the first time in his life, it is a large event to him, as all of you know by your own experience. You never can receive letters enough from famous men afterward to obliterate that one, or dim the memory of the pleasant surprise it was, and the gratification it gave you.

"Unconscious Plagiarism"
Mark Twain's Speeches (1923), p. 77

The Presidency can't add anything to Grant; he will shine on without it. It is ephemeral; he is eternal.

Mark Twain, a Biography, Paine, II, p. 691

[About Kipling]: He is a stranger to me, but he is a most remarkable man—and I am the other one. Between us, we cover all knowledge; he knows all that can be known, and I know the rest.

Mark Twain in Eruption, p. 311

[About Kipling]: He was a stranger to me and to all the world, and remained so for twelve months, then he became suddenly known, and universally known. From that day to this he has held this unique distinction—that of being the only living person, not head of a nation, whose voice is heard around the world the moment it drops a remark; the only such voice in existence that does not go by slow ship and rail, but always travels first class—by cable.

Mark Twain, a Biography, Paine, II, p. 881

FAMILIARITY
Familiarity breeds contempt—and children.

Mark Twain's Notebook, p. 237

Familiarity breeds contempt. How accurate that is. The reason we hold truth in such respect is because we have so little opportunity to get familiar with it.

Ibid., p. 345

FAMILY, MARK TWAIN'S *See* MORALS, MOTHER, MARK TWAIN'S, MUSIC, SANTA CLAUS, ROYALTY, TALK

FARM
[About Key West]: There is no soil upon it of any con-

sequence, and so I do not see how they can manage to grow anything. I did not hear of any farm or vegetable gardens around. If a man wanted to start a farm there, he would have to bring one in a ship.

Mark Twain's Travels with Mr. Brown, p. 69

[A letter written to the Secretary of Agriculture]:

New York, April 6, 1893.

To the Hon. J. Sterling Morton,—Dear Sir: Your petitioner, Mark Twain, a poor farmer of Connecticut—indeed, the poorest one there, in the opinion of many—desires a few choice breeds of seed corn (maize), and in return will zealously support the Administration in all ways honorable and otherwise.

To speak by the card, I want these things to hurry to Italy to an English lady. She is a neighbor of mine outside of Florence, and has a great garden and thinks she could raise corn for her table if she had the right ammunition. I myself feel a warm interest in this enterprise, both on patriotic grounds and because I have a key to that garden, which I got made from a wax impression. It is not very good soil, still I think she can grow enough for one table and I am in a position to select a table. If you are willing to aid and abet a countryman (and Gilder thinks you are) please find the signature and address of your petitioner below.

Respectfully and truly yours. Signed, Mark Twain.

P. S. A handful of choice (southern) watermelon seeds would pleasantly add to that lady's employments and give my table a corresponding lift.

Mark Twain's Letters, II, p. 582

. . . you couldn't raise a watermelon on this farm with a derrick.

"A New Planet"
Europe and Elsewhere, p. 356

He was a very inferior farmer when he first began, but a prolonged and unflinching assault upon his agricultural difficulties has had its effect at last, and he is now fast rising from affluence to poverty.

"Rev. Henry Ward Beecher's Farm"
A Curious Dream, p. 139

In my [column], the farmer will always find full market reports and complete instructions about farming from grafting of the seed to the harrowing of the matured crop.

The Curious Republic of Gondour, p. 22

Switzerland is simply a large, humpy, solid rock, with a thin skin of grass pressed over it. . . .

In Switzerland the farmer's plow is a wide shovel, which scrapes up and turns over the thin earthly skin of his native rock—and there the man of the plow is a hero. Now here, by our St. Nicholas road, was a grave, and it had a tragic story. A plowman was skinning his farm one morning,—not the steepest part of it, but still a steep part—that is, he was not skinning the front of his farm but the roof of it, near the eaves,—when he absentmindedly let go of the plow-handles to moisten his hands, in the usual way; he lost his balance and fell out of his farm backwards; poor fellow, he never touched anything till he struck bottom, 1,500 feet below.*

*This was on a Sunday—M. T.

We throw a halo of heroism around the life of the soldier and the sailor, because of the deadly dangers they are facing all the time. But we are not used to looking upon farming as a heroic occupation. This is because we have not lived in Switzerland.

A Tramp Abroad, II, Chapt. XIII, p. 175

FASHION

At General G—'s reception the other night, the most fashionably dressed lady was Mrs. G. C. She wore a pink satin dress, plain in front but with a good deal of rake to it—to the train, I mean; it was said to be two or three yards long. One could see it creeping along the floor some little time after the woman was gone. Mrs. C. wore also a white bodice, cut bias, with Pompadour sleeves, flounced with ruches; low neck, . . . with white kid gloves. She had on a pearl necklace, which glinted lonely, high up the midst of that barren waste of neck and shoulders. Her hair was frizzled into a tangled chaparral, forward of her ears, aft it was drawn together, and compactly bound and plaited into a stump like a pony's tail, and furthermore was canted upward at a sharp angle, and ingeniously supported by a red velvet crupper, whose forward extremity was made fast with a half-hitch around a hairpin on the top of her head. Her whole top hamper was neat and becoming. She had a beautiful complexion when she first came, but it faded out by degrees in an unaccountable way. However, it is not lost for good. I found the most of it on my shoulder afterwards. (I stood near the door when she squeezed out with the throng.)

"A Fashion Item"
Sketches New and Old, p. 197

And I also noticed that the ladies did not dress in full fashion—which is a thing that always distresses me. No woman can look as well out of fashion as in it.

Mark Twain's Travels with Mr. Brown, p. 142

I am persuaded that a coldly-thought-out and independent verdict upon a fashion in clothes, or manners, or literature, or politics, or religion, or any other matter that is projected into the field of our notice and interest, is a most rare thing—if it has indeed ever existed.

. . . An Empress introduced the hoop skirt, and we know the result . . . A nobody introduced the bloomer, and we know the result. If Eve should come again, in her ripe renown, and reintroduce her quaint style—well, we know what would happen. And we should be cruelly embarrassed, along at first.

"Corn-Pone Opinions"
Europe and Elsewhere, p. 400

. . . Writing fashion articles, like wet nursing, can only be done properly by women.

"The Lick House Ball"
The Washoe Giant In San Francisco, p. 35

FATE

The only thing Fate proves to me is that what has been was.

Mark Twain and I, Opie Read, p. 62

FATHER   *See also* ANCESTOR

My father and I were always on the most distant terms when I was a boy—a sort of armed neutrality, so to speak. At irregular intervals this neutrality was broken, and suffering ensued; but I will be candid enough to say that the breaking and suffering were always divided with strict impartiality between us—which is to say, my father did the breaking and I did the suffering.

"Memoranda,"
The Galaxy Magazine, Aug. 1870, p. 286

[Mark Twain's answer, when solicited for a gift tale to be sold for the benefit of abused children]:

"Why should I want a 'Society for the Prevention of Cruelty to Children' to prosper when I have a baby downstairs that kept me awake several hours last night with no pretext but a desire to make trouble? This occurs every night and it embitters me, because I see how needless it was to put in the other burglar alarm, a costly and complicated contrivance which cannot be depended upon, because it's always getting out of order and won't go! Whereas the baby is always getting out of order, too, but can nevertheless be depended on, for the reason that the more it gets out of order, the more it does go.

"Yes, I am embittered against your society, for I think the idea of it is all wrong, but if you will start a society for the prevention of cruelty to fathers, I will write you a whole book."

"A Letter from Mark Twain,"
The Youth's Companion, May 18, 1882

It is a wise child that knows its own father, and an unusual one that unreservedly approves of him.

More Maxims of Mark, p. 9

When I was a boy of 14, my father was so ignorant I

could hardly stand to have the old man around. But when I got to be 21, I was astonished at how much he had learned in 7 years.

Source Undetermined

FAULT *See also* MANNERS

Always acknowledge a fault frankly. This will throw those in authority off their guard and give you opportunity to commit more.

More Maxims of Mark, p. 5

It is easy to find fault, if one has that disposition. There was once a man who, not being able to find any other fault with his coal, complained that there were too many prehistoric toads in it.

"Pudd'nhead Wilson's Calendar,"
Pudd'nhead Wilson, Chapt. IX, p. 82

. . . none are so ready to find fault with others as those who do things worthy of blame themselves.

Personal Recollections of Joan of Arc,
I, Book II, Chapt. IV, p. 139

FEAR *See also* COURAGE, FLEA, STUPIDITY

Fear of lightning is a particularly distressing infirmity, for the reason that it takes the sand out of a person to an extent which no other fear can, and it can't be *reasoned* with, and neither can it be shamed out of a person. A woman who could face the very devil himself—or a mouse —loses her grip and goes all to pieces in front of a flash of lightning.

"Mrs. McWilliams and the Lightning,"
The American Claimant, p. 299

"Bedouins!" Every man shrunk up and disappeared in his clothes like a mud-turtle. My first impulse was to dash forward and destroy the Bedouins. My second was to dash to the rear to see if there were any coming in that direction. I acted on the latter impulse. So did all the others.

The Innocents Abroad, II, Chapt. XXVIII, p. 369

. . . Each man is afraid of his neighbor's disapproval—a thing which, to the general run of the race, is more dreaded than wolves and death.

> "The United States of Lyncherdom,"
> *Europe and Elsewhere*, p. 244

. . . we are not afraid of dynamite until we get acquainted with it.

> *Following the Equator*, II, Chapt. XXIV, p. 283

[Approaching an area of lawless Arabs]: . . . what would *you* have done? Acknowledged that you were afraid and backed shamefully out? Hardly. It would not be human nature, where there were so many women. You would have done as we did: said you were not afraid of a million Bedouins—and made your will and proposed quietly to yourself to take up an unostentatious position in the rear of the procession.

> *The Innocents Abroad*, II, Chapt. XXVIII, p. 367

He was afraid . . . and skipped and dodged and scrambled around like a woman who has lost her mind on account of the arrival of a bat.

> *Personal Recollections of Joan of Arc*,
> II, Book II, Chapt. XXXVII, p. 81

[Riding horseback]: The place was so steep that at times [the horse] stood straight up on his tip-toes and clung by his forward toe-nails, with his back to the Pacific Ocean and his nose close to the moon—and thus situated we formed an equestrian picture which was as uncomfortable to me as it may have been picturesque to the spectator. You may think I was afraid, but I was not. I knew I could stay on him as long as his ears did not pull out.

> *Letters from the Sandwich Islands*, p. 45

FEELINGS *See also* DICTIONARY, REASONING

Sometimes my feelings are so hot that I have to take the pen and put them out on paper to keep them from setting me afire inside; then all that ink and labor are wasted because I can't print the results.

> *Mark Twain, a Biography*, Paine, II, p. 724

We all do no end of feeling, and we mistake it for thinking.

"Corn-Pone Opinions,"
Europe and Elsewhere, p. 406

FICTION   *See* TRUTH

FIGHT

In an instant both boys were rolling and tumbling in the dirt, gripped together like cats; and for the space of a minute they tugged and tore at each other's hair and clothes, punched and scratched each other's noses, and covered themselves with dust and glory.

The Adventures of Tom Sawyer, p. 10

It is a worthy thing to fight for one's own country. It is another sight finer to fight for another man's.

Mark Twain's Letters, II, p. 663

FIRE   *See also* MIND, STOVE

[Mark Twain calls on some new neighbors]: My name is Clemens; we ought to have called on you before, and I beg your pardon for intruding now in this informal way, but your house is on fire.

Mark Twain, a Biography, Paine, I, p. 413

We boast a good deal in America of our fire departments, the most efficient and wonderful in the world, but they have something better than that to boast of in Europe —a rational system of building which makes human life safe from fire and renders fire departments needless. We boast of a thing which we ought to be ashamed to require.

Mark Twain's Autobiography, Paine, I, p. 226

. . . then the fire-boys mounted to the hall and flooded it with water enough to annihilate forty times as much fire as there was there; for a village fire company does not often get a chance to show off, and so when it does get a chance it makes the most of it. Such citizens of that village as were of a thoughtful and judicious temperament did not insure against fire; they insured against the fire company.

Pudd'nhead Wilson, Chapt. XI, p. 114

Mrs. A. lighted the fire with kerosene oil on Wednesday morning: the handles of her coffin cost $13.50.

Catalog of American Humor Exhibit

One is not allowed to build unstable, unsafe, or unsightly houses in Berlin; the result is this comely and conspicuously stately city, with its security from conflagrations and breakdowns. It is built of architectural Gibraltars. The building commissioners inspect while the building is going up. It has been found that this is better than to wait till it falls down. These people are full of whims.

. . .

Everything is orderly. The fire brigades march in ranks curiously uniformed, and so grave is their demeanor that they look like a Salvation Army under conviction of sin. People tell me that when a fire alarm is sounded, the firemen assemble calmly, answer to their names when the roll is called, then proceed to the fire. There they are ranked up, military fashion, and told off in detachments by the chief, who parcels out to the detachments the several parts of the work which they are to undertake in putting out that fire. This is all done with low-voiced propriety, and strangers think these people are working a funeral. As a rule, the fire is confined to a single floor in these great masses of bricks and masonry, and consequently there is little or no interest attaching to a fire here for the rest of the occupants of the house.

"The German Chicago,"

The American Claimant, Etc., p. 506

[Description of a forest fire]: The ground was deeply carpeted with dry pine-needles, and the fire touched them off as if they were gunpowder. It was wonderful to see with what fierce speed the tall sheet of flame traveled! . . .

Within half an hour all before us was a tossing, blinding tempest of flame! It was surging up adjacent ridges—sur-

179

mounted them and disappeared in the canyons beyond—burst into view upon higher and farther ridges, presently—shed a grander illumination abroad and dove again—flamed out again, directly, higher and still higher up the mountainside—threw out skirmishing parties of fire here and there, and sent them trailing their crimson spirals away among remote ramparts and ribs and gorges, till as far as the eye could reach the lofty mountain-fronts were webbed as it were with a tangled network of red lava streams. Away across the water the crags and domes were lit with a ruddy glare, and the firmament above was a reflected hell!

Every feature of the spectacle was repeated in the glowing mirror of the lake! Both pictures were sublime, both were beautiful; but that in the lake had a bewildering richness about it that enchanted the eye and held it with the stronger fascination.

Roughing It, I, Chapt. XXIII, p. 190

All agreed that a campfire was what would come nearest to saving us, now, and so we set about building it. We could find no matches, and so we tried to make shift with the pistols. Not a man in the party had ever tried to do such a thing before, but not a man in the party doubted that it *could* be done, and without any trouble—because every man in the party had read about it in books many a time and had naturally come to believe it, with trusting simplicity, just as he had long ago accepted and believed *that other* common book-fraud about Indians and lost hunters making a fire by rubbing two dry sticks together.

We huddled together on our knees in the deep snow, and the horses put their noses together and bowed their patient heads over us; and while the feathery flakes eddied down and turned us into a group of white statuary, we proceeded with the momentous experiment. We broke twigs from the sage-brush and piled them on a little cleared place in the shelter of our bodies. In the course of ten or fifteen minutes all was ready, and then, while conversation ceased and our pulses beat low with anxious suspense, Ollendorff applied his revolver, pulled the trigger and blew the pile clear out of the county! It was the flattest failure that ever was.

Roughing It, I, Chapt. XXXII, p. 254

[Mark Twain's comment after learning that a St. Louis Harbor boat had been christened *Mark Twain*]: May my namesake follow in my righteous footsteps, then neither of us will need any fire insurance.

Mark Twain, a Biography, Paine, III, p. 1424

FISH   *See also* CLAM, FROG, OYSTER

[Mark Twain's answer to a letter from a would-be writer]: "Young Author"—Yes, Agassiz *does* recommend authors to eat fish, because the phosphorus in it makes brain. So far you are correct. But I cannot help you to a decision about the amount you need to eat—at least not with certainty. If the specimen composition you send is about your fair usual average, I suggest that perhaps a couple of whales would be all you would want for the present. Not the largest kind, but simply good middling-sized whales.

"Answers to Correspondents,"
Sketches New and Old, p. 83

Do not tell fish stories where the people know you; but particularly, don't tell them where they know the fish.

More Maxims of Mark, p. 7

. . . the wonderful transparence of Lake Tahoe! I speak of the north shore of Tahoe, where one can count the scales on a trout at a depth of a hundred and eighty feet. I have tried to get this statement off at par here, but with no success; so I have been obliged to negotiate it at fifty per cent discount. At this rate I find some takers; perhaps the reader will receive it on the same terms—sheriff's-sale prices. As far as I am privately concerned, I abate not a jot of the original assertion that in those strangely-magnifying waters one may count the scales on a trout (a trout of the large kind) at a depth of a hundred and eighty feet —may see every pebble on the bottom—might even count a paper of dray-pins.

The Innocents Abroad, I, Chapt. XX, p. 262

[A hand-shake]: The King took the hand with a poorly disguised reluctance, and let go of it as willingly as a lady lets go of a fish.

A Connecticut Yankee in King Arthur's Court,
Chapt. XXXII, p. 289

When you fish for love, bait with your heart, not your brain.

Mark Twain's Notebook, p. 346

FLAG *See also* PATRIOTISM

And our flag—another pride of ours, our chiefest! . . . When we have seen it in far lands—glimpsing it unexpectedly in that strange sky, waving its welcome and benediction to us—we have caught our breaths, and uncovered our heads, and couldn't speak, for a moment, for the thought of what it was to us and the great ideals it stood for.

"To the Person Sitting in Darkness,"
Europe and Elsewhere, p. 271

While everybody gazed, [a stately ship] swept superbly by and flung the Stars and Stripes to the breeze! Quicker than thought, hats and handkerchiefs flashed in the air, and a cheer went up! She was beautiful before—she was radiant now. Many a one on our deck knew then for the first time how tame a sight his country's flag is at home compared to what it is in a foreign land. To see it is to see a vision of home itself and all its idols, and feel a thrill that would stir a very river of sluggish blood.

The Innocents Abroad, I, Chapt. VII, p. 98

. . . we were fighting for flags we loved; and when men fight for these things, and under these convictions, with nothing sordid to tarnish their cause, that cause is holy, the blood spilled for it is sacred, the life that is laid down for it is consecrated.

"On Lincoln's Birthday,"
Mark Twain's Speeches (1923), p. 230

FLEA *See also* COURAGE

Fleas can be taught nearly anything that a congressman can.

What Is Man? and Other Essays, Chapt. VI, p. 82

Nelson would have been afraid of ten thousand fleas, but a flea wouldn't be afraid of ten thousand Nelsons.

More Maxims of Mark, p. 11

Now you begin to see, don't you, that *distance* ain't the thing to judge by, at all; it's the time it takes to go the distance *in* that *counts* . . .

It's a matter of *proportion,* that's what it is; and when you come to gauge a thing's speed by its size, where's your bird and your man and your railroad alongside of a flea? The fastest man can't run more than about ten miles in an hour—not much more than 10,000 times his own length. But all the books says any common ordinary third-class flea can jump a hundred and fifty times his own length; yes, and he can make five jumps a second too—seven hundred and fifty times his own length, in one little second— for he don't fool away any time stopping and starting—he does them both at the same time; you'll see, if you try to put your finger on him. Now that's the common, ordinary, third-class flea's gait; but you take an Eyetalian *first*-class flea, that's been the pet of the nobility all his life and hasn't ever knowed what want or sickness or exposure was, and he can jump more than three hundred times his own length and keep it up all day, five jumps every second, which is fifteen hundred times his own length. Well, suppose a man could go fifteen hundred times his own length in a second—say, a mile and a half. It's ninety miles a minute; it's considerably more than five thousand miles an hour. Where's your man *now?*—yes, and your bird, and your railroad, and your balloon? Laws, they don't amount to much 'longside of a flea. A flea is just a comet, b'iled down small.

Tom Sawyer Abroad, Etc., Chapt. VII, p. 64

The cayote is a living, breathing allegory of Want. He is *always* hungry. He is always poor, out of luck and friendless. The meanest creatures despise him and even the flea would desert him for a velocipede.

Roughing It, I, Chapt. V, p. 48

A gentle, old-maidish person and a sweet young girl of seventeen sat right in front of us that night at the Mannheim Opera. These people talked, between the acts, and I understood them, though I understood nothing that was uttered on the distant stage. At first they were guarded in their talk, but after they had heard my agent and me conversing in English they dropped their reserve and I picked up many of their little confidences; no, I mean many of *her* little confidences—meaning the elder party—for the young girl only listened, and gave assenting nods, but never said a word. How pretty she was, and how sweet she was! I wished she would speak. But evidently she was absorbed in her own thoughts, her own young-girl dreams, and found a dearer pleasure in silence. But she was not dreaming sleepy dreams,—no, she was awake, alive, alert, she could not sit still a moment. She was an enchanting study. Her gown was of a soft white silky stuff that clung to her round young figure like a fish's skin, and it was rippled over with the gracefullest little fringy films of lace; she had deep, tender eyes, with long, curved lashes; and she had peachy cheeks, and a dimpled chin, and such a dear little dewy rosebud of a mouth; and she was so dove-like, so pure, and so gracious, so sweet and bewitching. For long hours I did mightily wish she would speak. And at last she did; the red lips parted, and out leaped her thought—and with a guileless and pretty enthusiasm, too: "Auntie, I just *know* I've got five hundred fleas on me!"

A Tramp Abroad, I, Chapt. IX, p. 81

FLOWER *See also* AGE

In the most forlorn and arid and dismal [place] of all, where the racked and splintered debris was thickest, where the ancient patches of snow lay against the very path, where the wind blew bitterest and the general aspect was mournfulest and dreariest, and furthest from any suggestion of cheer or hope, I found a solitary wee forget-me-not, flour-

ishing away, not a droop about it anywhere, but holding
its bright blue star up with the prettiest and gallantest air
in the world, the only happy spirit, the only smiling thing,
in all that grisly desert. She seemed to say, "Cheer up!—
As long as we are here, let us make the best of it."

Ibid., II, Chapt. V, p. 65

The Langdons had a "run" on the hot house for a day
or two—which is to say, an unusual lot of people died and
their friends came to get roses and things to decorate the
coffins with. . . . One day, later, I said to Livy: "I have
been in the conservatory, and there is a perfect *world* of
flowers in bloom—and we haven't a confounded corpse!"

The Love Letters of Mark Twain, p. 85

FLY   *See also* DIRT, SIMILES

One fly makes a summer.

"Pudd'nhead Wilson's Calendar,"
The Man That Corrupted Hadleyburg, Etc., p. 157

Nothing is made in vain, but the fly came near it.

More Maxims of Mark, p. 10

Nothing seems to please a fly so much as to be mistaken
for a huckleberry, and if it can be baked in a cake and
palmed off on the unwary as a currant, it dies happy.

Connecticut Courant Supplement,
Jan. 10, 1878, p. 7

In the midst of the prayer a fly had lit on the back of the
pew in front of Tom and tortured his spirit by calmly rubbing its hands together, embracing its head with its arms,
and polishing it so vigorously that it seemed to almost part
company with the body, and the slender thread of a neck
was exposed to view.

The Adventures of Tom Sawyer, Chapt. V, p. 50

FOOD   *See also* COFFEE, DIET, EGG, ENGLAND, GOD, MORALS,
   SCENERY, TASTER

On the Continent, you can't get a rare beefsteak—everything is as overdone as a martyr.

Mark Twain's Notebook, p. 330

Last spring I stopped frolicking with mince pie after midnight; up to then I had always believed it wasn't loaded.

Mark Twain's Speeches (1923), p. 257

Photographs fade, bric-a-brac gets lost, busts of Wagner get broken, but once you absorb a Bayreuth-restaurant meal it is your possession and your property until the time comes to embalm the rest of you . . . It is believed among scientists that you could examine the crop of a dead Bayreuth pilgrim anywhere in the earth and tell where he came from. But I like this ballast. I think a "Hermitage" scrape-up at eight in the evening, when all the famine-breeders have been there and laid in their mementoes and gone, is the quietest thing you can lay on your keelson except gravel.

"The Shrine of St. Wagner,"
What Is Man? and Other Essays, p. 223

Ours was a reasonably comfortable ship, with the customary seagoing fare—plenty of good food furnished by the Deity and cooked by the devil.

Following the Equator, I, Chapt. I, p. 16

Bacon would improve the flavor of an angel.

Remembered Yesterdays, Robert U. Johnson, p. 320

I ate one of those rolls—I would have eaten it if it had killed me—and said to myself: "It is on my stomach; 'tis well; if it were on my conscience, life would be a burden to me."

Letters from the Sandwich Islands, p. 147

There *must* be cream in Europe somewhere, but it is not in the cows; they have been examined.

"Down the Rhone,"
Europe and Elsewhere, p. 141

FOOL   *See also* LIGHTNING

Let us be thankful for the fools. But for them the rest of us could not succeed.

"Pudd'nhead Wilson's New Calendar,"
Following the Equator, I, Chapt. XXVII, p. 277

Ah, well, I am a great and sublime fool. But then I am God's fool, and all His work must be contemplated with respect.

Mark Twain, a Biography, Paine, II, p. 609

The idea that no gentleman ever swears is all wrong; he can swear and still be a gentleman if he does it in a nice and benevolent and affectionate way. The historian, John Fiske, whom I knew well and loved, was a spotless and most noble and upright Christian gentleman, and yet he swore once. Not exactly that, maybe; still he—but I will tell you about it.

One day, when he was deeply immersed in his work, his wife came in, much moved and profoundly distressed, and said: "I am sorry to disturb you, John, but I must, for this is a serious matter, and needs to be attended to at once."

Then, lamenting, she brought a grave accusation against their little son. She said: "He has been saying his Aunt Mary is a fool and his Aunt Martha is a damned fool." Mr. Fiske reflected upon the matter a minute, then said: "Oh, well, it's about the distinction I should make between them myself."

"Taxes and Morals,"
Mark Twain's Speeches (1923), p. 279

[Rev. Rising]: "I should try to say, 'Forgive them, Father, they know not what they do.' "

[Mark Twain]: "Oh, well! If you put it on the ground that they are just fools, that alters the case, as I am one of that class myself. Come in and we'll try to forgive them and forget about it."

Mark Twain, a Biography, Paine, I, p. 215

July 4. Statistics show that we lose more fools on this day than on all the other days of the year put together. This proves, by the number left in stock, that one Fourth of July per year is now inadequate, the country has grown so.

"Pudd'nhead Wilson's Calendar,"
Pudd'nhead Wilson, Chapt. XVII, p. 164

April 1. This is the day upon which we are reminded of

what we are on the other three hundred and sixty-four.

> "Pudd'nhead Wilson's Calendar,"
> *Ibid.*, Chapt. XXI, p. 206

Hain't we got all the fools in town on our side? And ain't that a big enough majority in any town?

> *The Adventures of Huckleberry Finn,*
> Chapt. XXVI, p. 234

FORBID   *See also* PROHIBITION

There is a charm about the forbidden that makes it unspeakably desirable . . .

> *Mark Twain's Notebook*, p. 275

Adam was but human—this explains it all. He did not want the apple for the apple's sake, he wanted it only because it was forbidden. The mistake was in not forbidding the serpent; then he would have eaten the serpent.

> "Pudd'nhead Wilson's Calendar,"
> *Pudd'nhead Wilson*, Chapt. II, p. 19

. . . the more things are forbidden, the more popular they become.

> *Mark Twain's Notebook*, p. 257

FOREIGNER   *See* NATION, POLITENESS, SPELLING, UNDER-
STANDING

FORGETFULNESS   *See also* BOYHOOD

Once, in the course of his talk, [Mark Twain] forgot a word and denounced his poor memory:

"I'll forget the Lord's middle name sometime, right in the midst of a storm, when I need all the help I can get."

> *Mark Twain, a Biography*, Paine, III, p. 1545

[In Australia]: We saw . . . the slender native bird of modest plumage and the eternally-forgettable name—the bird that is the smartest among birds, and can give a parrot thirty to one in the game and then talk him to death. I think it begins with M. I wish it began with G or something that a person can remember.

> *Following the Equator*, I, Chapt. XXIII, p. 230

To forget pain is to be painless; to forget care is to be rid of it; to go abroad is to accomplish both.

> *Mark Twain's Autobiography*, Paine, II, p. 234

FORMALITY

In statesmanship get the formalities right, never mind about the moralities.

> "Pudd'nhead Wilson's New Calendar,"
> *Following the Equator*, II, Chapt. XXIX, p. 341

FOURTH OF JULY *See also* DOG, UNCLE

Eight grown Americans out of ten dread the coming of the Fourth, with its pandemonium and its perils, and they rejoice when it is gone—if still alive.

> *Ibid.*, I, Chapt. XVI, p. 165

July 4. Statistics show that we lose more fools on this day than in all the other days of the year put together. This proves, by the number left in stock, that one Fourth of July per year is now inadequate, the country has grown so.

> "Pudd'nhead Wilson's Calendar,"
> *Pudd'nhead Wilson*, Chapt. XVII, p. 164

We have got a double Fourth of July—a daylight Fourth and a midnight Fourth. During the day in America . . . we keep the Fourth of July properly in a reverent spirit. We devote it to teaching our children patriotic things— reverence for the Declaration of Independence . . . when night shuts down, that pandemonium will begin, and there will be noise . . . there will be people crippled, there will be people killed . . . all through that permission which we give to irresponsible boys to play with firearms and fire-crackers, and all sorts of dangerous things.

> "Independence Day,"
> *Mark Twain's Speeches* (1923), p. 347

FRANCE *See also* DUELING, GOVERNMENT, GRAMMAR, MAS-SACRE, NOISE, PARIS, RUSSIA, SOAP, VIRTUE, WATER

France has neither winter nor summer nor morals—apart

from these drawbacks it is a fine country.

Mark Twain's Notebook, p. 153

FRANKLIN, BENJAMIN *See* WORDS

FRANKNESS

Frankness is a jewel; only the young can afford it.

Mark Twain's Letters, I, p. 16

We write frankly and fearlessly but then we "modify" before we print.

Life on the Mississippi, Chapt. XIV, p. 119

FREEDOM *See also* PROSPERITY, LABOR

It is by the goodness of God that in our country we have those three unspeakably precious things: freedom of speech, freedom of conscience, and the prudence never to practice either of them.

"Pudd'nhead Wilson's New Calendar,"
Following the Equator, I, Chapt. XX, p. 198

. . . all gentle cant and philosophizing to the contrary notwithstanding, no people in the world ever did achieve their freedom by goody-goody talk and moral suasion, it being immutable law that all revolutions that will succeed must *begin* in blood, whatever may answer afterward. If history teaches anything, it teaches that.

A Connecticut Yankee in King Arthur's Court,
Chapt. XX, p. 161

None but the dead have free speech.

Mark Twain's Notebook, p. 393

FRENCH LANGUAGE *See also* SERMON, SOAP

Angelo speaks French—a French which he could get a patent on, because he invented it himself; a French which no one can understand; a French which resembles no other confusion of sounds heard since Babel, a French which curdles the milk. He prefers it to his native Italian . . . It makes no difference what language he is addressed in, his reply is in French, his peculiar French, his grating uncanny French, which sounds like shoveling anthracite down a coal chute.

> *Mark Twain's Autobiography*, Paine, I, p. 230

This gentleman's article is an able one (as articles go, in the French, where they always tangle up everything to that degree that when you start into a sentence you never know whether you are going to come out alive or not.)

> "The Jumping Frog,"
> *Sketches New and Old*, p. 25

Lord Houghton told a number of delightful stories. He told them in French, and I lost nothing of them but the nubs.

> *Mark Twain's Autobiography*, Paine, II, p. 233

But French is different; *French* ain't anything. I ain't any more afraid of French than a tramp's afraid of pie.

> *A Tramp Abroad*, I, Chapt. XXVII, p. 289

There are some alleged French Protestants in Paris, and they built a nice little church on one of the great avenues that lead away from the Arch of Triumph, and proposed to listen to the correct thing, preached in the correct way, there, in their precious French tongue, and be happy. But their little game did not succeed. Our people [the Americans] are always there ahead of them Sundays, and take up all the room. When the minister gets up to preach, he finds his house full of devout foreigners, each ready and waiting with his little book in his hand—a morocco-bound Testament, apparently. But only apparently; it is Mr. Bellow's admirable and exhaustive little French-English dictionary, which in look and binding and size is just like a Testament—and those people are there to study French. The building has been nicknamed: "The Church of the Gratis French Lessons."

> "Paris Notes,"
> *Tom Sawyer Abroad, Etc.*, p. 378

I told [the Frenchman] in French . . . He said he could not understand me. I repeated. Still, he did not understand. He appeared to be very ignorant of French.

> *The Innocents Abroad*, I, Chapt. X, p. 135

It has always been a marvel to me—that French language; it has always been a puzzle to me. How beautiful that language is! How expressive it seems to be! How full of grace it is!

And when it comes from lips like those [of Sarah Bernhardt], how eloquent and how limpid it is! And, oh, I am always deceived—I always think I am going to understand it.

Mark Twain, a Biography, Paine, III, p. 1254

FRENCH PEOPLE   *See also* ANCESTOR, DUELING, HUMOR, MANNERS, PRAISE, TITLES

Their gesticulations are so out of proportion to what they are saying.

Mark Twain's Notebook, p. 216

The French are polite, but it is often mere ceremonious politeness. A Russian imbues his polite sayings with a heartiness, both of phrase and expression, that compels belief in their sincerity.

The Innocents Abroad, II, Chapt. X, p. 123

M. de Lamester's new French Dictionary just issued in Paris defines virtue as: "A woman who has only one lover and don't steal."

A Bibliography of Mark Twain, Merle Johnson, p. 178

I like to look at a Russian or a German or an Italian—I even like to look at a Frenchman if I ever have the luck to catch him engaged in anything that ain't indelicate.

"Extract from Captain Stormfield's Visit to Heaven," *The Mysterious Stranger, Etc.*, p. 271

. . . I found the brave fellow steeped in a profound French calm. I say French calm, because French calmness and English calmness have points of difference. He was moving swiftly back and forth among the *debris* of his furniture, now and then staving some sharp fragment of it across the room with his foot; grinding a constant grist of curses through his set teeth; and halting every little while to deposit another handful of his hair on the pile which he had been building of it on the table.

A Tramp Abroad, I, Chapt. VIII, p. 63

A severe-looking fidgety man . . . began to fire French questions at me in such a liquid form that I could not detect the joints between his words . . .

"Playing Courier,"
The American Claimant, p. 484

I thought I would practice my French on him, but he wouldn't have that either. It seemed to make him particularly bitter to hear his own tongue.

Ibid., p. 493

Jim: "Is a Frenchman a man? *Well* den! Dad blame it, why doan he talk like a man?"

The Adventures of Huckleberry Finn, p. 114

A joke in Chicago, you know, is a riddle in Paris.

Abroad with Mark Twain and Eugene Field,
Fisher, p. 92

FRIEND *See also* CONSCIENCE, DOG, ENEMY, IDEA, MEMORY, OPINION, PROSPERITY

The proper office of a friend is to side with you when you are in the wrong. Nearly anybody will side with you when you are in the right.

Mark Twain's Notebook, p. 344

The Impartial Friend: Death—the only immortal who treats us all alike, whose pity and whose peace and whose refuge are for all—the soiled and the pure—the rich and the poor—the loved and the unloved.

Moments with Mark Twain, Paine, p. 299

When you climb the hill of happiness may you never meet a friend.

Mark Twain's Notebook, p. 373

Everybody in the world, little and big, has one *special* friend, a friend that he's *glad* to do favors to—not sour about it, but *glad*—glad clear to the marrow. And so, I don't care where you start, you can get at anybody's ear that you want to—I don't care how low you are, nor how high he is. And it's so simple: you've only to find the *first* friend, that is all; that ends your part of the work. He finds the next friend himself, and that one finds the third, and so on, friend after friend, link after link, like a chain; and you can go up it or down it, as high as you like or as low as you like.

"Two Little Tales,"
The Man That Corrupted Hadleyburg, Etc., p. 198

An enemy can partly ruin a man, but it takes a good-natured injudicious friend to complete the thing and make it perfect.

Pudd'nhead Wilson, Chapt. V, p. 52

A man must not hold himself aloof from the things which his friends and his community have at heart if he would be liked.

A Connecticut Yankee in King Arthur's Court,
Chapt. IX, p. 70

He made himself old friends with me at once.

Source Undetermined

She waved a good-bye every now and then till her figure faded out in the plain, joining that interminable procession of friends made and lost in an hour that drifts past a man's life from cradle to grave and returns on its course no more.

"Down the Rhone,"
Europe and Elsewhere, p. 161

FRIENDSHIP *See also* MEMORY

The holy passion of Friendship is of so sweet and steady and loyal and enduring a nature that it will last through a whole lifetime, if not asked to lend money.

"Pudd'nhead Wilson's Calendar,"
Pudd'nhead Wilson, Chapt. VIII, p. 68

People talk about beautiful friendships between two persons of the same sex. What is the best of that sort, as compared with the friendship of man and wife, where the best impulses and highest ideals of both are the same. There is no place for comparison between the two friendships; the one is earthly, the other divine.

A Connecticut Yankee in King Arthur's Court,
Chapt. XLI, p. 369

FRIGHT   *See also* HURRY, SIMILES

My heart jumped up amongst my lungs . . . If I trod on a stick and broke it, it made me feel like a person had cut one of my breaths in two and I only got half, and the short half, too.

The Adventures of Huckleberry Finn,
Chapt. VIII, p. 65

I went away from there. I do not say that I went away in any sort of a hurry but I simply went—that is sufficient. I went out at the window, and I carried the sash along with me. I did not need the sash, but it was handier to take it than it was to leave it, and so I took it. I was not scared but I was considerably agitated.

The Innocents Abroad, I, Chapt. XVIII, p. 231

[The burglar-alarm] was the size of a wash-bowl, and was placed above the head of our bed . . .

. . . Rip went that gong! The first time this happened I thought the last day was come sure. I didn't think it *in* bed—no, but out of it,—for the first effect of that frightful gong is to hurl you across the house, and slam you against the wall, and then curl you up, and squirm you like a spider on a stove lid . . . When that thing wakes you, it doesn't merely wake you in spots; it wakes you all over, conscience and all, and you are booked for eighteen hours of wide-awakeness subsequently . . .

"The McWilliamses and the Burglar Alarm,"
The Mysterious Stranger, Etc., p. 318

. . . all of a sudden I catched my breath and grabbed Tom's arm, and all of my livers and lungs and things fell down into my legs.

"Tom Sawyer, Detective,"
Tom Sawyer Abroad, Etc., p. 185

I came to a sitting posture in an instant with my kidneys

195

in my throat, my hair on end.

Life on the Mississippi, p. 416

FROG

Smiley'd give him a little punch behind, and the next minute you'd see that frog whirling in the air like a dough-nut, see him turn one summerset, or may be a couple, if he got a good start, and come down flat-footed and all right, like a cat. . . . Smiley said all a frog wanted was educa-tion, and he could do most anything—and I believe him. Why, I've seen him set Dan'l Webster down here on this floor—Dan'l Webster was the name of the frog—and sing out, "Flies, Dan'l flies!" and quicker'n you could wink, he'd spring straight up, and snake a fly off'n the counter there, and flop down on the floor again as solid as a gob of mud, and fall to scratching the side of his head with his hind foot as indifferent as if he hadn't no idea he'd been doin' any more'n any frog might do. You never see a frog so modest and straightfor'ard as he was, for all he was so gifted.

The Jumping Frog of Calaveras County, p. 14

FRUIT *See also* SIMILES, TRAINING

[In India]: There was one tree in the compound, and a monkey lived in it. At first I was strongly interested in the tree, for I was told that it was the renowned *peepul*—the tree in whose shadow you cannot tell a lie. This one failed to stand the test, and I went away from it disappointed . . .

I wonder if the dorian, if that is the name of it, is an-other superstition like the peepul tree. There was a great abundance and variety of tropical fruit, but the dorian was never in evidence. It was never the season for the dorian. It was always going to arrive from Burmah sometime or other, but it never did. By all accounts, it was a most strange fruit, and incomparably delicious to the taste, but not to the smell. Its rind was said to exude a scent of so atrocious a nature that when a dorian was in the room even the presence of a polecat was a refreshment. We found many who had eaten the dorian, and they all spoke of it was a sort of rapture. They said that if you could hold your nose until the fruit was in your mouth a sacred joy would suffuse you from head to foot that would make you oblivious to the smell of the rind, but if your grip slipped and you caught the smell of the rind before the fruit was in your mouth, you would faint. There is a fortune in that rind. Some day somebody will import it into Europe and sell it for cheese.

> *Following the Equator,* II, Chapt. XIV, p. 171

If the old masters had labeled their fruits, one wouldn't be so likely to mistake pears for turnips.

> *Mark Twain, a Biography,* Paine, III, p. 634

FUMIGATE   *See* SOAP

FUN

. . . a good and wholesome thing is a little harmless fun in this world; it tones a body up and keeps him human and prevents him from souring.

> *Personal Recollections of Joan of Arc,*
> I, Book II, Chapt. XXI, p. 290

On one of his many voyages . . . [Mark Twain] was sitting on deck in a steamer-chair when two little girls stopped before him. One of them said, hesitatingly:

"Are you Mr. Mark Twain?"

"Why, yes, dear, they call me that."

"Won't you please say something funny?"

And for the life of him he couldn't make the required remark.

> *Mark Twain, a Biography,* Paine, II, p. 1046

There is no lasting quality to humor unless it's based on real substance. Being funny doesn't mean anything unless there is an underlying human note.

People don't realize that this requires the same powers of observation, analysis, and understanding as in serious writing.

> *Celebrities Off Parade,* Orcutt, p. 147

FUNERAL   *See also* BIRTHDAY, HONESTY, JOY, POLITICS, RO-
MANCE, SERMON

I've written a letter to everybody who has a single drop
of my blood in his veins and whose funeral I may ever have
to go to, and I have asked them *all* to come and settle right
down here within a radius of two blocks and just *stay* until
they all die, so I won't ever have to go out of town to
attend their funerals!

A Lifetime with Mark Twain, Lawton, p. 212

Somebody has said that in order to know a community,
one must observe the style of its funerals and know what
manner of men they bury with most ceremony.

Roughing It, II, Chapt. VI, p. 59

I *did* attend one or two funerals—maybe a dozen—out
there [on the borders of California]; funerals of desperadoes who had tried to purify society by exterminating other
desperadoes—and *did* accomplish the purification, though
not according to the program which they laid out for this
office.

Mark Twain's Autobiography, Paine, I, p. 350

FUTURE   *See also* PAST

The future is as absolutely fixed as the past.

Mark Twain, a Biography, Paine, III, p. 1270

G

GAMES *See also* SHIP

The English never play any game for amusement. If they can't make something or lose something—they don't care which—they won't play.

"The Million-Pound Bank Note,"
The American Claimant, Etc., p. 355

A permanent and intense interest is acquirable in baccarat, or in any other game, but you have to buy it. You don't get it by standing around and looking on.

. . . money and chips are flung upon the table, and the game seems to consist in the croupier's reaching for these things with a flexible oar, and raking them home. It appeared to be a rational enough game for him, and if I could have borrowed his oar I would have stayed, but I didn't see where the entertainment of the others came in. This was because I saw without perceiving, and observed without understanding.

"Aix, Paradise of Rheumatics,"
Europe and Elsewhere, p. 103

There are few things that are so unpardonably neglected in our country as poker. The upper class knows very little about it. Now and then you find ambassadors who have sort of a general knowledge of the game, but the ignorance of the people is fearful. Why, I have known clergymen, good men, kind-hearted, liberal, sincere, and all that, who did not know the meaning of a "flush." It is enough to make one ashamed of one's species.

A Bibliography of Mark Twain, Merle Johnson, p. 140

GAS *See* COMPLAINT, LIGHT

GENIUS *See also* ART, HUNGER
 Genius itself succeeds only by arduous self-training.

Mark Twain-Howells Letters, II, p. 157

Genius—an infinite capacity for overcoming the opposition of mediocrity.

 Holograph in a copy of *The Million Pound Bank-Note*

Genius is not born with sight, but blind; and it is not itself that opens its eyes, but the subtle influences of a myriad of stimulating exterior circumstances.

"St. Joan of Arc,"
The $30,000 Bequest, p. 153

Perhaps one must concede that genius has no youth, but starts with the ripeness of age and old experience.

Mark Twain, a Biography, Paine, II, p. 1089

[Mark Twain spoke of how great literary minds usually came along in company]: Now and then, on the stream of time, small gobs of that thing which we call genius drift down, and a few of these lodge at some particular point, and others collect about them and make a sort of intellectual island—a towhead, as they say on the river—such an accumulation of intellect we call a group, or a school, and name it.

Ibid., Paine, III, p. 1457

Genius lives in a world of its own, in palaces of enchantment . . . Everybody lives, but only Genius lives richly, sumptuously, imperially.

My Father • Mark Twain, Clara Clemens, p. 272

Genius is not very likely to ever discover himself; neither is he very likely to be discovered by his intimates; in fact I think I may put it in stronger words and say it is impossible that a genius—at least a literary genius—can ever be discovered by his intimates; they are so close to him that he is out of focus to them and they can't get at his proportions; they cannot perceive that there is any considerable difference between his bulk and their own. They can't get a perspective on him, and it is only by perspective that the difference between him and the rest of their limited circle can be perceived.

Mark Twain in Eruption, p. 359

He was a good enough sort of cretur, and hadn't no harm in him, and was just a genius, as the papers said, which wasn't his fault. We can't all be sound; we've got to be the way we're made. As near as I can make out, geniuses think they know it all, and so they won't take people's advice, but always go their own way, which makes everybody forsake them and despise them, and that is perfectly natural. If they was humbler, and listened and tried to learn, it would be better for them.

Tom Sawyer Abroad, Etc., Chapt. II, p. 20

. . . these execrable eccentricities of instinct and conduct are only the *evidence of* genius, not the *creators of* it.

"The Late Benjamin Franklin,"
Sketches New and Old, p. 215

GENTLEMAN   *See also* FOOL, ROOSEVELT

I don't remember that I ever defined a gentleman, but it seems to me that if any man has just, merciful and kindly instincts he would be a gentleman, for he would need nothing else in the world.

"Layman's Sermon,"
Mark Twain's Speeches (1923), p. 283

No real gentleman will tell the naked truth in the presence of ladies.

"A Double-Barreled Detective Story,"
The Man That Corrupted Hadleyburg, Etc., p. 311

Patrick was a gentleman, and to him I would apply the lines:

"So may I be courteous to men, faithful to friends,

True to my God, a fragrance in the path I trod."
Mark Twain's Autobiography, Paine, II, p. 203

I am a border-ruffian from the state of Missouri, and I am a Connecticut Yankee by adoption. In me, you have Missouri morals, Connecticut culture; this, gentlemen, is the combination which makes the perfect man.
"Plymouth Rock and the Pilgrims,"
Mark Twain's Speeches (1923), p. 88

GEOGRAPHY

George Ade and I would have been born in adjacent States if the damned geographers had not maliciously thrust Illinois between Indiana and Missouri.
One Afternoon With Mark Twain, Ade, p. 8

GERMAN LANGUAGE   See also DENTISTRY, FIRE, GRAMMAR, LANGUAGE, VOCABULARY, WORDS

It's awful undermining to the intellect, German is; you want to take it in small doses, or first you know your brains all run together, and you feel them flapping around in your head same as so much drawn butter.
A Tramp Abroad, II, Chapt. XXVII, p. 289

A dream . . . I was trying to explain to St. Peter, and was doing it in the German tongue, because I didn't want to be too explicit.
Mark Twain's Speeches (1923), p. 247

The longest German word:
Hottentotenstrottelmutterattentäterlattengitterwetterkotterbeutelratte.
Mark Twain's Autobiography, Paine, I, p. 166

[In Munich]: Our little children talk German as glibly as they do English, now, but the rest of us are mighty poor German scholars, I can tell you. Rev. Twichell (who was over here with me awhile) conceived a pretty correct average of *my* German. When I was talking, (in my native tongue,) about some rather private matters in the hearing of some Germans one day, Twichell said, "Speak in German, Mark,—some of these people may understand English."

Many a time when teachers and dictionaries fail to unravel knotty paragraphs, we wish we could fly to you for succor; we even go so far as to believe you can read a German newspaper and understand it; and in moments of deep irritation I have been provoked into expressing the opinion that you are the only foreigner except God who *can* do that thing. I would not rob you of your food or your clothes or your umbrella, but if I caught your German out I would take it. But I don't study any more,—I have given it up.

"A Letter to Mr. Bayard Taylor,"
American Literature, March, 1936, p. 50

[In Berlin]: Thirty days sick abed—full of interest—read the debates (in the German newspapers) and get excited over them, but don't *versteh*. By reading keep in a state of excited ignorance, like a blind man in a house afire; flounder around, immensely but unintelligently interested; don't know how I got in and can't find the way out, but I'm having a booming time all to myself.

Don't know what a Schelgesetzentwurf is, but I keep as excited over it and as worried about it as if it were my own child. I simply *live* on the Sch.; it is my daily bread. I wouldn't have the question settled for anything in the world.

Mark Twain, a Biography, Paine, II, p. 939

I went often to look at the collection of curiosities in Heidelberg Castle, and one day I surprised the keeper of it with my German. I spoke entirely in that language. He was greatly interested; and after I had talked awhile he said my German was very rare, possibly a "unique"; and wanted to add it to his museum.

If he had known what it had cost me to acquire my art, he would also have known that it would break any collector to buy it . . . A person who has not studied German can form no idea of what a perplexing language it is.

Surely there is not another language that is so slipshod and systemless, and so slippery and elusive to the grasp. One is washed about in it, hither and thither, in the most helpless way; and when at last he thinks he has captured a rule which offers firm ground to take a rest on amid the general rage and turmoil of the ten parts of speech, he turns over the page and reads, "Let the pupil make careful note of the following *exceptions.*" He runs his eye down and finds that there are more exceptions to the rule than instances of it. So overboard he goes again, to hunt for another Ararat and find another quicksand. Such has been, and continues to be my experience . . .

. . .

There are ten parts of speech, and they are all troublesome. An average sentence, in a German newspaper, is a sublime and impressive curiosity; it occupies a quarter of a column; it contains all the ten parts of speech—not in regular order, but mixed; it is built mainly of compound words constructed by the writer on the spot, and not to be found in any dictionary—six or seven words compacted into one, without joint, or seam—that is without hyphens; it treats of fourteen or fifteen different subjects, each enclosed in a parenthesis of its own with here and there extra parentheses which re-enclose three or four of the minor parentheses, making pens within pens: finally, all the parentheses and reparentheses are massed together between a couple of king-parentheses, one of which is placed in the first line of the majestic sentence and the other in the middle of the last line of it—*after which comes the VERB*, and you find out for the first time what the man has been talking about; and after the verb—merely by way of ornament, as far as I can make out,—the writer shovels in *"haben sind gewesen gehabt haben geworden sein,"* or words to that effect, and the monument is finished. I suppose that this closing hurrah is in the nature of the flourish to a man's signature— not necessary, but pretty. German books are easy enough to read when you hold them before the looking-glass, or stand on your head,—so as to reverse the construction . . .

. . .

Now observe the Adjective. Here was a case where simplicity would have been an advantage; therefore, for no other reason, the inventor of this language complicated it all he could. When we wish to speak of our "good friend or friends" in our enlightened tongue, we stick to the one form and have no trouble or hard feeling about it; but with the German tongue it is different. When a German gets his hands on an adjective, he declines it and keeps on declining it until the common sense is all declined out of it . . .

. . . I heard a Californian student in Heidelberg say, in one of his calmest moods, that he would rather decline two drinks than one German adjective.

.   .   .

In my note-book I find this entry—

July 1—In the hospital yesterday, a word of thirteen syllables was successfully removed from a patient, a North-German from near Hamburg; but as most unfortunately the surgeon had opened him in the wrong place, under the impression that he contained a panorama, he died. The sad event has cast a gloom over the whole community.

That paragraph furnishes a text for a few remarks about one of the most curious and notable features of my subject —the length of German words. Some German words are so long that they have a perspective.

.   .   .

. . . There are people in the world who will take a great deal of trouble to find out the faults in a religion or a language, and then go blandly about their business without suggesting any remedy. I am not that kind of person. I have shown that the German language needs reforming. Very well, I am ready to reform it . . .

In the first place, I would leave out the Dative Case . . . It confuses the plurals; and besides, nobody ever knows when he is in the Dative Case except he discover it by accident,—and then he does not know when or where it was that he got into it, or how long he has been in it, or how he is ever going to get out of it again. The Dative Case is but an ornamental folly,—it is better to discard it.

In the next place, I would move the Verb further up to

the front. You may lead up with ever so good a Verb, but I notice that you never really bring down a subject with it at the present German range,—you only cripple it. So I insist that this important part of speech should be brought forward to a position where it may be easily seen with the naked eye.

Thirdly I would import some strong words from the English tongue,—to swear with, and also to use in describing all sorts of vigorous things in a vigorous way.

Fourthly, I would reorganize the sexes—(in German, a young lady has no sex, while a turnip has. Think what overwrought reverence that shows for the turnip, and what careless disrespect for the girl.)—and distribute them according to the will of the Creator. This as a tribute of respect, if nothing else.

Fifthly, I would do away with those great long compounded words; or require the speaker to deliver them in sections, with intermissions for refreshments. To wholly do away with them would be best, for ideas are more easily received and digested when they come one at a time than when they come in bulk. Intellectual food is like any other; it is pleasanter and more beneficial to take it with a spoon than with a shovel.

Sixthly, I would require a speaker to stop when he is done, and not hang a string of those useless "haben sind gewesen gehabt haben geworden sein" to the end of his oration. This sort of gewgaws undignify a speech, instead of adding a grace. They are, therefore, an offense, and should be discarded.

Seventhly, I would discard the Parenthesis. Also the re-parenthesis, the re-re-parenthesis . . . and likewise the final wide-reaching, all-enclosing King-parenthesis. I would require every individual, be he high or low, to unfold a plain straightforward tale, or else coil it and sit on it and hold his peace . . .

And eighthly and last, I would retain "Zug" and "Schlag" with their pendants, and discard the rest of the vocabulary. This would simplify the language.

My philological studies have satisfied me that a gifted person ought to learn English (barring spelling and pronouncing) in thirty hours, French in thirty days, and German in thirty years. It seems manifest, then, that the latter tongue ought to be trimmed down and repaired. If it is to remain as it is, it ought to be gently and reverently set aside among the dead languages, for only the dead have time to learn it.

> "The Awful German Language,"
> *A Tramp Abroad,* II, Appendix D, p. 303

I can *understand* German as well as the maniac that invented it, but I *talk* it best through an interpreter.

> *Ibid.,* I, Chapt. XIV, p. 122

[A speech to the Vienna Press Club, November 24th, 1897]:

I am indeed the truest friend of the German language—and not only now, but from long since—yes, before twenty years already. And never have I the desire had the noble language to hurt; to the contrary, only wished she to improve—I would her only reform. It is the dream of my life been. I have already visits by the various German governments paid and for contracts prayed . . . I would only the language method—the luxurious, elaborate construction compress, the eternal parenthesis suppress, do away with, annihilate; the introduction of more than thirteen subjects in one sentence forbid; the verb so far to the front pull that one it without a telescope discover can. With one word, my gentlemen, I would your beloved language simplify so that, my gentlemen, when you her prayer need, One her yonder-up understands.

> "The Horrors of the German Language,"
> *Mark Twain's Speeches* (1923), p. 171

[Learning to ride the bicycle]: The steps of one's progress are distinctly marked. At the end of each lesson he knows he has acquired something, and he also knows what that something is, and likewise that it will stay with him. It is not like studying German, where you mull along, in a groping, uncertain way, for thirty years; and at last, just as you think you've got it, they spring the subjunctive on you, and there you are. No—and I see now, plainly enough, that the great pity about the German language is, that you can't fall off it and hurt yourself. There is nothing like that feature to make you attend strictly to business. But I also see, by what I have learned of bicycling, that the right and only sure way to learn German is by the bicycling method. That is to say, take a grip on one villainy of it at a time, and learn it—not ease up and shirk to the next, leaving that one half learned.

"Taming the Bicycle,"
What Is Man? and Other Essays, p. 288

A dog is "der Hund"; a woman is "die Frau"; a horse is "das Pferd"; now you put that dog in the genitive case, and is he the same dog he was before? No, sir; he is "des Hundes"; put him in the dative case and what is he? Why, he is "dem Hund." Now you snatch him into the accusative case and how is it with him? Why, he is "den Hunden." But suppose he happens to be twins and you have to pluralize him—what then? Why, they'll swat that twin dog around through the 4 cases until he'll think he's an entire international dog-show all in his own person. I don't like dogs, but I wouldn't treat a dog like that—I wouldn't even treat a borrowed dog that way. Well, it's just the same with a cat. They start her in at the nominative singular in good health and fair to look upon, and they sweat her through all the 4 cases and the 16 the's and when she limps out through the accusative plural you wouldn't recognize her for the same being. Yes, sir, once the German language gets hold of a cat it's good-bye cat. That's about the amount of it.

Mark Twain's Notebook, p. 139

The Germans have an inhuman way of cutting up their verbs. Now a verb has a hard time enough of it in this world when it's all together. It's downright inhuman to split it up. But that's just what those Germans do. They take part of a verb and put it down here, like a stake, and they take the other part of it and put it away over yonder like another stake, and between these two limits they just shovel in German.

"Disappearance of Literature"
Mark Twain's Speeches (1923), p. 209

In early times some sufferer had to sit up with a toothache, and he put in the time inventing the German language.

Mark Twain's Notebook, p. 141

. . . without a doubt Berlin is the place to come to finish your medical education, for certainly it is a luminous center of intelligence—a place where the last possibilities of attainment in all the sciences are to be had for the seeking. Berlin is a wonderful city for that sort of opportunity. They teach everything here. I don't believe there is anything in the whole earth that you can't learn in Berlin except the German language.

Ibid., p. 218

I was gradually coming to have a mysterious and shuddery reverence for this girl; nowadays whenever she pulled out from the station and got her train fairly started on one of those horizonless transcontinental sentences of hers, it was borne in upon me that I was standing in the awful presence of the Mother of the German Language. I was so impressed with this, that sometimes when she began to empty one of these sentences on me I unconsciously took the very attitude of reverence, and stood uncovered; and if words had been water, I had been drowned, sure. She had exactly the German way; whatever was in her mind to be delivered, whether a mere remark, or a sermon, or a cyclopedia, or the history of a war, she would get it into a single sentence or die. Whenever the literary German dives into a sentence, that is the last you are going to see of him till he emerges on the other side of his Atlantic with his verb in his mouth.

A Connecticut Yankee in King Arthur's Court,
Chapt. XXII, p. 190

That sentence is Germanic, and shows I am acquiring that sort of mastery of the art and spirit of the language which enables a man to travel all day in one sentence without changing cars.

> *Christian Science,* Book I, Chapt. I, p. 4

It is easier for a cannibal to enter the Kingdom of Heaven through the eye of a rich man's needle than it is for any other foreigner to read the terrible German script.

> *Mark Twain's Notebook,* p. 346

GERMAN PEOPLE   *See also* HOUSE, LAUNDRY, NEWSPAPER, REPUBLIC

. . . there is nothing the Germans like so much as opera.

> *A Tramp Abroad,* I, Chapt. IX, p. 81

When and how did we get the idea that the Germans are a stolid, phlegmatic race? In truth, they are widely removed from that. They are warm-hearted, emotional, impulsive, enthusiastic, their tears come at the mildest touch, and it is not hard to move them to laughter. They are the very children of impulse. We are cold and self-contained, compared to the Germans.

> *Ibid.,* I, Chapt. X, p. 87

In one place we saw a nicely-dressed German gentleman without any spectacles. Before I could come to anchor he had got away . . . The captain comforted me for my loss, however, by saying that the man was without any doubt a fraud who had spectacles, but kept them in his pocket in order to make himself conspicuous.

> *Ibid.,* I, Chapt. XV, p. 130

[The German stove]:
"Who is buried here?"
"Nobody."
"Then why the monument?"
"It is not a monument. It is a stove."

We had reverently removed our hats. We now put them on again. Stove eight feet high—very ornamental, around the top.

> *Mark Twain's Notebook,* p. 135

The Germans are exceedingly fond of Rhine wines; they are put up in tall, slender bottles, and are considered a pleasant beverage. One tells them from vinegar by the label.

A Tramp Abroad, I, Chapt. XV, p. 130

To carve fowls in the German fashion: Use a club, and avoid the joints.

Ibid., II, Chapt. XX, p. 266

GERMANY   *See* ANCESTOR, EARTHQUAKE, GRAMMAR, HOUSE, LAUNDRY, LIGHT, MUSIC, OPERA, RHEUMATISM, SMELL, TALK, TITLE

GIBBET   *See* PLATFORM

GIFT   *See* DEATH, PLEASURE

GIRL   *See also* CHILD, COMPLIMENT, FLEA, HAIR, MARRIAGE, SIMILES, SMELL

The average American girl possesses the valuable qualities of naturalness, honesty, and inoffensive straightforwardness; she is nearly barren of troublesome conventions and artificialities; consequently, her presence and her ways are unembarrassing, and one is acquainted with her and on the pleasantest terms with her before he knows how it came about.

The American Claimant, Etc., Chapt. XX, p. 170

They say God made man in his effigy. I don't know about that, but I'm quite sure that he put a lot of divinity into the American girl.

Abroad with Mark Twain and Eugene Field, Fisher, p. 212

Every time "the Bay" discontinues a pronunciation, and enters upon the correct form of pronouncing that word, never to retreat from it again, and never again to charm our ears with the music that was in the old lame sound of it, we feel that something that was precious has gone from us to return no more; a subtle, elusive, but nevertheless *real* sense of loss—and when we analyze it we find that the meaning of it is, that we are losing our *baby*—she is becoming a little girl, to blend with the vast and arid wastes of unindividualized little-girlhood and cease to be a centre

of wondering admiration, a rich unfailing source of daily
and hourly surprises.

Mark Twain to Mrs. Fairbanks, p. 193

. . .

GLACIER

[In the Alps]: My men being restored to health and
strength, my main perplexity, now, was how to get them
down the mountain again. I was not willing to expose the
brave fellows to the perils, fatigues, and hardships of that
fearful route again if it could be helped. First I thought
of balloons, but, of course, I had to give that idea up, for
balloons were not procurable. I thought of several other
expedients, but upon consideration discarded them, for
cause. But at last I hit it. I was aware that the movement
of glaciers is an established fact, for I had read it in Baedeker; so I resolved to take passage for Zermatt on the
great Gorner Glacier.

. . .

I marched the Expedition down the steep and tedious
mule-path and took up as good a position as I could upon
the middle of the glacier—because Baedeker said the middle
part travels the fastest. As a measure of economy, however,
I put some of the heavier baggage on the shoreward parts,
to go as slow freight.

I waited and waited, but the glacier did not move. Night
was coming on, the darkness began to gather—still we did
not budge. It occurred to me then, that there might be a
time-table in Baedeker; it would be well to find out the
hours of starting. I called for the book—it could not be
found . . . Very well, I must make the best of the situation.
So I pitched the tents, picketed the animals, milked the
cows, had supper, paregoricked the men, established the
watch, and went to bed—with orders to call me as soon
as we came in sight of Zermatt.

I awoke about half-past ten next morning, and looked
around. We hadn't budged a peg! At first I could not
understand it; then it occurred to me that the old thing
must be aground. So I cut down some trees and rigged

a spar on the starboard and another on the port side, and fooled away upwards of three hours trying to spar her off. But it was no use. She was half a mile wide and fifteen or twenty miles long, and there was no telling just whereabouts she *was* aground . . .

Presently Baedeker was found again, and I hunted eagerly for the time-table. There was none. The book simply said the glacier was moving all the time. This was satisfactory, so I shut up the book and chose a good position to view the scenery as we passed along. I stood there some time enjoying the trip, but at last it occurred to me that we did not seem to be gaining any on the scenery. I said to myself, "This confounded old thing's aground again, sure,"—and opened Baedeker to see if I could run across any remedy for these annoying interruptions. I soon found a sentence which threw a dazzling light upon the matter. It said, "The Gorner Glacier travels at an average rate of a little less than an inch a day." I have seldom felt so outraged. I have seldom had my confidence so wantonly betrayed. I made a small calculation: One inch a day, say 30 feet a year, estimated distance to Zermatt, 3–1/18 miles. Time required to go by glacier, *a little over five hundred years!* I said to myself, "I can *walk* it quicker—and before I will patronize such a fraud as this, I will do it."

When I revealed to Harris the fact that the passenger-part of this glacier—the central part—the lightning-express part, so to speak—was not due in Zermatt till the summer of 2378, and that the baggage, coming along the slow edge, would not arrive until some generations later, he burst out with:

"That is European management all over! An inch a day —think of that! Five hundred years to go a trifle over three miles! But I am not a bit surprised. It's a Catholic glacier. You can tell by the look of it. And the management."

I said, no, I believed nothing but the extreme end of it was in a Catholic canton.

"Well, then, it's a government glacier," said Harris. "It's all the same . . ."

. . . After a reflective pause, Harris added, "A little less than an inch a day, a little less than an *inch*, mind you. Well, I'm losing my reverence for glaciers."

A Tramp Abroad, II, Chapt. X, p. 142

. . . a man who keeps company with glaciers comes to feel tolerably insignificant by and by. The Alps and the glaciers together are able to take every bit of conceit out of a man and reduce his self-importance to zero if he will only remain within the influence of their sublime presence long enough to give it a fair and reasonable chance to do its work.

Ibid., II, Chapt. XI, p. 158

GLADNESS *See* DICTIONARY

GLASS *See* WINDOWS

GOD *See also* ARK, CONVICTION, CRITIC, FIGHT NOAH, POS-
SESSION, LAW, MAN, MONEY, WAR

Man proposes, but God blocks the game.

From an unpublished letter to Jean Clemens, June 19, 1908

If God is what people say there can be no one in the universe so unhappy as He; for He sees unceasingly myriads of His creatures suffering unspeakable miseries—and besides this foresees how they are going to suffer during the remainder of their lives. One might well say: "As unhappy as God."

Mark Twain's Notebook, p. 182

God pours out love upon all with a lavish hand—but He reserves vengeance for His very own.

Ibid., p. 237

God's inhumanity to man makes countless thousands mourn.

Ibid., p. 344

I dreamed that the visible universe is the physical person of God; that the vast worlds that we see twinkling millions of miles apart in the fields of space are the blood corpuscles

in his veins; and that we and the other creatures are the
microbes that charge with multitudinous life the corpuscles.

Following the Equator, I, Chapt. XII, p. 132

No man that ever lived has ever done a thing to please
God—primarily. It was done to please himself, *then* God
next.

The Being who, to me is the real God is the one who
created this majestic universe and rules it. He is the only
originator, the only originator of thoughts; thoughts suggested from within, not from without. The originator of
colors and of all their possible combinations; of forces and
the laws that govern them; of forms and shapes of *all* forms
—man has never invented a new one. He is the only originator. He made the materials of all things; he made the laws
by which, and by which only, man may combine them into
the machines and other things which outside influences
suggest to him. He made character—man can portray it but
not "create" it, for He is the only creator.

He is the perfect artisan, the perfect artist.

Mark Twain, a Biography, Paine, II, p. 1083

If I had been helping the Almighty when He created
man I would have had Him begin at the other end, and
start human beings with old age. How much better it
would have been to start old and have all the bitterness
and blindness of age in the beginning! One would not mind
then if he were looking forward to a joyful youth. Think of
the joyous prospect of growing young instead of old! Think
of looking forward to eighteen instead of eighty! Yes, the
Almighty made a poor job of it. I wish He had invited my
assistance.

Ibid., III, p. 1440

Without the grace of God I could do nothing.

Personal Recollections of Joan of Arc,
II, Book III, Chapt. VII, p. 167

If I were going to construct a God I would furnish Him
with some ways and qualities and characteristics which the
Present [Bible] lacks. He would not stoop to *ask* for any

man's compliments, praises, flatteries; and He would be far above *exacting* them. I would have Him as self-respecting as the better sort of man in these regards.

He would not be a merchant, a trader. He would not buy these things. He would not sell, or offer to sell, temporary benefits or the joys of eternity for the product called worship. I would have Him as dignified as the better sort of man in this regard.

He would value no love but the love born of kindnesses conferred; not that born of benevolences contracted for. Repentance in a man's heart for a wrong done would cancel and annul that sin, and no verbal prayers for forgiveness be required or desired or expected of that man.

In His Bible there would be no Unforgivable Sin. He would recognize in Himself the Author and Inventor of Sin and Author and Inventor of the Vehicle and Appliances for its commission; and would place the whole responsibility where it would of right belong: upon Himself, the only Sinner.

He would not be a jealous God—a trait so small that even men despise it in each other.

He would not boast.

He would keep private His admirations of Himself; He would regard self-praise as unbecoming the dignity of His position.

He would not have the spirit of vengeance in His heart. Then it could not issue from His lips.

There would not be any hell—except the one we live in from the cradle to the grave.

There would not be any heaven—of the kind described in the world's Bibles.

He would spend some of His eternities in trying to forgive Himself for making man unhappy when he could have made him happy with the same effort and he would spend the rest of them in studying astronomy.

Mark Twain's Notebook, p. 301

You never saw a bigoted, opinionated, stubborn, narrow-minded, self-conceited *almighty mean man* in your life but he had stuck in one place ever since he was born and thought God made the world and dyspepsia and bile for *his* especial comfort and satisfaction.

> "The American Vandal"
> *Mark Twain's Speeches* (1923), p. 30

God puts *something* good and something lovable in every man His hands create.

> *Ibid.*

A pathetic sort of old lady arrived who wished to pour out her adoration for Mark Twain and his works. Before leaving, she begged permission to kiss [Mark Twain's] hand in reverence. Quite seriously and sympathetically he submitted to this trying compliment. At the door she said, "How God must love you!"

"I hope so," he said, but when the door had closed behind her, he added, with a wishful light in his eye, "I guess she hasn't heard of our strained relations."

> *My Father • Mark Twain,* Clara Clemens, p. 259

I believe in God the Almighty.

> *Mark Twain, a Biography,* Paine, III, p. 1583

I doubt if God has given us any refreshment which, taken in moderation, is unwholesome, except microbes. Yet there are people who strictly deprive themselves of each and every eatable, drinkable, and smokable which has in any way acquired a shady reputation. They pay this price for health. And health is all they get for it. How strange it is! It is like paying out your whole fortune for a cow that has gone dry.

> *Mark Twain's Autobiography,* Paine, I, p. 98

To trust the God of the Bible is to trust an irascible, vindictive, fierce and ever fickle and changeful master; to trust the true God is to trust a Being who has uttered no promises, but whose beneficent, exact, and changeless ordering of the machinery of His colossal universe is proof that He is at least steadfast to His purposes; whose unwritten laws, so far as they affect man, being equal and impartial, show that he is just and fair; these things, taken together, suggest that if he shall ordain us to live hereafter, he will still be steadfast, just, and fair toward us. We shall not need to require anything more.

Mark Twain, a Biography, Paine, I, p. 412

I am built so, being made merely in the image of God, but not otherwise resembling him enough to be mistaken for him by anybody but a very near-sighted person.

Love Letters of Mark Twain, p. 254

When the Lord finished the world, he pronounced it good. That is what I said about my first work. But Time, I tell you, Time takes the confidence out of these incautious early opinions. It is more than likely that He thinks about the world, now, pretty much as I think about the "Innocents Abroad." The fact is, there is a trifle too much water in both. [Nov. 6, 1886]

The Adventures of Mark Twain,
Jerry Allen, p. xi

"Fear God and dread the Sunday School" exactly described that old feeling I used to have, but I couldn't have formulated it.

Mark Twain's Letters, I, p. 274

The suns and planets that form the constellations of the billion billion solar systems and go pouring, a tossing flood of shining globes, through the viewless arteries of space are the blood corpuscles in the veins of God; and the nations are the microbes that swarm and wiggle and brag in each, and to think God can tell them apart at that distance and has nothing better to do than try. *This*—the entertainment of an eternity. Who so poor in his ambitions as to consent to be God on those terms? Blasphemy? No, it is not blasphemy. If God is as vast as that, he is above blasphemy; if He is as little as that, He is beneath it.

Mark Twain, a Biography, Paine, III, p. 1354

GODS *See* CONDUCT

GOLD *See* MAN, MONEY, UNCLE

GOLDEN RULE *See also* LAW, RULE

Golden Rule: Made of hard metal so it could stand severe wear, it not being known at that time that butter would answer.

More Maxims of Mark, p. 8

GOLF

I've been studying this game of golf pretty considerably. I guess I understand now how it's played. . . . You take a small ball into a big field and you try to hit it—the ball, not the field. At the first attempt you hit the field and not the ball. After that you probably hit the air or else the boy who is carrying your bag of utensils. When you've gone on long enough you possibly succeed in obtaining your original object. If the boy's alive you send him off to look for the ball. If he finds it the same day, you've won the game.

From an unidentified English newspaper clipping, circa 1872

GOODNESS *See also* AGE, CONSCIENCE, GOD, PEOPLE

To be good is noble; but to show others how to be good is nobler and no trouble.

"Pudd'nhead Wilson's New Calendar,"
Flyleaf of *Following the Equator*

BE GOOD, BE GOOD

Be good, be good, be always good,
    And now and then be clever,
And don't you ever be *too* good,
    Nor ever be too clever;

For each as be too awful good
    The awful lonely are,
And such as often clever be
    Get cut and stung and trodden on by
persons of lesser mental capacity, for
this kind do by a law of their construction
regard exhibitions of superior intellectuality
as an offensive impertinence levelled at

their lack of this high gift, and are
prompt to resent such-like exhibitions
in the manner above indicated—and are
they justifiable? alas, alas they

(It is best not to go on; I think the line is already longer
than it ought to be for real true poetry.)

To Margaret
Privately printed, New York, 1931

There is *far* more goodness than ungoodness in man; for
if it were not so man would have exterminated himself
before this.

Love Letters of Mark Twain, p. 253

Be good and you will be lonesome.

"Pudd'nhead Wilson's New Calendar,"
Flyleaf of *Following the Equator*

. . . they bore within them the divine something in
whose presence the evil in people fled away and hid itself,
while all that was good in them came spontaneously forward out of the forgotten walls and corners in their systems
where it was accustomed to hide.

Mark Twain's Letters, I, p. 304

GOSPEL   *See* POLITICS

GOSSIP

. . . gossip of any kind and about anybody is one of the
most toothsomely Christian dishes I know of.

My Father • Mark Twain, Clara Clemens, p. 53

He gossips habitually; he lacks the common wisdom to
keep still that deadly enemy of a man, his own tongue.

Letters from the Sandwich Islands, p. 116

GOULD, JAY   *See* HISTORY

GOVERNMENT   *See also* BOUNTY, CITIZENSHIP, COUNTRY, DEMOCRACY, MAN, MASSES, MONARCHY, PATRIOTISM, PEO-

There is a phrase which has grown so common in the
world now that it has come to seem to have sense and
meaning—the sense and meaning implied when it is used;
that is the phrase which refers to this or that or the other
nation as possibly being "capable of self-government"; and
the implied sense of it is, that there has been a nation somewhere, some time or other, which *wasn't* capable of it—
wasn't as capable to govern it as some self-appointed spe-
cialists were or would be to govern it . . . even the best-
governed and most free and most enlightened monarchy is
still behind the best condition attainable by its people; . . .
the same is true of kindred governments of lower grades,
all the way down to the lowest.

A Connecticut Yankee in King Arthur's Court,
Chapt. XXV, p. 219

. . . no country can be well governed unless its citizens
as a body keep religiously before their minds that they are
the guardians of the law, and that the law officers are only
the machinery for its execution, nothing more.

The Gilded Age, I, Chapt. XXIX, p. 322

The mania for giving the Government power to meddle
with the private affairs of cities or citizens is likely to cause
endless trouble, through the rivalry of schools and creeds
that are anxious to obtain official recognition, and there is
great danger that our people will lose our independence
of thought and action which is the cause of much of our
greatness, and sink into the helplessness of the Frenchman
or German who expects his government to feed him when
hungry, clothe him when naked, to prescribe when his child
may be born and when he may die, and, in fine, to regulate
every act of humanity from the cradle to the tomb, including the manner in which he may seek future admission to
paradise.

"Official Physic,"
The Twainian, Nov. 1943, p. 5

[Mark Twain coins the term "New Deal"]: And now

here I was, in a country where a right to say how the country should be governed was restricted to six persons in each thousand of its population. For the nine hundred and ninety-four to express dissatisfaction with the regnant system and propose to change it, would have made the whole six shudder as one man. . . . It seemed to me that what the nine hundred and ninety-four dupes needed was a new deal.

A Connecticut Yankee in King Arthur's Court,
Chapt. XIII, p. 105

Concentration of power in a political machine is bad.

Ibid., Chapt. XVIII, p. 142

Unlimited power *is* the ideal thing when it is in safe hands. The despotism of heaven is the one absolutely perfect government. An earthly despotism would be the absolutely perfect earthly government, if the conditions were the same, namely, the despot the perfectest individual of the human race, and his lease on life perpetual. But as a perishable perfect man must die, and leave his despotism in the hands of an imperfect successor, an earthly despotism is not merely a bad form of government, it is the worst form that is possible.

Ibid., Chapt. X, p. 79

We have a form of government which gives each man a fair chance and no favor. With us no individual is born with a right to look down upon his neighbor and hold him in contempt.

Mark Twain's Speeches (1910), p. 415

Wherefore being all of one mind, we do highly resolve that government of the grafted by the grafter for the grafter shall not perish from the earth.

More Maxims of Mark, p. 14

GRAFT *See* GOVERNMENT

GRAMMAR *See also* ENGLAND, GERMAN LANGUAGE, GRANT, ULYSSES S., METAPHOR, PUNCTUATION, SIMILES, TALK, TEACHER, WORDS

Cast-iron rules will not answer . . . what is one man's comma is another man's colon.

Life As I Find It, p. 189

As soon as the Jubilee was over we went to what is called in English "an hotel." If we could have afforded an horse and an hackney cab we could have had an heavenly time flitting around.

Europe and Elsewhere, p. 213

To misplace an adverb is a thing which I am able to do with frozen indifference; it can never give me a pang.

Mark Twain-Howells Letters, II, p. 880

Perfect grammar—persistent, continuous, sustained—is the fourth dimension, so to speak; many have sought it, but none has found it. . . I know grammar by ear only, not by note, not by the rules. A generation ago I knew the rules—knew them by heart, word for word, though not their meanings—and I still know one of them: the one which says—which says—but never mind, it will come back to me presently.

Mark Twain's Autobiography, I, p. 173

. . . great books are weighed and measured by their style and matter and not by the trimmings and shadings of their grammar.

Mark Twain, a Biography, Paine, III, p. 1652

[Studying Italian]: Examination and inquiry showed me that the adjectives and such things were frank and fair-minded and straight-forward, and did not shuffle; it was the Verb that mixed the hands, it was the Verb that lacked stability, it was the Verb that had no permanent opinion about anything, it was the Verb that was always dodging the issue and putting out the light and making all the trouble.

. . .

I had noticed, in other foreign languages, that verbs are bred in families, and that the members of each family have certain features or resemblances that are common to that family and distinguish it from the other families—the other kin, the cousins and what not. I have noticed that this family-mark is not usually the nose or the hair, so to speak, but the tail—the Termination,—and that these tails are quite definitely differentiated; insomuch that an expert can tell a Pluperfect from a Subjunctive by its tail as easily and as certainly as a cowboy can tell a cow from a horse by the like process, the result of observation and culture. I should explain that I am speaking of legitimate verbs, those verbs which in the slang of the grammar are called Regular. There are others—I am not meaning to conceal this; others called Irregulars, born out of wedlock, of unknown and uninteresting parentage, and naturally destitute of family resemblances, as regards all features, tails included. But of these pathetic outcasts I have nothing to say.

> "Italian with Grammar,"
> *The $30,000 Bequest, Etc.*, p. 186

Harris said that if the best writer in the world once got the slovenly habit of doubling up his "have's" he could never get rid of it while he lived. That is to say, if a man gets the habit of saying "I should have liked to have known more about it" instead of saying simply and sensibly, "I should have liked to know more about it," that man's disease is incurable. Harris said that this sort of lapse is to be found in every copy of every newspaper that has ever been printed in English, and in almost all of our books.

> *A Tramp Abroad*, I, Chapt. XXIII, p. 226

"Pretty much" may not be elegant English, but it is high time it was. There is no elegant word or phrase which means just what it means.

> *Ibid.*, II, Chapt. IX, p. 130

In due course of time our journey came to an end at Kawaehae (usually pronounced To-a-*hi*—and before we find fault with this orthographical method of arriving at such an ostentatious result, let us lop off the ugh from our word "though").

> *Roughing It*, II, Chapt. XXXV, p. 311

It has a historical side.

I do not say "an" historical side, because I am speaking

the American language. I do not see why our cousins [the English] should continue to say "an" hospital, "an" historical fact, "an" horse. . . I think "an" is having a little too much to do with it. It comes of habit, which accounts for many things.

Mark Twain's Speeches (1923), p. 187

[A French guide for the American in Paris]: . . . "I speaky ze Angleesh pairfaitemaw."

He would have done well to have stopped there, because he had that much by heart and said it right off without making a mistake. But his self-complacency seduced him into attempting a flight into regions of unexplored English, and the reckless experiment was his ruin. Within ten seconds he was so tangled up in a maze of mutilated verbs and torn and bleeding forms of speech that no human ingenuity could ever have gotten him out of it with credit. It was plain enough that he could not "speaky" the English quite as "pairfaitemaw" as he had pretended he could.

The Innocents Abroad, I, Chapt. XIII, p. 163

Damn the subjunctive. It brings all our writers to shame.

Mark Twain's Notebook, p. 303

As to the Adjective: When in doubt, strike it out.

"Pudd'nhead Wilson's Calendar,"

Pudd'nhead Wilson, Chapt. XI, p. 96

In spite of myself, how awkwardly I do jumble words together; and how often I do use three words where one would answer—a thing I am always trying to guard against. I shall become as slovenly a writer as Charles Francis Adams, if I don't look out. (That is said in jest; because of course I do not seriously fear getting so bad as that. I never shall drop so far toward his and Bret Harte's level as to catch myself saying, "It must have been wiser to have believed that he might have accomplished it if he could have felt that he would have been supported by those who should have, &c, &c, &c".)

Mark Twain's Letters, I, p. 266

. . . You need not expect to get *your* book right the first time. Go to work and revamp or rewrite it. God only exhibits his thunder and lightning at intervals, and so they always command attention. These are God's adjectives. You thunder and lightning too much; the reader ceases to get under the bed, by and by.

Ibid., p. 324

As a rule, the grammar was leaky, and the construction more or less lame; but I did not mind these things. They are common defects of my own, and one mustn't criticize other people on grounds where he can't stand perpendicular himself.

A Connecticut Yankee in King Arthur's Court,
Chapt. XXVI, p. 240

If I were asked an opinion I would call this an ungrammatical nation. There is no such thing as perfect grammar, and I don't always speak good grammar myself. But I have been foregathering for the past few days with professors of American universities and I've heard them all say things like this: "He don't like to do it." . . . When these men take pen in hand they write with as good grammar as any. But the moment they throw the pen aside they throw grammatical morals aside with it.

Mark Twain's Speeches (1910), p. 99

The Germans do not seem to be afraid to repeat a word when it is the right one. . . But in English, when we have used a word a couple of times in a paragraph, we imagine we are growing tautological, and so we are weak enough to exchange it for some other word which only approximates exactness, to escape what we wrongly fancy is a greater blemish. Repetition may be bad, but surely inexactness is worse.

"The Awful German Language,"
A Tramp Abroad, II, Appendix D, p. 303

He understands all the languages, and talks them all, too. With an accent like gritting your teeth, it is true, and with a grammar that is no improvement on blasphemy—still, with practice you get at the meat of what he says, and it serves.

"A Horse's Tale,"
The Mysterious Stranger, Etc., p. 182

GRANT, ULYSSES S. *See also* FAME, HANDSHAKE, MONEY, WAR

General Grant had a fine memory for all kinds of things, including even names and faces. . . The first time I ever saw him was early in his first term as President. I had just arrived in Washington from the Pacific Coast, a stranger and wholly unknown to the public . . . when I met a friend, a Senator from Nevada. He asked me if I would like to see the President. I said I should be very glad; so we entered. . . General Grant got slowly up from his table, put his pen down, and stood before me with the iron expression of a man who had not smiled for seven years, and was not intending to smile for another seven. He looked me steadily in the eye—mine lost confidence and fell. I had never confronted a great man before, and was in a miserable state of funk and inefficiency. The Senator said:

"Mr. President, may I have the privilege of introducing Mr. Clemens?"

The President gave my hand an unsympathetic wag and dropped it. He did not say a word, but just stood. In my trouble I could not think of anything to say, I merely wanted to resign. There was an awkward pause, a dreary pause, a horrible pause. Then I thought of something, and looked up into that unyielding face, and said timidly:

"Mr. President, I—I am embarrassed. Are you?"

His face broke—just a little—a wee glimmer, the momentary flicker of a summer-lightning smile, seven years ahead of time—and I was out and gone as soon as *it* was.

Ten years passed away before I saw him the second time. Meantime I was become better known; and was one of the people appointed to respond to toasts at the banquet given to General Grant in Chicago by the Army of the Tennessee when he came back from his tour around the world . . .

. . .

General Grant was looking exactly as he had looked upon that trying occasion of ten years before—all iron and bronze self-possession. Mr. Harrison came over and led me to the

General and formally introduced me. Before I could put together the proper remark, General Grant said:

"Mr. Clemens, I am not embarrassed. Are you?"—And that little seven-year smile twinkled across his face again.

Following the Equator, I, Chapt. II, p. 29

Lately a great and honored author, Matthew Arnold, has been finding fault with General Grant's English. . .

Mr. Breen makes this discriminating remark: "To suppose that because a man is a poet or an historian, he must be correct in his grammar, is to suppose that an architect must be a joiner, or a physician a compounder of medicine." Mr. Breen's point is well taken. If you should climb the mighty Matterhorn to look out over the kingdoms of the earth it might be a pleasant incident to find strawberries up there. But Great Scott! you don't climb the Matterhorn for strawberries!

. . .

There is that about the sun which makes us forget his spots, and when we think of General Grant our pulses quicken and his grammar vanishes; we only remember that this is the simple soldier who, all untaught of silken phrase makers, linked words together with an art surpassing the art of the schools and put into them a something which will still bring to American ears, as long as America shall last, the roll of his vanished drums and the tread of his marching hosts. What do we care for grammar when we think of those thunderous phrases "unconditional and immediate surrender," . . . "I propose to fight it out on this line if it takes all summer." . . . And finally we have a gentler phrase, that one which shows you another true side of the man, shows you that in his soldier heart there was room for other than glory war mottoes and in his tongue the gift to fitly phrase them—"Let us have peace."

"General Grant's Grammar,"
Mark Twain's Speeches (1923), p. 135

It was while Grant was still in the West that Mr. Lincoln [upon hearing that Grant drank] said he wished he could find out what brand of whiskey that fellow used, so he could furnish it to some of the other generals.

Mark Twain's Letters, I, p. 458

Once General Grant was asked a question about a matter which had been much debated by the public and the newspapers; he answered the question without any hesitancy. "General, who planned the march through Georgia?" "The enemy." He added that the enemy usually makes your plans for you. He meant that the enemy by neglect or through force of circumstances leaves an opening for you, and you see your chance and take advantage of it.

Circumstances do the planning for us all, no doubt, by help of our temperament.

"The Turning Point of My Life,"
What Is Man? and Other Essays, p. 137

Struck by the beauty of Adelina Patti [the popular opera singer and contemporary of Grant], Twain said:

I would rather sleep with her *stark naked* than with General Grant in full uniform.

Mark Twain, Family Man, p. 122

GRATITUDE *See also* ADAM, DOG, TREACHERY

. . . gratitude is a debt which usually goes on accumulating like blackmail; the more you pay, the more is exacted. In time, you are made to realize that the kindness done you is become a curse and you wish it had not happened.

Mark Twain's Autobiography, Paine, I, p. 257

I don't care much for gratitude of the noisy, boisterous kind. Why, when some men discharge an obligation, you can hear the report for miles around.

Best Stories of the World, Masson, p. 135

GRAVEL

You never notice how commonplace and unpoetic gravel is until you bite into a layer of it in a pie.

What Is Man? and Other Essays, p. 363

GREATNESS *See also* COUNTRY, DOG, PEOPLE, RECOGNITION, WORDS

Mark Twain to Speaker of the House, Joseph Cannon:
You're no different in the chair from what you are in real life. Methinks thou art truly great, for only a big man can afford to be natural.

New York Herald, Jan. 30, 1906

GREEKS *See* VIRTUE

GREELEY, HORACE
I met Mr. Horace Greeley only once and then by accident. It was in 1871, in the (old) *Tribune* office. I climbed one or two flights of stairs and went to the wrong room. . . I rapped lightly on the door, pushed it open and stepped in. There sat Mr. Greeley, busy writing, with his back to me. . . It was not a pleasant situation, for he had the reputation of being pretty plain with strangers who interrupted his train of thought. The interview was brief. Before I could pull myself together and back out, he whirled around and glared at me through his great spectacles and said:
"Well, what in hell do *you* want!"
"I was looking for a gentlem—"
"Don't keep them in stock—clear out!"
I could have made a very neat retort but didn't, for I was flurried and didn't think of it till I was downstairs.

Mark Twain in Eruption, p. 347

Depew told this . . .: "Greeley turned on the man who was collecting money 'to save millions of your fellow creatures from going to hell,' and remarked 'I won't give you one damned cent. There don't half enough of them go there now.'"

Mark Twain's Notebook, p. 191

GRIEF *See also* JOY
My grief is always tempered with the satisfaction of knowing that for the one that goes, the hard, bitter struggling of life is ended.

Mark Twain, a Biography, Paine, III, p. 1499

GRIN

He merely gave me a large, cold, sarcastic grin, such as an ostensibly seven-year old horse gives you when you lift his lip and find he is fourteen.

"The Private History of a Campaign that Failed,"
The American Claimant, p. 243

GROWTH *See* LAW

GRUDGE *See* VACUUM

GUIDE *See also* PAINTING

[In Europe]: There is one remark . . . which never yet has failed to disgust these guides. We use it always when we can think of nothing else to say. After they have exhausted their enthusiasm pointing out to us and praising the beauties of some ancient bronze image or broken-legged statue we look at it stupidly and in silence for five, ten, fifteen minutes—as long as we can hold out, in fact—and then ask:

"Is—is he dead?"

That conquers the serenest of them.

The Innocents Abroad, I, Chapt. XXVII, p. 373

That guide or that courier or that dragoman never yet lived upon earth who had in him a faintest appreciation of a joke, even though that joke were so broad and so ponderous that if it fell on him it would flatten him out like a postage stamp.

Ibid., II, Chapt. XXII, p. 276

The guide told us these things, and he would hardly try so hazardous an experiment as the telling of a falsehood, when it is all he can do to speak the truth in English without getting the lockjaw.

Ibid., I, Chapt. XIX, p. 240

GUN

[He had] a venerable gun, which was long enough to

club any game with that came within shooting distance. . .

"Curious Relics for Sale,"
The Curious Republic of Gondour, p. 45

I was armed to the teeth with a pitiful little Smith and Wesson's seven-shooter, which carried a barrel like a homeopathic pill, and it took the whole seven to make a dose for an adult. But I thought it was grand. It appeared to me to be a dangerous weapon. It had only one fault—you could not hit anything with it.

Roughing It, I, Chapt. II, p. 19

[Along the stagecoach route]: He said the Apaches used to annoy him all the time down there, and that he came as near as anything to starving to death in the midst of abundance, because they kept him so leaky with bullet holes that he "couldn't hold his vittles." This person's statements were not generally believed.

Ibid., Chapt. IX, p. 75

[Advice to youth]: . . . don't . . . meddle with old unloaded firearms; they are the most deadly and unerring things that have ever been created by man. You don't have to take any pains at all with them; you don't have to have a rest, you don't have to have any sights on the gun, you don't have to take aim, even. No, you just pick out a relative and bang away, and you are sure to get him. A youth who can't hit a cathedral at thirty yards with a Gatling gun in three-quarters of an hour, can take up an old empty musket and bag his grandmother every time, at a hundred.

"Advice to Youth,"
Mark Twain's Speeches (1923), p. 107

Pa's got a few buckshot in him; but he don't mind it 'cuz he don't weigh much, anyway.

The Adventures of Huckleberry Finn,
Chapt. XVIII, p. 150

[Man has] made continual progress. Cain did his murder with a club. The Hebrews did their murders with javelins and swords; the Greeks and Romans added protective armor and the fine arts of military organization and generalship; the Christian has added guns and gunpowder; a few cen-

turies from now he will have so greatly improved the deadly
effectiveness of his weapons of slaughter that all men will
confess that without Christian civilization war must have
remained a poor and trifling thing to the end of time.

The Mysterious Stranger, Etc., Chapt. VIII, p. 110

Every time the "Devastation" let off one of her thirty-
five-ton guns it seemed as if an entire London fog issued
from her side, and the report was so long coming that if
she were to shoot a man he would be dead before he heard
it, and would probably go around wondering through all
eternity what it was that happened to him.

"O'Shah,"
Europe and Elsewhere, p. 77

[He freckled] me with bullet-holes till my skin
[wouldn't] hold my principles.

"Journalism in Tennessee,"
Sketches New and Old, p. 52

The law of probability decreed me guiltless of his blood;
for in all my small experience with guns I have never hit
anything I have tried to hit, and I knew I had done my best
to hit him.

"The Private History of a Campaign that Failed,"
The American Claimant, Etc., p. 255

Fifty years ago an old farmer and his wife, Brown by
name, were living near Hartford. Above their kitchen man-
telpiece an eighteenth-century Blunderbuss had hung since
the British war of 1812. A grandson came to spend Christmas with the Browns, and teased the old folk out of their
lives to be allowed to let it off. One morning after breakfast, Brown said, "Now Tommy, you will have a great
treat: I'm going to fire off that gun." So saying, he took it
down, cocked it, and thrust the barrel out of the window.
Mrs. Brown hurried up, and stood looking over his shoulder,
while Tommy danced about the kitchen in high glee.
Brown shut his eyes, and pulled the trigger. There was a
fearful explosion, and both the old people fell senseless.
From the fact that two of Mrs. Brown's front teeth were
found embedded in her husband's skull it was conjectured

that he stepped with some celerity. Would you believe it? The only remark Tommy made when reproached with causing his grandfather's death was, "I thought she'd kick some!"

East and West magazine, Aug. 1911, p. 8

If you shoot at your wife in the dark for a burglar you always kill her, but you can't hit a burglar. You can always kill a relative with a gun that isn't loaded.

Mark Twain's Notebook, p. 169

H

HABIT   *See also* AGE, DUTY, GRAMMAR, OYSTER, SMOKING

Old habit of mind is one of the toughest things to get away from in the world. It transmits itself like physical form and feature; and for a man, in those days, to have had an idea that his ancestors hadn't had, would have brought him under suspicion of being illegitimate.

A Connecticut Yankee in King Arthur's Court,
Chapt. XXII, p. 187

I had been confined to my bed several days with lumbago. My case refused to improve. Finally the doctor said:

"My remedies have no fair chance. Consider what they have to fight, besides the lumbago. You smoke extravagantly . . . take coffee immoderately . . . and . . . tea . . . you eat all kinds of things that are dissatisfied with each other's company . . . you drink two hot Scotches every night, don't you? . . .

"Yes."

". . . We can't make progress the way the matter stands. You must make a reduction in these things; you must cut down your consumption of them considerably for some days."

"I can't doctor."

"Why can't you?"

"I lack the will-power. I can cut them off entirely, but I can't merely moderate them."

He said that that would answer, and said he would come around in twenty-four hours and begin work again. He was taken ill himself and could not come; but I did not need him. I cut off all those things for two days and nights; in fact, I cut off all kinds of food, too, and all drinks except water, and at the end of forty-eight hours the lumbago was discouraged and left me. I was a well man; so I gave thanks and took to those delicacies again.

It seemed a valuable medical course, and I recommended it to a lady. She had run down and down and down, and had at last reached a point where medicines no longer had any helpful effect upon her. I said I knew I could put her upon her feet in a week. It brightened her up, it filled her with hope, and she said she would do everything I told her to do. So I said she must stop swearing and drinking and smoking and eating for four days, and then she would be all right again. And it would have happened just so, I know it; but she said she could not stop swearing and smoking and drinking, because she had never done those things. So there it was. She had neglected her habits, and hadn't any. Now that they would come good, there were none in stock. She had nothing to fall back on. She was a sinking vessel, with no freight in her to throw overboard and lighten ship withal. Why, even one or two little bad habits could have saved her, but she was just a moral pauper.

Following the Equator, I, Chapt. I, p. 22

Habit is habit, and not to be flung out of the window by any man, but coaxed down-stairs a step at a time.

"Pudd'nhead Wilson's Calendar,"
Pudd'nhead Wilson, Chapt. VI, p. 56

Nothing so needs reforming as other people's habits.

"Pudd'nhead Wilson's Calendar,"
Ibid., Chapt. XV, p. 145

We know all about the habits of the ant, we know all about the habits of the bee, but we know nothing at all about the habits of the oyster. It seems almost certain that we have been choosing the wrong time for studying the oyster.

"Pudd'nhead Wilson's Calendar,"
Ibid., Chapt. XVI, p. 158

We have no permanent habits until we are forty. Then they begin to harden, presently they petrify, then business begins.

"Seventieth Birthday,"
Mark Twain's Speeches (1923), p. 257

A man may have no bad habits and have worse.

"Pudd'nhead Wilson's New Calendar,"
Following the Equator, I, Chapt. I, p. 15

. . . I feel better than I would if I was dead, I reckon. And, besides, they say I am going to build up now and come right along and be all right. I am not saying anything, but I wish I had enough of my diseases back to make me aware of myself, and enough of my habits to make it worthwhile to live. To have nothing the matter with you and no habits is pretty tame, pretty colorless. It is just the way a saint feels, I reckon; it is at least the way he looks.

"Marienbad—A Health Factory,"
Europe and Elsewhere, p. 119

HAIR   *See also* FASHION, FRENCH PEOPLE, RIVER

When red-headed people are above a certain social grade their hair is auburn.

A Connecticut Yankee in King Arthur's Court,
Chapt. XVIII, p. 152

A lady in Milwaukee . . . who has been joked about her red hair until she goes around and shoots the last few thousand who make ancient remarks about it, says she heard a new thing on red hair . . . A friend from the East said . . . "I rather like this Skeneateles hair of yours." She didn't like to ask questions, but finally curiosity got the best of her, and she asked, "Well, what in the name of the thirteen apostles is Skeneateles hair?"

"Oh," says he . . . Skeneateles is about forty miles beyond Auburn, you know."

He is now carried in a sling . . .

"Warm Hair,"
Mark Twain's Library of Humor, p. 8

"What a lovely little snowdrop that is," said a friend to Mark Twain as a blonde beauty with flowing tresses passed them on Broadway.

"A snowdrop! I should say she was a hair-belle" (harebell), said Twain.

Hartford Courant, Feb. 2, 1870

[Bermuda]: The deep peace and quiet of the country sink into one's body and bones and give his conscience a rest, and chloroform the legion of invisible small devils that are always trying to white wash his hair.

"Rambling Notes of an Idle Excursion,"
Punch, Brothers, Punch, p. 89

HALLEY'S COMET

I came in with Halley's Comet in 1835. It is coming again next year (1910), and I expect to go out with it. It will be the greatest disappointment of my life if I don't go out with Halley's Comet. The Almighty has said, no doubt: "Now here are these two unaccountable freaks; they came in together, they must go out together."

Mark Twain, a Biography, Paine, III, p. 1511

[*The perihelion of Halley's Comet in 1835 was on November 16th; Twain was born on November 30, 1835. In 1910, the perihelion occurred on April 20. Twain died on April 21, 1910*].

HALO   *See* COMPLIMENT, DEED

HANDSHAKE   *See also* FISH

[Grant at a reception]—He reminded me irresistibly of a new hand catching bricks—determined to catch every brick that came, or perish in the attempt.

The Twainian, May–June 1948, p. 5

HANGING *See* KILLING, MOTHER

HANNIBAL, MO. *See* LIQUOR, MINSTRELS, NEGRO, PIL-
GRIMS, PRINTING, PUNISHMENT, RIVER

HAPPINESS *See also* DOUBT, FRIEND, HEAVEN, MARTYRDOM,
PEACE, STAGE COACH, TIME, TRAVEL, WANT
There are people who can do all fine and heroic things
but one: keep from telling their happinesses to the unhappy.
"Pudd'nhead Wilson's New Calendar,"
Following the Equator, I, Chapt. XXVI, p. 258
Happiness [isn't] a *thing in itself*—it's only a *contrast*
with something that [isn't] pleasant.
"Extract from Captain Stormfield's Visit to Heaven,"
The Mysterious Stranger, Etc., p. 242
. . . the one sole condition that makes spiritual happi-
ness and that preserves it is the absence of doubt.
Mark Twain in Eruption, p. 339
Leavin' me as happy as a dog with two tails.
The Adventures of Thomas Jefferson Snodgrass, p. 43
Happiness is a Swedish sunset—it is there for all, but
most of us look the other way and lose it.
Mark Twain's Notebook, p. 371
To be *busy* is man's only happiness.
Mark Twain's Letters, I, p. 151
I am happy—few are so happy—but I get none of this
happiness from knowing more of the unknowable than I
knew before.
Mark Twain and the Happy Island,
Wallace, p. 137
Both marriage and death ought to be welcome: the one
promises happiness, doubtless the other assures it.
Mark Twain's Letters, II, p. 501
[She looked] as happy as if she was on salary.
The Adventures of Huckleberry Finn,
Chapt. XXI, p. 189
No sane man can be happy, for to him life is real, and
he sees what a fearful thing it is. Only the mad can be

happy, and not many of those. The few that imagine themselves kings or gods are happy, the rest are no happier than the sane.

The Mysterious Stranger, Etc., Chapt. X, p. 130

Every man is a suffering-machine and a happiness-machine combined. The two functions work together harmoniously with a fine and delicate precision, on the give-and-take principle. For every happiness turned out in the one department the other stands ready to modify it with a sorrow or a pain—maybe a dozen. In most cases the man's life is about equally divided between happiness and unhappiness.

The Mysterious Stranger, Etc., Chapt. VII, p. 77

Peace . . . happiness . . . brotherhood . . . that is what we want in this world

Abroad with Mark Twain and Eugene Field,
Fisher, p. 42

Happiness seeks obscurity to enjoy itself.

Mark Twain and I, Opie Read, p. 62

HARDSHIP

It is poison—rank poison to knuckle down to care and hardships. They must come to us all, albeit in different shapes—and we may not escape them—it is not possible—but we may swindle them out of half of their puissance with a stiff upper lip.

Mark Twain's Letters to Will Bowen, p. 15

HARMONY   See DEMOCRACY

HARNESS   See HORSE

HARTE, BRET   See GRAMMAR, PLAY, PRINTING

HARTFORD, CONN.   See also COMPLAINT, DOG, INTRODUCTION, LIGHT, MIRACLE, MISSIONARY, TELEPHONE

[The City's Motto]: There are some things that are nexter to Godliness than even cleanliness.

Hartford's health being as good as that of any large town in the State, there is no need to better it. When a man is partially clean, it is a waste of energy to wash.

"Sabbath Meditations of a Hartford Politician,"
From an unpublished manuscript, Chapt. II, Verse XIV
[Unmailed letters and imaginary reply]:
(The madam squelched this, as being an undignified and unjustifiable attempt to drag a private grievance before the public. Right, as usual, confound it. S.L.C.)

Hartford, Oct. 16, 1888

My Dear Kinney:

I would very much like to be at the Foot Guard dinner, but I am not able to be away from home at that hour. If I lived up a back lane like Forest Street, where no life ever stirs after 4 in the afternoon, I should be all right, because that little stockingleg of a street has four splendid electric suns blazing in it; but for style I live in the great Avenue, where there is much going and coming at night, and consequently the Street Board have made a tunnel of it.

Last week they removed the only light that was within a quarter of a mile of me—in order that the chipmunks of Forest Street may the better see how to play. So they say. But you know that is an error, because chipmunks don't play at night. I say *you* know it, I am not charging that the Street Board know it. I am not charging that the Street Board know anything. For it would not be right to make a charge like that; it couldn't be sustained. I do not even charge that the Street Board didn't know it hadn't any right to move that light away from the mouth of Gillette Street. Why, good land, *they* don't know anything; that's what they are hired for.

Now when you live in a tunnel and haven't any chipmunks, or any pets in the Board, and the tunnel and its region are a notorious resort of burglars, and has only one policeman, and he can't cover his beat twice a night without a bicycle, what is the thing for you to do? Why, for humanity's sake, in the first place, you must provide some proper protection for that policeman. And in the next place, you must provide a light to find him by. These things I have not undertaken to do, at my private expense, for I am a humane man, although a sinner, just like all of us. I have undertaken to electric-light the darkest part of the tunnel; during the interval required to string the wires and put up the posts, I am going to personally patrol the tunnel with the policeman, and have a private watchman to patrol my yard. I come on watch at 6 P.M.—your dinner hour. Of course if I should come; and anything should happen to the policeman, there it is, you see—a good and faithful man hurt, in order that I might have a pleasant hour. Why, I should feel like a Street Board.

But there's another way. Don't you think you could come out to the tunnel, and fetch the dinner? You can easily find my place if you start before dark. Come; you are soldiers and you won't be afraid. Fetch the dinner out—do, it isn't far; I've got a lantern; you borrow another one, and we'll have a good time. Borrow it of the Board.

Yours, in eager expectancy,

Mark Twain.
Foot Guard Headquarters,
Hartford, Oct. 16, 3 P.M.

Dear Mark:

There are a good many words which I can't make out. If we send out a detail to take care of the policeman, can't you come to the dinner and read it yourself?

J. C. Kinney, Major in Command.
Oct. 16, 4 P.M.

Dear Kinney—

Certainly. That covers the ground. But pick the man.

M.T.

P.S. And would you be kind enough to order them to stay with the policeman and not wander? There is a river at the end of the tunnel. People and cats get drowned there every night.

M.T.

P.P.S. You want to be particular about this. It isn't a good river to get drowned in. For economy's sake the city empties a lot of sewers into it, right under our noses. It's unpleasant, of course—the "bouquet," I mean—but it saves telegraphing. The hotels in New York never require Hartford people to telegraph for rooms; no, they say, "Open a car window as you come along—that'll answer." It's a hint, you know, that they are aware that the richest city in the world for its size, can't afford sewers, and uses hog troughs. We get all of New Britain's sewage, you know; but did you know that we're going to have West Hartford's too, right away? And I've been told they are going to siphon the Farmington sewage over the hill to us. Some think it isn't a good idea; still, it saves telegraphing.

From an unpublished manuscript

HAT *See also* VANITY

. . . never run after your own hat—others will be delighted to do it. Why spoil their fun?

Abroad with Mark Twain and Eugene Field,
Fisher, p. 101

He landed a cobblestone on the side of my head which raised a bump there so large that I had to wear two hats for a time.

Mark Twain's Autobiography, Paine, II, p. 284

[In Carson City, Nevada]: . . . tradition says the reason there are so many bald people there, is, that the wind blows the hair off their heads while they are looking skyward after their hats. Carson streets seldom look inactive on summer afternoons, because there are so many citizens skipping around their escaping hats, like chambermaids trying to head off a spider.

Roughing It, I, Chapt. XXI, p. 171

HATE

To hate her is an unspeakable luxury.

My Father • Mark Twain, Clara Clemens, p. 84

It was distinction to be loved by such a man but it was a much greater distinction to be hated by him, because he loved scores of people; but he didn't sit up nights to hate anybody but me.

Life on the Mississippi, Chapt. L, p. 371

HAWAII [THE SANDWICH ISANDS]   *See* CONSCIENCE, LANGUAGE, LIE, MISSIONARY, MOSQUITO, POETRY, PUNS, RIGHT, ROBBER, SMELL, SMOKING, VOLCANO

HAWLEY, GENERAL JOSEPH   *See* POLITICS

HEAD   *See also* HAIR, IDEA

Do not undervalue the headache. While it is at its sharpest it seems a bad investment; but when relief begins, the unexpired remainder is worth $4 a minute.

"Pudd'nhead Wilson's New Calendar,"
Following the Equator, II, Chapt. XVIII, p. 215

Most men in California are bald. [1867] . . . of a Sunday when it rains, and the women cannot go out, a church congregation looks like a skating pond . . . on account of the shiny bald heads . . .

Mark Twain's Travels with Mr. Brown, p. 88

HEALING   *See* ILLNESS

HEALTH   *See also* DICTIONARY, GOD, ILLNESS, MONEY, OSTEOPATHY, TRUTH

Mrs. Clemens arrived . . . with a sprained ankle at one end of her and despondency at the other.

Mark Twain-Howells Letters, II, p. 661

I was always told that I was a sickly and precarious and tiresome and uncertain child, and lived mainly on alopathic medicines during the first seven years of my life. I asked my mother about this, in her old age—she was in her eighty-eighth year—and said:

"I suppose that during all that time you were uneasy about me?"

"Yes, the whole time."

"Afraid I wouldn't live?"

After a reflective pause—ostensibly to think out the facts

—"No—afraid you would."

Mark Twain's Autobiography, Paine, I, p. 108
[May 29, 1870]:

[On a holiday with the Twichells in the Adirondacks]:
Not that I mean to lead a stupid, useless life in the woods—
by no means. I shall exert myself in every way that promises to harden my muscles and toughen and strengthen my
frame. I shall use method in my exercises too. I shall change
and change about—not lying under one tree until injury
from over-exertion sets in, but changing to another now
and then. And I shall not "sit around" until overheated but
will watch my pulse and go to bed as soon as I find I am
crowding my powers. Some people ruin their health by
pure injudiciousness—but you never catch me ripping and
tearing around. That is the reason why I never break myself down.

Mark Twain to Mrs. Fairbanks, p. 131

HEART *See also* LOVE, ELOQUENCE, LETTERS, PREACHER,
RICHES, YOUTH, VALUE

One learns peoples through the heart, not the eyes or
the intellect.

"What Paul Bourget Thinks of Us,"
Literary Essays, p. 145

You can't reason with your heart; it has its own laws and
thumps about things which the intellect scorns.

A Connecticut Yankee in King Arthur's Court,
Chapt. XX, p. 162

When a man stands on the verge of seventy-two you
know perfectly well that he never reached that place without knowing what this life is—heartbreaking bereavement.

"Books, Authors, and Hats,"
Mark Twain's Speeches, p. 341

. . . the same spirit which moved them to put their
hands down through their hearts into their pockets in those
places . . . will answer "Here!" when its name is called
in this one.

Mark Twain's Letters, II, p. 638

HEAT *See also* DOG, WEATHER

Hot! The sky was an oven,—and a sound one, too, with no cracks in it to let in any air.

> *A Tramp Abroad,* I, Chapt. XXIV, p. 236

. . . the sun-flames shot down like the shafts of fire that stream out before a blowpipe.

> *The Innocents Abroad,* II, Chapt. XVIII, p. 212

The room [is] shut up as tight as a drum, and [is] so hot the mosquitoes are trying to get out.

> "Those Extraordinary Twins,"
> *Pudd'nhead Wilson,* p. 316

Fort Yuma is probably the hottest place on earth. The thermometer stays at one hundred and twenty in the shade there all the time—except when it varies and goes higher. It is a U. S. Military Post, and its occupants get so used to the terrific heat that they suffer without it. There is a tradition . . . that a very, very wicked soldier died there once, and of course, went straight to the hottest corner of perdition,—and the next day he *telegraphed back for his blankets.* There can be no doubt about the truth of this statement . . . I have seen the place where that soldier used to board.

> *Roughing It,* II, Chapt. XV, p. 153

. . . the tropical sun was beating down and threatening to cave the top of my head in, and I was literally dripping with perspiration and profanity.

> *Letters from the Sandwich Islands,* p. 35

Some people are malicious enough to think that if the devil were set at liberty and told to confine himself to Nevada Territory, he would . . . get homesick and go back to hell again.

> *Mark Twain, a Biography,* Paine, I, p. 190

HEAVEN *See also* EARTH, GOVERNMENT, HUMOR, OPINION, PRESBYTERIAN, SEX, SIMILES, TRAVEL

A man's got to be in his own heaven to be happy.

> *The Mysterious Stranger,* p. 236

I have never seen what to me seemed an atom of truth

that there is a future life . . . and yet—I am strongly inclined to expect one.

Mark Twain, a Biography, Paine, III, p. 1431

Heaven for climate, and hell for society.

Mark Twain's Speeches (1910), p. 117

[A man] . . . worked hard all his life to acquire heaven and when he got there the first person he met was a man he had been hoping all the time was in hell—so disappointed and outraged . . . he inquired the way to hell and took up his satchel and left.

Mark Twain's Notebook, p. 168

The ranches are very scattering—as scattering, perhaps, as lawyers in heaven.

The Washoe Giant in San Francisco, p. 62

[Bermuda]: I said it was like being in heaven. The Reverend rebukingly and rather pointedly advised me to make the most of it, then.

"Rambling Notes of an Idle Excursion,"
Tom Sawyer Abroad, Etc., p. 280

Singing hymns and waving palm branches through all eternity is pretty when you hear about it in the pulpit, but it's as poor a way to put in valuable time as a body could contrive.

"Extract from Captain Stormfield's Visit to Heaven,"
The Mysterious Stranger, Etc., p. 241

When I reflect upon the number of disagreeable people who I know have gone to a better world, I am moved to lead a different life.

"Pudd'nhead Wilson's Calendar,"
Pudd'nhead Wilson, Chapt. XIII, p. 123

HELL   *See also* HEAT, HEAVEN, LETTERS, OPINION, PRESBYTERIAN

HEREAFTER   *See* MOVING

HEREDITY   *See also* DEMOCRACY, MONEY, TITLES

We Americans worship the almighty dollar! Well, it is a worthier god than Hereditary Privilege.

Mark Twain's Notebook, p. 209

HERO *See* MAN

HEROINE

Heroine: Girl who is perfectly charming to live with, in a book.

More Maxims of Mark, p. 8

HISTORY *See also* FREEDOM, HUMAN RACE, MEMORY, NEWSPAPER, PROPHECY, WATER

Dates are difficult things to acquire; and after they are acquired it is difficult to keep them in the head. But they are very valuable . . . Dates are hard to remember because they consist of figures; figures are monotonously unstriking in appearance, and they don't take hold, they form no pictures, and so they give the eye no chance to help. Pictures can make dates stick. They can make nearly anything stick—particularly *if you make the pictures yourself.*

"How to Make History Dates Stick,"
What Is Man? and Other Essays, p. 141

. . . history can carry on no successful competition with *news,* in the matter of sharp interest.

Mark Twain's Autobiography, Paine, I, p. 322

The storm of worshiping gratitude which welcomed [Jay Gould's contribution of $5000 in 1878 for the relief of yellow fever victims in Tennessee] might have persuaded a stranger that for a millionaire American to give [money] to the dead and dying poor—when he could have bought a circuit judge with it—was the noblest thing in American history, and the holiest.

Mark Twain in Eruption, p. 74

The very ink with which all history is written is merely fluid prejudice.

Following the Equator, II, Chapt. XXXIII, p. 392

Herodotus says, "Very few things happen at the right time, and the rest do not happen at all: The conscientious historian will correct these defects."

> Acknowledgments for "A Horse's Tale,"
> *The Mysterious Stranger, Etc.* [1922], p. 143

HOBBY

A person should always have a hobby. Observe how a sweetheart fills every waking moment to the brim and makes life a jubilation. Observe the miser and the successful stock speculator and proprietor of vast money-making industries. Observe the student in his specialty—in bees, ants, bugs, fossils—*any* specialty that is absorbing. But the hobby must not be the *result*—no, only the pleasure of working *for* the result, and the final trial of accomplishing it.

> *Mark Twain's Notebook,* p. 188

HOLE

Today I have been having an experience—and it results in this maxim: To man all things are possible but one—he cannot have a hole in the seat of his breeches and keep his fingers out of it.

> *Mark Twain-Howells Letters,* I, p. 237

HOLIDAY   *See also* HEALTH

He began the day wishing he had had no intervening holiday, it made the going into captivity and fetters again so much more odious.

> *The Adventures of Tom Sawyer,* p. 55

[1908] I have retired from labor for good . . . and have entered upon a holiday whose other end is the cemetery.

> *Mark Twain-Howells Letters,* II, p. 838

HOLY LAND   *See also* BOOK, HORSE, MONEY, NOAH, PALESTINE, STREET, TOMB

Jerusalem is as knobby with countless little domes as a prison door is with bolt-heads.

> *The Innocents Abroad,* II, p. 327

HOME *See also* HOUSE, SHIP

. . . the Americans are the only race in the whole earth who have great and fine and dainty and perfect taste in the distribution of color and polish and richness and harmony in an interior; and it is just these things that make the divine home, the enchanted home. How poor and shabby and gawky and lubberly and shammy and stupid Europe is, when it comes to living!

My Father • Mark Twain, Clara Clemens, p. 106

A home without a cat—and a well-fed, well-petted and properly revered cat—may be a perfect home, perhaps, but how can it prove title?

Pudd'nhead Wilson, Chapt. I, p. 12

Our house was not unsentient matter—it had a heart, and a soul, and eyes to see us with; and approvals, and solicitudes, and deep sympathies; it was of us, and we were in its confidence, and lived in its grace and in the peace of its benediction. We never came home from an absence that its face did not light up and speak out its eloquent welcome —and we could not enter it unmoved.

Mark Twain's Letters, II, p. 641

HOMELINESS *See also* BEAUTY, WOMAN

[A homely woman] winds up sticking out a slipper like a horse trough, with a criminal attempt at grace.

Travels with Mr. Brown, p. 86

A woman who looks . . . homely at a first glance will often so improve upon acquaintance as to become really beautiful before the month is out.

Letters from the Sandwich Islands, p. 206

HONESTY *See also* DEATH, EXPRESSION, INSINCERITY, PAST

An honest man in politics shines more than he would elsewhere.

A Tramp Abroad, I, Chapt. IX, p. 81

Honesty is the best policy, but it is not the cheapest.

Mark Twain-Howells Letters, I, p. 57

He hadn't been honest but a short time. I was attending his funeral.

Mark Twain and I, Opie Read, p. 22

None of these visitors was at ease, but being honest people, they didn't pretend to be.

Pudd'nhead Wilson, Chapt. VI, p. 59

Every man is wholly honest to himself and to God, but not to anyone else.

More Maxims of Mark, p. 7

Honesty: The best of all the lost arts.

Ibid., p. 8

Aren't there a dozen kinds of honesty which can't be measured by the money-standard? . . . When a person is disloyal to any confessed duty, he is plainly and simply dishonest, and knows it; knows it, and is privately troubled about it and not proud of himself . . .

. . . Each person . . . is honest in one or several ways, but no [one] is honest in all the ways required by—by what? *By his own standard* . . .

Yes, even I am dishonest. Not in many ways, but in some. Forty-one, I think it is.

Mark Twain's Letters, II, p. 768

HONOR   *See also* COUNTRY, POLITICS

. . . honor is a harder master than the law. It cannot compromise for less than 100 cents on the dollar and its debts never outlaw.

Mark Twain, a Biography, Paine, II, p. 1007

On the whole it is better to deserve honors and not have them than to have them and not deserve them.

Mark Twain's Notebook, p. 380

A man that never believes in anybody's word or anybody's honorableness, . . . ain't got none of his own.

Tom Sawyer Abroad, Etc., Chapt. X, p. 99

Public shows of honor are pleasant, but private ones are

pleasanter, because they are above suspicion.

Mark Twain's Letters to Will Bowen, p. 26

HOPE *See also* AGE, DUTY, EXAGGERATION

. . . it is a blessed provision of nature that at times like these, as soon as a man's mercury has got down to a certain point there comes a revulsion, and he rallies. Hope springs up, and cheerfulness along with it, and then he is in good shape to do something for himself, if anything can be done.

A Connecticut Yankee in King Arthur's Court,
Chapt. VI, p. 47

HORSE *See also* FEAR, GRIN, INDIAN, SIMILES, SPEED, STORM,
TRAVEL

. . . I am not an expert in horses and do not speak with assurance. I can always tell which is the front end of a horse, but beyond that my art is not above the ordinary.

Mark Twain, a Biography, Paine, II, p. 938

The landlord . . . said the party had been gone nearly an hour, but that he could give me my choice of several horses that could overtake them. I said, never mind—I preferred a safe horse to a fast one—I would like to have an excessively gentle horse—a horse with no spirit whatever—a lame one, if he had such a thing. Inside of five minutes I was mounted, and perfectly satisfied with my outfit . . . I could see that he had as many fine points as any man's horse, and so I hung my hat on one of them, behind the saddle, and swabbed the perspiration from my face and started. I named him after this island, "Oahu" (pronounced O-waw-hee). The first gate he came to he started in; I had neither whip nor spur, and so I simply argued the case with him. He resisted argument, but ultimately yielded to insult and abuse. He backed out of that gate and steered for another one on the other side of the street. I triumphed by my former process. Within the next six hundred yards he crossed the street fourteen times and attempted thirteen gates, and in the meantime the tropical sun was beating down and threatening to cave the top of my head in, and

I was literally dripping with perspiration. He abandoned the gate business after that and went along peaceably enough, but absorbed in meditation. I noticed this latter circumstance, and it soon began to fill me with apprehension. I said to myself, this creature is planning some new outbreak, some fresh deviltry or other—no horse ever thought over a subject so profoundly as this one is doing just for nothing. The more this thing preyed upon my mind the more uneasy I became, until the suspense became almost unbearable, and I dismounted to see if there was anything wild in his eye—for I had heard that the eye of this noblest of our domestic animals is very expressive. I cannot describe what a load of anxiety was lifted from my mind when I found that he was only asleep. I woke him up and started him into a faster walk, and then the villainy of his nature came out again. He tried to climb over a stone wall, five or six feet high. I saw that I must apply force to this horse, and that I might as well begin first as last. I plucked a stout whip from a tamarind tree, and the moment he saw it, he surrendered. He broke into a convulsive sort of a canter, which had three short steps in it and one long one, and reminded me alternately of the clattering shake of the great earthquake, and the sweeping plunge of the *Ajax* in a storm.

Roughing It, II, Chapt. XXIII, p. 212

[I] spurred my animated trance up alongside . . .

"A Curious Relic for Sale"
The Curious Republic of Gondour, p. 51

[How to harness a horse, continental fashion]: The man stands up the horses on each side of the thing that projects from the front end of the wagon, and then throws the tangled mess of gear on top of the horses, and passes the thing that goes forward through a ring and hauls it aft, and passes the other thing through the other ring and hauls it aft on the other side of the other horse, opposite to the first one, after crossing them and bringing the loose end back, and then buckles the other thing underneath the horse and takes another thing and wraps it around the thing I spoke of before, and puts another thing over each horse's head, with broad flappers to it to keep the dust out of his eyes, and puts the iron thing in his mouth for him to grit his teeth on, uphill, and brings the ends of these things aft over his back, after buckling another one around under his neck to hold his head up, and hitching another thing on a thing that goes over his shoulders to keep his head up when he is climbing a hill, and then takes the slack of the thing which I mentioned a while ago and fetches it aft and makes it fast to the thing that pulls the wagon, and hands the other things up to the driver to steer with. I never have buckled up a horse myself, but I do not think we do it that way.

A Tramp Abroad, II, Chapt. II. p. 29

I had never seen an English hunter before, and it seemed to me that I could hunt a fox safer on the ground. I had always been diffident about horses, anyway, even those of the common altitudes, and I did not feel competent to hunt on a horse that went on stilts.

Following the Equator, I, Chapt. XX, p. 200

During the preceding night an ambushed savage had sent a bullet through the pony-rider's jacket, but he had ridden on, just the same, because pony-riders were not allowed to stop and inquire into such things except when killed.

Roughing It, I, Chapt. IX, p. 75

. . . he had a steam-engine . . . which he was very proud of . . . and was always showing . . . to visitors. One day one of these asked him what its capacity was—how many horse-power?

"Horse-power, h—ll!" he says, "it goes by steam!"

Mark Twain's Travels with Mr. Brown, p. 127

. . . the horse darted away like a telegram.

Roughing It, I, Chapt. XXIV, p. 196

The urbane livery-stable keeper furnished me with a solemn, short-bodied, long-legged animal—a sort of animated counting-house stool, as it were—which he called a

"Morgan" horse. He told me who the brute was "sired" by, and was proceeding to tell me who he was "dammed" by but I gave him to understand that I was competent to damn the horse myself . . .

"The Great Prize Fight"
The Washoe Giant in San Francisco, p. 26

I would have been a Rough-Rider if I could have gone to war on an automobile, but not on a horse . . . there is no place where a horse is comfortable.

Mark Twain's Speeches (1923), p. 201

[At the Thirteenth Annual Reunion of the Army of the Potomac, June 8, 1881]:

How often you see the remark that General So-and-So in such and such a battle had two or three horses shot under him.—General Burnside . . . has justly characterized this as a wanton waste of projectiles, and he . . . observed that if you can't aim a horse so as to hit the general with it, shoot it over him and you may bag somebody on the other side, whereas a horse shot under a general does no sort of damage. I agree cordially with General Burnside and Heaven knows I shall rejoice to see the artillerists of this land and all lands cease from this wicked and idiotic custom.

Ibid., p. 101

[In the Holy Land]: I have a horse now by the name of "Jericho." He is a mare. I have seen remarkable horses before, but none so remarkable as this. I wanted a horse that could shy, and this one fills the bill. I had an idea that shying indicated spirit. If I was correct, I have got the most spirited horse on earth. He shies at everything he comes across, with the utmost impartiality. He appears to have a mortal dread of telegraph poles, especially; and it is fortunate that these are on both sides of the road, because as it is now, I never fall off twice in succession on the same side. If I fell on the same side always, it would get to be monotonous after a while. This creature has scared at everything he has seen today, except a haystack. He walked up to that with an intrepidity and a recklessness that were astonishing. And it would fill any one with admiration to see how he preserves his self-possession in the presence of a barley-sack. This dare-devil bravery will be the death of this horse some day.

He is not particularly fast, but I think he will get me through the Holy Land. He has only one fault. His tail has been chopped off or else he has sat down on it too hard, some time or other, and he has to fight the flies with his heels. This is all very well, but when he tries to kick a fly off the top of his head with his hind foot, it is too much variety. He is going to get himself into trouble that way some day. He reaches around and bites my legs, too. I do not care particularly about that, only I do not like to see a horse too sociable.

I think the owner of this prize had a wrong opinion about him. He had an idea that he was one of those fiery, un-tamed steeds, but he is not of that character. I know the Arab had this idea, because when he brought the horse out for inspection in Beirout, he kept jerking at the bridle and shouting in Arabic, 'Whoa! will you? Do you want to run away, you ferocious beast, and break your neck?" when all the time the horse was not doing anything in the world, and only looked like he wanted to lean up against some-thing and think. Whenever he is not shying at things, or reaching after a fly, he wants to do that yet. How it would surprise his owner to know this.

The Innocents Abroad, II, Chapt. XIV, p. 181

It were not best that we should all think alike; it is difference of opinion that makes horse-races.

"Pudd'nhead Wilson's Calendar"
Pudd'nhead Wilson, Chapt. XIX, p. 182

HORSE-CAR *See* TRAVEL

HOTEL *See also* MOUNTAIN, SMELL

I stopped at the Benton House. It used to be a good

hotel, but that proves nothing—I used to be a good boy, for that matter. Both of us have lost character of late years . . . Perdition is full of better hotels than the Benton.

> *The Innocents Abroad,* II, Chapt. XXX, p. 401

[Family Hotels]: They are a London specialty, God has not permitted them to exist elsewhere . . . All the modern inconveniences are furnished, and some that have been obsolete for a century . . . The bedrooms are hospitals for incurable furniture.

> *Mark Twain's Letters,* II, p. 700

We tarried overnight at . . . The Grand Hotel . . . There was nothing grand about it but the bill.

> "Letters from Satan"
> *Europe and Elsewhere,* p. 218

Hotels are the only proper places for lectures. When I am ill-natured I so enjoy the freedom of a hotel where I can ring up a domestic and give him a quarter and then break furniture over him . . .

> *My Father • Mark Twain,* Clara Clemens, p. 52

HOUSE *See also* ABROAD, CHANGE, HOME, MONOTONY, MOVING

Our Hartford house was built with the kitchen toward the street so the servants could see the circus go by without running out into the front yard.

> *Mark Twain, a Biography,* Paine, I, p. 521

O NEVER revamp a house! Leave it just as it was, and then you can economise in profanity.

> To Edward H. House, Oct. 4, 1881,
> *Manuscript*

The house is full of carpenters and decorators whereas, what we really need here, is an incendiary.

> *Mark Twain's Letters,* I, p. 404

That kind of so-called housekeeping where they have six Bibles and no corkscrew.

> *Mark Twain's Notebook,* p. 210

When we returned in the fall, the house was as empty

as a beer closet in premises where painters have been at work.

"The McWilliamses and the Burglar-Alarm"
The Mysterious Stranger, Etc., p. 323

The frame house and log house molder and pass away even in the builder's time, and this makes a proper bond of sympathy and fellowship between the man and his home; but the stone house remains always the same to the person born in it; in his old age it is still as hard, and indifferent, and unaffected by time . . . The stone house is not of his evanescent race, it has no kinship with him, nor any interest in him.

"Down the Rhone"
Europe and Elsewhere, p. 146

[The numbering of Berlin houses]: There has never been anything like it since original chaos . . . At first one thinks it was done by an idiot; but there is too much variety about it for that; an idiot could not think up so many different ways of making confusion and propagating blasphemy.

There are a good many suicides in Berlin; . . . There is always a deal of learned and laborious arguing and ciphering going on as to the cause of this state of things. If they will set to work and number their houses in a rational way perhaps they will find out what was the matter.

"The German Chicago"
The American Claimant, Etc., p. 510

HUMAN BEING   *See also* HUMAN RACE, SOCIETY

Damn these *human beings;* if I had invented them I would go hide my head in a bag!

Mark Twain-Howells Letters, II, p. 695

Human life is maliciously planned with one principal object in view: to make you do the different kinds of things you particularly don't want to do.

Ibid., I, p. 242

The average human being is a perverse creature; and when he isn't that, he is a practical joker. The result to the

other person concerned is about the same; that is, he is
made to suffer.

Following the Equator, I, Chapt. IV, p. 67

HUMAN NATURE   *See also* ARK, BRUTALITY, FXPERIENCE,
   MONARCHY, NOAH, SUCCESS

. . . human nature is all alike; . . . we like to know what
the big people are doing, so that we can envy them . . .
The big personage of a village bears the same proportion
to the little people of the village that the President of the
United States bears to the nation . . . *conspicuousness* is
the only thing necessary in a person to command our interest, and in a larger or smaller sense, our worship. We
recognize that there are *no* trivial occurrences in life if we
get the right focus on them.

Mark Twain's Autobiography, Paine, II, p. 248

I wish here to mention an inscription I have seen . . .

"Glory to God in the highest, peace on earth *to men of
good will!*" It is not good scripture, but it is sound Catholic
and human nature.

The Innocents Abroad, II, Chapt. I, p. 18

[In Venice]: Human nature is *very* much the same all
over the world; and it is so like my dear native home to see
a Venetian lady go into a store and buy ten cents' worth of
blue ribbon and have it sent home in a scow.

Ibid., I, Chapt. XXIII, p. 297

HUMAN RACE   *See also* ARK, BRUTALITY, EXPERIENCE,
   HEAVEN, INSANITY, MAN, MONARCHY, MONOTONY, NOAH,
   POLITICS, PRIEST, ROYALTY, SOCIETY, SUCCESS, VARIETY

Every man is in his own person the whole human race,
with not a detail lacking. . . . I have studied the human
race with diligence and strong interest all these years in
my own person; in myself I find in big or little proportion
every quality and every defect that is findable in the mass
of the race. . . . What a coward every man is! and how
surely he will find it out if he will just let other people

alone and sit down and examine himself. The human race is a race of cowards; and I am not only marching in that procession but carrying a banner. [Sept. 4, 1907]

Mark Twain in Eruption, p. xxix

Why *was* the human race created? Or at least why wasn't something creditable created in place of it?

Mark Twain, a Biography, Paine, II, p. 1096

Etiquette requires us to admire the human race.

More Maxims of Mark, p. 7

The symbol of the race ought to be a human being carrying an ax, for every human being has one concealed about him somewhere, and is always seeking the opportunity to grind it.

Mark Twain, a Biography, Paine, II, p. 564

It is not worthwhile to try to keep history from repeating itself, for man's character will always make the preventing of the repetitions impossible.

Mark Twain in Eruption, p. 66

The human being is a curious and interesting invention. It takes a Cromwell and some thousands of preaching and praying soldiers and parsons ten years to raise the standards of English official and commercial morals to a respectworthy altitude, but it takes only one Charles II a couple of years to pull them down into the mud again.

Ibid., p. 81

I wish I could learn to remember that it is unjust and dishonorable to put blame upon the human race for any of its acts. For it did not make itself, it did not make its nature, it is merely a machine, it is moved wholly by outside influences.

Mark Twain's Letters, II, p. 764

Human beings seem to be a poor invention. If they are the noblest works of God where is the ignoblest?

Mark Twain's Notebook, p. 276

I have been reading the morning paper. I do it every morning—well knowing that I shall find in it the usual depravities and basenesses and hypocrisies and cruelties that make up civilization, and cause me to put in the rest

of the day pleading for the damnation of the human race.
Mark Twain's Letters, II, p. 678

Mrs. Eddy . . . knows that if you wish to confer upon
a human being something which he is not sure he wants,
the best way is to make it apparently difficult for him to
get—then he is no son of Adam if that apple does not assume an interest in his eye which it lacked before.
Christian Science, Book II, Chapt. VII, p. 177

However, such is the human race. Often it does seem
such a pity that Noah and his party did not miss the boat.
Ibid., p. 200

[The human race] is made up of sheep. It is governed
by minorities, seldom or never by majorities. It suppresses
its feelings and its beliefs and follows the handful that
makes the most noise. Sometimes the noisy handful is right,
sometimes wrong; but no matter, the crowd follows it.
The Mysterious Stranger, Etc., Chapt. IX, p. 117

The human race consists of the damned and the ought-
to-be-damned.
Mark Twain's Notebook, p. 346

"There spoke the race!" he said; "always ready to claim
what it hasn't got, and mistake its ounce of brass filings
for a ton of gold-dust."
The Mysterious Stranger, Etc., Chapt. X, p. 131

The human race consists of the dangerously insane and
such as are not.
Mark Twain's Notebook, p. 380

Is the human race a joke? Was it devised and patched
together in a dull time when there was nothing important
to do?

"The Czar's Soliloquy,"
The North American Review, March 1905, p. 326

HUMBLENESS *See* SHIP

HUMBUG *See* ANT, LAUGHTER, PRESS

HUMILIATION *See* ASSASSINATION, CRIMES

HUMOR

HUMOR *See also* COMEDY, CRITIC, DICTIONARY, DISEASE,
   FUN, GOD, LAUGHTER, NONSENSE, NOVEL, WIT

Humor is mankind's greatest blessing.
> *Mark Twain, a Biography*, Paine, III, p. 1556

I value humor highly, and am constitutionally fond of
it, but I should not like it as a steady diet. For its own best
interests, humor should take its outings in grave company;
its cheerful dress gets heightened color from the proximity
of sober hues . . . I think I have seldom deliberately set
out to be humorous, but have nearly always allowed the
humor to drop in or stay out according to its fancy . . . I
have never tried to write a humorous lecture; I have only
tried to write serious ones—it is the only way not to succeed.
> *Ibid.*, II, p. 1100

The humorous story is American, the comic story is
English, the witty story is French. The humorous story
depends for its effect upon the *manner* of the telling; the
comic story and the witty story upon the *matter*.

The humorous story may be spun out to great lengths,
and may wander around as much as it pleases, and arrive
nowhere in particular; but the comic and witty stories must
be brief and end with a point. The humorous story bubbles
gently along, the others burst.

The humorous story is strictly a work of art—high and
delicate art—and only an artist can tell it; but no art is
necessary in telling the comic and the witty story; anybody
can do it. The art of telling a humorous story—understand,
I mean by word of mouth, not print—was created in America, and has remained at home.

The humorous story is told gravely; the teller does his
best to conceal the fact that he even dimly suspects that
there is anything funny about it; but the teller of the comic
story tells you beforehand that it is one of the funniest
things he has ever heard, then tells it with eager delight,
and is the first person to laugh when he gets through. And
sometimes, if he has had good success, he is so glad and
happy that he will repeat the "nub" of it and glance around
from face to face, collecting applause, and then repeat it

again. It is a pathetic thing to see.

Very often, of course, the rambling and disjointed humorous story finishes with a nub, point, snapper or whatever you like to call it. Then the listener must be alert, for in many cases the teller will divert attention from that nub by dropping it in a carefully casual and indifferent way, with the pretense that he does not know it is a nub . . .

But the teller of the comic story does not slur the nub; he shouts it at you every time. And when he prints it, in England, France, Germany, and Italy, he italicizes it, puts some whooping exclamation-points after it, and sometimes explains it in a parenthesis. All of which is very depressing, and makes one want to renounce joking and lead a better life.

"How to Tell a Story,"
Literary Essays, p. 7

A synopsis of a humorous lecture holds up all the jokes, in a crippled condition for the world to remember . . . to take the points out of a humorous lecture is the same as taking the raisins out of a fruit cake . . .

And further, the charm of a humorous remark or still more, an elaborate succession of humorous remarks, *cannot* be put upon paper—and whosoever reports a humorous lecture *verbatim,* necessarily leaves the *soul* out of it, and no more presents that lecture to the reader than a person presents a *man* to you when he ships you a corpse.

The Love Letters of Mark Twain, p. 116

Everything human is pathetic. The secret source of humor itself is not joy but sorrow. There is no humor in heaven.

"Pudd'nhead Wilson's New Calendar,"
Following the Equator, I, Chapt. X, p. 119

Humorists of the "mere" sort cannot survive. Humor is only a fragrance, a decoration . . . Humor must not professedly teach, and it must not professedly preach, but it must do both if it would live forever. By forever, I mean thirty years. With all its preaching it is not likely to outlive so long a term as that. The very things it preaches about, and which are novelties when it preaches about them, can cease to be novelties and become commonplaces in thirty years. Then that sermon can thenceforth interest no one.

I have always preached. That is the reason that I have lasted thirty years. If the humor came of its own accord and uninvited, I have allowed it a place in my sermon. But I was not writing the sermon for the sake of the humor.

Mark Twain in Eruption, p. 202

I have no sense of humor. In illustration of this fact I will say this—by way of confession—that if there is a humorous passage in the Pickwick Papers I have never been able to find it.

Mark Twain's Notebook, p. 184

. . . those riches which are denied to no nation on the planet—humor and feeling.

Mark Twain's Letters, II, p. 798

[Humor] is the good-natured side of any truth.

Mark Twain and I, Opie Read, p. 34

Humor must be one of the chief attributes of God. Plants and animals that are distinctly humorous in form and characteristics are God's jokes.

Mark Twain, a Biography, Paine, III, p. 1556

Laughter without a tinge of philosophy is but a sneeze of humor. Genuine humor is replete with wisdom.

Mark Twain and I, Opie Read, p. 17

[Humor] sets the Thinking Machinery in motion.

Mark Twain's Speeches (1910), p. 131

. . . humor is the great thing, the saving thing, after all. The minute it crops up all our hardnesses yield, all our irritations and resentments slip away, and a sunny spirit takes their place.

"What Paul Bourget Thinks of Us," *Literary Essays,* p. 163

HUNGER

Hunger is the handmaid of genius.

"Pudd'nhead Wilson's New Calendar," *Following the Equator,* II, Chapt. VII, p. 76

. . . hunger is pride's master.
>*The Prince and the Pauper,* Chapt. XVIII, p. 175

HURRY *See also* AMERICA, CREATION, FRIGHT, GOD
[Seeing a dead man] I went away from there. I do not say that I went away in any sort of a hurry but I simply went—that is sufficient. I went out at the window, and I carried the sash along with me. I did not need the sash, but it was handier to take it than it was to leave it, and so I took it. I was not scared, but I was considerably agitated.
>*The Innocents Abroad,* I, Chapt. XVIII, p. 231

[Quoted by Mark Twain from McClintock's *The Enemy Conquered; or, Love Triumphant*]:
"And to what purpose will all this bustle of life, these agitations and emotions of the heart have conduced, if it leave behind it nothing of utility, if it leave no traces of improvement?"
>"The Enemy Conquered; or, Love Triumphant,"
>*The American Claimant, Etc.,* p. 432

HYMN-BOOK
When a Sunday school superintendent makes his customary little speech, a hymn-book in the hand is as necessary as is the inevitable sheet of music in the hand of a singer who stands forward on the platform and sings a solo at a concert—though why, is a mystery: for neither the hymn-book nor the piece of music is ever referred to by the sufferer.
>*The Adventures of Tom Sawyer,* Chapt. IV, p. 38

[A letter to Andrew Carnegie]: My dear Mr. Carnegie, —I see by the papers that you are very prosperous. I want to get a hymn-book. It costs six shillings. I will bless you, God will bless you, and it will do a great deal of good. Yours truly, Mark Twain.

P.S.—Don't send me the hymn-book; send me the six shillings.
>*Mark Twain in Eruption,* p. 35

Then my father died, leaving his family in exceedingly straitened circumstances; wherefore my book-education came to a standstill forever, and I became a printer's apprentice, on board and clothes, and when the clothes failed I got a hymn-book in place of them. This for summer wear, probably.

"Is Shakespeare Dead?"
What Is Man? and Other Essays, p. 329

HYPOCRITE

This nation is like all the others that have been spewed upon the earth—ready to shout for any cause that will tickle its vanity or fill its pocket. What a hell of a heaven it will be when they get all these hypocrites assembled there!

Mark Twain's Letters, II, p. 705

The first man was a hypocrite and a coward, qualities which have not yet failed in his line; it is the foundation upon which all civilizations have been built.

The Mysterious Stranger, Etc., Chapt. VIII, p. 112

I

ICE-STORM   *See also* BEAUTY

If we hadn't our bewitching autumn foliage, we should still have to credit the weather for one feature which compensates for all its bullying vagaries—the ice-storm: when a leafless tree is clothed with ice from the bottom to the top—ice that is as bright and clear as crystal; when every bough and twig is strung with icebeads, frozen dewdrops, and the whole tree sparkles cold and white like the Shah of Persia's diamond plume. Then the wind waves the branches and the sun comes out and turns all those myriads of beads and drops to prisms that glow and burn and flash with all manner of colored fires, which change and change again with inconceivable rapidity from blue to red, from red to green, and green to gold—the tree becomes a spraying fountain, a very explosion of dazzling jewels; and it stands there the acme, the climax, the supremest possibility in art or nature, of bewildering, intoxicating, intolerable magnificence. One cannot make the words too strong.

"The Weather,"
Mark Twain's Speeches (1923), p. 56

. . . The Taj has had no rival among the temples and palaces of men, none that even remotely approached it—it was man's architectural ice-storm.

Following the Equator, II, Chapt. XXXIII, p. 277

IDEA   *See also* BRAINS, HABIT

I haven't had an idea or a fancy for two days now—an excellent time to write to friends who have plenty of ideas and fancies of their own, and so will prefer the offerings of the heart before those of the head.

Mark Twain's Letters, I, p. 224

As a reformer, I know that ideas must be driven home again and again.

Ibid., p. 802

If a timid man had lived all his life in a community of human rabbits, had never read of brave deeds . . . had never heard any one praise them nor express envy of the heroes that had done them, he would have had no more idea of bravery than Adam had of modesty, and it could never . . . have occurred to him to *resolve* to become brave. He *could not originate the idea*—it had to come to him from the *outside*.

What Is Man? and Other Essays, Chapt. I, p. 10

There is no such thing as a new idea. It is impossible. We simply take a lot of old ideas and put them into a sort of mental kaleidoscope. We give them a turn and they make new and curious combinations. We keep on turning and making new combinations indefinitely; but they are the same old pieces of colored glass that have been in use through all the ages.

Mark Twain, a Biography, Paine, III, p. 1343

The man with a new idea is a crank until the idea succeeds.

"Pudd'nhead Wilson's New Calendar,"
Following the Equator, I, Chapt. XXXII, p. 311

The king looked puzzled—he wasn't a very heavy weight, intellectually. His head was an hour-glass; it could stow an idea, but it had to do it a grain at a time, not the whole idea at once.

A Connecticut Yankee in King Arthur's Court,
Chapt. XXVIII, p. 255

For an idea went ripping through my head that tore my

brains to rags—and land, but I felt gay and good!

"Tom Sawyer, Detective,"
Tom Sawyer Abroad, Etc., p. 157

The slowness of one section of the world about adopting the valuable ideas of another section of it is a curious thing and unaccountable. This form of stupidity is confined to no community, to no nation; it is universal. The fact is the human race is not only slow about borrowing valuable ideas —but sometimes persists in not borrowing them at all.

. . .

I think that as a rule we develop a borrowed European idea forward and that Europe develops a borrowed American idea backwards.

"Some National Stupidities,"
Europe and Elsewhere, p. 175

. . . suddenly a red-hot new idea came whistling down into my camp, and exploded with such comprehensive effectiveness as to sweep the vicinity clean of rubbishy reflections . . .

"Mental Telegraphy,"
The American Claimant, Etc., p. 370

What is the trouble with you? . . . It could not be your brain. Possibly it is your skull; you want to look out for that. Some people, when they get an idea, it pries the structure apart . . . Your skull was not made to put ideas in, it was made to throw potatoes at.

"An Unmailed Letter,"
Mark Twain's Letters, II, p. 475

. . . there was about a page used up in turning this idea around and round and exposing it in different lights.

Ibid., II, p. 475

I think I have struck a good idea. It is to reduce a series of big maps to mere photographic fly-specks and sell them together with a microscope of one quarter to one inch focal distance. [Oct. 3, 1885] [*This idea came into practical use during World War I*].

Mark Twain's Notebook, p. 188

IDEAL *See also* ADVICE

It is at our mother's knee that we acquire our noblest and truest and highest ideals, but there is seldom any money in them.

> *Mark Twain, a Biography*, Paine, III, p. 1513

Inestimably valuable is training, influence, education, in right directions . . . *training one's self-approbation to elevate its ideals.*

> *What Is Man? and Other Essays*, p. 9

Good friends, good books and a sleepy conscience: this is the ideal life.

> *Mark Twain's Notebook*, p. 347

IDIOT *See also* CONGRESSMAN, SCHOOL

[The superstition of the bees]: Jim said bees wouldn't sting idiots; but I wouldn't believe that, because I have tried them lots of times myself, and they wouldn't sting me.

> *The Adventures of Huckleberry Finn,*
> Chapt. VIII, p. 71

. . . We are all erring creatures, and mainly idiots, but God made us so and it is dangerous to criticise.

> *Mark Twain's Letters*, II, p. 726

IGNORANCE *See also* AGE, ART, MODESTY, STUPIDITY, SUCCESS

Nothing is so ignorant as a man's left hand, except a lady's watch.

> "Pudd'nhead Wilson's New Calendar,"
> *Following the Equator*, I, Chapt. XXII, p. 217

. . . we never knew an ignorant person yet but was prejudiced.

> *The Innocents Abroad*, I, Chapt. X, p. 135

. . . his ignorance covered the whole earth like a blanket, and there was hardly a hole in it anywhere.

> *Mark Twain in Eruption*, p. 180

[You are as] ignorant as the unborn babe! ignorant as unborn *twins!*

> *Roughing It*, II, Chapt. XXXVI, p. 321

[In Europe]: He said that between—fools and guide-books, a man could acquire ignorance enough in twenty-four hours in a country like this to last him a year.

A Tramp Abroad, I, Chapt. XXVIII, p. 295

I would rather have my ignorance than another man's knowledge, because I have got so much more *of* it.

Mark Twain's Letters, I, p. 250

. . . one should be gentle with the ignorant, for they are the chosen of God.

Ibid., II, p. 680

An ignorance so shining and conspicuous as yours—now I have it—go on a jury. That is your place.

New York Weekly, July 14, 1873

That is just the way with some people. They get down on a thing when they don't know nothing about it.

The Adventures of Huckleberry Finn,
Chapt. I, p. 16

Such mullet-headed ignorance!

Tom Sawyer Abroad, Etc., Chapt. I, p. 16

The man means well; his ignorance is his misfortune—not his crime.

Letters from the Sandwich Islands, p. 113

. . . If you had made the acquiring of ignorance the study of your life, you could not have graduated with higher honors than you could to-day.

"How I Edited an Agricultural Paper,"
Sketches New and Old, p. 313

When I was a boy of 14, my father was so ignorant I could hardly stand to have the old man around. But when I got to be 21, I was astonished at how much he had learned in 7 years.

Source Undetermined

ILLNESS *See also* DEATH, DOCTOR, EXPERIENCE, HABIT, HEALTH, HUMOR, MAN, MEDICINE, OPINION, SHIP

The doctor says I am on the verge of being a sick man. Well, that may be true enough while I am lying abed all day trying to persuade his cantankerous, rebellious medicines to agree with each other; but when I come out at night and get a welcome like this I feel as young and happy as anybody, and as for being on the verge of being a sick man I don't take any stock in that. I have been on the verge of being an angel all of my life, but it's never happened yet.

Mark Twain, a Biography, Paine, II, p. 1010

Man was made at the end of the week's work when God was tired.

Ibid., III, p. 1195

. . . my notion is, that no art of healing is the best for *all* ills. I should distribute the ailments around: surgery cases to the surgeon; lupus to the actinic-ray specialist; nervous prostration to the Christian Scientist; most ills to the allopath and the homeopath; and (in my own particular case) rheumatism, gout, and bronchial attacks to the osteopathist.

Ibid.

[A reply to letters recommending remedies]: Dear Sir (or Madam):—I try every remedy sent to me. I am now on No. 67. Yours is 2,653. I am looking forward to its beneficial results.

My Father • Mark Twain, Clara Clemens, p. 287

Thus I escaped. I am now lying in a very critical condition. At least I am lying anyway—critical or not critical. I am hurt all over, but I cannot tell the full extent yet, because the doctor is not done taking inventory. He will make out my manifest this evening. However, thus far he thinks only sixteen of my wounds are fatal. I don't mind the others.

"Niagara,"
Sketches New and Old, p. 80

I was in bed, trying to amuse the bronchitis.

Mark Twain's Speeches (1923), p. 298

. . . man starts in as a child and lives on diseases to the end as a regular diet.

Mark Twain, a Biography, Paine, III, p. 1362

One should not bring sympathy to a sick man. It is always kindly meant, and of course it has to be taken—but it isn't much of an improvement on castor oil. One who has a sick man's true interest at heart will forbear spoken sympathy, and bring him surreptitious soup and fried oysters and other trifles that the doctor has tabooed.

Mark Twain to Mrs. Fairbanks, p. 22

I have had a high old bilious colic, sailing through forty-eight hours of sin and misery, and coming ashore weak and helpless. [July 1903]

Mark Twain-Howells Letters, II, p. 773

I have a boil on one side of my nose and a cold on the other, and whether I sneeze or blow it is all one; I get the lockjaw anyhow. [Oct. 1868]

The Twainian, Mar.–Apr. 1949, p. 5

Mrs. Clemens had a long and wasting spell of sickness last spring, and is still proportioned like the tongs, but she is pulling up, now, and by and by will get some cushions on her, I reckon. I hope so, anyway.—it's been like sleeping with a bed full of baskets.

Mark Twain-Howells Letters, I, p. 435

ILLUSION *See also* DIGNITY

Don't part with your illusions. When they are gone you may still exist but you have ceased to live.

"Pudd'nhead Wilson's New Calendar,"
Following the Equator, II, Chapt. XXIII, p. 266

IMAGINATION *See also* READER

You can't depend on your judgment when your imagination is out of focus.

Mark Twain's Notebook, p. 344

Against a diseased imagination demonstration goes for nothing.

"The Private History of a Campaign that Failed,"
The American Claimant, Etc., p. 256

IMITATION

. . . any strange and much-talked-of event is always followed by imitation, the world being so well supplied with excitable people who only need a little stirring up to make them lose what is left of their heads and do mad things which they would not have thought of ordinarily.

"The United States of Lyncherdom,"
Europe and Elsewhere, p. 241

IMMORTALITY

Let us believe in it! . . . It had been the belief of the wise and thoughtful of many countries for three thousand years; let us accept their verdict; we cannot frame one that is more reasonable or probable.

My Father • Mark Twain, Clara Clemens, p. 177

One of the proofs of the immortality of the soul is that myriads have believed it. They also believed the world was flat.

Mark Twain's Notebook, p. 379

IMPRESSION

[A naval salute]: if the Shah was not impressed he must be the offspring of a mummy.

"O'Shah,"
Europe and Elsewhere, p. 52

. . . like many another man who produces a favorable impression by an introductory remark replete with wisdom, he followed it up with a vain and unnecessary question.—Would we take a drink?

"The Launch of the Steamer Capital,"
The Celebrated Jumping Frog of Calaveras County, p. 154

IMPROMPTU   *See* SPEECH

IMPULSE

[Man's] . . . sole impulse [is] to content his own inner spirit and [win] its approval.

What Is Man? and Other Essays, Chapt. I, p. 12

From his cradle to his grave a man never does a single

thing without any *first* and *foremost* object but one—to secure peace of mind, spiritual comfort, for *himself*.

Ibid., Chapt. II, p. 15

INCONSISTENCY *See* RESPECT

INDELICACY

. . . To the unconsciously indelicate all things are delicate.

A Connecticut Yankee in King Arthur's Court,
Chapt. IV, p. 39

Delicacy—a sad, sad false delicacy—robs literature of the best two things among its belongings. Family-circle narrative and obscene stories.

Mark Twain's Letters, I, p. 310

I finished my book yesterday and the Madam edited this stuff out of it—on the ground that the first part is not delicate and that the last part is indelicate.

Suppressed Chapter of Following the Equator

INDEPENDENCE

There are certain sweet-smelling sugar-coated lies current in the world which all politic men have apparently tacitly conspired together to support and perpetuate. One of these is, that there is such a thing in the world as independence: independence of thought, independence of opinion, independence of action. Another is, that the world loves to *see* independence—admires it, applauds it.

. . . Surely if anything *is* proven by whole oceans and continents of evidence, it is that the quality of independence was almost wholly left out of the human race. The scattering exceptions to the rule only emphasize it, light it up, make it glare. The whole population of New England meekly took their turns, for years, in standing up in the railway trains without so much as a complaint above their breath, till at last these uncounted millions were able to produce exactly one single independent man, who stood to his rights and made the railroad give him a seat.

Mark Twain's Autobiography, Paine, II, p. 8

I shall . . . endeavor to be as independent as a wood-sawyer clerk.

Mark Twain's Letters, I, p. 24

. . . a [steamboat] pilot, in those days, was the only unfettered and entirely independent human being that lived in the earth. . . . In truth, every man and woman and child has a master, and worries and frets in servitude; but, in the day I write of, the Mississippi pilot had *none* . . . His movements were entirely free; he consulted no one, he received commands from nobody, he promptly resented even the merest suggestions . . . I think pilots were about the only people I ever knew who failed to show, in some degree, embarrassment in the presence of traveling foreign princes. But then, people in one's own grade of life are not usually embarrassing objects.

Life on the Mississippi, Chapt. XIV, p. 119

INDIA *See also* FRUIT, KIPLING, LIE, MARRIAGE, MONKEY, MOUNTAIN, PLEASURE, RIVER, SNAKE, TASTER, WEATHER

There is only one India! It is the only country that has a monopoly of grand and imposing specialties. When another country has a remarkable thing, it cannot have it all to itself—some other country has a duplicate. But India—that is different. Its marvels are its own . . .

India has 2,000,000 gods, and worships them all. In religion all other countries are paupers; India is the only millionaire.

With her everything is on a giant scale—even her poverty; no other country can show anything to compare with it . . .

India [has] eighty languages and more custom-houses than cats.

Following the Equator, II, Chapt. VII, p. 83

A man is an idiot who can't earn a living in India. [1896]

Ibid., II, Chapt. XIII, p. 156

INDIAN *See also* INSTINCT

[Going west by stage-coach]: During the preceding night an ambushed savage had sent a bullet through the pony-rider's jacket, but he had ridden on just the same, because pony-riders were not allowed to stop and inquire into such things except when killed. As long as they had life enough left in them they had to stick to the horse and ride, even if the Indians had been waiting for them a week, and were entirely out of patience . . . [Our driver] said the place to keep a man "huffy" was down on the Southern Overland, among the Apaches, before the company moved the stage line up on the northern route. He said the Apaches used to annoy him all the time down there, and that he came as near as anything to starving to death in the midst of abundance, because they kept him so leaky with bullet holes that he "couldn't hold his vittles." This person's statements were not generally believed.

Roughing It, I, Chapt. IX, p. 75

It isn't worth while, in these practical times, for people to talk about Indian poetry—there never was any in them— except in the Fenimore Cooper Indians. But *they* are an extinct tribe that never existed.

The Innocents Abroad, Chapt. XX, Vol. I

[General Connor] has shown that he knows how to fight the kind of Indians that God made, but I suppose the humanitarians want somebody to fight the Indians that J. Fenimore Cooper made. There is just where the mistake is. The Cooper Indians are dead—died with their creator. The kind that are left are of altogether a different breed, and cannot be successfully fought with poetry, and sentiment, and soft soap, and magnanimity.

"The Indian Row,"
Mark Twain's Travels with Mr. Brown, p. 266

People say Tahoe means Silver Lake—Limpid Water, Falling Leaf. Bosh! It means grasshopper soup, the favorite dish of the Digger Tribe.

The Innocents Abroad, I, Chapt. XX, p. 263

Ours is a progressive land . . . a land which has developed . . . a United States Army which conquered sixty

Indians in eight months by tiring them out—which is much better than uncivilized slaughter, God knows.
Sketches New and Old, p. 235

I said there was nothing so convincing to an Indian as a general massacre. If he could not approve of the massacre, I said the next surest thing for an Indian was soap and education. Soap and education are not as sudden as a massacre, but they are more deadly in the long run; because a half-massacred Indian may recover, but if you educate him and wash him, it is bound to finish him some time or other.
"Facts Concerning the Recent Resignation,"
Sketches New and Old, p. 350

Indians at dinner with whites. One ate a spoonful of mustard; another one said: "What crying about?"

"Thinking about the good old chief that died."

Number two ate a spoonful of mustard—number one asked:

"What you crying about?"

"Thinking what a pity you didn't die when the old chief did."
Mark Twain's Notebook, p. 127

INDIGESTION   *See* CLAM, FOOD, SLEEP

INDIVIDUAL   *See* COUNTRY

INFIDEL   *See also* SIMILES
So we cut him open and found nothing in him but darkness. So we diagnosed his case as infidelity . . .
Mark Twain's Speeches (1910), p. 336

INFLUENCE   *See also* WASHINGTON, GEORGE
Whatsoever a man is, is due to his *make*, and to the *influences* brought to bear upon him by his heredities, his habitat, his associations. He is moved, directed, commanded by *exterior* influences—*solely*. He *originates* nothing, not

even a thought.

>*What Is Man?* and Other Essays, Chapt. I, p. 5

No single outside influence can make a man do a thing which is at war with his training. The most it can do is to start his mind on a new [track] and open it to the reception of *new* influences . . .

>*Ibid.,* Chapt. IV, p. 60

It is not the *single* outside influence that does the work, but only the *last* one of a long and disintegrating accumulation of them.

>*Ibid.,* Chapt. IV, p. 61

INFORMATION   *See also* TRUTH

I think it is best to put up with information the way you get it; and seem satisfied with it, and surprised at it, and grateful for it, and say, "My word!" and never let on.

>*Following the Equator,* I, Chapt. XXIII, p. 229

Often, the surest way to convey misinformation is to tell the strict truth.

>"Pudd'nhead Wilson's New Calendar,"
>*Ibid.,* II, Chapt. XXXIII, p. 266

[About *Roughing It*]: Yes, take it all around, there is quite a good deal of information in the book. I regret this very much, but really it could not be helped: information appears to stew out of me naturally, like the precious ottar of roses out of the otter. Sometimes it has seemed to me that I would give worlds if I could retain my facts; but it cannot be. The more I calk up the sources and the tighter I get, the more I leak wisdom.

>*Roughing It,* V, Prefatory, p. v

INHERITANCE

Inherited ideas are a curious thing, and interesting to observe and examine . . . the man who [would propose] to divert them by reason and argument would have . . . a long contract on his hands.

>*A Connecticut Yankee in King Arthur's Court,*
>Chapt. VIII, p. 66

. . . there isn't anything you can't stand, if you are only born and bred to it.

Ibid., Chapt. VIII, p. 68

INK *See* PREJUDICE

INNOCENCE *See* SIMILES

INSANITY *See also* LAW, MADNESS, MOUNTAIN, OPINION, RULE

. . . It was [Cain's] misfortune to live in a dark age that knew not the beneficent Insanity Plea.

Mark Twain's Letters, I, p. 188

. . . we know that in all matters of mere *opinion* that [every] man is insane—just as insane as we are . . . we know exactly where to put our finger upon his insanity: *it is where his opinion differs from ours.*

That is a simple rule, and easy to remember. When I, a thoughtful and unbiased Presbyterian, examine the Koran, I know that beyond any question every Mohammedan is insane; not in all things, but in religious matters. When a thoughtful and unbiased Mohammedan examines the Westminster Catechism, he knows that beyond any question I am spiritually insane. I cannot prove to him that he is insane, because you never can prove anything to a lunatic— for that is a part of his insanity and the evidence of it. He cannot prove to me that I am insane, for my mind has the same defect that afflicts his. All Democrats are insane, but not one of them knows it. None but the Republicans. All the Republicans are insane, but only the Democrats can perceive it. The rule is perfect: *in all matters of opinion our adversaries are insane.*

Christian Science, Book I, Chapt. V, p. 40

[People] abuse the spiritualists unsparingly, but I can remember when Methodist camp meetings and Campbellite revivals used to stock the asylums with religious lunatics . . . We don't cut up when mad men are bred by the old legitimate regular stock religions, but we can't allow wild-cat religions to indulge in such disastrous experiments.

. . .

I do not take any credit to my better-balanced head because I never went crazy on Presbyterianism. We go too slow for that. You never see us ranting and shouting and tearing up the ground. You never heard of a Presbyterian going crazy on religion. Notice us, and you will see how we do. We get up of a Sunday morning and put on the best harness we have got and trip cheerfully down town; we subside into solemnity and enter the church; we stand up and duck our heads and bear down on a hymn book propped on the pew in front when the minister prays; we stand up again while our hired choir are singing, and look in the hymn book and check off the verses to see that they don't shirk any of the stanzas; we sit silent and grave while the minister is preaching, and count the waterfalls and bonnets furtively, and catch flies; we grab our hats and bonnets when the benediction is begun; when it is finished, we shove, so to speak. No frenzy, no fanaticism—no skirmishing; everything perfectly serene. You never see any of us Presbyterians getting in a sweat about religion and trying to massacre the neighbors. Let us all be content with the tried and safe old regular religions, and take no chances on wildcat.

"The New Wildcat Religion,"
The Washoe Giant in San Francisco, p. 133

The human race consists of the dangerously insane and such as are not.

Mark Twain's Notebook, p. 380

Heaven knows insanity was disreputable enough, long ago; but now that the lawyers have got to cutting every gallows rope and picking every prison lock with it, it is become a sneaking villainy that ought to hang and keep on hanging its sudden possessors until evil-doers should conclude that the safest plan was to never claim to have it until they came by it legitimately. The very calibre of the people the lawyers most frequently try to save by the insanity subterfuge ought to laugh the plea out of the courts, one would think.

"Unburlesquable Things,"
The Galaxy Magazine, July 1870, p. 137

INSINCERITY

The *insincerity* of man—all men are liars, partial or hiders of facts, half tellers of truths, shirks, moral sneaks. When a merely honest man appears he is a comet—his fame is eternal—needs no genius, no talent—mere honesty—Luther, Christ, etc.

Mark Twain's Notebook, p. 181

INSOLENCE   *See* PROSPERITY

INSOMNIA   *See* MOUSE, SOCK

INSPIRATION   *See also* ART

. . . inspiring is an art which does not improve with practice.

Christian Science, Book II, Appendix C, p. 305

He is useless on top of the ground; he ought to be under it, inspiring the cabbages.

"Pudd'nhead Wilson's Calendar,"
Pudd'nhead Wilson, Chapt. XXI, p. 206

INSTINCT

Now my idea of the meaningless term "instinct" is, that it is merely *petrified thought;* solidified and made inanimate by habit; thought which was once alive and awake but is become unconscious—walks in its sleep, so to speak.

What Is Man? and Other Essays, Chapt. IV, p. 77

The nomadic instinct is a human instinct. It was born with Adam and transmitted through the patriarchs, and after thirty centuries of steady effort, civilization has not educated it entirely out of us yet. It has a charm which, once tasted, a man will yearn to taste again. The nomadic instinct cannot be educated out of an Indian at all.

The Innocents Abroad, II, Chapt. XXVIII, p. 366

. . . it shows that for all the brag you hear about knowledge being such a wonderful thing, instink is worth forty of it for real unerringness.

Tom Sawyer Abroad, Etc., Chapt. XIII, p. 131

INSTITUTION

Monarchies, artistocracies, and religions are all based upon that large defect in the human race—the individual's distrust of his neighbor, and his desire . . . to stand well in his neighbor's eye. These institutions will always remain, and always oppress . . . affront . . . degrade him, because he will always be and remain a slave of minorities. There was never a country where the majority of the people were in their secret hearts loyal to any of these institutions.

The Mysterious Stranger, p. 118

INSULT   *See also* ROYALTY

As sure to do you ultimate insult and injury as a supplicating sufferer whom you have helped out of his distress.

Mark Twain's Notebook, p. 131

INSURANCE   *See also* MORALS

This is a poor old ship, and ought to be insured and sunk.

Following the Equator, II, Chapt. II, p. 23

Certainly there is no nobler field for human effort than the insurance line of business—especially accident insurance. Ever since I have been a director in an accident-insurance company I have felt that I am a better man. Life has seemed more precious. Accidents have assumed a kindlier aspect. Distressing special providences have lost half their horror. I look upon a cripple now with affectionate interest —as an advertisement. I do not seem to care for poetry any more. I do not care for politics—even agriculture does not excite me. But to me now there is a charm about a railway collision that is unspeakable.

I will remark here, by way of advertisement, that that noble charity which we have named the "Hartford Accident Insurance Company" is an institution which is peculiarly to be depended upon. A man is bound to prosper who gives it his custom. No man can take out a policy in it and not get crippled before the year is out. Now there was one indigent man who had been disappointed so often with other companies that he had grown disheartened, his appetite left him, he ceased to smile—said life was but a weariness. Three weeks ago I got him to insure with us, and now he is the brightest, happiest spirit in this land—has a good steady income and a stylish suit of new bandages every day, and travels around on a shutter.

Mark Twain's Speeches (1923), p. 80

INTELLECT *See also* GENIUS, GERMAN LANGUAGE, HEART,
  IDEA, PROPHECY, RICHES, VALUE, WORK

Intellectual food is like any other; it is pleasanter and more beneficial to take it with a spoon than with a shovel.

A Tramp Abroad, II, Appendix D, p. 291

On [a long sea] voyage, with its eternal monotonies, people's intellects deteriorate . . . The mind gradually becomes inert, dull, blunted; it loses its accustomed interest in intellectual things; nothing but horse-play can rouse it.

Following the Equator, I, Chapt. IV, p. 61

. . . What a bare, glittering ice-berg is mere intellectual greatness.

Mark Twain's Margins in Thackeray's "Swift," p. 55

. . . as for the contents of his skull, they could have changed place with the contents of a pie, and nobody would have been the worse off for it but the pie.

Life on the Mississippi, Chapt. LIV, p. 406

The gods offer no rewards for intellect. There was never one yet that showed any interest in it . . .

Mark Twain's Notebook, p. 379

A man's brain (intellect) is stored powder; it cannot touch itself off; the fire must come from the outside.

Ibid., p. 365

Puns cannot be allowed a place in this department . . .
No circumstance, however dismal, will ever be considered
a sufficient excuse for the admission of that last and saddest
evidence of intellectual poverty, the pun.

> *Mark Twain, a Biography,* Paine, I, p. 403

INTEMPERANCE *See* TEMPERANCE

INTEREST

One always feels an abiding interest in any heroic thing
which has entered into his own experience.

> *Mark Twain's Autobiography,* Paine, I, p. 360

. . . you can't come here at eleven o'clock, or any other
hour, and catch me without a new interest—a perfectly fresh
interest—because I have either been reading the infernal
newspapers and got it there, or I have been talking with
somebody; and in either case the new interest is present . . .

> *Ibid.,* Paine, I, p. 327

A great and priceless thing is a new interest! How it takes
possession of a man! how it clings to him, how it rides him!

> *A Tramp Abroad,* II, Chapt. VI, p. 73

Do I seem to be seeking the good of the world? That is
the idea. It is my public attitude; privately I am merely
seeking my own profit. We all do it, but it is sound and it
is virtuous, for no public interest is anything other or nobler
than a massed accumulation of private interests.

> *Mark Twain's Speeches* (1923), p. 316

We take a natural interest in novelties, but it is against
nature to take an interest in familiar things.

> *Following the Equator,* I, Chapt. XVIII, p. 180

The things which interest us when we travel are, first,
the people; next, the novelties; and finally the history of
the places and countries visited.

> *Ibid.,* I, Chapt. XVI, p. 166

There ain't anything that is so interesting to look at as
a place that a book has talked about.

> *Tom Sawyer Abroad, Etc.,* Chapt. VII, p. 68

INTERRUPTION *See also* EXPERIENCE, TALK
Oh, never mind Charley Warner, he would interrupt the raising of Lazarus.

Mark Twain's Letters, II, p. 663

INTERVIEW *See also* DEATH, NEWSPAPER, TALK
. . . Interviewing a man in the first person, . . . is an altogether wrong way to interview him. It is entirely wrong because none of you, I, or anybody else, could interview a man—could listen to a man talking any length of time and then go off and reproduce that talk in the first person. It can't be done.

"The Savage Club Dinner,"
Mark Twain's Speeches (1923), p. 353

What I say in an interview loses its character in print . . . all its life and personality. The reporter realizes this himself, and tries to improve upon me, but he doesn't help matters any.

Mark Twain's Letters, II, p. 503

I think the very poorest article I ever wrote and destroyed was better worth reading than any interview with me that was ever published.

A Bibliography of Mark Twain, Merle Johnson, p. 146

Whenever you give an interviewer a fact give him another fact that will contradict it. Then he'll go away with a jumble that he can't use at all.

"The Robert Fulton Fund,"
Mark Twain's Speeches (1910), p. 300

INTOLERANCE *See also* TOLERANCE
Intolerance is everything for oneself, and nothing for the other person.

Mark Twain's Autobiography, Paine, II, p. 13

INTRODUCTION *See also* POLITICS
It was my introduction to an audience to which I lectured in a log schoolhouse. There were no ladies there. I wasn't famous then. They didn't know me. Only the miners

were there, with their breeches tucked into their boot-tops and with clay all over them. They wanted someone to introduce me, and they selected a miner who protested, saying:

"I don't know anything about this man. Anyhow, I only know two things about him. One is, he has never been in jail, and the other is, I don't know why."

Mark Twain's Speeches (1923), p. 370

INVALID

How little confirmed invalids appreciate their advantages. I was able to read . . . the Greville "Memoirs" through without interruption, take my meals in bed, neglect all business without a pang, and smoke eighteen cigars a day.

Mark Twain's Letters, I, p. 247

INVENTION *See also* ARMY, MISSIONARY, POST-OFFICE, WAR

Every great invention takes a livelihood away from 50,000 men—and within ten years *creates* a livelihood for *half a million*. [1888]

Mark Twain-Howells Letters, II, p. 597

[*Twain's description of his own invention, a spiral hat pin*]:

It looks like a sea serpent going for a missionary.

Mark Twain, a Biography, Paine, III, p. 1151

An inventor is a poet—a true poet . . . therefore his noblest pleasure dies with the stroke that completes the creature of his genius, just as the painter's and the sculptor's and other poets' highest pleasure ceases with the touch that finishes their work—and so only he can understand or appreciate the *legitimate* "success" of his achievement, little minds being able to get no higher than a comprehension of a vulgar moneyed success.

Mark Twain, Business Man, p. 114

We are called the nation of inventors. And we are. We could still claim that title and wear its loftiest honors if we

287

had stopped with the first thing we ever invented—which
was human liberty.

Mark Twain's Speeches (1923), p. 152

. . . what I wish to put on record now, is my new invention . . . It is this—*a self-pasting scrap-book*—good enough
idea if some juggling tailor does not come along and ante-
date me a couple of months, as in the case of [my] elastic
vest-strap.

Mark Twain's Letters, II, p. 196

Name the greatest of all inventors: Accident.

Mark Twain's Notebook, p. 374

It is another great step when England adopts our sewing-
machines without claiming the invention—as usual.

"After-Dinner Speech,"
Sketches New and Old, p. 234

[Mark Twain's letter to an author who had written a book
calculated to assist inventors and patentees]: Dear Sir,—
I have, as you say, been interested in patents and patentees.
If your book tells how to exterminate inventors send me
nine editions. Send them by express. Very truly yours, S. L.
Clemens.

Mark Twain, a Biography, Paine, II, p. 996

That's just the way things go. A man invents a thing
which could revolutionize the arts, produce mountains of
money, and bless the earth, and who will bother with it or
show any interest in it?—and so you are just as poor as you
were before. But you invent some worthless thing to amuse
yourself with, and would throw it away if let alone, and all
of a sudden the whole world makes a snatch for it and out
crops a fortune.

The American Claimant, Etc., Chapt. XXIV, p. 211

[Inventors] are the creators of the world—after God.

Mark Twain, the Man and His Work,
Wagenknecht, p. 126

INVITATION

[*In one of his dyspeptic moments in London, Twain*

wrote his friend, Henry Lee, explaining his inability to accept an invitation. His note has remained unpublished for obvious reasons]:

Dear Lee—I can't. I am in a family way with three weeks undigested dinners in my system, and shall just roost here and diet and purge till I am delivered. Shall I name it after you. Yr. friend, Sam'l L. Clemens. [1872]

Miscellaneous Papers,
New York Public Library

IRISHMEN *See also* NATION, CONGRESSMAN, DOG

Sir,—The word "patricide" in your issue of this morning . . . was an error. You meant it to describe the slayer of a father; you should have used "parricide" instead. Patricide merely means the killing of an Irishman—any Irishman, male or female.

Mark Twain, a Biography, Paine, II, p. 870

. . . Mr. [Andrew] Carnegie is no smaller than was Napoleon; he is no smaller than were several other men supremely renowned in history but for some reason or other he looks smaller than he really is . . . always when I see Carnegie I am reminded of a Hartford incident of the long, long ago . . . There was a little wee bit of a lawyer there by the name of Clarke who was famous for two things: his diminutiveness and his persecuting sharpness in cross-questioning witnesses. It was said that always when he got through with a witness there was nothing left of that witness, nothing but a limp and defeated and withered rag. Except once. Just that one time the witness did not wither. The witness was a vast Irishwoman and she was testifying in her own case. The charge was rape. She said she awoke in the morning and found the accused lying beside her, and she discovered that she had been outraged. The lawyer said, after elaborately measuring her great figure impressively with his eye, "Now, Madam, what an impossible miracle you are hoping to persuade this jury to believe! If one may take so preposterous a thing as that seriously, you might even charge it upon me. Come now, suppose you should wake up and find me lying beside you? What would you think?"

She measured him critically and at her leisure, with a calm, judicious eye, and said, "I'd think I'd had a miscarriage!"

Mark Twain in Eruption, p. 43

A random remark connecting Irishmen and beer brought this nugget of information out of him:

"They don't drink it, sir. They *can't* drink it, sir. Give an Irishman lager for a month, and he's a dead man. An Irishman is lined with copper and the beer corrodes it; but whiskey polishes the copper and is the saving of him, sir."

Life on the Mississippi, Chapt. XXIII, p. 188

. . . when Providence shapes a mouth especially for the accommodation of a potato you can detect that fact at a glance when that mouth is in repose—foreign travel can never remove *that* sign.

The Gilded Age, II, Chapt. II, p. 28

IRREVERENCE   *See also* PRESS, PRINTING, REVERENCE

When a thing is sacred to me it is impossible for me to be irreverent toward it. I cannot call to mind a single instance where I have ever been irreverent, except towards the things which were sacred to other people.

"Is Shakespeare Dead?"

What Is Man? and Other Essays, p. 367

We are always canting about people's "irreverence," always charging this offense upon somebody or other, and thereby intimating that we are better than that person and do not commit that offense ourselves. Whenever we do this we are in a lying attitude and our speech is cant; for none of us are reverent—in a meritorious way; deep down in our hearts we are all irreverent. There is probably not a single exception to this rule in the earth. There is probably not one person whose reverence rises higher than respect for his *own* sacred things; and therefore, it is not a thing to boast about and be proud of, since the most degraded savage has that—and, like the best of us, has nothing higher.

> *Following the Equator,* II, Chapt. XVII, p. 212

. . . a discriminating irreverence is the creator and protector of human liberty.

> *The American Claimant, Etc.,* Chapt. X, p. 80

Our papers have one peculiarity—it is American—their irreverence. They are irreverent toward pretty much everything, but where they laugh one good king to death, they laugh a thousand cruel and infamous shams and superstitions into the grave, and the account is squared. Irreverence is the champion of liberty and its only sure defense.

> *Mark Twain's Notebook,* p. 195

True irreverence is disrespect for another man's god.

> *Following the Equator,* II, p. 203

ISCARIOT, JUDAS

I never can think of Judas Iscariot without losing my temper. To my mind he was nothing but a low, mean, premature Congressman.

> *Life As I Find It,* p. 166

ISLAND *See* DIRECTION, GOD, OCCUPATION, RIVER

ITALIAN LANGUAGE *See also* GRAMMAR, SPELLING

The existing [Italian] phrase-books are inadequate. They are well enough as far as they go, but when you fall down and skin your leg they don't tell you what to say.

> "Italian Without a Master"
> *The $30,000 Bequest, Etc.,* p. 185

I cannot speak the language; I am too old now to learn how, also too busy when I am busy, and too indolent when I am not; wherefore some will imagine that I am having a dull time of it. But it is not so. The "help" are all natives; they talk Italian to me, I answer in English; I do not understand them, they do not understand me, consequently no harm is done, and everybody is satisfied. In order to be just and fair, I throw in an Italian word when I have one, and this has a good influence. I get the word out of the morning

paper. I have to use it while it is fresh, for I find that
Italian words do not keep in this climate. They fade towards night, and next morning they are gone . . . As a
rule my words and phrases are good for one day and train
only . . .

> "Italian Without a Master"
> *Ibid.*, p. 171

ITALY *See also* DIRT, GRAMMAR, LIBERTY, MICHELANGELO,
MOVING, OLD MASTERS, PAINTING, POLICEMAN, ROME,
SAINT, SMOKING, SOAP, SOUL, WORK

We reached Venice at eight in the evening and entered
a hearse . . . At any rate, it was more like a hearse than
anything else, though, to speak by the card, it was a
gondola . . . What a funny old city this Queen of the
Adriatic is! Narrow streets, vast, gloomy marble palaces,
black with the corroding damps of centuries, and all partly
submerged; no dry land visible anywhere, and no sidewalks
worth mentioning; if you want to go to church, to the
theater, or to the restaurant, you must call a gondola. It
must be a paradise for cripples, for verily a man has no
use for legs here.

For a day or two the place looked so like an overflowed
Arkansas town, because of the currentless waters laving
the very doorsteps of all the houses . . . that I could not
get rid of the impression that there was nothing the matter
here but a spring freshet, and that the river would fall in
a few weeks and leave a dirty high-water mark on the
houses, and the streets full of mud and rubbish.

> *The Innocents Abroad,* I, Chapt. XXII, p. 279

Italy has achieved the dearest wish of her heart and
become an independent state—and in so doing she has
drawn an elephant in the political lottery. She has nothing
to feed it on . . . She squandered millions of francs on a
navy which she did not need, and the first time she took
her new toy into action she got it knocked higher than
Gilderoy's kite—to use the language of the Pilgrims.

> *Ibid.*, I, Chapt. XXV, p. 326

Medicis are good enough for Florence. Let her plant Medicis and build grand monuments over them to testify how gratefully she was wont to lick the hand that scourged her.

Ibid., I, Chapt. XXIV, p. 313

ITCH   *See also* FLEA

If you are with the quality, or at a funeral, or trying to go to sleep when you ain't sleepy—if you are anywhere where it won't do for you to scratch, why, you will itch all over in upwards of a thousand places.

The Adventures of Huckleberry Finn, Chapt. II, p. 20

[In a suit of armor]: Well, you know, when you perspire that way, in rivers, there comes a time when you—when you—well, when you itch. You are inside, your hands are outside; so there you are; nothing but iron between. It is not a light thing, let it sound as it may. First it is one place; then another; then some more; and it goes on spreading and spreading, and at last the territory is all occupied, and nobody can imagine what you feel like, nor how unpleasant it is.

A Connecticut Yankee in King Arthur's Court,
Chapt. XII, p. 95

J

JACKASS *See* ASS

JAIL *See* INTRODUCTION

JAPAN

[The settlement of the Russian-Japanese war in 1905]:
I hope I am mistaken, yet in all sincerity I believe that this
peace is entitled to rank as the most conspicuous disaster
in political history.

Mark Twain, a Biography, Paine, III, p. 1243

JESUS *See* CHRISTIAN

JEWEL *See* DICTIONARY

JEWS

A few years ago a Jew observed to me that there was no
uncourteous reference to his people in my books, and asked
how it happened. It happened because the disposition was
lacking.

. . .

If the statistics are right, the Jews constitute but *one*

percent. of the human race. It suggests a nebulous dim puff of star dust lost in the blaze of the Milky Way. Properly the Jew ought hardly to be heard of; but he is heard of, has always been heard of . . . His contributions to the world's list of great names in literature, science, art, music, finance, medicine, and abstruse learning are also away out of proportion to the weakness of his numbers. He has made a marvelous fight in this world, in all the ages; and has done it with his hands tied behind him. He could be vain of himself, and be excused for it.

"Concerning the Jews"
Literary Essays, p. 251

The difference between the brain of the average Christian and that of the average Jew—certainly in Europe—is about the difference between a tadpole's and an Archbishop's. It's a marvelous race—by long odds the most marvelous that the world has produced, I suppose.

Mark Twain's Letters, II, p. 647

Sampson was a Jew—therefore not a fool. The Jews have the best average brain of any people in the world. The Jews are the only race who work wholly with their brains and never with their hands . . . They are peculiarly and conspicuously the world's intellectual aristocracy.

Mark Twain's Notebook, p. 151

Jewish persecution is not a religious passion, it is a business passion.

"Concerning the Jews"
Literary Essays, p. 274

JINGLE   *See* MIND

JOAN OF ARC   *See* LITERARY CRITICISM, SERIOUSNESS, TEMPERAMENT

JOB

. . . my great and infallible scheme for finding work for the unemployed . . . it is one of my high prides that I invented it, and that in basing it upon what I conceived to be a fact of human nature I estimated that fact of human nature accurately . . .

Go [to the place of your choice] and say that you want work . . . that you are tired of being idle; that you are not used to being idle, and can't stand it; that you just merely want the refreshment of work and require nothing in return.

[After you have been accepted] the terms are that you are to stay right there; do your work just as if you were getting the going wages for it. You are never to make any complaints; you are never to indicate that you would like to have wages or board. This will go on one, two, three, four, five, six days, according to the make of [your employer]. Some [employers] would break down under the strain in a couple of days. There are others who would last a week. It would be difficult to find one who could stand out a whole fortnight without getting ashamed of himself and offering you wages.

. . .

The scheme [works].

Mark Twain's Autobiography, Paine, II, p. 257

JOKE   *See also* HUMOR, GUIDES

It seemed peculiarly sad to sit here . . . and listen again to poor, flat, worm-eaten jokes that had given me the dry gripes when I was a boy . . . It about convinced me that there isn't any such thing as a new joke possible. Everybody laughed at these antiquities—but then they always do . . . the only right way to classify the majestic ages of some of those jokes was by geologic periods.

A Connecticut Yankee in King Arthur's Court,
Chapt. IV, p. 37

I was a stranger and he liked to have a fresh market for his jokes, the most of them having reached that state of wear where the teller has to do the laughing himself while the other person looks sick.

Ibid., Chapt. IX, p. 74

When a person of mature age perpetrates a practical joke

it is fair evidence, I think, that he is weak in the head and hasn't enough heart to signify.

Mark Twain in Eruption, p. 142

When grown-up persons indulge in practical jokes, the fact gauges them. They have lived narrow, obscure and ignorant lives, and at full manhood they still retain and cherish a job lot of leftover standards and ideals that would have been discarded with their boyhood if they had then moved out into the world and a broader life.

Mark Twain's Autobiography, Paine, II, p. 305

At the end of two months the fact that he had been played upon with a joke had managed to bore itself, like another Hoosac Tunnel, through the solid adamant of his understanding.

Roughing It, I, Chapt. XXXIV, p. 272

Riley has a ready wit . . . and a counterance that is as solemn and as blank as the back side of a tombstone when he is delivering a particularly exasperating joke.

"Riley—Newspaper Correspondent"
Sketches New and Old, p. 203

JOURNAL   *See* BOYHOOD, NOTEBOOK

At certain periods it becomes the dearest ambition of a man to keep a faithful record of his performances in a book; and he dashes at this work with an enthusiasm that imposes on him the notion that keeping a journal is the veriest pastime in the world, and the pleasantest. But if he only lives twenty-one days, he will find out that only those rare natures that are made up of pluck, endurance, devotion to duty for duty's sake, and invincible determination, may hope to venture upon so tremendous an enterprise as the keeping of a journal and not sustain a shameful defeat.

. . .

If you wish to inflict a heartless and malignant punishment upon a young person, pledge him to keep a journal a year.

The Innocents Abroad, I, Chapt. IV, p. 69

JOURNALISM *See* NEWSPAPER, OBSERVER, PUBLIC OPINION

JOYS *See also* PEOPLE

And the joy that went with it was like the light that flows across the land when an eclipse is receding from the face of the sun.

Joan of Arc, II, Chapt. XXXII, p. 32

Why is it that we rejoice at a birth and grieve at a funeral? Because we are not the person involved.

"Pudd'nhead Wilson's Calendar"
Pudd'nhead Wilson, Chapt. IX, p. 82

Grief can take care of itself; but to get full value of a joy you must have somebody to divide it with.

"Pudd'nhead Wilson's New Calendar"
Following the Equator, II, Chapt. XII, p. 138

An earthquake of sudden joy shook him from dome to cellar.

Mark Twain in Eruption, p. 92

JUBILEE

[Queen Victoria's Jubilee, 1897]: It was a sort of allegorical suggestion of the Last Day, and some who live to see that day will probably recall this one if they are not too much disturbed in mind at the time.

"Queen Victoria's Jubilee"
Europe and Elsewhere, p. 207

[The Jubilee Singers]: I think that in the Jubilees and their songs America has produced the perfect flower of the ages; and I wish it were a foreign product, so that she would worship it and lavish money on it and go properly crazy over it.

Mark Twain's Letters, II, p. 646

JUDGE *See* HISTORY

JUDGMENT *See also* IMAGINATION, PERSEVERANCE

You can't depend on your judgment when your imagination is out of focus.

Mark Twain's Notebook, p. 344

. . . I could not consent to deliver judgment upon *any* one's manuscript, because an individual's verdict [is] worthless . . . The great public [is] the only tribunal competent to sit in judgment upon a literary effort . . .

"Concerning the Carnival of Crime in Connecticut"
Tom Sawyer Abroad, Etc., p. 309

No man has an appreciation so various that his judgment is good upon all varieties of literary work.

My Father • Mark Twain, Clara Clemens, p. 47

JULY   *See* FOURTH OF JULY

JURY   *See also* IGNORANCE, INSANITY

We have a criminal jury system which is superior to any in the world; and its efficiency is only marred by the difficulty of finding twelve men every day who don't know anything and can't read.

"After-Dinner Speech"
Sketches New and Old, p. 235

The jury system puts a ban upon intelligence and honesty, and a premium upon ignorance, stupidity and perjury. It is a shame that we must continue to use a worthless system because it *was* good a thousand years ago . . . I desire to tamper with the jury law. I wish to so alter it as to put a premium on intelligence and character, and close the jury box against idiots, blacklegs, and people who do not read newspapers.

Roughing It, II, Chapt. VII, p. 76

Our admirable jury system enabled the persecuted ex-officials to secure a jury of nine gentlemen from a neighboring asylum and three graduates from Sing Sing, and presently they walked forth with characters vindicated.

The Gilded Age, II, Chapt. II, p. 25

The humorist who invented trial by jury played a colossal practical joke upon the world, but since we have the system we ought to try to respect it. A thing which is not thoroughly easy to do, when we reflect that by command of the law a criminal juror must be an intellectual vacuum attached to a melting heart and perfectly macaronian bowels of compassion . . .

Life As I Find It, p. 167

JUSTICE
The feet of the avenging deities are shod with wood. Justice is lame—slow but sure.

Inscription on a fly-leaf of
The Age of Fable—Bulfinch

K

KELLER, HELEN *See also* LITERARY CRITICISM

The assemblage . . . sat down to luncheon. I had to go away before it was over, and as I passed by Helen I patted her lightly on the head . . . she said at once, "Oh, it's Mr. Clemens." Perhaps some one can explain this miracle . . . Could she feel the wrinkles in my hand through her hair? *Three years later Twain found a rather amusing solution. Meeting Helen again, it occurred to him to ask her how she had recognized him that morning in what had seemed a marvelous way. She remembered and said with a smile:* "I smelled you."

> *Mark Twain, a Biography,* Paine, III, p. 1274

I must mention that beautiful creature, Helen Keller, whom I have known for these many years. I am filled with the wonder of her knowledge, acquired because shut out from all distractions. If I could have been deaf, dumb, and blind I also might have arrived at something.

> *Mark Twain's Speeches* (1910), p. 100

When Mr. Dooley exclaimed,—"God, how dull it must be for her, every day the same and every night the same as the day."

Mark Twain:—"You're damned wrong there. Blindness is

an exciting business, I tell you; if you don't believe it get up some dark night on the wrong side of your bed when the house is on fire and try to find the door."

Midstream, Helen Keller, p. 48

Watching [Helen's] teacher spelling out to [her, Mark Twain] drawled, "Can you spell into Helen's left hand and tell her the truth?"

Ibid., p. 57

[Helen Keller's impression of Mark Twain]: I feel the twinkle of his eye in his handshake. He makes you feel his heart is a tender Iliad of human sympathy.

The Story of My Life, Helen Keller, p. 139

KILLING

In five or six thousand years five or six high civilizations have risen, flourished, commanded the wonder of the world, then faded out and disappeared; and not one of them except the latest ever invented any sweeping and adequate way to kill people. They all did their best—to kill being the chiefest ambition of the human race and the earliest incident in its history—but only the Christian civilization has scored a triumph to be proud of. Two or three centuries from now it will be recognized that all the competent killers are Christians; then the pagan world will go to school to the Christian—not to acquire his religion, but his guns.

The Mysterious Stranger, Etc., Chapt. VIII, p. 111

. . . there was no way to convince one of those people but to kill him, and even then he doubted.

Personal Recollections of Joan of Arc,
I, Book II, Chapt. XXII, p. 300

If the desire to kill and the opportunity to kill came always together, who would escape hanging?

"Pudd'nhead Wilson's New Calendar"
Following the Equator, II, Chapt. X, p. 111

KINDNESS

Never refuse to do a kindness unless the act would work

great injury to yourself, and never refuse to take a drink—
under any circumstances.

Mark Twain's Notebook, p. 12

. . . A man . . . made out of the condensed milk of human
kindness.

The American Claimant, Etc., Chapt. XXV, p. 227

KINGS *See also* BARBER, FISH, ROYALTY

Let us take the present male sovereigns of the earth—
and strip them naked. Mix them with 500 naked mechanics,
and then march the whole around a circus ring . . . and
desire the audience to pick out the sovereigns.

They couldn't. You would have to paint them blue. You
can't tell a king from a cooper except you differentiate
their exteriority. [1888]

Mark Twain's Notebook, p. 198

KIPLING, RUDYARD *See also* FAME, POETRY, TALK

He is a stranger to me, but he is a most remarkable man—
and I am the other one. Between us we cover all knowledge; he knows all that can be known, and I know the rest.

Mark Twain in Eruption, p. 311

In those days you could have carried Kipling around in
a lunchbasket; now he fills the world.

Mark Twain, a Biography, Paine, II, p. 1086

[From a letter to Kipling, August 16, 1895]: Dear Kipling: . . . Years ago you came from India to Elmira to visit
me, as you said at the time. It has always been my purpose
to return that visit and that great compliment some day. I
shall arrive next January, and you must be ready. I shall
come riding my Ayah, with his tucks adorned with silver
bells and ribbons, and escorted by a troop of native How-
dahs, richly clad and mounted upon a herd of wild bun-
galows, and you must be on hand with a few bottles of
ghee, for I shall be thirsty.

Mark Twain's Notebook, p. 248

KITCHEN *See* HOUSE

KNIGHT

Knight-errantry is a most chuckle-headed trade, and it is tedious hard work, too, . . . A successful whirl in the knight-errantry line—now what is it when you blow away the nonsense and come down to the cold facts? It's just a corner in pork, that's all, and you can't make anything else out of it. You're rich—yes, suddenly rich—for about a day, maybe a week; then somebody corners the market on *you* and down goes your bucket-shop . . .

> *A Connecticut Yankee in King Arthur's Court,*
> Chapt. XIX, p. 156

As a rule, a knight is a lummox and sometimes even a labrick and hence open to pretty poor arguments . . .

> *Ibid.,* Chapt. XXX, p. 269

KNOWLEDGE *See also* EDUCATION, ETERNITY, EXPERIENCE, IGNORANCE, KIPLING, MAN, WISDOM

You try to tell *me* anything about the newspaper business! Sir! I have been through it from Alpha to Omaha, and I tell you that the less a man knows the bigger the noise he makes and the higher the salary he commands.

> "How I Edited an Agricultural Paper"
> *Sketches New and Old,* p. 314

When one reads Bibles, one is less surprised at what the Deity knows than at what He doesn't know.

> *Mark Twain's Notebook,* p. 385

All schools, all colleges, have two great functions: To confer, and to conceal valuable knowledge. The Theological knowledge which they conceal cannot justly be regarded as less valuable than that which they reveal. That is, if, when man is buying a basket of strawberries, it can profit him to know that the bottom half of it is rotten.

> *Ibid.,* p. 398

If there wasn't anything to find out, it would be dull. Even trying to find out and not finding out is just as inter-

esting as trying to find out and finding out, and I don't
know but more so.

"Eve's Diary"
The $30,000 Bequest, Etc., p. 306

I don't see any use in finding out things and clogging up
my head with them when I mayn't ever have any occasion
to use 'em.

Tom Sawyer Abroad, Etc., Chapt. I, p. 14

I was gratified to be able to answer promptly and I did.
I said I didn't know.

Life on the Mississippi, Chapt. VI, p. 57

. . . it is my thought that if one keeps to the things he
knows and not trouble about the things that he cannot be
sure about, he would have the steadier mind for it—and
there is profit in that.

Personal Recollections of Joan of Arc,
I, Book I, Chapt. II, p. 27

But we are all that way: when *we* know a thing we have
only scorn for other people who don't happen to know it.

Ibid., I, Book II, Chapt. XXIII, p. 308

You may have noticed that the less I know about a
subject the more confidence I have, and the more new
light I throw on it.

A Bibliography of Mark Twain, Merle Johnson, p. 165

When a man has been fifty years at sea he necessarily
knows nothing of men, nothing of the world but its surface,
nothing of the world's thought, nothing of the world's
learning but its ABC, and that blurred and distorted by
the unfocused lenses of an untrained mind. Such a man is
only a gray and bearded child.

"Rambling Notes of an Idle Excursion"
Tom Sawyer Abroad, Etc., p. 271

If it would not look too much like showing off, I would
tell the reader where New Zealand is; for he is as I was;
he thinks he knows. And he thinks he knows where Her-
zegovina is; and how to pronounce *pariah;* and how to use
the word *unique* without exposing himself to the derision

of the dictionary. But in truth, he knows none of these things. There are but four or five people in the world who possess this knowledge, and these make their living out of it. They travel from place to place, visiting literary assemblages, geographical societies, and seats of learning, and springing sudden bets that these people do not know these things . . .

All people think that New Zealand is close to Australia or Asia, or somewhere, and that you cross to it on a bridge. But that is not so. It is not close to anything, but lies by itself, out in the water. It is nearest to Australia, but still not near. The gap between is very wide. It will be a surprise to the reader, as it was to me, to learn that the distance from Australia to New Zealand is really twelve or thirteen hundred miles, and that there is no bridge.

Following the Equator, I, Chapt. XXVI, p. 258

L

LABOR *See also* ADAM, WORK

The highest pleasure to be got out of freedom, and having nothing to do, is labor. Therefore I labor. But I take my time about it.

Mark Twain's Letters, I, p. 430

LADY *See* COWARDICE, WOMAN

LAKE *See also* BEAUTY, FISH, LIE, PERFECTION, WATER

The Sea of Galilee [Gennesaret] is not so large a sea as Lake Tahoe—about two-thirds as large. It is no more to be compared to Tahoe than a meridian of longitude is to a rainbow. . . . The solitude of one is as cheerful and fascinating as the solitude of the other is dismal and repellent.

The Innocents Abroad, II, Chapt. XXI, p. 264

[At Virginia City, Nevada]: . . . further away the snowy mountains rose up and stretched their long barrier to the filmy horizon . . . beyond a lake that burned in the desert like a fallen sun. . . . At rare intervals . . . there were clouds in our skies, and then the setting sun would gild and flush and glorify this mighty expanse of scenery with a bewildering pomp of color that held the eye like a spell and moved the spirit like music.

Roughing It, II, Chapt. II, p. 30

(Lake Tahoe): . . . a sea whose royal seclusion is guarded by a cordon of sentinel peaks that lift their frosty fronts nine thousand feet above the level world; a sea whose every aspect is impressive, whose belongings are all beautiful, whose lonely majesty types the Deity!

The Innocents Abroad, I, Chapt. XX, p. 263

At eventide when everything seems to slumber, and the music of the vesper bells comes stealing over the water, one almost believes that nowhere else than on the Lake of Como can there be found such a paradise of tranquil repose.

Ibid., p. 259

Three months of camp life on Lake Tahoe would restore an Egyptian mummy to his pristine vigor, and give him an appetite like an alligator. I do not mean the oldest and driest mummies, of course, but the fresher ones.

Roughing It, I, Chapt. XXII, p. 183

LAND

The reason arable land is so scarce in Spain is because the people squander so much of it on their persons, and then when they die it is improvidently buried with them.

"A Royal Compliment,"
The Curious Republic of Gondour, p. 63

LAND, THE HOLY See BOOK, CAMEL, HORSE, MONEY, NOAH, PALESTINE, SMELL, STREET, TOMB, TRAVEL

LANGUAGE See also DICTIONARY, FRENCH LANGUAGE, GERMAN LANGUAGE, GRAMMAR, ITALIAN LANGUAGE, SLANG, TEETH, WORDS, WRITING

[In Hawaii]: The native language is soft and liquid and flexible, and in every way efficient and satisfactory—till you get mad; then there you are; there isn't anything in it to swear with. Good judges all say it is the best Sunday language there is. But then all the other six days in the week it just hangs idle on your hands; it isn't any good for business and you can't work a telephone with it. Many a time the attention of the missionaries has been called to this defect, and they are always promising they are going to fix it; but no, they go fooling along and fooling along and nothing is done.

"Welcome Home,"
Mark Twain's Speeches (1923), p. 147

He appears to have his own opinion of a sea voyage, and if it were put into language and the language solidified, it would probably essentially dam the widest river in the world.

The Innocents Abroad, II, Chapt. XXXII, p. 426

There is no such thing as the "Queen's English." The property has gone into the hands of a joint stock company and we own the bulk of the shares!

"Pudd'nhead Wilson's New Calendar,"
Following the Equator, I, Chapt. XXIV, p. 236

But language is a treacherous thing, a most unsure vehicle, and it can seldom arrange descriptive words in such a way that they will not inflate the facts—by help of the reader's imagination, which is always ready to take a hand and work for nothing, and do the bulk of it at that.

Ibid., II, Chapt. XXXIII, p. 270

. . . a gifted person ought to learn English (barring spelling and pronouncing) in thirty hours, French in thirty days, and German in thirty years. . . If [German] is to remain as it is, it ought to be gently and reverently set aside among the dead languages, for only the dead have time to learn it.

"The Awful German Language,"
A Tramp Abroad, II, Appendix D, p. 305

He understands all the languages and talks them all, too, with an accent like gritting your teeth, it is true, and with a grammar that is no improvement on blasphemy—still,

with practice you get at the meat of what he says, and
it serves.

"A Horse's Tale,"
The Mysterious Stranger, Etc., p. 182

If V. were as hopelessly bad as his English pronunciation, nothing but a special intervention of Providence could
save him from perdition hereafter.

Letters from the Sandwich Islands, p. 93

I thought I would like the translation best, because
Greek makes me tired.

"The Jumping Frog,"
Literary Essays, p. 121

Hicks had no imagination. I had a double supply. He
was born calm. I was born excited. No vision could start
a rapture in him and he was constipated as to language,
anyway, but if I saw a vision I emptied the dictionary onto
it and lost the remnant of my mind into the bargain.

Mark Twain in Eruption, p. 120

I have a prejudice against people who print things in a
foreign language and add no translation. When I am the
reader, and the author considers me able to do the translating myself, he pays me quite a nice compliment—but if
he would do the translating for me, I would try to get
along without the compliment.

Moments with Mark Twain, Paine, p. 139

To any foreigner, English is exceedingly difficult. Even
the angels speak it with an accent.

"Pudd'nhead Wilson's Calendar,"
Written in Clara Clemens' copy of *Pudd'nhead Wilson*

Four persons in the house speak Italian and nothing else,
one person speaks German and nothing else, the rest of
the talk is in French, English and profane languages.

Mark Twain's Autobiography, Paine, I, p. 230

He was constipated as to language . . . anyway.

Mark Twain in Eruption, p. 121

LAST *See* WORDS

LAUGHTER *See also* DOG, HUMOR, WORDS

Then the fountains of my great deeps were broken up, and I rained laughter for forty days and forty nights for as much as three minutes.

> *Mark Twain, a Biography*, Paine, III, p. 1300

[The human race] in its poverty, has unquestionably one really effective weapon—laughter. Power, money, persuasion, supplication, persecution—these can lift at a colossal humbug—push it a little, weaken it a little, century by century; but only laughter can blow it to rags and atoms at a blast. Against the assault of laughter nothing can stand.

> *The Mysterious Stranger, Etc.*, Chapt. X, p. 132

When he laughs it sounds like rasping two stones together, and he always starts it off with a cheery screech like raking a nail across a window-pane.

> "A Curious Dream,"
> *Sketches New and Old*, p. 261

Catherine was like to die, for pure enjoyment. She didn't laugh loud—we, of course, wished she would—but kept in the shelter of a fan, and shook until there was danger that she would unhitch her ribs from her spine.

> *Joan of Arc*, I, Chapt. XV, p. 237

. . . Sherburn sort of laughed; not the pleasant kind, but the kind that makes you feel like when you are eating bread that's got sand in it.

> *The Adventures of Huckleberry Finn*,
> Chapt. XXII, p. 196

Then he busted out, and had another of them forty-rod laughs of his'n.

> "Tom Sawyer, Detective,"
> *Tom Sawyer Abroad, Etc.*, p. 196

Such a laugh was money in a man's pocket, because it cut down the doctor's bill like everything.

> *The Adventures of Tom Sawyer*, Chapt. XXX, p. 268

. . . Quaking with a gentle ecstasy of laughter.

> "First Interview with Artemus Ward,"
> *Sketches New and Old*, p. 368

. . . sometimes when a bright remark was made at one end of the procession and started on its travels toward the other, you could note its progress all the way by the sparkling spray of laughter it threw off from its bows as it ploughed along. . .

A Connecticut Yankee in King Arthur's Court,
Chapt. XXI, p. 772

. . . and then alongside my head there burst out the most inhuman explosion of laughter that ever rent the drum of a person's ear . . . it was LaHire; and he stood there with his gauntlets on his hips and his head tilted back and his jaws spread to that degree to let out his hurricanes and his thunders that it amounted to indecent exposure, for you could see everything that was in him.

Personal Recollections of Joan of Arc,
I, Book II, Chapt. XV, p. 245

I am never more tickled than when I laugh at myself.

Mark Twain and I, Opie Read, p. 60

LAUNDRY

German laundry could not have acquired this perfect ignorance of how to do up a shirt without able instruction—one easily sees England in it. Your collar is like a horse-collar; your shirt can stand alone and when you get into it you feel ready for crime. It is a wonder they do not have more crime here, but it is increasing as adoption of clean shirts spreads among the social democrats.

Mark Twain's Notebook, p. 141

LAW   *See also* COVETOUSNESS, CUSTOM, HEAVEN, INSANITY, IRISHMEN, PRESS, PRINCIPLE, SIMILES, WAGE, WORK

A diplomat of full age ought surely to know this pair of simple things! that a country's laws are written upon paper, and that its customs are engraved upon brass. One may play with the one but not with the other. It is less risky for a stranger to dance upon our Constitution in the public square than to affront one of our solidified customs. The one is merely eminently respectable, the other is sacred. [re Gorky's visit with his mistress to the U.S. in 1906]

S.L.C. to C.T., p. 11

[Regarding the plea of insanity]: Really, what we want now, is not laws against crime, but a law against *insanity.*

"A New Crime,"
Sketches New and Old, p. 250

. . . in the matter of the sexual relations man's statutory regulations of it [are] a distinct interference with a higher law, the law of Nature. . . I [can't] call to mind a written law of any kind that had been promulgated in any age of the world in any statute book or any Bible for the regulation of man's conduct in *any* particular, from assassination all the way up to Sabbath-breaking, that [isn't] a violation of the law of Nature, which I regard as the highest of laws, the most peremptory and absolute of all laws—Nature's laws being in my belief plainly and simply the laws of God, since He instituted them . . . we [are] the servants of convention; we [can] not subsist, either in a savage or a civilized state, without conventions; . . . we must accept them and stand by them, even when we [disapprove] of them; . . . while the laws of Nature, that is to say the laws of God, plainly [make] every human being a law unto himself, we must steadfastly refuse to obey those laws, and we must as steadfastly stand by the conventions which ignore them, since the statutes furnish us peace, fairly good government and stability, and therefore are better for us than the laws of God, which would soon plunge us into confusion and disorder and anarchy, if we should adopt them.

Mark Twain in Eruption, p. 315

They live in the midst of a country [America] where there is no end to the laws and no beginning to the execution of them.

"Temperance and Woman's Rights,"
Europe and Elsewhere, p. 27

A crime persevered in a thousand centuries ceases to be

a crime, and becomes a virtue. This is the law of custom, and custom supersedes all other forms of law. Christian governments are as frank today, as open and above-board, in discussing projects for raiding each other's clothes-lines as ever they were before the Golden Rule came smiling into this inhospitable world and couldn't get a night's lodging anywhere.

Following the Equator, II, Chapt. XXVII, p. 322

. . . the administration of law can never go lax where every individual sees to it that it grows not lax in his own case, or in cases which fall under his eyes.

Mark Twain's Notebook, p. 140

To succeed in the other trades, capacity must be shown; in the law, concealment of it will do.

"Pudd'nhead Wilson's New Calendar,"
Following the Equator, II, Chapt. I, p. 11

If we only had some God in the country's laws, instead of being in such a sweat to get him into the Constitution, it would be better all around.

Mark Twain's Letters, I, p. 262

Those people . . . early stricken of God, intellectually— the departmental *interpreters* of the laws in Washington . . . can always be depended on to take any reasonably good law and interpret the common sense all out of it.

Ibid., II, p. 481

What is the most rigorous law of our being? *Growth*.

Mark Twain's Speeches (1923), p. 121

. . . honor is a harder master than the law.

Mark Twain, a Biography, Paine, II, p. 1007

The Constitution has made America an asylum for the poor and oppressed of all nations.

"The Disgraceful Persecution of a Boy,"
Sketches New and Old, p. 145

I believe you keep a lawyer. I have always kept a lawyer, too, though I have never made anything out of him. It is service to an author to have a lawyer. There is something so disagreeable in having a personal contact with a pub-

lisher. So it is better to work through a lawyer—and lose
your case.

"Author's Club,"
Mark Twain's Speeches (1923), p. 186

. . . they all laid their heads together like as many
lawyers when they are gettin' ready to prove that a man's
heirs ain't got any right to his property.

"A Thomas Jefferson Snodgrass Letter,"
The Iowa Journal of History and Politics,
July 1929, p. 441

From everlasting . . . this is the law: the sum of wrong
and misery shall always keep exact step with the *sum* of
human blessedness. No civilization, no advance, has ever
modified these proportions by even the shadow of a shade,
nor ever can, while our race endures.

Mark Twain, a Biography, Paine, III, p. 1469

LAZY *See also* DIRT, DIPLOMAT, HEALTH, SLOWNESS, WORK

I am not as lazy as I was—but I am lazy enough yet for
two people.

Mark Twain to Mrs. Fairbanks, p. 8

It was an awful drudgery for a lazy man, and I was born
lazy. I am no lazier now than I was forty years ago, but
that is because I reached the limit forty years ago. You
can't go beyond possibility.

Mark Twain in Eruption, p. 256

I am too lazy, now, in my sere and yellow leaf, to be
willing to work for anything but love.

Mark Twain's Letters, I, p. 416

LEARNING *See also* ACQUIREMENT, EDUCATION, EXPERI-
ENCE, TALK, WOMAN

A little learning makes the whole world kin.—Proverbs
xxxii, 7.

"The Awful German Language,"
A Tramp Abroad, II, Appendix D, p. 290

Learning softeneth the heart and breedeth gentleness and charity.

The Prince and the Pauper, Chapt. IV, p. 40

Supposing is good, but finding out is better.

Mark Twain in Eruption, p. 324

A man who can't learn stands in his own light.

"An Entertaining Article,"
The $30,000 Bequest, Etc., p. 226

To do a thing you must learn how; . . . to play a fiddle it is not merely necessary to take a bow and fiddle with it.

Mark Twain-Howells Letters, I, p. 157

LECTURING *See also* HUMOR, MEMORY, PLATFORM, READER, SPEECH, WOMAN

The same old practising on audiences still goes on—the same old feeling of pulses and altering manner and matter to suit the symptoms. [1871]

Love Letters of Mark Twain, p. 162

Written things are not for speech; their form is literary; they are stiff, inflexible, and will not lend themselves to happy and effective delivery with the tongue—where their purpose is to merely entertain, not instruct; they have to be limbered up, broken up, colloquialized, and turned into the common forms of unpremeditated talk—otherwise they will bore the house, not entertain it.

Mark Twain in Eruption, p. 216

I never made a success of a lecture delivered in a church yet. People are afraid to laugh in church.

Mark Twain's Letters, I, p. 189

Lecturing is gymnastics, chest-expander, medicine, mind-healer, blues-destroyer, all in one.

The Eccentricities of Genius, Pond, p. 225

LEISURE *See also* SUNDAY

Sunday is the only day that brings unbearable leisure. I hope you will be in New York another winter; then I shall know what to do with these foretastes of eternity.

Mark Twain's Letters, II, p. 679

LETTERS *See also* COMPLAINT, FAME, KIPLING, RUDYARD,
MOTHER, STRANGER, TELEPHONE, TYPEWRITER, WRONG

I am going to write you . . . but not now, for I haven't
anything to do and I can't write letters except when I am
rushed.

> "My Author's League with Mark Twain,"–D. Quick,
> *The North American Review,* Summer, 1938, p. 319

. . . how wonderful are old letters in bringing a dead
past back to life and filling it with movement and stir of
figures clothed in ruddy flesh! It all seems more real and
present than it does in a novel, and one feels it more and
is more a part of it, with the joylight in one's eyes, and
one's own heart on the skewer.

> *My Father • Mark Twain,* Clara Clemens, p. 228

[From a letter to Karl Gerhardt and his wife, 1881]:

We want you both to write us just as often as you can
and thus keep the bridge strong and firm between your
hearts and ours–don't let it fall to decay and leave the
affections without a highway to cross on.

> *From a hitherto unpublished letter*

[A negro in Kentucky boasting about his grandson]:
"My little grandson goes to (school). The other day he
wrote a letter to his aunt, up in Cincinnati. He has an uncle
way up in New York, but he can't write that far yet."

> *Mark Twain and I,* Opie Read, p. 25

One only has to leave home to learn how to write an
interesting letter to an absent friend when he gets back.

> *Mark Twain's Letters,* I, p. 30

Pamela, you wouldn't do for a local reporter–because you
don't appreciate the interest that attaches to *names.* An
item is of no use unless it speaks of some *person* and not
then, unless that person's *name* is distinctly mentioned. The
most interesting letter one can write, . . . is one that treats
of *persons* he has been acquainted with rather than the
public events of the day.

> *Ibid.,* I, p. 89

The most useful and interesting letters we get here from
home are from children seven or eight years old . . . they

tell all they know, and then stop.

"A Complaint about Correspondents,"
The Celebrated Jumping Frog of Calaveras County, p. 31

When you get an exasperating letter what happens? If you are young, you answer it promptly, instantly—and mail the thing you have written. At forty what do you do? By that time you have found out that a letter written in a passion is a mistake in ninety-nine cases out of a hundred. . .

. . .

To this day I lose my balance and send an overwarm letter—or more frequently telegram—two or three times a year. But that is better than doing it a hundred times a year, as I used to do years ago. Perhaps I write about as many as ever, but I pigeonhole them. They ought not to be thrown away. Such a letter a year or so old is as good as a sermon to the man who wrote it. It makes him feel small and shabby, but—well, that wears off. Any sermon does; but the sermon does some little good, anyway. An old cold letter . . . makes you wonder how you could ever have got into such a rage about nothing.

Mark Twain, a Biography, Paine, II, p. 860

Ah, in that sweeter, lovelier, peacefuler hell, there is no letterwriting.

My Father • Mark Twain, Clara Clemens, p. 101

Letters are like a plum pudding—you never know when you might come across a plum, and though sometimes you might crack your tooth on a bit of nut-shell that got in by mistake, the succulent plums quite make up for any temporary inconvenience.

Enchantment, Dorothy Quick, p. 93

If there's anything that makes me mad and likely to refuse a request it's a long rambling letter that wears you out before you get to the point.

Ibid., p. 94

[*Letter to Twichell, 1880*]: Somebody may be reading *this* letter 80 years hence—(you pitying snob, who are holding this yellow-paper in your hand in 1960—I know how

pathetically trivial our small concerns will seem to you).
Mark Twain's Letters, I, p. 385

LIBERTY *See also* INVENTION, IRREVERENCE, POLITICS, PRESS, RELIGION

Rome's liberties were not auctioned off in a day, but were bought slowly, gradually, furtively, little by little; first with a little corn and oil for the exceedingly poor and wretched, later with corn and oil for voters who were not quite so poor, later still with corn and oil for pretty much every man that had a vote to sell—exactly our own history over again.

Mark Twain in Eruption, p. 68

LIBRARY *See* BOOK

Jane Austen's books, too, are absent from this library. Just that one omission alone would make a fairly good library out of a library that hadn't a book in it.
Following the Equator, II, Chapt. XXVI, p. 312

But the truth is, that when a Library expels a book of mine and leaves an unexpurgated Bible lying around where unprotected youth and age can get hold of it, the deep unconscious irony of it delights me and doesn't anger me.
Mark Twain's Letters, II, p. 805

LIE *See also* CAT, COLD, CONVINCING, ENGLAND, FRUIT, INDE-PENDENCE, MOUNTAIN, NEWSPAPER, RAILROAD, SLANDER, TOLERANCE, TRAVEL, TRUTH, WASHINGTON, GEORGE, WEAKNESS

Note that venerable proverb: Children and fools *always* speak the truth. The deduction is plain: adults and wise persons *never* speak it.
"On the Decay of the Art of Lying,"
Tom Sawyer Abroad, Etc., p. 356

The men in that far country were liars, every one. Their mere howdy-do was a lie, because *they* didn't care how you did, except they were undertakers.

Ibid., p. 357

The highest perfection of politeness is only a beautiful edifice, built, from the base to the dome, of graceful and gilded forms of charitable and unselfish lying.

Ibid., p. 358

Figures often beguile, particularly when I have the arranging of them myself. The remark attributed to Disraeli would apply—"There are three kinds of lies—lies, damned lies and statistics."

Mark Twain's Autobiography, I, p. 246

Carlyle said "A lie cannot live." It shows that he did not know how to tell them.

Mark Twain in Eruption, p. 131

George Washington couldn't tell a lie. I can; but I won't.

Mark Twain, Henderson, p. 187

Never waste a lie; you never know when you may need it.

Ibid., p. 189

. . . it was necessary to watch this man all the time . . . He told me such a monstrous lie once that it swelled my left ear up, and spread it so that I was actually not able to see out around it; it remained so for months, and people came miles to see me fan myself with it.

Life on the Mississippi, Chapt. XXXIV, p. 276

He is not a liar, but he will become one if he keeps on. He told me once that he used to crack cocoanuts with his teeth when he was a boy; and when I asked how he got them into his mouth, he said he was upwards of six feet high at that time, and had an unusual mouth. And when I followed him up and asked him what had become of that other foot, he said a house fell on him and he was never able to get his stature back again. Swervings like these from the strict line of fact often beguile a truthful man on and on until he eventually becomes a liar.

Following the Equator, II, Chapt. XXIV, p. 291

[In the Sandwich Islands]: It is said by some, and believed, that Kanakas won't lie, but I know they *will* lie— like auctioneers—lie like lawyers—lie like patent-medicine advertisements—they will *almost* lie like *newspaper* men. They will lie for a dollar when they could get a dollar and a half for telling the truth. They never tell a traveler the right road or right distance to a place. Christian Kanakas will go into court and swear on the Bible and then stand up and lie till the lights burn blue around them, and then go home and go through a lot of purifying idolatrous ceremonies and the thing is all straight.

"The Sandwich Islands,"
Mark Twain's Speeches (1923), p. 7

A white man cannot drink the water of Mono Lake for it is nearly pure lye. It is said that the Indians in the vicinity drink it sometimes, though. It is not improbable, for they are among the purest liars I ever saw. (There will be no additional charge for this joke, except to parties requiring an explanation of it. This joke has received high commendation from some of the ablest minds of the age.)

Roughing It, I, Chapt. XXXVIII, p. 296

He was a falsehood done in flesh and blood . . .

The Gilded Age, II, Chapt. XXVII, p. 293

The only difference . . . between a silent lie and a spoken one is, that the silent lie is a less respectable one than the other. And it can deceive, whereas the other can't—as a rule.

Following the Equator, II, Chapt. III, p. 40

There was one tree in the compound, and a monkey lived in it. At first I was strongly interested in the tree, for I was told that it was the renowned *peepul*—the tree in whose shadow you cannot tell a lie. This one failed to stand the test, and I went away from it disappointed.

Ibid., II, Chapt. XIV, p. 171

Jo Bowers . . . was a huge, harmless brag . . . an experienced, industrious, ambitious, and often quite picturesque liar, and yet not a successful one, for he had had no intelligent training, but was allowed to come up just any way.

"The Private History of a Campaign that Failed,"
The American Claimant, p. 238

The glory which is built upon a lie soon becomes a most unpleasant incumbrance. . . . How easy it is to make people believe a lie, and how hard it is to undo that work again!

> *Mark Twain in Eruption,* p. 128

In all lies there is wheat among the chaff.

> *A Connecticut Yankee in King Arthur's Court,*
> Chapt. XI, p. 84

There are 869 different forms of lying, but only one of them has been squarely forbidden. Thou shalt not bear false witness against thy neighbor.

> "Pudd'nhead Wilson's New Calendar,"
> *Following the Equator,* II, Chapt. XIX, p. 224

It is often the case that the man who can't tell a lie thinks he is the best judge of one.

> "Pudd'nhead Wilson's Calendar,"
> *Pudd'nhead Wilson,* Conclusion, p. 223

When he slept, he snored a lie; when he awoke, he blinked a falsehood.

> *Mark Twain and I,* Opie Read, p. 54

A wise man does not waste so good a commodity as lying for naught.

> *The Prince and the Pauper,* Chapt. XVIII, p. 172

The most outrageous lies that can be invented will find believers if a man only tells them with all his might.

> *Mark Twain's Travels with Mr. Brown,* p. 175

Like the rest of the village, she could tell every-day lies fast enough and without taking any precautions against fire and brimstone on their account; but this was a new kind of lie, and it had a dangerous look because she hadn't had any practice in it. After a week's practice it wouldn't have given her any trouble. It is the way we are made.

> *The Mysterious Stranger, Etc.,* Chapt. V, p. 40

Only rigid cultivation can enable a man to find truth in a lie.

> *A Tramp Abroad,* I, Chapt. XXIV, p. 243

He was not a direct liar, but he would subtly convey untruths. He never dealt in any but large things, if you let him tell it. If by accident his trousers got stained in diverse tints, he would explain it by no actual lie, yet he would leave you with the impression that he got it sliding down a rainbow.

Mark Twain's Notebook, p. 325

Never tell a lie—except for practice.

Mark Twain, Henderson, p. 188

Lies told to injure a person and lies told to profit yourself are not justifiable, but lies told to help another person, and lies told in the public interest—ah well, that's quite another matter.

"Traveling with a Reformer,"
Literary Essays, p. 100

Pond is not an interesting liar; it is the only fault he has. He is destitute of the sense of proportion, and he has no imagination. These are fatal defects in a liar.

Mark Twain's Letters, II, p. 704

An awkward, feeble, leaky lie is a thing which you ought to make it your unceasing study to avoid; such a lie . . . has no more real permanence than an average truth. Why, you might as well tell the truth at once and be done with it.

Mark Twain's Speeches (1923), p. 106

There are certain sweet-smelling sugar-coated lies current in the world which all politic men have apparently tacitly conspired together to support and perpetuate. One . . . is, that there is such a thing in the world as independence . . . of thought, of opinion, of action. Another is, that the world loves to *see* independence—admires it, applauds it. Another . . . that there is such a thing in the world as toleration—in religion, in politics, and such . . . and that toleration is admired and applauded. Out of these trunk-lies spring many branch ones: to wit, the lie that not all men are slaves; the lie that men are glad when other men succeed . . . that there is heroism in man . . . that there is something about him that ought to be perpetuated —in heaven, or hell, or somewhere . . . that conscience, man's moral medicine chest, is not only created by the Creator, but is put into man ready charged with the right

and only true and authentic correctives of conduct . . .
that we are units, individuals, and have natures of our own,
instead of being the tail end of a tapeworm eternity of
ancestors extending in linked procession back and back . . .
to our source in the monkeys, with this so-called individu-
ality of ours a decayed and rancid mush of inherited instincts and teachings derived, atom by atom . . . from the
entire line of that sorry column, and not so much new and
original matter in it as you could balance on a needle point
and examine under a microscope.

Mark Twain's Autobiography, Paine, II, p. 8

You take the lies out of him, and he'll shrink to the size
of your hat.

Life on the Mississippi, Chapt. XXIV, p. 196

There never was such a country for wandering liars; and
they were of both sexes . . . the masters of the castle were
three stupendous brothers, each with four arms and one eye
—the eye in the center of the forehead, and as big as a
fruit. Sort of fruit not mentioned; their usual slovenliness in
statistics.

A Connecticut Yankee in King Arthur's Court,
Chapt. XI, p. 83

The silent colossal National Lie that is the support and
confederate of all the tyrannies and shams and inequalities
and unfairnesses that afflict the peoples—that is the one to
throw bricks and sermons at.

"My First Lie, and How I Got Out of It,"
The Man That Corrupted Hadleyburg, Etc., p. 156

LIFE *See also* AGE, AMERICA, CONSCIENCE, DEATH, DREAM,
DUTY, GENIUS, MYSTERY, PREDESTINATION, ROMANCE, ROY-
ALTY, THOUGHT, TIME, UNDERTAKER, YOUTH

It's an epitome of life—The first half of it consists of the
capacity to enjoy without the chance; the last half consists
of the chance without the capacity.

Mark Twain's Letters, II, p. 709

Grand result of a hard-fought, successful career and

blameless life: Piles of money, tottering age, and a broken heart.

Mark Twain to Mrs. Fairbanks, p. 199

It is life. Like soap-bubbles . . . we are blown upon the world; we float buoyantly . . . then vanish with a little puff.

"Chapters from My Autobiography,"
The North American Review, May 3, 1907, p. 3

What is human life? The first third a good time; the rest remembering about it.

More Maxims of Mark, p. 14

Life is too long and too short. Too long for the weariness of it; too short for the work to be done.

Mark Twain, a Biography, Paine, III, p. 1502

. . . the events of life are mainly small events—they only seem large when we are close to them. By and by they settle down and we see that one doesn't show above another. They are all about one general low altitude, and inconsequential.

Mark Twain's Autobiography, Paine, I, p. 282

All say, "How hard it is that we have to die"—a strange complaint to come from the mouths of people who have had to live.

"Pudd'nhead Wilson's Calendar,"
Pudd'nhead Wilson, Chapt. IV, p. 39

An autobiography that leaves out the little things and enumerates only the big ones is no proper picture of the man's life at all; his life consists of his feelings and his interests, with here and there an incident apparently big or little to hang the feelings on.

Mark Twain's Autobiography, Paine, I, p. 288

All life demands change, variety, contrast,—else there is small zest to it.

"New York Weather,"
Mark Twain's Travels with Mr. Brown, p. 195

Life's on'y a fleetin' show . . . as the sayin' is. We've all got to go, sooner or later. To go with a clean record's the

main thing. Fact is, it's the on'y thing worth strivin' for . . .
"Rambling Notes of an Idle Excursion,"
Tom Sawyer Abroad, Etc., p. 257

We recognize that there are no trivial occurrences in life if we get the right focus on them.
Mark Twain's Autobiography, Paine, II, p. 249

[Quoted by Mark Twain from McClintock's *The Enemy Conquered; or, Love Triumphant*]:

And to what purpose will all this bustle of life, these agitations and emotions of the heart have conduced, if it leave behind it nothing of utility, if it leave no traces of improvement?
"The Enemy Conquered; or, Love Triumphant,"
The American Claimant, Etc., p. 432

Such is life, and the trail of the serpent is over us all.
The Innocents Abroad, II, Chapt. XXII, p. 286

It is not likely that any complete life has ever been lived which was not a failure in the secret judgment of the person who lived it.
More Maxims of Mark, p. 9

LIGHT

In Frankfort, hotel chandelier with 9 burners but you had to light 8 of them in order to see the other 1. Bad gas has no nationality.
Mark Twain's Notebook, p. 136

There are only two forces that can carry light to all corners of the globe—only two—the sun in the heavens and the Associated Press down here. I may seem to be flattering the sun, but I do not mean it so; I am meaning to be just and fair all around.
Mark Twain's Speeches (1923), p. 315

[The candle was] extinguished at 11 at night and so were all the . . . lamps except one or two, which were left burning to help the passenger see how to break his neck trying to get around in the dark.
"About All Kinds of Ships,"
The American Claimant, Etc., p. 462

. . . There was a tin lantern freckling the floor with little spots of light . . .

> *Pudd'nhead Wilson*, Chapt. IX, p. 83

. . . outside it was as dark and dreary as if the world had been lit with Hartford gas.

> "The Loves of Alonzo FitzClarence
> and Rosannah Ethelton,"
> *Tom Sawyer Abroad, Etc.*, p. 426

Mrs. D. overlooks Central Park and a far-reaching sweep of fallen constellations—that is acres of interlacing webs of gas-lights and electrics.

> *My Father • Mark Twain*, Clara Clemens, p. 106

LIGHTNING   *See also* FEAR, GRAMMAR, RAFTSMAN, STORM, WEATHER, WORDS

The lightning glared out . . . One second you couldn't see your hand before you, and the next you could count the threads in your coat sleeve.

> *Tom Sawyer Abroad*, p. 43

The trouble isn't that there are too many fools, but that the lightning isn't distributed right.

> *More Maxims of Mark*, p. 13

[In New England]: The lightning there is peculiar; it is so convincing, that when it strikes a thing it doesn't leave enough of that thing behind for you to tell whether—Well, you'd think it was something valuable, and a Congressman had been there.

> "The Weather,"
> *Mark Twain's Speeches* (1923), p. 55

Thunder is good, thunder is impressive; but it is the lightning that does the work.

> *Mark Twain's Letters*, II, p. 818

[Too many lightning rods]: By actual count, the lightning struck at my establishment seven hundred and sixty-four times in forty minutes, but tripped on one of those fateful rods every time, and slid down the spiral-twist and shot into the earth before it probably had time to be surprised at the way the thing was done . . . one whole day and night not a member of my family stuck his head out the window but he got the hair snatched off it as smooth as a billiard-ball.

> "Political Economy,"
> *Sketches New and Old,* p. 23

LIKING

. . . I'm all admiration for him on account of his character and liking naturally follows admiration, you know.

> *The American Claimant, Etc.,* Chapt. XXII, p. 189

I do not believe I could ever learn to like her except on a raft at sea with no other provisions in sight.

> *Mark Twain in Eruption,* p. 293

He liked to like people, therefore people liked him.

> *Personal Recollections of Joan of Arc,*
> I, Book II, Chapt. XVI, p. 255

He made me like him, and did it without trouble . . . He made me better satisfied with myself than I had ever been before.

> *Following the Equator,* I, Chapt. XXV, p. 248

LIQUOR *See also* CHARITY, COLD, DRINK, GERMAN PEOPLE, IRISHMEN, KINDNESS, MUSIC, OCCUPATION, PLEDGE, PROHIBITION, SABBATH, WATER, WINE

Six stages of inebriety: 1—Verboso, 2—Jocoso, 3—Moroso, 4—Bellicoso, 5—Lachrymoso, 6—Comatoso.

> *Holograph in a copy of Following the Equator*

I find that two glasses of champagne are an admirable stimulant to the tongue. . . . I have never seen the time when I could write to my satisfaction after drinking even one glass of wine.

> *The Twainian,* Mar.–Apr. 1950, p. 1

John Wagner, the oldest man in Buffalo [is] one hundred and four years old . . . and yet has never tasted a drop of liquor in his life—unless—unless you count whiskey.

> "A Fine Old Man,"
> *Sketches New and Old,* p. 205

After supper pap took the jug, and said he had enough

whiskey there for two drunks and one delirium tremens.

The Adventures of Huckleberry Finn,
Chapt. VI, p. 50

The fact that this young woman had never moistened the selvedge edge of her soul with a less plebeian tipple than champagne, had a marked and subduing effect upon Harris. He believed she belonged to the royal family. But I had my doubts.

A Tramp Abroad, II, Chapt. II, p. 32

We dined in the inn . . . and our driver ought to have dined there, too, but he would not have had time to dine and get drunk both, so he gave his mind to making a masterpiece of the latter, and succeeded.

Ibid., I, Chapt. IV, p. 54

Temperate temperance is best. Intemperate temperance injures the cause of temperance, while temperate temperance helps it in its fight against intemperate intemperance.

Fanatics will never learn that, though it be written in letters of gold across the sky.

Mark Twain's Notebook, p. 310

Hannibal always had a weakness for the Temperance cause. I joined the Cadets [of Temperance] myself, although they didn't allow a boy to smoke, or drink or swear, but I thought I never could be truly happy till I wore one of those stunning red scarfs and walked in procession when a distinguished citizen died. I stood it four months, but never an infernal distinguished citizen died during the whole time; and when they finally pronounced old Dr. Norton convalescent (a man I had been depending on for seven or eight weeks), I just drew out . . . in disgust, and pretty much all the distinguished citizens in the camp died within the next three weeks.

Mark Twain's Travels with Mr. Brown, p. 146

[In Congress] they prohibit [liquor] save in the committee rooms—[they] carry it in in demijohns [and] carry it out in demagogues.

Mark Twain's Notebook, p. 114

. . . to make a *pledge* of any kind is to declare war

against nature . . . [a pledge] does not strike at the root of the trouble . . . The root is not the *drinking*, but the *desire* to drink. These are very different things. The one merely requires will—and a great deal of it, both as to bulk and staying capacity—the other merely requires watchfulness—and for no long time . . . When the desire intrudes it should be at once banished out of the mind . . . A desire constantly repulsed for a fortnight should die, then. That should cure the drinking habit. The system of refusing the mere *act* of drinking and leaving the *desire* in full force, is unintelligent war tactics, it seems to me.

Following the Equator, I, Chapt. I, p. 20

[The Grand Hotel Des Bains]: This . . . was a good enough hotel, and comfortable, but there was nothing grand about it but the bill . . . Except in the case of one item— Scotch whiskey. I ordered a sup of that, for I always take it at night as a preventive of toothache. I have never had the toothache; and what is more, I never intend to have it. They charged me a dollar and a half . . . for half a pint . . . for that wee little mite—really hardly enough to break a pledge with.

"Letters to Satan,"
Europe and Elsewhere, p. 218

How solemn and beautiful is the thought that the earliest pioneer of civilization, the van-leader of civilization is never the steamboat, never the railroad, never the newspaper, never the Sabbath-school, never the missionary—but always whiskey.

Life on the Mississippi, Chapt. LX, p. 446

He hadn't a vice, unless a large and grateful sympathy with Scotch whiskey may be called by that name. I didn't regard it as a vice, because he was a Scotchman, and Scotch whiskey to a Scotchman is as innocent as milk is to the rest of the human race.

Mark Twain in Eruption, p. 353

LITERARY CRITICISM *See also* BOOK, GERMAN LANGUAGE,

GRAMMAR, JUDGMENT, LIBRARY, PLAGIARISM, SCOTT, WALTER, SIMILES, WORDS, WRITING

I like Joan of Arc best of all my books and it *is* the best, I know it perfectly well. And besides, it furnished me seven times the pleasure afforded me by any of the others; twelve years of preparation and two years of writing. The others needed no preparation, and got none.

Mark Twain, a Biography, Paine, II, p. 1034

. . . you make all the motives and feelings perfectly clear without analyzing the guts out of them the way George Eliot does . . . George Eliot and Hawthorne . . . tire me to death. As for *The Bostonians* [by James], I would rather be damned to John Bunyan's heaven than read that.

"A Letter to William Dean Howells,"
Mark Twain's Letters, II, p. 455

To me [Poe's] prose is unreadable—like Jane Austen's. No, there is a difference. I could read his prose on a salary, but not Jane's.

Ibid., II, p. 830

When I take up one of Jane Austen's books . . . I feel like a barkeeper entering the kingdom of heaven. I know what his sensation would be and his private comments. He would not find the place to his taste, and he would probably say so.

Mark Twain, a Biography, Paine, III, p. 1500

I bored through *Middle March* . . . with its labored and tedious analyses of feelings and motives, its paltry and tiresome people . . . and nearly died from the overwork.

I did try to read one other—*Daniel Deronda*. I dragged through three chapters, losing flesh all the time, and then was honest enough to quit . . .

Mark Twain's Letters, II, p. 454

. . . The American Miscellany . . . that . . . literary fatty degeneration of the heart . . .

The Gilded Age, II, Chapt. V, p. 62

. . . there is another word of praise due to this ship's library: it contains no copy of the *Vicar of Wakefield*, that strange menagerie of complacent hypocrites and idiots, of theatrical cheap-john heroes and heroines, who are always showing off, of bad people who are not interesting, and good people who are fatiguing. A singular book. Not a sincere line in it, and not a character that invites respect; a book which is one long waste-pipe discharge of goody-goody puerilities and dreary moralities . . .

Following the Equator, II, Chapt. XXVI, p. 312

[About Helen Keller]: When she writes an essay . . . her English is fine and strong, her grasp of the subject is the grasp of one who *knows,* and her page is electric with light.

Ibid., II, Chapt. XXV, p. 303

[Your] quiet style resembles Goldsmith's *Citizen of the World,* and *Don Quixote*—which are my *beau ideals* of fine writing.

Mark Twain's Letters, I, p. 45

[The Mormon Bible] is chloroform in print. If Joseph Smith composed this book, the act was a miracle—keeping awake while he did it was, at any rate.

Roughing It, I, Chapt. XVI, p. 132

It is hard to make a choice of the most beautiful passage in a book which is so jammed with beautiful passages as the Bible; but it is certain that not many things within its lids may take rank above the exquisite story of Joseph. Who taught those ancient writers their simplicity of language, their felicity of expression, their pathos, and above all, their faculty of sinking themselves entirely out of sight of the reader and making the narrative stand out alone and seem to tell itself? Shakespeare is always present when one reads his book; Macaulay is present when we follow the march of his stately sentences; but the Old Testament writers are hidden from view.

The Innocents Abroad, II, Chapt. XX, p. 245

. . . it was worth the journey to India to qualify myself to read *Kim* understandingly and to realize how great a book it is.

Mark Twain in Eruption, p. 312

[Elinor Glynn]: I talked with her with daring frankness, frequently calling a spade a spade instead of coldly symbolizing it as a snowshovel; and on her side she was equally frank.

Ibid., p. 315

It was on this wise (which is a favorite expression of great authors, and a very neat one, too, but I never hear anybody *say* on this wise when they are talking) . . .

Roughing It, I, Chapt. XVII, p. 145

[Cooper's] scholarly savages in the *Last of the Mohicans* . . . are fittingly associated with backwoodsmen who divide each sentence into two equal parts; one part critically grammatical, refined, and choice of language, and the other part just such an attempt to talk like a hunter or a mountaineer as a Broadway clerk might make after eating an edition of Emerson Bennett's works and studying frontier life at the Bowery Theatre a couple of weeks. . . .

Ibid., I, Chapt. XIX, p. 157

. . . The *Deerslayer* is just simply a literary delirium tremens.

"Fenimore Cooper's Literary Offenses,"
Literary Essays, p. 96

No man has an appreciation so various that his judgment is good upon all varieties of literary work.

My Father • Mark Twain, Clara Clemens, p. 47

. . . great books are weighed and measured by their style and matter, and not by the trimmings and shadings of their grammar.

Mark Twain, a Biography, Paine, III, p. 1652

LITERARY HOAX

[One of Mark Twain's literary hoaxes]: It was a crisp and spicy morning in early October. The lilacs and laburnums, lit with the glory-fires of autumn, hung burning and flashing in the upper air, a fairy bridge provided by kind Nature for the wingless wild things that have their home in the tree-tops and would visit together; the larch and the pomegranate flung their purple and yellow flames in brilliant broad splashes along the slanting sweep of the woodland; the sensuous fragrance of innumerable deciduous flowers rose upon the swooning atmosphere; far in the empty sky a solitary oesophagus slept upon motionless wing; everywhere brooded stillness, serenity, and the peace of God.

"A Double-Barreled Detective Story,"
The Man That Corrupted Hadleyburg, Etc., p. 312

LITERATURE *See also* FACT, INDELICACY

In literature imitations do not imitate.

More Maxims of Mark, p. 8

I love all literature, and as long as I am a doctor of literature . . . I mean to doctor everybody else's.

Mark Twain's Speeches (1923), p. 354

. . . High and fine literature is wine, and mine is water; but everybody likes water.

Mark Twain's Letters, II, p. 485

I have noticed, in such literary experiences as I have had, that one of the most taking things to do is to conceal your meaning when you are *trying* to conceal it. Whereas, if you go at literature with a free conscience and nothing to conceal you can turn out a book, every time, that the very elect can't understand.

The American Claimant, Etc., Chapt. V, p. 49

LOCUST *See* NATURE

LOGIC

. . . the world will not stop and think . . . It has no reflection, no logic, no sense of proportion. With it, figures go for nothing; to it, figures reveal nothing, it cannot reason upon them rationally; it would say, for instance, that China is being swiftly and surely Christianized since nine Chinese Christians are being made every day; and it would fail, with him, to notice that the fact that 33,000 pagans are *born* there every day, damages the argument.

"The United States of Lyncherdom,"
Europe and Elsewhere, p. 239

Logic is logic; and by disregarding its laws even Emperors . . . can be beguiled into making charges which should not be ventured upon except in the shelter of plenty of lightning-rods.

Mark Twain's Letters, II, p. 668

LONELINESS *See also* EDEN, GARDEN OF
It was . . . as lonesome as Sunday.

A Connecticut Yankee in King Arthur's Court,
Chapt. I, p. 19

Be good and you will be lonesome.

"Pudd'nhead Wilson's New Calendar,"
Flyleaf of *Following the Equator*

LONGITUDE *See* RAFTSMEN, TIME

LOST *See also* DIRECTION, SOCK, TEMPER
The porter . . . made our course so plain that we should never be able to get lost without high-priced outside help.

A Tramp Abroad, II, Chapt. IV, p. 53

I might have had [a good night's sleep] last night if I hadn't lost my temper, for I was loaded up high with fatigue; but at two this morning I had a W.C. call and jumped up in the dark and ran in my night-shirt and without a candle—for I believed I knew my way. This hotel d'Angleterre must be a congeries of old dwellings—if it isn't, it is built up in a series of water-tight compartments, like the American liners, that go clear to the top. You can't get out of your own compartment. There is only your one hall; it has four rooms on each side of it and a staircase in the midst; would you think a person could get lost in such a place? I assure you it is possible; for a person of talent.

We are on the second floor from the ground. There is a

W.C. on the floor *above* us and one on the floor *below* us. Halls pitch dark, I groped my way and found the upper W.C. Starting to return, I went upstairs instead of down, and went to what I supposed was my room, but I could not make out the number in the dark and was afraid to enter it. Then I remembered that I—no, my mind lost confidence and began to wander. I was no longer sure as to what floor I was on, and the minute I realized that, the rest of my mind went. One cannot stand still in a dark hall at two in the morning, lost, and be content. One must move and go on moving, even at the risk of getting worse lost. I groped up and down a couple of those flights, over and over again, cursing to myself. And every time I thought I heard somebody coming, I shrank together like one of those toy balloons when it collapses. You see, I was between two fires; I could not grope to the top floor and start fresh and count down to my own, for it was all occupied by young ladies and a dangerous place to get caught in, clothed as I was clothed, and not in my right mind. I could not grope down to the ground floor and count *up*, for there was a ball down there. A ball, and young ladies likely to be starting up to bed about this time. And so they were. I saw the glow of their distant candles, I felt the chill of their distant cackle. I did not know whether I was on a W.C. floor or not, but I had to take a risk. I groped to the door that ought to be it—right where you turn down the stairs; and it was it. I entered it grateful, and stood in its dark shelter with a beating heart and thought how happy I should be to live there always, in that humble cot, and go out no more among life's troubles and dangers. Several young ladies applied for admission, but I was not receiving. Thursdays being my day. I meant to freeze out the ball if it took a week. And I did. When the drone and burr of its music had ceased for twenty minutes and the house was solidly dead and dark, I groped down to the ground floor, then turned and counted my way up home, all right.

Then straightway my temper went up to 180 in the shade and I began to put it into form. Presently an admiring voice said—"When you are through with your prayers, I would like to ask where you have been, all night."

Mark Twain's Notebook, p. 238

LOVE   *See also* FISH, HEART, LANGUAGE, MARRIAGE

Love seems the swiftest, but it is the slowest of all growths. No man or woman really knows what perfect love is until they have been married a quarter of a century.

Ibid., p. 235

How vapid and inefficient the loves of the gods of mythology—the loves of Jove and Juno—must have been, for when the music of love woke its grand symphony in their hearts, there was none above them to thank.

My Father · Mark Twain, Clara Clemens, p. 13

True love is the only heart disease that is best left to "run on"—the only affection of the heart for which there is no help, and none desired.

Mark Twain's Notebook, p. 371

We pay as we can, in love; and in this coin practising no economy.

Mark Twain's Letters, II, p. 642

When you fish for love, bait with your heart, not your brain.

Mark Twain's Notebook, p. 346

She has loved me in those old days—this is my security; for whom one has loved, one cannot betray.

The Prince and the Pauper, Chapt. XXVI, p. 236

Man will do many things to get himself loved, he will do all things to get himself envied.

"Pudd'nhead Wilson's New Calendar"
Following the Equator, I, Chapt. XXI, p. 207

LOYALTY   *See also* CONSCIENCE, COUNTRY, PATRIOTISM, ROYALTY, VOTING

The same men who enthusiastically preach loyal consistency to church and party are always ready and willing and anxious to persuade a Chinaman or an Indian or a Kanaka to desert *his* church, or a fellow-American to desert *his* party. The man who deserts to them is all that is high and pure and beautiful—apparently; the man who deserts from them is all that is foul and despicable. This is consistency with a capital C.

Mark Twain's Speeches (1923), p. 129

Loyalty to petrified opinions never yet broke a chain or freed a human soul in *this* world—and never *will*.

Ibid., p. 130

Loyalty is a word which has worked vast harm; for it has been made to trick men into being "loyal" to a thousand iniquities, whereas the true loyalty should have been to themselves—in which case there would have ensued a rebellion, and the throwing off of that deceptive yoke.

Mark Twain's Notebook, p. 199

The first thing I want to teach is *disloyalty* [in *A Connecticut Yankee*] till they get used to disusing that word *loyalty* as representing a virtue. This will beget independence—which is loyalty to one's best self and principles, and this is often disloyalty to the general idols and fetishes.

Ibid., p. 199

LUCK   *See also* EXAGGERATION, VALUE

. . . the hand of Providence is in it somewhere. You can depend upon it. I never yet had what seemed at the time to be a particular aggravating streak of bad luck but that it revealed itself to me later as a piece of royal good fortune. Who am I . . . that I should take it upon myself what is good fortune and what is evil? For about a week, Providence headed me off at every turn. The real object of it and the real result, may not transpire till you and I are old, and these days forgotten—and therefore is it not premature, now, to call it bad luck? We *can't* tell yet.

Mark Twain to Mrs. Fairbanks, p. 79

Persons who think there is no such thing as luck—good or bad—are entitled to their opinion.

Mark Twain's Autobiography, Paine, II, p. 140

I was to talk to a lot of Young Men's Christian Associations in the Majestic Theater on a Sunday afternoon. My secretary and I entered the place by the stage door and sat down in a box and looked out over a desert expanse of empty benches—wondering. My secretary presently went to the main entrance in the other street, to see what the matter was; just as she started the Young Christians came pouring in like a tidal wave; she plowed through the wave and by the time she reached the main door the place was full and the police, mounted and on foot, were struggling with a multitude of remaining Young Christians and keeping them back. The doors were being closed against the people. There was one last man, of course—there always is. He almost got his body into the closing door but was pushed back by a big officer. He realized that his chance was gone. He was mute for a moment while his feelings were rising in him, then he said: "I have been a member of the Young Men's Christian Association in good standing for seven years and never got any reward for it, and here it is again—just my God damned luck!"

Mark Twain in Eruption, p. 7

My father . . . "kept store" . . . several years but had no luck, except that I was born to him.

Mark Twain's Autobiography, Paine, I, p. 96

It did not occur to the citizens that brains were at the bottom of his luck.

The Gilded Age, I, Chapt. V, p. 65

M

MADNESS *See also* INSANITY

When we remember that we are all mad, the mysteries disappear and life stands explained.

Mark Twain's Notebook, p. 345

. . . in one way or another all men are mad. Many are mad for money . . . Love is a madness . . . it can grow to a frenzy of despair . . . All the whole list of desires, predilections, aversions, ambitions, passions, cares, griefs, regrets, remorses, are incipient madness, and ready to grow, spread and consume, when the occasion comes. There are no healthy minds, and nothing saves any man but accident— the accident of not having his malady put to the supreme test.

One of the commonest forms of madness is the desire to be noticed, the pleasure derived from being noticed. Perhaps it is not merely common, but universal.

"The Memorable Assassination"
What Is Man? and Other Essays p. 170

MAIL

It seemed as if I never could begin the burden of clearing off the accumulated mail. But at last I went at it with determination . . . and accomplished it in five minutes without a pen-stroke. By help of the fire. It shows what native talent, unobstructed by principle, can do, when duty calls.

Letters to Mary, p. 89

MAJORITY   *See also* HUMAN RACE, FOOL

Whenever you find that you are on the side of the majority, it is time to reform (or pause and reflect).

Mark Twain's Notebook, p. 393

MALICE

Of all the creatures [man] . . . is the only one—the solitary one—that possesses malice.

. . . He is the only creature that inflicts pain for sport, knowing it to *be* pain . . . *all* creatures kill . . . man is the only one . . . that kills in malice, the only one that kills for revenge.

Mark Twain's Autobiography, Paine, II, p. 7

Malice and malignity faded out of me—or maybe I *drove* them out of me, knowing that a malignant book would hurt nobody but the fool who wrote it.

Mark Twain's Letters, I, p. 414

She was loaded to the eyelids with cold malice.

A Connecticut Yankee in King Arthur's Court,
Chapt. XVI, p. 127

MAN   *See also* ARK, BROTHERHOOD, CLOTHES, COWARDICE,
   DOG, DUTY, EQUALITY, GOD, HAPPINESS, HUMAN BEING,
   HUMAN NATURE, HUMAN RACE, ILLNESS, IMPULSE, IN-
   FLUENCE, INSINCERITY, LOVE, NATURE, OPINION, SEX,
   SHEEP, UNIVERSE, WAR, WEAKNESS, WISDOM, WORSHIP

Man was made at the end of the week's work, when God was tired.

Mark Twain's Notebook, p. 381

. . . no man ever does a duty for duty's sake, but only for the sake of the satisfaction he personally gets out of doing the duty, or for the sake of avoiding the personal discomfort he would have to endure if he shirked that duty.

Mark Twain in Eruption, p. 240

Man adapted to the earth? Why, he can't sleep out-of-doors without freezing to death or getting rheumatism or the malaria; he can't keep his nose under water over a minute without being drowned; he can't climb a tree without falling out and breaking his neck. Why, he's the poorest, clumsiest excuse of all the creatures that inhabit this earth. He has got to be coddled and housed and swathed and bandaged and upholstered to be able to live at all. He is a rickety sort of a thing, anyway you take him, a regular British Museum of infirmities and inferiorities. He is always undergoing repairs . . .

Think of the lion and the tiger and the leopard, and then think of man—that poor thing!—the animal of the wig, the ear-trumpet, the glass eye, the porcelain teeth, the wooden leg, the trepanned skull, the silver windpipe—a creature that is mended and patched all over from top to bottom. If he can't get renewals of his bric-a-brac in the next world what will he look like? He has just that one stupendous superiority—his imagination, his intellect.

Mark Twain, a Biography, Paine, III, p. 1361

Man is the Only Animal that Blushes. Or needs to.

"Pudd'nhead Wilson's New Calendar"
Following the Equator, I, Chapt. XXVII, p. 264

I believe that our Heavenly Father invented man because he was disappointed in the monkey.

Mark Twain in Eruption, p. 372

Every man is in his own person the whole human race, with not a detail lacking.

Ibid., p. xxix

It is a *solemn thought:* Dead, the noblest man's meat is inferior to pork.

More Maxims of Mark, p. 9

Unconsciously we all have a standard by which we measure other men, and if we examine closely we find that this standard is a very simple one, and is this: we admire them, we envy them, for great qualities which we ourselves lack. Hero-worship consists in just that. Our heroes are the men who do things which we recognize, with regret, and sometimes with a secret shame, that we cannot do. We find not much in ourselves to admire, we are always privately wanting to be like somebody else. If everybody was satisfied with himself, there would be *no* heroes.

Mark Twain's Autobiography, Paine, I, p. 263

The noblest work of God? Man.

Who found it out? Man.

Ibid., II, p. 316

[Mark Twain's answer to a minister's expression of belief that man is the chief love and delight of God]: Land, it is just for the world the way I feel about it myself, sometimes, even when dry. And when not dry, even those warm words are not nearly warm enough to get up to what I am feeling, when I am holding on to something and blinking affectionately at myself in the glass, and recollecting that I'm it.

And when I am feeling historical, there is nothing that ecstatifies like hunting the Chief Love and Delight of God around and around just here on this tiny earth and watching him perform. I watch him progressing and progressing— always progressing—always mounting higher and higher, sometimes by means of the Inquisition, sometimes by means of the Terror, sometimes by eight hundred years' of witch-burning, sometimes by help of a St. Bartholomew's, sometimes by spreading hell and civilization in China, sometimes by preserving and elevating the same at home by a million soldiers and a thousand battleships; and when he gets down to today I still look at him spread out over a whole page of the morning paper, grabbing in Congress, grabbing in Albany, grabbing in New York and St. Louis and all around, lynching the innocent, [slobbering] hypocrisies, reeking, dripping, unsavory, but always recognizable as the same old Most Sublime Existence in all the range of non-divine Being, the Chief Love and Delight of God; and then I am more gladder than ever that I am it.

Mark Twain in Eruption, p. 383

[Man is] a mere coffee-mill [that is] neither [permitted] to supply the coffee nor turn the crank, his sole and piteously humble function being to grind coarse or fine, according to his make, outside impulses doing all the rest.

What Is Man? and Other Essays Conclusion, p. 102

Moralizing, I observed, then, that "all that glitters is not gold." Mr. Ballou said I could go further than that, and lay it up among my treasures of knowledge that *nothing* that glitters is gold. So I learned then, once for all, that gold in its native state is but dull unornamental stuff, and that only low-born metals excite the admiration of the ignorant with an ostentatious glitter. However, like the rest of the world, I still go on underrating men of gold and glorifying men of mica. Commonplace human nature cannot rise above that.

Roughing It, I, Chapt. XXVIII, p. 228

Man is . . . a poor joke—the poorest that was ever contrived.

Mark Twain's Letters, II, p. 676

We seem so delicately made, so destructible, so insubstantial; yet it is easier to reduce a granite statue to ashes than it is to do that with a man's body.

Personal Recollections of Joan of Arc,
II, Book III, Chapt. XX, p. 270

That government is not best which secures mere life and property—there is a more valuable thing—manhood.

Mark Twain's Notebook, p. 210

The only very marked difference between the average civilized man and the average savage is that the one is gilded and the other painted.

Ibid., p. 392

Concerning the difference between man and the jackass: some observers hold that there isn't any. But this wrongs the jackass.

Ibid., p. 347

The timid man yearns for full value and demands a

tenth. The bold man strikes for double value and compromises on par.

"Pudd'nhead Wilson's New Calendar"
Following the Equator, I, Chapt. XIII, p. 136

MANNERS   *See also* BATH, POLITENESS

They always go for our *manners*. Damn our manners—we claim no superiority there; we don't travel on our manners; they are no better than French ones.

We have tremendous faults, colossal faults, and they need lashing and deserve it; and we will take it, too, without a whimper; but *bother* our manners, they are of no consequence—we are interested in far more serious, far more dignified matters. We have enormous merits, enormous claims upon the world's respect, and even gratitude; but our manners are not of these.

The French for manners. They have contributed little else to this world—those and millinery styles—let them continue—for so God has willed.

But talk to us of our invention, energy, enterprise, and things that we brag about and are proud of—and of our infamous politics, trolleys, governmental inanities and crimes—and give it to us.

Hitherto unpublished manuscript

MARRIAGE   *See also* LOVE

Punch's advice to persons about to marry—"Don't"—was a thousand years old when Punch was born.

Mark Twain's Notebook, p. 164

I was married a month ago, and so have cast away the blue goggles of bachelordom and now look at the world through the crystal lenses of my new estate.

The Hannibal Courier Post, March 6, 1935

[In India]: [The bridegroom] and the bride were to entertain company every night and nearly all night for a week or more, then get married, if alive.

Following the Equator, II, Chapt. VI, p. 70

There are two or three solemn things in life and a happy

marriage is one of them, for the terrors of life are all to come.

Mark Twain, a Biography, Paine, III, p. 1524

. . . both marriage and death ought to be welcome: the one promises happiness, doubtless the other assures it.

Mark Twain's Letters, II, p. 501

It is stated with a show of authority that diamond engagement rings are rapidly going out of fashion, and emeralds, opals, or pearls taking their place. . . . If the idea be followed up faithfully . . . matrimony will be brought within the reach of all.

"Memoranda"
The Galaxy Magazine, May, 1870, p. 726

[A letter to a friend who was engaged to be married]: How well I know the feeling! Know it to the uttermost delicious pang of discovery and surprise. There is nothing in the world that approaches it; all other enthusiasms, heart-leapings, exultations are pale beside it; it's as if you had struck gas. . . .

Yes, indeed, I know all about it—all. We who have our home in this divine far country, spread wide its hospitable gates to you and say out of heart and mouth, enter in, ye are welcome!

My Father • Mark Twain, Clara Clemens, p. 236

Marriage—yes, it *is* the supreme felicity of life. I concede it. And it is also the supreme tragedy of life. The deeper the love the surer the tragedy. And the more disconsolating when it comes.

Mark Twain's Letters, II, p. 811

There are three things which come to my mind which I consider excellent advice:

First, girls, don't smoke—that is, don't smoke to excess. I am seventy-three and a half years old, and I have been smoking seventy-three of them. But I never smoke to excess—that is, I smoke in moderation, only one cigar at a time.

Second, don't drink—that is, don't drink to excess.

Third, don't marry—I mean, to excess.

"Advice to Girls"
Mark Twain's Speeches (1910), p. 107

MARTYRDOM *See also* SIMILES
Martyrdom covers a multitude of sins.

Mark Twain's Notebook, p. 381
Martyrdom is the luckiest fate that can befall some people. Louis XVI did not die in his bed, consequently history is very gentle with him. . . .
Martyrdom made a saint of Mary Queen of Scots three hundred years ago, and she has hardly lost all of her saintship yet. Martyrdom made a saint of the trivial and foolish Marie Antoinette, and her biographers still keep her fragrant with the odor of sanctity to this day. . . .

A Tramp Abroad, I, Chapt. XXVI, p. 265
On the Continent, you can't get a rare beefsteak—everything is as overdone as a martyr.

Mark Twain's Notebook, p. 330
Martyrdom gilded with notoriety has its fascinations.

"A Scrap of Curious History"
What is Man? and Other Essays, p. 187

MASSACRE *See also* INDIAN
For 1,000 years this savage nation [France] indulged itself in massacre; every now and then a big massacre or a little one. The spirit is peculiar to France—I mean in Christendom—no other state has had it.

Mark Twain, a Biography, Paine, II, p. 644

MASSES *See also* COUNTRY, PFOPLE
The pitifulest thing out is a mob; that's what an army is—a mob; they don't fight with courage that's born in them, but with courage that's borrowed from their mass, and from their officers. But a mob without any *man* at the head of it is *beneath* pitifulness.

The Adventures of Huckleberry Finn, Chapt. XXII, p. 197

The master minds of all nations, in all ages, have sprung in affluent multitude from the mass of the nations, and from the mass of the nation only—not from its privileged classes; . . .

A Connecticut Yankee in King Arthur's Court,
Chapt. XXV, p. 220

MASTERS, THE OLD   *See also* ANGEL, PAINTING
[In Rome]: Livy and Clara Spaulding are having a royal time worshiping the old Masters, and I as good a time gritting my ineffectual teeth over them.

Mark Twain's Letters, I, p. 339
If the old masters had labeled their fruit one wouldn't be so likely to mistake pears for turnips.

Mark Twain, a Biography, Paine, II, p. 634
Perhaps the reason I used to enjoy going to the Academy of Fine Arts in New York was because there were but a few hundred paintings in it, and it did not surfeit me to go through the list. I suppose the Academy was bacon and beans in the Forty-Mile Desert, and a European Gallery is a state dinner of thirteen courses. One leaves no sign after him of the one dish, but the thirteen frighten away his appetite and give him no satisfaction.

The Innocents Abroad, II, Chapt. I, p. 15

MAXIMS   *See also* HOLE
It is more trouble to make a maxim than it is to do right.
"Pudd'nhead Wilson's New Calendar"
Following the Equator, I, Chapt. III, p. 41
The proper proportions of a maxim: a minimum of sound to a maximum of sense.

A Mark Twain holograph, written Dec. 12, 1897

MEANNESS   *See also* EARLY, EXAGGERATION, OPINION, SEA
It is better to be a mean *live* man than a stick—even a gold-headed stick.

Life As I Find It, p. 42

MEASUREMENT

[In Australia]: The road lay through the middle of an empty space which seemed to me to be a hundred yards wide between the fences. I was not given the width in yards, but only in chains and perches—and furlongs, I think. I would have given a good deal to know what the width was, but I did not pursue the matter. . . . It was a wide space; I could tell you how wide, in chains and perches and furlongs and things, but that would not help you any. Those things sound well, but they are shadowy and indefinite, like troy weight and avoirdupois; nobody knows what they mean. When you buy a pound of a drug and the man asks you which you want, troy or avoirdupois, it is best to say, "Yes," and shift the subject.

Following the Equator, I, Chapt. XXIII, p. 229

MEDICINE   *See also* CONSCIENCE, HABIT, ILLNESS

I was always told that I was a sickly and precarious and tiresome and uncertain child, and lived mainly on allopathic medicines during the first seven years of my life. I asked my mother about this, in her old age—she was in her eighty-eighth year—and said:

"I suppose that during all that time you were uneasy about me?"

"Yes, the whole time."

"Afraid I wouldn't live?"

After a reflective pause—ostensibly to think out the facts —"No—afraid you would."

Mark Twain's Autobiography, Paine, I, p. 108

[The doctors] could not hide it from themselves that every time they emptied a fresh drug store into him he got worse.

"Two Little Tales"

The Man That Corrupted Hadleyburg, Etc., p. 199

In my boyhood, every old woman gathered her own medicines in the woods. She knew how to compound doses that would stir the vitals of a cast-iron dog.

Mark Twain's Autobiography, Paine, I, p. 107

[The] whale-ships carry no doctor . . . The captain is provided with a medicine-chest, with the medicines numbered instead of named. A book of directions goes with this. It describes diseases and symptoms, and says, "Give a teaspoonful of No. 9 once an hour," or "Give ten grains of No. 12 every half-hour," etc. One of our sea captains came across a skipper in the North Pacific who was in a state of great surprise and perplexity. Said he:

"There's something rotten about this medicine-chest business. One of my men was sick—nothing much the matter. I looked in the book: it said, give him a teaspoonful of No. 15. I went to the medicine-chest, and I see I was out of No. 15. I judged I'd got to get up a combination somehow that would fill the bill; so I hove into the fellow half a teaspoonful of No. 8 and half a teaspoonful of No. 7, and I'll be hanged if it didn't kill him in fifteen minutes! There's something about this medicine-chest system that's too many for me!"

"Rambling Notes of an Idle Excursion"
Tom Sawyer Abroad, Etc., p. 270

. . . My literary relic . . . is a *Dictionary of Medicine,* by Dr. James of London, assisted by Mr. Boswell's Dr. Samuel Johnson, and is a hundred and fifty years old, it having been published at the time of the rebellion of '45. If it had been sent against the Pretender's troops there probably wouldn't have been a survivor. In 1861 this deadly book was still working the cemeteries—down in Virginia. For three generations and a half it had been going quietly along, enriching the earth with its slain.

"A Majestic Literary Fossil"
The American Claimant, Etc., p. 526

Galen could have come into my sick-room at any time during my first seven years—I mean any day when it wasn't fishing weather, and there wasn't any choice but school or sickness—and he could have sat down there and stood my doctor's watch without asking a question. He would have smelt around among the wilderness of cups and bottles and vials on the table and the shelves, and missed not a stench that used to glad him two thousand years before, nor discovered one that was of a later date.

> "A Majestic Literary Fossil"
> *Ibid.*, p. 525

The doctor asked for a few sheets of paper and a pen, and said he would write a prescription; which he did. It was one of Galen's; in fact, it was Galen's favorite, and had been slaying people for sixteen thousand years. Galen used it for everything, applied it to everything, said it would remove everything from warts all the way through to lungs—and it generally did."

> "Those Extraordinary Twain"
> *Pudd'nhead Wilson*, p. 305

After forty years of public effort I have become just a target for medicines. [1910]

> *Mark Twain, a Biography*, Paine, III, p. 1571

MEDIOCRITY   *See* GENIUS

MEMORY   *See also* FORGETFULNESS, GRANT, GENERAL ULYSSES S., TRAVEL, TRUTH

. . . no confidence in a memory which . . . you wouldn't even venture to trust with the Latin motto of the United States, lest it mislay it and the country suffer.

> *The Twainian*, Mar.–Apr. 1948, p. 2

. . . a grown person's memory-tablet is a palimpsest, with hardly a bare place upon which to engrave a phrase.

> *Mark Twain's Letters*, II, p. 732

The eye has a good memory.

> *Mark Twain, a Biography*, Paine, II, p. 753

. . . my memory was never loaded with anything but blank cartridges.

> *Life on the Mississippi*, Chapt. VI, p. 59

Thirty years ago I was delivering a memorized lecture every night, and every night I had to help myself with a page of notes to keep from getting myself mixed. The notes consisted of beginnings of sentences, and were eleven in number, and they ran something like this:

"In that region the weather—"
"At that time it was a custom—"
"But in California one never heard—"

When my mother got to be eighty-five years old her memory failed her. She forgot little threads that hold life's patches of meaning together.

"Morals and Memory,"
Mark Twain's Speeches (1923), p. 287

A pair of connected little incidents of that month have served to keep the memory of it green for me all this time; incidents of no consequence and not worth embalming, yet my memory has preserved them carefully and flung away things of real value to give them space and make them comfortable. The truth is, a person's memory has no more sense than his conscience, and no appreciation whatever of values and proportions.

Mark Twain in Eruption, p. 118

This memory of ours stores up a perfect record of the most useless facts and anecdotes and experiences. And all the things that we ought to know—that we need to know— that we'd profit by knowing—it casts aside with the careless indifference of a girl refusing her true lover.

"Morals and Memory,"
Mark Twain's Speeches (1910), p. 225

. . . I remember you and recall you *without effort, without exercise of will;*—that is, by *natural impulse,* undictated by a sense of duty, or of obligation. And that, I take it, is the only sort of remembering worth the having. When we think of friends, and call their faces out of the shadows, and their voices out of the echoes that faint along the corridors of memory, and do it without knowing *why* save that we *love* to do it, we content ourselves that that friendship is a Reality, and not a Fancy—that it is builded upon a rock, and not upon the sands that dissolve away with the ebbing tides and carry their monuments with them. [Feb. 27, 1869]

> *Mark Twain to Mrs. Fairbanks,* p. 80

When I was younger I could remember anything, whether it happened or not; but I am getting old, and soon I shall remember only the latter.

> *Mark Twain, a Biography,* Paine, III, p. 1269

It isn't so astonishing, the number of things that I can remember, as the number of things I can remember that aren't so.

> *Ibid.,* Paine, III, p. 1269

MEND

It is never too late to mend. There is no hurry.

> *Holograph on a photo,* Aug. 1903

MENDICANCY *See* BEGGAR

MENTAL TELEGRAPHY *See* MENTAL TELEPATHY

MENTAL TELEPATHY

Certainly mental telegraphy is an industry which is always silently at work—oftener than otherwise, perhaps, when we are not suspecting that it is affecting our thought. . . . I imagine that we get most of our thoughts out of somebody else's head, by mental telegraphy—and not always out of heads of acquaintances, but, in the majority of cases, out of the heads of strangers; strangers far removed. . . .

> *Mark Twain's Autobiography,* Paine, II, p. 221

MERIDIANS *See* RAFTSMEN

MERIT

I am prouder to have climbed up to where I am just by sheer natural merit than I would be to ride the very sun in the zenith and have to reflect that I was nothing but a poor little accident, and got shot up there out of somebody else's catapult. To me, merit is everything—in fact, the only thing. All else is dross.

Personal Recollections of Joan of Arc,
I, Book II, Chapt. XXIV, p. 320

METAPHOR   *See also* SIMILE
(*Finding Dan Beard to illustrate Connecticut Yankee*):
It was a fortunate hour that I went netting for lightning bugs and caught a meteor.

Mark Twain's Letters, II, p. 511

. . . the water, small-poxed with rain-splashes.

Ibid., II, p. 711

You taught me in my callow days, let me pay back the debt now in my old age out of a thesaurus with wisdom smelted from the golden ores of experience.

Ibid., II, p. 767

The wheel flew to port so fast that the spokes blended into a spider web.

The Gilded Age, I, Chapt. IV, p. 48

The boats go stuttering by with a good deal of frequency.

Mark Twain's Notebook, p. 335

I . . . have the controversial lead myself, always getting eight feet . . . often nine, sometimes even quarterless Twain—as I believed; but always "no bottom," as *he* said.

Is Shakespeare Dead?, p. 13

METHUSELAH   *See also* EDUCATION
Mrs. Duncan is really older than Methuselah because she knows a lot of things that Methuselah never heard of. What did Methuselah know about a barbed-wire fence?

Mark Twain, a Biography, Paine, I, p. 328

[From an address to a graduating class]:
Methuselah lived to be 969 years old but what of that? There was nothing doing. He might as well have lived to be a thousand. You boys and girls will see more in the next

fifty years than Methuselah saw in his whole lifetime.

Autobiography with Letters,
William Lyon Phelps, p. 67 ·

[A letter to William Dean Howells]:

. . . goodbye, and a short life and a merry one be yours. Poor old Methuselah, how did he manage to stand it so long?

Mark Twain's Letters, I, p. 355

A poet has said, "Better fifty years of England than all the cycles of Cathay." But I say better one decade of this period than the 900 years of Methuselah. There is more done now in a year than he ever saw in all his life. Methuselah lived over 900 years but he never saw a barbed wire fence.

"Mark Twain in Iowa,"
The Iowa Journal of History and Politics,
Oct. 1929, p. 538

MICHELANGELO   *See also* POPULARITY

I used to worship the mighty genius of Michael Angelo— that man who was great in poetry, painting, sculpture, architecture—great in everything he undertook. But I do not want Michael Angelo for breakfast—for luncheon—for dinner—for tea—for supper—for between meals. I like a change, occasionally. In Genoa, he designed everything; in Milan, he or his pupils designed everything . . . In Florence, he painted everything, designed everything, nearly, and what he did not design he used to sit on a favorite stone and look at, and they showed us the stone. In Pisa he designed everything but the old shot-tower and they would have attributed that to him if it had not been so awfully out of the perpendicular. . . . He designed St. Peter's; he designed the Pope; he designed the Pantheon, the uniform of the Pope's soldiers, the Tiber, the Vatican, the Coliseum, the Capitol . . . the eternal bore designed the Eternal City, and unless all men and books do lie, he painted everything in it! Dan said the other day to the guide, "Enough,

enough, enough! Say no more! Lump the whole thing! say that the Creator made Italy from designs by Michael Angelo!"

I never felt so fervently thankful, so soothed, so tranquil, so filled with a blessed peace, as I did yesterday when I learned that Michael Angelo was dead.

The Innocents Abroad, I, Chapt. XXVII, p. 365

MICROBE   *See also* GOD, UNIVERSE, WALLACE, ALFRED
. . . every man is born crammed with sin microbes, and the only thing that can extirpate these sin microbes is morals.

"Seventieth Birthday,"
Mark Twain's Speeches (1923), p. 261
God works through man . . . just about as much as a man works through his microbes.

Mark Twain, a Biography, Paine, III, p. 1271
. . . he could hear his microbes gnaw, the place was so still.

The Man That Corrupted Hadleyburg, Etc.,
Chapt. I, p. 44

MILLIONAIRE   *See* MONEY

MIND   *See also* BRAINS, CHRISTIAN SCIENCE, MASSES, MENTAL TELEPATHY, SHIP, WALL
The wise change their minds when they perceive that they have been in error.

Personal Recollections of Joan of Arc,
I, Book II, Chapt. I, p. 108
At the last moment six or seven had sufficient decision of character to make up their minds to go, and did go, and I felt a sense of relief at once—it was forever too late, now, and I could make up my mind at my leisure, not to go. I must have a prodigious quantity of mind; it takes me as much as a week, sometimes, to make it up.

The Innocents Abroad, I, Chapt. VII, p. 100
But the Mayor said he saw nothing suspicious about me,

and that I seemed a harmless person and nothing the matter with me but a wandering mind, and not much of that. . . .

. . .

I didn't finish, because my mind was getting to be in a good deal of a whirl, and when you are that way you think you have finished a sentence when you haven't, and you go mooning and dreaming away, and the first thing you know you get run over by a dray or a cow or something.

"Playing Courier,"
The American Claimant, Etc., p. 486

[Comment by Paine]: "Why is [Mark Twain's] mind like a railroad timetable? Because it is subject to change without notice."

Mark Twain's Notebook, p. 395

The mood of writing . . . [Mark Twain was known to say] always attacked him when some "mentally dead people brought their corpses with them for a long visit."

My Father • Mark Twain, Clara Clemens, p. 42

The mind that becomes soiled in youth can never again be washed clean. I know this by my own experience, and to this day I cherish an unappeasable bitterness against the unfaithful guardians of my young life, who not only permitted but compelled me to read an unexpurgated Bible through before I was 15 years old. None can do that and ever draw a clean, sweet breath again this side of the grave.

Mark Twain, a Biography, Paine, III, p. 1280

We were speaking of presence of mind in accidents. . .
. . . I had great presence of mind once. It was at a fire. An old man leaned out of a four-story building calling for help. Everybody in the crowd below looked up, but nobody did anything. The ladders weren't long enough. Nobody had any presence of mind—nobody but me. I came to the rescue. I yelled for a rope. When it came I threw the old man the end of it. He caught it and I told him to tie it around his waist. He did so, and I pulled him down.

Mark Twain, a Biography, Paine, III, p. 149

I am different from other women; my mind changes

oftener. People who have no mind can easily be steadfast and firm, but when a man is loaded down to the guards with it, as I am, every heavy sea of foreboding or inclination, maybe of indolence, shifts the cargo.

Mark Twain's Letters, I, p. 190

. . . a full belly is little worth where the mind is starved, and the heart.

The Prince and the Pauper, Chapt. IV, p. 39

. . . the mind is independent of the man. He has no control over it; it does as it pleases. . .

. . . At some time or other you have been captivated by a ridiculous rhyme-jingle . . . [such as]

"I saw Esau kissing Kate
And she saw I saw Esau;
I saw Esau, he saw Kate,
And she saw—"

And so on. My mind went mad with joy over it. I repeated it all day and all night for a week in spite of all I could do to stop it, and it seemed to me that I must surely go crazy.

And the new popular song . . . with the taking melody sings through one's head day and night, asleep and awake, till one is a wreck. There is no getting the mind to let it alone.

. . . Yes, asleep as well as awake. The mind is quite independent. It is master.

What Is Man? and Other Essays, Chapt. V, p. 65

. . . where is the use of making up your mind in this world? It is usually a waste of time to do it.

Following the Equator, I, Chapt. III, p. 50

Will the reader please to cast his eye over the following lines, and see if he can discover anything harmful in them?

"Conductor, when you receive a fare,
Punch in the presence of the passenjare!
A blue trip slip for an eight-cent fare,
A buff trip slip for a six-cent fare,
A pink trip slip for a three-cent fare,
Punch in the presence of the passenjare!

Chorus:

Punch, brothers! Punch with care!

Punch in the presence of the passenjare!

I came across these jingling lines in a newspaper a little while ago, and read them a couple of times. They took instant and entire possession of me. All through breakfast they went waltzing through my brain; and when, at last, I rolled up my napkin, I could not tell whether I had eaten anything or not . . . I took up my pen, but all I could get it to say was, "Punch in the presence of the passenjare." . . . The day's work was ruined—I could see that plainly enough. I gave up and drifted down-town, and presently discovered that my feet were keeping time to that relentless jingle. . . . By sunrise I was out of my mind, and everybody marveled and was distressed at the idiotic burden of my ravings—"Punch! Oh, punch! Punch in the presence of the passenjare!"

Two days later, on Saturday morning, I arose, a tottering wreck. . .

. . .

Why did I write this article? It was for a worthy, even a noble purpose. It was to warn you, reader, if you should come across those rhymes, to avoid them—avoid them as you would a pestilence!

"Punch, Brothers, Punch,"
Tom Sawyer Abroad, Etc., p. 334

Mind is plainly an ass, but it will be many ages before it finds it out, no doubt.

Mark Twain, a Biography, Paine, III, p. 1670

. . . he would come in and say he had changed his mind,—which was a gilded figure of speech, because he hadn't any. . .

"The Old-Fashioned Printer,"
Mark Twain's Speeches (1923), p. 139

[Mind-cure]: Any mummery will cure if the patient's faith is strong in it.

A Connecticut Yankee in King Arthur's Court,
Chapt. XXVI, p. 234

Somehow I continue to feel sure of that cult's colossal future. . . I am selling my Lourdes stock already and buying Christian Science trust. I regard it as the Standard Oil of the future.

Mark Twain, a Biography, Paine, II, p. 1076

Christian Science is humanity's boon . . . [Mrs. Eddy] has organized and make available a healing principle that for two thousand years has never been employed, except as the merest kind of guesswork. She is the benefactor of the age.

Ibid., Paine, III, p. 1271

MINING *See also* EXAGGERATION, MAN

The aged Professor Silliman took the homely-looking specimen of New Jersey coal, and said he would make a test and determine its quality. The next day the owners of the grand discovery waited on him again, eager to hear the verdict which was to make or mar their fortunes. The Professor said, with that impressive solemnity which always marked his manner:

"Gentlemen, I understand you to say that this property is situated upon a hill-top—consequently the situation is prominent. It is valuable—immensely valuable—though as a coal mine I am obliged to observe that it is a failure. Fence it in, gentlemen—fence it in, and hold to it through good and evil fortune till the Last Day; for I am convinced that it will be the best point from which to view the sublime spectacle of the final conflagration. I feel satisfied that if any part of the earth shall remain uninjured after that awful fire, it will be this coal-mine of yours!"

"Memoranda,"

The Galaxy Magazine, May 1870, p. 726

The pick and shovel are the only claims I have any confidence in now.

Mark Twain, a Biography, Paine, I, p. 198

MINISTER *See* CLERGYMAN, FOOL, PREACHER

MINORITY *See* HUMAN RACE

MINSTRELS

I remember the first Negro musical show I ever saw. It must have been in the early forty's. It was a new institution. In our village of Hannibal we had not heard of it before, and it burst upon us as a glad and stunning surprise.

The show remained a week and gave a performance every night. Church members did not attend these performances, but all the worldlings flocked to them and were enchanted. Church members did not attend shows out there in those days. . .

One of these things, which always delighted the audience of those days until the minstrels wore it threadbare was "Bones's" account of the perils which he had once endured during a storm at sea. The storm lasted so long that in the course of time all the provisions were consumed. Then the middle man would inquire anxiously how the people managed to survive.

"Bones" would reply, "We lived on eggs."

"You lived on eggs! Where did you get eggs?"

"Every day, when the storm was so bad, the Captain laid *to*."

During the first five years that joke convulsed the house, but after that the population of the United States had heard it so many times that they respected it no longer and always received it in a deep and reproachful and indignant silence, along with others of its caliber which had achieved disfavor by long service.

The minstrel troops had good voices and both their solos and their choruses were a delight to me as long as the negro show continued in existence. . .

As I have said, it was the worldlings that attended that first minstrel show in Hannibal. Ten or twelve years later the minstrel show was as common in America as the Fourth of July but my mother had never seen one. She was about 60 years old by this time and she came down to St. Louis with a dear and lovely lady of her own age, an old citizen of Hannibal, Aunt Betsey Smith. . .

Like my mother, Aunt Betsey Smith had never seen a negro show. She and my mother were very much alive; their age counted for nothing; they were fond of excitement . . . they were always ready . . . for any and every kind of dissipation that could not be proven to have anything irreligious about it—and they never missed a funeral.

In St. Louis they were eager for novelties and they applied to me for help. They wanted something exciting and proper. I told them I knew of nothing in their line except a Convention which was to meet in the great hall of the Mercantile Library and listen to an exhibition and illustration of native African music by fourteen missionaries who had just returned from that dark continent. I said that if they actually and earnestly desired something instructive and elevating, I would recommend the Convention, but that if at bottom they really wanted something frivolous, I would look further. But no, they were charmed with the idea of the Convention and were eager to go. I was not telling them the strict truth and I knew it at the time, but it was no great matter; it is not worthwhile to strain one's self to tell the truth to people who habitually discount everything you tell them, whether it is true or isn't.

The alleged missionaries were the Christy Minstrel troupe, in that day one of the most celebrated of such troops and also one of the best. We went early and got seats in the front bench. By and by when all the seats on that spacious floor were occupied, there were sixteen hundred persons present. When the grotesque negroes came filing out on the stage in their extravagant costumes, the old ladies were almost speechless with astonishment. I explained to them that the missionaries always dressed like that in Africa. . .

. . . I said that they could see by looking around that the best people in St. Louis were present and that certainly they would not be present if the show were not of the proper sort.

They were comforted and also quite shamelessly glad to be there. They were happy now and enchanted with the novelty of the situation; all that they needed was a pretext of some kind or other to salve their consciences, and their consciences were quiet now, quiet enough to be dead. They gazed on that long curved line of artistic mountebanks with devouring eyes. The middle man began. Presently he led up to that old joke which I was telling about a while ago. Everybody in the house except my novices had heard it a hundred times; a frozen and solemn and indignant silence settled down upon the sixteen hundred, and poor "Bones" sat there in that depressing atmosphere and went through with his joke. It was brand new to my venerable novices and when he got to the end and said, "We lived on eggs" and followed it by explaining that every day during the storm the Captain "laid *to*," they threw their heads back and went off into heart-whole cackles and convulsions of laughter that so astonished and delighted that great audience that it rose in a solid body to look, and see who it might be that had not heard that joke before. The laughter of my novices went on and on until their hilarity became contagious, and the whole sixteen hundred joined in and shook the place with the thunders of their joy.

Aunt Betsey and my mother achieved a brilliant success for the Christy minstrels that night, for all the jokes were as new to them as they were old to the rest of the house. They received them with screams of laughter and passed the hilarity on, and the audience left the place sore and weary with laughter and full of gratitude to the innocent pair that had furnished to their jaded souls that rare and precious pleasure.

Mark Twain in Eruption, p. 110

It seems to me that to the elevated mind and the sensitive spirit, the hand organ and the nigger show are a standard and a summit to whose rarefied altitude the other forms of musical art may not hope to reach.

Ibid., p. 110

MIRACLE *See also* ANGEL, BEAUTY, CHEATING, MISSIONARY

It was a deep and satisfying pleasure to see the sun create the new morning, and gradually, patiently, lovingly, clothe it on with splendor after splendor, and glory after glory, till the miracle was complete.

A Tramp Abroad, I, Chapt. XIV, p. 124

When you are going to do a miracle for an ignorant race, you want to get in every detail that will count; you want to make all the properties impressive to the public eye . . . then you can turn yourself loose and play your effects for all they are worth. I know the value of these things, for I know human nature. You can't throw too much style into a miracle.

A Connecticut Yankee in King Arthur's Court,
Chapt. XXIII, p. 197

There is nothing more awe-inspiring than a miracle, except the credulity that can take it at par.

Mark Twain's Notebook, p. 393

[Captain Hurricane Jones explains the miracle of the Bible]:

First, you see, I read and read, and thought and thought, till I got to understand what sort of people they were in the old Bible times, and then after that it was all clear and easy. Now this was the way I put it up concerning Isaac* and the prophets of Baal. There was some mighty sharp men among the public characters of that old ancient day, and Isaac was one of them. Isaac had his failings—plenty of them, too; it ain't for me to apologize for Isaac; he played it on the prophets of Baal, and like enough, he was justifiable, considering the odds that was against him. No, all I say is, 'twarn't any miracle, and that I'll show you so's't you can see it yourself.

Well, times had been getting rougher and rougher for prophets—that is, prophets of Isaac's denomination. There was four hundred and fifty prophets of Baal in the community, and only one Presbyterian; that is, if Isaac *was* a Presbyterian, which I reckon he was, but it don't say.

Naturally, the prophets of Baal took all the trade . . . [Isaac] begins to throw out hints that the other parties are this and that and t'other. . . The king asked Isaac what he meant by his talk. Says Isaac, "Oh, nothing particular; only, can they pray down fire from heaven on an altar? It ain't much, maybe, your majesty, only can they *do* it? That's the idea."

So the king was a good deal disturbed and he went to the prophets of Baal and they said, pretty airy, that if he had an altar ready *they* were ready; and they intimated he better get it insured, too.

Well, the prophets of Baal prayed along the best they knew how all the afternoon, and never raised a spark. At last, about sundown, they were all tuckered out, and they owned up and quit.

What does Isaac do now? He steps up and says to some friends of his there, "Pour four barrels of water on the altar!" Everybody was astonished; for the other five had prayed at it dry, you know, and got whitewashed. They poured it on. Says he, "Heave on four more barrels." Then he says, "Heave on four more." Twelve barrels, you see, all together. The water ran all over the altar, and all down the sides, and filled up a trench around it that would hold a couple of hogsheads—"measures," it says; I reckon it means about a hogshead. Some of the people were going to put on their things and go, for they allowed he was crazy. They didn't know Isaac. Isaac knelt down and began to pray; he strung along, and strung along . . . till everybody had got tired and gone to thinking about something else, and then, all of a sudden, when nobody was noticing, he outs with a match and rakes it on the underside of his leg, and pff! up the whole thing blazes like a house afire! Twelve barrels of *water*? *Petroleum*, sir, PETROLEUM! That's what it was!

Yes, sir, the country was full of it. Isaac knew all about that. You read the Bible. Don't you worry about the tough places. They ain't tough when you come to think them out and throw light on them. There ain't a thing in the Bible

but what is true; all you want is to go prayerfully to work and cipher out how 'twas done.
* This was the Captain's mistake.

"Rambling Notes of an Idle Excursion,"
Tom Sawyer Abroad, Etc., p. 273

I had been used to chromos for years, and I saw now that without my suspecting it a passion for art had got worked into the fabric of my being, and was become a part of me. It made me homesick to look around over this proud and gaudy but heartless barrenness and remember that in our house in East Hartford, all unpretending as it was, you couldn't go into a room but you would find an insurance-chromo, or at least a three-color God-Bless-Our-Home over the door; and in the parlor we had nine. But here, even in my grand room of state, there wasn't anything in the nature of a picture except a thing the size of a bed-quilt, which was neither woven or knitted (it had darned places in it), and nothing in it was the right color or the right shape; and as for proportion, even Raphael himself couldn't have botched them more formidably after all his practice on those nightmares they call his "celebrated Hampton Court cartoons." Raphael was a bird. We had several of his chromos; one was his "Miraculous Draught of Fishes," where he puts in a miracle of his own—puts three men into a canoe which wouldn't have held a dog without upsetting. I always admired to study R.'s art, it was so fresh and unconventional.

A Connecticut Yankee in King Arthur's Court,
Chapt. VII, p. 55

MIRROR   *See* RIDDLE, VANITY

MISERY

Dear, dear, a body don't know what real misery is till he is thirsty all the way through and is certain he ain't ever going to come to any water any more.

Tom Sawyer Abroad, Etc., Chapt. VIII, p. 75

. . . the *sum* of wrong and misery shall always keep

exact step with the *sum* of human blessedness.

Mark Twain, a Biography, Paine, III, p. 1469

MISFORTUNE

. . . the size of a misfortune is not determinable by an outsider's measurement of it, but only by the measurement applied to it by the person specially affected by it. The king's lost crown is a vast matter to the king, but of no consequence to the child. The lost toy is a great matter to the child, but in the king's eyes it is not a thing to break the heart about.

Mark Twain's Autobiography, Paine, II, p. 40

MISSIONARY *See also* BLUSH, GOD, RELIGION

With the best intentions the missionary has been laboring in China for eighty years. . . The evil result is—that nearly a hundred thousand Chinamen have acquired our Civilization.

And the good result is—that by the compassion of God four hundred millions have escaped it.

"The Dervish and the Offensive Stranger,"
Europe and Elsewhere, p. 313

[In Hawaii]: Near by is an interesting ruin—the meager remains of an ancient temple—a place where human sacrifices were offered up in those old bygone days . . . long, long before the missionaries braved a thousand privations to come and make [the natives] permanently miserable by telling them how beautiful and how blissful a place heaven is, and now nearly impossible it is to get there; and showed the poor native how dreary a place perdition is and what unnecessarily liberal facilities there are for going to it; showed him how, in his ignorance, he had gone and fooled away all his kinsfolk to no purpose; showed him what rapture it is to work all day long for fifty cents to buy food for next day with, as compared with fishing for a pastime and lolling in the shade through eternal summer, and eating of the bounty that nobody labored to provide but Nature.

How sad it is to think of the multitudes who have gone to their graves in this beautiful island and never knew there was a hell.

Roughing It, II, Chapt. XXIII, p. 216

Don't make it for today or tomorrow, but collect the money on the spot.

We are all creatures of sudden impulse. We must be worked up by steam, as it were . . . Fifteen or twenty years ago I had an experience I shall never forget. I got into a church which was crowded by a sweltering and panting multitude. The city missionary of our town—Hartford—made a telling appeal for help. He told of personal experiences among the poor in cellars and top lofts requiring instances of devotion and help. The poor are always good to the poor. When a person with . . . millions gives a hundred thousand dollars it makes a great noise in the world, but he does not miss it; it's the widow's mite that makes no noise but does the best work.

I remembered on that occasion in the Hartford church the collection was being taken up. The appeal had so stirred me that I could hardly wait for the hat or plate to come my way. I had four hundred dollars in my pocket, and I was anxious to drop it in the plate and wanted to borrow more. But the plate was so long in coming my way that the fever-heat of beneficence was going down lower and lower—going down at the rate of a hundred dollars a minute. The plate was passed too late. When it finally came to me, my enthusiasm had gone down so much that I kept my four hundred dollars—and stole a dime from the plate. So you see, time sometimes leads to crime.

"Votes for Women,"
Mark Twain's Speeches (1923), p. 222

. . . missionarying was a better thing in those days than it is in ours. All you had to do was to cure the head savage's sick daughter by a miracle—a miracle like the miracle of Lourdes in our day, for instance—and immediately that head savage was your convert, and filled to the eyes with a new convert's enthusiasm. You could sit down and make yourself easy now. He would take the ax and convert the rest of the nation himself.

"Switzerland, the Cradle of Liberty,"
What Is Man? and Other Essays, p. 198

[*Twain's invention—a spiral hat-pin*]: It looks like a sea serpent going for a missionary.

Manuscript in Huntington Library

Twenty or thirty years ago, when missionary enterprise was in its infancy among the islands of the South Seas, Capt. Summers anchored his sloop-of-war off one of the Marquesas, I think it was. The next morning he saw an American flag floating from the beach, union down. This excited him fearfully, of course, and he sent off a boat at once to inquire into the matter. Presently the boat returned, and brought a grave-looking missionary. The Captain's anxiety ran high. He said:

"What's the trouble out there—quick!"

"Well, I am grieved to say, sir," said the missionary, "that the natives have been interrupting our sacerdotal exercises."

"No!—blast their yaller hides. I'll—what—what was it you said they'd been doing?"

"It pains me, sir, to say that they have been interrupting our sacerdotal exercises."

"Interrupting your—your—h—l! Man them starboard guns! Stand by, now, to give 'em the whole battery!"

The astounded clergyman hastened to protest against such excessive rigorous measures, and finally succeeded in making the old tar understand that the natives had only been breaking up a prayer-meeting.

"Oh, devil take it, man, is that all? I thought you meant that they'd stopped your grog!"

"A Character,"
Mark Twain's Travels with Mr. Brown, p. 257

O kind missionary, O compassionate missionary, leave China! Come home and convert these Christians!

"The United States of Lyncherdom,"
Europe and Elsewhere, p. 249

A missionary is a man who is pretty nearly all heart. . .
"To My Missionary Critics,"
Europe and Elsewhere, p. 295

We are all missionaries (propagandists of *our* views).
Each of us disapproves of the other missionaries. . . .
Mark Twain's Notebook, p. 393

MISSISSIPPI RIVER *See also* CREATION, DISCOVERY, INDE-
PENDENCE, PILOTING, RACING, RIVER, WATER

These dry details . . . give me an opportunity of introducing one of the Mississippi's oddest peculiarities—that of
shortening its length from time to time. If you will throw
a long, pliant appleparing over your shoulder, it will pretty
fairly shape itself into an average section of the Mississippi
River; that is the nine or ten hundred miles stretching from
Cairo, Ill., southward to New Orleans, the same being
wonderfully crooked, with a brief straight bit here and
there at wide intervals. . .

.   .   .

At some forgotten time in the past, cut-offs were made. . .
These shortened the river, in the aggregate, seventy-seven
miles.

Since my own day on the Mississippi, cut-offs have been
made at Hurricane Island, at Island 100, at Napoleon, Ark.,
at Walnut Bend, and at Council Bend. These shortened the
river, in the aggregate, sixty-seven miles. . .

Therefore the Mississippi between Cairo and New Orleans was twelve hundred and fifteen miles long one hundred and seventy-six years ago. It was eleven hundred and
eighty after the cut-off of 1722. . . . Consequently its
length is only nine hundred and seventy-three miles at
present.

Now, if I wanted to be one of those ponderous scientific
people, and "let on" to prove what had occurred in the
remote past by what had occurred in a given time in the
recent past, or what will occur in the far future by what
has occurred in late years, what an opportunity is here!
Geology never had such a chance, nor such exact data to

argue from! Nor, "development of species," either!

In the space of one hundred and seventy-six years the lower Mississippi has shortened itself two hundred and forty-two miles. That is an average of a trifle over one mile and a third per year. Therefore, any calm person, who is not blind or idiotic, can see that in the Old Oölitic Silurian Period, just a million years ago next November, the Lower Mississippi River was upward of one million three hundred thousand miles long, and stuck out over the Gulf of Mexico like a fishing-rod. And by the same token any person can see that seven hundred and forty-two years from now the Lower Mississippi will be only a mile and three-quarters long, and Cairo and New Orleans will have joined their streets together, and be plodding comfortably along under a single mayor and a mutual board of aldermen. There is something fascinating about science. One gets such wholesale returns of conjecture out of such a trifling investment of fact.

> *Life on the Mississippi,* Chapt. XVII, p. 149

[Piloting on the Mississippi]: The face of the water, in time became a wonderful book—a book that was a dead language to the uneducated passenger, but which told its mind to me without reserve, delivering its most cherished secrets as clearly as if it uttered them with a voice. And it was not a book to be read once and thrown aside, for it had a new story to tell every day.

> *Ibid.,* Chapt. IX, p. 82

The military engineers of the [United States River Commission] have taken upon their shoulders the job of making the Mississippi over again—a job transcended in size by only the original job of creating it. They are building wing-dams here and there, to deflect the current; and dikes to confine it in narrower bounds; and other dikes to make it stay there . . .

[Uncle Mumford's impressions of the Commission]: "You turn one of those little European rivers over to this Commission with its hard bottom and clear water, and it would just be a holiday job for them to wall it, and pile it, and dike it, and tame it down, and boss it around, and make it go wherever they wanted it to, and stay where they put it, and do just as they said, every time. But this ain't that kind of a river. They have started in here with big confidence, and the best intentions in the world; but they are going to get left. What does Ecclesiastes VII, 13, say? Says enough to knock *their* little game galley-west, don't it?"

[Ecclesiastes VII, 13: "Consider the work of God; for who can make that straight which he hath made crooked?"]

Ibid., Chapt. XXVIII, p. 220

Mississippi steamboating was born about 1812; at the end of thirty years it had grown to mighty proportions; and in less than thirty more it was dead. A strangely short life for so majestic a creature. Of course it is not absolutely dead; neither is a crippled octogenarian who could once jump twenty-two feet on level ground; but as contrasted with what it was in its prime vigor, Mississippi steamboating may be called dead.

Life on the Mississippi, Chapt. XXII, p. 185

Your true pilot cares nothing about anything on earth but the river, and his pride in his occupation surpasses the pride of kings.

Ibid., Chapt. VII, p. 63

When I find a well-drawn character in fiction or biography I generally take a warm personal interest in him, for the reason that I have known him before—met him on the river.

Ibid., Chapt. XVII, p. 158

[Several islands were washed away] . . . The Mississippi is a just and equitable river; it never tumbles one man's farm overboard without building a new farm just like it for that man's neighbor. This keeps down hard feelings.

Ibid., Chapt. XXV, p. 203

[On the upper Mississippi]: The majestic bluffs that overlook the river, along through this region, charm one with the grace and variety of their forms, and the soft

beauty of their adornment . . . And then you have the
shining river, winding here and there and yonder, its sweep
interrupted at intervals by clusters of wooded islands
threaded by silver channels; and you have glimpses of distant villages, asleep upon capes; and of stealthy rafts slip-
ping along in the shade of the forest walls; and of white
steamers vanishing around remote points. And it is all as
tranquil and reposeful as dreamland, and has nothing this-
worldly about it—nothing to hang a fret or a worry upon.

Until the unholy train comes tearing along,—which it
presently does, ripping the sacred solitude to rags and tat-
ters with its devil's war-whoop and the roar and thunder
of its rushing wheels—and straightway you are back in this
world . . .

Ibid., Chapt. LVIII, p. 432

MISSOURI   *See also* GENTLEMAN, HANNIBAL, PILGRIMS
[Mark Twain's parents]: . . . their first crop of children
was born [in Tennessee]. I was postponed to Missouri.
Missouri was an unknown new state and needed attractions.
Mark Twain's Autobiography, Paine, I, p. 87
The armorial crest of my own state consisted of two dis-
solute bears holding up the head of a dead and gone cask
between them and making the pertinent remark, "UNITED,
WE STAND—(hic)—DIVIDED WE FALL." It was always
too figurative for the author of this book.
Roughing It, I, Chapt. XIII, p. 114

MISTAKE   *See also* ADVICE
[From a letter to Professor E. T. Evans]: . . . from one
who lives a life made half of mistakes, and the other half
of apologies for them; but who is
Sincerely yours, S. L. Clemens.
From a hitherto unpublished letter,
in University of Michigan Library

MOB   *See* MASSES

MODESTY *See also* GOVERNMENT, IGNORANCE, NEWSPAPER, RULE, VOTING

If his modesty equaled his ignorance he would make a violet seem stuck-up.

> "From a Brooklyn Lecture,"
> *The Twainian,* Jan.–Feb. 1946, p. 4

Modesty antedates clothes and will be resumed when clothes are no more.

> *Mark Twain, a Biography,* Paine, III, p. 1514

Modesty died when clothes were born.

> *Ibid.*

The man who is ostentatious of his modesty is twin to the statue that wears a fig-leaf.

> "Pudd'nhead Wilson's New Calendar,"
> *Following the Equator,* II, Chapt. XIV, p. 168

I was born modest; not all over, but in spots.

> *A Connecticut Yankee in King Arthur's Court,*
> Chapt. XVI, p. 129

[He] went swaggering around in his bandages showing off like an innocent big child . . . He was prouder of being wounded than a really modest person would be of being killed.

> *Personal Recollections of Joan of Arc,*
> I, Book II, Chapt. XXVII, p. 338

The statue that advertises its modesty with a fig-leaf brings its modesty under suspicion.

> *Mark Twain,* Henderson, p. 115

I was born modest, but it didn't last.

> "Layman's Sermon,"
> *Mark Twain's Speeches* (1910), p. 137

MOMENT *See* TIME

MONARCHY *See also* COUNTRY, DEMOCRACY, REPUBLIC, ROYALTY

If there is any valuable difference between being an American and a monarchist it lies in the theory that the

American can decide for himself what is patriotic and
what isn't.

Mark Twain, a Biography, Paine, II, p. 779

[Mark Twain prophesies a monarchy]: Because of a
special and particular reason? Yes. Two special reasons and
one condition.

1. It is the nature of man to want a definite something
to love, honor, reverently look up to, and obey: God and
King, for example.

2. Little republics have lasted long, protected by their
poverty and insignificance, but great ones have not.

3. The Condition: vast power and wealth, which breed
commercial and political corruption and incite public favorites to dangerous ambitions.

. . .

For fifty years our country has been a constitutional
monarchy, with the Republic party sitting on the throne.
Mr. Cleveland's couple of brief interruptions do not count;
they were accidents and temporary, they made no permanent inroad upon Republican supremacy. [1908]

Mark Twain in Eruption, p. 1

I shall vote for the continuance of the monarchy. That
is to say, I shall vote for Mr. Taft. If the monarchy could
be permanently abolished and the republic restored to us
by electing Mr. Bryan, I would vote the Democratic ticket;
but it could not happen. The monarchy is here to stay.
[1908]

Ibid., p. 34

Human nature being what it is, I suppose we must expect
to drift into monarchy by and by. It is a saddening thought
but we cannot change our nature—we are all alike, we
human beings; and in our blood and bone, and ineradicably,
we carry the seeds out of which monarchies and aristocra-
cies are grown: worship of gauds, titles, distinctions, power.
We have to worship these things and their possessors, we
are all born so and we cannot help it. We have to be despised by somebody whom we regard as above us or we

are not happy; we have to have somebody to worship and envy or we cannot be content. In America we manifest this in all the ancient and customary ways. In public we scoff at titles and hereditary privilege but privately we hanker after them, and when we get a chance we buy them for cash and a daughter . . .

Like all the other nations, we worship money and the possessors of it—they being our aristocracy, and we have to have one.

. . .

I suppose we must expect that unavoidable and irresistible Circumstances will gradually take away the powers of the State and concentrate them in the central government, and that the republic will then repeat the history of all time and become a monarchy; but I believe that if we obstruct these encroachments and steadily resist them the monarchy can be postponed for a while yet.

Mark Twain in Eruption, p. 64

Monarchy has speech, and by it has been able to persuade man that it differs somehow from the rattlesnake, has something valuable about it somewhere, something worth preserving, something even good and high and fine, when properly "modified," something entitling it to protection from the club of the first comer who catches it out of its hole.

Mark Twain's Letters, II, p. 536

Strip the human race, absolutely naked, and it would be a real democracy. But the introduction of even a rag of tiger skin, or a cow tail, could make a badge of distinction and be the beginning of a monarchy.

Mark Twain's Notebook, p. 337

The first gospel of all monarchies should be Rebellion; the second should be Rebellion; and the third and all gospels and the only gospel in any monarchy should be Rebellion against Church and State.

Ibid., p. 217

Men write many fine and plausible arguments in support of monarchy, but the fact remains that where every man

in a state has a vote, brutal laws are impossible.
>> *A Connecticut Yankee in King Arthur's Court,*
>> Chapt. XXV, p. 219

MONEY   *See also* BOAT, CRIME, FRIEND, MISSIONARY, MON-
ARCHY, MOTTO, PLUMBER, NOBILITY, POVERTY, PROSPER-
ITY, RICHES, UNCLE, VALUE, WAGES, WALL STREET,
WOMAN, WORSHIP

[He] had no more conscience than a millionaire.
>> "When in Doubt, Tell the Truth,"
>> *Mark Twain's Speeches* (1923), p. 295

The lack of money is the root of all evil.
>> *More Maxims of Mark,* p. 10

The low level which commercial morality has reached in
America is deplorable. We have humble God-fearing Christian men among us who will stoop to do things for a million
dollars that they ought not to be willing to do for less than
2 millions.
>> *Ibid.,* p. 10

The real yellow peril: GOLD.
>> *Ibid.,* p. 12

You are always ciphering out how much a man's health
is injured, and how much his intellect is impaired, and how
many pitiful dollars and cents he wastes in the course of
ninety-two years' indulgence in the fatal practice of smoking; and in the equally fatal practice of drinking coffee; and
in playing billiards occasionally; and in taking a glass of
wine at dinner, etc., etc., etc. . . . You are blind to the
fact that most old men in America smoke and drink coffee,
although, according to your theory, they ought to have
died young; and that hearty old Englishmen drink wine
and survive it, and portly old Dutchmen both drink and
smoke freely, and yet grow older and fatter all the time.
And you never try to find out how much solid comfort,
relaxation, and enjoyment a man derives from smoking in
the course of a lifetime . . . Of course you can save money
by denying yourself all those little vicious enjoyments for
fifty years; but then what can you do with it? What can you

put it to? Money can't save your infinitesimal soul. All the use that money can be put to is to purchase comfort and enjoyment in this life . . . You people who have no petty vices are never known to give away a cent . . .

"Answers to Correspondents,"
Sketches New and Old, p. 81

We Americans worship the almighty dollar! Well, it is a worthier god than Hereditary Privilege.

Mark Twain's Notebook, p. 209

In my experience, previously counted chickens never *do* hatch . . . It is much better to hedge disappointment by not counting. Unexpected money is a delight. The same sum is a bitterness when you expected more.

Mark Twain's Letters (1923), p. 324

I was out of money [1867], and I went down to Washington to see if I could earn enough there to keep me in bread and butter . . . I remember a time . . . we had to have three dollars before the close of the day. . . . I wandered around the streets for an hour, trying to think up some way to get that money, but nothing suggested itself. At last I lounged into the big lobby of the Ebbitt House, which was then a new hotel, and sat down. Presently a dog came loafing along. He paused, glanced up at me and said with his eyes, "Are you friendly?" and I answered with my eyes that I was. He gave his tail a grateful wag and came forward and rested his jaw on my knee and lifted his brown eyes to my face in a winningly affectionate way. . . . Pretty soon Brig.-Gen. Miles, the hero of the land, came strolling by in his blue and gold splendors with everybody's admiring gaze upon him. He saw the dog and stopped, and there was a light in his eye which showed that he had a warm place in his heart for dogs like this gracious creature; then he came forward and patted the dog and said:

"He is very fine—he is a wonder; would you sell him?"

I was greatly moved . . . I said, "Yes."

The General said, "What do you ask for him?"

"Three dollars."

The General was manifestly surprised. He said . . .
"Only three dollars? Why that dog . . . can't possibly be
worth less than fifty . . . Reconsider your price if you
like, I don't wish to wrong you."

But if he had known me he would have known that I was
no more capable of wronging him than he was of wronging
me. I responded with the same quiet decision as before,
"No, three dollars. That is his price."

"Very well, since you insist upon it," said the General,
and he gave me three dollars and led the dog away . . .
upstairs.

In about ten minutes a gentle-faced, middle-aged gentleman came along, and began to look around . . . under
tables and everywhere, and I said to him, "Is it a dog you
are looking for?"

His face had been sad, before, and troubled; but it lit up
gladly now, and he answered, "Yes—have you seen him?"

"Yes," I said, "he was here a minute ago, and I saw him
follow a gentleman away. I think I could find him for you
if you would like me to try."

I have seldom seen a person look so grateful . . . I said
I would do it with great pleasure but that as it might take
a little time I hoped he would not mind paying me something for my trouble. He said he would do it most gladly
. . . and asked me how much. I said, "Three dollars."

He looked surprised, and said, "Dear me, it is nothing!
I will pay you ten, quite willingly."

But I said, "No, three is the price," and I started for the
stairs without . . . further argument . . . When I reached
the room I found the General there caressing his dog, and
quite happy. I said, "I am sorry, but I have to take the
dog again."

He seemed very much surprised and said, "Take him
again? Why, he is my dog; you sold him to me . . ."

"Yes," I said, "it is true—but I have to have him, because
the man . . . that owns him . . . wants him again . . .
he wasn't my dog."

The General looked even more surprised . . . "Do you

mean to tell me that you were selling another man's dog—and knew it?"

"Yes, I knew it wasn't my dog. . . . Put yourself in my place. Suppose you had sold a dog that didn't belong to you . . ."

"Oh," he said, "don't muddle my brains any more . . . Take him along, and give me a rest."

So I paid back the three dollars and led the dog downstairs and passed him over to his owner, and collected three dollars for my trouble.

I went away then with a good conscience, because I had acted honorably; I never could have used the three that I sold the dog for, because it was not rightly my own, but the three I got for restoring him to his rightful owner was righteously and properly mine, because I had earned it. . . . My principles have remained to this day what they were then. I was always honest . . . I was never able to persuade myself to use money which I had acquired in questionable ways.

Mark Twain in Eruption, p. 353

The world seems to think that the love of money is "American"; and that the mad desire to get suddenly rich is "American." I believe that both of these things are merely and broadly human, not American monopolies at all. The love of money is natural to all nations, for money is a good and strong friend. I think that this love has existed everywhere, ever since the Bible called it the root of all evil.

I think that the reason why we Americans seem to be so addicted to trying to get rich suddenly is merely because the *opportunity* to make promising efforts in that direction has offered itself to us with a frequency out of all proportion to the European experience.

"What Paul Bourget Thinks of Us,"
Literary Essays, p. 155

[The rightful earl] merely wanted to borrow money. I never knew an American earl that didn't.

Mark Twain, a Biography, Paine, II, p. 673

In an age when we would rather have money than health,

and would rather have another man's money than our own, he lived and died unsordid. . .

"Samuel Erasmus Moffett,"
Europe and Elsewhere, p. 354

A young half-breed with a complexion like a yellow-jacket asked me if I would like to have my boots blacked. It was at the Salt Lake house this morning after we arrived. I said yes, and he blacked them. Then I handed him a silver five-cent piece, with the benevolent air of a person who is conferring wealth and blessedness upon poverty and suffering. The yellow-jacket took it with what I judged to be suppressed emotion, and laid it reverently down in the middle of his broad hand. Then he began to contemplate it, much as a philosopher contemplates a gnat's ear in the ample field of his microscope. . . Presently the yellow-jacket handed the half dime back to me and told me I ought to keep my money in my pocketbook instead of in my soul, and then I wouldn't get it cramped and shriveled up so!

Roughing It, I, Chapt. XVII, p. 145

[In the Holy Land]: . . . if you hire a man to sneeze for you here, and another man chooses to help him, you have got to pay both. They do nothing whatever without pay. How it must have surprised these people to hear the way of salvation offered to them *"without money and without price."* If the manners, the people, or the customs of this country have changed since the Savior's time, the figures and metaphors of the Bible are not the evidences to prove it by.

The Innocents Abroad, II, Chapt. XXIII, p. 290

[Simple rules for saving money]: To save half, when you are fired by an eager impulse to contribute to a charity, wait and count forty. To save three-quarters, count sixty. To save it all, count sixty-five.

"Pudd'nhead Wilson's New Calendar,"
Following the Equator, II, Chapt. XI, p. 125

Spending one's capital is feeding a dog on his own tail.

Mark Twain's Notebook, p. 345

381

(MONEY)

We used to trust in God. I think it was in 1863 that some genius suggested that ["In God we trust"] be put upon the gold and silver coins which circulated among the rich. They didn't put it upon the nickels and coppers because they didn't think the poor folks had any trust in God.

Good citizenship would teach accuracy of thinking and accuracy of statement. Now, that motto on the coin is an overstatement. Those Congressmen had no right to commit this whole country to a theological doctrine. But since they did, Congress ought to state what our creed should be.

"Education and Citizenship"
Mark Twain's Speeches (1923), p. 378

"Your friend Rogers is a good fellow," someone said to Mark Twain of H. H. Rogers of Standard Oil fame. "It's a pity his money is tainted."

"It's twice tainted," drawled Mark. "Tain't yours and tain't mine."

Francis Wilson's Life of Himself, Wilson, p. 299

I'm opposed to millionaires, but it would be dangerous to offer me the position.

The American Claimant, Etc., Chapt. XIV, p. 121

. . . you will have to modify your installment system to meet the emergency of a constipated purse; for if you should need to borrow any more money I would not know how or where to raise it.

Mark Twain, a Biography, Paine, II, p. 921

[On February 27, 1886, the Charles L. Webster and Co. [Mark Twain's company] paid $200,000 to Mrs. [Ulysses S.] Grant [for the *Autobiography of Ulysses S. Grant*], the largest single royalty check in the history of book-publishing.]

Mark Twain's Letters, II, p. 464

Vast wealth, to the person unaccustomed to it, is a bane. It eats into the flesh and bone of his morals.

The $30,000 Bequest, Etc., Chapt. VI, p. 33

. . .

MONKEY *See also* MAN

I believe . . . our Heavenly Father invented man because he was disappointed in the monkey.

Mark Twain in Eruption, p. 372

[At Delhi]: Two of these creatures came into my room in the early morning, through a window whose shutters I had left open, and when I woke one of them was before the glass brushing his hair, and the other one had my note-book, and was reading a page of humorous notes and crying. I did not mind the one with the hairbrush but the conduct of the other one hurt me: it hurts me yet. I threw some-thing at him, and that was wrong, for my host had told me that the monkeys were best left alone. They threw everything at me that they could lift, and then went into the bathroom to get some more things, and I shut the door on them.

Following the Equator, II, Chapt. XXIV, p. 284

MONOTONY *See also* INTELLECT, MICHELANGELO, MIND, MUSIC, YODELING

The human race was always interesting, and we know by its past that it will always continue so. Monotonously. It is always the same; it never changes. Its circumstances change from time to time, for better or worse, but the race's *character* is permanent, and never changes . . .

It is not worth while to try to keep history from repeating itself, for man's character will always make the preventing of the repetitions impossible.

Mark Twain in Eruption, p. 66

[In Nevada]: It was a dreadful trip. But Oliver did not complain. The horses dragged the wagon two miles from town and then gave out. Then we three pushed the wagon seven miles, and Oliver moved ahead and pulled the horses after him by the bits. We complained, but Oliver did not. The ground was frozen, and it froze our backs while we slept; the wind swept across our faces and froze our noses. Oliver did not complain . . . Fifteen days of hardship and fatigue brought us to the end of the two hundred miles, and the judge had not complained. We wondered if anything *could* exasperate him. We built a Humboldt house. It is done in this way. You dig a square in the steep base of the mountain, and set up two uprights and top them with two joists. Then you stretch a great sheet of "cotton domestic" from the joint where the joists join the hillside down over the joists to the ground; this makes the roof and the front of the mansion; the sides and back are the dirt walls your digging has left. A chimney is easily made by turning up one corner of the roof. Oliver was sitting alone in this dismal den, one night, by a sage-brush fire, writing poetry; he was very fond of digging poetry out of himself—or blasting it out when it came hard. He heard an animal's footsteps close to the roof; a stone or two and some dirt came through and fell by him. He grew uneasy and said: "Hi!—clear out from there, can't you!"—from time to time. But by and by he fell asleep where he sat, and pretty soon a mule fell down the chimney! The fire flew in every direction, and Oliver went over backwards. About ten nights after that he recovered confidence enough to go to writing poetry again. Again he dozed off to sleep, and again a mule fell down the chimney. This time, about half of that side of the house came in with the mule. Struggling to get up, the mule kicked the candle out and smashed most of the kitchen furniture, and raised considerable dust. These violent awakenings must have been annoying to Oliver, but he never complained. He moved to a mansion on the opposite side of the canyon, because he had noticed the mules did not go there. One night about eight o'clock he was endeavoring to finish his poem, when a stone rolled in—then a hoof appeared below the canvas—then part of a cow—the after part. He leaned back in dread and shouted "Hooy! Hooy! get out of this!" and the cow struggled manfully,—lost ground steadily—dirt and dust streamed down, and before Oliver could get well away, the entire cow crashed through on to the table and made a shapeless wreck of everything! Then, for the first time in his life, I think, Oliver complained. He said: *"This thing is growing monotonous!"*

The Innocents Abroad, I, Chapt. XXVII, p. 362

When a cackling hen is far away and is saying K-k-k-k-k-k-KWACKO! you hear nothing but the first syllable of her last word—just a single strenuous note, pitched on a high key, all the rest is lost in the intervening distance. At a distance this fiend-owl's note sounds like that. Close by it is soft and dovelike and it is not so very unlike a flute note. It is quadruple time—one utterance to the bar, followed by three-quarter note rests, . . . the monotony of it is maddening. You beat time to it, and count the hoots and the rests—you cannot help it. You count till your reason reels. Low and soft as the note is, it is marvelously penetrating; it bores into the skull like an auger. It can distress you when it is 150 yards away; at a third of that distance it is unendurable. When you have counted fifty hoots and 150 rests you have reached the limit of human endurance. You must turn and drive the creature away or your mind will go to ruin.

Mark Twain's Notebook, p. 234

If you interrupted her she would either go right along without noticing, or answer with a couple of words, and go back and say the sentence over again. So, interruptions only did harm; and yet I had to interrupt, and interrupt pretty frequently, too, in order to save my life; a person would die if he let her monotony drip on him right along all day.

A Connecticut Yankee in King Arthur's Court,
Chapt. XV, p. 114

. . . take a condition which is present all the time, and the results of that condition will be uniform; this uniformity of result will in time become monotonous; monotonousness, by the law of its being, is fatiguing.

Personal Recollections of Joan of Arc,
I, Book II, Chapt. XXIV, p. 319

MONTH *See* FOOL, FOURTH OF JULY, SPECULATION

MOOD

It is right and wholesome to have those light comedies and entertaining shows, and I shouldn't wish to see them diminished. But none of us is *always* in the comedy spirit; we have our graver moods; they come to us all; the lightest of us cannot escape them. These moods have their appetites —healthy and legitimate appetites—and there ought to be some way of satisfying them.

"About Play-Acting"
The Man That Corrupted Hadleyburg, Etc., p. 213

MOON *See also* EXAGGERATION, EXPERIENCE, STARS

Every one is a moon, and has a dark side which he never shows to anybody.

Following the Equator, II, Chapt. XXX, p. 350

At half eclipse the moon was like a gilded acorn in its cup.

Ibid., I, Chapt. IV, p. 60

But the magic of the moonlight is a vanity and a fraud; and whoso putteth his trust in it shall suffer sorrow and disappointment.

The Innocents Abroad, II, Chapt. XXII, p. 287

MORALS *See also* ANCESTOR, BRUTALITY, CHILD, FOR-
MALITY, FRANCE, GOODNESS, HABIT, LIBRARY, LIQUOR,
MAN, MICROBE, MONEY, NEWSPAPER, OPTIMISM, RELIGION,
RIGHT, STEALING, TYPEWRITER, VIRTUE, WRONG

I used to be an honest man. I am crumbling. No—I have crumbled. When they assessed me at $75,000 a fortnight ago I went out and tried to borrow the money and couldn't; then when I found they were letting a whole crop of millionaires live in New York at a third of the price they were charging me, I was hurt, I was indignant, and said: "This is the last feather. I am not going to run this town all by myself." In that memorable moment—I began to crumble . . . In fifteen minutes I had become just a mere moral sandpile; and I lifted up my hand along with those seasoned and experienced deacons and swore off every rag of per-

sonal property I've got in the world, clear down to cork
leg, glass eye, and what is left of my wig.

"Taxes and Morals"
Mark Twain's Speeches (1923), p. 278

Morals consist of political morals, commercial morals, ec-
clesiastical morals, and morals.

More Maxims of Mark, p. 10

[About George W. Cable]: You know that when it comes
down to moral honesty, limpid innocence, and utterly
blemishless piety, the apostles were mere policemen to
Cable. . . .

Mark Twain, a Biography, Paine, II, p. 743

. . . the moral idea [is] undergoing constant change . . .
what was considered justifiable in an earlier day [is] regarded as highly immoral now . . . even the Decalogue
[makes] no reference to lying, except in the matter of
bearing false witness against a neighbor . . . There [is] a
commandment against covetousness, though covetousness
to-day is the basis of all commerce . . . The morals of the
Lord have been the morals of the beginning; the morals
of the first-created man . . . the morals of necessity; . . . the
morals of mankind have kept pace with necessity, whereas
those of the Lord have remained unchanged.

Ibid., Paine, III, p. 1357

Morals are not the important thing—nor enlightenment—
nor civilization. A man can do absolutely well without them,
but he can't do without *something to eat.* The supremest
thing is the *need of the body,* not of the mind and spirit.

Ibid., Paine, III, p. 1514

It has always been a peculiarity of the human race that
it keeps two sets of morals in stock—the private and real,
and the public and artificial.

Mark Twain in Eruption, p. 382

As for [Grover] Cleveland, his private life may be no
worse than that of most men, but as an enemy of that
contemptible, hypocritical, lopsided morality which says a
woman shall suffer all the shame of unchastity and man

none, I want to see him destroyed politically by his past. The men who defend him would take their wives to the White House if he were president, but if he married his concubine—"made her an honest woman"—they would not go near him. I can't stand that.

"A Letter to William Dean Howells"
Mark Twain's Letters, II, p. 444

In our well-meant effort to lift up the Filipino to our own moral attitude with a musket, we have slipped on the ice and fallen down to his.

"The Dervish and the Offensive Stranger"
Europe and Elsewhere, p. 313

[Mark Twain's daughter Susie once said]:
"The difference between papa and mama is, that mama loves morals and papa loves cats."

Mark Twain, a Biography, Paine, II, p. 684

No matter how healthy a man's morals may be when he enters the White House, he comes out again with a pot-marked soul.

My Father • Mark Twain, Clara Clemens, p. 238

The most permanent lessons in morals are those which come, not of booky teachings but of experience.

A Tramp Abroad, II, Chapt. XVIII, p. 239

As by the fires of experience, so by commission of crime, you learn real morals. Commit all the crimes, familiarize yourself with all sins, take them in rotation (there are only two or three thousand of them), stick to it, commit two or three every day and by-and-by you will be proof against them. When you are through you will be proof against all sins and morally perfect. You will be vaccinated against every possible commission of them. This is the only way.

"Theoretical and Practical Morals"
Mark Twain's Speeches (1923), p. 191

Morals are an acquirement—like music, like a foreign language, like piety, poker, paralysis—no man is born with them. I wasn't myself, I started poor. I hadn't a single moral. There is hardly a man in this house that is poorer than I was then. Yes, I started like that—the world before me, not a moral in the slot. Not even an insurance moral. I can remember the first one I ever got . . . it was an old moral, an old second-hand moral, all out of repair, and didn't fit anyway. But if you are careful with a thing like that, and keep it in a dry place, and save it for processions, and Chautauquas, and World's Fairs, and so on, and disinfect it now and then, and give it a fresh coat of whitewash once in a while, you will be surprised to see how well she will last and how long she will keep sweet, or at least inoffensive. When I got that mouldy old moral, she had stopped growing, because she hadn't any exercise; but I worked her hard, I worked her Sundays and all. Under this cultivation she waxed in might and stature beyond belief, and served me well and was my pride and joy for sixty-three years. Then she got to associating with insurance presidents, and lost flesh and character, and was a sorrow to look at and no longer competent for business. She was a great loss to me.

"Seventieth Birthday"
Mark Twain's Speeches (1923), p. 260

Commercial morals, especially, are bad. There is no gainsaying that Greek, Turkish, and Armenian morals consist only in attending church regularly on the appointed Sabbaths, and in breaking the ten commandments all the balance of the week. It comes natural to them to lie and cheat in the first place, and then they go on and improve on nature until they arrive at perfection.

The Innocents Abroad, II, Chapt. VII, p. 93

It's my opinion that every one I know has morals, though I wouldn't like to ask. I know I have. But I'd rather teach them than practice them any day. "Give them to others"— that's my motto.

"Morals and Memory"
Mark Twain's Speeches (1923), p. 284

The children's theatre is the only teacher of morals and conduct and high ideals that never bores the pupil, but always leaves him sorry when the lesson is over.

Mark Twain's Letters, II, p. 819

There are two kinds of Christian morals, one private and the other public. These two are so distinct, so unrelated, that they are no more akin to each other than are archangels and politicians. During three hundred and sixty-three days in the year the American citizen is true to his Christian private morals, and keeps undefiled the nation's character at its best and highest; then in the other two days of the year he leaves his Christian private morals at home and carries his Christian public morals to the tax office and the polls, and does the best he can to damage and undo his whole year's faithful and righteous work.

"Taxes and Morals"
Mark Twain's Speeches (1923), p. 276

There is a Moral Sense, and there is an Immoral Sense. History shows us that the Moral Sense enables us to perceive morality and how to avoid it, and that the Immoral Sense enables us to perceive immorality and how to enjoy it.

"Pudd'nhead Wilson's New Calendar"
Following the Equator, I, Chapt. XVI, p. 162

Bill Styles, lobbying in behalf of a candidate for U.S. Senator—in the legislature—spoke of the low grade of legislative morals, "kind of discouragin', you see, it's so hard to find men of so high type of morals that they'll *stay bought.*"

Mark Twain's Notebook, p. 213

He hasn't any more principle than a blue jay; and as for morals, he's empty.

"A Horse's Tale"
The Mysterious Stranger, Etc., p. 193

It is not best that we use our morals week days; it gets them out of repair for Sundays.

Mark Twain's Notebook, p. 345

A man should not be without morals; it is better to have bad morals than none at all.

Ibid., p. 237

The Moral Sense teaches us what is right, and how to avoid it—when unpopular.

"The United States of Lyncherdom"
Europe and Elsewhere, p. 244

MORMONS *See also* BIBLE, LITERARY CRITICISM, SNORING, WOMAN

[We] hurried on to the home of the Latter-Day Saints, the stronghold of the prophets, the capital of the only absolute monarchy in America—Great Salt Lake City. [1861]
Roughing It, I, Chapt. XII, p. 111

My idea, when I began this chapter, was to say something about desperadoism in the "flush times" of Nevada. To attempt a portrayal of that era and that land, and leave out the blood and carnage, would be like portraying Mormondom and leaving out polygamy.
Ibid., II, Chapt. VII, p. 77

MOSQUITO *See also* HEAT

[In Honolulu]: Mosquitoes, 2 kinds—day and night.
Mark Twain's Notebook, p. 20

[Go to bed], then wait, and suffer, till all the mosquitoes have crawled in under the bar, then slip out quickly, and shut them in and sleep peacefully on the floor till morning.
Roughing It, II, Chapt. XXII, p. 209

He was an austere man, and had the reputation of being singularly unworldly, for a river man. Among other things, he said that Arkansas had been injured and kept back by generations of exaggerations concerning the mosquitoes there. One may smile, said he, and turn the matter off as being a small thing; but when you come to look at the effects produced, in the way of discouragement of immigration and diminished values of property, it was quite the opposite of a small thing, or thing in any wise to be coughed down or sneered at. These mosquitoes had been persistently represented as being formidable and lawless; whereas "the truth is, they are feeble, insignificant in size, diffident to a fault, sensitive"—and so on, and so on; you would have supposed he was talking about his family. But if he was soft on the Arkansas mosquitoes, he was hard enough on the mosquitoes of Lake Providence to make up for it—"those Lake Providence colossi," as he finely called them. He said that two of them could whip a dog, and that four of them could hold a man down; and except help come, they would kill him—"butcher him," as he expressed it. Referred in a sort of casual way—and yet significant way, to "the fact that the life policy in its simplest form is unknown in Lake Providence—they take out a mosquito policy besides." He told many remarkable things about those lawless insects. Among others, said he had seen them try to *vote*. Noticing that this statement seemed to be a good deal of a strain on us, he modified it a little; said he might have been mistaken as to that particular, but knew he had seen them around the polls "canvassing."

Life on the Mississippi, Chapt. XXXIV, p. 274

[In Italy]: The mosquitoes are not a trouble. There are very few of them, they are not noisy, and not much interested in their calling. A single unkind word will send them away; if said in English, which impresses them because they do not understand it, they come no more that night. . . . I have got some of the eggs to take home. If this breed can be raised in our climate they will be a great advantage.

Mark Twain's Autobiography, Paine, I, p. 228

MOTHER *See* IDEALS

MOTHER, MARK TWAIN'S *See also* HEALTH, MEMORY, MINSTRELS, NEGRO, PUNISHMENT, SUSPICION, TRUTH, WATER, WORDS

My venerable mother is a tolerably good correspondent—she is above the average, at any rate. She puts on her spectacles and takes her scissors and wades into a pile of newspapers, and slashes out column after column—editorials, hotel arrivals, poetry, telegraph news, advertisements, novelettes, old jokes, recipes for making pies, cures for "biles"—any thing that comes handy; it don't matter to her; she is entirely impartial; she slashes out a column, and runs her eye down it over her spectacles—(she looks over them because she can't see through them, but she prefers them to her more serviceable ones because they have got gold rims to them)—runs her eye down the column, and says, "Well, it's from a St. Louis paper, anyway," and jams it into the envelope along with her letter. She writes about everybody I ever knew or ever heard of; but unhappily, she forgets that when she tells me that "J. B. is dead," and that "W. L. is going to marry T. D." and that "B. K. and R. M. and L. P. J. have gone to New Orleans to live," it is more than likely that years of absence may have so dulled my recollection of once familiar names, that their unexplained initials will be as unintelligible as Hebrew unto me. She never writes a name in full, and so I never know whom she is talking about. Therefore, I have to guess—and this was how it came that I mourned the death of Bill Kribben when I should have rejoiced over the dissolution of Ben Kenfuron.

"A Complaint About Correspondents"
The Celebrated Jumping Frog of Calaveras County, p. 30
[Jane Clemens, Mark Twain's mother]: Her sense of pity was abnormal. . . . She would drown the young kittens, when necessary, but warmed the water for the purpose.

Mark Twain, a Biography, Paine, I, p. 36
[Jane Clemens advised]: "Never learn to do anything. If you don't learn you'll always find some one else to do it for you."

Mark Twain, the Man and His Work, p. 10
Jane Clemens never seemed to look over a letter and correct it. Once . . . in a letter to [her son], she meant to say "Kiss Susy for me" and instead wrote "Kill Susy for me." She told Pamela [her daughter], what a funny mistake she had made. "But you didn't send it, did you?" asked Pamela, naturally shocked. "Oh, yes," her mother answered calmly, "Sam will understand what I meant."

Sam's answer came promptly. He wrote: "I said to Livy

'It is a hard thing to ask of loving parents, but Ma is getting old and her slightest whim must be our law'; so I called in Downey [the coachman], and Livy and I held the child with the tears streaming down our faces while he sawed her head off." His mother's reaction to that letter was outraged indignation at the method by which the child had been dispatched. "Sawed her head off!" she kept saying. "*Sawed her head off!*"

> *Mark Twain, Business Man*, p. 16

[A motto of Jane Clemens]: "People born to be hanged are safe in water."

> *Mark Twain, a Biography*, Paine, I, p. 35

MOTTO *See also* MONEY

When we have been abroad . . . for even so brief a time as a year, the first thing we notice when we get back home is the wanton and unprovoked discourtesies that assail us at every turn . . . You will step into the trolley with your heart so full of thankfulness to be at home again that you can't speak. . . . Then the conductor bawls out "Come, step lively, will you!" and you realize that you are [at home once more]. . . . We have never claimed to be the Uncourteous Nation, the Unpolite Nation, . . . Is it because we are also the Too-Modest Nation? Probably. Is that why we still keep that old, quiet, courtly uninsolent, uncharacteristic *E Pluribus Unum* for our national motto, instead of replacing it with an up-to-date one, full of national character, "Come, *step* lively!"

> "Introducing Doctor Van Dyke"
> *Mark Twain's Speeches* (1923), p. 300

Everybody's private motto: It's better to be popular than right.

> *More Maxims of Mark*, p. 7

I noticed in the papers this afternoon a despatch from Washington, saying that Congress would immediately pass a bill restoring to our gold coinage the motto "In God We Trust." I'm glad of that. . . . I was troubled when that motto was removed. Sure enough, the prosperities of the whole nation went down in a heap [in the Panic of 1907] when we ceased to trust in God in that conspicuously advertised way. [1908]

"Dinner to Whitelaw Reid"
Mark Twain's Speeches (1923), p. 382

[*The Man That Corrupted Hadleyburg* by Mark Twain tells how a town changed the motto on its official seal, from "Lead us not into Temptation" to "Lead us into Temptation."]

Our public motto is "In God We Trust" and when we see those gracious words on the trade-dollar (worth sixty cents) they always seem to tremble and whimper with pious emotion . . .

Mark Twain in Eruption, p. 382

One thing at a time, is my motto—and just play that thing for all it is worth, even if it's only two pair and a jack.

A Connecticut Yankee in King Arthur's Court,
Chap. II, p. 25

MOUNTAIN *See also* FARM, GLACIER, LAKE, PLEASURE, SIMILES, STORM, YODELING

But we are all insane, anyway. Note the mountain-climbers.

Mark Twain's Notebook, p. 368

O Switzerland! . . . Those mountains had a soul; they thought; they spoke,—one couldn't hear it with the ears of the body, but what a voice it was!—and how real. Deep down in my memory it is sounding yet. Alp calleth unto Alp!—that stately old Scriptural wording is the right one for God's Alps and God's ocean. How puny we were in that awful presence—and how painless it was to be so; how fitting and right it seemed, and how stingless was the sense of our unspeakable insignificance. And Lord how pervading were the repose and peace and blessedness that poured out of the heart of the invisible Great Spirit of the Mountains.

Now what *is* it? There are mountains and mountains and mountains in this world—but only these take you by the heart-strings.

Mark Twain's Letters, I, p. 351

This is the right condition of mind and body . . . stepping with metaphorically uncovered head into the presence of the most impressive mountain mass that the globe can show—the Jungfrau. The stranger's first feeling, when suddenly confronted by that towering and awful apparition wrapped in its shroud of snow, is breath-taking astonishment. It is as if heaven's gates had swung open and exposed the throne.

"Switzerland, the Cradle of Liberty"
What Is Man? *and Other Essays*, p. 194

[The Matterhorn]: Its strange form, its august isolation, and its majestic unkinship with its own kind, make it,—so to speak,—the Napoleon of the mountain world. "Grand, gloomy, and peculiar," is a phrase which fits it as aptly as it fitted the great captain.

A Tramp Abroad, II, Chapt. VII, p. 99

[Albert Smith's lectures on Mont Blanc] made people as anxious to see it as if it owed them money.

Ibid., II, Chapt. XIV, p. 193

. . . every now and then some ermined monarch of the Alps swung magnificently into view for a moment, then drifted past an intervening spur and disappeared . . .

Ibid., II, Chapt. II, p. 34

The Rigi-Kulm is an imposing Alpine mass, 6,000 feet high, which stands by itself, and commands a mighty prospect of blue lakes, green valleys, and snowy mountains—a compact and magnificent picture three hundred miles in circumference. The ascent is made by rail, or horseback, or on foot, as one may prefer. I and my agent panoplied ourselves in walking costume . . .

We were soon tramping leisurely up the leafy mule-path. . . . All the circumstances were perfect—and the anticipations, too, for we should soon be enjoying, for the first time, that wonderful spectacle, an Alpine sunrise—the object of our journey . . .

At ten minutes past six we reached the Kaltbad station, where there is a spacious hotel with great verandas which command a majestic expanse of lake and mountain scenery. We were pretty well fagged out, now, but as we did not wish to miss the Alpine sunrise, we got through with our dinner as quickly as possible˙ and hurried off to bed. It was unspeakably comfortable to stretch our weary limbs between the cool, damp sheets. And how we did sleep!— for there is no opiate like Alpine pedestrianism.

In the morning we both awoke and leaped out of bed at the same instant and ran and stripped aside the window curtains; but we suffered a bitter disappointment . . .; it was already half past three in the afternoon.

We dressed sullenly and in ill spirits, each accusing the other of oversleeping. Harris said if we had brought the courier along, as we ought to have done, we should not have missed these sunrises. I said he knew very well that one of us would have had to sit up and wake the courier . . .

. . .

We climbed, and climbed; and we kept on climbing; we reached about forty summits, but there was always another one ahead. It came on to rain, and it rained in dead earnest. We were soaked through and it was bitter cold . . .

[We arrived at] the Rigi-Kulm hotel—the one that occupies the extreme summit, and whose remote little sparkle of lights we had often seen glinting high aloft among the stars from our balcony away down yonder in Lucerne . . .

. . .

Supper warmed us, and we went immediately to bed, . . .

We curled up in the clammy beds, and went to sleep without rocking. We were so sodden with fatigue that we never stirred nor turned over till the blooming blasts of the Alpine horn aroused us. It may well be imagined that we did not lose any time. We snatched a few odds and ends of clothing, cocooned ourselves in the proper red blankets, and plunged along the halls and out into the whistling wind bareheaded. We saw a tall wooden scaffolding on the very peak of the summit, a hundred yards away, and made for it. We rushed up the stairs to the top of this scaffolding, and stood there, above the vast outlying world, with hair flying and ruddy blankets waving and cracking in the fierce breeze.

"Fifteen minutes too late, at last!" said Harris, in a vexed voice. "The sun is clear above the horizon."

"No matter," I said, "it is a most magnificent spectacle, and we will see it do the rest of its rising, anyway."

In a moment we were deeply absorbed in the marvel before us, and dead to everything else. The great cloud-barred disk of the sun stood just above a limitless expanse of tossing white-caps,—so to speak,—a billowy chaos of massy mountain domes and peaks draped in imperishable snow, and flooded with an opaline glory of changing and dissolving splendors, while through rifts in a black cloud-bank above the sun, radiating lances of diamond dust shot to the zenith. The cloven valleys of the lower world swam in a tinted mist which veiled the ruggedness of their crags and ribs and ragged forests, and turned all the forbidding region into a soft and rich and sensuous paradise.

We could not speak. We could hardly breathe. We could only gaze in drunken ecstasy and drink it in. Presently Harris exclaimed:

"Why, —nation, it's going *down!*"

Perfectly true. We had missed the *morning* horn-blow, and slept all day. This was stupefying.

Harris said:

"Look here, the sun isn't the spectacle,—it's *us*,—stacked up here on top of this gallows, in these idiotic blankets, and two hundred and fifty well dressed men and women down here gawking up at us and not caring a straw whether the sun rises or sets, as long as they've got such a ridiculous spectacle as this to set down in their memorandum books. They seem to be laughing their ribs loose, and there's one girl there that appears to be going all to pieces. I never

saw such a man as you before. I think you are the very
last possibility in the way of an ass."

"What have *I* done?" I answered with heat.

"What have you done? You've got up at half past seven
in the evening to see the sun rise, that's what you've done."

"And have you done any better, I'd like to know? I
always used to get up with the lark, till I came under the
petrifying influence of your turgid intellect."

"*You* used to get up with the lark,—Oh, no doubt,—you'll
get up with the hangman one of these days. But you ought
to be ashamed to be jawing here like this, in a red blanket,
on a forty-foot scaffold on top of the Alps . . ."

And so the customary quarrel went on. When the sun
was fairly down, we slipped back to the hotel in the
charitable gloaming, and went to bed again. We had en-
countered the horn-blower on the way, and he had tried to
collect compensation, not only for announcing the sunset,
which we did see, but for the sunrise, which we had totally
missed; but we said no, we only took our solar rations on
the "European plan"—pay for what you get. He promised
to make us hear his horn in the morning, if we were alive.

He kept his word. We heard his horn and instantly got
up. It was dark and cold and wretched. As I fumbled
around for the matches, knocking things down with my
quaking hands, I wished the sun would rise in the middle
of the day, when it was warm and bright and cheerful, and
one wasn't sleepy. We proceeded to dress by the gloom
of a couple of sickly candles, but we could hardly button
anything, our hands shook so. I thought of how many
happy people there were in Europe, Asia, and America,
and everywhere, who were sleeping peacefully in their
beds, and did not have to get up and see the Rigi sunrise,—
people who did not appreciate their advantage, as like as
not, but would get up in the morning wanting more boons
of Providence. While thinking these thoughts I yawned, in
a rather ample way, and my upper teeth got hitched on
a nail over the door, and whilst I was mounting a chair to
free myself, Harris drew the window curtain and said:

"Oh, this is luck! We shan't have to go out at all,—yonder are the mountains, in full view."

That was glad news, indeed. It made us cheerful right away. One could see the grand Alpine masses dimly outlined against the black firmament, and one or two faint stars blinking through rifts in the night. Fully clothed, and wrapped in blankets, we huddled ourselves up, by the window, with lighted pipes, and fell into chat. . . . By and by a delicate, spiritual sort of effulgence spread itself by imperceptible degrees over the loftiest altitudes of the snowy wastes,—but there the effort seemed to stop. I said, presently:

"There is a hitch about this sunrise somewhere. It doesn't seem to go. What do you reckon is the matter with it?"

"I don't know. It appears to hang fire somewhere. I never saw a sunrise act like that before. Can it be that the hotel is playing anything on us?"

"Of course not. The hotel merely has a property interest in the sun, it has nothing to do with the management of it. . . . Now what can be the matter with this sunrise?"

Harris jumped up and said:

"I've got it! I know what's the matter with it! We've been looking at the place where the sun *set* last night!"

"It is perfectly true! Why couldn't you have thought of that sooner. Now we've lost another one! . . ."

A *Tramp Abroad*, I, Chapts. XXVIII, XXIX, pp. 292–309

[Mountains around Lake Lucerne]: Not snow-clad mountains, these, yet they climbed high enough toward the sky to meet the clouds and veil their foreheads in them.

Ibid., I, Chapt. XXVII, p. 279

. . . in the Black Hills, . . . Laramie Peak . . . [loomed] vast and solitary—a deep, dark rich indigo blue in hue, so portentously did the old colossus frown under his beetling brows of storm-cloud.

Roughing It, I, Chapt. IX, p. 75

[The Rocky Mountains]: These Sultans of the fastness were turbaned with tumbled volumes of cloud, which shredded away from time to time and drifted off fringed

and torn, trailing their continents of shadow after them;
and catching presently on an intercepting peak, wrapped
it about and brooded there—then shredded away again
and left the purple peak, as they had left the purple domes,
downy and white with new-laid snow.

Ibid., I, Chapt. XII, p. 103

[At Darjeeling]: Up there we found a fairly comfortable
hotel, the property of an indiscriminate and incoherent
landlord, who looks after nothing, but leaves everything to
his army of Indian servants. No, he does look after the bill
—to be just to him—and the tourist cannot do better than
follow his example. I was told by a resident that the summit
of Kinchinjunga is often hidden in the clouds, and that
sometimes a tourist has waited twenty-two days and then
been obliged to go away without a sight of it. And yet went
not disappointed; for when he got his hotel bill he recognized that he was now seeing the highest thing in the
Himalayas. But this is probably a lie.

Following the Equator, II, Chapt. XIX, p. 231

There is a high mountain I have come across that is so
cold that people who have been there find it impossible to
tell the truth. I know that's a fact—because—I've been—
there myself.

Mark Twain, Henderson, p. 104

MOUSE

We were in bed by ten, for we wanted to be up and away
on our tramp homeward with the dawn. I hung fire, but
Harris went to sleep at once. I hate a man who goes to
sleep at once; there is a sort of indefinable something about
it which is not exactly an insult, and yet is an insolence;
and one which is hard to bear, too. I lay there fretting over
this injury, and trying to go to sleep, but the harder I tried,
the wider awake I grew. I got to feeling very lonely in the
dark, with no company but an undigested dinner. My mind
got a start by and by, and began to consider the beginning
of every subject which has ever been thought of; but it
never went further than the beginning; it was touch and

go; it fled from topic to topic with a frantic speed. At the end of an hour my head was in a perfect whirl and I was dead tired, fagged out.

The fatigue was so great that it presently began to make some head against the nervous excitement; while imagining myself wide awake, I would really doze into momentary unconsciousnesses, and come suddenly out of them with a physical jerk which nearly wrenched my joints apart—the delusion of the instant being that I was tumbling backwards over a precipice. After I had fallen over eight or nine precipices and thus found out that one-half of my brain had been asleep eight or nine times without the wide-awake, hard-working other half suspecting it, the periodical unconsciousnesses began to extend their spell gradually over more of my brain-territory, and at last I sank into a drowse which grew deeper and deeper and was doubtless just on the very point of becoming a solid, blessed, dreamless stupor, when—what was that?

My dulled faculties dragged themselves partly back to life and took a receptive attitude. Now, out of an immense, a limitless distance, came a something which grew and grew, and approached, and presently was recognizable as a sound—it had rather seemed to be a feeling, before. This sound was a mile away, now—perhaps it was the murmur of a storm; and now it was nearer—not a quarter of a mile away; was it the muffled rasping and grinding of distant machinery? No, it came still nearer; was it the measured tramp of a marching troop? But it came nearer still, and still nearer—and at last it was right in the room: it was merely a mouse gnawing the woodwork. So I had held my breath all that time for such a trifle.

Well, what was done could not be helped; I would go to sleep at once and make up the lost time. That was a thoughtless thought. Without intending it—hardly knowing it—I fell to listening intently to that sound, and even unconsciously counting the strokes of the mouse's nutmeg-grater. Presently I was deriving exquisite suffering from this employment, yet maybe I could have endured it if the mouse had attended steadily to his work; but he did not do that; he stopped every now and then, and I suffered more while waiting and listening for him to begin again than I did while he was gnawing. Along at first I was mentally offering a reward of five—six—seven—ten—dollars for that mouse; but toward the last I was offering rewards which were entirely beyond my means. I close-reefed my ears,—that is to say, I bent the flaps of them down and furled them into five or six folds, and pressed them against the hearing-orifice—but it did no good: the faculty was so sharpened by nervous excitement that it was become a microphone and could hear through the overlays without trouble.

My anger grew to a frenzy. I finally did what all persons before me have done, clear back to Adam—resolved to throw something. I reached down and got my walking-shoes, then sat up in bed and listened, in order to exactly locate the noise. But I couldn't do it; it was as unlocatable as a cricket's noise; and where one thinks that that is, is always the very place where it isn't. So I presently hurled a shoe at random, and with a vicious vigor. It struck the wall over Harris's head and fell down on him; I had not imagined I could throw so far. It woke Harris, and I was glad of it until I found he was not angry; then I was sorry. He soon went to sleep again, which pleased me; but straightaway the mouse began again, which roused my temper once more. I did not want to wake Harris a second time, but the gnawing continued until I was compelled to throw the other shoe. This time I broke a mirror—there were two in the room—I got the largest one, of course. Harris woke again, but did not complain, and I was sorrier than ever. . . .

The mouse eventually retired, and by and by I was sinking to sleep, when a clock began to strike; I counted till it was done, and was about to drowse again when another clock began; I counted; then the two great Rathhaus clock angels began to send forth soft, rich, melodious blasts from their long trumpets. I had never heard anything that was so lovely, or weird, or mysterious—but when they got to blowing the quarter-hours, they seemed to me to be over-doing the thing. Every time I dropped off for a moment, a new noise woke me. Each time I woke I missed my coverlet, and had to reach down to the floor and get it again.

At last all sleepiness forsook me. I recognized the fact that I was hopelessly and permanently wide-awake. Wide-awake, and feverish and thirsty. When I had lain tossing there as long as I could endure it, it occurred to me that it would be a good idea to dress and go out in the great square and take a refreshing wash in the fountain, and smoke and reflect there until the remnant of the night was gone.

A Tramp Abroad, I, Chapt. XIII, p. 110

MOVING *See also* HOUSE

Livy appoints me to finish this; but how can a headless man perform an intelligent function? I have been bully-ragged all day by the builder, by his foreman, by the architect, by the tapestry devil who is to upholster the furniture, by the idiot who is putting down the carpets, by the scoundrel who is setting up the billiard-table (and has left the balls in New York), by the wildcat who is sodding the ground and finishing the driveway (after the sun went down), by a book *agent*, whose body is in the back yard and the coroner notified. Just think of this thing going on the whole day long, and I a man who loathes details with all his heart!

Mark Twain, a Biography, Paine, I, p. 520

I should wish the Countess to move out of Italy, out of Europe, out of the planet. I should want her bonded to retire to her place in the next world, and inform me which of the two it was, so that I could arrange for my own hereafter.

Ibid., Paine, III, p. 1213

The packing and fussing and arranging have begun, for the removal to America, and, by consequence, the peace of life is marred and its contents and satisfactions are departing. There is not much choice between a removal and a funeral; in fact, a removal is a funeral, substantially, and I am tired of attending them.

Ibid., Paine, II, p. 1110

MUGWUMP *See* POLITICS

MULE *See also* MONOTONY

Sam Clemens was a "Marion Ranger" during the Civil War. He developed a painful boil, and needed assistance to mount a small yellow mule [which he had nicknamed "Paint Brush"]. The mule refused to cross the river, so Ab Grimes took the coil of rope, hitched one end of it to his own saddle and the other end to Paint Brush's neck. Grimes was mounted on a big horse, and when he started it was necessary for Paint Brush to follow. Arriving at the farther bank, Grimes looked around, and was horrified to see that the end of the rope led down in the water with no horse and rider in view. He spurred up the bank, and the hat of Lieutenant Clemens and the ears of Paint Brush appeared.

"Ab," said Clemens, as he mopped his face, "do you know that that little devil *waded* all the way across?"

Mark Twain, a Biography, Paine, I, p. 166

Mules and donkeys and camels have appetites that anything will relieve temporarily, but nothing satisfy.

Roughing It, I, Chapt. III, p. 32

[1861]: Shortly after noon the farmers began to arrive from several directions, with mules and horses for our use, and these they lent us for as long as the war might last, which they judged would be about three months. The animals were of all sizes, all colors, and all breeds. They were mainly young and frisky, and nobody in the command could stay on them long at a time; for we were town boys, and ignorant of horsemanship. The creature that fell to my share was a very small mule, and yet so quick and active that it could throw me without difficulty; and it did this whenever I got on it. Then it would bray—stretching its neck out, laying its ears back, and spreading its jaws till you could see down to its works. It was a disagreeable animal in every way. If I took it by the bridle and tried to lead it off the grounds, it would sit down and brace back, and no one could budge it. However, I was not entirely destitute of military resources, and I did presently manage to spoil this game; for I had seen many a steamboat aground in my time, and knew a trick or two which even a grounded mule would be obliged to respect. There was a well by the corn-crib; so I substituted thirty fathom of rope for the bridle, and fetched him home with the windlass.

> "The Private History of a Campaign that Failed,"
> *The American Claimant, Etc.*, p. 241

MUMMY *See also* LAKE

Rheumatism? Why a man can't any more start a case of rheumatism in this house than he can shake an opinion out of a mummy!

> *The Gilded Age*, I, Chapt. VII, p. 91

. . . and if the Shah was not impressed he must be the offspring of a mummy.

> "O'Shah,"
> *Europe and Elsewhere*, p. 52

MURDER *See* IRISHMEN, ASSASSINATION, KILLING

MUSIC *See also* CRITIC, ECSTASY, JUBILEE, LAKE, MINSTRELS, OPERA, SINGING, VOICE, WORK

It is 2:30 in the morning and I am writing because I can't sleep. I can't sleep because a professional pianist is coming tomorrow *to play for me*. My God! I wouldn't allow Paderewski or Gabrilowitsch to do that. I would rather have a leg amputated.

> *Mark Twain, a Biography*, Paine, III, p. 1561

[General Sickles'] talk is full of interest and bristling with points, but as there are no emphases scattered through it anywhere, and as there is no animation in it, it soon becomes oppressive by its monotony and it makes the listeners drowsy. . . . The late Bill Nye once said, "I have been told that Wagner's music is better than it sounds." That felicitous description of a something which so many people have tried to describe, and couldn't, does seem to fit the general's manner of speech exactly. His talk is much better than it is.

Mark Twain's Autobiography, Paine, I, p. 337

We often feel sad in the presence of music without words; and often more than that in the presence of music without music.

More Maxims of Mark, p. 14

The choir hurled its soul into a "voluntary"—one of those things where the melodeon pumps, and strains, and groans and wails a bit, and then the soprano pipes a reedy solo, the alto drops in a little after, then the bass bursts in, then the pealing tenor—then a wild chase, one trampling on the heels of the other—then a grand discordant confusion that sets one's teeth on edge—and finally a triumphant "Oh, praise the L-o-r-d!" in a unison of unutterable anguish— and the crime is consummated. It was Herod's slaughter set to music.

My Father • Mark Twain, Clara Clemens, p. 10

Tunes are good remembrancers.

Ibid., p. 23

A Southerner talks music.

Life on the Mississippi, Chapt. XLIV, p. 332

. . . Then the fiddlers laid themselves out, and went at it like forty millions of wood sawyers at two dollars and a half a cord.

The Adventures of Thomas Jefferson Snodgrass, p. 6

[At Baden-Baden]: There was a vast crowd in the public grounds that night to hear the band play the "Fremersberg" . . .

I suppose the Fremersberg is very low-grade music; I know, indeed, that it *must* be low-grade music, because it so delighted me, warmed me, moved me, stirred me, uplifted me, enraptured me, that I was full of cry all the time, and mad with enthusiasm. My soul had never had such a scouring out since I was born . . . it seemed to me that nothing but the very lowest of low-grade music *could* be so divinely beautiful. The great crowd which the Fremersberg had called out was another evidence that it was low-grade music; for only the few are educated up to a point where high-grade music gives pleasure. I have never heard enough classic music to be able to enjoy it. I dislike the opera because I want to love it and can't.

I suppose there are two kinds of music,—one kind which one feels, just as an oyster might, and another sort which requires a higher faculty, a faculty which must be assisted and developed by teaching. Yet if base music gives certain of us wings, why should we want any other? But we do. We want it because the higher and better like it. But we want it without giving it the necessary time and trouble; so we climb into that upper tier, that dress circle, by a lie; we *pretend* we like it. I know several of that sort of people —and I propose to be one of them myself when I get home with my fine European education.

A *Tramp Abroad,* I, Chapt. XXIV, p. 241

So then the gracious Queen imagined and contrived that simple and witching costume [for Joan of Arc] . . . which I cannot think of even now in my dull age without being moved just as rhythmical and exquisite music moves one; for *that* was music, that dress—that is what it was—music that one saw with the eyes and felt in the heart. Yes, she was a poem, she was a dream, she was a spirit when she was clothed in that.

Personal Recollections of Joan of Arc,
I, Book II, Chapt. VI, p. 162

Ah, that shows you the power of music, that magician of magicians, who lifts his wand and says his mysterious word and all things real pass away and the phantoms of your mind walk before you clothed in flesh.

Ibid., II, Book II, Chapt. XXXVI, p. 67

And the minute the words were out of his mouth somebody over in the crowd struck up the doxolojer, and everybody joined in with all their might, and it just warmed you up and made you feel as good as church letting out. Music *is* a good thing; and after all that soul-butter and hogwash I never see it freshen up things so, and sound so honest and bully.

The Adventures of Huckleberry Finn,
Chapt. XXV, p. 219

There is a villain over the way, yonder, who has been playing "Get out of the Wilderness" on a flute . . . sometimes fast, sometimes slow, and always skipping the first note in the second bar—skipping it so uniformly that I have got to waiting and painfully looking out for it latterly. Human nature cannot stand this sort of torture. I wish his funeral was to come off at half-past eleven o'clock to-morrow and I had nothing to do. I would attend it.

Letters from the Sandwich Islands, p. 86

The early twilight of a Sunday evening in Hamilton, Bermuda, is an alluring time. There is just enough of whispering breeze, fragrance of flowers, and sense of repose to raise one's thoughts heavenward; and just enough amateur piano music to keep him reminded of the other place. There are many venerable pianos in Hamilton, and they all play at twilight. Age enlarges and enriches the powers of some musical instruments—notably those of the violin—but it seems to set a piano's teeth on edge. Most of the music in vogue there is the same that those pianos prattled in their innocent infancy; and there is something very pathetic about it when they go over it now, in their asthmatic second childhood, dropping a note here and there, where a tooth is gone.

"Rambling Notes of an Idle Excursion,"
Tom Sawyer Abroad, Etc., p. 290

I have attended operas, whenever I could not help it, for fourteen years now; I am sure I know of no agony comparable to the listening to an unfamiliar opera. I am enchanted with the airs of "Trovatore" and other old operas which the hand-organ and the music-box have made entirely familiar to my ear. I am carried away with delightful enthusiasm when they are sung at the opera. But oh, how far between they are! And what long, arid, heartbreaking and headaching "between-times" of that sort of intense but incoherent noise which always so reminds me of the time the orphan asylum burned down.

Mark Twain, a Biography, Paine, II, p. 624

[Told by Mark Twain's daughter, Clara]: When we were children, Susy and I had spent much of our leisure time studying music. . . . Father gave us performances of darky songs which he sang while he accompanied himself on the piano. He had a curious way of playing with his fingers stretched straight out over the keys, so that each time he played a chord it seemed as if a miracle had happened. He always cleared his throat many times before he began, and then sang quite loudly with his head thrown back and his eyes fixed on the ceiling. We thought he looked very "cute." He interrupted himself constantly to correct wrong chords, but usually in vain, for he could not find the right ones. Then, with some display of temper he would change to another song. His two favorites were "Swing Low, Sweet Chariot," and "Go Chain the Lion Down," which he rendered in a truly impressive way, despite the fact that musically certain lacks were noticeable. When he sang "Rise and Shine and Give God the Glory, Glory," he gave out so much fervor of spirit that one could never forget it.

My Father • Mark Twain, Clara Clemens, p. 188

If it please your neighbor to break the sacred calm of night with the snorting of an unholy trombone, it is your duty to put up with his wretched music and your privilege to pity him for the unhappy instinct that moves him to delight in such discordant sounds. I did not always think thus: This consideration for musical amateurs was born of certain disagreeable personal experiences that once followed the development of a like instinct in myself. Now this infidel over the way, who is learning to play on the trombone, and the slowness of whose progress is almost miraculous, goes on with his harrowing work every night, uncursed by me, but tenderly pitied. Ten years ago, for the same offense, I would have set fire to his house. At that time I was a prey to an amateur violinist for two or three weeks, and the sufferings I endured at his hands are inconceivable. He played "Old Dan Tucker," and he never played anything else; but he performed that so badly that he could throw me into fits with it if I were awake, or into a nightmare if I were asleep. As long as he confined himself to "Dan Tucker" though, I bore with him and abstained from violence; but when he projected a fresh outrage, and tried to do "Sweet Home," I went over and burnt him out. My next assailant was a wretch who felt a call to play the clarionet. He only played the scale, however, with his distressing instrument, and I let him run the length of his tether also; but finally, when he branched out into a ghastly tune, I felt my reason deserting me under the exquisite torture, and I sallied forth and burnt him out likewise. During the next two years I burnt out an amateur cornet player, a bugler, a bassoon-sophomore, and a barbarian whose talents ran in the base-drum line.

I would certainly have scorched this trombone man if he had moved into my neighborhood in those days. But as I said before, I leave him to his own destruction now, because I have had experience as an amateur myself, and I feel nothing but compassion for that kind of people. Besides, I have learned that there lies dormant in the souls of all men a penchant for some particular musical instrument, and an unsuspected yearning to learn to play on it, that are bound to wake up and demand attention some day. Therefore, you who rail at such as disturb your slumbers with unsuccessful and demoralizing attempts to subjugate a fiddle, beware! for sooner or later your own time will come. . . .

After a long immunity from the dreadful insanity that moves a man to become a musician in defiance of the will of God that he should confine himself to sawing wood, I finally fell a victim to the instrument that they call the accordeon. At this day I hate that contrivance as fervently as any man can, but at the time I speak of I suddenly acquired a disgusting and idolatrous affection for it. I got one of powerful capacity, and learned to play "Auld Lang Syne" on it. It seems to me, now, that I must have been gifted

with a sort of inspiration to be enabled, in the state of
ignorance in which I then was, to select out of the whole
range of musical composition the one solitary tune that
sounds vilest and most distressing on the accordeon. I do
not suppose there is another tune in the world with which
I could have afflicted so much anguish upon my race as I
did with that one during my short musical career.

After I had been playing "Lang Syne" about a week, I
had the vanity to think I could improve the original melody,
and I set about adding some little flourishes and variations
to it, but with rather indifferent success, I suppose, as it
brought my landlady into my presence with an expression
about her of being opposed to such desperate enterprises.
Said she, "Do you know any other tune but that, Mr.
Twain?" I told her, meekly, that I did not. "Well, then,"
said she, "stick to it just as it is; don't put any variations to
it, because it's rough enough on the boarders the way it
is now."

The fact is . . . it was altogether too rough; half of them
left, and the other half would have followed, but Mrs.
Jones saved them by discharging me from the premises.

I only staid one night at my next lodging-house. Mrs.
Smith was after me early in the morning. . . . I could see
that [she] took no delight in music, and I moved to Mrs.
Brown's.

For three nights in succession I gave my new neighbors
"Auld Lang Syne," plain and unadulterated, save by a few
discords that rather improved the general effect than otherwise. But the first time I tried the variations the boarders
mutinied. I never did find anybody that would stand those
variations. I was very well satisfied with my efforts in that
house, however, and I left it without any regrets; I drove
one boarder as mad as a March hare, and another one tried
to scalp his mother. . . .

I went to board at Mrs. Murphy's. . . . The very first
time I struck up the variations, a haggard, care-worn, cadaverous old man walked into my room and stood beaming

upon me a smile of ineffable happiness. Then he placed his hand upon my head, and looking devoutly aloft, he said with feeling unction, and in a voice trembling with emotion, "God bless you, young man! God bless you! For you have done that for me which is beyond all praise. For years I have suffered from an incurable disease, and knowing my doom was sealed and that I must die, I have striven with all my power to resign myself to my fate, but in vain—the love of life was too strong within me. But heaven bless you, my benefactor! for since I heard you play that tune and those variations, I do not want to live any longer—I am entirely resigned—I am willing to die—in fact, I am anxious to die."

. . .

My passion for the accordeon finally spent itself and died out, and I was glad when I found myself free from its unwholesome influence. While the fever was upon me, I was a living, breathing calamity wherever I went, and desolation and disaster followed in my wake . . . I did incalculable harm . . . and yet to atone for it all, I did but one single blessed act, in making that weary old man willing to go to his long home. Still, I derived some little benefit from that accordeon; for while I continued to practice on it, I never had to pay any board—landlords were always willing to compromise, on my leaving before the month was up.

"A Touching Story of George Washington's Boyhood,"
The Celebrated Jumping Frog of Calaveras County, p. 132

Cousin Susy Warner . . . played that other deep, rich, noble Beethoven piece—the one where all along . . . half a dozen of the bass notes keep rolling back down-stairs a little way—only to the first landing; and then get up again and roll down again, and are the darling of the piece and the charm of it.

Love Letters of Mark Twain, p. 252

When Clara Kellogg comes here I will drink four bottles of lager and then sing . . . for her—for I never can get any ease or expression into music without a good backing of inspiration. She will admire that song, then.

Mark Twain-Howells Letters, I, p. 104

There's no music like the bugle to stir the blood, in the still solemnity of the morning twilight, with the dim plain stretching away to nothing and the spectral mountains slumbering against the sky.

"A Horse's Tale,"
The Mysterious Stranger, p. 183

I have a strong liking for music and a decided preference for sombre and solemn music over the other kinds. . . .

A man with either humor *or* music in him is half-good and half-bad; he must lack both, to be wholly bad, he must contain both to be wholly good, perfectly good, unqualifiedly good. I contain both.

From an original letter in the Berg Collection, New York Public Library

MYSTERY   *See also* MADNESS

Some things you *can't* find out; but you will never know you can't by guessing and supposing; no, you have to be patient and go on experimenting until you find out that you can't find out. And it is delightful to have it that way, it makes the world so interesting. If there wasn't anything to find out, it would be dull. Even trying to find out and not finding out is just as interesting as trying to find out and finding out, and I don't know but more so.

"Eve's Diary,"
The $30,000 Bequest, p. 306

N

NAKEDNESS   *See* GRANT, U. S., MONARCHY

NAME   *See also* ADAM, EXPERIENCE, FORGETFULNESS, LET-
TERS, PARIS, PUNISHMENT, SMITH, SNODGRASS, TWAIN,
MARK

There are three little rabbits and they are about the size
of mice. . . . I have named them Dorothy. One name is
enough for all of them. They are so little. (1907)

Enchantment, p. 78

Adam [is] a man who comes down to us without a stain
upon his name, unless it was a stain to take one apple when
most of us would have taken the whole crop. I stand up
for him on account of his sterling private virtues, and not
because he happens to be a connection of mine.

"On Adam,"

Mark Twain's Speeches (1923), p. 97

[Dunlap] did the bravest thing that can be imagined—a
thing to make one shiver when one remembers how the
world is given to resenting shams and affectations: he began
to write his name so: *d'Un Lap.*

"A Private History of a Campaign That Failed,"

The American Claimant, Etc., p. 237

What remarkable names those diseases have! It makes me envious of the man that has them all.

> "Osteopathy,"
> *Mark Twain's Speeches* (1923), p. 232

Hang these names . . . they warp my jaw.

> "A Horse's Tale,"
> *The Mysterious Stranger, Etc.*, p. 192

The minute we get reconciled to a person, how willing we are to throw aside little needless punctilios and pronounce his name right.

> "The Shrine of St. Wagner,"
> *What Is Man? and Other Essays*, p. 216

[From a Quintus Curtius Snodgrass letter]:

. . . it must be intensely annoying to the spirit of a defunct warrior to know that, after having laid down his life for fame, his name has been misspelt in the papers.

> *The Twainian*, June 1942, p. 1

The name "Mark Twain," has proven the greatest *nom de plume* ever chosen. . . .

> *Mark Twain, a Biography*, Paine, I, p. 222

Names are not always what they seem. The common Welsh name Bzjxxllwcp is pronounced Jackson.

> "Pudd'nhead Wilson's New Calendar,"
> *Following the Equator*, I, Chapt. XXXVI, p. 339

The great god Vishnu has 108 . . . special [names]—108 peculiarly holy ones—names just for Sunday use only. I learned the whole of Vishnu's 108 by heart once, but they wouldn't stay; I don't remember any of them now but John W.

> *Ibid.*, II, Chapt. III, p. 35

We called him Barney for short. We couldn't use his real name, there wasn't time.

> *Ibid.*, II, Chapt. VIII, p. 90

NARRATIVE

Most people who have the narrative gift—that great and rare endowment—have with it the defect of telling their choice things over the same way every time, and this in-

jures them and causes them to sound stale and wearisome
after several repetitions. . . .

Personal Recollections of Joan of Arc,
I, Book II, Chapt. VII, p. 172

. . . I have made several attempts to do [my] autobiography in one way or another with a pen, but the result
was not satisfactory; it was too literary. With the pen in
one's hand, narrative is a difficult art; narrative should flow
as flows the brook down through the hills and the leafy
woodlands, its course changed by every bowlder it comes
across and by every grass-clad gravelly spur that projects
into its path; its surface broken, but its course not stayed
by rocks and gravel on the bottom in the shoal places; a
brook that never goes straight for a minute, but *goes*, and
goes briskly, sometimes ungrammatically, and sometimes
fetching a horseshoe three-quarters of a mile around, and
at the end of the circuit flowing within a yard of the path
it traversed an hour before; but always *going*, and always
following at least one law, always loyal to that law, the law
of the *narrative, which has no law*.

With a pen in hand the narrative stream is a canal; it
moves slowly, smoothly, decorously, sleepily, it has no
blemish except that it is all blemish. It is too literary, too
prim, too nice; the gait and style and movement are not
suited to narrative. That canal stream is always reflecting;
it is its nature, it can't help it. Its slick shiny surface is
interested in everything it passes along the banks—cows,
foliage, flowers, everything. And so it wastes a lot of time
in reflections.

Mark Twain's Autobiography, Paine, I, p. 237

NATION *See also* LOYALTY, MASSES, MOTTO, PATRIOTISM,
WAGES

Nations do not *think*, they only *feel*. They get their feelings at second hand through their temperaments, not their
brains. A nation can be brought—by force of circumstances,
not argument—to reconcile itself to *any kind of government
or religion that can be devised;* in time it will fit itself to

the required conditions; later, it will prefer them and will fiercely fight for them.

> *What Is Man? and Other Essays*, p. 108

A nation is only an individual multiplied.

> "The Turning-Point of My Life,"
> *Ibid.*, p. 138

A foreigner can photograph the exteriors of a nation, but I think that is as far as he can get. No foreigner can report its interior—its soul, its life, its speech, its thought.

> "What Paul Bourget Thinks of Us,"
> *Literary Essays*, p. 145

The English, the arrogant nation. The Americans the material nation, the Germans the patient nation, the Russians the unclassifiable nation, the French the volatile nation, the Scotch the thrifty nation, the Italians the hot-blooded kind-hearted nation, the Irish the nation of chaste women.

> *Mark Twain's Notebook*, p. 185

[In Switzerland]: For the struggle here throughout the centuries has not been in the interest of any private family, or any church, but in the interest of the whole body of the nation, and for shelter and protection of all forms of belief.

> "Switzerland, the Cradle of Liberty,"
> *What Is Man? and Other Essays*, p. 194

NATIONALITY *See* NATURE, PAINTING

NATURE *See also* COMPENSATION, HOPE, LAW, PLEDGE, PROVIDENCE

There are some natures which never grow large enough to speak out and say a bad act *is* a bad act, until they have inquired into the politics or the nationality of the man who did it.

> *The Galaxy Magazine*, May 1870, p. 726

Nature makes the locust with an appetite for crops; man would have made him with an appetite for sand—I mean a man with the least little bit of common sense.

> *Mark Twain's Notebook*, p. 347

Architects cannot teach nature anything.

"Memorable Midnight Experience,"
Europe and Elsewhere, p. 4

The man who is born stingy can be taught to give liberally—with his hands; but not with his heart. The man born kind and compassionate can have that disposition crushed down out of sight by embittering experience; but if it were an organ the postmortem would find it still in his corpse.

Christian Science, Book II, Chapt. X, p. 262

[The mob] had but obeyed a law of our nature—an irresistible law—to enjoy and applaud a spirited and promptly delivered retort, no matter who makes it.

Personal Recollections of Joan of Arc,
II, Book III, Chapt. XX, p. 275

We speak of nature; it is folly; there is no such thing as nature; what we call by that misleading name is merely heredity and training. We have no thoughts of our own; no opinions of our own; they are transmitted to us, trained into us. All that is original in us, and therefore fairly creditable or discreditable to us, can be covered up and hidden by the point of a cambric needle, all the rest being atoms contributed by, and inherited from, a procession of ancestors that stretches back a billion years to the Adam-clam or grasshopper or monkey from whom our race has been so tediously and ostentatiously and unprofitably developed. And as for me, all that I think about in this plodding sad pilgrimage, this pathetic drift between the eternities, is to look out and humbly live a pure and high and blameless life, and save that one microscopic atom in me that is truly *me:* the rest may land in Sheol and welcome for all I care.

A Connecticut Yankee in King Arthur's Court,
Chapt. XVIII, p. 144

It is strange and fine—Nature's lavish generosities to her creatures. At least to all of them except man. For those that fly she has provided a home that is nobly spacious—a home which is forty miles deep and envelopes the whole globe, and has not an obstruction in it. For those that swim she has provided a more than imperial domain—a domain which is miles deep and covers four-fifths of the globe. But as for man, she has cut him off with the mere odds and ends of the creation. She has given him the thin skin, the meager skin which is stretched over the remaining one-fifth—the naked bones stick up through it in most places. On the one-half of this domain he can raise snow, ice, sand, rocks, and nothing else. So the valuable part of his inheritance really consists of but a single fifth of the family estate; and out of it he has to grub hard to get enough to keep him alive and provide kings and soldiers and powder to extend the blessings of civilization with. Yet man, in his simplicity and complacency and inability to cipher, thinks Nature regards him as the important member of the family—in fact, her favorite. Surely, it must occur to even his dull head, sometimes, that she has a curious way of showing it.

Following the Equator, II, Chapt. XXVI, p. 311

If one desires to be stirred by a poem of nature wrought in the happily commingled graces of picturesque rocks, glimpsed distances, foliage, color, shifting lights and shadows, and falling water, that tears almost come into his eyes so potent is the charm exerted, he need not go away from America to enjoy such an experience. The Rainbow Fall, in Watkins Glen (N.Y.) . . . is an example.

Roughing It, II, Chapt. XXXV, p. 310

Nature knows no indecencies; man invents them.

Mark Twain's Notebook, p. 288

NECESSITY *See also* CIVILIZATION

Necessity is the mother of "taking chances."

Roughing It, II, Chapt. I

NEEDY

How far should a community go in giving assistance to the needy? It seems to me that if you do too much for them you make them lazy . . . the community is upsetting one of the most essential of all human habits, the habit of looking out for yourself.

Mark Twain and I, p. 31

NEGRO   *See also* BIBLE, EPITAPH, MINSTRELS

He was always the gratefullest nigger I ever see, for any little thing you done for him. He was only nigger outside; inside he was as white as you be.

Tom Sawyer Abroad, Etc., Chapt. XI, p. 113

We had a little slave boy . . . there in Hannibal. . . . He was a cheery spirit, innocent and gentle, and the noisiest creature that ever was, perhaps. All day long he was singing, whistling, yelling, whooping, laughing—it was maddening, devastating, unendurable. At last, one day, I lost my temper, and went raging to my mother and said Sandy had been singing for an hour without a single break, and I couldn't stand it, and *wouldn't* she please shut him up. The tears came into her eyes and her lip trembled and she said . . .:

"Poor thing, when he sings it shows that he is not remembering, and that comforts me; but when he is still I am afraid he is thinking, and I cannot bear it. He will never see his mother again; if he can sing, I must not hinder it, but be thankful for it. If you were older, you would understand me; then that friendless child's noise would make you glad."

Mark Twain's Autobiography, Paine, I, p. 101

Mark Twain paid two colored students' way through college. He considered this as partial reparation "due from every white man to every black man."

Mark Twain, a Biography, Paine, II, p. 701

In the South Mark Twain once met an exceedingly old "darky" who claimed to have crossed the Delaware with Washington.

"Were you with Washington," asked Mark Twain mischievously, "when he took that hack at the cherry tree?"

This was a poser for the old darky; his pride was appealed to, his character was at stake. After an awkward hesitation. . . . "Lord, boss, I was dar. In cose I was. I was with Marse George at dat very time. In fac—I done druv dat hack myself."|

> *Mark Twain,* Henderson, p. 187

Why not educate the negroes more zealously and above all give them a *good* example?

. . .

In the case of the negro. . . . The majority of us do not like his features, or his color, and we forget to notice that his heart is often a damned sight better than ours.

> *My Husband · Gabrilowitsch,* Clara Clemens, p. 16

[The last word on slavery]:
". . . We blowed out a cylinder-head."
"Good gracious! Anybody hurt?"
"No'm. Killed a nigger."
"Well, it's lucky; because sometimes people do get hurt."

> *The Adventures of Huckleberry Finn,*
> Chapt. XXXII, p. 287

NERVOUSNESS
Our guide fidgeted about as if he had swallowed a spring mattress.

> *The Innocents Abroad,* I, Chapt. XXVII, p. 369

NEVADA *See* BEAUTY, BILLIARDS, CLIMATE, COLD, HAT, LAKE, MINING, MONOTONY, MOSQUITO, NIGHT, SAGE-BRUSH, TUNNEL, WATER

Some people are malicious enough to think that if the devil were set at liberty and told to confine himself to Nevada Territory, he would come . . . and look sadly around awhile, and then get homesick and go back to hell again.

> *Mark Twain, a Biography,* Paine, I, p. 190

To attempt a portrayal of that era and that land (Nevada) and leave out the blood and carnage would be like portraying Mormondom and leaving out polygamy.

> *Roughing It,* II, p. 77

NEW DEAL *See* GOVERNMENT

NEW ENGLAND *See also* INDEPENDENCE, PILGRIMS, SCEN-
ERY, WEATHER

Now as to the *size* of the weather in New England—
lengthways, I mean. It is utterly disproportioned to the size
of that little country. Half the time, when it is packed as
full as it can stick, you will see that New England weather
sticking out beyond the edges and projecting around hundreds and hundreds of miles over the neighboring States.
She can't hold a tenth part of her weather. You can see
cracks all about where she has strained herself trying to do
it. I could speak volumes about the inhuman perversity of
the New England weather, but I will give but a single specimen. I like to hear rain on a tin roof. So I covered part of
my roof with tin, with an eye to that luxury. Well, sir, do
you think it ever rains on that tin? No, sir; skips it every
time.

"The Weather,"
Mark Twain's Speeches (1923), p. 56

I heard . . . many . . . unhappy provincialisms which
warned me that many New England people have gone
westward and are going to mar the ancient purity of the
Missourian dialect if somebody don't put a stop to it.

"Notable Things in St. Louis,"
Mark Twain's Travels with Mr. Brown, p. 142

NEW JERSEY *See* MINING

NEW ORLEANS *See also* NEWSPAPER

But the people cannot have wells, and so they take rain-
water. Neither can they conveniently have cellars or graves,
the town being built upon "made ground"; so they do without both, and few of the living complain, and none of the
others.

Life on the Mississippi, Chapt. XLI, p. 318

NEW YORK CITY and NEW YORK STATE *See also*
MORALS, NATURE, OLD MASTERS, OSTEOPATHY

When your foreigner makes disagreeable comments on New York by daylight, float him down the river at night. [1900]

"Municipal Government,"
Mark Twain's Speeches (1910), p. 124

. . . when the [steam-ship] passenger lands on our side he lands on the American side of the river, not in the provinces. As a very learned man said . . .: "When we land a passenger on the American side there's nothing betwixt him and his hotel but hell and the hackman."

"An Undelivered Speech,"
Ibid. (1923), p. 166

There is something about this ceaseless buzz, and hurry, and bustle, that keeps a stranger in a state of unwholesome excitement all the time, and makes him restless and uneasy, and saps from him all capacity to enjoy anything or take a strong interest in any matter whatever—a something which impels him to try to do everything, and yet permits him to do nothing. He is a boy in a candy-shop—could choose quickly if there were but one kind of candy, but is hopelessly undetermined in the midst of a hundred kinds. A stranger feels unsatisfied, here, a good part of the time.

"New York,"
Mark Twain's Travels with Mr. Brown, p. 260

All men in New York insult you—there seem to be no exceptions. There are exceptions of course—*have* been—but they are probably dead. I am speaking of all persons there who are clothed in a little brief authority. [1885]

Mark Twain's Notebook, p. 185

NEW ZEALAND *See* KNOWLEDGE, RAILROAD

NEWSPAPER *See also* ASSASSINATION, COMPLIMENT, EDITOR, GERMAN LANGUAGE, HUMAN RACE, INTEREST, INTERVIEW, KNOWLEDGE, LIE, NAME, PRAYER, PRESS, PRINTING, REPUTATION, REVERENCE, SPELLING, STUPIDITY

Together, William Swinton and I invented a scheme for our mutual sustenance; we became the fathers and originators of what is a common feature in the newspaper world now, the syndicate. We became the old original first Newspaper Syndicate on the planet . . . We had twelve journals on our list; they were all weeklies, all obscure and poor and all scattered far away among the back settlements. It was a proud thing for those little newspapers to have a Washington correspondence, and a fortunate thing for us . . . Each of the twelve took two letters a week from us, at a dollar per letter; each of us wrote one letter per week, and sent off six duplicates of it to these benefactors, thus acquiring twenty-four dollars a week to live on, which was all we needed in our cheap and humble quarters.

Mark Twain in Eruption, p. 352

News is history in its first and best form, its vivid and fascinating form, and . . . history is the pale and tranquil reflection of it.

Mark Twain's Autobiography, Paine, I, p. 326

The grand stand was well filled with the beauty and the chivalry of New Orleans. That phrase is not original with me. It is the Southern reporter's. He has used it for two generations. He uses it twenty times, or twenty thousand times a day, or a million times a day—according to the exigencies. He is obliged to use it a million times a day, if he have occasion to speak of respectable men and women that often; for he has no other phrase for such service except that single one. He never tires of it; it always has a fine sound to him. There is a kind of swell, medieval bulliness and tinsel about it that pleases his gaudy, barbaric soul. If he had been in Palestine in the early times, we should have had no reference to "much people" out of him. No, he would have said "the beauty and the chivalry of Galilee" assembled to hear the Sermon on the Mount. . . .

The New Orleans . . . average correspondent . . . knows other methods of handling statistics. He just throws off all restraint and wallows in them:

"On Saturday, early in the morning, the beauty of the place graced our cabin, and proud of her fair freight the gallant boat glided up the bayou."

Twenty-two words to say the ladies came aboard and the boat shoved out up the creek, is a clean waste of ten good words, and is also destructive of compactness of statement.

The trouble with the Southern reporter is—Women. They unsettle him; they throw him off his balance. He is plain, and sensible, and satisfactory, until woman heaves in sight. Then he goes all to pieces; his mind totters, becomes flowery and idiotic. From reading the above extract, you would imagine that this student of Sir Walter Scott is an apprentice and knows next to nothing about handling a pen.

Life on the Mississippi, Chapt. XLV, p. 340

It seems to me that just in the ratio that our newspapers increase, our morals decay. The more newspapers the worse morals. Where we have one newspaper that does good, I think we have fifty that do harm. We *ought* to look upon the establishment of a newspaper of the average pattern in a virtuous village as a calamity.

"License of the Press,"
Mark Twain's Speeches (1923), p. 47

. . . if during fifty years the institutions of the old world could be exposed to the fire of a flouting and scoffing press like ours, monarchy and its attendant crimes would disappear from Christendom.

The American Claimant, Etc., Chapt. X, p. 79

. . . and so the paper came out without any novel in it. It was but a feeble, struggling, stupid journal, and the absence of the novel probably shook public confidence; at any rate, before the first side of the next issue went to press, the *Weekly Occidental* died as peacefully as an infant.

An effort was made to resurrect it, with the proposed advantage of a telling new title, and Mr. F. said that *The Phenix* would be just the name for it, because it would give the idea of a resurrection from its dead ashes in a new and undreamed of condition of splendor; but some low-priced smarty on one of the dailies suggested that we call it the

Lazarus; and inasmuch as the people were not profound in Scriptural matters, but thought the resurrected Lazarus and the dilapidated mendicant that begged in the rich man's gateway were one and the same person, the name became the laughing-stock of the town, and killed the paper for good and all.

> *Roughing It,* II, Chapt. X, p. 105

He was as shy as a newspaper is when referring to its own merits.

> "Pudd'nhead Wilson's New Calendar,"
> *Following the Equator,* II, Chapt. VI, p. 80

The old Saw says, "Let a sleeping dog lie." Right. Still when there is much at stake it is better to get a newspaper to do it.

> "Pudd'nhead Wilson's New Calendar,"
> *Ibid.,* II, Chapt. VIII, p. 87

[528 A.D.]: I dropped a nickel out of the window and got my paper; the Adam-newsboy of the world went around the corner to get my change; is around the corner yet.

> *A Connecticut Yankee in King Arthur's Court,*
> Chapt. XXVI, p. 235

There is an abundance of newspapers in Berlin, and there was also a newsboy, but he died.

> "The German Chicago,"
> *The American Claimant, Etc.,* p. 507

. . . the most important function of a public journal in any country [is] the propagating of national feeling and pride in the national name—the keeping the people in love with *their* country and *its* institutions, and shielded from the allurements of alien and inimical systems.

> *Ibid.,* Chapt. X, p. 78

[Mark Twain is offended by inaccuracies in a newspaper article about him]: They put words into my mouth. I'd rather they had put street sweepings.

> *Mark Twain, the Man and His Work,*
> Wagenknecht, p. 67

I would recognize the fact that for Gen. Grant to sue the [*New York*] *"World"* would be an enormously valuable advertisement for that daily issue of unmedicated closet-paper.

Mark Twain, Business Man, Webster, p. 323

NIAGARA FALLS *See also* READER

The hack fares are so much higher than the Falls that the Falls appear insignificant.

Hartford, *Connecticut Times,* Sept. 7, 1869

I had to visit Niagara fifteen times before I succeeded in getting my imaginary Falls gauged to the actuality and could begin to sanely and wholesomely wonder at them for what they were, not what I had expected them to be. When I first approached them it was with my face lifted toward the sky, for I thought I was going to see an Atlantic ocean pouring down thence, over cloud-vexed Himalayan heights, a sea-green wall of water sixty miles front and six miles high, and so, when the toy reality came suddenly into view—that beruffled little wet apron hanging out to dry— the shock was too much for me, and I fell with a dull thud.

Yet slowly, surely, steadily, in the course of my fifteen visits, the proportions adjusted themselves to the facts, and I came at last to realize that a water-fall a hundred and sixty-five feet high and a quarter of a mile wide was an impressive thing. It was not a dipperful to my vanished great vision, but it would answer.

Following the Equator, II, Chapt. XXIII, p. 275

You can descend a staircase here a hundred and fifty feet down, and stand at the edge of the water. After you have done it, you will wonder why you did it; but you will then be too late.

. . .

On the Canada side you drive along the chasm between long ranks of photographers standing guard behind their cameras, ready to make an ostentatious frontispiece of you . . . and a diminished and unimportant background of sublime Niagara; and a great many people *have* the incredible effrontery or the native depravity to aid and abet this sort of crime.

There is no actual harm in making Niagara a background whereon to display one's marvelous insignificance in a good strong light, but it requires a sort of superhuman self-complacency to enable one to do it.

"Niagara,"
Sketches New and Old, p. 75

[Adam]: "I was thinking about the Falls, and I said to myself, 'How wonderful it is to see that vast body of water tumble down there!' Then in an instant a bright thought flashed into my head, and I let it fly, saying, 'It would be a deal more wonderful to see it tumble *up* there!'—and I was just about to kill myself with laughing at it when all nature broke loose in war . . . and I had to flee for my life. 'There,' [Eve] said in triumph, 'that is just it; the Serpent mentioned that very jest, and called it the First Chestnut, and said it was coeval with the creation.' Alas, I am indeed to blame. Would that I were not witty . . ."

"Extracts from Adam's Diary,"
The Man That Corrupted Hadleyburg, Etc., p. 268

NIGHT   *See also* PILOTING, SIMILES

[At Carson City, Nevada]: Night came . . . not with a lingering twilight, but with a sudden shutting down like a cellar door.

Roughing It, I, Chapt. XXXI, p. 252

NOAH   *See also* BED, PROVIDENCE, SHIP

. . . such is the human race. Often it does seem such a pity that Noah and his party did not miss the boat.

Christian Science, Book II, Chapt. VII, p. 200

We spoke to Noah about [the dinosaurs]; he colored and changed the subject. Being brought back to it—and pressed a little—he confessed that in the matter of stocking the Ark the stipulations had not been carried out with absolute strictness—that is, in minor details, unessentials. There were some irregularities. He said the boys were to blame for this—the boys mainly, his own fatherly indulgence partly.

They were in the giddy heyday of their youth at the time, the happy springtime of life; their hundred years sat upon them lightly, and—well, he had once been a boy himself, and he had not the heart to be too exacting with them. And so—well, they did things they shouldn't have done, and he—to be candid, he winked. But on the whole they did pretty faithful work, considering their age. They collected and stowed a good share of the really useful animals; and also, when Noah was not watching, a multitude of useless ones, such as flies, mosquitoes, snakes, and so on, but they did certainly leave ashore a good many creatures which might possibly have had value some time or other, in the course of time. Mainly these were vast saurians a hundred feet long, and monstrous mammals, such as the megatherium and that sort, and there was really some excuse for leaving them behind, for two reasons: (1) it was manifest that some time or other they would be needed as fossils for museums and (2) there had been a miscalculation, the Ark was smaller than it should have been and so there wasn't room for those creatures.

. . . As for the dinosaur—But Noah's conscience was easy; it was not named in his cargo list and he and the boys were not aware that there was such a creature. He said he could not blame himself for not knowing about the dinosaur, because it was an American animal, and America had not then been discovered.

"Adam's Soliloquy,"
Europe and Elsewhere, p. 378

I remembered that on the river an apprentice pilot not only got nothing in the way of salary but he also had to pay some pilot a sum in cash which he didn't have—a large sum. It was what I had done myself. I had paid Bixby a hundred dollars and it was borrowed money. I was told by a person who said he was studying for the ministry that even Noah got no salary for the first six months—partly on account of the weather and partly because he was learning navigation.

Mark Twain in Eruption, p. 165

[In the Holy Land]: . . . we passed through an Arab

village of stone dry-goods boxes (they look like that), where Noah's tomb lies under lock and key. . . .

Noah's tomb is built of stone, and is covered with a long stone building. Bucksheesh let us in. The building had to be long, because the grave of the honored old navigator is two hundred and ten feet long itself! It is only about four feet high, though. He must have cast a shadow like a lightning-rod. The proof that this is the genuine spot where Noah was buried can only be doubted by uncommonly incredulous people. The evidence is pretty straight. Shem, the son of Noah, was present at the burial, and showed the place to his descendants, who transmitted the knowledge to their descendants, and the lineal descendants of these introduced themselves to us to-day. It was pleasant to make the acquaintance of members of so respectable a family. It was a thing to be proud of. It was the next thing to being acquainted with Noah himself.

The Innocents Abroad, II, Chapt. XV, p. 184

NOAH'S ARK   *See also* ARK, BED
[To Susie for her 3rd birthday], a Noah's Ark from me, containing 200 wooden animals such as only a human being could create and only God call by name without referring to the passenger list.

Mark Twain's Letters, I, p. 252

NOBILITY   *See also* EQUALITY, RIDICULE, ROYALTY
The law of work does seem utterly unfair—but there it is, and nothing can change it: the higher the pay in enjoyment the worker gets out of it, the higher shall be his pay in cash, also. And it's also the very law of those transparent swindles, transmissible nobility and kingship.

A Connecticut Yankee in King Arthur's Court,
Chapt. XXVIII, p. 257

I will say this much for the nobility: that, tyrannical, murderous, rapacious, and morally rotten as they were, they were deeply and enthusiastically religious. Nothing could divert them from the regular and faithful performance of the pieties enjoined by the Church. More than once I had seen a noble, who had gotten his enemy at a disadvantage, stop to pray before cutting his throat. . . .

Ibid., Chapt. XVII, p. 131

[In Europe]: I think it is a great thing to say that in two and a half years I met only one person who had fallen a victim to the shams—I think we may call them shams—of nobilities and of heredities.

"Lotus Club Dinner"
Mark Twain's Speeches (1923, p. 163

A monarch when good is entitled to the consideration which we accord to a pirate who keeps Sunday School between crimes; when bad he is entitled to none at all. But if you cross a king with a prostitute the resulting mongrel perfectly satisfies the English idea of nobility.

Mark Twain's Notebook, p. 196

"But I thought you were opposed to nobilities?"

"Transmissible ones, yes. But that's nothing. I'm opposed to millonaires, but it would be dangerous to offer me the position."

The American Claimant, Etc., Chapt. XIV, p. 121

Essentially, nobilities are foolishness, but if I were a citizen where they prevail I would do my best to get a title, for the consideration it furnishes—that is what we want. In Republics we strive for it with the surest means we have —money.

Mark Twain's Notebook, p. 367

NOISE   *See also* BIBLE, FRIGHT, KNOWLEDGE

You don't have to hear noise unless you want to. The only time I hear the Elevated [in New York] is—when it —stops.

Life As I Find It, p. 344

(Jim's opinion of King Sollermun and his harem):

Mos' likely dey has rackety times in de nussery. 'En I reckon de wives quarrels considable; 'en dat 'crease de racket . . . . would a wise man want to live in de mids er sich a blim-blammin all de time? . . . A wise man 'ud take 'en buil' a biler-factory; 'en den he could shet *down* de biler-factory when he want to res'.

> *The Adventures of Huckleberry Finn,* p. 111

Noise proves nothing. Often a hen who has merely laid an egg cackles as if she had laid an asteroid.

> "Pudd'nhead Wilson's New Calendar"
> *Following the Equator,* I, Chapt. V, p. 72

. . . it is no harm to bark, if one stops there and does not bite. . . .

> *Personal Recollections of Joan of Arc,*
> I, Book II, Chapt. III, p. 126

W. never heard any noise of any kind after his eyes were shut. Some people thought he never did when they were open, either.

> *The Gilded Age,* II, Chapt. VII, p. 77

[At Aix]: . . . that billiard table of a market place, and that church are able, on a bet, to turn out more noise to a cubic yard at the wrong time than any other similar combination in the earth or out of it. In the street you have the skull-bursting thunder of the passing hack, a volume of sound not producible by six hacks anywhere else; on the hack is a lunatic with a whip which he cracks to notify the public to get out of his way. This crack is as keen and sharp and penetrating and ear-splitting as a pistol shot at close range, and the lunatic delivers it in volleys, not single shots. You think you will not be able to live till he gets by, and when he does get by he leaves only a vacancy for the bandit who sells *Le Petit Journal* to fill with his strange and awful yell. He arrives with the early morning and the market people, and there is a dog that arrives at about the same time and barks steadily at nothing till he dies, and they fetch another dog just like him. The bark of this breed is the twin of the whip volley, and stabs like a knife. By and by, what is left of you the church bell gets. There are many bells, and apparently six or seven thousand town clocks, and as they are all five minutes apart probably by law—there are no intervals. Some of them are striking all the time,—at least, after you go to bed they are. There is one clock that strikes the hour and then strikes it over again to see if it was right. Then for evenings and Sundays there is a chime—a chime that starts in pleasantly and musically, then breaks into a frantic roar, and boom, and crash of warring sounds that make you think Paris is up and the Revolution come again. And yet, as I have said, one sleeps here—sleeps like the dead. . . . Yes, there is indeed something in this air that is death to insomnia.

"Aix, the Paradise of Rheumatics"
Europe and Elsewhere, p. 101

NONSENSE
There is no more sin in publishing an entire volume of nonsense than there is in keeping a candy-store with no hardware in it. It lies wholly with the customer whether he will injure himself by means of either, or will derive from them the benefits which they will afford him if he uses their possibilities judiciously.

Mark Twain's Speeches (1910), Preface

NOSE   *See also* EYES, TRAVEL, WISDOM
The Popes have long been the patrons and preservers of art, just as our new, practical Republic is the encourager and upholder of mechanics. In their Vatican is stored up all that is curious and beautiful in art; in our Patent Office is hoarded all that is curious or useful in mechanics. When a man invents a new style of horse-collar or discovers a new and superior method of telegraphing, our government issues a patent to him that is worth a fortune; when a man digs up an ancient statue in the Campagna, the Pope gives him a fortune in gold coin. We can make something of a guess at a man's character by the style of nose he carries on his face. The Vatican and the Patent Offices are governmental noses, and they bear a deal of character about them.

The Innocents Abroad, II, Chapt. I, p. 17
There warn't no other sound but the scraping of the feet on the floor and blowing noses—because people always

blows them more at a funeral than they do at other places except church.

The Adventures of Huckleberry Finn,
Chapt. XXVII, p. 238

NOTE-BOOK *See also* JOURNAL

We were at sea now, for a very long voyage. . . .

We were all lazy and satisfied . . . as the meager entries in my note-book (that sure index, to me, of my condition) prove. What a stupid thing a note-book gets to be at sea, anyway.

The Innocents Abroad, II, Chapt. XXXII, p. 425

NOTICE *See also* MADNESS

. . . when we do a liberal and gallant thing it is but natural we should wish to see notice taken of it.

Personal Recollections of Joan of Arc,
I, Book II, Chapt. VII, p. 175

NOTORIETY *See* ASSASSINATION

NOVEL

Almost the whole capital of the novelist is the slow accumulation of *un*conscious observation—absorption.

"What Paul Bourget Thinks of Us"
Literary Essays, p. 146

[From a letter to William Dean Howells]:
I can't write a novel—for I lack the faculty.

Mark Twain's Letters, I, p. 346

And when a thousand able novels have been written, *there* you have the soul of the people, the life of the people, the speech of the people; and not anywhere else can these be had.

"What Paul Bourget Thinks of Us"
Literary Essays, p. 147

There is only one expert who is qualified to examine the

souls and the life of a people and make a valuable report—
the native novelist.

"What Paul Bourget Thinks of Us"
Ibid., p. 145

There are those who say a novel should be a work of
art solely, and you must not preach in it, you must not teach
in it. That may be true as regards novels but it is not true
as regards humor.

Mark Twain in Eruption, p. 202

NOVELTY

Unquestionably, the popular thing in this world is
novelty.

A Connecticut Yankee in King Arthur's Court,
Chapt. XXXIX, p. 354

NURSE

After a series of wet-nurses for Clara [Twain's third
baby], the family hired Maria McLaughlin, wife of a
worthless Irishman—who was apparently Irish, herself, with
a powerful strain of Egyptian in her—and she staid a year
till the Baby was weaned. Thus No. 5 ended the procession
—and in great style, too.

There was never any wet-nurse like that one—the unique,
the sublime, the unapproachable! She stood six feet in her
stockings, she was perfect in form and contour, raven-
haired, dark as an Indian, stately, carrying her head like
an empress. She had the martial port and stride of a grena-
dier, and the pluck and strength of a battalion of them. In
professional capacity the cow was a poor thing compared
to her, and not even the pump was qualified to take on
airs where she was. . . . She was healthy as iron, she had
the appetite of a crocodile, the stomach of a cellar, and the
digestion of a quartz-mill. Scorning the adamantine law
that a wet-nurse must partake of delicate things only, she
devoured anything and everything she could get her hands
on, shoveling into her person fiendish combinations of fresh
pork, lemon pie, boiled cabbage, ice cream, green apples,

pickled tripe, raw turnips, and washing the cargo down with freshets of coffee, tea, brandy, whiskey, . . . anything that was liquid; she smoked pipes, cigars, cigarettes, she whooped like a Pawnee and swore like a demon; and then she would go upstairs loaded as described and perfectly delight the baby with a banquet which ought to have killed it at thirty yards, but which only made it happy and fat and boozy. No child but this one ever had such grand and wholesome service. . . . In addition to the great quantities of strong liquors which she bought down town every day and consumed, she drank 256 pint bottles of beer in our house in one month, and that month the shortest one of the year . . . She was a wonder, a portent, that Egyptian.

Maria arrived home about eleven o'clock one night, as full as an egg and as unsteady on end. But the Bay was as empty as *she* was full; so after a steady pull of twenty minutes the Bay's person was level full of milk punch constructed of lager beer, cheap whiskey, rum and wretched brandy, flavored with chewing tobacco, cigar smoke and profanity and the pair were regally "sprung" and serenely happy. The Bay never throve so robustly on any nurse's milk as she did on Maria's for no other milk had so much substance to it.

Mark Twain, Family Man, p. 17

O

OBITUARY *See also* EPITAPH, EXAGGERATION

I forgot to state that Mr. Wakeman is dead. That is the reason why I have to write an obituary about him. He would not be so particular if he were not departed.

Mark Twain to Mrs. Fairbanks, p. 128

OBLIGATION

When some men discharge an obligation you can hear the report for miles around.

Source Undetermined

OBSCURITY *See also* HAPPINESS

Obscurity and a competence—that is the life that is best worth living.

Mark Twain's Notebook, p. 298

OBSERVER

A good journalist is a trained observer.

Mark Twain and I, Opie Read, p. 1

The Observer of Peoples has to be a Classifier, a Grouper, a Deducer, a Generalizer, a Psychologizer, and first and last a Thinker.

"What Paul Bourget Thinks of Us"
Literary Essays, p. 141

OCCUPATION *See also* CHEERFULNESS, MISSISSIPPI RIVER

. . . I had gained a livelihood in various vocations, but had not dazzled anybody with my successes; still the list was before me, and the amplest liberty in the matter of choosing, provided I wanted to work—which I did not. . . . I had once been a grocery clerk, for one day, but had consumed so much sugar in that time that I was relieved from further duty by the proprietor; said he wanted me outside, so that he could have my custom. I had studied law an entire week, and then given it up because it was so prosy and tiresome. I had engaged briefly in the study of blacksmithing, but wasted so much time trying to fix the bellows so that it would blow itself, that the master turned me adrift in disgrace, and told me I would come to no good. I had been a bookseller's clerk for a while, but the customers bothered me so much I could not read with any comfort, and so the proprietor gave me a furlough and forgot to put a limit on it. I had clerked in a drug store part of a summer, but my prescriptions were unlucky, and we appeared to sell more stomach pumps than soda water. So I had to go. I had made of myself a tolerable printer, under the impression that I would be another Franklin some day, but somehow had missed the connection thus far. . . . I was a good average St. Louis and New Orleans pilot and by no means ashamed of my abilities in that line; wages were two hundred and fifty dollars a month and no board to pay, and I did long to stand behind a wheel again and never roam any more. . . . I had been a private secretary, a silver miner and a silver mine operative, and amounted to less than nothing in each, and now—What to do next?

Roughing It, II, Chapt. IX, p. 15

It seems to me that the occupation of Unbiased Traveler Seeking Information is the pleasantest and most irresponsible trade there is. The traveler can always find out anything he wants to, merely by asking. He can get at all the facts, and more. . . . Anybody who has an old fact in stock that is no longer negotiable in the domestic market will let him have it at his own price. . . . They cost almost nothing and they bring par in the foreign market. Travelers . . . always freight up with the same old nursery tales that their predecessors selected, and they carry them back and always work them off without any trouble in the home market.

Following the Equator, I, Chapt. IX, p. 113

[Said of immigrants to Mauritius]: "The first year they gather shells; the second year they gather shells and drink; the third year they do not gather shells."

Ibid., II, Chapt. XXVII, p. 324

OFFICE   *See also* SIMILES

Washington seems to be made up of people who want offices. . . . These office-seekers are wonderfully importunate, and super-naturally gifted with "cheek." They fasten themselves to influential friends like barnacles to whales, and never let go until they are carried into the pleasant waters of office or scraped off against a protruding hotel bill.

The Twainian, July–Aug. 1947, p. 5

OLD MASTERS   *See* PAINTING

OPERA   *See also* MUSIC, POLITICS, PROFANITY, SINGING

We went to Mannheim and attended a shivaree—otherwise an opera—the one called Lohengrin. The banging and slamming and booming and crashing were something beyond belief. The racking and pitiless pain of it remains stored up in my memory alongside the memory of the time that I had my teeth fixed. . . .

. . .

. . . There was little of that sort of customary thing where the tenor and the soprano stand down by the footlights, warbling, with blended voices, and keep holding out their arms toward each other and drawing them back and spreading both hands over first one breast and then the other with a shake and a pressure—no, it was every rioter for himself and no blending. Each sang his indictive narrative in turn, accompanied by the whole orchestra of sixty instruments, and when this had continued for some time, and one was hoping they might come to an understanding and modify the noise, a great chorus composed entirely of maniacs would suddenly break forth, and then during two minutes, and sometimes three, I lived over again all that I had suffered the time the orphan asylum burned down.

We only had one brief little season of heaven and heaven's sweet ecstasy and peace during all this long and diligent and acrimonious reproduction of the other place. This was while a gorgeous procession of people marched around and around, in the third act, and sang the Wedding Chorus. To my untutored ear that was music,—almost divine music. While my seared soul was steeped in the healing balm of those gracious sounds, it seemed to me that I could almost re-suffer the torments which had gone before, in order to be so healed again. There is where the deep ingenuity of the operatic idea is betrayed. It deals so largely in pain that its scattered delights are prodigiously augmented by the contrasts.

> *A Tramp Abroad,* I, Chapt. IX, p. 78

This present opera was "Parsifal."

The first act of the three occupied two hours, and I enjoyed that in spite of the singing.

> "The Shrine of St. Wagner,"
> *What Is Man?* and Other Essays, p. 214

. . . there isn't often anything in [a] Wagner opera that one would call by such a violent name as acting; as a rule all you would see would be a couple of . . . people, one of them standing still, the other catching flies. Of course I do not really mean that he would be catching flies; I only mean that the usual operatic gestures which consist in reaching first one hand out into the air then the other might suggest the sport I speak of if the operator attended strictly to business. . . .

. . .

. . . Singing! It does seem the wrong name to apply to it. Strictly described, it is a practising of difficult and unpleasant intervals, mainly. An ignorant person gets tired of listening to gymnastic intervals in the long run, no matter how pleasant they may be. In "Parsifal" there is a hermit named Gurnemanz who stands on the stage in one spot and practises by the hour, while first one and then another character of the cast endures what he can of it and then retires to die.

"The Shrine of St. Wagner,"
Ibid., p. 213

Yesterday they played the only operatic favorite I have ever had—an opera which has always driven me mad with ignorant delight whenever I have heard it—"Tannhauser."

[In] the last act of "Tannhauser" . . . Presently that noble chorus of men's voices was heard approaching, and from that moment until the closing of the curtain it was music, just music—music to make one drunk with pleasure, music to make one take scrip and staff and beg his way round the globe to hear it.

"The Shrine of St. Wagner,"
Ibid., p. 216

. . . some of Wagner's operas bang along for six whole hours on a stretch! . . . A German lady in Munich told me that a person could not like Wagner's music at first, but must go through the deliberate process of learning to like it,—then he would have his sure reward; for when he had learned to like it he would hunger for it and never be able to get enough of it. She said that six hours of Wagner was by no means too much. . . . she said that Wagner's operas differed from all others in one notable respect, and that was that they were not merely spotted with music here and there, but were *all* music, from the first strain to the last. This surprised me. I said I had attended one of his insurrections, and found hardly *any* music in it except the Wedding Chorus. She said Lohengrin was noisier than Wagner's other operas, but that if I would keep on going to see it I would find by and by that it was all music, and therefore would then enjoy it. I *could* have said, "But would you advise a person to deliberately practice having the toothache in the pit of his stomach for a couple of years in order that he might then come to enjoy it?" But I reserved that remark.

A Tramp Abroad, I, Chapt. X, p. 84

San Francisco was Paradise to me. I lived at the best hotel, exhibited my clothes in the most conspicuous places, infested the opera, and learned to seem enraptured with music which oftener afflicted my ignorant ear than enchanted it, if I had had the vulgar honesty to confess it. However, I suppose I was not greatly worse than the most of my countrymen in that.

Roughing It, II, Chapt. XVII, p. 161

We have the grand opera; and I have witnessed and greatly enjoyed the first act of everything which Wagner created, but the effect on me has always been so powerful that one act was quite sufficient; whenever I have witnessed two acts I have gone away physically exhausted; and whenever I have ventured an entire opera the result has been the next thing to suicide. But if I could have the nigger show back again in its pristine purity and perfection, I should have but little further use for opera.

Mark Twain in Eruption, p. 110

OPINION *See also* ECHO, EVIDENCE, INSANITY, SIZE, TALK, THOUGHT

Is a person's public and private opinion the same? It is thought there have been instances.

More Maxims of Mark, p. 9

We are discreet sheep; we wait to see how the drove is going, and then go with the drove. We have two opinions: one private, which we are afraid to express; and another one—the one we use—which we force ourselves to wear to please Mrs. Grundy, until habit makes us comfortable in it, and the custom of defending it presently makes us love it, adore it, and forget how pitifully we came by it. Look at it in politics.

Mark Twain's Autobiography, Paine, II, p. 10

It were not best that we should all think alike; it is difference of opinion that makes horse-races.

"Pudd'nhead Wilson's Calendar,"
Pudd'nhead Wilson, Chapt. XIX, p. 182

I am glad the American . . . goes abroad. It does him good. It makes a better man of him. It rubs out a multitude of his old unworthy biases and prejudices. It aids his religion, for it enlarges his charity and his benevolence, it broadens his views of men and things; it deepens his generosity and his compassion for the failings and shortcomings of his fellow creatures. Contact with men of various nations and many creeds teaches him that there are *other* people in the world besides his own little clique, and other opinions as worthy of attention and respect as his own. He finds that he and *his* are not the most momentous matters in the universe. Cast into trouble and misfortune in strange lands and being mercifully cared for by those he never saw before, he begins to learn that best lesson of all—that one which culminates in the conviction that God puts *something* good and something lovable in every man his hands create —that the world is *not* a cold, harsh, cruel, prison-house, stocked with all manner of selfishness and hate and wickedness. It *liberalizes* [one] to travel. You never saw a bigoted, opinionated, stubborn, narrow-minded, self-conceited, *almighty mean man* in your life but he had stuck in one place ever since he was born and thought God made the world and dyspepsia and bile for *his* especial comfort and satisfaction.

"The American Vandal,"
Mark Twain's Speeches (1923), p. 29

Their opinions were all just green with prejudice.

"Seventieth Birthday,"
Mark Twain's Speeches (1923), p. 255

Opinions based upon theory, superstition, and ignorance are not very precious.

Mark Twain's Letters, II, p. 695

In all matters of opinion our adversaries are insane.

Christian Science, Book I, Chapt. V, p. 41

Asked what he thought about the existence of heaven or hell, Mark Twain replied: "I don't want to express an opinion. You see, I have friends in both places."

Mark Twain, Henderson, p. 109

Loyalty to petrified opinions never yet broke a chain or freed a human soul in *this* world—and never *will*.

"Consistency,"
Mark Twain's Speeches (1923), p. 130

OPPORTUNITY   *See also* KILLING

Anyone who is old, who has really lived and felt this life, he knows the pathos of lost opportunity.

Mark Twain's Speeches (1923), p. 265

Some of us cannot be optimists, but by judiciously utilizing the opportunities Providence puts in our way we can all be bigamists.

Ibid., p. 246

OPTIMIST   *See also* ASS, PESSIMIST

That optimism of yours is always ready to turn hell's backyard into a play-ground.

Mark Twain, a Biography, Paine, III, p. 1502

Optimist: Day-dreamer more elegantly spelled.

More Maxims of Mark, p. 11

Optimist: Person who travels on nothing from nowhere to happiness.

Ibid., p. 11

Sixty years ago optimist and fool were not synonymous terms. This is a greater change than that wrought by science and invention. It is the mightiest change that was ever wrought in the world in any sixty years since creation. [Jan. 1905]

Mark Twain's Notebook, p. 395

Tom Reed was invited to lecture to the Ladies' Society for the Procreation or Procrastination, or something, of Morals, I don't know what it was—advancement, I suppose, of pure morals—he had the immoral indiscretion to begin by saying that some of us can't be optimists, but by judiciously utilizing the opportunities that Providence puts in our way we can all be bigamists.

"Sixty-Seventh Birthday,"
Mark Twain's Speeches (1923), p. 246

ORGANIZATION

Organization is necessary in all things. It is even necessary in reform.

"Layman's Sermon,"
Mark Twain's Speeches (1923), p. 281

It's because the fiftieth fellow and his pals are organized and the other forty-nine are not that the dirty one rubs it into the clean fellows every time.

"Municipal Corruption,"
Ibid., p. 218

ORIENT

. . . in the Oriental countries . . . every separate and individual devil of them's got the ophthalmia! It's as natural to them as noses are—and sin. It's born with them, it stays with them, it's all that some of them have left when they die.

The Gilded Age, I, Chapt. VIII, p. 99

Oriental scenes look best in steel engravings. I cannot be imposed upon any more by that picture of the Queen of Sheba visiting Solomon. I shall say to myself, You look fine, madam, but your feet are not clean, and you smell like a camel.

The Innocents Abroad, II, Chapt. XXIV, p. 310

ORIGINALITY *See also* ADAM, GOD, IDEA, NATURE

It is an astonishing thing that after all these ages the world goes on thinking the human brain machinery can originate a thought.

It can't. It never has done it. In all cases, little and big, the thought is born of a suggestion; and in *all* cases the suggestions come to the brain from the outside. The brain never acts except from exterior impulse.

Mark Twain's Letters, II, p. 813

OSTEOPATHY *See also* ILLNESS

[In 1901, Mark Twain appeared before the Assembly Committee in Albany, N.Y., in favor of the Seymour bill legalizing the practice of osteopathy]:

The State stands as a mighty Gibraltar clothed with power. It stands between me and my body, and tells me what kind of a doctor I must employ. When my soul is sick unlimited spiritual liberty is given me by the State. Now then, it doesn't seem logical that the State shall depart from this great policy, the health of the soul, and change about and take the other position in the matter of smaller consequences—the health of the body.

The Bell bill limitations would drive the osteopaths out of the State. Oh, dear me! when you drive somebody out of the State you create the same condition as prevailed in the Garden of Eden. You want the thing that you can't have . . .

I know how Adam felt in the Garden of Eden about the prohibited apple. Adam didn't want the apple till he found out he couldn't have it, just as he would have wanted osteopathy if he couldn't have it.

Whose property is my body? Probably mine. I so regard it. If I experiment with it, who must be answerable? I, not the State. If I choose injudiciously, does the State die? Oh, no.

. . .

. . . At a time during my younger days my attention was attracted to a picture of a house which bore the inscription, "Christ Disputing the Doctors."

I could attach no other meaning to it than that Christ was actually quarrelling with the doctors. So I asked an old slave, who was a sort of a herb doctor in a small way— unlicensed, of course—what the meaning of the picture was. "What has he done?" I asked. And the colored man replied: "Humph, he ain't got no license."

"Osteopathy,"
Mark Twain's Speeches (1923), p. 232

To ask a doctor's opinion of osteopathy is equivalent to going to Satan for information about Christianity.

Mark Twain's Notebook, p. 344

OUT

It is easier to stay out than get out.

Mark Twain's Notebook, p. 347

OYSTER   *See also* CLAM

We all know about the habits of the ant, we know all about the habits of the bee, but we know nothing at all about the habits of the oyster. It seems certain that we have been choosing the wrong time for studying the oyster.

"Pudd'nhead Wilson's Calendar,"
Pudd'nhead Wilson, Chapt. XVI, p. 158

[Lord Kelvin says he thinks the world] isn't more than a hundred million years old, and he thinks the human race has inhabited it about thirty thousand years of that time. Even so, it was 99,970,000 years getting ready, impatient as the Creator doubtless was to see man and admire him. That was because God first had to make the oyster . . .

Now an oyster has hardly any more reasoning power than a man has, so it is probable this one jumped to the conclusion that the nineteen million years was a preparation for *him.* That would be just like an oyster . . .

Mark Twain, a Biography, Paine, III, p. 1358

P

PAGE

By his look he was good natured; by his gait he was satisfied with himself. He was pretty enough to frame. He arrived, looked me over with a smiling and impudent curiosity, and informed me he was a page.

"Go 'long!" I said, "you ain't more than a paragraph!"

A Connecticut Yankee in King Arthur's Court,
Chapt. II, p. 23

PAIN *See also* DENTISTRY, FORGETFULNESS

Our consciences take *no* notice of pain inflicted upon others until it reaches a point where it gives pain to *us*. In *all* cases without exception we are absolutely indifferent to another person's pain until his sufferings make us uncomfortable.

What Is Man? and Other Essays, Chapt. II, p. 28

PAINTING *See also* MICHELANGELO, MIRACLE, RENAISSANCE, SAINT

That is the kind of pictures to have—full of human interest and good fellowship; it is worth an acre of smirking saints stuck full of arrows and lugging skulls around for baggage. How sick and goody-goody and tiresome they do look in the tedious galleries of the snuffling Old Masters.

My Father • Mark Twain, Clara Clemens, p. 131

It is much better to label a portrait when you first paint it, then there is no uncertainty in your mind and you can get bets out of the visitor and win them.

"Instructions in Art,"
Europe and Elsewhere, p. 315

. . . I had seen the "Mona Lisa" only a little while before, and stood two hours in front of that painting, repeating to myself: "People come from around the globe to stand here and worship. What is it they find in it?" To me it was merely a serene and subdued face, and there an end. There might be more in it, but I could not find it. The complexion was bad; in fact, it was not even human; there are no people of that color. I finally concluded that maybe others still saw in the picture faded and vanished marvels which had been there once and were now forever vanished.

"Down the Rhone,"
Ibid., p. 142

It occurs to me now that I have never seen the ice-storm put upon canvas, and have not heard that any painter has tried to do it. I wonder why that is. Is it that paint cannot counterfeit the intense blaze of a sun-flooded jewel?

Following the Equator, II, Chapt. XXIII, p. 279

[In Rome]: I cannot write about the Vatican . . . of its wilderness of statues, paintings, and curiosities of every description and every age. The "old masters" . . . fairly swarm there . . . I think I shall never remember anything I saw there distinctly but the mummies, and the Transfiguration, by Raphael. . . . I shall remember the Transfiguration partly because it was placed in a room almost by itself; partly because it is acknowledged by all to be the first oil-painting in the world; and partly because it was wonderfully beautiful. The colors are fresh and rich, the "expression," I am told, is fine, the "feeling" is lively, the "tone" is good, the "depth" is profound, and the width is about four and a half feet, I should judge. . . . It is fine enough to be a *Renaissance*. . . . It is not possible that the reason I find such charms in this picture is because it is out of the crazy chaos of the galleries? If some of the others were set apart, might not they be beautiful? If this were set in the midst of the tempest of pictures one finds in the vast galleries of the Roman palaces, would I think it so handsome? If, up to this time, I had seen only one "old master" in each palace, instead of acres and acres of walls and ceilings fairly papered with them, might I not have a more civilized opinion of the old masters than I have now? I think so.

The Innocents Abroad, II, Chapt. I, p. 14

Why, Mars Tom, if you knowed what chuckle-heads dem painters is, you'd wait a long time before you'd fetch one er *dem* in to back up a fac'. I's gwine to tell you, den you kin see for you'self. I see one of 'em a-paintin' away, one day, down in ole Hank Wilson's back lot, en I went down to see, en he was paintin' dat old brindle cow wid de near horn gone—you knows de one I means. En I ast him what he's paintin' her for, en he say when he git her painted, de picture's wuth a hundred dollars. Mars Tom, he could a got de cow for fifteen, en I *tole* him so. Well, sah, if you'll b'lieve me, he jes' shuck his head, dat painter did, en went on a-dobbin'. Bless you, Mars Tom, *dey* don't know nothin'.

Tom Sawyer Abroad, Etc., Chapt. III, p. 32

Here, in Milan, in an ancient tumble-down ruin of a church, is the mournful wreck of the most celebrated painting in the world—"The Last Supper," by Leonardo da Vinci. . . . "The Last Supper" is painted on the dilapidated wall of what was a little chapel attached to the main church in ancient times, I suppose. It is battered and scarred in every direction, and stained and discolored by time, and Napoleon's horses kicked the legs off most the disciples when they (the horses, not the disciples) were stabled there more than half a century ago.

. . .

The colors are dimmed with age; the countenances are

scaled and marred, and nearly all expression is gone from them; the hair is a dead blur upon the wall, and there is no life in the eyes. Only the attitudes are certain.

People come here from all parts of the world, and glorify this masterpiece. They stand entranced before it with bated breath and parted lips, and when they speak, it is only in the catchy ejaculations of rapture . . .

I only envy these people; I envy them their honest admiration, if it be honest—their delight, if they feel delight. I harbor no animosity toward any of them. But at the same time the thought *will* intrude itself upon me, How can they see what is not visible? . . . What would you think of a man who stared in ecstasy upon a desert of stumps and said: "Oh, my soul, my beating heart, what a noble forest is here!"

. . .

Anyone who is acquainted with the old masters will comprehend how much the Last Supper is damaged when I say that the spectator cannot really tell, now, whether the disciples are Hebrews or Italians. These ancient painters never succeeded in denationalizing themselves. The Italian artists painted Italian Virgins, the Dutch painted Dutch Virgins, the Virgins of the French painters were Frenchwomen—none of them ever put into the face of the Madonna that indescribable something which proclaims the Jewess, whether you find her in New York, in Constantinople, in Paris, Jerusalem, or in the Empire of Morocco . . .

The Innocents Abroad, I, Chapt. XIX, p. 246

We have seen famous pictures until our eyes are weary with looking at them and refuse to find interest in them any longer. . . . We have seen pictures of martyrs enough, and saints enough, to regenerate the world . . .

. . . We have seen thirteen thousand St. Jeromes, and twenty-two thousand St. Marks, and sixteen thousand St. Matthews, and sixty thousand St. Sebastians, and four millions of assorted monks, undesignated, and we feel encouraged to believe that when we have seen some more of these various pictures, and had a larger experience, we shall begin to take an absorbing interest in them like our cultivated countrymen from *Amerique*.

Ibid., XXIII, p. 303

PALESTINE

Of all the lands there are for dismal scenery, I think Palestine must be the prince. . . . It is a hopeless, dreary, heart-broken land.

. . .

Palestine sits in sackcloth and ashes. Over it broods the spell of a curse that has withered its fields and fettered its energies. Where Sodom and Gomorrah reared their domes and towers, that solemn sea now floods the plain, in whose bitter waters no living thing exists—over whose waveless surface the blistering air hangs motionless and dead—about whose borders nothing grows but weeds, and scattering tufts of cane, and that treacherous fruit that promises refreshment to parching lips, but turns to ashes at the touch. Nazareth is forlorn; . . . Jericho the accursed lies a moldering ruin to-day, even as Joshua's miracle left it more than three thousand years ago; Bethlehem and Bethany, in their poverty and their humiliation, have nothing about them now to remind one that they once knew the high honor of the Saviour's presence. . . . Renowned Jerusalem itself, the stateliest name in history, has lost all its ancient grandeur, and is become a pauper village; . . . Magdala is the home of beggared Arabs . . .

Palestine is desolate and unlovely. And why should it be otherwise? Can the *curse* of the Deity beautify a land?

Palestine is no more of this work-day world. It is sacred to poetry and tradition—it is dream-land.

The Innocents Abroad, II, Chapt. XXIX, p. 392

. . . "Kings" and "kingdoms" were as thick in Britain as they had been in little Palestine in Joshua's time, when people had to sleep with their knees pulled up because they couldn't stretch out without a passport.

A Connecticut Yankee in King Arthur's Court,
Chapt. XVI, p. 126

PALIMPSEST *See* MEMORY

PARIS *See also* FRANCE

Being now wealthy and distinguished, Mr. O'Reily, still bearing the legislative "Hon." attached to his name (for titles never die in America, although we *do* take a republican pride in poking fun at such trifles), sailed for Europe with his family. They traveled all about, turning their noses up at everything, and not finding it a difficult thing to do, either, because nature had originally given those features a cast in that direction; and finally they established themselves in Paris, that Paradise of Americans of their sort. They stayed there two years and learned to speak English with a foreign accent. . . . Finally they returned home and became ultra-fashionables. They landed here as the Hon. Patrique Oreillé and family, and so are known unto this day.

The Gilded Age, II, Chapt. II, p. 25

PARTY *See* COUNTRY, POLITICS, VOTING

PASSION *See* CONSCIENCE

PAST

I said there was but one solitary thing about the past worth remembering and that was the fact that it *is* past—can't be restored.

Mark Twain's Letters, I, p. 290

"I wonder why we hate the past so?"

"It's so damned humiliating," which is what any man would say of his past if he were honest; but honest men are few when it comes to themselves.

My Mark Twain, William Dean Howells, p. 30

PATENT *See also* INVENTION

. . . the first official thing I did . . . was to start a patent office; for I knew a country without a patent office and

454

good patent laws was just a crab, and couldn't travel any way but sideways or backways.

A Connecticut Yankee in King Arthur's Court,
Chapt. IX, p. 70

Patents are not frequently born in singles. . . . they are always twins or triplets. The Patent Office is a vast lying-in hospital for such.

Mark Twain-Howells Letters, II, p. 767

PATHOS *See also* HUMOR, OPPORTUNITY

The two most pathetic, moving things in the English tongue to me are these—1. A refrain from a long-ago forgotten song, "In the days when we went gypsying, a long time ago." The other—"Departed this life," on a gravestone.

Mark Twain's Notebook, p. 319

By some subtle law all tragic human experiences gain in pathos by the perspective of time.

"My Literary Debut,"
The Man That Corrupted Hadleyburg, p. 84

PATIENCE

Some things you *can't* find out; but you will never know you can't by guessing and supposing; no, you have to be patient and go on experimenting until you find out that you can't find out. . . . Even trying to find out and not finding out is just as interesting as trying to find out and finding out, and I don't know but more so.

"Eve's Diary,"
The $30,000 Bequest, p. 306

PATIENT *See* TALK

PATRIOTISM *See also* CHRISTIANITY, COUNTRY, FIGHT,
FLAG, POLITICS, VOTING

We teach [our boys] to take their patriotism at second-hand; to shout with the largest crowd without examining into the right or wrong of the matter—exactly as boys under monarchies are taught and have always been taught. We teach them to regard as traitors, and hold in aversion and contempt, such as do not shout with the crowd, and so here in our democracy we are cheering a thing which of all things is most foreign to it and out of place—the delivery of our political conscience into somebody else's keeping. This is patriotism on the Russian plan.

Mark Twain, a Biography, Paine, III, p. 1118

Patriotism is merely a religion—love of country, worship of country, devotion to the country's flag and honor and welfare.

"As Regards Patriotism,"
Europe and Elsewhere, p. 301

I would not voluntarily march under this country's flag, or any other, when it was my private judgment that the country was in the wrong. If the country *obliged* me to shoulder the musket, I could not help myself, but I would never volunteer. To volunteer would be the act of a traitor to myself, and consequently traitor to my country. If I refused to volunteer, I should be *called* a traitor, I am well aware of that—but that would not make me a traitor. The unanimous vote of the sixty millions could not make me a traitor. I should still be a patriot, and, in my opinion, the only one in the whole country.

Mark Twain's Autobiography, Paine, II, p. 18

. . . patriotism is usually the refuge of the scoundrel. He is the man who talks the loudest.

"Education and Citizenship,"
Mark Twain's Speeches (1923), p. 378

The soul and substance of what customarily ranks as patriotism is moral cowardice—and always has been.

Mark Twain's Notebook, p. 394

[Patriotism] . . . is a word which always commemorates a robbery. There isn't a foot of land in the world which doesn't represent the ousting and re-ousting of a long line of successive "owners" who each in turn, as "patriots," with proud swelling hearts defended it against the next gang of "robbers" who came to steal it and *did*—and became swelling-hearted patriots in *their* turn.

Ibid., p. 295

A man can be a Christian *or* a patriot, but he can't legally be a Christian *and* a patriot—except in the usual way: one of the two with the mouth, the other with the heart. The spirit of Christianity proclaims the brotherhood of the race and the meaning of that strong word has not been left to guesswork, but made tremendously definite—the Christian must forgive his brother man all crimes he can imagine and commit, and all insults he can conceive and utter—forgive these injuries how many times?—seventy times seven—another way of saying there shall be no limit to this forgiveness. That is the spirit and the law of Christianity. Well—patriotism has *its* laws. And it also is a perfectly definite one, there are no vaguenesses about it. It commands that the brother over the border shall be sharply watched and brought to book every time he does us a hurt or offends us with an insult. Word it as softly as you please, the spirit of patriotism is the spirit of the dog and the wolf. The moment there is misunderstanding about a boundary line or a hamper of fish or some other squalid matter, see patriotism rise, and hear him split the universe with his war-whoop. The spirit of patriotism being in its nature jealous and selfish, is just in man's line, it comes natural to him—he can live up to all its requirements to the letter; but the spirit of Christianity is not in its entirety possible to him.

The prayer concealed in what I have been saying is, not that patriotism should cease and not that the talk about universal brotherhood should cease, but that the incongruous firm be dissolved and each limb of it be required to transact business by itself, for the future.

Mark Twain's Notebook, p. 332

. . . majority Patriotism is the customary Patriotism.

"As Regards Patriotism,"
Europe and Elsewhere, p. 303

Patriotism is Patriotism. Calling it Fanaticism cannot de-

457

grade it. Even though it be a political mistake . . . it is honorable—always honorable, always noble—and privileged to hold its head up and look the nations in the face.

Following the Equator, I, Chapt. XXXV

In the beginning of a change the patriot is a scarce man, and brave, and hated and scorned. When his cause succeeds, the timid join him, for then it costs nothing to be a patriot.

Mark Twain's Notebook, p. 394

. . . the modern patriotism, the true patriotism, the only rational patriotism is loyalty to the *nation* all the time, loyalty to the government when it deserves it.

"The Czar's Soliloquy,"
The North American Review, March 1905, p. 324

PAUSE, THE   *See also* READER, WORDS

A person who does not appreciate the exceeding value of pauses, and does not know how to measure their duration judiciously, cannot render the grand simplicity and dignity of a composition like [the Lord's Prayer] effectively.

A Tramp Abroad, II, Chapt. VII, p. 93

The pause is not of much use to the man who is reading from a book because he cannot know what the exact length of it ought to be; he is not the one to determine the measurement—the audience must do that for him. He must perceive by their faces when the pause has reached the proper length, but his eyes are not on the faces, they are on the book; therefore he must determine the proper length of the pause by guess; he cannot guess with exactness and nothing but exactness, absolute exactness, will answer.

. . . For one audience the pause will be short, for another a little longer . . . the performer must vary the length . . . to suit the shades of difference between audiences . . .

I used to play with the pause as other children play with a toy . . . In the negro ghost story of "The Golden Arm" one of these pauses occurs just in front of the closing remark. Whenever I got the pause the right length, the remark that followed it was sure of a satisfactorily startling effect, but if the length of the pause was wrong by the five-millionth of an inch, the audience had had time in that infinitesimal fraction of a moment to wake up from its deep concentration in the grisly tale and foresee the climax, and be prepared for it before it burst upon them—and so it fell flat.

Mark Twain in Eruption, p. 225

PEACE *See also* WAR

The gospel of peace is always making a deal of noise, always rejoicing in its progress but always neglecting to furnish statistics. There are no peaceful nations now.

. . . All Christendom is a soldier-camp. The poor have been taxed in some nations to the starvation point to support the giant armaments which Christian governments have built up, each to protect itself from the rest of the Christian brotherhood, and incidentally to snatch any scrap of real estate left exposed by a weaker owner.

Mark Twain, a Biography, Paine, III, p. 1467

Perpetual peace we cannot have on any terms, I suppose; but I hope we can gradually reduce the war strength of Europe till we get it down to where it ought to be—20,000 men, properly armed. Then we can have all the peace that is worth while, and when we want a war anybody can afford it. [1899]

Mark Twain's Letters, II, p. 674

If I never learnt nothing else out of pap, I learnt that the best way to get along with his kind of people is to let them have their own way.

The Adventures of Huckleberry Finn,
Chapt. XIX, p. 171

Peace—happiness—brotherhood—that is what we want in this world.

Abroad with Mark Twain and Eugene Field, Fisher, p. 42

. . . how pervading were the repose and peace and

blessedness that poured out of the heart of the invisible Great Spirit of the Mountains.

Mark Twain's Letters, I, p. 351

PEDESTRIAN *See* TALK

PEN *See also* VIRTUE

I am trying a new fountain pen—the "Yale"—(1886), and am weak from the loss of profanity.

Mark Twain-Howells Letters, II, p. 552

PEOPLE *See also* AMERICA, CIVILIZATION, DOG, HUMAN RACE, LIKING, MOON, NATURE, NOVEL

. . . in my experience hard-hearted people are very rare everywhere.

Mark Twain's Autobiography, I, p. 125

One learns peoples through the heart, not the eyes or the intellect.

There is only one expert who is qualified to examine the souls and the life of a people and make a valuable report— the native novelist.

"What Paul Bourget Thinks of Us,"
Literary Essays, p. 145

All the talk used to be about doing people good, now it is about doing people.

More Maxims of Mark, p. 5

There are three kinds of people—Commonplace Men, Remarkable Men, and Lunatics.

Following the Equator, I, Chapt. XIII, p. 148

. . . the more you join in with people in their joys and their sorrows, the more nearer and dearer they come to be to you. . . .

But it is sorrow and trouble that brings you the nearest. . . .

Tom Sawyer Abroad, Etc., Chapt. XI, p. 104

We make little account of that vague, formless, inert mass, that mighty underlying force which we call "the people"—an epithet which carries contempt with it. It is a strange attitude; for at bottom we know that the throne which the people support stands, and that when that support is removed nothing in this world can save it.

Personal Recollections of Joan of Arc,
II, Book II, Chapt. XXXIII, p. 37

I believe that some day it will be found out that peasants are people. Yes, being in a great many respects like ourselves. And I believe that some day *they* will find this out, too—and then! Well, then I think they will rise up and demand to be regarded as part of the race. . . .

Ibid., II, Book II, Chapt. XXXVII, p. 77

When I reflect on the number of disagreeable people who I know have gone to a better world, I am moved to lead a different life.

"Pudd'nhead Wilson's Calendar,"
Pudd'nhead Wilson, Chapt. XIII, p. 123

. . . the high court of The People, from whose decision there is no appeal.

"The Evidence,"
The Washoe Giant in San Francisco, p. 77

There is a great deal of human nature in people.

"The Broadway Bridge,"
Mark Twain's Travels with Mr. Brown, p. 185

Keep away from people who try to belittle your ambitions. Small people always do that, but the really great make you feel that you, too, can become great.

Morally We Roll Along, MacLaren, p. 66

PERFECTION *See also* BEAUTY

One's admiration of a perfect thing always grows, never declines, and this is the surest evidence to him that it *is* perfect.

A Tramp Abroad, II, Chapt. XX, p. 254

A body ought to have a moral lapse of *some* kind to keep from being perfection . . .

Mark Twain to Mrs. Fairbanks, p. 223

Lake Annecy. It is a revelation. It is a miracle. It brings the tears to a body's eyes. It is so enchanting. That is to say, it affects you just as all other things that you instantly recognize as perfect affect you—perfect music, perfect eloquence, perfect art, perfect joy, perfect grief.

Mark Twain, a Biography, Paine, II, p. 922

None of us like mediocrity, but we all reverence perfection. This girl's music was perfection in its way; it was the worst music that had ever been achieved on our planet by a mere human being.

A Tramp Abroad, II, Chapt. III, p. 39

PERJURY

They are all caked with perjury, many layers thick. Iron clad, so to speak.

The $30,000 Bequest, p. 238

PERSEVERANCE   *See also* EXAGGERATION

[Quoted by Mark Twain from McClintock's *The Enemy Conquered; or, Love Triumphant*]:

Perseverance is a principle that should be commendable in those who have judgment to govern it.

"The Enemy Conquered; or, Love Triumphant,"
The American Claimant, Etc., p. 427

PERSPIRATION

[Climbing a mountain]: . . . the perspiration was flowing from me, washing boulders down the hill.

Mark Twain's Notebook, p. 335

I perspired so much that mother put a life-preserver to bed with me.

"Osteopathy,"
Mark Twain's Speeches (1910), p. 254

PERSISTENCE

It is a thing which happens with the persistency of sunrise.

Mark Twain-Howells Letters, II, p. 767

PESSIMIST

Pessimists are born not made; optimists are born not

made; but no man is born either pessimist wholly or optimist wholly, perhaps; he is pessimistic along certain lines and optimistic along certain others. That is my case.

Mark Twain's Letters, II, p. 785

Pessimist: The optimist who didn't arrive.

More Maxims of Mark, p. 12

The man who is a pessimist before 48 knows too much; if he is an optimist after it, he knows too little.

Mark Twain's Notebook, p. 380

. . . the man who *isn't* a pessimist is a d–d fool.

Mark Twain, a Biography, Paine, III, p. 1508

We would have shone at a wake, but not at anything more festive.

The Innocents Abroad, I, Chapt. II, p. 59

There is no sadder sight than a young pessimist, except an old optimist.

Mark Twain's Notebook, p. 385

PHILIPPINES *See* MORALS

PHILOSOPHY

[The philosophy of *The Man That Corrupted Hadleyburg:* Every man is strong until his price is named.]

Laughter without a tinge of philosophy is but a sneeze of humor.

Mark Twain and I, Opie Read, p. 17

[Quoted by Mark Twain from McClintock's *The Enemy Conquered; or, Love Triumphant*]:

. . . the end of true philosophy is to proportion our wants to our possessions.

The American Claimant, Etc., p. 456

Philosophy is a David with the sling of truth in his hand, killing the giants of error.

Mark Twain and I, Opie Read, p. 27

PHONOGRAPH

[*In 1888, Mark Twain ordered a phonograph from the Edison Co., and gave it a fair trial for dictation.*]

You can't write literature with it because it hasn't any ideas and it hasn't the gift for elaboration, or smartness of talk, or vigor of action, or felicity of expression, but is just matter-of-fact, compressive, unornamental, and as grave and unsmiling as the devil.

Mark Twain's Letters, I, p. 544

PHOTOGRAPH *See also* COMPLIMENT, IDEA

I think a photograph is a most important document, and there is nothing more damning to go down to posterity than a silly, foolish smile caught and fixed forever.

Mark Twain and the Happy Island, Wallace, p. 34

. . . no photograph ever was good, yet, of anybody—hunger and thirst and utter wretchedness overtake the out-law who invented it! It transforms into desperadoes the meekest of men; depicts sinless innocence upon the pictured faces of ruffians; gives the wise man the stupid leer of a fool, and a fool an expression of more than earthly wisdom. . . . The sun never looks through the photographic instrument that it does not print a lie. The piece of glass it prints it on is well named a "negative"—a contradiction—a misrepresentation—a falsehood. I speak feelingly of this matter, because by turns the instrument has represented me to be a lunatic, a Solomon, a missionary, a burglar and an abject idiot, and I am neither.

Letters from the Sandwich Islands, p. 130

PHYSICIAN *See* DOCTOR

PICTURE *See* HISTORY, MEMORY, PAINTING

PILGRIMS *See also* SHIP

[At a dinner celebrating the landing of the Pilgrims]: Celebrating their landing! What was there remarkable about it, I would like to know? . . . Why, those Pilgrims had been at sea three or four months. It was the very middle of winter: it was as cold as death off Cape Cod there. Why shouldn't they come ashore? If they *hadn't* landed there would be some reason for celebrating the fact. It would have been a case of monumental leatherheadedness which the world would not willingly let die. . . .

. . .

People may talk as they like about that Pilgrim stock, but, after all's said and done, it would be pretty hard to improve on those people; and, as for me, I don't mind coming out flatfooted and saying there ain't any way to improve on them—except having them born in Missouri!

"Plymouth Rock and the Pilgrims,"
Mark Twain's Speeches (1923), p. 87

PILOTING *See also* BRAINS, INDEPENDENCE, MISSISSIPPI
RIVER, RACING

A pilot must have a memory; but there are two higher qualities . . . He must have good and quick judgment and decision, and a cool, calm courage that no peril can shake. . . . Judgment is a matter of brains, and a man must *start* with a good stock of that article or he will never succeed as a pilot.

Life on the Mississippi, Chapt. XIII, p. 114

[Bixby]: "There's only one way to be a pilot and that is to get this entire river by heart. You have to know it just like A.B.C."

Mark Twain's Notebook, p. 3

[Bixby]: ". . . you've got to know the *shape* of the river perfectly. It is all there is left to steer by on a very dark night. . . ."

[Twain]: "How on earth am I ever going to learn it, then?"

[Bixby]: "How do you follow a hall at home in the dark? Because you know the shape of it. You can't see it."

Life on the Mississippi, Chapt. VIII, p. 71

PIPE

He was smoking the "humbliest" pipe I ever saw—a dingy, funnel-shaped, red-clay thing, streaked and grimed with oil and years of tobacco, and with all the different

kinds of dirt there are, and thirty per cent of them peculiar
and indigenous to Endor and perdition. And rank? I never
smelt anything like it. It withered a cactus that stood lifting
its prickly hands aloft beside the trail. It even woke up my
horse.

"A Curious Relic For Sale,"
Life As I Find It, p. 57

PIRACY
[*Re Canadian pirates of literary property*]: Possible suits
for damages and felony would be no more restraint upon
them, I think, than would the presence of a young lady
upon a stud-horse who had just found a mare unprotected
by international copyright.

Letter to James Osgood, Oct. 28, 1881,
Mark Twain's Letters to His Publishers, p. 144

PITY *See* DEATH

PLACE *See* CUSTOM

PLAGIARISM *See also* PLAY, READER
Perhaps no poet is a conscious plagiarist; but there seems
to be warrant for suspecting that there is no poet who is
not at one time or another an unconscious one.

Following the Equator, I, Chapt. VIII, p. 105
. . . all our phrasings are spiritualized shadows cast
multitudinously from our readings. . . .

Mark Twain's Autobiography, I, p. 241
I knew one thing—that a certain amount of pride always
goes along with a teaspoonful of brains, and that this pride
protects a man from deliberately stealing other people's
ideas. That is what a teaspoonful of brains will do for a
man—and admirers had often told me I had nearly a basketful—though they were rather reserved as to the size of
the basket.

"Unconscious Plagiarism,"
Mark Twain's Speeches (1923), p. 78

I never charge anyone with plagiarism, for to do so would prove me incapable of gratitude for the highest compliment a man can pay me.

Belnap Collection, Connecticut
State Library at Hartford, p. 16

The kernel, the soul—let us go further and say the substance, the bulk, the actual and valuable material of *all* human utterances—is plagiarism. . . . When a great orator makes a great speech you are listening to ten centuries and ten thousand men—but we call it *his* speech, and really some exceedingly small portion of it *is* his. But not enough to signify. . . .

. . . . a grown person's memory-tablet is a palimpsest, with hardly a bare space upon which to engrave a phrase.

Mark Twain's Letters, II, p. 731

PLAN *See* VALUE

PLANET *See* EARTH

PLATFORM *See also* ANCESTORS, EXPERIENCE, LECTURING
I did not think I should ever stand on a platform again until the time was come for me to say "I die innocent." [1877]

Thomas Nast, Paine, p. 367

I hate the platform; it scares me. I know it might do good. It might do good to cut off my head, but I would rather do good some other way.

"Mark Twain in the Adirondacks"—W. H. Larom,
The Bookman, Jan. 1924, p. 537

PLAY *See also* SHAKESPEARE
[The play *Ah Sin* by Mark Twain and Bret Harte]: This is a . . . remarkable play. The construction . . . and . . . development of the story are the result of great research, and erudition and genius and invention—and plagiarism . . . When our play was finished, it was so long, and so broad and so deep—in places—that it would have taken a week

to play it. . . . The manager . . . cut out and cut out and —the more he cut the better the play got . . . it would have been one of the very best plays in the world if his strength had held out so that he could cut out the whole of it.

A *Bibliography of Mark Twain*, Merle Johnson, p. 139

The managers . . . always said [my plays] wouldn't act. . . . I judge the trouble is that the literary man is thinking of the style and quality . . . while the playwright thinks only of how it will play. One is thinking how it will sound, the other of how it will look.

Mark Twain, a Biography, Paine, III, p. 1414

PLAYFULNESS *See* RAFTSMEN, WORK

PLEASURE *See also* AUTHOR, DENTISTRY, GOD

. . . the exercise of an extraordinary gift is the supremest pleasure in life. . . .

The American Claimant, Etc., Chapt. VI, p. 51

There is probably no pleasure equal to the pleasure of climbing a dangerous Alp; but it is a pleasure which is confined strictly to people who can find pleasure in it. I have not jumped to this conclusion; I have traveled to it per gravel train, so to speak. . . .

A Tramp Abroad, II, Chapt. VII, p. 101

What is it that confers the noblest delight? What is that which swells a man's breast with pride above that which any other experience can bring to him? Discovery! To know that you are walking where none others have walked; that you are beholding what human eye has not seen before; that you are breathing a virgin atmosphere. To give birth to an idea—to discover a great thought—an intellectual nugget, right under the dust of a field that many a brain-plow had gone over before. To find a new planet, to invent a new hinge, to find the way to make the lightnings carry your messages. To be the *first*—that is the idea. To do something, say something, see something, before *anybody* else— these are the things that confer a pleasure compared with which other pleasures are tame and commonplace, other ecstasies cheap and trivial. Morse . . . Fulton . . . Jenner . . . Howe . . . Daguerre . . . Columbus . . . These are the men who have really *lived*—who have crowded long life-times of ecstasy into a single moment.

The Innocents Abroad, I, Chapt. XXVI, p. 338

We traveled up hill by the regular train five miles to the summit, then changed to a little canvas-canopied hand-car for the 35-mile descent. . . .

Mr. Pugh waved his flag and started, like an arrow from a bow, and before I could get out of the car we were gone too. I had previously had but one sensation like the shock of that departure, and that was the gaspy shock that took my breath away the first time that I was discharged from the summit of a toboggan slide. But in both instances the sensation was pleasurable—intensely so; it was a sudden and immense exaltation, a mixed ecstasy of deadly fright and unimaginable joy. I believe that this combination makes the perfection of human delight.

. . .

For rousing, tingling, rapturous pleasure there is no holi-day trip that approaches the bird-flight down the Himalayas in a hand-car. It has no fault, no blemish, no lack, except that there are only thirty-five miles of it instead of five hundred.

Following the Equator, II, Chapt. XX, p. 235

PLEDGE *See also* DRINK, LIQUOR, PROHIBITION, SMOKING

. . . to make a *pledge* of any kind is to declare war against nature; for a pledge is a chain that is always clank-ing and reminding the wearer of it that he is not a free man.

Following the Equator, I, Chapt. I, p. 20

Taking the pledge will not make bad liquor good, but it will improve it.

More Maxims of Mark, p. 13

PLUMBER *See also* PRAYER, THANKSGIVING

When we were finishing our house, we found we had a

little cash left over, on account of the plumber not knowing it.

"The McWilliamses and the Burglar Alarm,"
The Mysterious Stranger, Etc., p. 315

. . . there had been times, not many generations past, when the office of taster had its perils, and was not a grandeur to be desired. Why they did not use a dog or a plumber seems strange.

The Prince and the Pauper, Chapt. VII, p. 64

POETIC PROSE   *See also* BEAUTY, CALIFORNIA, MOUNTAIN, PALESTINE, RAFTSMEN, ROYALTY, SPHYNX, STAGECOACH

When I'm playful I use the meridians of longitude and parallels of latitude for a seine, and drag the Atlantic Ocean for whales! I scratch my head with lightning and purr myself to sleep with thunder.

Life on the Mississippi, Chapt. III, p. 33

. . . that is a pair of most striking and remarkable girls to look at, with a most indescribable sort of beauty. They fasten one's eyes like a magnet—or a baby—or a wood-fire in the twilighted room.

My Father • Mark Twain, Clara Clemens, p. 105

[The Sandwich (Hawaiian) Islands]: For me its balmy airs are always blowing, its summer seas flashing in the sun; the pulsing of its surf is in my ear; I can see its garlanded crags, its leaping cascades, its plumy palms drowsing by the shore, its remote summits floating like islands above the cloud-rack; I can feel the spirit of its woody solitudes, I hear the plashing of the brooks; in my nostrils still lives the breath of flowers that perished twenty years ago.

Mark Twain, a Biography, Paine, II, p. 879

Laramie Peak . . . [loomed] vast and solitary—a deep, dark, rich indigo blue in hue, so portentously did the old colossus frown under his beetling brows of storm-cloud.

Roughing It, I, Chapt. IX, p. 75

POETRY   *See also* BOOK, BROWNING, PALESTINE, SPHYNX

It was a terrible moment when he placed that pistol against his forehead. He [pulled the trigger] and cleaned out all the gray matter in his brains. It carried the poetic faculty away, and now he's a useful member of society.

"University Settlement"
Mark Twain's Speeches (1910), p. 142

The poetry of [the desert is] all in the anticipation—there is none in the reality.

Roughing It, I, Chapt. XVIII, p. 150

I am not fond of all poetry, but there's something in Kipling that appeals to me. I guess he's just about my level.

Mark Twain, a Biography, Paine, III, p. 1440

Let us hope there is a hell, for this poet's [Townsend's] sake, who carries his bowels in his skull, and when they operate works the discharge into rhyme and prints it.

Mark Twain-Howells Letters, II, p. 488

Prose wanders around with a lantern and laboriously schedules and verifies the details and particulars of a valley and its frame of crags and peaks, then Poetry comes, and lays bare the whole landscape with a single splendid flash.

Ibid., p. 800

POLICEMAN   *See also* POLITICS

[The Roman soldier who stood at his post during the destruction of Pompeii]: Being a soldier, he stayed—because the warrior instinct forbade him to fly. Had he been a policeman he would have stayed, also—because he would have been asleep.

The Innocents Abroad, II, Chapt. IV, p. 52

These were all the speeches that were made, and I recommend them to parties who present policemen with gold watches, as models of brevity and point.

Ibid., II, Chapt. X, p. 123

If there were an earthquake in Berlin the police would take charge of it and conduct it in that sort of orderly way that would make you think it was a prayer-meeting. That is what an earthquake generally ends in, but this one would be different from those others; it would be kind of soft and self-contained, like a republican praying for a mugwump.

"The German Chicago"
The American Claimant, Etc., p. 509

POLITENESS *See also* CHILDREN, DEATH

. . . [as] polite as three-dollar clerks in government offices.

A Tramp Abroad, I, Chapt. XXI, p. 198

The American characteristic is Uncourteousness. We are the Impolite Nation. . . .

We are called the Inventive Nation—but other nations invent. And we are called the Bragging Nation—but other nations brag. And we are called the Energetic Nation—but there are other energetic nations. It is only in uncourteousness, incivility, impoliteness, that we stand alone—until hell shall be heard from.

Mark Twain's Notebook, p. 298

Even the foreigner loses his kindly politeness as soon as we get him Americanized.

"Introducing Doctor Van Dyke"
Mark Twain's Speeches (1923), p. 300

Our national impoliteness is not natural but acquired. It would be a curious study, *how* and from whom we acquired it.

Mark Twain's Notebook, p. 136

POLITICS *See also* CAIN, COUNTRY, EARTHQUAKE, GOVERN-
MENT, HONESTY, MORALS, NATURE, RELIGION, VOTING,
WASHINGTON, D.C.

I am a mugwump and a mugwump is pure from the marrow out.

Mark Twain, a Biography, Paine, II, p. 823

. . . one of the first achievements of the legislature was to institute a ten-thousand-dollar agricultural fair to show off forty dollars' worth of pumpkins in—however, the Territorial legislature was usually spoken of as the "asylum."

Roughing It, II, Chapt. XIV, p. 136

To lodge all power in one party and keep it there is to insure bad government and *the sure and gradual deterioration of the public morals.*

> *Mark Twain's Autobiography,* Paine, II, p. 14

[From a letter to Jules Hart, Dec. 17, 1901]:

When politics enter into municipal government, nothing resulting therefrom in the way of crimes and infamies is then incredible. It actually enables one to accept and believe the impossible. . . .

> *From a manuscript hitherto unpublished*

Mark Twain used his pungent pen to attack the shady schemes of Tammany. The death of a Tammany leader inspired one of Twain's famed quips: "I refused to attend his funeral. But I wrote a very nice letter explaining that I approved of it."

> *From an unidentified newspaper clipping*

The New Political Gospel: Public office is private graft.

> *More Maxims of Mark,* p. 10

Senator: Person who makes laws in Washington when not doing time.

> *Ibid.,* p. 12

. . . the average American citizen is true to his Christian principles three hundred and sixty-three days in the year . . . on the other two days of the year he [leaves] those principles at home and [goes] to the tax-office and the voting-booths, and [does] his best to damage and undo his whole year's faithful and righteous work.

> *Mark Twain, a Biography,* Paine, III, p. 1272

If we would learn what the human race really *is* at bottom, we need only observe it in election times.

> *Mark Twain's Autobiography,* Paine, II, p. 11

I do not know much about politics, and am not sitting up nights to learn.

> *Mark Twain, a Biography,* Paine, I, p. 399

. . . a man's first duty is to his own conscience and honor; the party and country come second to that, and never first.

> *Ibid.,* II, p. 780

I think I can say, and say with pride, that we have

legislatures that bring higher prices than any in the world.
"After-Dinner Speech"
Sketches New and Old, p. 235

[In *The Galaxy Magazine*]: I shall not often meddle with
politics, because we have a political Editor who is already
excellent and only needs to serve a term or two in the
penitentiary to be perfect.
Mark Twain, a Biography, Paine, I, p. 388

. . . policemen and politicians . . . are the dust-licking
pimps and slaves of the scum . . . in America.
Roughing It, II, Chapt. XIII, p. 135

[In 1881 Gen. Joseph R. Hawley, of Connecticut, addressed an immense Republican ratification meeting at Elmira. . . . He was introduced by Mark Twain]:

"I see I am advertised to introduce the speaker of the
evening . . . and I see it is the report that I am to make a
political speech. Now, I must say this is an error. I wasn't
constructed to make stump speeches. . . . Gen. Hawley
was President of the Centennial Commission. He was a
gallant soldier in the war. He has been Governor of Connecticut, member of Congress, and was President of the
convention that nominated Abraham Lincoln."

Gen. Hawley: "That nominated Grant."

Twain: "He says it was Grant, but I know better. He is
a member of my church at Hartford and the author of
'Beautiful Snow.' Maybe he will deny that. But I am only
here to give him a character from his last place. As a pure
citizen, I respect him; as a personal friend of years, I have
the warmest regard for him; as a neighbor whose vegetable
garden adjoins mine, why—why, I watch him. That's nothing; we all do that with any neighbor. Gen. Hawley keeps
his promises not only in private but in public. . . . He is
broad-souled, generous, noble, liberal, alive to his moral and
religious responsibilities. Whenever the contribution box
was passed I never knew him to take out a cent. He is a
square, true, honest man in politics, and I must say he
occupies a mighty lonesome position. . . . He is an American
of Americans. Would we had more such men! So broad, so

bountiful is his character that he never turned a tramp empty handed from his door, but always gave him a letter of introduction to me. . . . Pure, honest, incorruptible, that is Joe Hawley. Such a man in politics is like a bottle of perfumery in a glue factory—it may modify the stench if it doesn't destroy it. And now, in speaking thus highly of the speaker of the evening, I haven't said any more of him than I would say of myself. Ladies and gentlemen, this is Gen. Hawley."

> *Latter part of speech from unidentified*
> *newspaper clipping dated 1881*
> *Mark Twain, a Biography,* Paine, II p. 709

. . . get out of that sewer—party politics.

> *Mark Twain Letters,* II, p. 761

. . . the citizen who thinks he sees that the commonwealth's political clothes are worn out, and yet holds his peace and does not agitate for a new suit, is disloyal; he is a traitor.

> *A Connecticut Yankee in King Arthur's Court,*
> Chapt. XIII, p. 105

Concentration of power in a political machine is bad . . . it is an enemy to human liberty.

> *Ibid.,* Chapt. XVIII, p. 142

Somebody told him to keep up the dodge of pretending to belong to both parties—it was first-rate Washington policy to carry water on both shoulders. George said as long as he only had to carry the water on his shoulders he could stand it, but he was too good a Democrat to carry any in his stomach!

> "Personal"
> *Mark Twain's Travels with Mr. Brown,* p. 157

A pretty air in an opera is prettier there than it could be anywhere else, I suppose, just as an honest man in politics shines more than he would elsewhere.

> *A Tramp Abroad,* I, Chapt. IX, Vol. I

St. Patrick had no politics; his sympathies lay with the right—that was politics enough. When he came across a reptile, he forgot to inquire whether he was a democrat or a republican, but simply exalted his staff and "let him have it."

"Letter Read at a Dinner of the Knights of St. Patrick"
Tom Sawyer Abroad, Etc., p. 438

PONY EXPRESS

In a little while all interest was taken up in stretching our necks and watching for the "pony-rider"—the fleet messenger who sped across the continent from St. Joe to Sacramento, carrying letter nineteen hundred miles in eight days! Think of that for perishable horse and human flesh and blood to do! . . . There was no idling-time for a pony-rider on duty. He rode fifty miles without stopping, by daylight, moonlight, starlight, or through the blackness of darkness . . . He rode a splendid horse that was born for a racer . . . kept him at his utmost speed for ten miles, and then, as he came crashing up to the station where stood two men holding fast a fresh, impatient steed, the transfer of rider and mail-bag was made in the twinkling of an eye, and away flew the eager pair and were out of sight before the spectator could get hardly the ghost of a look. Both rider and horse went "flying light." The rider's dress was thin, and fitted close . . . He carried no arms—he carried nothing that was not absolutely necessary, for even the postage on his literary freight was worth *five dollars a letter.* . . . There were about eighty pony-riders in the saddle all the time, night and day, stretching in a long, scattering procession from Missouri to California . . . Now we were expecting one along every moment . . . . the driver exclaims: "HERE HE COMES!" Every neck is stretched further, and every eye strained wider. Away across the endless dead level of the prairie a black speck appears against the sky, and it is plain that it moves. . . . In a second or two it becomes a horse and rider, rising and falling . . . sweeping toward us . . . nearer and nearer, and the flutter of hoofs comes faintly to the ear—another instant a whoop and a hurrah from our upper deck, a wave of the rider's hand, but no reply, and man and horse burst past our excited faces, and go winging away like a belated fragment of a storm!

Roughing It, I, Chapt. VIII, p. 69

PONY RIDER   *See* HORSE, INDIAN, PONY EXPRESS

POPULARITY

Even popularity can be overdone. In Rome along at first you are full of regrets that Michelangelo died; but by and by you only regret that you didn't see him do it.

"Pudd'nhead Wilson's Calendar"
Pudd'nhead Wilson, Chapt. XVII, p. 164

Everybody's private motto: It's better to be popular than right.

More Maxims of Mark, p. 7

POPULATION   *See also* SAN FRANCISCO

The village of Florida, Mo. contained 100 people and I increased the population by 1%. It is more than many of the best men in history could have done for a town. It may not be modest in me to refer to this, but it is true. There is no record of a person doing as much—not even Shakespeare. But I did it for Florida and it shows I could have done it for any place—even London, I suppose.

Mark Twain's Autobiography, Paine, I, p. 95

PORPOISES

Schools of porpoises come streaking in to the ship from out the black distances like luminous sea serpents. A porpoise 8 feet long would look like a glorified serpent 30 to 50 ft. long, every curve of the tapering long body perfect and the whole snake dazzingly illuminated by the phosphorescent splendors in the waters. . . . The night was so dark that the actual surface of the sea was not distinguishable, and so it was a weird sight to see this spiral ghost come suddenly flashing along out of the solid gloom and streak past like a meteor.

Mark Twain's Notebook, p. 251

POSSESSION

They . . . were always wrenching the conversation out of its groove . . . so that they could say "my horse" here, and "my horse" there and yonder and all around, and taste the words and lick their chops over them, and spread their legs and hitch their thumbs in their armpits, and feel as the good God feels when He looks out on His fleets of constellations plowing the awful deeps of space and reflects with satisfaction that they are His—all His.

Personal Recollections of Joan of Arc,
II, Book II, Chapt. XXXVI, p. 65

Each person is born to one possession which outvalues all his others—his last breath.

"Pudd'nhead Wilson's New Calendar"
Following the Equator, II, Chapt. VI, p. 69

POST-OFFICE

[In 1899] Mark Twain invented a postal-check, more simple than the money-orders, because they could be bought in any quantity and denomination and kept on hand for immediate use. One could make them individually payable merely by writing in the name of the payee. He remarked: "The government officials would probably not care to buy it as soon as they found they couldn't kill Christians with it."

Mark Twain, a Biography, Paine, II, p. 1076

POVERTY   *See also* VALUE, RICHES

Let us adopt geological time, then time being money,— there will be no poverty.

Mark Twain's Notebook, p. 393

Honest poverty is a gem that even a King might feel proud to call his own, but I wish to sell out. I have sported that kind of jewelry long enough. I want some variety. I wish to become rich, so that I can instruct the people and glorify honest poverty a little, like those kind-hearted, fat, benevolent people do.

Mark Twain's Travels with Mr. Brown, p. 236

The offspring of poverty: Greed, sordidness, envy, hate, malice, cruelty, meanness, lying, shirking, cheating, stealing, murder.

Mark Twain, a Biography, Paine, III, p. 1194

POWER   *See also* GOVERNMENT, POLITICS
It always makes me feel a little sad to see . . . something meant to be great that doesn't know its own power. . . . And people are like that . . . They don't know their own possibilities and so they perform just as the elephant does for someone else's bidding, while all the time within them is the driving power of the universe.

Enchantment, Dorothy Quick, p. 160

The human race dearly envies a lord . . . on two accounts, I think: its Power and its Conspicuousness.

"Does the Race of Man Love a Lord?"
The $30,000 Bequest, Etc., p. 270

PRAISE   *See also* COMPLIMENT
It is human to like to be praised; one can even notice it in the French.

"What Paul Bourget Thinks of Us"
Literary Essays, p. 152

There is no satisfaction in the world's praise anyhow, and it has no worth to me save in the way of business.

Mark Twain's Letters, I, p. 128

PRAYER   *See also* SEX, WAR, WEATHER
Leaving out the gamblers, the burglars, and the plumbers, perhaps we do put our trust in God after a fashion. But, after all, it is an overstatement.

If the cholera or black plague should come to these shores, perhaps the bulk of the nation would pray to be delivered from it, but the rest would put their trust in The Health Board. . . .

"Education and Citizenship"
Mark Twain's Speeches (1923), p. 379

Prayer alone cannot change the unalterable Truth, or

give us an understanding of it; but prayer coupled with a fervent habitual desire to know and do the will of God will bring us into all Truth. Such a desire has little need of audible expression. It is best expressed in thought and life.

Christian Science, Book II, Appendix D, p. 321

There was a temple devoted to prayers for rain—and with fine sagacity it was placed at a point so well up on the mountain side that if you prayed twenty four times a day you would be likely to get it every time. You would seldom get to your Amen before you would have to hoist your umbrella.

Roughing It, II, Chapt. XXXI, p. 280

Pray for me! I reckon if she knowed me she'd take a job that was more nearer her size . . . but . . . she had the grit to pray for Judas if she took the notion—there warn't no back-down to her, I judge.

The Adventures of Huckleberry Finn,
Chapt. XXVIII, p. 250

. . . it would be kind of soft and self-contained like a republican praying for a mugwump.

"The German Chicago"
The American Claimant, Etc., p. 509

Uncle Silas he peeled off one of his bulliest old-time blessings, with as many layers to it as an onion, and whilst the angels was hauling in the slack of it I was trying to study up what to say.

"Tom Sawyer, Detective"
Tom Sawyer Abroad, Etc., p. 174

[Aboard ship]: There they are . . . praying for fair winds —when they know . . . this is the only ship going east this time of the year, but there's a thousand coming west— what's a fair wind for us is a *head* wind to them—the Almighty's blowing a fair wind for a thousand vessels, and this tribe wants Him to turn it clear around so as to accommodate *one,*—and she a steamship at that? It ain't good sense, it ain't good reason, it ain't good Christianity, it ain't common human charity.

The Innocents Abroad, I, Chapt. IV, p. 76

[In Tibet]: The prayer wheel was a frequent feature. It brought me near to these people and made them seem kinfolk of mine. Through our preacher we do much of our praying by proxy. We do not whirl him around on a stick, as they do, but that is merely a detail.

Following the Equator, II, Chapt. XIX, p. 233

I have been reading the morning paper. I do it every morning—well knowing that I shall find in it the usual depravities and basenesses and hypocrisies and cruelties that make up civilization, and cause me to put in the rest of the day pleading for the damnation of the human race. I cannot seem to get my prayers answered, yet I do not despair.

Mark Twain's Letters, II, p. 678

PREACHER *See also* CHURCH, CLERGYMAN, COMEDY, DOC-
TOR, FOOL, PRINTING, SERMON

[To be a preacher]: It was the most earnest ambition I ever had. . . . Not that I ever really wanted to be a preacher, but because it never occurred to me that a preacher could be damned. It looked like a safe job.

Mark Twain, a Biography, Paine, I, p. 84

. . . he was a preacher, too . . . and never charged nothing for his preaching, and it was worth it, too.

The Adventures of Huckleberry Finn,
Chapt. XXXIII, p. 294

[Mark Twain to Rev. Joseph Twichell]: "Joe, that's a clever trick of yours to pound the pulpit extra hard when you haven't anything to say."

[Rev. Twichell]: "Mark, it was clever of you to discover it."

My Father • Mark Twain, Clara Clemens, p. 26

. . . send on the professional preachers—there are none I like better to converse with. If they're not narrow-minded and bigoted they make good companions.

Mark Twain's Letters, I, p. 126

I have always preached. . . . If the humor came of its own accord and uninvited, I have allowed it a place in my sermon, but I was not writing the sermon for the sake of the humor. I should have written the sermon just the same whether any humor applied for admission or not.

Mark Twain in Eruption, p. 202

In Hartford, Twain heard Twichell preach one of his best sermons. Afterward he said: "I enjoyed your sermon this morning. I welcomed it as an old friend, for I have a book in my library that contains every word of it."

"Why, that can't be, Clemens. I should certainly like to see that book."

"All right, you shall have it," replied the humorist.

The next morning the rector received with Twain's compliments, a dictionary.

An unidentified news clipping

It is not a new thing for a thoroughly good and well-meaning preacher's soft heart to run away with his soft head.

"Temperance and Woman's Rights"
Europe and Elsewhere, p. 30

PREDESTINATION *See also* PROVIDENCE

When the first living atom found itself afloat on the great Laurentian sea the first act of that first atom led to the *second* act of that first atom, and so on down through the succeeding ages of all life, until, if the steps could be traced, it would be shown that the first act of that first atom has led inevitably to the act of my standing here . . . at this instant . . .

Mark Twain, a Biography, I, p. 397

. . . nothing can change the order of [one's] life after the first event has determined it.

The Mysterious Stranger, Etc., Chapt. VII, p. 81

It shows how foolish people are when they blame themselves for anything they have done . . . nothing happens that your first act hasn't arranged to happen and made inevitable; and so, of your own motion you can't ever alter the scheme or do a thing that will break a link.

Ibid., Chapt. VIII, p. 100

PREFACE

[Preface to the Uniform Edition of Mark Twain's writings]: Prefaces wear many disguises, call themselves by various names, and pretend to come on various businesses . . . but their errand is always the same; they are there to apologize for the book; in other words, furnish reasons for its publication. . . .

Aside from the ordinary commercial reasons I find none that I can offer with dignity. . . . I find no reason which I can offer without immodesty except the rather poor one that I should like to see a Uniform Edition myself. It is nothing; a cat could say it about her kittens. Still, I believe I will stand upon that.

The Innocents Abroad, I, p. xxxv

PREJUDICE   *See also* HISTORY, IGNORANCE, LANGUAGE, PRINCIPLE, SATAN, SOCIETY, TEETH, TRAVEL

Put aside prejudice—prejudice is nobody's sure friend.

Letters to Mary, p. 107

Travel is fatal to prejudice.

The Innocents Abroad, II, Conclusion. p. 444

We are chameleons, and our partialities and prejudices change places with an easy and blessed facility, and we are soon wonted to the change and happy in it.

Mark Twain's Speeches (1923), p. 316

The very ink with which history is written is merely fluid prejudice.

"Pudd'nhead Wilson's New Calendar,"
Following the Equator, II, Chapt. XXXIII, p. 392

PRESBYTERIAN   *See also* CONVICTION, INSANITY, RELIGION, SIMILES, WEATHER

Presbyterianism without infant damnation would be like the dog on the train that couldn't be identified because it had lost its tag.

Mark Twain, a Biography, Paine, III, p. 1534

. . . the door opened and Mrs. Hay, gravely clad, gloved,

bonneted, and just from church, and fragrant with the odors of Presbyterian sanctity, stood in it.

Mark Twain's Autobiography, Paine, I, p. 233

[H.] is biased. You find me a Presbyterian that isn't, if you think you can.

"Adam's Soliloquy,"
Europe and Elsewhere, p. 380

I was a Presbyterian, and I knew . . . that in Biblical times, if a man committed a sin, the extermination of the whole surrounding nation—cattle and all—was likely to happen.

Mark Twain in Eruption, p. 261

The heaven and hell of the wildcat religions are vague and ill-defined but there is nothing mixed about the Presbyterian heaven and hell. The Presbyterian hell is all misery; the heaven all happiness—nothing to do. But when a man dies on a wildcat basis, he will never rightly know hereafter which department he is in—but he will think he is in hell anyhow, no matter which place he goes to; because in the good place they pro-gress, pro-gress, pro-gress —study, study, study, all the time—and if this isn't hell I don't know what is; and in the bad place he will be worried by remorse of conscience. Their bad place is preferable, though, because eternity is long, and before a man got half through it he would forget what it was he had been so sorry about. Naturally he would then become cheerful again; but the party who went to heaven would go on progressing and progressing, and studying and studying until he would finally get discouraged and wish he were in hell, where he wouldn't require such a splendid education.

"Reflections on the Sabbath,"
The Washoe Giant in San Francisco, p. 116

It has taken a weary long time to persuade American Presbyterians to give up infant damnation and try to bear it the best they can.

"Is Shakespeare Dead?"
What Is Man? and Other Essays, p. 366

. . . mine was a trained Presbyterian conscience and

knew but the one duty—to hunt and harry its slave upon all pretexts and on all occasions, particularly when there was no sense nor reason in it.

Mark Twain's Autobiography, Paine, I, p. 131

PRESIDENT *See* CLEVELAND, GRANT, ROOSEVELT

PRESS *See also* IRREVERENCE, LIBERTY, LIGHT, NEWSPAPER
The license of the press has scorched every individual of us in our time.

Mark Twain's Speeches (1923), p. 50
It is a free press. . . . There are laws to protect the freedom of the press's speech, but none that are worth anything to protect the people from the press.

"License of the Press,"
Ibid., p. 43
. . . the *liberty* of the Press is called the Palladium of Freedom, which means, in these days, the liberty of being deceived, swindled, and humbugged by the Press and paying hugely for the deception.

"From Author's Sketch Book, Nov. 1870,"
The Twainian, May 1940, p. 2
. . . our press . . . [is] distinctively and preciously American, its frank and cheerful irreverence being by all odds the most valuable of all its qualities . . . its mission . . . is to stand guard over a nation's liberties, not its humbugs and shams.

The American Claimant, Etc., Chapt. X, p. 79
I have a sort of vague general idea that there is too much liberty of the press in this country, and that through the absence of all wholesome restraint the newspaper has become in a large degree a national *curse*, and will probably damn the Republic yet.

"License of the Press,"
Mark Twain's Speeches (1923), p. 52

PRETENSE *See* HONESTY, SHAM

PRIDE *See also* HUNGER, PLAGIARISM, POSSESSION, SHIP, TRAVEL

Human pride is not worth while; there is always something lying in wait to take the wind out of it.

> *Following the Equator,* II, Conclusion, p. 409

. . . I felt as proud as Pierpont Morgan on discovering a Fifteenth Century missal and buying it for five dollars.

Abroad with Mark Twain and Eugene Field, Fisher, p. 134

. . . although [my father] left us a sumptuous legacy of pride in his fine Virginian stock and its national distinction, I presently found that I could not live on that alone without occasional bread to wash it down with.

> *Roughing It,* II, Chapt. I, p. 15

We are a race of lightning-shod Mercuries, and proud of it—instead of being, like our ancestors, a race of plodding crabs, and proud of that.

> "A Majestic Literary Fossil,"
> *The American Claimant, Etc.,* p. 525

The pride of profession is one of the boniest bones of existence, if not the boniest.

> "The Bee,"
> *What Is Man? and Other Essays,* p. 284

PRIEST *See also* RELIGION

The old monks are wise. They know how to drive a stake through a pleasant tradition that will hold it to its place forever.

> *The Innocents Abroad,* II, Chapt. XXIII, p. 294

[I had] for comrade, a Catholic priest who was better than I was, but didn't seem to know it. . . . He will rise. He will be a Bishop some day. Later an Archbishop. Later a Cardinal. Finally an Archangel, I hope. And then he will recall me when I say, "Do you remember that trip we made from Ballarat to Bendigo, when you were nothing but Father C., and I was nothing to what I am now?"

> *Following the Equator,* I, Chapt. XXV, p. 245

La Trappe must have known the human race well. The

scheme which he invented hunts out everything that a man wants and values—and withholds it from him. . . .

· · ·

If he had consulted you or me he would have been told that his scheme lacked too many attractions; that it was impossible; that it could never be floated. . . .

· · ·

. . . But La Trappe knew the race. He knew the powerful attraction of unattractiveness: he knew that no life could be imagined, howsoever comfortless and forbidding, but somebody would want to try it.

Ibid., II, Chapt. XXIX, p. 345

[He] was a canon of the cathedral of Paris. I do not know what a canon of a cathedral is, but that is what he was. He was nothing more than a sort of a mountain howitzer, likely, because they had no heavy artillery in those days.

The Innocents Abroad, I, Chapt. XV, p. 191

PRINCIPLE *See also* BIRD, PROSPERITY

. . . a troublesome old rip, with no more principle than an Injun. . . .

"Rambling Notes of an Idle Excursion,"
Tom Sawyer Abroad, Etc., p. 287

. . . freckles me with bullet-holes till my skin won't hold my principles.

"Journalism in Tennessee,"
Sketches New and Old, p. 52

. . . if he's short of facts, he invents them. He hasn't any more principle than a blue-jay.

"A Horse's Tale,"
The Mysterious Stranger, Etc., p. 193

[Adam]: "I was obliged to eat [the apples], I was so hungry. It was against my principles, but I find that principles have no real force except when one is well fed. . . ."

"Extracts from Adam's Diary,"
The Man That Corrupted Hadleyburg, Etc., p. 266

You cannot have a theory without principles. Principles is another name for prejudices.

"Literature,"
Mark Twain's Speeches (1923), p. 207

Principles aren't of much account anyway, except at election time. After that you hang them up to let them season.

"Municipal Corruption,"
Ibid., p. 220

We all live in the protection of certain cowardices which we call our principles.

More Maxims of Mark, p. 14

[Choate, a lawyer] was engaged as a young man with a gentle Hebrew, in the process of skinning the client. The main part in that business is the collection of the bill for services in skinning the man. "Services" is the term used in that craft for the operation of that kind—diplomatic in its nature.

Choate's [partner] made out a bill for five hundred dollars for his services, so called. But Choate told him he better leave the matter to him, and the next day he collected the bill for services and handed the Hebrew five thousand dollars, saying, "That's your half of the loot," and inducing that memorable response: "Almost thou persuadest me to become a Christian."

. . . the principle underlying that anecdote . . . the principle of give and take—give one and take ten—the principle of diplomacy.

"The Dinner to Mr. Choate,"
Mark Twain's Speeches (1923), p. 242

PRINTING

I set (or sat) type alongside of his father . . . more than fifty years ago when none but the pure of heart were in that business.

Mark Twain, a Biography, Paine, III, p. 1208

[An incident which occurred when Mark Twain and Wales McCormick were printer's apprentices in Hannibal, Missouri]:

I have said that Wales was reckless, and he was. . . .
Among his shining characteristics was the most limitless
and adorable irreverence . . .

Once the celebrated founder of . . . the new and wide-
spread sect called Campbellites arrived in our village from
Kentucky, and it made a prodigious excitement. The farmers and their families drove or tramped into the village
from miles around to get a sight of the illustrious Alexander
Campbell and to have a chance to hear him preach.

He preached a sermon on one of these occasions which
he had written especially for that occasion. All the Campbellites wanted it printed . . .

We set up the great book in pages—eight pages to a form
—and by help of a printer's manual we managed to get the
pages in their apparently crazy but really sane places on
the imposing-stone. . . . Wales read the proof, and presently he was aghast, for he had struck a snag. And it was a
bad time to strike a snag, because it was Saturday; it was
approaching noon; Saturday afternoon was our holiday, and
we wanted to get away and go fishing. . . . Wales . . .
showed us what had happened. He had left out a couple
of words in a thin-spaced page of solid matter and there
wasn't another break-line for two or three pages ahead.
What in the world was to be done? Overrun all those pages
in order to get in the two missing words? Apparently there
was no other way. It would take an hour to do it. Then a
revise must be sent to the great minister; we must wait for
him to read the revise; . . . It looked as if we might lose
half the afternoon before we could get away. Then Wales
had one of his brilliant ideas. In the line in which the "out"
had been made occurred the name Jesus Christ. Wales re-
duced it in the French way to J.C. It made room for the
missing words, but it took 99 per cent of the solemnity out
of a particularly solemn sentence. We sent off the revise
and waited. We were not intending to wait long. In the
circumstances we meant to get out and go fishing before
that revise should get back, but we were not speedy enough.
Presently that great Alexander Campbell appeared at the

far end of that sixty-foot room, and his countenance cast a gloom over the whole place. He strode down to our end and what he said was brief, but it was very stern, and it was to the point. He read Wales a lecture. He said, "So long as you live, don't you ever diminish the Saviour's name again. Put it *all* in." He repeated this admonition a couple of times to emphasize it, then he went away.

. . . So [Wales] imposed upon himself the long and weary and dreary task of over-running all those three pages in order to improve upon his former work and incidentally and thoughtfully improve upon the great preacher's admonition. He enlarged the offending J.C. into Jesus H. Christ. Wales knew that that would make prodigious trouble, and it did. But it was not in him to resist it. He had to succumb to the law of his make. I don't remember what his punishment was, but he was not the person to care for that. He had already collected his dividend.

Mark Twain's Autobiography, Paine, II, p. 279

(I began to set type when I was 13 years old, and have always had a right respect and reverence for that art.)

There is not a material marvel of this marvelous age in which we live whose fatherhood cannot be traced distinctly back to a single point, a single remote germ, a single primal source—the movable types of Gutenberg and Faust. That invention, of 538 years ago, was the second supreme event in the globe's creative history; for by an unstrained metaphor one may say that on that day God said again, Let there be light—and there was light. From that faint and far source, divergent threads of light stretch down through the centuries, as from some star-sun, glinting out of dim solitudes of space, to each and every precious and wonderful achievement of man's inventive genius which goes to make up to-day the sum of what we rightly call the most extraordinary age the world has ever seen. Each of these achievements is the result of the ray that came to it from that star-sun; this age is the result of that fan of rays; without that star-sun this age had not been.

What changes have not these movable types witnessed—

and wrought—in 538 years! They have seen the implements
of war so changed that an army corps of today, with its
Gatling guns, and bombs, and rifled cannon and other
deadly things would hold a field against the combined
armies of Europe of Gutenberg's time, and a single iron-
clad of today sweep her fleets from the sea. They have seen
methods of travel so changed that a citizen of to-day could
give Gutenberg a couple of years' start and beat him around
the world. They have seen facility of speech so changed by
the telephone that even a truth may travel farther in two
minutes to-day than a lie could in a week in his day. They
have seen methods of written communication so changed
that a New Yorker may send a message to China now
quicker than Gutenberg could have carried it up stairs to
his wife. They have seen methods of printing so changed
that a press of today will turn off a job in a year which a
customer of Gutenberg's would have had to wait nearly
five centuries for—and then get it, perhaps, when interest
in that publication had pretty much died out, and he would
wish he hadn't ordered it. They have seen the science of
medicine and surgery so immeasurably changed that a doctor of today would save three patients in less time than it
would take *his* doctor to kill three hundred. They have
seen industrial methods so amazingly accelerated by machinery that today a body of men would manufacture the
stuffs and clothe and shoe a whole nation while a like body
of Gutenberg's contemporaries were doing the same for its
capital city. In a word, those movable types, in these 538
years, have changed, and marvelously accelerated and advanced and improved every art and every industry known
to men; they have utterly changed the face of art and industry in this whole world; so that not one single thing is
done to-day as men saw it done in the day of Gutenberg
and Faust.

But no, I am wrong. There is one thing which they have
not changed; one thing which remains just what it was in
the year 1348*, unchanged, unadvanced, unimproved. The
movable type has taught the whole world something: it

has taught itself nothing. Isn't that a curious thing? Isn't it striking? Isn't it an actually stupefying thought? The typesetting art is the one solitary art in this world which has stood stock-still for five hundred years. It is the art creative of arts, yet it can create nothing for itself. Truly it is a sun; it is the source and impulse of all intellectual life, but it stands still. Imagine, if you please, the people of Gutenberg's day suddenly snatched out of their graves and set down in New York, without a cent. What a strange new world it would be to them; what a strange and hopeless place for them. Poor fellows, they would apply here, they would apply there, they would apply yonder; but all to no use, they could get no work; they would find that the trades they learned five hundred years ago were worthless to them now, so sweeping has been the change in methods. Within one week that entire host would be in the poor house. With only one exception—old Gutenberg. He would be subbing somewhere. Yes, it is a most curious thing—that which I have been talking about. And the more one thinks it over, the more strange and curious it seems. I confess to you, fellow-craftsmen, that I control one of the hundred and one devices and inventions for setting type by machinery, but do not be uneasy, I did not come here to advertise it. I only came to disgorge some grave and thoughtful thoughts, that is all; and you have done me the grace to receive them in a less depreciative spirit than the foremen used to do in an office where I was a reporter twenty years ago.

When I brought in that sort of copy, one of them used to say, in printers' parlance, "Here he comes with some more hell-matter," and the other said in a parlance of his own, "Here he comes with some more hogwash." Printers are strangely frank in the matter of literary criticism.

*[Mark Twain's error; Gutenberg lived 1398–1468.]

From an unpublished speech manuscript, 1886

[Bret Harte]: His duties as editor required him to read proof. Once a galley slip was laid before him which consisted of one of those old-time obituaries which were so dismally popular all over the United States when we were still a soft-hearted and sentimental people. There was half a column of the obituary . . . it was made up of superlatives . . . closing with that remark which was never missing from the regulation obituary: "Our loss is her eternal gain."

In the proof Harte found this observation: "Even in Yreka her chastity was conspicuous." Of course that was a misprint for "charity," but Harte didn't think of that; he knew a printer's mistake had been made and he also knew that a reference to the manuscript would determine what it was; therefore he followed proofreader custom and with his pen indicated [this] . . . he drew a black line under the word chastity, and in the margin he placed a question mark enclosed in parentheses. . . . But there is another proofreader law which he overlooked. That law says that when a word is not emphatic enough you must draw a line under it, and this will require the printer to reinforce it by putting it in italics.

When Harte took up the paper in the morning and looked at that obituary he took only one glance; then he levied on a mule that was not being watched and cantered out of town, knowing well that in a very little while there was going to be a visit from the widower, with his gun. In the obituary the derelict observation now stood in this form: "Even in Yreka her *chastity* was conspicuous(?)"—a form which turned the thing into a ghastly and ill-timed sarcasm!

Mark Twain in Eruption, p. 288

PRIVILEGE *See also* DEMOCRACY

[Near Scott's Bluff Pass]: It was along here somewhere that we first came across genuine and unmistakable alkali water in the road, and we cordially hailed it as a first-class curiosity, and a thing to be mentioned with éclat in letters to the ignorant at home. This water gave the road a soapy appearance. . . . I think the strange alkali water excited us as much as any wonder we had come upon yet, and I know we felt very complacent and conceited, and better satisfied with life after we had added it to our list of things which *we* had seen and some other people had not.

Roughing It, I, Chapt. VIII, p. 72

. . . it seemed to me he had not bought a villa, but only a privilege—the privilege of building it over again and making it humanly habitable.

Mark Twain's Autobiography, Paine, I, p. 215

PROCRASTINATION *See also* WORK

I am a natural procrastinaturalist.

Mark Twain-Howells Letters, I, p. 50

Do not put off till tomorrow what can be put off till day-after-tomorrow just as well.

More Maxims of Mark, p. 7

PROFANITY *See also* ANGER, BOAT, CLERGYMAN, COM-
PLAINT, FOOL, HOUSE, LANGUAGE, LUCK, RAILROAD, RE-
FORM, TAXES, TEMPER

He called me a quadrilateral astronomical incandescent son of a bitch.

Mark Twain-Howells Letters, II, p. 765

Sir to you, I would like to know what kind of a goddam government this is that discriminates between two common carriers and makes a goddam railroad charge everybody equal and lets a goddam man charge any goddam price he wants to for his goddam opera box. [Oct. 1907]

Ibid., II, p. 827

I little judicious profanity helps out an otherwise ineffectual sketch or poem remarkably.

Ibid., I, p. 59

By the humping, jumping Jesus!

My Father • Mark Twain, Clara Clemens, p. 26

[After learning to ride the bicycle, Mark Twain declared] that he invented all the new bicycle profanity that has since come into general use.

Mark Twain, a Biography, Paine, II, p. 767

There ought to be a room in this house to swear in. It's

dangerous to have to repress an emotion like that.

> *Ibid.*, III, p. 1301

[The captain] wove a glittering streak of profanity through his garrulous fabric that was refreshing to a spirit weary of the dull neutralities of undecorated speech.

> "Rambling Notes of an Idle Excursion,"
> *Tom Sawyer Abroad, Etc.*, p. 272

[Mark Twain used to conceal his profanity from his wife. One morning she overheard him. When he came into her room she repeated to him his last terrific remark. The humor of it struck him.]

"Livy," he said, "did it sound like that?"

"Of course it did," she said, "only worse. I wanted you to hear just how it sounded."

"Livy," he said, "it would pain me to think that when I swear it sounds like that. You got the words right, Livy, but you don't know the tune."

> *Mark Twain, a Biography*, Paine, I, p. 559

[The captain] considered swearing blameless because sailors would not understand an order unillumined by it.

> "The Captain's Story,"
> *Literary Essays*, p. 194

In certain trying circumstances, urgent circumstances, desperate circumstances profanity furnishes a relief denied even to prayer.

> *Mark Twain, a Biography*, Paine, I, p. 214

I have some new sleeve buttons . . . beautiful anticussers. You can put them in and take them out without a change of temper. . . . They are tumblebugs of cornelian . . . with patent antiblasphemers attached on the under side.

> *My Father • Mark Twain*, Clara Clemens, p. 121

. . . what a lie it is to call this a free country, where none but the unworthy and undeserving may swear.

> "On Speech-Making Reform,"
> *Mark Twain's Speeches* (1923), p. 6

. . . [Finally] he was empty. You could have drawn a

seine through his system and not caught curses enough to disturb your mother.

Life on the Mississippi, Chapt. VI, p. 59

I sent down . . . and hired an artist by the week to sit up nights and curse that stranger, and give me a lift occasionally in the daytime when I came to a hard place.

"A Mysterious Visit,"
Sketches New and Old, p. 421

Profanity is more necessary to me than is immunity from colds. [To Orion Clemens, 1877]

Seen in manuscript

. . . I was . . . blaspheming my luck in a way that made my breath smell of brimstone.

Roughing It, I, Chapt. VII, p. 62

The two American miners . . . are poor yet, and they take turn about in getting up early in the morning to curse those Mexicans—and when it comes down to pure ornamental cursing, the native American is gifted above the sons of men.

Ibid., II, Chapt. XIX, p. 183

The governor's temper got afire, and he delivered an oath . . . that knocked up the dust where it struck the ground . . .

Personal Recollections of Joan of Arc,
I, Book II, Chapt. III, p. 128

If I cannot swear in heaven I shall not stay there.

Mark Twain's Notebook, p. 345

[Accomplished profanity]: There is nothing like listening to an artist—all his passions passing away in lava, smoke, thunder, lightning, and earthquake.

Mark Twain's Speeches (1910), p. 292

Let us swear while we may, for in heaven it will not be allowed.

Mark Twain's Notebook, p. 344

Going down on an elevator, a man stepped in from one of the floors swearing violently. Clemens leaning over to Hall, with his hand to his mouth and in a whisper audible to every one, said: "Bishop of Chicago." The man, with a

quick glance, recognized his fellow-passenger and subsided.
> *Mark Twain, a Biography,* Paine, II, p. 965

The spirit of wrath—not the words—is the sin; and the spirit of wrath is cursing. We begin to swear before we can talk.
> "Pudd'nhead Wilson's New Calendar,"
> *Following the Equator,* I, Chapt. XXXI, p. 303

PROFESSION *See also* PRIDE

The loftiest of all human vocations—medicine and surgery. Relief from physical pain and physical distress. Next comes the pulpit, which solaces mental distress: soothes the sorrows of the soul. The two are the great professions, the noble professions. The gap between them and the next is wide—an abyss.
> *Mark Twain's Notebook,* p. 251

PROGRESS *See also* GUN

. . . the 19th century made progress—the first progress after "ages and ages"—colossal progress. In what? Materialities. Prodigious acquisitions were made in things which add to the comfort of many and make life harder for as many more. But the addition to righteousness? Is that discoverable? I think not. The materialities were not invented in the interest of righteousness . . .
> *Mark Twain's Letters,* II, p. 769

(*In Munich*): I have written 900 pages of manuscript on my book; it is half done; Livy and Clara have learned half of the German language together so they are half done; the children have learned how to speak German, drink beer and break the Sabbath like the natives, so they are half-done. We are all a half-way lot, like the rest of the world; but we are progressing toward the great goal, Completion, Perfection—which has also another name, the Unattainable.
> *Samuel Langhorne Clemens,* p. 10

PROHIBITION *See also* LIQUOR

What do I think of Prohibition? Nothing, for the simple

reason that there is no such thing. When men want drink, they'll have it in spite of all the laws ever passed; when they don't want it, no drink will be sold.

Mark Twain's Notebook, p. 257

What marriage is to morality, a properly conducted liquor traffic is to sobriety.

In fact, the more things are forbidden, the more popular they become.

Ibid., p. 257

It is the *prohibition* that *makes* anything precious.

Ibid., p. 275

Evidence . . . proves that prohibition only drives drunkenness behind doors and into dark places, and does not cure it or even diminish it.

"Miscellaneous,"
Mark Twain's Travels with Mr. Brown, p. 248

PROMISE

. . . alas! I never could keep a promise . . . It is likely that such a very liberal amount of space was given to the organ which enables me to *make* promises, that the organ which should enable me to keep them was crowded out. But I grieve not. I like no half-way things. I had rather have one faculty nobly developed than two faculties of mere ordinary capacity.

The Innocents Abroad, I, Chapt. XXIII, p. 306

Better a broken promise than none at all.

More Maxims of Mark, p. 6

PROMPTNESS   *See* KNOWLEDGE

PRONUNCIATION   *See*   CHILDREN,   DRINK,   LANGUAGE, NAME, SPELLING, TEETH

PROPHECY

It seems to me the prophets fooled away their time when they prophesied the destruction of the cities—old Time would have fixed that, easy enough.

Mark Twain's Notebook, p. 107

A prophet doesn't have to have any brains. They are good to have, of course, for the ordinary exigencies of life, but they are no use in professional work. It is the restfulest vocation there is. When the spirit of prophecy comes upon you, you merely cake your intellect and lay it off in a cool place for a rest, and unship your jaw and leave it alone; it will work itself: the result is prophecy.

> *A Connecticut Yankee in King Arthur's Court,*
> Chapt. XXVII, p. 249

There is no prophecy in our day but history. But history is a trustworthy prophet.

> *Christian Science,* Book II, Chapt. VII, p. 213

. . . prophecies boldly uttered never fall barren on superstitious ears.

> *Personal Recollections of Joan of Arc,*
> I, Book II, Chapt. IV, p. 133

. . . a prophecy is a grisly and awful thing whether one thinks it ascends from hell or comes down from heaven.

> *Ibid.,* II, Book III, Chapt. IV, p. 184

Prophecy: Two bull's eyes out of a possible million.

> *More Maxims of Mark,* p. 12

PROPORTION

Consider well the proportions of things. It is better to be a young June-bug than an old bird of paradise.

> "Pudd'nhead Wilson's Calendar,"
> *Pudd'nhead Wilson,* Chapt. VIII, p. 68

PROSE   *See* POETRY

PROSPERITY   *See also* DOG, FRIEND, WAGE, WOMAN

Only he who has seen better days and lives to see better days again knows their full value.

> *Mark Twain's Notebook,* p. 379

Few of us can stand prosperity. Another man's I mean.

> "Pudd'nhead Wilson's New Calendar,"
> *Following the Equator,* II, Chapt. IV, p. 50

There is an old time toast which is golden for its beauty.

"When you ascend the hill of prosperity may you not meet a friend."

> "Pudd'nhead Wilson's New Calendar,"
> *Ibid.*, II, Chapt. V, p. 60

Prosperity is the surest breeder of insolence I know of.

> "What Six Years Have Wrought,"
> *Mark Twain's Travels with Mr. Brown*, p. 110

Prosperity is the best protector of principle.

> "Pudd'nhead Wilson's New Calendar,"
> *Following the Equator*, II, Chapt. II, p. 23

In prosperity we are popular; popularity comes easy in that case, but when the other thing comes our friends are pretty likely to turn against us.

> *The American Claimant, Etc.*, Chapt. XII, p. 104

It does rather look as if in a republic where all are free and equal prosperity and position constitute *rank*.

> *Ibid.*, Chapt. XII, p. 105

. . . what a vast respect Prosperity commands.

> *Mark Twain's Letters*, I, p. 43

PROVERB   *See* LEARNING

PROVIDENCE   *See also* DOG, FATE, IRISHMEN, LUCK

I never count any prospective chickens when I know that Providence knows where the nest is.

> *Mark Twain-Howells Letters*, I, p. 445

I have a boil on one side of my nose and a cold on the other, and whether I sneeze or blow it is all one; I get the lockjaw anyhow. I never fully comprehended the ways of Providence. For my feeble finite wisdom is utter stumped with the simple problem of what great and good end is to be accomplished by the conferring of this boil and this cold on me both at the same time, but Providence understands it easy enough. The ways of Providence are too inscrutable for the subscriber.

> Letter to the *Alta California*, Oct. 28, 1868,
> *The Twainian*, Mar.–Apr. 1949, p. 5

A cultivated bootblack happily accounted for the absence

of all apparent fear on the part of both Daniel and the lion, in a picture representing the prophet in the den:

"Humph! the lion don't give a damn for Dan'l, and Dan'l don't give a damn for the lion—both of 'em relies on the protection o' Prov'dence."

Mark Twain's Travels with Mr. Brown, p. 224

. . . there [is] no such thing as an accident: . . . it was all forewritten in the day of the beginning; . . . every event, however slight, was embryonic in that first instant of created life, and immutably timed to its appearance in the web of destiny.

Mark Twain, a Biography, Paine, II, p. 628

. . . consider Noah's flood—I wish I knew the real reason for playing that cataclysm on the public; like enough, somebody that liked dry weather wanted to take a walk. That is probably the whole thing—and nothing more to it.

My Father • Mark Twain, Clara Clemens, p. 54

Providence leaves nothing to go by chance. All things have their uses and their part and proper place in Nature's economy: the ducks eat the flies—the flies eat the worms—the Indians eat all three—the wild cats eat the Indians—the white folks eat the wild cats—and thus all things are lovely.

Roughing It, I, Chapt. XXXVIII, p. 297

We are accustomed to seeing the hand of Providence in everything. . . . When Providence washes one of his worms into the sea in a tempest, then starves him and freezes him on a plank for thirty-four days, and finally wrecks him again on an uninhabited island, where he lives on shrimps and grasshoppers and other shellfish for three months, and is at last rescued by some old whisky-soaked, profane, and blasphemous infidel of a tramp captain, and carried home gratis to his friends, the worm forgets that it was Providence that washed him overboard, and only remembers that Providence rescued him.

Mark Twain's Autobiography, Paine, I, p. 209

Special Providence! That phrase nauseates me—with its implied importance of mankind and triviality of God. In

my opinion these myriads of globes are merely the blood
corpuscles ebbing and flowing through the arteries of God
and we but animalculae that infest them, disease them,
pollute them, and God does not know we are there and
would not care if He did.

Mark Twain's Notebook, p. 190

There is this trouble about special providences—namely,
there is so often a doubt as to which party was intended to
be the beneficiary. In the case of the children, the bears,
and the prophet, the bears got more real satisfaction out of
the episode than the prophet did, because they got the
children.

"Pudd'nhead Wilson's Calendar,"
Pudd'nhead Wilson, Chapt. IV, p. 38

. . . the partialities of Providence do seem to me to be
slathered around . . . without that gravity and attention to
detail which the real importance of the matter would seem
to suggest.

Mark Twain's Letters, I, p. 247

The government's official report, showing that our rail-
ways killed twelve hundred persons last year [1905] and
injured sixty thousand, convinces me that under present
conditions one Providence is not enough properly and effi-
ciently to take care of our railroad business.

Mark Twain, a Biography, Paine, III, p. 1229

. . . a while ago, while Providence's attention was absorbed in disordering some time-tables so as to break up a
trip of mine to Mr. C's on the Hudson, that Johnstown dam
got loose. I swear I was afraid to pray, for fear I should
laugh.

Mark Twain's Letters, II, p. 512

. . . any man of judgment cannot but think well of his
modesty in only relying on Providence to save the ship, but
looking out for his carpet sack himself. If we would always
do our share many things would be accomplished that never
are accomplished.

"Noon, 16th,"
Mark Twain's Travels with Mr. Brown, p. 17

There are many scapegoats for our sins but the most popular is Providence.

Mark Twain's Notebook, p. 347

PUBLIC   *See also* INTEREST, POLITICS
A man *can't* hold public office and be honest.

Mark Twain's Letters, I, p. 68

The public is merely a multiplied "me."

Christian Science, Book I, Chapt. VI, p. 66

His Christianity is of no use to him and has no influence upon him when he is acting in a public capacity. He has sound and sturdy private morals, but he has no public ones.

Ibid., Book II, Conclusion, p. 359

Public servant: Persons chosen by the people to distribute the graft.

More Maxims of Mark, p. 12

PUBLIC OPINION   *See also* FEELING, OPINION
That awful power, the public opinion of a nation, is created in America by a horde of ignorant, self-complacent simpletons who failed at ditching and shoemaking and fetched up in journalism on their way to the poorhouse.

"License of the Press,"
Mark Twain's Speeches (1923), p. 49

. . . if he *thinks* it is principle he may be mistaken; a close examination may show it is only bowing to the tyranny of public opinion.

Mark Twain's Letters, I, p. 326

American public opinion is a delicate fabric. It shrivels like webs of morning at the lightest touch.

Mark Twain, a Biography, Paine, III, p. 1285

PUBLIC SPEAKING   *See* LECTURING, SPEECH

PUBLISHER   *See also* LAW, NONSENSE
All publishers are Columbuses. The successful author is their America. The reflection that they—like Columbus—didn't discover what they expected to discover . . . doesn't

trouble them. All they remember is that they discovered America; they forget that they started out to discover some patch or corner of India.

Mark Twain in Eruption, p. 186

The bare suggestion of scarlet fever in the family makes me shudder; I believe I would almost rather have Osgood publish a book for me.

Mark Twain's Letters, II, p. 439

How often we recall, with regret, that Napoleon once shot at a magazine editor and missed him and killed a publisher. But we remember with charity, that his intentions were good.

Ibid., II, p. 800

. . . publishers are not accountable to the laws of heaven and earth in any country . . .

A Bibliography of Mark Twain, Merle Johnson, p. 160

PUN *See also* GERMAN LANGUAGE, LIE, MONEY, PAGE, VIRTUE, WATER

Since England and America have been joined in Kipling, may they not be severed in Twain.

Mark Twain, a Biography, Paine, II, p. 1087

[At Key West]: I know why they call this the trimonthly line of steamers . . . It's because they go down to Greytown one month, and then they try all next month to get back again.

"Brown Delivered of a Joke,"
Mark Twain's Travels with Mr. Brown, p. 60

Poi [is] an inseductive mixture . . . almost tasteless before it ferments and too sour for a luxury afterward. . . . When solely used, however, it produces acrid humors, a fact which sufficiently accounts for the humorous character of the Kanakas.

Roughing It, II, Chapt. XXV, p. 230

. . . no circumstances, however dismal, will ever be considered a sufficient excuse for the admission of that last and saddest evidence of intellectual poverty, the Pun.

Mark Twain, a Biography, Paine, I, p. 403

"A Cat-Tale," told by Mark Twain to his young daughters:

Once there was a noble big cat, whose Christian name was Catasqua . . . but she did not have any surname, because she was a short-tailed cat—being a Manx—and did not need one. . . . Well, Catasqua had a beautiful family of catlings . . . Cattaraugus, the eldest, was white, and he had high impulses and a pure heart; Catiline, the youngest, was black . . . he was vain and foolish . . . Catasqua built a new house . . . behind it she constructed a splendid large catadrome, and enclosed it with a caterwaul about nine feet high, and in the center was a spacious grass plot . . . for cat fights, three-cornered cat, and all that sort of thing . . . It had a hedge of dainty little catkins around it, and right in the center was a . . . great categorematic in full leaf . . . The front garden was a spectacle of . . . bewildering magnificence. A stately row of flowering catalpas stretched . . . clear to the gate, wreathed from stem to stem with the delicate tendrils . . . of the cat's-foot ivy, whilst ever and anon the enchanted eye wandered from congeries of lordly cattails and kindred catapetalous blooms . . . only to encounter the still more entrancing vision of catnip without number. . . . Hither to the north boiled the majestic cataract . . . and thither to the south sparkled the gentle catadupe . . .

"A Cat-Tale,"
Letters from the Earth, p. 125

PUNCH *See* MIND

PUNCTUATION

Grammar is a science that was always too many for yours truly; but I like my punctuation respected.

Mark Twain, the Man and His Work,
Wagenknecht, p. 75

My punctuation . . . is the one thing I am inflexibly particular about. . . . It's got more real variety about it than any other accomplishment I possess, and I reverence it accordingly.

Ibid., p. 75

[My manuscript] was small-poxed with corrections of my punctuation. Then my volcano turned itself loose. . . . I said I didn't care if [the proof-reader] was an Archangel imported from Heaven, he couldn't puke his ignorant impudence over *my* punctuation.

Love Letters of Mark Twain, p. 273

PUNISHMENT

All crimes should be punished with humiliations—public exposure in ridiculous and grotesque situations—and never in any other way. Death makes a hero of the villain, and he is envied by some spectators and by imitators.

Mark Twain's Notebook, p. 193

If *I* were to suggest what ought to be done to him, I should be called extravagant—but what does the sixteenth chapter of Daniel say? Aha!

Roughing It, I, Chapt. XX, p. 167

It used to take me all vacation to grow a new hide in place of the one they flogged off me during the school term.

"Foolishness,"

Mark Twain's Travels with Mr. Brown, p. 244

When my mother came in and saw the bowl lying on the floor in fragments, she was speechless for a minute. I allowed that silence to work; I judged it would increase the effect. I was waiting for her to ask, "Who did that?"—so that I could fetch out my news [that Henry did it]. But it was an error of calculation. When she got through with her silence she didn't ask anything about it—she merely gave me a crack on the skull with her thimble that I felt all the way down to my heels. Then I broke out with my injured innocence, expecting to make her very sorry that she had punished the wrong one. . . . I told her that I was not the one—it was Henry. But there was no upheaval. She said, without emotion: "It's all right. It isn't any matter. You deserve it for something you've done that I didn't know about; and if you haven't done it, why then you deserve it for something that you are going to do that I shan't hear about."

Mark Twain's Autobiography, Paine, II, p. 94

Some seventeen or eighteen centuries ago, the ignorant men of Rome were wont to put Christians in the arena of the Coliseum . . . and turn the wild beasts in upon them for a show. It was for a lesson as well. It was to teach the people to abhor and fear the new doctrine the followers of Christ were teaching. The beasts tore the victims limb from limb and made poor mangled corpses of them in the twinkling of an eye. But when the Christians came into power, when the holy Mother Church became mistress of the barbarians, she taught them the error of their ways by no such means. No, she put them in this pleasant Inquisition and pointed to the Blessed Redeemer, who was so gentle and so merciful toward all men, and they urged the barbarians to love him; and they did all they could to persuade them to love and honor him—first by twisting their thumbs out of joint with a screw; then by nipping their flesh with pincers—red-hot ones, because they are the most comfortable in cold weather; then by skinning them alive a little, and finally by roasting them in public. They always convinced those barbarians. The true religion properly administered, as the good Mother Church used to administer it, is very, very soothing.

The Innocents Abroad, I, Chapt. XXVI

[At Mrs. Horr's school in Hannibal, Missouri]: . . . I presently broke the rule again and Mrs. Horr told me to go out and find a switch and fetch it. I was glad she appointed me, for I believed I could select a switch suitable to the occasion with more judiciousness than anybody else.

In the mud I found a cooper's shaving . . . I carried it to Mrs. Horr, presented it, and stood before her in an attitude of meekness and resignation. . . . She divided a long look of strong disapprobation equally between me and the shaving; then she called me by my entire name, Samuel Langhorne Clemens—probably the first time I ever heard it all strung together in one procession—and said she was ashamed of me. I was to learn later that when a teacher calls a boy by his entire name it means trouble. She said she would try and appoint a boy with a better judgment than mine in the matter of switches, and it saddens me yet to remember how many faces lighted up with the hope of getting that appointment. Jim Dunlap got it, and when he returned with the switch of his choice I recognized that he was an expert.

Mark Twain in Eruption, p. 107

PURE

To the pure all things are impure.

Mark Twain's Notebook, p. 372

PURGE   *See* ELEVATOR, INVITATION

PURPOSE   *See* SOUL

R

RABBIT *See also* NAME

[The "jackass rabbit"]: He is well named. He is just like any other rabbit, except that he is from one-third to twice as large, has longer legs in proportion to his size, and has the most preposterous ears that ever were mounted on any creature *but* the jackass. When he is sitting quiet, thinking about his sins, or is absent-minded . . . his majestic ears project above him conspicuously; but the breaking of a twig will scare him nearly to death, and then he tilts his ears back gently and starts for home. . . . But one must shoot at this creature once, if he wishes to see him throw his heart into his heels, and do the best he knows how . . . he lays his long ears down on his back, straightens himself out like a yard-stick every spring he makes, and scatters miles behind him with an easy indifference that is enchanting.

. . . The Secretary started him with a shot from the Colt. . . . He dropped his ears, set up his tail, and left for San Francisco at a speed which can only be described as a flash and a vanish! Long after he was out of sight we could hear him whiz.

Roughing It, I, Chapt. III, p. 29

RACE *See* SOCIETY

RACING

I think that much the most enjoyable of all races is a steamboat race. . . . Two red-hot steamboats raging along, neck-and-neck, straining every nerve,—that is to say, every rivet in the boilers,—quaking and shaking and groaning from stem to stern, spouting white steam from the pipes, pouring black smoke from the chimneys, raining down sparks, parting the river into long breaks of hissing foam— that is sport that makes a body's very liver curl with enjoyment.

> *Life on the Mississippi,* Chapt. XLV, p. 344

[A small private nautical race]: . . . he threw his whole heart into his little, useless oars, and we moved off at the rate of a mile a week.

> *Europe and Elsewhere,* p. 72

RADICAL

The radical of one century is the conservative of the next. The radical invents the views. When he has worn them out the conservative adopts them.

> *Mark Twain's Notebook,* p. 344

RAFT *See* STARS

RAFTSMEN

[The braggadocia of a raftsman who called himself *"The Child of Calamity"*]: "Whoo-oop! I'm the old original iron-jawed, brass-mounted, copper-bellied corpse-maker from the wilds of Arkansaw! . . . I'm the man they call Sudden Death and General Desolation! Sired by a hurricane, dam'd by an earthquake, half-brother to the cholera, nearly related to the small-pox on the mother's side! . . . I take nineteen alligators and a bar'l of whiskey for breakfast when I'm in robust health, and a bushel of rattlesnakes and a dead body when I'm ailing. I split the everlasting rocks with my glance, and I squench the thunder when I speak!

Whoo-oop! Stand back and give me room according to my strength. Blood's my natural drink, and the wails of the dying is music to my ear! . . .

When I'm playful I use the meridians of longitude and parallels of latitude for a seine, and drag the Atlantic Ocean for whales! I scratch my head with the lightning and purr myself to sleep with the thunder! When I'm cold, I bile the Gulf of Mexico and bathe in it; when I'm hot I fan myself with an equinoctial storm; when I'm thirsty I reach up and suck a cloud dry like a sponge; when I range the earth hungry, famine follows in my tracks! Whoo-oop! . . . I put my hand on the sun's face and make it night in the earth; I bite a piece out of the moon and hurry the seasons; I shake myself and crumble the mountains! . . . The boundless vastness of the great American desert is my enclosed property, and I bury my dead on my own premises! . . . Whoo-oop! bow your neck . . . for the Pet Child of Calamity's a-coming!"

Life on the Mississippi, Chapt. III, p. 32

RAILROAD *See also* ACCIDENT, CLERGYMAN, LIE, PROVIDENCE

There isn't a mountain in Switzerland now that hasn't a ladder railroad or two up its back like suspenders.

"Switzerland, the Cradle of Liberty,"
What Is Man? p. 193

[It was a] hard trip, because it was one of those trains that get tired every seven minutes and stops to rest three quarters of an hour. . . . Next year we will walk.

Mark Twain's Letters, II, p. 568

[In Egypt]: I shall not speak of the railway, for it is like any other railway—I shall only say that the fuel they use for the locomotive is composed of mummies three thousand years old, purchased by the ton or by the graveyard for that purpose, and that sometimes one hears the profane engineer call out pettishly, "D—n these plebeians, they don't burn worth a cent—pass out a King!"

The Innocents Abroad, II, Chapt. XXXI, p. 421

One has no difficulty in remembering his sins while the train is creeping down this bridge . . .

A Tramp Abroad, I, Chapt. XXIX, p. 314

[The slowness of the New Zealand railway service]: . . . He advised the conductor to put the cowcatcher on the other end of the train because we are not going to overtake any cows, but there is no protection against their climbing aboard at the other end and biting the passengers.

Mark Twain's Notebook, p. 299

[About 1900]: I refer with effusion to our railway system, which consents to let us live, though it might do the opposite, being our owners. It only destroyed three thousand and seventy lives last year by collisions, and twenty-seven thousand two hundred and sixty by running over heedless and unnecessary people at crossings. The companies seriously regretted the killing of these thirty thousand people, and went so far as to pay for some of them —voluntarily, of course, for the meanest of us would not claim that we possess a court treacherous enough to enforce a law against a railway company. But, thank Heaven, the railway companies are generally disposed to do the right and kindly thing without compulsion. I know of an instance which greatly touched me at the time. After an accident the company sent home the remains of a dear distant old relative of mine in a basket, with the remark, "Please state what figure you hold him at—and return the basket." Now there couldn't be anything friendlier than that.

"After-Dinner Speech,"
Sketches New and Old, p. 235

Any detail of railroading that is not troublesome cannot honorably be described as continental.

Following the Equator, I, Chapt. XIV, p. 150

A railroad is like a lie—you have to keep building to it to make it stand.

"Hannibal—By a Native Historian,"
Mark Twain's Travels with Mr. Brown, p. 146

[From a letter to Thomas Nast]:
Be piously grateful . . . that you are permitted to remain

512

with your household . . . and do all your praying now, for a time is coming when you will have to go railroading and platforming, and then you will find you cannot pray any more, because you will have only just time to swear enough.

Th. Nast, His Period and His Pictures, Paine, p. 513

RAIN *See* WEATHER

RAINBOW *See also* LIE

[At Elmira]: One evening a rainbow spanned an entire range of hills with its mighty arch, and from a black hub resting upon the hill-top in the exact centre, *black* rays diverged upward in perfect regularity to the rainbow's arch and created a very strongly defined and altogether the most majestic, magnificent and startling half-sunk wagon wheel you can imagine. After that, a world of tumbling and prodigious clouds came drifting up out of the West and took to themselves a wonderfully rich and brilliant *green* color —the decided green of new spring foliage. Close by them we saw the intense blue of the skies, through rents in the cloud-rack, and away off in another quarter were drifting clouds of a delicate pink color. . . . And the stupendous wagon wheel was still in the supremacy of its unspeakable grandeur. So . . . the colors present in the sky at once and the same time were blue, green, pink, black, and the varicolored splendors of the rainbow. . . . I don't know whether this weird and astounding spectacle most suggested heaven, or hell. The wonder, with its constant, stately, and always surprising changes, lasted upwards of two hours, and we all stood on the top of the hill . . . till the final miracle was complete and the greatest day ended that we ever saw.

Mark Twain's Letters, I, p. 282

We have not the reverent feeling for the rainbow that a savage has, because we know how it is made. We have lost as much as we gained by prying into that matter.

A Tramp Abroad, II, Chapt. XIV, p. 282

RANK *See* PROSPERITY

READER *See also* CHURCH, CLASSIC, PAUSE, The

It is so unsatisfactory to read a noble passage and have
no one at hand to share the happiness with you. And it is
unsatisfactory to read to one's self anyhow—for the uttered
voice so heightens the expression . . .

My Father • Mark Twain, Clara Clemens, p. 21

. . . in reading from the book you are telling another
person's tale at secondhand; you are a mimic, and not the
person involved; you are an artificiality, not a reality;
whereas in telling the tale without the book you absorb the
character and presently become the man himself, just as in
the case with the actor.

The greatest actor would not be able to carry his audience by storm with a book in his hand; reading from the
book renders the nicest shadings of delivery impossible. . . .

When a man is reading from a book on the platform, he
soon realizes that there is one powerful gun in his battery
of artifice that he can't work with an effect proportionate
to its caliber: that is the *pause*—that impressive silence, that
eloquent silence, that geometrically progressive silence
which often achieves a desired effect where no combination
of words howsoever felicitous could accomplish it.

Mark Twain in Eruption, p. 224

I don't believe any of you have ever read *Paradise Lost,*
and you don't want to. That's something that you just
want to take on trust. It's a classic . . . something that
everybody wants to have read and nobody wants to read.

"Disappearance of Literature"

Mark Twain's Speeches (1910), p. 194

I am a careless reader, I suppose—an *impressionist* reader;
an impressionist reader of what is *not* an impressionist
picture; a reader who overlooks the informing details or
masses their sum improperly, and gets only a large, splashy,
general effect—an effect which is not correct, and which
is not warranted by the particulars placed before me—particulars which I did not examine, and whose meanings I
did not cautiously and carefully estimate. It is an effect
which is some thirty-five or forty times finer than the reality,

and is therefore a great deal better and more valuable than the reality; and so, I ought never to hunt up the reality, but stay miles away from it, and thus preserve undamaged my own private mighty Niagara tumbling out of the vault of heaven, and my own ineffable Taj, built of tinted mists upon jeweled arches of rainbows supported by colonnades of moonlight. It is a mistake for a person with an unregulated imagination to go and look at an illustrious world's wonder.

Following the Equator, II, Chapt. XXIII, p. 275

[From a letter to Mary Hallock Foote]:

Now when you come to think of it, wasn't it a curious idea—I mean for a dozen ladies of (apparently) high intelligence to elect me their Browning reader? Of course you think I declined at first; but I didn't. I'm not the declining sort. I would take charge of the constellations if I were asked to do it. All you need in this life is ignorance and confidence; then success is sure. I've been Browning reader forty-two weeks, now, and my class has never lost a member by desertion. What do you think of that for a man in a business he wasn't brought up to?

. . . I used to explain Mr. Browning—but the class won't stand that. They say my reading imparts clear comprehension—and that is a good deal of a compliment, you know; but they say the poetry never gets obscure till I begin to explain it—which is only frank, and that is the softest you can say about it. So I've stopped being expounder, and thrown my heft on the reading. Yes, and with vast results —nearly unbelievable results. I don't wish to flatter anybody, yet I will say this much: Put me in the right condition and give me room according to my strength, and I can read Browning so Browning himself can understand it. It sounds like stretching, but it's the cold truth. Moral: don't explain your author, read him right and he explains himself.

When Huck Finn Went Highbrow, Casseres, p. 7

The lazy bed was infinitely preferable. I had many an exciting day, subsequently, lying on it reading the statutes and the dictionary, and wondering how the characters would turn out.

Roughing It, I, Chapt. II, p. 27

I'm disgusted with these mush-and-milk preacher travel [books], . . . they're the flattest reading—they are sicker than the smart things children say in the newspapers.

Letters from the Sandwich Islands, p. 151

. . . all our phrasings are spiritualized shadows cast multitudinously from our readings . . .

Mark Twain's Autobiography, Paine, I, p. 241

REASONING   *See also* ENVIRONMENT, LOGIC

But·that is the way we are made: we don't reason, where we feel; we just feel.

A Connecticut Yankee in King Arthur's Court,
Chapt. XI, p. 88

We always get at second hand our notions about systems of government . . . and prohibition and anti-prohibition, and the holiness of peace and the glories of war; and codes of honor and codes of morals . . . and approval . . . and beliefs . . . and ideas . . . and preferences . . . We get them all at second hand, we reason none of them out for ourselves . . . In morals, conduct, and beliefs we take the color of our environment and associations, and it is a color that can safely be warranted to wash.

"Is Shakespeare Dead"
What Is Man? and Other Essays, p. 364

If religions were got by reasoning, we should have the extraordinary spectacle of an American family with a Presbyterian in it, and a Baptist, a Methodist, a Catholic, a Mohammedan, a Buddhist, and a Mormon. A Presbyterian family does not produce Catholic families or other religious brands, it produces its own kind; and not by intellectual processes, but by association.

Christian Science, Book I, Chapt. IX, p. 93

Does the human being reason? No; he thinks, muses, reflects, but does not reason. Thinks *about* a thing; rehearses its statistics and its parts and applies to them what other people on his side of the question have said about them, but he does not compare the parts himself, and is not capable of doing it.

That is, in the two things which are the peculiar domain of the heart, not the mind,—politics and·religion. He doesn't want to know the other side. He wants arguments and statistics for his own side, and nothing more.

Mark Twain's Notebook, p. 307

RECKLESSNESS *See* COURAGE

RECOGNITION
Greatness may be classed as the ability to win recognition.

Mark Twain and I, Opie Read, p. 11

RECREATION *See* WORK

REFINEMENT
She was not quite what you would call refined. She was not quite what you would call unrefined. She was the kind of person that keeps a parrot.

"Pudd'nhead Wilson's New Calendar"
Following the Equator, II, Chapt. XXI, Vol. II
There are no people who are quite so vulgar as the over-refined ones.

"Pudd'nhead Wilson's New Calendar"
Ibid., II, Chapt. XXVI, p. 308

REFLECTION *See also* STEALING
. . . reflection is the beginning of reform. If you don't reflect when you commit a crime then that crime is of no use; it might just as well have been committed by some one else. You must reflect or the value is lost; you are not vaccinated against committing it again.

"Theoretical Morals"
Mark Twain's Speeches (1910), p. 133
By temperament I was the kind of person that *does* things. Does them, and reflects afterward. . . . I have been punished many and many a time, and bitterly, for doing

things and reflecting afterward, but these tortures have been of no value to me: I still do the thing commanded by Circumstance and Temperament, and reflect afterward. Always violently. When I am reflecting, on those occasions, even deaf persons can hear me think.

"The Turning-Point of My Life"
What Is Man? and *Other Essays*, p. 134

REFORM   *See also* BOYHOOD, CHURCH, GERMAN LANGUAGE, IDEA, ORGANIZATION, SPELLING, VICE

. . . I will speak to him, though at bottom I think hanging would be more lasting.

"A Horse's Tale"
The Mysterious Stranger, Etc., p. 195

Swore off from profanity early this morning. I was on deck in the peaceful dawn, the calm and holy dawn. Went down dressed, bathed, put on white linen, shaved—a long, hot, troublesome job, and no profanity. Then started to breakfast. Remembered my tonic—first time in three months without being told—poured it in a measuring-glass, held bottle in one hand, it in the other, the cork in my teeth—reached up and got a tumbler—measuring-glass sprang out of my fingers—got it, poured out another dose, first setting the tumbler on washstand—just got it poured, ship lurched, heard a crash behind me—it was the tumbler, broken into millions of fragments, but the bottom hunk whole—picked it up to throw out of the open port, threw out the measuring-glass instead—then I released my voice. Mrs. C. behind me in the door: "Don't reform any more, it isn't any improvement."

Mark Twain's Notebook, p. 268

You can straighten a worm, but the crook is in him and only waiting.

More Maxims of Mark, p. 14

[Spelling]: . . . look at the "pneumatics" and the "pneumonias" and the rest of them. A real reform would settle them once and for all, and wind up by giving us an alphabet that we wouldn't have to spell with at all. Why, there isn't a man who doesn't have to throw out about fifteen hundred words a day when he writes his letters because he can't spell them! It's like trying to do a St. Vitus's dance with wooden legs.

Now, if we had an alphabet that was adequate and competent . . . things would be different. Spelling reform has only made it baldheaded and unsightly. There is the whole tribe of them, "Row" and "read" and "lead"—a whole family who don't know who they are. I ask you to pronounce s-o-w, and you ask me what kind of a one.

If we had a sane, determinate alphabet, instead of a hospital of comminuted eunuchs, you would know whether one referred to the act of a man casting the seed over the ploughed land or whether one wished to recall the lady hog and the future ham.

"The Alphabet and Simplified Spelling"
Mark Twain's Speeches (1923), p. 365

Then, in natural order, followed riot, insurrection, and the wrack and restitutions of war. It was bound to come, and it would naturally come in that way. It has been the manner of reform since the beginning of the world.

"A Scrap of Curious History"
What Is Man? and Other Essays, p. 192

Nothing so needs reforming as other people's habits.

"Pudd'nhead Wilson's Calendar"
Pudd'nhead Wilson, Chapt. XV, p. 45

The judge . . . said he reckoned a body could reform the old man with a shotgun, maybe, but he didn't know no other way.

The Adventures of Huckleberry Finn, Chapt. V, p. 43

RELATIONS *See* GOD

RELIGION *See also* CHRISTIANITY, CHURCH, CONFIDENCE, CONVICTION, DOCTRINE, ENVIRONMENT, GOD, INSANITY, MINISTER, PRAYER, PREACHER, PRESBYTERIAN, PRIEST, PUNISHMENT, REASONING, REVERENCE

Your ancestors broke forever the chains of political slav-

ery, and gave the vote to every man in this wide land,
excluding none!—none except those who did not belong to
the orthodox church. Your ancestors—yes, they were a hard
lot; but, nevertheless, they gave us religious liberty to worship as they required us to worship, and political liberty to
vote as the church required.

"Plymouth Rock and the Pilgrims"
Mark Twain's Speeches (1923), p. 89

I could have given my own sect the preference and made
everybody a Presbyterian without any trouble, but that
would have been to affront a law of human nature: spiritual
wants and instincts are as various in the human family as
are physical appetites, complexions, and features, and a
man is only at his best, morally, when he is equipped with
the religious garment whose color and shape and size most
nicely accommodate themselves to the spiritual complexion,
angularities, and stature of the individual who wears it. . . .

A Connecticut Yankee in King Arthur's Court,
Chapt. X, p. 78

In Bombay I was told by an American missionary that in
India there are 640 Protestant missionaries at work. . . .
A force of 640 in Benares alone would have its hands over-
full with 8,000 Brahmin priests for adversary. Missionaries
need to be well equipped with hope and confidence. . . .
It enables [them] to get a favorable outlook out of statistics
which might add up differently with other mathematicians.
For instance:

"During the past few years competent observers declare
that the number of pilgrims to Benares has increased."

And then [they] add up this fact and get this conclusion:

"But the revival, if so it may be called, has in it the marks
of death. It is a spasmodic struggle before dissolution."

In this world we have seen the Roman Catholic power
dying, upon these same terms, for many centuries. Many
a time we have gotten all ready for the funeral and found
it postponed again, on account of the weather or something.
Taught by experience, we ought not to put on our things

for this Brahminical one till we see the procession move. Apparently one of the most uncertain things in the world is the funeral of a religion. [1895]

> *Following the Equator*, II, Chapt. XIV, p. 175

So much blood has been shed by the Church because of an omission from the Gospel: "Ye shall be *indifferent* as to what your neighbor's religion is." Not merely tolerant of it, but indifferent to it. Divinity is claimed for many religions; but no religion is great enough or divine enough to add that new law to its code.

> *Mark Twain, a Biography*, Paine, III, p. 1537

The easy confidence with which I know another man's religion is folly teaches me to suspect that my own is also.

I would not interfere with any one's religion, either to strengthen it or to weaken it. I am not able to believe one's religion can affect his hereafter one way or the other, no matter what that religion may be. But it may easily be a great comfort to him in this life—hence it is a valuable possession to him.

> *Ibid.*, III, p. 1584

. . . the city of Benares is in effect just a big church, a religious hive, whose every cell is a temple, a shrine, or a mosque, and whose every conceivable earthly and heavenly good is procurable under one roof, so to speak—a sort of Army and Navy Stores, theologically stocked.

> *Following the Equator*, II, Chapt. XV, p. 179

. . . the religious folly you are born in you will *die* in, no matter what apparently reasonabler religious folly may seem to have taken its place; meanwhile abolished and obliterated it.

> *Mark Twain, a Biography*, Paine, II, p. 764

. . . he was a man who would have called brother a cannibal king who had eaten a Jesuit, while he would have mobilized the whole British fleet against savages who dined off an Episcopalian.

> *Abroad with Mark Twain and Eugene Field*,
> Fisher, p. 151

Zeal and sincerity can carry a new religion further than any other missionary except fire and sword.

Christian Science, Book I, Chapt. VII, p. 82

[Nicodemus Dodge on religion]:

"What is your own religion?"

"Well, boss, you've kind o' got me, thar—and yit you hain't got me so mighty much, nuther. I think't if a feller he'ps another feller when he's in trouble, and don't cuss, and don't do no mean things, nur noth'n' he ain' no business to do, and don't spell the Saviour's name with a little g, he ain't runnin' no resks—he's about as saift as if he b'longed to a church."

A Tramp Abroad, I, Chapt. XXIII, p. 230

Man . . . is kind enough when he is not excited by religion.

"A Horse's Tale"
The Mysterious Stranger, Etc., p. 206

Religion consists in a set of things which the average man thinks he believes, and wishes he was certain.

Mark Twain's Notebook, p. 153

We must have a *religion*—it goes without saying—but my idea is, to have it cut up into forty free sects, so that they will police each other, as had been the case in the United States . . . Concentration of power in a political machine is bad; and an Established Church is only a political machine; it was invented for that; it is nursed, cradled, preserved for that; it is an enemy to human liberty, and does no good which it could not better do in a split-up and scattered condition.

A Connecticut Yankee in King Arthur's Court,
Chapt. XVIII, p. 142

It is agreed, in this country [U.S.A.], that if a man can arrange his religion so that it perfectly satisfies his conscience, it is not incumbent upon him to care whether the arrangement is satisfactory to anyone else or not.

"As Regards Patriotism"
Europe and Elsewhere, p. 301

A list of sects is not a record of *studies,* searchings, seek-ings after light; it mainly (and sarcastically) indicates what *association* can do. If you know a man's nationality you can come within a split hair of guessing the complexion of his religion.

What Is Man? and Other Essays, p. 44

I tried some experiments of my own. These . . . proved that the ant is peculiarly intelligent in the higher concerns of life. I constructed four miniature houses of worship—a Mohammedan mosque, a Hindu temple, a Jewish synagogue, and a Christian cathedral, and placed them in a row. I then marked 15 ants with red paint and turned them loose. They made several trips to and fro, glancing in at the several places of worship, but not entering. I turned loose 15 more, painted blue. They acted just as the red ones had done. I now gilded 15 and turned them loose. No change in result: the 45 traveled back and forth in an eager hurry, persistently and continuously, visiting each fane but never entering. This satisfied me that these ants were without religious prejudices—just what I wished; for under no other condition would my next and greater experiment be valuable.

I now placed a small square of white paper within the door of each fane; upon the mosque paper I put a pinch of putty, upon the temple paper a dab of tar, upon the synagogue paper a trifle of turpentine, and upon the cathedral paper a small cube of sugar. First I liberated the red ants. They examined and rejected the putty, the tar and the turpentine, and then took to the sugar with zeal and apparently sincere conviction. I next liberated the blue ants, they did exactly as the red ones had done. The gilded ants followed. The preceding results were precisely repeated. This seemed to prove beyond question that ants destitute of religious prejudices will always prefer Christianity to any of the other great creeds.

However, to make sure I removed the ants and put putty in the cathedral and sugar in the mosque. I now liberated the ants in a body and they rushed tumultuously to the cathedral. I was very much touched and gratified and went in the back room to write down the event; but when I came back the ants had all apostatized and gone over to the Mohammedan communion. I said I had been too hasty in my conclusions . . . I went on with the test . . . placed the sugar first in one house of worship, then another, till I had tried them all. With this result: that whatever church I put the sugar in, that was the one the ants straightway joined. This was true . . . that in religious matters the ant is the opposite of man: for man cares for but one thing, to find the Only True Church; whereas the ant hunts for the one with the sugar in it.

Mark Twain's Notebook, p. 284

REMARK

Often a quite assified remark becomes sanctified by use and petrified by custom; it is then a permanecy, its term of activity a geologic period.

"Does the Race of Man Love a Lord"
The $30,000 Bequest, Etc., p. 268

REMEDY *See* HABIT, ILLNESS

REMORSE

Conscience kept me awake all night, oozing remorse at every pore.

"Concerning the Recent Carnival of Crime in Connecticut"
Tom Sawyer Abroad, Etc., p. 317

My remorse does not deceive me. (1896) I know that if Susy were back I should soon be neglectful of her as I was before—it is our way. We think we would do better, because of our lesson. But it is a fallacy. Our natures would go back to what they had always been and our conduct would obey their commands.

My Father • Mark Twain, Clara Clemens, p. 175

RENAISSANCE

Who is this Renaissance? Where did he come from? Who gave him permission to cram the Republic with his exe-

crable daubs? . . . The guide said that after Titian's time
. . . high art declined; then it partially rose again . . . and
these shabby pictures were the result. . . . I said, in my
heat, I wished to goodness high art had declined five
hundred years sooner. The Renaissance pictures suit me
very well, though sooth to say its school were too much
given to painting real men and did not indulge enough
in martyrs.

The Innocents Abroad, I, Chapt. XXIII, p. 307

REPENTANCE   *See also* DUTY

When we repent of a sin, we do it perfunctorily, from
principle, coldly and from the head; but when we repent
of a good deed the repentance comes hot and bitter and
straight from the heart. . . . In my time I have done eleven
good deeds. I remember all of them, four . . . with crystal
clearness. These four I repent of whenever I think of them
—and it is not seldomer than fifty-two times a year. I repent
of them in the same old original furious way, undiminished,
always. . . . I have not repented of any sin with the un-
modifying earnestness and sincerity with which I have repented of these four gracious and beautiful good deeds.

Letters from the Earth, p. 167

My repentances were very real, very earnest; and after
each tragedy they happened every night for a long time.
But as a rule they could not stand the daylight. They faded
out and shredded away and disappeared in the glad splendor of the sun. . . . In all my boyhood life I am not sure
that I ever tried to lead a better life in the daytime—or
wanted to . . . But in my age, as in my youth, night brings
me many a deep remorse. . . . When "Injun Joe" died . . .
But never mind. Somewhere I have already described what
a raging hell of repentance I passed through then. I believe that for months I was as pure as the driven snow.
After dark.

Mark Twain's Autobiography, Paine, I, p. 134

In church last Sunday I listened to a charity sermon. My
first impulse was to give $350; I repented of that and re-

duced it $100; repented of that and reduced it another hundred; repented of that and reduced it another hundred; repented of that and reduced the remaining fifty to twenty-five; repented of that and came down to fifteen; repented of that and dropped to $2.50; when the plate came around, I repented once more and contributed 10¢ . . . when I got home, I did wish to goodness I had that 10¢ back again.

"The Carnival of Crime in Connecticut"
Tom Sawyer Abroad, p. 318

REPORTER *See also* NEWSPAPER
[*In his reporting days, Mark Twain was instructed by an editor never to state anything as a fact that he could not verify. Sent out to cover an important social event soon afterward, he turned in the following story*]:
A woman giving the name of Mrs. James Jones, who is reported to be one of the society leaders of the city, is said to have given what purported to be a party yesterday to a number of alleged ladies. The hostess claims to be the wife of a reputed attorney.

Source undetermined

REPUBLIC *See also* CITIZENSHIP, DEMOCRACY, MONARCHY, PROSPERITY
Down there (on earth) they talk of the heavenly King—and that is right—but then they go right on speaking as if heaven was a republic and everybody was on a dead-level with everybody else. How are you going to have a republic at all, where the head of the government is absolute, holds his place forever, and has no parliament, no council to meddle or make in his affairs, nobody voted for, nobody elected, nobody in the whole universe with a voice in the government, nobody asked to take a hand in its matters, and nobody *allowed* to do it.

"Captain Stormfield's Visit to Heaven"
The Mysterious Stranger, p. 259
. . . there is plenty good enough material for a republic in the most degraded people that ever existed—even the

Russians; plenty of manhood in them—even in the Germans
—if one could but force it out of its timid and suspicious
privacy, to overthrow and trample in the mud any throne
that ever was set up and any nobility that ever supported it.
> *A Connecticut Yankee in King Arthur's Court,*
> Chapt. XXX, p. 277

What keeps a republic on its legs is good citizenship.
> "Layman's Sermon"
> *Mark Twain's Speeches* (1923), p. 281

REPUTATION

Reputation is a hall-mark: it can remove doubt from pure
silver, and it can also make the plated article pass for pure.
> *Mark Twain's Letters,* II, p. 472

Unassailable certainty is the thing that gives a newspaper
the firmest and most valuable reputation.
> *Roughing It,* II, Chapt. I, p. 19

"Getting the reputation is the uphill time in most things,
Captain."

"It's so. It ain't enough to know how to reef a gasket, you
got to make the mate know you know it. That's reputation . . ."
> *The American Claimant, Etc.,* Chapt. XVI, p. 136

RESPECT *See also* ROYALTY

We are all inconsistent. We are offended and resent it
when people do not respect us; and yet no man, deep down
in the privacy of his heart, has any considerable respect
for *himself.*
> "Pudd'nhead Wilson's New Calendar"
> *Following the Equator,* I, Chapt. XXIX, p. 288

The truth is always respectable.
> *The Adventures of Tom Sawyer,*
> Chapt. XXIII, p. 216

REVERENCE *See also* IRREVERENCE, CHILDREN, RAINBOW

The ordinary reverence, the reverence defined and explained by the dictionary, costs nothing. Reverence for

one's own sacred things—parents, religion, flag, laws and respect for one's own beliefs—these are feelings which we cannot even help. They come natural to us; they are involuntary, like breathing. There is no personal merit in breathing. But the reverence which is difficult, and which has personal merit in it, is the respect which you pay, without compulsion, to the political or religious attitude of a man whose beliefs are not yours. You can't revere his gods or his politics, and no one expects you to do that, but you could respect his belief in them if you tried hard enough; and you could respect *him*, too, if you tried hard enough. But it is very, very difficult; it is next to impossible, and so we hardly ever try. If the man doesn't believe as we do, we say he is a crank, and that settles it. I mean it does nowadays, because we can't burn him.

Following the Equator, II, Chapt. XVII, p. 211

The Catholic Church says the most irreverent things about matters which are sacred to the Protestants, and the Protestant Church retorts in kind about the confessional and other matters which Catholics hold sacred, then both of these irreverences turn upon Thomas Paine and charge *him* with irreverence. This is all unfortunate, because it makes it difficult for students equipped with only a low grade of mentality to find out what Irreverence really *is*.

"Is Shakespeare Dead?"
What Is Man? and Other Essays, p. 369

I can go as far as the next man in genuine reverence of holy things, but this stretching the narrow garment of belief to fit the broad shoulders of a wish, 'tis too much for me.

Mark Twain's Notebook, p. 108

We have not the reverent feeling for the rainbow that a savage has, because we know how it is made. We have lost as much as we have gained by prying into that matter.

A Tramp Abroad, II, Chapt. XIV, Vol. II

Our papers have one peculiarity—it is American—their irreverence . . . They are irreverent toward pretty much everything, but where they laugh one good king to death, they laugh a thousand cruel and infamous shams and superstitions into the grave, and the account is squared. Irreverence is the champion of liberty and its only sure defense.

Mark Twain's Notebook, p. 195

True irreverence is disrespect for another man's god.

"Pudd'nhead Wilson's New Calendar"
Following the Equator, II, Chapt. XVII, p. 203

Who is to decide what ought to command my reverence —my neighbor or I? . . . you can't have reverence for a thing that doesn't command it. If you could do that, you could digest what you haven't eaten, and do other miracles and get a reputation.

Mark Twain, a Biography, Paine, III, p. 1313

REVIEW   *See* BABY

REVOLT   *See also* FREEDOM

Moral cowardice . . . is the commanding feature of the make-up of 9,999 men . . . (out of) 10,000. . . . No revolt against a public infamy or oppression has ever been begun but by one daring man in the 10,000.

"United States of Lyncherdom,"
Europe and Elsewhere, p. 243

REWARD

Reacting honorably for the sake of reward or approbation: I do. I want payment in coin for everything I do. If I can't get peace and joy in return for propping up my blatherskite of a crumbling soul, then, I'll let her rot, and the quicker the better.

My Father • Mark Twain, Clara Clemens, p. 180

RHEUMATISM   *See also* ILLNESS, MUMMY

People say that Germany, with her damp stone houses, is the home of rheumatism. If that is so, Providence must have foreseen it would be so and therefore filled the land with . . . healing baths.

A Tramp Abroad, I, Chapt. XXI, p. 197

RHODES, CECIL

There he stands, upon his dizzy summit . . . the marvel of the time, the mystery of the age, an Archangel with wings to half the world, Satan with a tail to the other half.

I admire him, I frankly confess it; and when his time comes I shall buy a piece of the rope for a keepsake.

Following the Equator, II, Chapt. XXXIII, p. 404

RHYME *See* MIND

RICHES *See also* DISASTER, POVERTY

I have no desire for riches. Honest poverty and a conscience torpid through virtuous inaction are more to me than corner lots and praise.

"A Cat-Tale,"
Letters from the Earth, p. 131

. . . a man wants riches in his youth, when the world is fresh to him. He wondered why Providence could not have reversed the usual process, and let the majority of men begin with wealth and gradually spend it, and die poor when they no longer needed it.

The Gilded Age, II, Chapt. XVIII, p. 204

. . . those riches which are denied to no nation on the planet—humor and feeling.

Mark Twain's Letters, II, p. 798

Like all the other nations, we worship money and the possessors of it—they being our aristocracy, and we have to have one. We like to read about rich people in the papers; the papers know it, and they do their best to keep this appetite liberally fed. They even leave out a football bull-fight now and then to get room for all the particulars of how—according to the display heading—"Rich Woman Fell Down Cellar—Not Hurt." The falling down the cellar is of no interest to us when the woman is not rich, but no rich woman can fall down cellar and we not yearn to know all about it and wish it was us.

"Chapters from My Autobiography,"
The North American Review, Jan. 4, 1907, p. 4

Pleasure, Love, Fame, Riches: they are but temporary disguises for lasting realities—Pain, Grief, Shame, Poverty.

"The Five Boons of Life,"
The $30,000 Bequest, Etc., p. 163

. . . it is in the heart that the values lie . . . a loving good heart is riches, and riches enough . . . without it intellect is poverty.

"Eve's Diary,"
Ibid., p. 295

. . . being rich ain't what it's cracked up to be. It's just worry and worry, and sweat and sweat, and a-wishing you was dead all the time.

The Adventures of Tom Sawyer, Chapt. XXXV, p. 317

The offspring of riches: Pride, vanity, ostentation, arrogance, tyranny.

Mark Twain, a Biography, Paine, III, p. 1194

If all men were rich, all men would be poor.

Mark Twain's Notebook, p. 344

RIDDLE

One says to the Other, "You can refuse me ten thousand requests but there is one which you will be obliged to grant. I ask that one now. Look in the glass."

The Other looked in the glass, and it was so.

Examine the glass and tell the result.

S.L.C. to C.T., p. 14

RIDICULE *See also* CHARACTER

You see, he was only just a man after all, and couldn't stand ridicule any better than other people.

Personal Recollections of Joan of Arc,
II, Book III, Chapt. XVI, p. 249

What is the chiefest privilege remaining to nobility? That you shall not laugh at it. No other class is exempt. If you would know how vast a privilege it is, observe that to accord it to any thing, or being, or idea, is to give it eternal life.

No god and no religion can survive ridicule. No church, no nobility, no royalty or other fraud, can face ridicule in a fair field and live.

Mark Twain's Notebook, p. 198

RIGHT   *See also* CONSISTENCY, FRIEND, HUMAN RACE, WRONG

Always do right. This will gratify some people, and astonish the rest.

Mark Twain in Eruption, Frontispiece

Do right and you will be conspicuous.

Mark Twain, a Biography, Paine, III, p. 1134

. . . I am persuaded that the world has been tricked into adopting some false and most pernicious notions about *consistency*—and to such a degree that the average man has turned the rights and *wrongs* of things entirely *around*, and is *proud* to be "consistent," unchanging, immovable, fossilized, where it should be his humiliation that he is so.

"Consistency,"
Mark Twain's Speeches (1923), p. 130

[Hawaii]: . . . in the islands you've got to do everything just wrong, or you can't stay there. You do it wrong to get it right, for if you do it right you get it wrong; there isn't any way to get it right *but* to do it wrong, and the wronger you do it the righter it is. The natives illustrate this every day . . . they never milk a cow on the starboard side, they always milk her on the larboard; it's why you see so many short people there—they've got their heads kicked off.

"Welcome Home,"
Ibid. (1923), p. 145

Do right *for your own sake*, and be happy in knowing that your *neighbor* will certainly share in the benefits resulting.

What Is Man? and Other Essays, Chapt. IV, p. 59

The fact that man knows right from wrong proves his *intellectual* superiority to the other creatures; but the fact that he can *do* wrong proves his *moral* inferiority to any creature that *cannot*.

> *Ibid.*, Chapt. VI, p. 89

There isn't a Parallel of Latitude but thinks it would have been the Equator if it had had its rights.

> "Pudd'nhead Wilson's New Calendar,"
> *Following the Equator*, II, Chapt. XXXIII, p. 392

With us no individual is born with a right to look down upon his neighbor and hold him in contempt.

> "Americans and the English,"
> *Mark Twain's Speeches* (1923), p. 36

Man has not a single right which is the product of anything but might.

Not a single right is indestructible: a new might can at any time abolish it, hence, man possesses not a single *permanent* right.

> *Mark Twain's Notebook*, p. 394

RIGHTS   *See also* EQUATOR

He cultivates respect for human rights by always making sure that he has his own.

> *My Father • Mark Twain*, Clara Clemens, p. 262

RISING   *See* EARLY RISING

RIVER   *See also* MISSISSIPPI RIVER, SHIP

Later I took a twilight tramp along the high banks of a moist ditch called the Guires River. If it was my river I wouldn't leave it outdoors nights, in this careless way, where any dog can come along and lap it up. It is a tributary of the Rhone when it is in better health.

> "Down the Rhône,"
> *Europe and Elsewhere*, p. 140

A great Indian river, at low water, suggests the familiar anatomical picture of a skinned human body, the intricate mesh of interwoven muscles and tendons to stand for water-channels, and the archipelagoes of fat and flesh inclosed by them to stand for the sandbars. . . . Curious rivers they are; low shores a dizzy distance apart, with nothing between but an enormous acreage of sandflats with sluggish little veins of water dribbling around amongst them; Saharas of sand, smallpox-pitted with footprints punctured in belts as straight as the equator clear from the one shore to the other (barring the channel-interruptions)—a dry-shod ferry, you see. Long railway bridges are required for this sort of rivers, and India has them. You approach Allahabad by a very long one. It was now carrying us across the bed of Jumna, a bed which did not seem to have been slept in for one while or more. It wasn't all river-bed—most of it was overflow ground.

Following the Equator, II, Chapt. XIII, p. 158

[At Hannibal, Missouri]: Bear Creek—so called, perhaps, because it was always so particularly bare of bears—is hidden out of sight now, under islands and continents of piled lumber, and nobody but an expert can find it. I used to get drowned in it every summer regularly, and be drained out, and inflated and set going again by some chance enemy; but not enough of it is unoccupied now to drown a person in. It was a famous breeder of chills and fever in its day. I remember one summer when everybody in town had this disease at once. Many chimneys were shaken down, and all the houses were so racked that the town had to be rebuilt. The chasm or gorge between Lover's Leap and the hill west of it is supposed by scientists to have been caused by glacial action. This is a mistake.

Life on the Mississippi, Chapt. LV, p. 412

A crowd of [Hindoo] men, women, and comely young maidens [were standing] waist deep in the water [of the Ganges River] . . . scooping it up in their hands and drinking it. . . . According to their creed, the Ganges water makes everything pure that it touches—instantly and utterly pure. The sewer water was not an offense to them, [a float-

ing] corpse did not revolt them; the sacred water had
touched both, and both were now snow-pure, and could
defile no one. The memory of that sight will always stay by
me; but not by request.

Following the Equator, II, Chapt. XVI, p. 192

When La Salle came down [the Mississippi] a century
and a quarter ago there was nothing on its banks but savages. He opened up this great river, and by his simple act
was gathered in this great Louisiana territory. I would have
done it myself for half the money.

"The St. Louis Harbor-Boat 'Mark Twain,'"
Mark Twain's Speeches (1910), p. 424

Warsaw, also on the banks of the Mississippi River—is an
emotional bit of the Mississippi . . . when it is low water
you have to climb up to it on a ladder, and when it floods
you have to hunt for it with a deep-sea lead. . . .

"Sixty-Seventh Birthday,"
Mark Twain's Speeches (1923), p. 249

We came to the shallow, yellow, muddy South Platte,
with its low banks and its scattering flat sand-bars and
pigmy islands—a melancholy stream straggling through the
center of the enormous flat plain, and only saved from
being impossible to find with the naked eye by its sentinel
rank of scattering trees standing on either bank. The Platte
was "up," they said—which made me wish I could see it
when it was down, if it could look any sicker and sorrier.
They said it was a dangerous stream to cross, now, because
its quick-sands were liable to swallow up horses, coach, and
passengers if an attempt was made to ford it. But the mails
had to go, and we made the attempt. Once or twice in
midstream the wheels sunk into the yielding sands so
threateningly that we half believed we had dreaded and
avoided the sea all our lives to be shipwrecked in a "mud-
wagon" in the middle of a desert at last. But we dragged
through and sped away toward the setting sun.

Roughing It, I, Chapt. VII

The Neckar is in many places so narrow that a person

can throw a dog across it, if he has one. . . . A hatful of rain makes high water in the Neckar, and a basketful produces an overflow.

A Tramp Abroad, I, Chapt. XIV, p. 121

The river Nile is lower than it has been for 150 years. This news will be chiefly interesting to parties who remember the former occasion.

A Bibliography of Mark Twain, Merle Johnson, p. 178

A river without islands is like a woman without hair. She may be good and pure, but one doesn't fall in love with her very often.

Mark Twain, His Life and Work, Will Clemens, p. 184

I've seen this river so wide that it had only one bank.

Mark Twain and I, Opie Read, p. 48

People accustomed to the monster mile-wide Mississippi, grow accustomed to associating the term "river" with a high degree of watery grandeur. Consequently, such people feel rather disappointed when they stand on the shores of the Humboldt or the Carson and find that a "river" in Nevada is a sickly rivulet which is just the counterpart of the Erie in all respects save that the canal is twice as long and four times as deep. One of the pleasantest and most invigorating exercises one can contrive is to run and jump across the Humboldt river till he is overheated, and then drink it dry.

Roughing It, I, Chapt. XXVIII, p. 222

ROAD   *See also* DIRECTIONS

The legislature sat sixty days, and passed private toll-road franchises all the time. When they adjourned it was estimated that every citizen owned about three franchises, and it was believed that unless Congress gave the Territory another degree of longitude there would not be room enough to accommodate the toll-roads. The ends of them were hanging over the boundary line everywhere like a fringe.

Roughing It, I, Chapt. XXV, p. 208

[In Bermuda]: Take any road you please . . . it curves always, which is a continual promise, whereas straight roads reveal everything at a glance and kill interest.

"Rambling Notes of an Idle Excursion,"
Tom Sawyer Abroad, Etc., p. 285

ROBBER

[Kamehameha]: He was a mere kinglet and of little or no consequence at the time of Captain Cook's arrival in 1788; but about four years afterward he conceived the idea of enlarging his sphere of influence. That is a courteous modern phrase which means robbing your neighbor—for your neighbor's benefit. . . .

Following the Equator, I, Chapt. III, p. 43

A robber is much more high-toned than what a pirate is—as a general thing. In most countries they're awful high up in the nobility—dukes and such.

The Adventures of Tom Sawyer, Chapt. XXXV, p. 318

ROMANCE *See also* BIOGRAPHY

. . . to be human is to have one's little modicum of romance secreted away in one's composition.

The Gilded Age, I, Chapt. X, p. 118

. . . the romance of life is the only part of it that is overwhelmingly valuable, and romance dies with youth. After that, life is a drudge, and indeed a sham.

Mark Twain's Letters to Will Bowen, p. 27

ROME, ITALY *See* NOSE, POPULARITY, PUNISHMENT

ROOSEVELT, THEODORE

Every time, in 25 years, that I have met Roosevelt the man, a wave of welcome has streaked through me with the hand-grip; but whenever (as a rule) I meet Roosevelt the statesman and politician, I find him destitute of morals and not respectworthy. It is plain that where his political self and his party self are concerned he has nothing resembling a conscience; that under those inspirations he is naively indifferent to the restraints of duty and even unaware of them; ready to kick the Constitution into the back yard whenever it gets in the way; and whenever he smells a vote, not only willing but eager to buy it, give extravagant rates for it and pay the bill—not out of his own pocket or the party's, but out of the nation's, by cold pillage. . . .

. . . Theodore the man is sane; in fairness we ought to keep in mind that Theodore, as statesman and politician, is insane and irresponsible.

Mark Twain's Letters, II, p. 766

Certainly [Roosevelt] is popular . . . and with the best of reasons. If the twelve apostles should call at the White House, he would say, "Come in, come in! I am delighted to see you. I've been watching your progress, and I admired it very much." Then if Satan should come, he would slap him on the shoulder and say, "Why, Satan, how *do* you do? I am so glad to meet you. I've read all your works and enjoyed every one of them." Anybody could be popular with a gift like that.

Mark Twain, a Biography, Paine, III, p. 1340

I am not jesting, but am in deep earnest, when I give it as my opinion that our President is *the* representative American gentleman—of today. I think he is as distinctly and definitely the representative American gentleman of today as was Washington the representative American gentleman of his day. Roosevelt is the whole argument for and against, in his own person. He represents what the American gentleman ought not to be, and does it as clearly, intelligibly, and exhaustively as he represents what the American gentleman *is.* We are by long odds the most ill-mannered nation, civilized or savage, that exists on the planet today, and our President stands for us like a colossal monument visible from all ends of the earth.

Mark Twain in Eruption, p. 33

ROYALTY *See also* CLOTHES, MONARCHY, NOBILITY, REPUBLIC, RIDICULE, VALUE

There was never a throne which did not represent a crime.

Mark Twain, a Biography, Paine, II, p. 874

We hold these truths to be self-evident—that all monarchs are usurpers and descendants of usurpers, for the reason that no throne was ever set up in this world by the will, freely exercised, of the only body possessing the legitimate right to set it up—the numerical mass of the nation.

Ibid., Paine, II, p. 890

[Mark Twain's daughter, Jean, comments on his invitation to dine with the Emperor of Germany]: "Papa, the way things are going, pretty soon there won't be anybody left for you to get acquainted with but God."

Mark Twain's Notebook, p. 242

[The assassination of Empress Elizabeth of Austria, 1898]: She was so blameless—the Empress; and so beautiful in mind and heart, in person and spirit; and whether with the crown upon her head, or without it and nameless, a grace to the human race, almost a justification of its creation; would be, indeed, but that the animal that struck her down re-establishes the doubt.

Mark Twain, a Biography, Paine, II, p. 1071

Well, never mind about the rightful earl; he merely wanted to borrow money. I never knew an American earl that didn't.

Ibid., Paine, II, p. 673

It was pitiful for a person born in a wholesome free atmosphere to listen to their humble and hearty outpourings of loyalty toward their king and Church and nobility; as if they had any more occasion to love and honor king and Church and noble than a slave has to love and honor the lash, or a dog has to love and honor the stranger that kicks him! Why, dear me, *any* kind of royalty, howsoever modified, *any* kind of aristocracy, howsoever pruned, is rightly an insult; but if you are born and brought up under that sort of arrangement you probably never find it out for yourself, and don't believe it when somebody else tells you.

A Connecticut Yankee in King Arthur's Court,
Chapt. VIII, p. 65

[Queen Victoria]: [She] was a model upon which many a humbler life was formed and made beautiful while she

lived . . . [hers] a life which finds its just image in the
star which falls out of its place in the sky and out of existence, but whose light still streams with unfaded luster
across the abysses of space long after its fires have been
extinguished at their source.

"Queen Victoria,"
Mark Twain's Speeches (1923), p. 387

Bonaparte instituted the setting of merit above birth, and
also so completely stripped the divinity from royalty that,
whereas crowned heads in Europe were gods before, they
are only men since, and can never be gods again, but only
figure-heads, and answerable for their acts like common
clay. Such benefactions as these compensate the temporary
harm which Bonaparte and the Revolution did, and leave
the world in debt to them for these great and permanent
services to liberty, humanity, and progress.

Life on the Mississippi, Chapt. XLVI, p. 346

I think it is not wise for an emperor, or a king, or a president, to come down into the boxing ring, so to speak, and
lower the dignity of his office by meddling in the small
affairs of private citizens.

Mark Twain in Eruption, p. 22

As a general thing, we have been shown through palaces
by some plush-legged, filigreed flunkey or other, who
charged a franc for it; but after talking with the company
half an hour, the Emperor of Russia and his family conducted us all through their mansion themselves. They made
no charge. They seemed to take a real pleasure in it.

We spent half an hour idling through the palace, admiring the cosy apartments and the rich but eminently homelike appointments of the place, and then the imperial family bade our party a kind good-bye, and proceeded to count
the spoons.

The Innocents Abroad, II, Chapt. X, p. 127

There are shams and shams; there are frauds and frauds,
but the transparentest of all is the sceptered one. We see
monarchs meet and go through solemn ceremonies, farces,
with straight countenances; but it is not possible to imagine

them meeting in private and not laughing in each other's faces.

Mark Twain's Notebook, p. 196

. . . there is nothing diviner about a king than there is about a tramp, after all. He is just a cheap and hollow artificiality when you don't know he is a king. But reveal his quality, and dear me it takes your very breath away to look at him. I reckon we are all fools. Born so, no doubt.

A Connecticut Yankee in King Arthur's Court,
Chapt. XXXIV, p. 320

I urged that kings were dangerous. He said, then have cats. He was sure that a royal family of cats would answer every purpose. They would be as useful as any other royal family, they would know as much, they would have the same virtues and the same treacheries, the same disposition to get up shindies with other royal cats, they would be laughably vain and absurd and never know it, they would be wholly inexpensive, finally, they would have as sound a divine right as any other royal house. . . . The worship of royalty being founded in unreason, these graceful and harmless cats would easily become as sacred as any other royalties, and indeed more so, because it would presently be noticed that they hanged nobody, beheaded nobody, imprisoned nobody, inflicted no cruelties or injustices of any sort, and so must be worthy of a deeper love and reverence than the customary human king, and would certainly get it.

Ibid., Chapt. XL, p. 363

This autobiography of mine is a mirror, and I am looking at myself in it all the time. Incidentally I notice the people that pass along at my back—I get glimpses of them in the mirror—and whenever they say or do anything that can help advertise me and flatter me and raise me in my own estimation, I set these things down in my autobiography. I rejoice when a king or a duke comes my way and makes himself useful to this autobiography, but they are rare customers, with wide intervals between. I can use them with good effect as lighthouses and monuments along my way, but for real business I depend upon the common herd.

Mark Twain's Autobiography, Paine, II, p. 312

All I say is, kings is kings, and you got to make allowances. Take them all around, they're a mighty ornery lot. It's the way they're raised.

The Adventures of Huckleberry Finn,
Chapt. XXIII, p. 206

The world is made wrong, kings should go to school to their own laws at times, and so learn mercy.

The Prince and the Pauper, Chapt. XXVII, p. 253

I liked the king, and *as* a king I respected him—respected the office; at least respected it as much as I was capable of respecting any unearned supremacy.

A Connecticut Yankee in King Arthur's Court,
Chapt. VIII, p. 69

Let us take the present male sovereigns of the earth—and strip them naked. Mix them with 500 naked mechanics, and then march the whole around a circus ring, charging suitable admission of course,—and desire the audience to pick out the sovereigns.

They couldn't. You would have to paint them blue. You can't tell a king from a cooper except you differentiate their exteriority.

Mark Twain's Notebook, p. 198

RULE   *See also* GRAMMAR

Without doubt modesty is nothing less than a holy feeling; and without doubt the person whose rule of modesty has been transgressed feels the same sort of wound that he would feel if something made holy to him by his religion had suffered a desecration. I say "rule of modesty" because there are about a million rules in the world, and this makes a million standards to be looked out for. . . . All human rules are more or less idiotic, I suppose. It is best so, no doubt. The way it is now, the asylums can hold the sane people, but if we tried to shut up the insane we should run out of building materials.

Following the Equator, II, Chapt. XIV, p. 170

What has become of the golden rule?

It exists, it continues to sparkle, and is well taken care of. It is Exhibit A in the Church's assets, and we pull it out every Sunday and give it an airing. . . . It is strictly religious furniture, like an acolyte, or a contribution-plate, or any of those things. It is never intruded into business; and Jewish persecution is not a religious passion, it is a business passion.

> "Concerning the Jews,"
> *Literary Essays*, p. 274

It is good to obey all the rules when you're young, so you'll have the strength to break them when you're old.

> "Mark Twain's Friendship Inspired Little
> Girl to Successful Career," Dorothy Quick,
> *Advance Magazine*, Feb. 1940, p. 2

RUMOR *See also* DEATH

. . . rumor will die itself if you will only give it three days. Start any rumor, and if the public can go with its curiosity unsatisfied for three days something else will spring up which will make the public forget all about the first one.

> *A Bibliography of Mark Twain*, Merle Johnson, p. 147

It has been reported that I was seriously ill—it was another man; dying—it was another man; dead—the other man again. . . . As far as I can see, nothing remains to be reported, except that I have become a foreigner. When you hear it, don't you believe it. And don't take the trouble to deny it. Merely just raise the American flag on our house in Hartford, and let it talk.

> *Mark Twain's Letters*, II, p. 650

RUSH *See* CREATION

RUSSIA *See also* ENGLAND, NATION, REPUBLIC, ROYALTY, SNEEZE

[At Yalta], the Emperor of Russia and his family conducted us all through their mansion themselves. They made no charge. They seemed to take a real pleasure in it.

We spent half an hour idling through the palace, admiring the cosy apartments and the rich but eminently homelike appointments of the place, and then the imperial family bade our party a kind goodbye, and proceeded to count the spoons.

The Innocents Abroad, II, Chapt. X, p. 126

And look at Russia. It spreads all around and everywhere, and yet ain't no more important in this world than Rhode Island is, and hasn't got half as much in it that's worth saving.

Tom Sawyer Abroad, Etc., Chapt. IX, p. 91

The French are polite, but it is often mere ceremonious politeness. A Russian imbues his polite things with a heartiness, both of phrase and expression, that compels belief in their sincerity.

The Innocents Abroad, II, Chapt. X, p. 123

I wish Europe would let Russia annihilate Turkey a little —not much, but enough to make it difficult to find the place again without a divining-rod or a diving-bell.

Ibid., II, Chapt. XV, p. 185

Some of us, even the white-headed, may live to see the blessed day when tsars and grand dukes will be as scarce there as I trust they are in heaven. [1906]

Mark Twain, a Biography, Paine, III, p. 1285

S

SABBATH *See also* SUNDAY

But we were good boys . . . we didn't break the Sabbath often enough to signify—once a week perhaps. . . . Anyway, we were good Presbyterian boys when the weather was doubtful; when it was fair, we did wander a little from the fold.

"Sixty-Seventh Birthday,"
Mark Twain's Speeches (1923), p. 251

We were all perfectly willing to keep the Sabbath day, but there are times when to keep the *letter* of a sacred law whose spirit is righteous, becomes a sin, and this was a case in point.

The Innocents Abroad, II, Chapt. XVI, p. 193

The day of rest comes but once a week, and sorry am I that it does not come oftener. Man is so constituted that he can stand more rest than this. I often think regretfully that it would have been so easy to have two Sundays in a week, and yet it was not so ordained. The omnipotent Creator could have made the world in three days just as easily as he made it in six, and this would have doubled the Sundays. Still it is not our place to criticize the wisdom of the Creator.

"Reflections on the Sabbath,"
The Washoe Giant in San Francisco, p. 115

I shall act as conscientiously as did the old Puritan lady who used to whip her beer barrel because the beer would work on the Sabbath day.

"To the Reading Public,"
The Twainian, May 1940, p. 2

SACRIFICE

. . . we have smuggled a word into the dictionary which ought not to be there at all—Self-Sacrifice. It describes a thing which does not exist. . . . We ignore and never mention the Sole Impulse which dictates and compels a man's every act: the imperious necessity of securing his own approval, in every emergency and at all costs.

What Is Man? and Other Essays, Chapt. II, p. 29

SAGE-BRUSH

[At Carson City, Nevada]: . . . in [this] infernal soil nothing but that fag-end of vegetable creation, "sage-brush," ventures to grow . . . When crushed, sage-brush emits an odor which isn't exactly magnolia and equally isn't exactly polecat—but it is a sort of compromise between the two.

Mark Twain's Letters, I, p. 54

It is an imposing monarch of the forest in exquisite miniature.

Roughing It, I, Chapt. III, p. 31

SAILOR *See* PROFANITY

SAINT *See also* HABIT

We have seen pictures of martyrs enough, and saints enough, to regenerate the world. . . . We have seen 13,000 St. Jeromes, 16,000 St. Matthews, 60,000 St. Sebastians, and four millions of assorted monks . . . and feel encouraged to believe that when we have seen more of these . . . and had larger experience we shall begin to take an absorbing interest in them like our cultivated countrymen from Amerique.

The Innocents Abroad, I, p. 304

St. Patrick had no politics; his sympathies lay with the right—that was politics enough. When he came across a reptile, he forgot to inquire whether he was a Democrat or a Republican, but simply exalted his staff and "let him have it."

"Letter Read at a Dinner of the Knights of St. Patrick,"
Tom Sawyer Abroad, Etc., p. 438

[In Genoa]: They also showed us a portrait of a Madonna which was painted by St. Luke, and it did not look half as old and smoky as some of the pictures by Rubens. We could not help admiring the Apostle's modesty in never once mentioning in his writings that he could paint.

The Innocents Abroad, I, Chapt. XVII, p. 218

SALARY *See* LITERARY CRITICISM

SALESMAN

A commercial traveler is about to unroll his samples:
Merchant (pettishly)—No, don't. I don't want to buy anything!

Drummer—If you please, I was only going to show you—
Merchant—But I don't wish to see them!

Drummer (after a pause, pleadingly)—But do you mind letting *me* look at them? I haven't seen them for three weeks!

A Tramp Abroad, II, Appendix F, p. 319

SALT LAKE CITY, UTAH *See* MONEY, MORMONS, TRUTH, WOMAN

SAMOA *See* DIRECTIONS

SAN FRANCISCO

I have done more for San Francisco than any other of its old residents. Since I left there it has increased its population fully 300,000. I could have done more—I could have left earlier—it was suggested.

Mark Twain, a Biography, Paine, III, p. 1248

SANTA CLAUS

[A letter from Mark Twain to his children]:
Letter from Santa Claus.   Palace of St. Nicholas
                                        In the Moon
  My dear Susie Clemens: Christmas morning

I have received and read all the letters which you and
your little sister have written me by the hand of your
mother and your nurses; I have also read those which you
little people have written me with your own hands—for
although you did not use any characters that are in grown
people's alphabet, you used the characters that all children
in all lands on earth and in the twinkling stars use; and as
all my subjects in the moon are children and use no characters but that, you will easily understand that I can read
your and your baby's sister's jagged and fantastic marks
without any trouble at all. But I had trouble with those
letters which you dictated through your mother and the
nurses, for I am a foreigner and cannot read English writing
well. You will find that I made no mistakes about the things
which you and the baby ordered in your *own* letters—I went
down your chimney at midnight when you were asleep and
delivered them all myself—and kissed both of you, too, because you are good children, well-trained, nice-mannered,
and about the most obedient little people I ever saw. But
in the letters which you dictated there are some words which
I could not make out for certain, and one or two small
orders which I could not fill because we ran out of stock.
Our last lot of Kitchen-furniture for dolls has just gone to a
very poor little child in the North Star away up in the cold
country above the Big Dipper. Your mama can show you
that star and you will say: "Little Snow Flake" (for that is
the child's name) "I'm glad you got that furniture, for you
need it more than I." That is, you must *write* that, with
your own hand, and Snow Flake will write you an answer.
If you only spoke it she wouldn't hear you. Make your

letter light and thin, for the distance is great and the postage very heavy.

There was a word or two in your mama's letter which I couldn't be certain of. I took it to be "a trunk full of doll's clothes." Is that it? I will call at your kitchen door about nine o'clock this morning to inquire. But I must not see anybody and I must not speak to anybody but you. When the kitchen door bell rings George must be blindfolded and sent to open the door. Then he must go back to the dining-room or the china closet and take the cook with him. You must tell George he must walk on tiptoe and not speak—otherwise he will die some day. Then you must go up to the nursery and stand on a chair or the nurse's bed and put your ear to the speaking tube that leads down to the kitchen and when I whistle through it you must speak in the tube and say, "Welcome, Santa Claus!" Then I will ask whether it was a trunk you ordered or not. If you say it was, I shall ask you what *color* you want the trunk to be. Your mama will help you to name a nice color and then you must tell me every single thing in detail which you want the trunk to contain. Then when I say "Good bye and a Merry Christmas to my little Susie Clemens," you must say "Goodbye, good old Santa Claus, I thank you very much and please tell that little Snow Flake I will look at her star tonight and she must look down here—I will be right in the West bay-window; and every fine night I will look at her star and say, 'I know somebody up there and *like* her, too.'" Then you must go down into the library and make George close all the doors that open into the mainhall, and everybody must keep still for a little while. I will go to the moon and get those things and in a few minutes I will come down the chimney that belongs to the fireplace that is in the hall—if it is a trunk you want—because I couldn't get such a thing as a trunk down the nursery chimney, you know.

People may talk if they want, until they hear my foot-steps in the hall. Then you tell them to keep quiet a little while till I go back up the chimney. Maybe you will not hear my footsteps at all—so you may go now and then and peep through the dining-room doors, and by and by you will see that thing which you want, right under the piano in the drawing-room—for I shall put it there. If I should leave any snow in the hall, you must tell George to sweep it into the fireplace, for I haven't time to do such things. George must not use a broom, but a rag—else he will die some day. You must watch George and not let him run into danger. If my boot should leave a stain on the marble, George must not holystone it away. Leave it there always in memory of my visit; and whenever you look at it or show it to anybody you must let it remind you to be a good little girl. Whenever you are naughty and somebody points to that mark which your good old Santa Claus's boot made on the marble, what will you say, little Sweetheart?

Goodbye for a few minutes, till I come down to the world and ring the kitchen door-bell.

Your loving

Santa Claus

Whom people sometimes call The Man in the Moon.

My Father • Mark Twain, Clara Clemens, p. 36

SATAN *See also* BRUTALITY, CHEATING, ROOSEVELT, THEODORE

Satan (impatiently) to New Comer. The trouble with you Chicago people is, that you think you are the best people down here; whereas you are merely the most numerous.

"Pudd'nhead Wilson's New Calendar,"

Following the Equator, II, Chapt. XXIV, p. 282

I have no special regard for Satan, but I can at least claim I have no prejudice against him. It may even be I lean a little his way, on account of his not having a fair show. All religions issue Bibles against him, and say the most injurious things about him, but we never hear *his* side. We have none but evidence for the prosecution and yet we have rendered the verdict. To my mind, this is irregular. It is un-English; it is un-American; it is French. Without this precedent Dreyfus could not have been condemned. Of course Satan has some kind of a case, it goes without saying. It may be a poor one, but that is nothing; that can be said about any of us. As soon as I can get at the facts I will undertake his rehabilitation myself, if I can find an unpolitic publisher. It is a thing we ought to be willing to do for anyone who is under a cloud. We may not pay him reverence, for that would be indiscreet, but we can at least respect his talents. A person who has for untold centuries maintained the imposing position of spiritual head of four-fifths of the human race, and political head of the whole of it, must be granted the possession of executive abilities of the loftiest order. In his large presence the other popes and politicians shrink to midges for the microscope. I would like to see him. I would rather see him and shake him by the tail than any other member of the European concert.

> "Concerning the Jews,"
> *Literary Essays,* p. 251

Satan must have been pretty simple, even according to the New Testament, or he wouldn't have led Christ up on a high mountain and offered him the world if he would fall down and worship him. That was a manifestly absurd proposition, because Christ, as the Son of God, already owned the world; and, besides, what Satan showed him was only a few rocky acres of Palestine. It is just as if some one should try to buy Rockefeller, the owner of all the Standard Oil Company, with a gallon of kerosene.

> *Mark Twain, a Biography,* Paine, III, p. 1469

SATIRE

One can deliver a satire with telling force through the insidious medium of a travesty, if he is careful not to overwhelm the satire with the extraneous interest of the travesty.

> "A Couple of Sad Experiences,"
> *Galaxy Magazine,* June 1870, p. 858

SATISFACTION   *See* MAN

SAVAGE *See also* MISSIONARY
There are many humorous things in the world: among
them the white man's notion that he is less savage than the
other savages.
>*Following the Equator*, I, Chapt. XXI, p. 216

The only very marked difference between the average
civilized man and the average savage is that the one is
gilded and the other painted.
>*Mark Twain's Notebook*, p. 392

SAWYER, TOM
If I went on, now, and took him into manhood, he would
just lie like all the one-horse men in literature and the
reader would conceive a hearty contempt for him.
>*Mark Twain's Letters*, I, p. 258

SAY *See* CONVICTION

SCANDAL *See* GOSSIP, SIMILES

SCENERY *See also* CALIFORNIA, HOLY LAND, LAKE
[Redding, Conn.]: [It] seemed it's best when all was
summer-green; later it seemed at its best when all around
was burning with the autumn splendors; and now once
more it seems at its best, with the trees naked and the
ground a painter's palette.
>*Mark Twain's Letters*, II, p. 822

Nothing helps scenery like ham and eggs.
>*Roughing It*, I, Chapt. XVII, p. 148

SCHOOL *See also* BOYHOOD, PUNISHMENT, TEACHER
. . . out of the public school grows the greatness of the
nation.
>"Public Education Association,"
>*Mark Twain's Speeches* (1923), p. 212

There are those who scoff at the school boy, calling him
frivolous and shallow. Yet it was a schoolboy who said:

"Faith is believing what you know ain't so."

> "Pudd'nhead Wilson's New Calendar,"
> *Following the Equator*, I, Chapt. XII, p. 132

All schools, all colleges, have two great functions: to confer, and to conceal valuable knowledge. The theological knowledge which they conceal cannot justly be regarded as less valuable than that which they reveal. That is, if, when a man is buying a basket of strawberries, it can profit him to know that the bottom half of it is rotten.

> *Mark Twain's Notebook*, p. 398

In the first place God made idiots. This was for practice. Then he made School Boards.

> "Pudd'nhead Wilson's New Calendar,"
> *Following the Equator*, II, Chapt. XXV, p. 295

I never let my schooling interfere with my education.

> *Source Undetermined*

SCIENCE   *See also* MISSISSIPPI RIVER

Scientists have odious manners, except when you prop up their theory; then you can borrow money of them.

> "The Bee,"
> *What Is Man?* and Other Essays, p. 283

SCIENCE, CHRISTIAN   *See* CHRISTIAN SCIENCE

SCOTT, SIR WALTER

Prof. Trent . . . said that Scott would outlive all his critics. I guess that's true. The fact of the business is, you've got to be one of two ages to appreciate Scott. When you're eighteen you can read *Ivanhoe*, and you want to wait until you are ninety to read some of the rest. It takes a pretty well-regulated abstemious critic to live 90 years.

> "Disappearance of Literature,"
> *Mark Twain's Speeches* (1923), p. 210

SEA   *See also* EQUATOR, INTELLECT, PRAYER, ROMANCE, SHIP

We hear all our lives about the "gentle stormless Pacific"

. . . Balboa . . . waved his country's banner and named his great discovery "Pacific"—thus uttering a lie which will go on deceiving generation after generation of students while the old ocean lasts. . . . If I had been there with my experience I would have said to this man Balboa . . . "You have jumped to a conclusion and christened this sleeping boy-baby by a girl's name, without stopping to inquire into the sex of it" . . . if [he] had named this ocean the "Four Months Pacific" he would have come nearer the mark.

Letters from the Sandwich Islands, p. 7

[Brown was seasick]: [The] rule of his present case was to seem to look like an allegory of unconditional surrender —hopeless, helpless and indifferent.

Ibid., p. 142

. . . a long sea-voyage not only brings out all the mean traits one has, and exaggerates them, but raises up others which he never suspected he possessed, and even creates new ones. A twelve months' voyage at sea would make an ordinary man a very miracle of meanness. On the other hand, if a man has good qualities, the spirit seldom moves him to exhibit them on shipboard, at least with any sort of emphasis.

The Innocents Abroad, II, Conclusion, p. 441

I was only seasick once. . . . It was on a little ship on which there were two hundred other passengers. I—was—sick. I was so sick that there wasn't any left for those other two hundred passengers.

Mark Twain's Speeches (1923), p. 303

SEAS, SOUTH *See* DIRECTIONS, MISSIONARY

SEASON *See also* CLIMATE

The land that has four well-defined seasons cannot lack beauty, or pall with monotony.

Roughing It, II, Chapt. XV, p. 150

France has neither winter, nor summer, nor morals.

Mark Twain, a Biography, Paine, II, p. 642

There are only two seasons in the region around Mono Lake—the breaking up of one winter and the beginning of the next.

Roughing It, I, Chapt. XXXVIII, p. 298

SECTS *See* RELIGION

SELF

. . . we do not deal much in fact when we are contemplating ourselves.

"Does the Race of Man Love a Lord?"
The $30,000 Bequest, Etc., p. 284

SELF-APPROVAL *See* CONSCIENCE

SELF-MADE

Self-made man, you know. They know how to talk. They do deserve more credit than any other breed of men, yes, that is true; and they are among the very first to find it out, too.

A Connecticut Yankee in King Arthur's Court,
Chapt. XXXII, p. 287

SELF-SACRIFICE *See* SACRIFICE

SELFISHNESS *See also* BENEVOLENCE

He had more selfish organs than any seven men in the world—all packed in the stern-sheets of his skull, of course, where they belonged. They weighed down the back of his head so that it made his nose tilt up in the air.

Life on the Mississippi, Chapt. XXIV, p. 196

. . . there may be two sorts of selfishness—brutal and divine; . . . he who sacrifices others to himself exemplifies the first, whereas he who sacrifices himself for others personifies the second—the divine contenting of his soul by serving the happiness of his fellow-men.

Mark Twain, a Biography, Paine, II, p. 744

SENATOR

SENATOR *See also* POLITICS
. . . the Senator's frank could convey a horse through the mails, if necessary.
The Gilded Age, I, Chapt. XXIV, p. 270

SERENITY
[He was] . . . full of . . . the serenity which a good conscience buttressed by a sufficient bank account gives.
Following the Equator, II, Chapt. XIII, p. 160

SERIOUSNESS
I shall never be accepted seriously over my own signature. —People always want to laugh over what I write and are disappointed if they don't find a joke in it. This [Joan of Arc] is to be a serious book. It means more to me than anything I have ever undertaken. I shall write it anonymously.
Mark Twain, a Biography, Paine, II, p. 959
The fire brigade march in rank, curiously uniformed, and so grave is their demeanor that they look like a Salvation Army under conviction of sin.
"The German Chicago,"
The American Claimant, Etc., p. 506

SERMON *See also* PREACHER, REPENTENCE, SUNDAY
It is said that once a man of small consequence died, and the Rev. T. K. Beecher was asked to preach the funeral sermon—a man who abhors the lauding of people, either dead or alive, except in dignified and simple language, and then only for merits which they actually possessed or possess, not merits which they merely ought to have possessed. The friends of the deceased got up a stately funeral. They must have had misgivings that the corpse might not be praised strongly enough, for they prepared some manuscript headings and notes in which nothing was left unsaid on that subject that a fervid imagination and unabridged dictionary could compile, and these they handed to the

minister as he entered the pulpit. They were merely intended as suggestions, and so the friends were filled with consternation when the minister stood up in the pulpit and proceeded to read off the curious odds and ends in ghastly detail and in a loud voice! And their consternation solidified to petrifaction when he paused at the end, contemplated the multitude reflectively, and then said, impressively:

"The man would be a fool who tried to add anything to that. Let us pray!"

"Post-Mortem Poetry,"
The $30,000 Bequest, Etc., p. 251

. . . and Uncle Silas he preached them the blamedest jumbledest idiotic sermons you ever struck, and would tangle you up so you couldn't find your way home in daylight: . . . by George, they give me the jim-jams and the fantods and caked up what brains I had, and turned them solid.

"Tom Sawyer, Detective,"
Tom Sawyer Abroad, Etc., p. 227

Few sinners are saved after the first twenty minutes of a sermon.

The Hannibal Courier-Post, March 6, 1935

. . . a French sermon is like a French speech—never names a hisorical event, but only the date of it; if you are not up on your dates, you get left.

"Paris Notes,"
Tom Sawyer Abroad, Etc., p. 378

This portion of Mr. Twichell's sermon made a great impression upon me, and I was grieved that some one hadn't wakened me earlier so that I might have heard what went before.

Mark Twain's Letters, I, p. 314

. . . a peculiarity that conspicuously marked and marred [school compositions] was the inveterate and intolerable sermon that wagged its crippled tail at the end of each.

The Adventures of Tom Sawyer, Chapt. XXI, p. 198

[He] . . . preached a prayer-meeting sermon that night

that gave him a rattling reputation, because the oldest man in the world couldn't a understood it.

The Adventures of Huckleberry Finn,
Chapt. XLII, p. 370

SERPENT *See* ADAM, EVE

SEX *See also* SIMILES

Of the delights of *this* world man cares *most* for sexual intercourse. He will go any length for it—risk fortune, character, reputation, life itself. And what do you think he has done? In a thousand years you would never guess—*He has left it out of his heaven! Prayer takes its place.*

Mark Twain's Notebook, p. 397

SHADOW *See* SIMILES

SHAKESPEARE, William *See* COMEDY, EXPRESSION

SHAM *See also* NAME, NOBILITY

. . . what sorry shows and shadows we are. Without our clothes and our pedestals we are poor things and much of a size; our dignities are not real, our pomps are shams. At our best and stateliest we are not suns, as we pretended, and teach, and believe, but only candles; and any bummer can blow us out.

"The Memorable Assassination"
What Is Man? and Other Essays, p. 170

We all have our shams—I suppose there is a sham somewhere about every individual, if we could manage to ferret it out.

The Gilded Age, II, Chapt. II, p. 28

SHAME

These were the darlingest words . . . for they whitewashed his shame for him, and that is a good service to have when you can't get the best of all verdicts: self-acquittal.

The American Claimant, Etc., Chapt. XIV, p. 120

SHEEP *See also* OPINION
To create man was a fine and original idea; but to add the sheep was tautology.

Mark Twain's Notebook, p. 379

SHELL *See* OCCUPATION

SHIP *See also* ARK, COLUMBUS, EXAGGERTION, INSURANCE,
NOAH, PUN, SEA, TWAIN, MARK
[Card-players aboard ship]: One night the storm suddenly culminated in a climax of unparalled fury; the vessel went down on her beam ends, and every thing let go with a crash—passengers, tables, cards, bottles. . . . In a moment fifty sore distressed and pleading voices ejaculated, "O Heaven! help us in our extremity!" and one voice rang out clear and sharp above the plaintive chorus and said, "Remember, boys, I played the tray for low!" . . .

"Remarkable Instances of Presence of Mind"
The Celebrated Jumping Frog of Calaveras County, p. 173
When the ship begins to roll sideways and kick up behind at the same time, I always know I am expected to perform a certain duty. I learned it years ago on the "Quaker City." You might suppose that I would have forgotten my part after so long a residence on shore. But there it is again. It's habit . . . you might confine me for 40 years in a Rhode Island corn patch, and at the end of that time I'd know just as well what to do when a ship begins to kick as I do at this moment. The darkest night never confuses me in the least. It's a little singular when you look at it, isn't it? But I presume it's attributable to the solemn steadfastness of the great deep.

Mark Twain, His Life and Works, Will Clemens, p. 129

[Aboard ship]: . . . the world is far, far away; it has ceased to exist for you—seemed a fading dream, along in the first days; has dissolved to an unreality now; it is gone from your mind with all its businesses and ambitions, its prosperities and disasters, its exultations and despairs, its joys and griefs and cares and worries. They are no concern of yours any more; they have gone out of your life; they are a storm which has passed and left a deep calm behind.

Following the Equator, II, Chapt. XXVI, p. 313

. . . they chartered a ship called *Mayflower* and set sail, and I have heard it said that they pumped the Atlantic Ocean through that ship sixteen times.

"To the Whitefriars"
Mark Twain's Speeches (1923), p. 181

[Columbus's ship]: . . . she was full of rats . . . the heavy seas made her seams open and shut like your fingers, and she leaked like a basket; where leakage is, there also, of necessity, is bilgewater; and where bilgewater is, only the dead can enjoy life. This is on account of the smell. In the presence of bilgewater, limburger cheese becomes odorless and ashamed.

"About All Kinds of Ships"
The American Claimant, Etc., p. 475

A ship is precisely a little village where gossips abound and where every man's business is his neighbor's.

Mark Twain's Notebook, p. 43

As far back as Noah's time it became law that ships must be constantly painted and fussed at when at sea; custom grew out of the law and at sea custom knows no death, this custom will continue until the sea goes dry.

Following the Equator, I, Chapt. IV, Vol. I

[Part of a speech delivered by Mark Twain at a farewell dinner tendered him by the Lord Mayor of Liverpool, July 10, 1907]:

Home is dear to us all, and now I am departing to my own home beyond the ocean. Oxford has conferred upon me the loftiest honor that has ever fallen to my share of this life's prizes. It is the very one I would have chosen, as outranking all and any others, the one more precious to me than any and all others, within the gift of man or state. During my four weeks' sojourn in England I have had another lofty honor, a continuous honor, an honor which has flowed serenely along, without halt or obstruction, through all these twenty-six days, a most moving and pulse-stirring honor—the heart-felt grip of the hand, and the welcome that does not descend from the pale-gray matter of the brain, but rushes up with the red blood from the heart. It makes me proud, and sometimes it makes me humble, too . . . Many and many a year ago I gathered an incident from Dana's *Two Years Before the Mast*. It was like this: There was a presumptuous little self-important skipper in a coasting sloop, engaged in the dried-apple and kitchen-furniture trade, and he was always hailing every ship that came in sight. He did it just to hear himself talk and to air his small grandeur. One day a majestic Indiaman came ploughing by with course on course of canvas towering into the sky, her decks and yards swarming with sailors, her hull burdened to the Plimsoll line with a rich freightage of precious spices, lading the breezes with gracious and mysterious odors of the orient. It was a noble spectacle, a sublime spectacle! Of course, the little skipper popped into the shrouds and squeaked out a hail, "Ship ahoy! What ship is that? And whence and whither?" In a deep and thunderous bass the answer came back through the speaking trumpet "The *Begum*, of Bengal, one hundred and forty-two days out from Canton, homeward bound. What ship is that?" Well, it just crushed that poor little creature's vanity flat, and he squeaked back most humbly, "Only the *Mary Ann*, fourteen hours out from Boston, bound for Kittery Point—with nothing to speak of!" Oh, what an eloquent word, that "only," to express the depths of his humbleness! That is just my case. During just one hour in the twenty-four—not more— I pause and reflect in the stillness of the night with the echoes of your English welcome still lingering in my ears, and then I am humble. Then I am properly meek, and for that little while I am only the *Mary Ann*, fourteen hours out, cargoed with vegetables and tinware; but during all the twenty-three hours my vain self-complacency rides high on the white crest of your approval, and then I am a stately Indiaman, ploughing the great seas under a cloud of canvas and laden with the kindest words that have ever been vouchsafed to any wandering alien in this world, I think; then my twenty-six fortunate days on this old mother soil seem to be multiplied by six, and *I* am the *Begum* of Bengal, one hundred and forty-two days out from Canton, homeward bound!

"The Last Lotus Club Speech"
Mark Twain's Speeches (1923), p. 372

We were six days going [by boat] from St. Louis to "St. Joe" . . . No record is left in my mind, now, concerning it, but a confused jumble of savage-looking snags, which we deliberately walked over with one wheel or the other; and of reefs which we butted and butted, and then retired from and climbed over in some softer place; and of sand-bars which we roosted on occasionally, and rested, and then got out our crutches and sparred over. In fact, the boat might almost as well have gone to St. Joe by land, for she was walking most of the time, anyhow—climbing over reefs and clambering over snags patiently and laboriously all day long. The captain said she was a "bully" boat, and all she wanted was more "shear" and a bigger wheel. I thought she wanted a pair of stilts, but I had the deep sagacity not to say so.

Roughing It, I, Chapt. I, p. 17

SHOES

I had on new shoes. They were No. 7's when I started, but were not more than 5's now, and still diminishing. . . . Everybody has worn tight shoes for two or three hours and known the luxury of taking them off in a retired place and seeing his feet swell up and obscure the firmament.

"Rambling Notes of an Idle Excursion"
Tom Sawyer Abroad, p. 292

SHUDDER

I cannot think of anything now more certain to make one shudder, than to have a soft-footed camel sneak up behind him and touch him on the ear with its old, flabby under lip.

The Innocents Abroad, II, Chapt XXIII, p. 289

SHYNESS *See also* NEWSPAPER

Hawthorne is shy; I am shy. "Oh, a couple of shysters!"

The Twainian, Mar.-Apr. 1959, p. 3

SICKNESS *See* ILLNESS, SHIP

SILENCE *See also* ASSASSINATION, MICROBE, READER, SIMILES, SLANDER

But I never said nothing . . . kept it to myself; it's the best way; then you don't have no quarrels, and don't get into no trouble.

The Adventures of Huckleberry Finn, Chapt. XIX, p. 170

Wilson stopped and stood silent. Inattention dies a quick and sure death when a speaker does that. The stillness gives warning that something is coming.

Pudd'nhead Wilson, Chapt. XXI, p. 214

A crowd like that can make a good deal of silence when they combine.

Mark Twain, a Biography, Paine, III, p. 1300

At the signal, the silence was torn to rags.

Personal Recollections of Joan of Arc,
I, Book II, Chapt. XXVII, p. 341

There was a pause—a silence of the sort that tortures one into stealing a glance to see how the situation looks.

Ibid., I, Book I, Chapt. XXI, p. 290

She didn't say a word, but her silence spoke with the voice of thunder.

Mark Twain in Eruption, p. 199

SIMILES *See also* EARTHQUAKE, EXPERIENCE, FOOD, GUIDE,

HAT, IGNORANCE, JOKE, LAW, MISSIONARY, POLITENESS, SMELL, SMILE, TAXES, TEETH

[The steamboat *Paul Jones*] . . . knocked her bottom out, and went down like a pot.

> *Life on the Mississippi*, Chapt XXV, p. 201

I gripped my jaws together, and calmed myself down till I was as cold as a capitalist.

> "The Million-Pound Bank Note"
> *The American Claimant, Etc.*, p. 359

His face was as blank as a target after a militia shooting-match.

> "Extract from Captain Stormfield's Visit to Heaven"
> *The Mysterious Stranger, Etc.*, p. 230

The silence of surprise held its own for a moment, then was broken by a just audible ripple of merriment which swept the sea of faces like the wash of a wave.

> *Life on the Mississippi*, Chapt. LVII, p. 424

[He has] no more sex than a tape-worm.

> *Mark Twain's Autobiography*, Paine, I, p. 75

You see, the charm about M. is, he is so catholic and unprejudiced that he fits in anywhere and everywhere. It makes him powerful good company, and as popular as scandal.

> *The American Claimant, Etc.*, Chapt. III, p. 30

. . . as dark as the inside of an infidel.

> "The McWilliamses and the Lightning"
> *The American Claimant, Etc.*, p. 301

[He] is as happy as a martyr when the fire won't burn.

> *Mark Twain, Business Man*, Webster, p. 123

When he got a-front of us he lifts his hat ever so gracious and dainty, like it was the lid of a box that had butterflies asleep in it and he didn't want to disturb them.

> *The Adventures of Huckleberry Finn*,
> Chapt. XXXIII, p. 295

. . . she set there, very impatient and excited and handsome, but looking kind of happy and eased-up, like a person that's had a tooth pulled out.

> *Ibid.*, Chapt. XXVIII, p. 245

[The Rock of Gibraltar]: It is pushed out into the sea on the end of a flat, narrow strip of land, and is suggestive of a "gob" of mud on the end of a shingle.

The Innocents Abroad, I, Chapt. VII, p. 99

Sometimes he smiled, and it was good to see; but when he straightened himself up like a liberty-pole, and the lightning begun to flicker out from under his eyebrows, you wanted to climb a tree first, and find out what the matter was afterwards.

The Adventures of Huckleberry Finn,
Chapt. XVIII, p. 146

. . . as innocent as a virgin . . . as innocent as an unborn virgin . . . [this] covered the ground.

"Joan of Arc"
Mark Twain's Speeches (1923), p. 274

. . . as regular as the Amens at a missionary caucus.

The Shotover Papers—Oxford University

Bedouins! Every man shrunk up and disappeared in his clothes like a mud-turtle.

The Innocents Abroad, II, Chapt. XXVIII, p. 369

I looked as out of place as a Presbyterian in hell.

Mark Twain, a Biography, Paine III, p. 1395

. . . outside it was as dark and dreary as if the world had been lit by Hartford gas.

"The Loves of Alonzo Fitzclarence and Rosannah Ethelton"
Tom Sawyer Abroad, Etc., p. 426

[Dutch flat poetry]: It is too smooth and blubbery; it reads like butter-milk gurgling from a jug.

"Answers to Correspondents"
Sketches New and Old, p. 86

. . . this one simple breakfast looms up in my memory like a shot-tower.

Roughing It, I, Chapt. XII, p. 108

. . . the horse darted away like a telegram.

Ibid., I, Chapt. XXIV, p. 196

I flattened myself out in the dust like a postage stamp.

Ibid., I, Chapt. XXVII, p. 291

[The flies at Mono Lake]: You can hold them under

water as long as you please—they do not mind it—they are only proud of it.

When you let them go, they pop up to the surface as dry as a patent-office report.

Ibid., I, Chapt. XXXVIII, p. 296

The evenings are as cool and balmy as a shroud.

The Twainian, Mar.-Apr. 1950, p. 3

His mouth opened up like a trunk.

The Adventures of Huckleberry Finn, p. 292

The flag flickered like a candle-flame.

Roughing It, II, Chapt. XIV, p. 145

. . . as scarce as lawyers in heaven.

"Information for the Millions"
The Celebrated Jumping Frog of Calaveras County, p. 144

He smiled all over his face and looked as radiantly happy as he will look some day when Satan gives him a Sunday vacation in the cold storage vault.

Mark Twain in Eruption, p. 75

He was as full of life as a watch spring.

Hartford Courant, Feb. 28, 1906

She is as homely as an oyster.

The Twainian, Sept.-Oct. 1947, p. 3

At a boat-race: They darted away as if they had been shot from a bow.

Ibid., Jan.-Feb. 1949, p. 3

I'm deep in a book . . . am grinding it out like a steam-mill.

Miscellaneous Papers in N.Y. Public Library

He fell out of an empty flatboat. . . . Being loaded with sin, he went to the bottom like an anvil.

Life on the Mississippi, Chapt. LIV, p. 398

In Washington: These office-seekers are . . . supernaturally gifted with "cheek." They fasten themselves to influential friends like barnacles to whales, and never let go until they are carried into the pleasant waters of office or scraped off against a protruding hotel bill.

The Twainian, July–Aug. 1947, p. 5

The Washoe tarantulas: Proud? Indeed, they would take up a straw and pick their teeth like a member of Congress.

Roughing It, I, Chapt. XXVI, p. 176

Riley . . . has a countenance that is as solemn and as blank as the backside of a tombstone.

"Riley—Newspaper Correspondent,"
Sketches New and Old, p. 203

The two-year-old: rips and tears around outdoors most of the time, and consequently is as hard as a pine-knot and as brown as an Indian.

Mark Twain, a Biography, I, p. 510

The young women smiled up over their shoulders, and the clerks smiled back . . . and all went merry as a marriage bell.

Galaxy magazine, May 1870, p. 719

Noon! . . . His shadder was just a blot around his feet.

Tom Sawyer Abroad, p. 62

Moonlight . . . his shadder laid on the sand by him like a puddle of ink.

Ibid., p. 68

The Shah had all his jewels on. He shone like a window with the westing sun on it.

"O'Shah,"
Europe and Elsewhere, p. 67

. . . gesticulating like a spider with the colic.

Following the Equator, II, Chapt. XXIV, p. 289

The boats go stuttering by with a good deal of frequency.

Mark Twain's Notebook, p. 335

The tamarind . . . pursed up my lips till they resembled the stem-end of a tomato . . . and sharpened my teeth till I could have shaved with them.

Roughing It, II, p. 209

The cat would lay down on our coats and snore like a steamboat.

Ibid., Chapt. XX, p. 186

. . . one walks over the soundless carpet of beaten yellow bark and dead spines of the foliage till he feels like a wandering spirit bereft of a footfall.

Ibid., II, Chapt. XV, p. 148

The buggy vanished past him like a thought.

Mark Twain's Letters, I, p. 306

In Honolulu . . . I ate several . . . tamarinds . . . They pursed up my lips, till they resembled the stem-end of a tomato, and I had to take my sustenance through a quill for twenty-four hours. They sharpened my teeth till I could have shaved with them, and gave them a "wire-edge" that I was afraid would stay; but a citizen said "no, it will come off when the enamel does"—which was comforting at any rate. I found, afterward, that only strangers eat tamarinds —but they only eat them once.

Roughing It, II, Chapt. XXII, p. 209

. . . she was as welcome as a corpse is to a coroner.

A Connecticut Yankee in King Arthur's Court,
Chapt. XI, p. 87

But lonely, conspicuous, and superb, rose that wonderful upright wedge, the Matterhorn. Its precipitous sides were powdered over with snow, and the upper half hidden in thick clouds which now and then dissolved to cobweb films and gave brief glimpses of the imposing tower as through a veil. A little later the Matterhorn took to himself the semblance of a volcano; he was stripped naked to his apex— around this circled vast wreaths of white cloud which strung slowly out and streamed away slantwise toward the sun, a twenty-mile stretch of rolling and tumbling vapor, and looking just as if it were pouring out of a crater. Later again, one of the mountain's sides was clean and clear, and another side densely clothed from base to summit in thick smoke-like cloud which feathered off and blew around the shaft's sharp edge like the smoke around the corners of a burning building. The Matterhorn is always experimenting, and always gets up fine effects, too. In the sunset, when all the lower world is palled in gloom, it points toward heaven out of the pervading blackness like a finger of fire. In the sunrise—well, they say it is very fine in the sunrise.

A Tramp Abroad, II, Chapt. IX, p. 138

It shriveled up the King's little soul like a raisin.
Personal Recollections of Joan of Arc,
I, Book II, Chapt. VIII, p. 181

. . . as happy as if she was on salary.
The Adventures of Huckleberry Finn,
Chapt. XXI, p. 189

[It] made you feel as good as church letting out.
Ibid., Chapt. XXV, p. 219

. . . the house was as empty as a beer closet in premises
where painters have been at work.
"The McWilliamses and the Burglar-Alarm,"
The Mysterious Stranger, Etc., p. 323

It wasn't any more labor to steer her than it is to count
the Republican vote in a South Carolina election.
Life on the Mississippi, Chapt. XXIV, p. 196

They could tell alligator water as far as another Christian
could tell whiskey.
Ibid., Chapt. XXIV, p. 193

[It was as natural] as it is to put a friend's cedar pencil
in your pocket . . .
The Innocents Abroad, II, Chapt. X, p. 131

SIN   *See* MICROBE, PROVIDENCE, SIMILES, SINNER

SINCERITY   *See* RELIGION

SINGING   *See also* MUSIC, OPERA
I was not able to detect in the vocal parts of "Parsifal"
anything that might with confidence be called rhythm, or
tune or melody; one person performed at a time—and a long
time, too—often in a noble, and always in a high-toned
voice; but he only pulled out long notes, then some short
ones, then another long one, then a sharp, quick, peremptory bark or two . . . and when he was done you saw
that the information which he had conveyed had not com-
pensated for the disturbance . . . The great master . . .
deals only in barren solos when he puts in the vocal parts.
It may be that he was deep, and only added the singing to
his operas for the sake of the contrast it would make with

the music.

"The Shrine of St. Wagner,"
What Is Man? and Other Essays, p. 214

When the young Sam Clemens was annoyed by the singing of the slave boy, Sandy, his mother said: "Poor thing,
when he sings it shows he is not remembering . . . but
when he is still I am afraid he is thinking . . . He will
never see his mother again. If he can sing, I must not hinder
it, but be thankful for it."

Mark Twain's Autobiography, Paine, I, p. 101

The venerable screech-owl . . . filed her saw all through
the hymn.

Atlantic Monthly, Dec. 1947, p. 71

. . . singing is one of the most entrancing . . . and eloquent of all vehicles . . . for conveying . . . feeling, but
it seems to me that the chief virtue in song is melody, air,
tune, rhythm, or what you please to call it, and that when
this feature is absent what remains is a picture with the
color left out.

"The Shrine of St. Wagner,"
What Is Man? and Other Essays, p. 214

The choir always tittered and whispered all through the
service. There was once a church choir that was not ill-
bred, but I have forgotten where it was, now.

The Adventures of Tom Sawyer, Chapt. V, p. 48

I think in the Jubilees and their songs America has produced the perfectest flower of the ages; and I wish it were
a foreign product, so that she could worship it and lavish
money on it and go properly crazy over it.

Mark Twain's Letters, II, p. 646

Congregational singing reminds one of nothing but the
dental chair.

Mark Twain's Notebook, p. 130

[The popular song nuisance, "Marching Through Georgia"]: If it had been all the same to General Sherman, I
wish he had gone around by way of the Gulf of Mexico,
instead of marching through Georgia.

Mark Twain's Letters, I, p. 112

SINNER   *See also* MICROBE, PROVIDENCE, SIMILES
. . . he [was] a cyclopedia of sin.
> *Personal Recollections of Joan of Arc,*
> I, Book II, Chapt. XII, p. 217

[The] sinners are so thick that you can't throw out your line without hooking several of them . . . the flattest old sermon a man can grind out is bound to corral half a dozen.
> "Important Correspondence,"
> *Sketches of the Sixties,* p. 167

[Near a volcano]: The smell of sulphur is strong, but not unpleasant to a sinner.
> *Roughing It,* II, Chapt. XXXIII, p. 301

. . . it is not the word that is the sin, it is the spirit back of the word.
> "Taxes and Morals,"
> *Mark Twain's Speeches* (1923), p. 279

SIZE   *See also* CHANGE, ENGLAND, HAT, IRISHMEN
I tried all the different ways I could think of to compel myself to understand how large St. Peter's [Cathedral] was, but with small success . . .

It is estimated that the floor of the church affords standing room for—for a large number of people; I have forgotten the exact figures. But it is no matter—it is near enough.
> *The Innocents Abroad,* I, Chapt. XXVI, p. 347

When we are young we generally estimate an opinion by the size of the person that holds it, but later we . . . realize . . . there are times when a hornet's opinion disturbs us more than an emperor's.
> "An Undelivered Speech,"
> *Mark Twain's Speeches* (1923), p. 165

They are so big it takes only eleven of them to make a dozen.
> *Mark Twain's Notebook* in manuscript,
> Oct. 24, 1890 to June 14, 1881

SKATING
There would be a power of fun in skating if you could

do it with somebody else's muscles.

Mark Twain's Letters, I, p. 240

When you are on skates you waddle off as stuffy and stupid and ungainly as a buzzard that's had half a horse for dinner.

New York Sunday Mercury, March 17, 1867

SKULL   *See also* COLUMBUS, TOMB

I'm going to leave my skull to Cornell University so the scientists can examine it and send me a report.

Mark Twain Tonight

SKY   *See* STARS

SLANDER

. . . it is not wise to keep the fires going under a slander unless you can get some large advantage out of keeping it alive. Few slanders can stand the wear of silence.

Mark Twain's Autobiography, Paine, I, p. 139

A feeble, stupid, preposterous lie will not live two years —except it be a slander upon somebody.

Mark Twain's Speeches (1923), p. 106

SLANG

Slang in a woman's mouth is not obscene, it only sounds so.

More Maxims of Mark, p. 12

SLAVE   *See also* NEGRO, SINGING

. . . you mustn't volunteer advice to a slave-driver unless you want to damage the cause you are arguing for.

A Connecticut Yankee in King Arthur's Court,
Chapt. XXXV, p. 322

The skin of every human being contains a slave.

Mark Twain's Notebook, p. 393

The blunting effects of slavery upon the slaveholder's moral perceptions are known and conceded, the world over; and a privileged class, an aristocracy is but a band

of slaveholders under another name.
A Connecticut Yankee in King Arthur's Court,
Chapt. XXV, p. 216

SLEEP   *See also* EARLY RISING, HORSE, MOUSE, WORK

Pretty soon, various kinds of bugs and ants and worms and things began to flock in out of the wet and crawl down inside my armor to get warm; and while some of them behaved well enough, and snuggled up amongst my clothes and got quiet, the majority were of a restless, uncomfortable sort, and never stayed still, but went on prowling and hunting for they did not know what; especially the ants, which went tickling along in wearisome procession from one end of me to the other by the hour, and are the kind of creatures which I never wish to sleep with again. It would be my advice to persons situated in this way, to not roll or thrash around, because this excites the interest of all the different sorts of animals and makes every last one of them want to turn out and see what is going on, and this makes things worse than they were before, and of course makes you objurgate harder, too, if you can. Still, if one did not roll and thrash around he would die; so perhaps it is as well to do one way as the other; there is no real choice. Even after I was frozen solid I could still distinguish that tickling, just as a corpse does when he is taking electric treatment. I said I would never wear armor after this trip.
A Connecticut Yankee in King Arthur's Court,
Chapt. XIII, p. 99

I am losing enough sleep to supply a worn-out army.
Mark Twain, a Biography, Paine, III, p. 1569

I hate a man who goes to sleep at once; there is a sort of indefinable something about it which is not exactly an insult, and yet is an insolence. I got to feeling very lonely, with no company but an undigested dinner.
A Tramp Abroad, I, Chapt. XIII, p. 110

SLOWNESS   *See also* RAILROAD, HORSE

I *have* seen slower people than I am—and more deliberate . . . and even quieter, and more listless, and lazier people than I am. But they were dead.

The Galaxy Magazine, Dec. 1870, "Memoranda," p. 884

For a long time I was on a boat that was so slow we used to forget what year it was we left port in.

Life on the Mississippi, Chapt. XVI, p. 145

SMELL *See also* DIRT, FRUIT, POLITICS, SHIP

[Christopher Columbus] blew out his flickering stencher and began to refresh his lungs with inverted sighs freighted with the rich odors of rancid oil and bilgewater. The sighs returned as snores.

"About All Kinds of Ships,"
The American Claimant, Etc., p. 476

. . . the smells zigzagged across the pavement and followed me like a rotten conscience.

Abroad with Mark Twain and Eugene Field, Fisher, p. 36

[I] never smelt anything like it. It was an insurrection in a gasometer.

A Connecticut Yankee in King Arthur's Court,
Chapt. XX, p. 166

The horse doctor came, a pleasant man and full of hope and professional interest in the case. In the matter of smell he was pretty aromatic—in fact, quite horsy—and I tried to arrange with him for absent treatment, but it was not in his line, so, out of delicacy, I did not press it.

Christian Science, Book I, Chapt. III, p. 27

The smell of sulphur is strong but not unpleasant to a sinner.

Roughing It, II, Chapt. XXXIII, p. 301

[Seeing a stranded whale along the beach]: The whale was not a long one, physically speaking—say thirty-five feet —but he smelt much longer; he smelt as much as a mile and a half longer, I should say, for we traveled about that distance beyond him before we ceased to detect his fragrance.

"Concerning the Answer to that Conundrum,"
Sketches of the Sixties, p. 128

[Honolulu girls]: . . . they fill the markets . . . with

their bright presences, and smell like thunder with their villainous cocoa-nut oil.

Letters from the Sandwich Islands, p. 53

[Inn at Heilbron]: The furniture was quaint old carved stuff, full four hundred years old, and some of the smells were over a thousand.

A Tramp Abroad, I, Chapt. XI, p. 101

[In Smyrna]: . . . superior to everything, and claiming the bulk of attention first, last and all the time—is a combination of Mohammedan stenches, to which the smell of even a Chinese quarter would be as pleasant as the roasting odors of the fatted calf to the nostrils of the returning Prodigal.

The Innocents Abroad, II, Chapt. XI, p. 141

[In the great bazaar of Stamboul]: . . . the only solitary thing one does not smell [there] is something which smells good.

Ibid., II, Chapt. VI, p. 30

SMILE *See also* SIMILES

Wrinkles should merely indicate where smiles have been.

"Pudd'nhead Wilson's New Calendar,"
Following the Equator, II, Chapt. XVI, p. 190

He received it with a smile, one of those large smiles which goes all around over, and has folds in it, and wrinkles, and spirals, and looks like the place where you have thrown a brick in a pond.

"The Million Pound Bank-Note,"
The American Claimant, Etc., p. 347

Butler is dismally and drearily homely, and when he smiles it is like the breaking up of a hard winter.

Mark Twain's Notebook, p. 116

. . . that smile faded gradually out of his countenance like breath off'n a razor.

A Tramp Abroad, I, Chapt. III, p. 28

SMITH *See also* ADAM, EXPERIENCE

[Mark Twain dedicates one of his books]: To John Smith, whom I have known in divers and sundry places about the world, and whose many and manifold virtues did always command my esteem, I dedicate this book. It is said that the man to whom a volume is dedicated always buys a copy. If this prove true in the present instance, a princely affluence is about to burst upon the author.

The Celebrated Jumping Frog of
Calaveras County, Dedication

SMOKING *See also* HABIT, MARRIAGE, MONEY

. . . when they use to tell me I'd shorten my life ten years by smoking, they little knew the devotée they were wasting their puerile words upon—they little knew how trivial and valueless I would regard a decade that had no smoking in it!

Mark Twain's Letters, I, p. 180

[In Genoa]: Never smoke any Italian tobacco. Never do it on any account. It makes me shudder to think what it must be made of. You cannot throw an old cigar "stub" down anywhere, but some vagabond will pounce upon it on the instant. I like to smoke a good deal, but it wounds my sensibilities to see one of these stub-hunters watching me out of the corners of his hungry eyes and calculating how long my cigar will be likely to last. It reminded me too painfully of that San Francisco undertaker who used to go to sick beds with his watch in his hand and time the corpse.

The Innocents Abroad, I, Chapt. XVII, p. 214

When I was a youth I used to take all kinds of pledges, and do my best to keep them, but I never could, because I didn't strike at the root of the habit—the *desire;* I generally broke down within the month. Once I tried limiting a habit. That worked tolerably well for a while. I pledged myself to smoke but one cigar a day. I kept the cigar waiting until bedtime, then I had a luxurious time with it. But desire persecuted me every day and all day long; so, within the week I found myself hunting for larger cigars than I had been used to smoke; then larger ones still, and still larger ones. Within the fortnight I was getting cigars *made* for me—on a yet larger pattern. They still grew and grew in size. Within the month my cigar had grown to such proportions that I could have used it as a crutch. It now seemed to me that a one-cigar limit was no real protection to a person, so I knocked my pledge on the head and resumed my liberty.

Following the Equator, I, Chapt. I, p. 24

The only cigars here [in Hawaii] are those trifling, insipid, tasteless, flavorless things they call Manilas—ten for twenty-five cents—and it would take a thousand of them to be worth half the money. After you have smoked about thirty-five dollars' worth of them in the forenoon, you feel nothing but a desperate yearning to go out somewhere and take a smoke.

Mark Twain's Letters, I, p. 112

SNAKE

There are narrow escapes in India. In the very jungle where I killed 16 tigers and all those elephants, a cobra bit me, but it got well; every one was surprised. This could not happen twice in ten years, perhaps. Usually death would result in fifteen minutes.

Following the Equator, II, Chapt. XXI, p. 246

Eve's calmness was perfectly noble. . . . Had [you] ever heard of another woman, who, being approached by a serpent, would not excuse herself and break for the nearest timber?

Is Shakespeare Dead?, p. 20

SNEEZE

The Autocrat of Russia possesses more power than any other man in the earth; but he cannot stop a sneeze.

"Pudd'nhead Wilson's New Calendar,"
Following the Equator, I, Chapt. XXXV, p. 332

SNOBBERY

Yes, we do so love our little distinctions! And then we

loftily scoff at a Prince for enjoying his larger ones; forgetting that if we only had his chance—ah! "Senator" is not a legitimate title. A Senator has no more right to be addressed by it than have you or I; but, in the . . . State capitals and in Washington, there are five thousand senators who take very kindly to that fiction, and who purr gratefully when you call them by it—which you may do quite unrebuked. Then those same Senators smile at the self-constructed majors and generals and judges of the south!

. . .

All the human race loves a lord—that is, it loves to look upon or be noticed by the possessor of Power or Conspicuousness; and sometimes animals, born to better things and higher ideals, descend to man's level in this matter. In the Jardin des Plantes I have seen a cat that was so vain of being the personal friend of an elephant that I was ashamed of her.

"Does the Race of Man Love a Lord?"
The $30,000 Bequest, Etc., p. 284

SNODGRASS

"Snodgrass! . . . What is his first name?"

"His—er—his initials are S. M."

"His initials. I don't care anything about his initials . . . what do they *stand* for?"

"Well, you see, his father was a physician, and he—he—well, he was an idolater of his profession, and he—well, he was a very eccentric man, and—"

"What do they *stand* for? What are you shuffling about?"

"They—well, they stand for Spinal Meningitis."

The American Claimant, Etc., Chapt. XXIV, p. 216

SNORING

At breakfast . . . I ventured for the first time to throw out a feeler, for all these days' silence made me a little uneasy and suspicious. I intimated that at home, I sometimes snored—not often, and not much, but a little—yet it might be possible that at sea, I—though I hoped—that is to say—

But I was most pleasantly interrupted at that point by a universal outburst of compliment and praise, with assurances that I made the nights enjoyable for everybody, and that they often lay awake hours to listen, and Mr. Rogers said it infused him so with comfortableness that he tried to keep himself awake by turning over and over in bed, so as to get more of it. Rice said it was not a coarse and ignorant snore. Colonel Payne said he was always sorry when night was over and he knew he had to wait all day before he could have some more; and Tom Reed said the reason he moved down into the coal bunkers was because it was even sweeter there, where he could get a perspective on it. This is very different from the way I am treated at home, where there is no appreciation of what a person does.

My Father • Mark Twain, Clara Clemens, p. 221

[Brigham Young's advice]: "Bless you, sir, at a time when I had seventy-two wives in this house, I groaned under the pressure of keeping thousands of dollars tied up in seventy-two bedsteads when the money ought to have been out at interest; and I just sold out the whole stock, sir, at a sacrifice, and built a bedstead seven feet long and ninety-six feet wide. But it was a failure, sir. I could *not* sleep. It appeared to me that the whole seventy-two women snored at once. The roar was deafening. And then the danger of it! That was what I was looking at. They would all draw in their breath at once, and you could see the walls of the house suck in—and then they would all exhale their breath at once, and you could see the walls swell out, and strain, and hear rafters crack, and the shingles grind together. My friend, take an old man's advice, and *don't* encumber yourself with a large family . . . ten or eleven wives is all you need."

Roughing It, I, Chapt. XV, p. 130

Jim begun to snore—soft and blubbery at first, then a long

rasp, then a stronger one, then a half dozen horrible ones like the last water sucking down the plug-hole of a bathtub, then the same with more power to it, and some big coughs and snorts flung in, the way a cow does that is choking to death; and when the person has got to that point he is at his level best, and can wake up a man that is in the next block with a dipperful of loddanum in him, but can't wake himself up although all that awful noise of his'n ain't but three inches from his own ears. And that is the curiousest thing in the world, seems to me. But you rake a match to light the candle, and that little bit of a noise will fetch him. I wish I knowed what was the reason of that, but there don't seem to be no way to find out.

Tom Sawyer Abroad, Etc., Chapt. X, p. 97

SOAP

[In Italy]: . . . they must keep epidemics away somehow or other, and fumigation is cheaper than soap. They must either wash themselves or fumigate other people.

The Innocents Abroad, I, Chapt. XX, p. 257

I said there was nothing so convincing to an Indian as a general massacre. If he could not approve of the massacre, I said the next surest thing for an Indian was soap and education. Soap and education are not as sudden as a massacre, but they are more deadly in the long run; because a half-massacred Indian may recover, but if you educate him and wash him, it is bound to finish him some time or other.

"Facts Concerning the Recent Resignation," *Sketches New and Old*, p. 350

My missionaries were . . . to explain to the lords and ladies what soap was; and if the lords and ladies were afraid of it, get them to try it on a dog. The missionary's next move was to get the family together and try it on himself; he was to stop at no experiment, however desperate, that could convince the nobility that soap was harmless; if any doubt remained, he must catch a hermit—the woods were full of them. . . . If a hermit could survive a wash, and that failed to convince a duke, give him up, let him alone.

A Connecticut Yankee in King Arthur's Court,
Chapt. XVI, p. 124

In Marseilles they make half the fancy toilet soap we consume in America, but the Marseillaise only have a vague theoretical idea of its use, which they have obtained from books of travel, just as they have acquired an uncertain notion of clean shirts, and the peculiarities of the gorilla, and other curious matters. This reminds me of poor Blucher's note to the land-lord in Paris:

"*Monsieur le* landlord—Sir: *Pourquoi* don't you *mettez* some *savon* in your bedchambers? *Est-ce que vous pensez* I will steal it? *La nuit passee* you charged me *pour deux chandelles* when I only had one; *hier vous avez* charged me *avec glace* when I had none at all; *tout les jours* you are coming some fresh game or other on me, *mais vous ne pouvez pas* play this *savon* dodge on me twice. *Savon* is a necessary *de la vie* to anybody but a Frenchman, *et je l'aurai hors de cet hotel* or make trouble. You hear me. *Allons.*

"Blucher"
The Innocents Abroad, I, Chapt. XIX, p. 245

SOBRIETY *See* PROHIBITION

SOCIETY

. . . heaven for climate; hell for society.

"Tammany and Croker"
Mark Twain's Speeches (1910), p. 117

We may not doubt that society in heaven consists mainly of undesirable persons.

Mark Twain's Notebook, p. 381

I am quite sure . . . I have no race prejudice . . . no color prejudices, nor caste . . . nor creed prejudices . . . I can stand any society. All I care to know is that a man is a human being—that is enough for me; he can't be any worse.

"Concerning the Jews"
Literary Essays, p. 251

There are no common people except in the highest spheres of society.

Abroad with Mark Twain and Eugene Field,
Fisher, p. 218

SOCK

I awoke at 3 this morning, and after raging to myself for 2 interminable hours, I gave it up. I rose, assumed a catlike stealthiness, to keep from waking Livy, and proceeded to dress in the pitch dark. Slowly but surely I got on garment after garment—all down to one sock; I had one slipper on and the other in my hand. Well, on my hands and knees I crept softly around, pawing and feeling and scooping along the carpet, and among chair-legs for that missing sock; I kept that up;—and still kept it up and *kept* it up. At first I only said to myself, "Blame that sock," but that soon ceased to answer; my expletives grew steadily stronger and stronger,—and at last, when I found I was *lost,* I had to sit flat down on the floor and take hold of something to keep from lifting the roof off with the profane explosion that was trying to get out of me. I could see the dim blur of the window, but of course it was in the wrong place and could give me no information as to where I was. But I had one comfort—I had not waked Livy; I believed I could find that sock in silence if the night lasted long enough. So I started again and softly pawed all over the place,—and sure enough at the end of half an hour I laid my hand on the missing article. I rose joyfully up and butted the wash-bowl and pitcher off the stand and simply raised ———— so to speak. Livy screamed, then said, "Who is that? What is the matter?" I said "There ain't anything the matter—I'm hunting for my sock." She said, "Are you hunting for it with a club?"

Mark Twain's Letters, I, p. 348

SOLDIER *See also* WAR

I could have become a soldier myself if I had waited.
I had got part of it learned; I knew more about retreating
then the man that invented retreating.

> "The Private History of a Campaign That Failed"
> *The American Claimant, Etc.,* p. 258

SOLEMNITY *See* JOKE

SOLITUDE *See* MISSISSIPPI RIVER

SOLOMON *See* BIBLE

SORROW *See* HUMOR, JOY, PEOPLE

SOUL *See also* BEES, BELIEF
Be careless in your dress if you must, but keep a tidy soul.

> "Pudd'nhead Wilson's New Calendar"
> *Following the Equator,* Chapt. XXIII, p. 227

. . . a great soul, with a great purpose, can make a weak
body strong and keep it so.

> *Personal Recollections of Joan of Arc,*
> I, Book II, Chapt. IV, p. 132

[They are a] couple of men whose small souls will escape
through their pores some day if they do not varnish their
hides.

> *Mark Twain, a Biography,* Paine, I, p. 402

It shriveled up the King's little soul like a raisin.

> *Personal Recollections of Joan of Arc,*
> I, Book II, Chapt. VIII, p. 181

[A Neopolitan audience hissed Frezzolini]: . . . what a
multitude of small souls were crowded into that theater.
. . . If the manager could have filled his theater with . . .
souls alone, without the bodies, he could not have cleared
less than ninety millions of dollars.

> *The Innocents Abroad,* II, Chapt. II, p. 25

SOUND *See also* BEES
I heard the dim hum of a spinning wheel wailing along

up and sinking along down again; and then I knowed for certain I wished I was dead—for that *is* the lonesomest sound in the whole world.

The Adventures of Huckleberry Finn,
Chapt. XXXII, p. 285

. . . the faint far sound of tolling bells . . . floated fitfully to us on the passing breeze . . . so faintly, so softly, that we hardly knew whether we heard it with our ears or with our spirits.

A Connecticut Yankee in King Arthur's Court,
Chapt. XXII, p. 181

SOUTH, THE   *See* MUSIC, NEWSPAPER, UNDERTAKER

SPAIN   *See* LAND

SPECTACLES   *See also* MOTHER, MARK TWAIN'S

It was on the 10th of May—1884—that I confessed to age by mounting spectacles for the first time, and in the same hour I renewed my youth, to outward appearance, by mounting a bicycle for the first time.

The spectacles stayed on.

"Speech"
Mark Twain's Speeches (1923), p. 109

[Aunt Polly's spectacles]: She seldom or never looked *through* them for so small a thing as a boy; they . . . were built for "style," not service—she could have seen through a pair of stove-lids just as well.

The Adventures of Tom Sawyer, Chapt. I, p. 1

SPECULATION

There are two times in a man's life when he should not speculate: when he can't afford it, and when he can.

"Pudd'nhead Wilson's New Calendar"
Following the Equator, II, Chapt. XX, p. 235

October. This is one of the peculiarly dangerous months to speculate in stocks in. The others are July, January, September, April, November, May, March, June, December, August and February.

"Pudd'nhead Wilson's Calendar"
Pudd'nhead Wilson, Chapt. XIII, p. 123

SPEECH *See also* EXPERIENCE, FREEDOM, LECTURING, MEM-
ORY, PAUSE, SHIP, SILENCE, TALK

There is nothing in the world like persuasive speech to fuddle the mental apparatus and upset the convictions and debauch the emotions of an audience not practiced in the tricks and delusions of oratory.

The Man that Corrupted Hadleyburg, Etc.,
Chapt. III, p. 55

[Chief Justice Turner]: He could charm an audience an hour on a stretch without ever getting rid of an idea.

Mark Twain in Eruption, p. 391

The advantage of a prepared speech is that you start when you are ready and stop when you get through.

Mark Twain, His Life and Work, Will Clemens, p. 158

Impromptu speaking. . . . That is a difficult thing. I used to do it in this way. I used to begin about a week ahead, and write out my impromptu speech and get it by heart . . . In order to do an impromptu speech as it should be done you have to indicate the places for pauses and hesitations. . . .

I do that kind of speech (I mean an offhand speech), and do it well, and make no mistake, in such a way to deceive the audience completely and make that audience believe it is an impromptu speech—that is art.

"To the Whitefriars"
Mark Twain's Speeches (1923), p. 182

A person who is to make a speech . . . owes it to himself and to his audience to write the speech out and memorize it.

Mark Twain in Eruption, p. 301

It is my custom to keep on talking until I get the audience cowed.

Mark Twain, a Biography, Paine, III, p. 1290

SPEED *See also* DOG, EXPERIENCE, FLEA, RABBIT, RACING,
STORM, STAGECOACH, TRAVEL

This was the most faultless piece of road in the mountains, and the driver said he would "let his team out." He did, and if the Pacific express trains whiz through there now any faster than we did then in the stage-coach, I envy the passengers the exhilaration of it. We fairly seemed to pick up our wheels and fly—and the mail matter was lifted up free from everything and held in solution!

Roughing It, I, Chapt. XII, p. 109

The buggy vanished past him like a thought.

Mark Twain's Letters, I, p. 306

After a gallop of sixteen miles the Californian youth and the Genuine Mexican Plug came tearing into town again, shedding foam-flakes like the spume-spray that drives before a typhoon. . . .

Roughing It, I, Chapt. XXIV, p. 197

SPEED *See also* DOG, EXPERIENCE, FLEA, RABBIT, RACING,
STAGESTORM, TRAVEL

I should like to know the name of the Lightning Express . . . for I owe a friend a dozen chickens, and I believe it will be cheaper to send eggs, instead, and let them develop on the road.

Mark Twain's Speeches (1910), p. 343

The speed of the railroad train . . . made a rail fence look like a fine tooth comb.

"Mark Twain in Iowa"—Fred Lorch
Iowa Journal, July 1929, p. 445

He is the alertest dog that ever was; . . . as to movement, he makes a white streak through the air thirty yards long when he is getting started; after that he is invisible.

Mark Twain, Business Man, p. 384

. . . . a man and horse burst past our excited faces, and [went] winging away like a belated fragment of a storm!

Roughing It, I, Chapt. VIII, p. 71

Nat Parsons' horse was put up, and he didn't know what *to* do. But just then along comes a darky driving an old ramshackly hack . . . He rushes out and shouts: "A half a

dollar if you git me to the Capitol in half an hour . . ."
Nat jumped in and slammed the door, and away they went
a-ripping and a-tearing over the roughest road a body ever
see, and the racket of it was something awful. Nat passed
his arms through the loops and hung on for life and death,
but pretty soon the hack hit a rock and flew up in the air,
and the bottom fell out, and when it come down Nat's feet
was on the ground, and he see he was in the most desperate
danger if he couldn't keep up with the hack. He was horrible scared, but he laid into his work for all he was worth,
and hung tight to the arm-loops and made his legs fairly
fly. He yelled and shouted to the driver to stop, and so did
the crowds along the street, for they could see his legs
spinning along under the coach, and his head and shoulders bobbing inside through the windows, and he was in
awful danger; but the more they all shouted the more the
darky whooped and . . . lashed the horses . . . He thought
they were all hurrying him up, and, of course, he couldn't
hear anything for the racket . . . And so they went ripping
along, . . . and when they got to the Capitol at last it was
the quickest trip that ever was made . . . The horses laid
down, and Nat dropped, all tuckered out, and he was all
dust and rags and barefooted; but he was in time . . .

Tom Sawyer Abroad, Chapt. I, p. 11

SPELLING   *See also* ALPHABET, REFORM, WORDS

People say that English spelling is that of Chaucer and
Spencer and Shakespeare and a lot of other people who do
not know how to spell anyway.

Mark Twain's Speeches (1923), p. 321

[An address to the Associated Press, Sept. 18, 1906]:
I am here to appeal to the nations in behalf of the simplified spelling. I have come here because they cannot all be
reached except through you. . . . I implore you to spell
. . . in our simplified forms. Do this daily, constantly, persistently, for three months—only three months—it is all I
ask. The infallible result?—victory, victory all down the line.
For by that time all eyes here and above and below will

have become adjusted to the change and in love with it, and the present clumsy and ragged forms will be grotesque to the eye and revolting to the soul. And we shall be rid of phthisis and phthisic and pneumonia and pneumatics, and diphtheria and pterodactyl, and all those other insane words which no man addicted to the simple Christian life can try to spell and not lose some of the bloom of his piety in the demoralizing attempt.

"Spelling and Pictures,"
Ibid. (1923), p. 315

. . . simplified spelling is all right, but, like chastity, you can carry it too far.

"Alphabet and Simplified Spelling,"
Ibid. (1923), p. 367

[Leonardo da Vinci]: They spell it Vinci and pronounce it Vinchy; foreigners always spell better than they pronounce.

The Innocents Abroad, I, Chapt. XIX, p. 239

SPHYNX

After years of waiting, it was before me at last. The great face was so sad, so earnest, so longing, so patient. There was a dignity not of earth in its mien, and in its countenance a benignity such as never anything human wore. It was stone, but it seemed sentient. If ever image of stone thought, it was thinking. It was looking toward the verge of the landscape, yet looking *at* nothing—nothing but distance and vacancy. It was looking over and beyond everything of the present, and far into the past. It was gazing out over the ocean of Time—over lines of century-waves which, further and further receding, closed nearer and nearer together, and blended at last into one unbroken tide, away toward the horizon of remote antiquity. It was thinking of the wars of departed ages; of the empires it had seen created and destroyed; of the nations whose birth it had witnessed, whose progress it had watched, whose annihilation it had noted; of the joy and sorrow, the life and death, the grandeur and decay, of five thousand slow revolving years. It was the type of an attribute of man—of the faculty of his heart and brain. It was MEMORY—RETROSPECTION— wrought into visible, tangible form. . . .

The Sphynx is grand in its loneliness; it is imposing in its magnitude; it is impressive in the mystery that hangs over its story. And there is that in the overshadowing majesty of this eternal figure of stone, with its accusing memory of the deeds of all ages, which reveals to one something of what he shall feel when he shall stand at last in the awful presence of God.

The Innocents Abroad, II, Chapt. XXXI, p. 417

SPIRIT   *See also* COVETOUSNESS, HEART
I will learn the spirit that goeth with burdens that have not honor. It is the spirit that stoopeth the shoulders . . . and not the weight; for armor is heavy, yet it is a proud burden, and a man standeth straight in it.

A Connecticut Yankee in King Arthur's Court,
Chapt. XXVIII, p. 256

[It was the] spirit which moved them to put their hands down through their hearts into their pockets.

Mark Twain's Letters, II, p. 638

STAGE-COACH   *See also* TRAVEL
The stage whirled along at a spanking gait, the breeze flapping curtains and suspended coats in a most exhilarating way; the cradle swayed and swung luxuriously, the pattering of the horses' hoofs, the cracking of the driver's whip, and his "Hi-yi g'lang!" were music; the spinning ground and the waltzing trees appeared to give us a mute hurrah as we went by, and then slack up and look after us with interest, or envy, or something; and as we lay and smoked the pipe of peace and compared all this luxury with the years of tiresome city life that had gone before it, we felt that there was only one complete and satisfying happiness in the world, and we had found it.

Roughing It, I, Chapt. III, p. 27

STANDARD *See also* MAN

The human being always looks down when he is examining another person's standard; he never finds one that he has to examine by looking up.

What Is Man? and Other Essays, Chapt. V, p. 63

STARS

It's lovely to live on a raft. We had the sky up there, all speckled with stars, and we used to lay on our backs and look up at them, and discuss about whether they was made or only just happened. Jim he allowed they was made, but I allowed they happened; I judged it would have took too long to *make* so many. Jim said the moon could a *laid* them; well, that looked kind of reasonable, so I didn't say nothing against it, because I've seen a frog lay most as many, so of course it could be done. We used to watch the stars that fell, too, and see them streak down. Jim allowed they'd got spoiled and was hove out of the nest.

The Adventures of Huckleberry Finn,
Chapt. XIX, p. 163

STATESMANSHIP

If we had less statesmanship, we would get along with fewer battleships.

From an unpublished Mark Twain notebook, 1905

[In statesmanship] get your formalities right—never mind about the moralities.

"Pudd'nhead Wilson's New Calendar,"
Following the Equator, II, Chapt. XXVII, p. 323

. . . the true statesman does not despise any wisdom, howsoever lowly may be its origin.

A Connecticut Yankee in King Arthur's Court,
Chapt. XXVI, p. 233

A statesman gains little by the arbitrary exercise of iron-clad authority upon all occasions that offer, for this wounds the just pride of his subordinates, and thus tends to undermine his strength. A little concession, now and then, where it can do no harm, is the wiser policy.

Ibid., Chapt. XVII, p. 135

By and by when each nation has 20,000 battleships and 5,000,000 soldiers we shall all be safe and the wisdom of statesmanship will stand confirmed.

More Maxims of Mark, p. 6

Statesmanship and Assmanship are spelt different.

From a hitherto unpublished note

STEALING   *See also* LAW

All the territorial possessions of all the political establishments in the earth—including America, of course—consist of pilferings from other people's wash. No tribe, howsoever insignificant, and no nation, howsoever mighty, occupies a foot of land that was not stolen.

Following the Equator, II, Chapt. XXVII, p. 321

[The first time I ever stole a watermelon]: I stole it out of a farmer's wagon while he was waiting on another customer. "Stole" is a harsh term. I withdrew—I retired that watermelon. I carried it to a secluded corner of a lumberyard. I broke it open. It was green—the greenest watermelon raised in the valley that year.

The minute I saw it was green I was sorry, and began to reflect—reflection is the beginning of reform. . . . I began to reflect. I said to myself: "What ought a boy to do who has stolen a green watermelon? What would George Washington do? . . . There is only one right, high, noble thing for any boy to do who has stolen a watermelon of that class: he must make restitution; he must restore that stolen property to its rightful owner." I said I would do it when I made that good resolution. I felt it to be a noble, uplifting obligation. I rose up spiritually stronger and refreshed. I carried that watermelon back—what was left of it—and restored it to the farmer, and made him give me a ripe one in its place.

"Theoretical Morals,"
Mark Twain's Speeches (1910), p. 133

STICK *See* MEANNESS

STORM *See also* LIGHTNING, WEATHER

Bless your heart, if you could only have seen my mare Margaretta; *there* was a beast!—*there* was lightning for you! Trot! Trot is no name for it—she flew! How she *could* whirl a buggy along! . . . I started her out about thirty or thirty-five yards ahead of the awfullest storm I ever saw in my life, and it chased us upwards of eighteen miles! It did, by the everlasting hills! And I'm telling you nothing but the un-varnished truth when I say that not one single drop of rain fell on me—not a single *drop,* sir! And I swear to it! But my dog was a-swimming behind the wagon all the way!

Roughing It, II, Chapt. XXXVI, p. 320

People boast a good deal about Alpine thunderstorms; but the storms which I have had the luck to see in the Alps were not the equals of some which I have seen in the Mississippi Valley. I may not have seen the Alps do their best, of course, and if they can beat the Mississippi, I don't wish to.

Life on the Mississippi, Chapt. LI, p. 375

STORY *See also* FISH, HUMOR

If you wish to lower yourself in a person's favor, one good way is to tell his story over again, the way *you* heard it.

Mark Twain's Notebook, p. 345

STOVE *See also* FIRE

In America we prefer to kindle the fire with the kerosene can and chance the inquest.

"Some National Stupidities,"
Europe and Elsewhere, p. 178

STOWE *See* CHILDREN

STRANGER

. . . my time is taken up answering letters of strangers.

. . . What does possess strangers to write so many letters?
I never could find that out. However, I suppose I did it
myself when I was a stranger.

Mark Twain's Letters, I, p. 405

. . . being a stranger, he was of course regarded as an
inferior person—for that has been human nature from Adam
down—and of course, also, he was made to feel unwelcome,
for this is the ancient law with man and the other animals.

"A Scrap of Curious History,"
What Is Man? and Other Essays, p. 184

STREET

[In Damascus]: The street called Straight is straighter
than a corkscrew, but not as straight as a rainbow. St.
Luke is careful not to commit himself; he does not say it is
the street which *is* straight, but the "street which is *called*
Straight." It is a fine piece of irony; it is the only facetious
remark in the Bible, I believe.

The Innocents Abroad, II, Chapt. XVII, p. 208

In Naples, the streets (sidewalks, too), . . . are not often
wide enough to pass a man on without caroming on him.

Ibid., II, Chapt. III, p. 31

STREET-CAR *See* TRAVEL

STRENGTH *See* SOUL

STRIVING *See* LIFE

STUPIDITY

[He] was endowed with a stupidity which by the least
little stretch would go around the globe four times and tie.

Mark Twain in Eruption, p. 168

. . . there are some things that can beat smartness and
foresight. Awkwardness and stupidity can. The best swordsman in the world doesn't need to fear the second best
swordsman in the world: no, the person for him to be

afraid of is some ignorant antagonist who has never had a sword in his hand before; he doesn't do the thing he ought to do, and so the expert isn't prepared for him.

> *A Connecticut Yankee in King Arthur's Court,*
> Chapt. XXXIV, p. 313

It has become a sarcastic proverb that a thing must be true if you saw it in a newspaper. That is the opinion intelligent people have of that lying vehicle in a nutshell. But the trouble is that the stupid people—who constitute the grand overwhelming majority of this and all other nations—*do* believe and *are* moulded and convinced by what they get out of a newspaper, and there is where the harm lies.

> "License of the Press,"
> *Mark Twain's Speeches* (1923), p. 47

STYLE   *See* WORDS

SUCCESS   *See also* FOOL, GENIUS, LAW

[From a letter to Mrs. Foote]:

All you need in this life is ignorance and confidence; then success is sure.

> *When Huck Finn Went Highbrow,* Casseres, p. 7

Human nature is the same everywhere; it deifies success, it has nothing but scorn for defeat.

> *Personal Recollections of Joan of Arc,*
> I, Book II, Chapt. VIII, p. 101

A successful book is not made of what is in it, but what is left out of it.

> *Mark Twain's Letters,* II, p. 644

SUFFERING   *See* HAPPINESS

SUICIDE   *See also* POETRY

I would commit suicide if I had the pluck and the outfit.

> *Mark Twain, a Biography,* Paine, III, p. 1221

SUN   *See also* MOUNTAIN

The sun had positive *weight* to it. Not a man could sit erect under it.

The Innocents Abroad, II, p. 378

SUNDAY *See also* LEISURE, SABBATH

The library at the British Museum I find particularly astounding. . . . And what a touching sight it is of a Saturday afternoon to see the poor careworn clergymen gathered together in that vast reading-room cabbaging sermons for Sunday.

"About London,"
Mark Twain's Speeches (1923), p. 39

I believe I see what the week is for: it is to give time to rest up from the weariness of Sunday.

Extracts from Adam's Diary, p. 29

It is not best that we use our morals week days; it gets them out of repair for Sunday.

Mark Twain's Notebook, p. 345

SUPERIORS *See* ADVICE

SUPERSTITION

Let me make the superstitions of a nation and I care not who makes its laws or its songs either.

"Pudd'nhead Wilson's New Calendar,"
Following the Equator, II, Chapt. XV, p. 179

SUPPOSING *See* LEARNING

SUPREMACY

Some instinct tells me that eternal vigilance is the price of supremacy.

Eve's Diary, p. 5

SURGERY *See* ADVICE

SURVIVAL

Christianity will doubtless still survive in the earth ten

centuries hence—stuffed and in a museum.

Mark Twain's Notebook, p. 346

SUSPICION

When one's character begins to fall under suspicion and disfavor, how swift, then, is the work of disintegration and destruction.

My Father • Mark Twain, Clara Clemens, p. 86

Ma says Axtele was above "suspition"—but I have searched through Webster's Unabridged, and can't find the word. However, it's of no consequence—I hope he got down safely.

Mark Twain's Letters, I, p. 68

SWEARING *See* PROFANITY

SWIMMING *See* MOTHER, MARK TWAIN'S

SWITZERLAND *See also* CLOCK, FARM, GLACIER, MOUNTAIN, YODELING

After trying the political atmosphere of the neighboring monarchies, it is healing and refreshing to come among people whose political history is great and fine.

"Switzerland—the Cradle of Liberty,"
What Is Man? and Other Essays, p. 194

There have always been Tells in Switzerland—people who would not bow.

"Switzerland, the Cradle of Liberty,"
Ibid., p. 196

SYMPATHY *See* ILLNESS

SYNDICATE *See* NEWSPAPER

T

TAJ MAHAL   *See* ICE-STORM, READER, WONDER

TALENT   *See also* LITERARY CRITICISM
We are always more anxious to be distinguished for a talent which we do not possess than to be praised for the fifteen which we do possess.

> *Mark Twain's Autobiography,* II, p. 139

If he can explain the rest of the $28, raising the dead is foolishness to *his* talent.

> *Mark Twain, Business Man,* Webster

TALK   *See also* CAIN, CHEERFULNESS, CHURCHILL, GERMAN
   LANGUAGE, SPEECH, WORDS
[From a letter to Edward W. Bok]:
For several quite plain and simple reasons, an "interview" must, as a rule, be an absurdity, and chiefly for this reason—It is an attempt to use a boat on land or a wagon on water, to speak figuratively. Spoken speech is one thing, written speech is quite another. Print is the proper vehicle for the latter, but it isn't for the former. The moment "talk" is put into print you recognize that it is not what it was when you heard it; you perceive that an immense something

has disappeared from it. That is its soul. You have nothing but a dead carcass left on your hands. Color, play of feature, the varying modulations of the voice, the laugh, the smile, the informing inflections, everything that gave that body warmth, grace, friendliness and charm and commended it to your affections—or, at least, to your tolerance—is gone and nothing is left but a pallid, stiff and repulsive cadaver.

Such is "talk" almost invariably, as you see it lying in state in an "interview." The interviewer seldom tries to tell one *how* a thing was said; he merely puts in the naked remark and stops there. . . .

. . . leave the whole interview out; it is rubbish. I wouldn't talk in my sleep if I couldn't talk better than that.

Mark Twain's Letters, II, p. 504

[Mark Twain's daughter, Susy, writes of her father]: "He doesn't like to go to church at all; why I never understood, until just now, he told us the other day that he couldn't bear to hear any one talk but himself, but that he could listen to himself talk for hours without getting tired. Of course he said this in a joke, but I've no [doubt] it was founded on truth."

Mark Twain's Autobiography, Paine, II, p. 83

[Mark Twain's daughter writes of her father]: "A lady acquaintance of his is rather apt to interrupt what one is saying, and papa told mamma that he thought he should say to the lady's husband, 'I am glad your wife wasn't present when the Deity said Let there be light.'"

Ibid., II, p. 83

. . . when you have talked a lot the emptier you get.

"Galveston Orphan Bazaar,"
Mark Twain's Speeches (1923), p. 204

[Charles Dana said about Wayne MacVeagh]: "Talk! He was born to talk. Don't let him get out with you; he'll skin you." I said, "I have been skinned, skinned, and skinned for years, there is nothing left." He said, "Oh, you'll find there is; that man is the very seed and inspiration of that proverb which says, 'No matter how close you skin an onion, a clever man can always peel it again.' "

"Sixty-Seventh Birthday,"
Ibid. (1923), p. 248

If animals don't talk, I miss *my* guess.

"A Horse's Tale,"
The Mysterious Stranger, Etc., p. 193

. . . my teeth were already loose from incessant speaking, and the very thought of adding a jabber at this time was a pain to me. . . .

Mark Twain in Eruption, p. 326

[It's a] terrible death to be talked to death.

Mark Twain, a Biography, Paine, I, p. 340

[Kipling] refreshed them with his talk—talk which . . . might be likened to footprints, so strong and definite was the impression which they left behind.

Ibid., Paine, II, p. 880

The rapidity of his utterance made a man drunk in a minute.

"To the Whitefriars,"
Mark Twain's Speeches (1923), p. 179

The Colonel's tongue was a magician's wand that turned dried apples into figs and water into wine as easily as it could change a hovel into a palace and present poverty into imminent future riches.

The Gilded Age, I, Chapt. VIII, p. 93

Now, the true charm of pedestrianism does not lie in the walking, or in the scenery, but in the talking. The walking is good to time the movement of the tongue by, and to keep the blood and the brain stirred up and active; the scenery and the woodsy smells are good to bear in upon a man an unconscious and unobtrusive charm and solace to eye and soul and sense; but the supreme pleasure comes from the talk. It is no matter whether one talks wisdom or nonsense, the case is the same, the bulk of the enjoyment lies in the wagging of the gladsome jaw and the flapping of the sympathetic ear.

A Tramp Abroad, I, Chapt. XXIII, p. 225

Learning began with talk and is therefore older than books. Our opinions really do not blossom into fruition until we have expressed them to someone else.

Mark Twain and I, Opie Read, p. 38

His tongue is in constant motion from eleven in the forenoon till four in the afternoon, and why it does not wear out is the affair of Providence, not mine.

Letters from the Sandwich Islands, p. 85

. . . the average man likes to hear himself talk, when he is not under criticism.

"On After-Dinner Speaking,"
Mark Twain's Speeches (1923), p. 84

He was bent on putting us at ease, and he had the right art; one could not remain doubtful and timorous where a person was so earnest and simple and gentle, and talked so alluringly as he did.

The Mysterious Stranger, Etc., Chapt. II, p. 11

Captain Tom Bowling was garrulous. He had that garrulous attention to minor detail which is born of scheduled farm life or life at sea on long voyages, where there is little to do and time no object.

"Rambling Notes of an Idle Excursion,"
Tom Sawyer Abroad, Etc., p. 267

[The patients at Marienbad]: Wherever you see two or a dozen people of ordinary bulk talking together, you know they are talking about their livers. When you first arrive here your new acquaintances seem sad and hard to talk to, but pretty soon you get the lay of the land and the hang of things, and after that you haven't any more trouble. You look into the dreary dull eye and softly say:

"Well, how's your liver?"

You will see that dim eye flash up with a grateful flame, and you will see that jaw begin to work, and you will recognize that nothing is required of you from this out but to listen as long as you remain conscious.

"Marienbad—A Health Factory,"
Europe and Elsewhere (1923), p. 125

. . . what an incredible gift of gabble! . . . never heard

anything like it; tongue journaled on ball-bearings!

"Meisterschaft: In Three Acts,"
The American Claimant, Etc., p. 320

So I finally opened the conversation myself [with a fellow passenger].

The Sphynx was a Sphynx no more! The fountains of her great deep were broken up, and she rained the nine parts of speech forty days and forty nights, metaphorically speaking, and buried us under a desolating deluge of trivial gossip that left not a crag or pinnacle of rejoinder projecting above the tossing waste of dislocated grammar and decomposed pronunciation!

Roughing It, I, Chapt. II, p. 23

But Jim was asleep. Tom looked kind of ashamed, because you know a person always feels bad when he is talking uncommon fine and thinks the other person is admiring, and that other person goes to sleep that way. Of course he oughtn't to go to sleep, because it's shabby; but the finer a person talks the certainer it is to make you sleep, and so when you come to look at it it ain't nobody's fault in particular; both of them's to blame.

Tom Sawyer Abroad, Etc., Chapt. X, p. 97

She was a quite biddable creature and good-hearted, but she had a flow of talk that was as steady as a mill, and made your head sore like the drays and wagons in a city. If she had had a cork she would have been a comfort. But you can't cork that kind; they would die. Her clack was going all day, and you would think something would surely happen to her works, by and by; but no, they never got out of order; and she never had to slack up for words. She could grind, and pump, and churn, and buzz by the week, and never stop to oil up or blow out. And yet the result was just nothing but wind. She never had any ideas, any more than a fog has.

A Connecticut Yankee in King Arthur's Court,
Chapt. XII, p. 96

[A man] was reproached by a friend, who said:

"I think it a shame that you have not spoken to your wife

for fifteen years. How do you explain it? How do you justify it?"

That poor man said:

"I didn't want to interrupt her."

"Chapters from My Autobiography,"
The North American Review, March 15, 1907, p. 569

. . . he was just the kind of person you could depend on to spoil a . . . thing . . . if you didn't warn him, his tongue was so handy, and his spirit so willing, and his information so uncertain.

Dowley was in fine feather, and I early got him started, and then adroitly worked him around onto his own history for a text and himself for a hero, and then it was good to sit there and hear him hum. Self-made man, you know. They know how to talk. They do deserve more credit than any other breed of men, yes, that is true; and they are among the very first to find it out, too.

A Connecticut Yankee in King Arthur's Court,
Chapt. XXXII, p. 287

People can always talk well when they are talking what they feel. This is the secret of eloquence.

Love Letters of Mark Twain, p. 53

. . . it is no harm to bark, if one stops there and does not bite. . . .

Personal Recollections of Joan of Arc,
I, Book II, Chapt. III

And when at last she had spread the cloth and loaded it with . . . all manner of country luxuries, Col. Sellers modified his harangue and for a moment throttled it down to the orthodox pitch for a blessing, and then instantly burst forth again as from a parenthesis, and clattered on with might and main till every stomach in the party was laden with all it could carry.

The Gilded Age, I, Chapt. V, p. 63

It is my custom to keep on talking until I get the audience cowed.

Mark Twain's Letters, II, p. 794

. . . they talk . . . till you are sick of . . . their relentless clack, and wish it had pleased Providence to leave the clapper out of their empty skulls.

"Back from 'Yurrup,'"
A Curious Dream, p. 104

What a talker he is. He could persuade a fish to come out and take a walk with him.

Mark Twain's Notebook, p. 232

We discussed . . . and disputed . . . at any rate *he* did, and I got in a word now and then when he slipped a cog and there was a vacancy.

"Is Shakespeare Dead?"
What Is Man? and Other Essays, p. 300

. . . *agreeing* with a person cripples controversy and ought not to be allowed.

"A Little Note to M. Paul Bourget,"
Literary Essays, p. 170

Colonel Greene . . . began a sentence and went on and on, dropping a comma in here and there at intervals of eighteen inches, never hesitating for a word, drifting straight along like a river at half bank with no reefs in it; the surface of his talk as smooth as a mirror; his construction perfect and fit for print without correction . . . And when the hammer fell, at the end of his ten minutes, he dumped in a period right where he was and stopped—and it was just as good there as it would have been anywhere else in that ten minutes' sentence.

Mark Twain's Autobiography, Paine, I, p. 299

TAMMANY *See* POLITICS

TASTER

I believe a salaried taster has to taste everything before the prince ventures it—an ancient and judicious custom in the East, which has thinned out the tasters a good deal, for of course it is the cook that puts the poison in. If I were an Indian prince I would not go to the expense of a taster, I would eat with the cook.

Following the Equator, II, Chapt. IV, p. 52

TAXES *See also* MORALS, POLITICS

What is the difference between a taxidermist and a tax
collector? The taxidermist takes only your skin.

> *Mark Twain's Notebook,* p. 379

[I] shall never use profanity except in discussing house
rent and taxes. Indeed, upon second thought, I will not
even use it then, for it is unchristian, inelegant, and degrading—though to speak truly I do not see how house rent
and taxes are going to be discussed worth a cent without it.

> "Two Mark Twain Editorials,"
> *Europe and Elsewhere,* p. 15

[In early Nevada]: . . . there was but little realty to
tax, and it did seem as if nobody was ever going to think
of the simple salvation of inflicting a money penalty on
murder.

> *Roughing It,* II, Chapt. XIV, p. 137

. . . a most prodigious fire-breathing dragon used to live
in that region, and made more trouble than a tax collector.

> *A Tramp Abroad,* I, Chapt. XVII, p. 148

I don't know of a single foreign product that enters this
country untaxed except the answer to prayer.

> "When in Doubt, Tell the Truth,"
> *Mark Twain's Speeches* (1923), p. 293

TEA *See* ENGLAND

TEACHER *See also* PUNISHMENT

It is noble to teach oneself; it is still nobler to teach
others—and less trouble.

> "Introducing Doctor Van Dyke,"
> *Mark Twain's Speeches* (1923), p. 296

The self-taught man seldom knows anything accurately,
and he does not know a tenth as much as he could have
known if he had worked under teachers, and, besides, he
brags, and is the means of fooling other thoughtless people
into going and doing as he himself has done.

> "Taming the Bicycle,"
> *What Is Man? and Other Essays,* p. 290

. . . in foreign languages you always begin with [the verb *Amare,* to love]. Why, I do not know. It is merely habit, I suppose; the first teacher chose it, Adam was satisfied, and there hasn't been a successor since with originality enough to start a fresh one.

"Italian with Grammar,"
The $30,000 Bequest, Etc., p. 188

They are making a great fuss in Springfield, Mass., because a young lady school teacher has unmercifully flogged one of her boy pupils. . . . The boy was getting the best of this one in Springfield, but she called for reinforcements, and another teacher came. They doubled teams on him. It is the old story. We had one of our old maids nearly flaxed out once—we had her to the edge of the well, and we would have got her in in another minute, but the unprincipled old harridan piped for assistance.

"Foolishness,"
Mark Twain's Travels with Mr. Brown, p. 244

TEETH   *See also* COLD, FRUIT, SIMILES

. . . her name is one of those nine-jointed Russian affairs, and there are not letters enough in our alphabet to hold out. I am not reckless enough to try to pronounce it when I am awake, but I make a stagger at it in my dreams, and get up with the lockjaw in the morning. . . . Her dear name haunts me still in my dreams. It is awful on teeth. It never comes out of my mouth but it fetches an old snag along with it. And then the lockjaw closes down and nips off a couple of the last syllables—but they taste good.

The Innocents Abroad, II, Chapt. XI, p. 146

[He was] a slim creature, with teeth which made his mouth look like a neglected churchyard.

Following the Equator, I, Chapt. XXXVI

[In New Zealand]: Bad teeth in the colonies. A citizen told me that they don't have teeth filled, but pull them out and put in false ones, and that now and then one sees a young lady with a full set. She is fortunate. I wish I had been born with false teeth and a false liver and false carbuncles. I should get along better.

Ibid., Chapt. XXXIV, p. 329

We are chameleons, and our partialities and prejudices change places with an easy and blessed facility, and we are soon wonted to the change and happy in it. We do not regret our old, yellow fangs and snags and tushes after we have worn nice, fresh, uniform store teeth a while.

"Spelling and Pictures,"
Mark Twain's Speeches (1910), p. 205

Adam and Eve had many advantages, but the principal one was, that they escaped teething.

"Pudd'nhead Wilson's Calendar,"
Pudd'nhead Wilson, Chapt. IV, p. 38

TELEPATHY, MENTAL *See* MENTAL TELEPATHY

TELEPHONE

The humblest hello-girl along ten thousand miles of wire could teach gentleness, patience, modesty, manners, to the highest duchess in Arthur's land.

A Connecticut Yankee in King Arthur's Court,
Chapt. XV, p. 115

It is my heart-warm and world-embracing Christmas hope and aspiration that all of us, the high, the low, the rich, the poor, the admired, the despised, the loved, the hated, the civilized, the savage (every man and brother of us all through-out the whole earth), may eventually be gathered together in a heaven of everlasting rest and peace and bliss, except the inventor of the telephone.

Seen in manuscript (1 page) circa 1878

The village [Dublin, New Hampshire] is bunched to-gether in its own place, but a good telephone service makes its markets handy to all those outliars. I have spelled it that way to be witty.

Mark Twain's Letters, II, p. 782

Confound a telephone, anyway. It is the very demon for conveying similarities of sound that are miracles of divergence from similarity of sense.

> *A Connecticut Yankee in King Arthur's Court,*
> Chapt. XXIV, p. 207

[The telephone] is a time-saving, profanity-breeding, useful invention, and in America is to be found in all houses except parsonages.

> "Letters to Satan,"
> *Europe and Elsewhere,* p. 216

[When the telephone annoyed him, Mark Twain wrote to the telephone management in Hartford, Conn.]: The time is coming very soon when the telephone will be a perfect instrument, when proximity will no longer be a hindrance to its performance, when, in fact, one will hear a man who is in the next block just as easily and comfortably as he would if that man were in San Francisco.

> *Mark Twain, a Biography,* Paine, II, p. 838

About the end of the year [1881] I put up a telephone wire from my house down to the *Courant* office, the only telephone wire in town, and the *first* one that was ever used in a private house in the world.

> *Ibid.,* p. 726

TEMPER   *See also* FRENCH PEOPLE, PROFANITY

That idiot (Whitmore) puts me in a rage; and while it lasts I recognize and concede that there is not another temper as bad as mine except God Almighty's. [1899]

> *Mark Twain-Howells Letters,* II, p. 710

Although his temper was slow to ignite, it was a reliable burner when well going.

> *Sam Clemens of Hannibal,* Wecter, p. 205

Yesterday a thunder-stroke fell upon me out of the most unsuspected of skies which for a moment ranged me breast to breast and comraded me as an equal, with all men who have suffered sudden and awful disaster: I found that all their lives my children have been afraid of me! have stood all their days in uneasy dread of my sharp tongue and uncertain temper. The accusing instances stretch back to their babyhood, and are burnt into their memories: and I never suspected, and the fact was never guessed by *anybody* until yesterday. Well, all the concentrated griefs of fifty years seemed colorless by the side of that pathetic revelation.

Mark Twain-Howells Letters, II, p. 575

It takes me a long time to lose my temper, but once lost I could not find it with a dog.

Mark Twain's Notebook, p. 240

. . . he was the angriest man in the State, and there wasn't a rag or remnant of an injurious adjective left in him anywhere.

"Chapters from My Autobiography,"
The North American Review, April 5, 1907, p. 679

Tom lost his temper. I notice a person 'most always does that's got laid out in an argument.

Tom Sawyer Abroad, Etc., Chapt. III, p. 33

My gun-powdery chief went off with a bang . . . and then went on loading and firing until he was out of adjectives.

I had learned long ago that he only carried just so many rounds of ammunition, and was sure to subside into a very placable and even remorseful old smooth-bore as soon as they were all gone.

Life on the Mississippi, Chapt. VIII, p. 70

TEMPERAMENT   *See also* BELIEF, REFLECTION, EXAGGERATION

. . . the temperament is *master of the man*, . . . he is its fettered and helpless slave and must in all things do as it commands. A man's temperament is born in him, and no circumstances can ever change it.

Mark Twain, a Biography, Paine, III, p. 1552

It seems to be conceded that there are a few human peculiarities that can be generalized and located here and there in the world and named by the name of the nation where they are found. I wonder what they are. Perhaps one of them is temperament. One speaks of French vivacity and German gravity and English stubbornness. There is no American temperament. The nearest that one can come at it is to say there are two—the composed Northern and the impetuous Southern; and both are found in other countries.

"What Paul Bourget Thinks of Us,"
Literary Essays, p. 153

. . . *temperament* is the man; the thing tricked out with clothes and named Man is merely its Shadow, nothing more. . . . I cannot help feeling disappointed in Adam and Eve. That is, in their temperaments. Not in *them,* poor helpless young creatures—afflicted with temperaments made out of butter; which butter was commanded to get into contact with fire and *be melted.* What I cannot help wishing is, that Adam and Eve had been postponed, and Martin Luther and Joan of Arc put in their place—that splendid pair equipped with temperaments not made of butter, but of asbestos. By neither sugary persuasions nor by hell fire could Satan have beguiled *them* to eat the apple.

There would have been results! Indeed, yes. The apple would be intact to-day; there would be no human race; there would be no *you;* there would be no *me.*

"The Turning Point of My Life,"
What Is Men? and Other Essays, p. 139

TEMPERANCE   *See also* LIQUOR

Temperate temperance is best. Intemperate temperance injures the cause of temperance, while temperate temperance helps it in its fight against intemperate intemperance. Fanatics will never learn that, though it be written in letters of gold across the sky.

Mark Twain's Notebook, p. 310

TEMPERATURE

I judge . . . it has cooled down, now, so a person is comparatively comfortable, with his skin off.

Here (in Elmira) when a person is going to die, he is

always in a sweat about where he is going; but in Keokuk of course they don't care, because they are fixed for everything.

Mark Twain's Letters, II, p. 470

TEMPTATION *See* COWARDICE

TERROR

Terror is an efficacious agent only when it doesn't last. In the long run there is more terror in threats than in execution, for when you get used to terror your emotions get dulled.

Abroad with Mark Twain, Fisher, p. 60

THANKSGIVING

Thanksgiving Day. Let all give humble, hearty and sincere thanks, now, but the turkeys. In the island of Fiji they do not use turkeys; they use plumbers. It does not become you and me to sneer at Fiji.

"Pudd'nhead Wilson's Calendar,"
Pudd'nhead Wilson, Chapt. XVIII, p. 167

[From a letter to his wife]:

Oh, think of Mrs. F.—a Pegasus harnessed with a dull brute of the field. Mated, but not matched—that must be the direst grief that can befall any poor human creature— and when I think how I have escaped it when so many that are worthier than I have suffered it, I am filled with a thankfulness to God which I can feel—that rare thankfulness that such as I feel all too seldom. It is at such times that one's heart lifts up its unspoken gratitude and no choicely worded eloquence of lip and brain is like unto it, or half so puissant.

My Father • Mark Twain, Clara Clemens, p. 210

Thanksgiving Day, 1905: Every year every person in America concentrates all his thoughts upon one thing, the cataloguing of his reasons for being thankful to the Deity for the blessings conferred upon him and upon the human race during the expiring 12 months.

This is well and as it should be; but it is too one-sided. No one seems to think of the Deity's side of it; apparently no one concerns himself to inquire how much or how little He has to be thankful for during the same period; apparently no one has had good feeling enough to wish He might have a Thanksgiving day too. There is nothing right about this.

Do you suppose everything has gone to His satisfaction during the year? Do you believe He is as sweepingly thankful as our nation is going to be . . . ?

One is justified in fearing that the Deity's Thanksgiving Day is not as rosy as ours will appear when the Thanksgiving sentiments blossom in our journals and that if He, now voiceless, should utter a sentiment it would be tinged with a pathetic regret.

The Washington Times, Nov. 27, 1905

THEORY *See also* FACT

. . . the trouble about arguments is, they ain't nothing but *theories*, after all, and theories don't prove nothing, they only give you a place to rest on, a spell, when you are tuckered out butting around and around trying to find out something there ain't no way *to* find out. . . .

There's another trouble about theories: there's always a hole in them somewheres, sure, if you look close enough.

Tom Sawyer Abroad, Etc., Chapt. IX, p. 90

THERMOMETER *See* COLD

THINGS *See also* EDUCATION

It was only a little thing to do, and no trouble; and it's the little things that smooths people's roads the most, down here below.

The Adventures of Huckleberry Finn,
Chapt. XXVIII, p. 249

(THINGS)

Many a small thing has been made large by the right kind of advertising.

> A *Connecticut Yankee in King Arthur's Court*,
> Chapt. XXII, p. 188

It's just the little things that makes a man to be looked up to and liked.

> *The Adventures of Huckleberry Finn*,
> Chapt. XXVII, p. 239

One thing at a time is my motto—and just play that thing for all it is worth, even if it's only two pair and a jack.

> A *Connecticut Yankee in King Arthur's Court*,
> Chapt. II, p. 25

A thing long expected takes the form of the unexpected when at last it comes.

> *Mark Twain's Notebook*, p. 236

THOUGHT *See also* AMERICA, BIOGRAPHY, ECHO, FEELING, OPINION, ORIGINALITY, TROUBLE

The utterer of a thought always utters a second-hand one.

> *What Is Man? and Other Essays*, Chapt. III, p. 30

You are but a *thought*—a vagrant thought, a useless thought, a homeless thought, wandering forlorn among the empty eternities.

> *The Mysterious Stranger, Etc.*, Chapt. XI, p. 140

His opinions are not the outcome of reflection, for he never thinks about anything, but heaves out the opinion that is on top in his mind, and which is often an opinion about some quite different thing and does not fit the case. But that is his way; his main idea is to get out an opinion, and if he stopped to think he would lose chances.

> *Following the Equator*, II, Chapt. II, p. 32

It is curious—the space-annihilating power of thought. For just one second, all that goes to make the *me* in me was in a Missourian village, on the other side of the globe, vividly seeing again these forgotten pictures of fifty years ago, and wholly unconscious of all things but those; and in the next second I was back in Bombay. . . .

Back to boyhood—fifty years; back to age again—another

fifty; and a flight equal to the circumference of the globe—
all in two seconds by the watch!

Ibid., I, Chapt. II, p. 29

At first the tumult of my own thoughts, summoned by
the danger-signal and swarming to the rescue from every
quarter of my skull, kept up such a hurrah and confusion
and fifing and drumming that I couldn't take in a word;
but presently when my mob of gathering plans began to
crystallize and fall into position and form line of battle, a
sort of order and quiet ensued and I caught the boom of
the king's batteries, as if out of remote distance.

A Connecticut Yankee in King Arthur's Court,
Chapt. XXXIV, p. 309

. . . a man's private thought can never be a lie; what he
thinks, is to him the truth, always.

Mark Twain's Letters, II, p. 498

. . . life does not consist mainly—or even largely—of facts
and happenings. It consists mainly of the storm of thoughts
that is forever blowing through one's head.

Mark Twain's Autobiography, Paine, I, p. 283

What a wee part of a person's life are his acts and words!
His real life is led in his head, and is known to none but
himself. All day . . . the mill of his brain is grinding, and
his *thoughts* . . . are his history.

Ibid., Paine, I, p. 2

Thought! You should not try to think. One cannot think
without the proper machinery.

"Playing Courier,"
The American Claimant, Etc., p. 488

The world will not stop and think—it never does, it is not
its way; its way is to generalize from a single sample.

"The United States of Lyncherdom,"
Europe and Elsewhere, p. 239

THUNDER   *See also* SILENCE

Thunder is good, thunder is impressive; but it is the
lightning that does the work.

Mark Twain's Letters, II, p. 818

TIBET *See* PRAYER

TIME *See also* AGE, CREATION, MISSIONARY, PAST, POVERTY, PROCRASTINATION, WATCH, WORK, YOUTH

[Sailing west across the Pacific]: To-morrow we shall be close to the center of the globe—the 180th degree of west longitude and 180th degree of east longitude.

And then we must drop out a day—lose a day out of our lives, a day never to be found again. We shall all die one day earlier than from the beginning of time we were foreordained to die. We shall be a day behindhand all through eternity. We shall always be saying to the other angels, "Fine day to-day," and they will be always retorting, "But it isn't to-day, it's to-morrow." We shall be in a state of confusion all the time and shall never know what true happiness is.

Following the Equator, I, Chapt. IV, p. 68

Mars Tom talkin' sich talk as dat! Choosday in one place en Monday t'other, bofe in the same day! Huck, dis ain't no place to joke. . . . Two days in one day! How you gwine to get two days inter one day? Can't git two hours inter one hour, kin you? . . . Can't git two gallons of whisky inter a one-gallon jug, kin you? No, sir, 'twould strain de jug. Yes, en even den you couldn't, *I* don't believe. . . . It's the beatenest rubbage!

Tom Sawyer Abroad, Etc., Chapt. III, p. 36

Do not put off till tomorrow what can be put off till day-after-tomorrow just as well.

More Maxims of Mark, p. 7

For the majority of us, the past is a regret; the future an experiment.

Mark Twain and I, Opie Read, p. 34

Let us adopt geological time, then time being money,—there will be no poverty.

Mark Twain's Notebook, p. 393

I am thrashing away at my new book, and am afraid I should not find time to write my own epitaph, in case I was suddenly called for.

Mark Twain, His Life and Work, Will Clemens, p. 11
There is in life only one moment and in eternity only one. It is so brief that it is represented by the fleeting of a luminous mote through the thin ray of sunlight—and it is visible but a fraction of a second. The moments that preceded it have been lived, are forgotten and are without value; the moments that have not been lived have no existence and will have no value except in the moment that each shall be lived. While you are asleep you are dead; and whether you stay dead an hour or a billion years the time to you is the same.

Mark Twain's Notebook, p. 323

TIMIDITY *See also* MAN
Sometimes daring—a bold front—will accomplish things that timidity would fail to accomplish.

Mark Twain's Autobiography, Paine, II, p. 207

TITLES *See also* DEMOCRACY, PARIS, PROSPERITY, VANITY
We adore titles and heredities with our hearts and ridicule them with our mouths. This is our democratic privilege.

Mark Twain's Autobiography, Paine, II, p. 350
In Germany they respect titles, in England they revere them, in France they adore them, that is, the French newspapers do.

Mark Twain's Notebook, p. 322
Titles—another artificiality—are a part of [man's] clothing. They and the [clothes] conceal the wearer's inferiority and make him seem great and a wonder, when at bottom there is nothing remarkable about him. They can move a nation to fall on its knees and sincerely worship an Emperor who, without his clothes and the title, would drop to the rank of the cobbler and be swallowed up and lost sight of in the massed multitude of the inconsequentials. No great title is efficient without clothes to support it.

"The Czar's Soliloquy,"
The North American Review, March 1905, p. 322
Titles of honor and dignity once acquired in a democ-

racy, even if by accident and properly usable for only forty-eight hours, are as permanent here as eternity is in Heaven . . . Once a Justice of the Peace for a week, always "judge" afterward.

Mark Twain's Autobiography, Paine, II, p. 350

TOLERANCE *See also* INTOLERANCE

All the talk about tolerance, in anything or anywhere, is plainly a gentle lie. It does not exist. It is in no man's heart; but it unconsciously, and by moss-grown inherited habit, drivels and slobbers from all men's lips.

Mark Twain's Autobiography, Paine, II, p. 12

TOMB

Right under the roof of [The Church of the Holy Sepulchre in Jerusalem] . . . Adam himself, the father of the human race, lies buried. There is no question that he is actually buried in the grave which is pointed out as his—there can be none—because it has never yet been proved that that grave is not the grave in which he is buried.

The tomb of Adam! How touching it was, here in a land of strangers, far away from home, and friends, and all who cared for me, thus to discover the grave of a blood relation. True, a distant one, but still a relation. The unerring instinct of nature thrilled its recognition. The fountain of my filial affection was stirred to its profoundest depths, and I gave way to tumultuous emotion. I leaned upon a pillar and burst into tears. I deem it no shame to have wept over the grave of my poor dead relative. . . . Noble old man—he did not live to see me—he did not live to see his child. And I—I—alas, I did not live to see *him.* Weighed down by sorrow and disappointment, he died before I was born—six thousand brief summers before I was born. But let us try to bear it with fortitude. . . . Let us take comfort in the thought that his loss is our eternal gain.

The Innocents Abroad, II, Chapt. XXVI, p. 337

TOMBSTONE *See* FACE

TOMORROW *See* TIME, WORK

TRAGEDY *See* MARRIAGE, PATHOS, YOUTH

TRAINING *See also* ARGUMENT

Training is everything. The peach was once a bitter almond; cauliflower is nothing but cabbage with a college education.

> "Pudd'nhead Wilson's Calendar,"
> *Pudd'nhead Wilson*, Chapt. V, p. 49

. . . a body that don't get *started* right when he's little ain't got no show—when the pinch comes there ain't nothing to back him up and keep him to his work, and so he gets beat.

> *The Adventures of Huckleberry Finn,*
> Chapt. XVI, p. 130

Everything has its limit—iron ore cannot be educated into gold.

> *What Is Man? and Other Essays,* Chapt. I, p. 4

It takes *training* to enable a person to be properly courteous when he is dying.

> *Mark Twain's Autobiography,* Paine, I, p. 345

TRAITOR *See* PATRIOTISM

TRANQUILLITY *See* MISSISSIPPI RIVER

TRANSLATION *See also* LANGUAGE

. . . translations always reverse a thing and bring an entirely new side of it into view, thus doubling the property and making two things out of what was only one thing before.

> "On After-Dinner Speaking"
> *Mark Twain's Speeches* (1923), p. 83

TRAVEL *See also* ABROAD, CLERGYMAN, INTEREST, MANNERS, OCCUPATION, OPINION, SALESMAN, SEA

We are at home again. We are exhausted. . . . We have full comfort in one reflection, however. Our experiences in Europe have taught us that in time this fatigue will be forgotten; the heat will be forgotten; the thirst, the tiresome volubility of the guide, the persecutions of the beggars—and then, all that will be left will be pleasant memories . . . memories we shall call up with always increasing interest as the years go by, memories which some day will become all beautiful when the last annoyance that incumbers them shall have faded out of our minds never again to return.

> *The Innocents Abroad,* II,
> Chapt. XXVII, p. 362

. . . nothing so liberalizes a man and expands the kindly instincts that nature put in him as travel and contact with many kinds of people.

> "The Traveller's Club"
> *Mark Twain's Travels with Mr. Brown,* p. 184

There is no unhappiness like the misery of sighting land (and work) again after a cheerful, careless voyage.

> *Mark Twain's Letters to Will Bowen,* p. 15

I have found out that there ain't no surer way to find out whether you like people or hate them than to travel with them.

> *Tom Sawyer Abroad, Etc.,* Chapt. XI, p. 103

There is the Sea of Galilee and this Dead Sea—neither of them twenty miles long or thirteen wide. And yet when I was in Sunday-school I thought they were sixty thousand miles in diameter.

Travel and experience mar the grandest pictures and rob us of the most cherished traditions of our boyhood.

> *The Innocents Abroad,* II, Chapt. XXVIII, p. 378

. . . we love the Old Travelers. We love to hear them prate and drivel and lie. We can tell them the moment we see them. They always throw out a few feelers: they never cast themselves adrift till they have sounded every individual and know that he has not traveled. Then they open

their throttle-valves, and how they do brag, and sneer, and
swell, and soar, and blaspheme the sacred name of Truth!
Their central idea, their grand aim, is to subjugate you,
keep you down, make you feel insignificant and humble
in the blaze of their cosmopolitan glory! . . . But still I
love the Old Travelers. I love them for their witless plati-
tudes; for their supernatural ability to bore; for their startling, their brilliant, their overwhelming mendacity!

Ibid., I, Chapt. XII, p. 154

Travel is fatal to prejudice, bigotry, and narrow-minded-
ness, and many of our people need it sorely on these accounts. Broad, wholesome, charitable views of men and
things cannot be acquired by vegetating in one little corner
of the earth all one's lifetime.

Ibid., II, Conclusion, p. 444

To be condemned to live as the average European family
lives would make life a pretty heavy burden to the average
American family.

On the whole, I think that short visits to Europe are
better for us than long ones. The former preserve us from
becoming Europeanized; they keep our pride of country
intact, and at the same time they intensify our affection for
our country and our people; whereas long visits have the
effect of dulling those feelings,—at least in the majority of
cases.

A Tramp Abroad, II, Chapt. XXI, p. 272

[A trip west by stage-coach]: As the sun went down and
the evening chill came on, we made preparation for bed.
We stirred up the hard leather letter-sacks, and the knotty
canvas bags of printed matter (knotty and uneven because
of projecting ends and corners of magazines, boxes and
books). We stirred them up and redisposed them in such a
way as to make our bed as level as possible. And we *did*
improve it, too, though after all our work it had an up-
heaved and billowy look about it, like a little piece of a
stormy sea. Next we hunted up our boots from odd nooks
among the mail bags where they had settled, and put them

on. Then we got down our coats, vests, pantaloons and heavy woolen shirts, from the arm-loops where they had been swinging all day, and clothed ourselves in them—for, there being no ladies either at the station or in the coach, and the weather being hot, we had looked to our comfort by stripping to our underclothing, at nine o'clock in the morning. All things being now ready, we stowed the uneasy Dictionary where it would lie as quiet as possible, and placed the water-canteen and pistols where we could find them in the dark. Then we smoked a final pipe, and swapped a final yarn; after which, we put the pipes, tobacco, and bag of coin in snug holes and caves along the mail-bags, and then fastened down the coach curtains all around and made the place as "dark as the inside of a cow," as the conductor phrased it in his picturesque way. It was certainly as dark as any place could be—nothing was even dimly visible in it. And finally, we rolled ourselves up like silk-worms, each person in his own blanket, and sank peacefully to sleep.

Whenever the stage stopped to change horses, we would wake up, and try to recollect where we were—and succeed —and in a minute or two the stage would be off again, and we likewise. We began to get into the country, now, threaded here and there with little streams. These had high, steep banks on each side, and every time we flew down one bank and scrambled up the other, our party inside got mixed somewhat. First we would all be down in a pile at the forward end of the stage, nearly in a sitting posture, and in a second we would shoot to the other end, and stand on our heads. And we would sprawl and kick, too, and ward off ends and corners of mail-bags that came lumbering over us and about us; and as the dust rose from the tumult, we would all sneeze in chorus, and the majority of us would grumble, and probably say some hasty thing, like: "Take your elbow out of my ribs!—can't you quit crowding?"

Every time we avalanched from one end of the stage to

the other, the Unabridged Dictionary would come too; and every time it came it damaged somebody. One trip it "barked" the Secretary's elbow; the next trip it hurt me in the stomach, and the third it tilted Bemis's nose up till he could look down his nostrils—he said . . . .

Still, all things considered, it was a very comfortable night. It wore gradually away, and when at last a cold gray light was visible through the puckers and chinks in the curtains, we yawned and stretched with satisfaction, shed our cocoons, and felt that we had slept as much as was necessary. By and by, as the sun rose up and warmed the world, we pulled off our clothes and got ready for breakfast. We were just pleasantly in time, for five minutes afterward the driver sent the weird music of his bugle winding over the grassy solitudes, and presently we detected a low hut or two in the distance. Then the rattling of the coach, the clatter of our six horses' hoofs, and the driver's crisp commands, awoke to a louder and stronger emphasis, and we went sweeping down on the station at our smartest speed. It was fascinating—that old Overland stage-coaching.

Roughing It, I, Chapt. IV, p. 35

I have traveled more than anyone else and I have noticed that even the angels speak English with an accent.

"Pudd'nhead Wilson's New Calendar"
Following the Equator, II, Conclusion, p. 406

Travel has no longer any charm for me. I have seen all the foreign countries I want to see except heaven and hell, and I have only a vague curiosity as concerns one of those. [1891]

Mark Twain's Letters, II, p. 548

Our trip around the earth ended at the Southampton pier, where we embarked thirteen months before. It seemed a fine and large thing to have accomplished—the circumnavigation of this great globe in that little time, and I was privately proud of it. For a moment. Then came one of those vanity-snubbing astronomical reports from the Observatory-people, whereby it appeared that another great body of light had lately flamed up in the remotenesses of space which was traveling at a gait which would enable it to do all that I had done in *a minute and a half*. Human pride is not worth while; there is always something lying in wait to take the wind out of it.

Following the Equator, II, Conclusion, p. 408

Brains are of no value when you are trying to navigate Berlin in a horse-car . . .

. . . A native tells me that when the first car was put on, thirty or forty years ago, the public had such a terror of it that they didn't feel safe inside of it or outside either. They made the company keep a man at every crossing with a red flag in his hand. Nobody would travel in the car except convicts on the way to the gallows. This made business in only one direction, and the car had to go back light. To save the company, the city government transferred the convict cemetery to the end of the line. This made traffic in both directions and kept the company from going under. This sounds like some of the information which traveling foreigners are furnished with in America. To my mind it has a doubtful ring about it.

"The German Chicago"
The American Claimant, Etc., p. 508

TREACHERY

Gratitude and treachery are merely the two extremities of the same procession. You have seen all of it that is worth staying for when the band and the gaudy officials have gone by.

"Pudd'nhead Wilson's Calendar"
Pudd'nhead Wilson, Chapt. XVIII, p. 167

TREE *See also* BEAUTY, CALIFORNIA, FRUIT, ICE-STORM, LIE

[In Bermuda]: There was exactly one mahogany tree on the island. I know this to be reliable because I saw a man who said he had counted it many a time and could not be mistaken. He was a man with a harelip and a pure heart, and everybody said he was as true as steel. Such men are all too few.

"Rambling Notes of an Idle Excursion"
Tom Sawyer Abroad, Etc., p. 299

. . . it is a soft and pensive foggy morning, . . . and the naked tree branches are tear-beaded, and Nature has the look of trying to keep from breaking down and sobbing . . .

My Father •Mark Twain, Clara Clemens, p. 227

The stage whirled along at a spanking gait, . . . the spinning ground and the waltzing trees appeared to give us a mute hurrah as we went by, and then slack up and look after us with interest, or envy . . .

Roughing It, I, Chapt. III, p. 27

Sometimes a limbless veteran of the forest stood aloof in his flowing vine-robes, like an ivy-clad tower of some old feudal ruin.

"An Unpeopled Paradise"
Mark Twain's Travels with Mr. Brown, p. 50

. . . there are frequent groves of palm; and an effective accent is given to the landscape by isolated individuals of this picturesque family, towering, clean-stemmed, their plumes broken and hanging ragged, Nature's imitation of an umbrella that has been out to see what a cyclone is like and is trying not to look disappointed.

Following the Equator, II, Chapt. XIX, p. 224

. . . in front of the London Bank of Australia, is a very handsome cottonwood. It is in opulent leaf, and every leaf perfect. The full power of the on-rushing spring is upon it, and I imagine I can see it grow. Alongside the bank and a little way back in the garden there is a row of soaring fountain-sprays of delicate feathery foliage quivering in the breeze, and mottled with flashes of light that shift and play through the mass like flash-lights through an opal—a most beautiful tree, and a striking contrast to the cottonwood. Every leaf of the cottonwood is distinctly defined—it is a kodak for faithful, hard, unsentimental detail; the other an impressionist picture, delicious to look upon, full of subtle and exquisite charm, but all details fused in a swoon of vague and soft loveliness.

> *Ibid.*, I, Chapt. XXIII, p. 227

TROUBLE *See also* MAXIMS

. . . drag your thoughts away from your troubles—by the ears, by the heels, or any other way, so you manage it; it's the healthiest thing a body can do.

> *The American Claimant, Etc.*, Chapt. XV, p. 132

[He] made more trouble than a tax-collector.

> *A Tramp Abroad*, I, Chapt. XVII, p. 148

. . . . You know the more you join with people in their joys and their sorrows, the more nearer and dearer they come to be to you.

> *Tom Sawyer Abroad, Etc.*, Chapt. XI, p. 104

We all like to see people in trouble, if it doesn't cost us anything.

> *Ibid.*, I, Chapt. XII, p. 140

TRUST *See* GOD, MONEY, PRAYER

TRUTH *See also* AUTOBIOGRAPHY, FAMILIARITY, HUMOR, LIE, MOUNTAIN

Truth is the most valuable thing we have. Let us economize it.

> "Pudd'nhead Wilson's New Calendar"
> *Following the Equator*, I, Chapt. VII, p. 89

Truth is stranger than fiction—to some people, but I am measurably familiar with it.

> "Pudd'nhead Wilson's New Calander"
> *Ibid.*, I, Chapt. XV, p. 155

Truth is stranger than fiction, but it is because Fiction is obliged to stick to possibilities; Truth isn't.

> "Pudd'nhead Wilson's New Calendar"
> *Ibid.*, I, Chapt. XV, p. 155

If you tell the truth you don't have to remember anything.

> *Mark Twain's Notebook*, p. 240

. . . all through my life my facts have had a substratum of truth, and therefore they were not without value. Any person who is familiar with me knows how to strike my average, and therefore knows how to get at the jewel of any fact of mine and dig it out of its blue-clay matrix. My mother knew that art. When I was seven or eight . . . a neighbor said to her, "Do you ever believe anything that that boy says?" My mother said, "He is the wellspring of truth, but you can't bring up the whole well with one bucket"—and she added, "I know his average, therefore he never deceives me. I discount him 90 per cent for embroidery, and what is left is perfect and priceless truth, without a flaw in it anywhere."

Mark Twain's Autobiography, Paine, I, p. 293

An injurious truth has no merit over an injurious lie. Neither should ever be uttered. The man who speaks an injurious truth, lest his soul be not saved if he do otherwise, should reflect that that sort of a soul is not strictly worth saving.

"On the Decay of the Art of Lying"
Tom Sawyer Abroad, Etc., p. 358

When in doubt, tell the truth.

Mark Twain's Notebook, p. 237

["When in doubt, tell the truth."] That maxim I did invent, but never expected it to be applied to me. I meant to say, "When *you* are in doubt"; When I am in doubt myself I use more sagacity.

"When in Doubt, Tell the Truth"
Mark Twain's Speeches (1923), p. 292

The truth is always respectable.

The Adventures of Tom Sawyer, Chapt. XXIII, p. 216

Never tell the truth to people who are not worthy of it.

More Maxims of Mark, p. 11

I have not professionally dealt in truth. Many when they come to die have spent all the truth that was in them, and enter the next world as paupers. I have saved up enough to make an astonishment there.

Mark Twain's Notebook, p. 371

None but the dead are permitted to speak the truth.

Ibid., p. 393

Homely truth is unpalatable.

The Adventures of Tom Sawyer, Chapt. XXI, p. 198

A man is never more truthful than when he acknowledges himself a liar.

Mark Twain and I, Opie Read, p. 34

Often, the surest way to convey misinformation is to tell the strict truth.

Following the Equator, II, Chapt. XXIII, p. 266

I never could tell a lie that anybody would doubt, nor a truth that anybody would believe.

Ibid., II, Chapt. XXVI, p. 310

We are always hearing of people who are around *seeking after Truth*. I have never seen a (permanent) specimen. I think he has never lived. But I have seen several entirely sincere people who *thought* they were (permanent) Seekers after Truth. They sought diligently, persistently, carefully, cautiously, profoundly, with perfect honesty and nicely adjusted judgment—until they believed that without doubt or question they had found the Truth. *That was the end of the search.* [They] spent the rest of [their lives] hunting up shingles wherewith to protect [their] Truth from the weather.

What Is Man? and Other Essays, Chapt. IV, p. 45

Tell the truth or trump—but get the trick!

"Pudd'nhead Wilson's Calendar"
Pudd'nhead Wilson, Chapt. I, p. 11

No real gentleman will tell the naked truth in the presence of ladies.

The Double-Barreled Detective Story
Chapt. IV, p. 53

Think what tedious years of study, thought, practice, experience, went to the equipment of that peerless old master who was able to impose upon the whole world the lofty and sounding maxim that "truth is might and will prevail" —the most majestic compound fracture of fact which any of woman born has yet achieved.

"Advice to Youth"
Mark Twain's Speeches (1923), p. 106

I don't know anything that mars good literature so completely as too much truth.

"The Savage Club Dinner"
Mark Twain's Speeches (1923), p. 354

Having found the Truth; perceiving that beyond question man has but one moving impulse—the contenting of his own spirit—and is merely a machine and entitled to no personal merit for anything he does, it is not humanly possible for me to seek further. The rest of my days will be spent in patching and painting and puttying and caulking my priceless possession and in looking the other way when an imploring argument or a damaging fact approaches.

What Is Man? and Other Essays, Chapt. V, p. 75

Salt Lake City was healthy—an extremely healthy city. They declared that there was only one physician in the place and he was arrested every week regularly and held to answer under the vagrant act for having "no visible means of support." They always give you a good substantial article of truth in Salt Lake, and good measure and good weight, too. Very often, if you wished to weigh one of their airiest little commonplace statements you would want the hay scales.

Roughing It, I, Chapt. XIII, p. 115

TUNNEL

[Jim Townsend] was a stockholder in the "Daly" mine, in Virginia City, and he heard that his Company had let a contract to run a tunnel two hundred and fifty feet to strike the ledge. He visited the premises, and found a man starting a tunnel in very near the top of a very sharp hill. He said:

"You're the man that's got the contract to run this tunnel, I reckon?"

"Yes."

"Two hundred and fifty feet, I hear?"

"Yes."

"Well, it's going to be a mighty troublesome tunnel—and expensive."

"Why?"

"Because you've got to build the last hundred and sixty-five feet of it on trestle-work—it's only eighty-five feet through the hill."

"Jim Townsend's Tunnel"
Mark Twain's Travels with Mr. Brown, p. 147

TURKS *See* VIRTUE

TWAIN, MARK *See also* DEBT, CLEMENS, SAMUEL L., DE-
SCRIPTION, HALLEY'S COMET PUNS

[The setting from which Samuel Clemens derived his *nom de plume;* on a Mississippi steamboat]: In another instant the *Boreas* plunged into what seemed a crooked creek. . . . Not a whisper was uttered, now, but the three men stared ahead into the shadows and two of them spun the wheel back and forth with anxious watchfulness while the steamer tore along. The chute seemed to come to an end every fifty yards, but always opened out in time. Now the head of it was at hand. George tapped the big bell three times, two leadsmen sprang to their posts, and in a moment their weird cries rose on the night air and were caught up and repeated by two men on the upper deck:

"No-o bottom!"

"De-e-p four!"

"Half three!"

"Quarter three!"

"Mark under wa-a-ter three!"

"Half twain!"

"Quarter twain!"—

Davis pulled a couple of ropes—there was a jingling of small bells far below, the boat's speed slackened, and the pent steam began to whistle and the gauge-cocks to scream:

"By the mark twain!"

"Quar-ter-*her*-er-*less* twain!"

"Eight *and* a half!"

"Eight feet!"

"Seven-ana-half!—"

Another jingling of little bells and the wheels ceased turning altogether. The whistling of the steam was something frightful, now—it almost drowned all other noises.

"Stand by to meet her!"

George had the wheel hard down and was standing on a spoke.

"All ready!'

The boat hesitated—seemed to hold her breath, as did the captain and the pilots—and then she began to fall away to starboard and every eye lighted:

"*Now* then!—meet her! meet her! Snatch her!"

The wheel flew to port so fast that the spokes blended into a spider-web—the swing of the boat subsided—she steadied herself—

"Seven feet!"

"Sev—six and a *half!*"

"*Six* feet! Six f—"

Bang! She hit bottom! George shouted through the tube:

"Spread her wide open! *Whale it at her!*"

Pow-wow-chow! The escape-pipes belched snowy pillars of steam aloft, the boat ground and surged and trembled—and slid over into—

"M-a-r-k twain!"

. . . Tap! tap! tap! (to signify "Lay in the leads.")

And away she went, flying up the willow shore, with the whole sea of the Mississippi stretching abroad on every hand.

The Gilded Age, I, Chapt. IV, p. 47

TWICHELL, Joseph   *See* HEALTH

TYPESETTING   *See* PRINTING

TYPEWRITER

In the year '74 [I hired a young woman, and she] copied a considerable part of a book of mine *on the machine*. . . . I have claimed that I was the first person in the world that ever had a telephone in his house for practical purposes; I will now claim—until dispossessed—that I was the first person in the world to *apply the typewriter to literature* . . .

The early machine was full of caprices, full of defects—devilish ones. It had as many immoralities as the machine of to-day has virtues. After a year or two I found that it was degrading my character, so I thought I would give it to Howells. . . . He took it home to Boston, and my morals began to improve, but his have never recovered.

He kept it six months, and then returned it to me. I gave it away twice after that, but it wouldn't stay; it came back. Then I gave it to our coachman, Patrick McAleer, who was very grateful, because he did not know the animal, and thought I was trying to make him wiser and better. As soon as he got wiser and better he traded it to a heretic for a side-saddle which he could not use, and there my knowledge of its history ends.

> "The First Writing Machines"
> *The $30,000 Bequest, Etc.*, p. 169

[To the Remington Rand Typewriter Co.]: Please do not use my name in any way. Please do not even divulge the fact that I own a machine. I have entirely stopped using the typewriter, for the reason that I never could write a letter with it to anybody without receiving a request by return mail that I would not only describe the machine, but state what progress I had made in the use of it, etc., etc. I don't like to write letters, and so I don't want people to know I own this curiosity-breeding little joker. [1875]

> *Mark Twain's Letters*, I, p. 256

U

UNCLE

[Concerning the danger of fire-works on Fourth of July]:
I have had relatives killed in that way. One was in Chicago
years ago—an uncle of mine, just as good an uncle as I
have ever had, and I had lots of them,—yes, uncles to burn,
uncles to spare. This poor uncle, full of patriotism, opened
his mouth to hurrah, and a rocket went down his throat.
Before that man could ask for a drink of water to quench
that thing, it blew up and scattered him all over the forty-
five States, and . . . twenty-four hours after that it was raining buttons, recognizable as his, on the Atlantic seaboard.
A person cannot have a disaster like that and be entirely
cheerful the rest of his life. I had another uncle, on an
entirely different Fourth of July, who was blown up that
way, and really it trimmed him as it would a tree. He had
hardly a limb left on him anywhere. All we have left now
is an expurgated edition of that uncle.

"Independence Day"
Mark Twain's Speeches (1923), p. 346

[To the Editors of the *New York Evening Post*]: I have
just seen your despatch from San Francisco . . . about "Gold
in Solution" in the Calistoga Springs, and about the proprietor's having "extracted $1,000 in gold of the utmost

fineness from ten barrels of water" during the past fortnight, by a process known only to himself. This will surprise
many of your readers, but it does not surprise me, for I
once owned those springs myself. What does surprise me,
however, is the falling off in the richness of the water. In my
time the yield was a dollar a dipperful. I am not saying this
to injure the property, in case a sale is contemplated; I am
only saying it in the interest of history.

It may be that this hotel proprietor's process in an inferior
one—yes, that may be the fault. Mine was to take my uncle
—I had an extra uncle at the time, on account of his parents
dying and leaving him on my hands—and fill him up, and
let him stand fifteen minutes to give the water a chance to
settle well, then insert him in an exhausted receiver, which
had the effect of sucking the gold out through his pores.
I have taken more than eleven thousand dollars out of that
old man in a day and a half. I should have held on to those
springs, but for the badness of the roads and the difficulty
of getting the gold to market.

New York Evening Post, Sept. 16, 1880

[Mrs. Eddy] is the sole person who, in the matter of
Christian Science exegesis, is privileged to exploit the Spiral
Twist.*

*That is a technicality—that phrase. I got it of an uncle
of mine. He had once studied in a theological cemetery, he
said, and he called the Department of Biblical Exegesis the
Spiral Twist "for short." He said it was always difficult to
drive a straight text through an unaccommodating cork, but
that if you twisted it it would go. He had kept bar in his
less poetical days.

Christian Science, II, Chapt. VII, p. 196

UNDERSTANDING *See also* ARK

English and Americans are foreigners, but in a lesser
degree than in the case with other peoples. Men and women
—even man and wife are foreigners. Each has reserves that
the other cannot enter into, nor understand. These have

the effect of frontiers.

Mark Twain's Notebook, p. 386

UNDERTAKER *See also* DOCTOR
In answer to an inquiry about his health: I am able to say that while I am not ruggedly well, I am not ill enough to excite an undertaker. Truly yours, S. L. Clemens.

Manuscript letter, Feb. 24, 1910

Let us endeavor so to live that when we come to die even the undertaker will be sorry.

"Pudd'nhead Wilson's Calendar,"
Pudd'nhead Wilson, Chapt. VI, p. 56

There is Bill Ferguson, the Redding undertaker. . . . Like my old Southern friend, he is one of the finest planters anywhere.

"Dr. Mark Twain, Farmeopath,"
Mark Twain's Speeches (1910), p. 335

UNIONS
[In the year 528 A.D.]: The masters are these: nobles, rich men, the prosperous generally. These few, who do no work, determine what pay the vast hive shall have who *do* work. . . . They're a "combine"—a trade union, to coin a new phrase—who band themselves together to force their lowly brother to take what they choose to give. Thirteen hundred years hence—so says the unwritten law—the "combine" will be the other way, and then how these fine people's posterity will fume and fret and grit their teeth over the insolent tyranny of trade unions!

A Connecticut Yankee in King Arthur's Court,
Chapt. XXXIII, p. 303

The unionized workman is here and he will remain. He is the greatest birth of the greatest age the nations of the world have known. You cannot sneer at him—that time has gone by. He has before him the most righteous work that was ever given into the hand of man to do; and he will do it. Yes, he is here; and the question is not—as it has been heretofore during a thousand ages—What shall we do with him? For the first time in history we are relieved of the necessity of managing his affairs for him. He is not a broken dam this time—he is the Flood! [1887]

Mark Twain, a Biography, Paine, II, p. 850

UNIVERSE

Mr. Wallace has proved that the universe was made for this world, and that this world was made for man. There being 22 billion microbes in each man, and feeding upon him, we now perceive who the whole outfit was made for.

From an unpublished Mark Twain notebook, Aug. 2, 1905

Wallace says that the whole universe was made to take care of and to keep steady this little floating mote in the center of it, which we call the world. It looks like a good deal of trouble for such a small result; but it's dangerous to dispute with a learned astronomer like Wallace. Still, I don't think we ought to decide too soon about it—not until the returns are all in.

Ibid., Paine, III, p. 1358

USEFULNESS

He is useless on top of the ground; he ought to be under it, inspiring the cabbages.

"Pudd'nhead Wilson's Calendar," *Pudd'nhead Wilson,* Chapt. XXI, p. 206

UTAH *See* MONEY, MORMONS, TRUTH, WOMAN

V

VACATION *See* HEALTH

VACUUM
. . . what little indignation he excited in me soon passed
and left nothing behind it but compassion. One cannot keep
up a grudge against a vacuum.

A Tramp Abroad, II, Chapt. IX, p. 135

VALUE *See also* BEAUTY, PREACHER, PROSPERITY, RICHES
It is easy to make plans in this world; even a cat can do
it; and when one is out in . . . remote oceans it is noticeable that a cat's plans and a man's are worth about the
same. There is much the same shrinkage in both, in the
matter of values.

Following the Equator, I, Chapt. III

It shames the average man to be valued below his own
estimate of his worth.

A Connecticut Yankee in King Arthur's Court,
Chapt. XXXV, p. 321

One values a thing when one can't afford it.

Christian Science, Book II, Chapt. VII, p. 178

The interest [in] a prince is different. It may be envy, it

may be worship, doubtless it is a mixture of both—and it does not satisfy its thirst with one view, or even noticeably diminish it. Perhaps the essence of the thing is the value which men attach to a valuable something which has come by luck and not been earned. A dollar picked up in the road is more satisfaction to you than the ninety-and-nine which you had to work for, and money won at faro or in stocks snuggles into your heart in the same way. A prince picks up grandeur, power, and a permanent holiday and gratis support by a pure accident, the accident of birth, and he stands always before the grieved eye of poverty and obscurity a monumental representative of luck. And then—supremest value of all—his is the only high fortune on the earth which is secure . . . By common consent of all the nations and all the ages the most valuable thing in this world is the homage of men, whether deserved or undeserved. It follows without doubt or question, then, that the most desirable position possible is that of a prince.

"The Shrine of St. Wagner,"
What Is Man? and Other Essays, p. 219

VANITY   *See also* ASSASSINATION, NOTORIETY
There are no grades of vanity, there are only grades of ability in concealing it.

Mark Twain's Notebook, p. 345
He had only one vanity, he thought he could give advice better than any other person.

The Man That Corrupted Hadleyburg, Etc.,
Chapt. I, p. 21
Forty years ago I was not so good-looking. A looking glass then lasted me three months. Now I can wear it out in two days.

Mark Twain's Autobiography, Paine, II, p. 202
W. was in his glory. In his obscure days his hat was number six and a quarter; in these latter days he was not able to get his head into a barrel.

Mark Twain in Eruption, p. 186

VARIETY

This uncertain climate has its pleasant features. All life demands change, variety, contrast—else there is small zest to it.

Mark Twain's Travels with Mr. Brown, p. 195

We of the North poke fun at the South for its fondness for titles—a fondness for titles pure and simple, regardless of whether they are genuine or pinchbeck. We forget that whatever a Southerner likes the rest of the human race likes, and that there is no law of predilection lodged in one people that is absent from another people. There is no variety in the human race. We are all children, all children of the one Adam, and we love toys.

"Does the Race of Man Love a Lord?"
The $30,000 Bequest, Etc., p. 282

VEGETABLE   *See* INSPIRATION, TRAINING, SAGE-BRUSH

VENGEANCE   *See* GOD

VERSE   *See* MIND

VICE

. . . you people who have no petty vices are never known to give away a cent . . .

Now, I don't approve of dissipation, and I don't indulge in it, either; but I haven't a particle of confidence in a man who has no redeeming petty vices.

"Answers to Correspondents,"
Sketches New and Old, p. 82

I used to vex myself with reforms, every now and then. And I never had occasion to regret these divergencies, for, whether the resulting deprivations were long or short, the rewarding pleasure which I got out of the vice when I returned to it always paid me for all that it cost.

Mark Twain's Autobiography, Paine, II, p. 102

VIGILANCE *See* SUPREMACY

VIRGIN *See* SIMILES

VIRGINIA *See* MEDICINE

VIRTUE *See also* LAW

I don't claim to have all the virtues—only nine or ten of them.

> "Osteopathy,"
> *Mark Twain's Speeches* (1923), p. 234

Be virtuous and you will be eccentric.

> "Mental Photographs,"
> *A Curious Dream,* p. 85

M. de L.'s new French dictionary just issued in Paris defines virtue as "A woman who has only one lover and don't steal."

> *A Bibliography of Mark Twain,* Merle Johnson, p. 178

None of us can have as many virtues as the fountain-pen, or half its cussedness; but we can try.

> "Pudd'nhead Wilson's New Calendar,"
> *Following the Equator,* II, Chapt. XXXII, p. 379

[The Nicaraguan damsels]: They are virtuous according to their lights, but I guess their lights are a little dim.

> *Mark Twain's Travels with Mr. Brown,* p. 41

Several Americans, long resident in Constantinople, contend that most Turks are pretty trustworthy, but few claim that the Greeks have any virtues that a man can discover—at least without a fire assay.

> *The Innocents Abroad,* II, Chapt. VII, p. 94

We stopped at the village of Bethany, an hour out from Jerusalem. They showed us the tomb of Lazarus. I had rather live in it than in any house in the town. And they showed us also a large "Fountain of Lazarus," and in the center of the village the ancient dwelling of Lazarus. Lazarus appears to have been a man of property. The legends of the Sunday-schools do him great injustice; they give one the impression that he was poor. It is because they get him confused with that Lazarus who had no merit but his virtue, and virtue never has been as respectable as money.

Ibid., II, Chapt. XXVIII, p. 368

[The moral of *The Man That Corrupted Hadleyburg*]: The weakest of all weak things is a virtue that has not been tested in the fire.

Mark Twain, Henderson, p. 192

VISIT

The mood to write always attacks me when some mentally dead people bring their corpses with them for a long visit.

My Father • Mark Twain, Clara Clemens, p. 42

VOCABULARY *See also* WORDS

. . . these archaics are a little *too* simple; the vocabulary is too limited, and so, by consequence, descriptions suffer in the matter of variety; they run too much to level Saharas of fact, and not enough to picturesque detail; this throws about them a certain air of the monotonous.

A Connecticut Yankee in King Arthur's Court,
Chapt. XV, p. 117

Reading German books shows in what a narrow groove of vocabulary authors travel—they use the same words all the time. Read a book of one and you can fluently read his others. Take up a book by another author and you have got to go for the dictionary. His vocabulary is all different.

Mark Twain's Notebook, p. 148

VOICE

Lord—there's nothing like the human organ to make words live and throb, and lift the hearer to the full altitudes of their meaning.

Mark Twain-Howells Letters, I, p. 279

He had a honey kind of voice—it would persuade a cast-iron dog to come down off a doorstep and lick his hand.

"A Curious Experience,"
The American Claimant, Etc., p. 271

His voice was the effortless deep bass of a church organ, and would disturb the tranquillity of a gas flame fifty yards away.

Ibid., Chapt. XVI, p. 136

. . . you know what a honey kind of a voice he's got when he talks; you know how it would persuade a cast-iron dog to come down off of a doorstep and lick his hand. Now if you'll take my word for it, sir, it ain't a circumstance to his singin'! Flute music is harsh to that boy's singin'! Oh, he just gurgles it out so soft and sweet and low, there in the dark, that it makes you think you are in heaven. . . . I don't care *what* he sings, it goes plum straight home to you —it goes deep down to where you *live*—and it fetches you every time!

"A Curious Experience," *Ibid.*, p. 271

George's voice was just "turning," and when he was singing a dismal sort of bass, it was apt to fly off the handle and startle everybody with a most discordant cackle on the upper notes. George didn't know the tunes, either, which was also a drawback to his performances. I said:

"Come, now, George *don't* improvise. It looks too egotistical. It will provoke remark. Just stick to 'Coronation,' like the others. It is a good tune—*you* can't improve it any, just off-hand, in this way."

"Why, I'm not trying to improve it—and I *am* singing like the others—just as it is in the notes."

And he honestly thought he was, too; and so he had no one to blame but himself when his voice caught on the center occasionally, and gave him the lockjaw.

The Innocents Abroad, I, Chapt. IV, p. 75

In the afternoon the ship's company assembled aft, on deck, under the awnings; the flute, the asthmatic melodeon, and the consumptive clarinet, crippled the Star Spangled Banner, the choir chased it to cover, and George came in with a peculiarly lacerating screech on the final note and slaughtered it. Nobody mourned.

Ibid., I, Chapt. X, p. 133

VOLCANO

With its streams of liquid and gorgeously brilliant fire, it looked like a colossal railroad map of the State of Massachusetts done in chain lightning on a midnight sky.

Roughing It, II, Chapt. XXXIII, p. 298

[The volcano of Kilauea]: Now and then the surging bosom of the [crater] lake . . . would calm down ominously and seem to be gathering strength for an enterprise; and then all of a sudden a red dome of lava of the bulk of an ordinary dwelling would heave itself aloft like an escaping balloon, then burst asunder, and out of its heart would flit a pale-green film of vapor, and float upward and vanish in the darkness—a released soul soaring homeward from captivity with the damned, no doubt.

Ibid., II, Chapt. XXXIV, p. 305

[In the crater bottom of Kilauea]: . . . we were surrounded with beds of rotten lava through which we could easily break and plunge down a thousand feet. I thought eight hundred would answer for me.

Ibid., II, Chapt. XXXIV, p. 303

I have seen Vesuvius since, but it was a mere toy, a child's volcano, a soup-kettle, compared to this [Kilauea].

Ibid., II, Chapt. XXXIII, p. 295

. . . we rested our elbows on the railing in front and looked abroad over the wide crater, and down over the sheer precipice at the seething fires beneath us. . . . I turned to see the effect on the balance of the company, and found the reddest-faced set of men I almost ever saw. In the strong light every countenance glowed like red-hot iron, every shoulder was suffued with crimson and shaded rearward into dingy shapeless obscurity! The place below looked like the infernal regions and these men like half-cooled devils just come up on a furlough.

Ibid., II, Chapt. XXXIII, p. 297

VOTING *See also* POLITICS

No party holds the privilege of dictating to me how I shall vote. If loyalty to party is a form of patriotism, I am no patriot. If there is any valuable difference between a monarchist and an American, it lies in the theory that the American can decide for himself what is patriotic and what isn't. I claim that difference. I am the only person in the sixty millions that is privileged to dictate my patriotism. [1884]

> *Mark Twain, a Biography,* Paine, II, p. 779

Vote: The only commodity that is peddleable without a license.

> *More Maxims of Mark,* p. 13

In our country it is always our first care to see that our people have the opportunity of voting for their choice of men to represent and govern them—we do not permit our great officials to appoint the little officials. We prefer to have so tremendous a power as that in our own hands. We hold it safest to elect our judges and everybody else. In our cities, the ward meetings elect delegates to the nominating conventions and instruct them whom to nominate. The publicans and their retainers rule the ward meetings (for everybody else hates the worry of politics and stays at home); the delegates from the ward meetings organize as a nominating convention and make up a list of candidates—one convention offering a democratic and another a republican list of—incorruptibles; and then the great meek public come forward at the proper time and make unhampered choice and bless Heaven that they live in a free land where no form of despotism can ever intrude.

> *The Gilded Age,* II, Chapt. II, p. 23

VOYAGE *See also* INTELLECT, SEA

There is no unhappiness like the misery of sighting land (and work) again after a cheerful, careless voyage.

> *Letters to Will Bowen,* p. 15

VULGARITY *See* REFINEMENT

W

WAGES

A man who hasn't had much experience, and doesn't think, is apt to measure a nation's prosperity or lack of prosperity by the mere size of the prevailing wages; if the wages be high, the nation is prosperous; if low, it isn't. Which is an error. It isn't what sum you get, it's how much you can buy with it, that's the important thing; and it's that that tells whether your wages are high in fact or only high in name.

A Connecticut Yankee in King Arthur's Court,
Chapt. XXXI, p. 279

There are written laws—they perish; but there are also unwritten laws—*they* are eternal. Take the unwritten law of wages; it says they've got to advance, little by little, straight through the centuries.

Ibid., Chapt. XXXIII, p. 301

WALK *See* TALK

WALL

[At Onteora]: The partitions of the houses were so thin we could hear the women occupants of adjoining rooms changing their minds.

Remembered Yesterdays, Robert U. Johnson, p. 324

WALL STREET

If you live in the country, buy at 80, sell at 40. Avoid all forms of eccentricity.

Mark Twain, a Biography, Paine, II, p. 706

WALLACE, ALFRED RUSSEL   *See also* UNIVERSE

Discussing Wallace's book, *Man's Place in the Universe:*
Such is the history of organic evolution. Man has been here 32,000 years. That it took a hundred million years to prepare the world for him is proof that that is what it was done for. I suppose it is. I dunno. If the Eiffel tower were now representing the world's age, the skin of paint on the pinnacle-knob at its summit would represent man's share of that age; and anybody would perceive that that skin was what the tower was built for. I reckon they would. I dunno.

Mark Twain-Howells Letters, II, p. 777

WANT

Now, look here, old friend, I know the human race; and I know that when a man comes to Washington, I don't care if it's from Heaven, it's because he *wants* something.

Source undetermined at date of publication

The cayote is a living, breathing allegory of Want. He is *always* hungry. He is always poor, out of luck and friendless.

Roughing It, I, Chapt. V, p. 48

[Quoted by Mark Twain from McClintock's *The Enemy Conquered; or, Love Triumphant*]:

The perfection of wisdom, and the end of true philosophy is to proportion our wants to our possessions, our ambitions to our capacities; we will then be a happy and a virtuous people.

"The Enemy Conquered; or, Love Triumphant,"
The American Claimant, Etc., p. 456

WAR   *See also* ENGLAND, FREEDOM, NATURE, PEACE, STATESMANSHIP

My ancestors came of patriotic stock . . . In the War of the Revolution, they were at the massacre of Bunker Hill. They were not persons to stand fooling around when a massacre was going on! One of them was wounded! He drove a baggage-wagon. He was kicked by a mule.

"Mark Twain as a Lecturer," W. H. Merrill,
Harper's Weekly, Feb. 10, 1906

[The Spanish American War, 1898]: It is a worthy thing to fight for one's freedom; it is another sight finer to fight for another man's. And I think this is the first time it has been done.

Mark Twain's Letters, II, p. 663

[The Boer War, 1900]: I notice that God is on both sides in this war; thus history repeats itself. But I am the only person who has noticed this; everybody here thinks He is playing the game for this side, and for this side only.

Ibid., II, p. 694

It was a time of great and exalting excitement. The country was up in arms, the war was on, in every breast burned the holy fire of patriotism . . .

Sunday morning came—next day the battalions would leave for the front; the church was filled . . .

Then came the "long" prayer. None could remember the like of it for passionate pleading and moving and beautiful language. The burden of its supplication was, that an ever-merciful and benignant Father of us all would watch over our noble young soldiers, and aid, comfort, and encourage them in their patriotic work; bless them, shield them in the day of battle . . .

An aged stranger entered and moved with slow and noiseless step up the main aisle, his eyes fixed upon the minister. . . . With all eyes following him and wondering, he made his silent way; without pausing, he ascended to the preacher's side and stood there, waiting . . . then in a deep voice he said:

"I come from the Throne—bearing a message from Almighty God!" The words smote the house with a shock . . .

"He has heard the prayer of His servant your shepherd, and will grant it if such shall be your desire after I, His messenger, shall have explained to you its import—that is to say, its full import. For it is like unto many of the prayers of men, in that it asks for more than he who utters it is aware of—except he pause and think.

"You have heard your servant's prayer—the uttered part of it. I am commissioned of God to put into words the other part of it—that part which the pastor—and also you in your hearts—fervently prayed silently . . .

"When you have prayed for victory you have prayed for many unmentioned results which follow victory—*must* follow it, cannot help but follow it. Upon the listening spirit of God the Father fell also the unspoken part of the prayer. He commandeth me to put it into words. Listen!

"O Lord our Father, our young patriots, idols of our hearts, go forth to battle—be Thou near them! With them—in spirit—we also go forth from the sweet peace of our beloved firesides to smite the foe. O Lord our God, help us to tear their soldiers to bloody shreds with our shells; help us to cover their smiling fields with the pale forms of their patriot dead; help us to drown the thunder of the guns with the shrieks of their wounded, writhing in pain; help us to lay waste their humble homes with a hurricane of fire; help us to wring the hearts of their unoffending widows with unavailing grief; help us to turn them out roofless with their little children to wander unfriended the wastes of their desolated land in rags and hunger and thirst, sports of the sun flames of summer and the icy winds of winter, broken in spirit, worn with travail, imploring Thee for the refuge of the grave and denied it—for our sakes who adore Thee, Lord, blast their hopes, blight their lives, protract their bitter pilgrimage, make heavy their steps, water their way with their tears, stain the white snow with the blood of their wounded feet! We ask it, in the spirit of love, of Him Who is the Source of Love, and Who is the ever-faithful refuge and friend of all that are sore beset and seek His aid with humble and contrite hearts. Amen."

(After a pause.) "Ye have prayed it; if ye still desire it, speak! The messenger of the Most High waits . . ."

"The War Prayer,"
Europe and Elsewhere, p. 394

. . . the idea is that these formidable new war-inventions will make war impossible by and by—but I doubt it. Man was created a bloody animal and I think he will always thirst for blood and will manage to have it. I think he is far and away the worst animal that exists; and the only untamable one.

My Father • *Mark Twain,* Clara Clemens, p. 264

As a military man, I wish to point out what seems to me to be military errors in the conduct of the campaign which we have just been considering [The Boer War]. I have seen active service in the field, and it was in the actualities of war that I acquired my training and my right to speak. I served two weeks in the beginning of our Civil war, and during all that time commanded a battery of infantry composed of twelve men. General Grant knew the history of my campaign, for I told it to him. I also told him the principle upon which I had conducted it; which was, to tire the enemy. I tired out and disqualified many battalions, yet never had a casualty myself nor lost a man. General Grant was not given to paying compliments, yet he said frankly that if I had conducted the whole war much bloodshed would have been spared, and that what the army might have lost through the inspiriting results of collision in the field would have been amply made up by the liberalizing influences of travel. Further endorsement does not seem to me to be necessary.

Following the Equator, II, Chapt. XXXI, p. 373

There has never been a just [war], never an honorable one—on the part of the instigator of the war. I can see a million years ahead, and this rule will never change in so many as half a dozen instances. The loud little handful—as usual—will shout for the war. The pulpit will—warily and cautiously—object—at first; the great, big, dull bulk of the nation will rub its sleepy eyes and try to make out why there should be a war, and will say, earnestly and indignantly, "It is unjust and dishonorable, and there is no necessity for it." Then the handful will shout louder. A few fair men on the other side will argue and reason against the war with speech and pen, and at first will have a hearing and be applauded; but it will not last long; those others will outshout them, and presently the anti-war audiences will thin out and lose popularity. Before long you will see this curious thing: the speakers stoned from the platform, and free speech strangled by hordes of furious men who in their secret hearts are still at one with those stoned speakers —as earlier—but do not dare to say so. And now the whole nation—pulpit and all—will take up the war-cry, and shout itself hoarse, and mob any honest man who ventures to open his mouth; and presently such mouths will cease to open. Next the statesmen will invent cheap lies, putting the blame upon the nation that is attacked, and every man will be glad of those conscience-soothing falsities, and will diligently study them, and refuse to examine any refutations of them; and thus he will by and by convince himself that the war is just, and will thank God for the better sleep he enjoys after this process of grotesque self-deception.

The Mysterious Stranger, Etc., Chapt. IX, p. 119

Peace by compulsion. That seems a better idea. . . . Peace by persuasion has a pleasant sound, but I think we should not be able to work it. We should have to tame the human race first, and history seems to show that that cannot be done. Can't we reduce the armaments little by little— on a pro rata basis—by concert of the powers? Can't we get four great powers to agree to reduce their strength 10 per cent a year and thrash the others into doing likewise?

Mark Twain's Letters, II, p. 672

. . . when I retired from the rebel army in '61 I retired upon Louisiana [Mo.] in good order; at least in good enough order for a person who had not yet learned how to retreat according to the rules of war, and had to trust to native genius. It seemed to me that for a first attempt at a retreat it was not badly done. I had done no advancing in all that campaign that was at all equal to it.

Life on the Mississippi, Chapt. LIII, p. 392

The Emperor sent his troops to the field with immense enthusiasm. He will lead them in person when they return.

"The European War,"

The Curious Republic of Gondour, p. 122

Grant remembered "Squibob" Derby (John Phoenix) at West Point very well. He said that Derby was always drawing caricatures of the professors and playing jokes on everybody. He told [this]: A professor questioning a class concerning certain particulars of a possible siege said, "Suppose a thousand men are besieging a fortress whose equipment of provisions is so-and-so; it is a military axiom that at the end of forty-five days the fort will surrender. Now, young men, if any of you were in command of such a fortress, how would you proceed?"

Derby held up his hand in token that he had an answer for that question. He said, "I would march out, let the enemy in, and at the end of forty-five days I would change places with him."

Mark Twain, a Biography, Paine, II, p. 712

WARD, ARTEMUS

Artemus looked like a glove-stretcher, his hair, red and brushed forward, reminded me of a divided flame. His nose rambled aggressively before his face with all the determination of a cow-catcher, while his red mustache, to follow out the simile, seemed not unlike the unfortunate cow.

The Saga of the Comstock Lode, Lyman, p. 258

WARNER, CHARLES D. *See* INTERRUPTION, WEATHER

WASHINGTON, D.C. *See also* LAW, OFFICE, POLITICS, SENATOR, SIMILES, WANT

(WASHINGTON, D. C.)

There is something good and motherly about Washington, the grand old benevolent National Asylum for the Helpless.

The Gilded Age, I, Chapt. XXIV, p. 269

. . . you ought not to go into the [Capitol] dome . . . because it would be utterly impossible to go up there without seeing the frescoes in it—and why should you be interested in the delirium tremens of art?

Ibid., I, Chapt. XXIV, p. 264

WASHINGTON, GEORGE *See also* LIE, NEGRO

He was ignorant of the commonest accomplishments of youth. He could not even lie.

"A Biographical Sketch of George Washington,"
The Washoe Giant in San Francisco, p. 107

. . . the real point in that story . . . is not that George said to his father, "Yes, father, I cut down the cherry-tree; I can't tell a lie," but that the little boy—only seven years old—should have his sagacity developed under such circumstances. He was a boy wise beyond his years. His conduct then was a prophecy of later years. Yes, I think he was the most remarkable man the country ever produced—up to my time, anyway.

Now then, little George realized that circumstantial evidence was against him. He knew that his father would know from the size of the chips that no full-grown hatchet cut that tree down, and that no man would have haggled it so. He knew that his father would send around the plantation and inquire for a small boy with a hatchet, and he had the wisdom to come out and confess it. Now, the idea that his father was overjoyed when he told little George that he would rather have him cut down a thousand cherry-trees than tell a lie is all nonsense. What did he really mean? Why, that he was absolutely astonished that he had a son who had the chance to tell a lie and didn't.

I admire old George—if that was his name—for his discernment. He knew when he said that his son couldn't lie that he was stretching it a good deal. . . . The way the old George Washington story goes down it doesn't do anybody any good. It only discourages people who can tell a lie.

"On Poetry, Veracity, Suicide,"
Mark Twain's Speeches (1910), p. 349

Did Washington's great value, then, lie in what he accomplished? No; that was only a minor value. His major value, his vast value, his immeasurable value to us and to the world and to future ages and peoples, lies in his permanent and sky-reaching conspicuousness as an *influence*.

"In Defense of General Funston,"
The North American Review, May 1902, p. 615

That George could refrain from telling the lie is not the remarkable feature, but that he could do it off-hand, that way.

More Maxims of Mark, p. 13

WATCH *See also* CLOCK

. . . the tedious hours did lag and drag and limp along with such cruel deliberation! It was so trying to give one's watch a good long undisturbed spell and then take it out and find that it had been fooling away the time and not trying to get ahead any!

Roughing It, I, Chapt. XVIII, p. 152

[The less a man could see a joke, the more determined was Mark Twain to joke with him.] One day he carried a very cheap, worthless watch to be repaired by [a] solemn little man [the watchmaker]:

"I am going to ask you to be particularly careful of this watch because it is a valuable one. The most valuable one I possess."

The watchmaker retorted in a half-hurt manner: "How can you say such a thing? The watch is not at all valuable. It is no good."

"But I gave six francs for it in Paris."

"Still, it is a cheap watch."

The little man remained doggedly serious and Mark Twain had to retreat.

> *My Father • Mark Twain,* Clara Clemens, p. 186

When your watch gets out of order you have the choice of two things to do: throw it in the fire or take it to the watch-tinker. The former is the quickest.

> "Pudd'nhead Wilson's New Calendar,"
> *Following the Equator,* II, Chapt. XXVIII, p. 329

My uncle William (now deceased, alas!) used to say that a good horse was a good horse until it had run away once, and that a good watch was a good watch until the repairers got a chance at it.

> "My Watch,"
> *Sketches New and Old,* p. 15

In a minor tournament I won the prize, which was a Waterbury watch. I put it in my trunk. In Pretoria, South Africa, nine months afterward, my proper watch broke down and I took the Waterbury out, wound it, set it by the great clock on the Parliament House (8.05), then went back to my room and went to bed, tired from a long railway journey. The parliamentary clock had a peculiarity which I was not aware of at the time—a peculiarity which exists in no other clock, and would not exist in that one if it had been made by a sane person; on the half-hour it strikes the succeeding *hour,* then strikes the hour *again* at the proper time. I lay reading and smoking awhile; then, when I could hold my eyes open no longer and was about to put out the light, the great clock began to boom, and I counted—ten. I reached for the Waterbury to see how it was getting along. It was marking 9.30. It seemed rather poor speed for a three-dollar watch, but I supposed that the climate was affecting it. I shoved it half an hour ahead, and took to my book and waited to see what would happen. At 10 the great clock struck ten *again.* I looked—the Waterbury was marking half-past ten. This was too much speed for the money, and it troubled me. I pushed the hands back a half hour, and waited once more; I had to, for I was vexed and restless now, and my sleepiness was gone.

By and by the great clock struck 11. The Waterbury was marking 10.30. I pushed it ahead half an hour, with some show of temper. By and by the great clock struck 11 again. The Waterbury showed up 11.30, now, and I beat her brains out against the bedstead. I was sorry next day, when I found out.

Following the Equator, I, Chapt. IV, p. 66

Young Mr. Blucher, who is from the Far West, and is on his first voyage, was a good deal worried by the constantly changing "ship time." He was proud of his new watch at first, and used to drag it out promptly when eight bells struck at noon, but he came to look after a while as if he were losing confidence in it. Seven days out from New York he came on deck, and said with great decision:

"This thing's a swindle!"

"What's a swindle?"

"Why, this watch. I bought her out in Illinois—gave $150 for her—and I thought she was good. And, by George, she *is* good on shore, but somehow she don't keep up her lick here on water—gets seasick, maybe. She skips; she runs along regular enough till half-past eleven, and then, all of a sudden, she lets down. I've set that old regulator up faster and faster, till I've shoved it clear around, but it don't do any good; she just distances every watch in the ship, and clatters along in a way that's astonishing till it is noon, but them eight bells always gets in about ten minutes ahead of her, anyway. I don't know what to do with her now. She's doing all she can—she's going her best gait, but it won't save her . . ."

The ship was gaining a full hour every three days, and this fellow was trying to make his watch go fast enough to keep up to her. . . . We sent him to the captain, and he explained to him the mystery of "ship time," and set his troubled mind at rest.

The Innocents Abroad, I, Chapt. V, p. 78

WATER *See also* BOOK, FISH, GOD, MISERY, MOTHER, POLITICS, PRIVILEGE

Ed said the muddy Mississippi water was wholesomer to drink than the clear water of the Ohio. He said if you let a pint of this yaller Mississippi water settle, you would have about a half . . . inch of mud in the bottom . . . and then it warn't no better than Ohio water—what you wanted to do was to keep it stirred up. . . . he said there was nutritiousness in the mud, and a man that drunk Mississippi water could grow corn in his stomach if he wanted to. . . . He says, "You look at the graveyards; that tells the tale. Trees won't grow worth shucks in a Cincinnati graveyard, but in a St. Louis graveyard they grow upwards of eight hundred foot high. It's all on account of the water the people drunk before they laid up. A Cincinnati corpse don't richen a soil any."

Life on the Mississippi, Chapt. II, p. 35

In Europe everywhere except in the mountains, the water is flat and insipid beyond the power of words to describe. . . . It is only good to wash with; I wonder it doesn't occur to the average inhabitant to try it for that.

A Tramp Abroad, II, Chapt. XVII, p. 220

I went to the chemist's on the corner, as per instructions, and asked for a glass of Challe water. It comes from a spring sixteen miles from here. It was furnished to me, but, perceiving that there was something the matter with it, I offered to wait till they could get some that was fresh, but they said it always smelled that way. They said that the reason that this was so much ranker than the sulphur water of the bath was that this contained thirty-two times as much sulphur as that. It is true, but in my opinion that water comes from a cemetery, and not a fresh cemetery, either. History says that one of the early Roman generals lost an army down there somewhere. If he could come back now I think this water would help him find it again. However, I drank the Challe, and have drunk it once or twice every day since. I suppose it is all right, but I wish I knew what was the matter with those Romans.

"Aix, the Paradise of Rheumatics,"
Europe and Elsewhere, p. 109

654

Europeans say ice-water impairs digestion. How do they know?—they never drink any.

     A Tramp Abroad, I, Chapt. XXVIII, p. 298

[Mono Lake] is two hundred feet deep, and its sluggish waters are so strong with alkali that if you only dip the most hopelessly soiled garment into them once or twice, and wring it out, it will be found as clean as if it had been through the ablest of washerwomen's hands. . . . If we threw the water on our heads and gave them a rub or so, the white lather would pile up three inches high. This water is not good for bruised places and abrasions of the skin. We had a valuable dog. He had raw places on him. He had more raw places on him than sound ones. He was the rawest dog I almost ever saw. He jumped overboard one day to get away from the flies. But it was bad judgment. In his condition, it would have been just as comfortable to jump into the fire. The alkali water nipped him in all the raw places simultaneously, and he struck out for the shore with considerable interest. He yelped and barked and howled as he went—and by the time he got to the shore there was no bark to him—for he had barked the bark all out of his inside, and the alkali water had cleaned the bark all off his outside, and he probably wished he had never embarked in any such enterprise. He ran around and round in a circle, and pawed the earth and clawed the air, and threw double somersaults, sometimes backward and sometimes forward, in the most extraordinary manner. He was not a demonstrative dog, as a general thing, but rather of a grave and serious turn of mind, and I never saw him take so much interest in anything before. He finally struck out over the mountains, at a gait which we estimated at about two hundred and fifty miles an hour, and he is going yet.

     Roughing It, I, Chapt. XXXVIII, p. 294

[At Aix]: The springs, the healing waters that gush up from under this hillside village, indeed are ancient. . . . They furnished a million gallons a day to wash the lake dwellers with, the same to wash the Caesars with, no less to wash Balzac with, and have not diminished on my

account.
> "Aix, the Paradise of Rheumatics,"
> *Europe and Elsewhere,* p. 98

Water taken in moderation cannot hurt anybody.
> *Mark Twain's Notebook,* p. 13

[Jim's opinion of a "myridge" (mirage)]: I tell you, sah, when three sees a thing, drunk or sober, it's *so.*
> *Tom Sawyer Abroad, Etc.,* Chapt. VIII, p. 77

[In the dining room of a Pacific steamship during a heavy sea]: The attentive waiters kept bringing water to Brown, who was always talking, and would not see the glass set down in time to make his remark heard: "Frank, don't bring me any water; have to drink it at a gulp to keep it from spilling, and I've had more'n enough already." And yet about once every two minutes some passenger opposite would put up his hands and shrink behind them and exclaim, "Your water, Mr. Brown! your water! Look out for your water!" and lo, the suffering Brown would find his glass once more replenished and canting dangerously to leeward. It would be instantly seized and emptied. At the end of a quarter of an hour Brown had accomplished nothing in the way of dinner, on account of these incessant watery interruptions. The boy Frank brought another glass of water, and said, "Will you have some beefsteak, Mr. Brown?" "Take that water and go to blazes with it! Beefsteak! *no!* I've drank eleven gallons of water in fifteen minutes, and there ain't room enough in me for a sirloin steak off'm a sand-fly!"
> *Letters from the Sandwich Islands,* p. 4

[Mark Twain's mother]: "People born to be hanged are safe in water."
> *Mark Twain, a Biography,* Paine, I, p. 35

I have no recollection of seeing a solitary gin-mill in a depot-building from St. Louis to New York. . . . At Cincinnati there were 250,000 people moderately drunk, but that was an accident. At a great fire, a large number of barrels of whiskey had been bursted open, and the stuff ran down to the river, got into an eddy, was pumped into the water-works and was distributed throughout the city in the form of weak whiskey punches. It was said that there was more water drank in Cincinnati that day than was ever drank there in one day before. It is likely.

"Progress and Prosperity,"
Mark Twain's Travels with Mr. Brown, p. 156

WATERMELON *See also* EVE, FARM, STEALING

It was during my first year's apprenticeship in the *Courier* office that I did a thing which I have been trying to regret for fifty-five years. It was a summer afternoon and just the kind of weather that a boy prizes for river excursions and other frolics, but I was a prisoner. The others were all gone holidaying, I was alone and sad. I had committed a crime of some sort and this was the punishment. I must lose my holiday, and spend the afternoon in solitude besides. I had the printing-office all to myself, there in the third story. I had one comfort, and it was a generous one while it lasted. It was the half of a long and broad watermelon, fresh and red and ripe. I gouged it out with a knife, and I found accommodation for the whole of it in my person—though it did crowd me until the juice ran out of my ears. There remained then the shell, the hollow shell. It was big enough to do duty as a cradle. I didn't want to waste it, and I couldn't think of anything to do with it which could afford entertainment. I was sitting at the open window which looked out upon the sidewalk of the main street three stories below, when it occurred to me to drop it on somebody's head. I doubted the judiciousness of this, and I had some compunctions about it, too, because so much of the resulting entertainment would fall to my share and so little to the other person. But I thought I would chance it. I watched out of the window for the right person to come along—the safe person—but he didn't come. Every time there was a candidate he or she turned out to be an unsafe one, and I had to restrain myself. But at last I saw the right one coming. It was my brother Henry. He was the best boy in the whole region. He never did harm to anybody, he never offended anybody. He was exasperatingly good. He had an overflowing abundance of goodness—but not enough to save him this time. I watched his approach with eager interest. He came strolling along, dreaming his pleasant summer dream and not doubting but that Providence had him in His care. If he had known where I was he would have had less confidence in that superstition. As he approached his form became more and more foreshortened. When he was almost under me he was so foreshortened that nothing of him was visible from my high place except the end of his nose and his alternately approaching feet. Then I poised the watermelon, calculated my distance, and let it go, hollow side down. The accuracy of that gunnery was beyond admiration. He had about six steps to make when I let that canoe go, and it was lovely to see those two bodies gradually closing in on each other. If he had had seven steps to make, or five steps to make, my gunnery would have been a failure. But he had exactly the right number to make, and that shell smashed down right on the top of his head and drove him into the earth up to the chin, the chunks of that broken melon flying in every direction like a spray. I wanted to go down there and condole with him, but it would not have been safe. He would have suspected me at once. I expected him to suspect me, anyway, but as he said nothing about this adventure for two or three days—I was watching him in the meantime in order to keep out of danger—I was deceived into believing that this time he didn't suspect me. It was a mistake. He was only waiting for a sure opportunity. Then he landed a cobblestone on the side of my head which raised a bump there so large that I had to wear two hats for a time.

Mark Twain's Autobiography, Paine, II, p. 282

WEAKNESS *See also* SOUL

. . . man's most universal weakness [is] lying.

Mark Twain and I, Opie Read, p. 34

. . . the man who had it in him to espouse the quarrel

of the weak out of inborn nobility of spirit was no mean timber whereof to construct a Christian.

Roughing It, II, Chapt. VI, p. 70

[The moral of *The Man That Corrupted Hadleyburg*]: The weakest of all weak things is a virtue which has not been tested in the fire.

Mark Twain, Henderson, p. 192

WEALTH *See* POVERTY, RICHES

WEAPON *See* DUELING, GUN, SEASON, STUPIDITY, WAR

WEATHER *See also* CLIMATE, COLD, HEAT, TEMPERATURE

[Robert Underwood Johnson, one-time editor of *The Century Magazine,* and a stickler for exactness, gives reliable evidence that Twain uttered the weather epigram]:

We all grumble about the weather—but—nothing is done about it.

Remembered Yesterdays, Robert U. Johnson, p. 322

[Those who claim Charles Dudley Warner authored the famous remark can point merely to an editorial in the *Hartford Courant,* Aug. 24, 1897, p. 8, which reads]:

"A well known American writer said once that, while everybody talked about the weather, nobody seemed to do anything about it."

[The quotation is too Twainesque in style to be considered that of Warner or any other writer].

The weather—consider the weather. The "sentiment" would be profane, so is withheld.

Holograph, Dec. 3, 1886

It is best to read the weather forecast before we pray for rain.

More Maxims of Mark, p. 8

He was so little interested—just as when people speak of the weather—that he did not notice whether I made him any answer or not.

"A Word of Explanation"
A Connecticut Yankee in King Arthur's Court, p. 11

Shut the door. Not that it lets in the cold but that it lets out the cozyness.

Mark Twain's Notebook, p. 346

When a person is accustomed to one hundred and thirty-eight in the shade, his ideas about cold weather are not valuable.

Following the Equator, II, Chapt. XVIII, p. 223

. . . in this hot weather . . . the only beverage in the ship that is passable, is the butter.

The Innocents Abroad, II, Chapt. IV, p. 57

I believe that in India "cold weather" is merely a conventional phrase and has come into use through the necessity of having some way to distinguish between weather which will melt a brass doorknob and weather which will only make it mushy.

Following the Equator, II, Chapt. XVIII, p. 223

We watched the weather all through that awful night and kept an eye on the barometer, to be prepared for the least change. There was not the slightest change recorded by the instrument, during the whole time. Words cannot describe the comfort that that friendly, hopeful, steadfast thing was to me in that season of trouble. It was a defective barometer, and had no hand but the stationary brass pointer, but I did not know that until afterward. If I should be in such a situation again, I should not wish for any barometer but that one.

A Tramp Abroad, II, Chapt. VIII, p. 115

In Arkansas they have a winter; in Sydney [Australia] they have the name of it, but not the thing itself. . . . In the matter of summer weather Arkansas has no advantage over Sydney, perhaps, but when it comes to winter weather, that is another affair. You could cut up an Arkansas winter into a hundred Sydney winters and have enough left for Arkansas and the poor.

Following the Equator, I, Chapt. IX, p. 114

I reverently believe that the Maker who made us all makes everything in New England but the weather. I don't know who makes that, but I think it must be raw apprentices in the weather-clerk's factory who experiment and learn how, in New England, for board and clothes, and then are promoted to make weather for countries that require a good article, and will take their custom elsewhere if they don't get it. There is a sumptuous variety about the New England weather that compels the stranger's admiration—and regret. The weather is always doing something there; always attending strictly to business; always getting up new designs and trying them on the people to see how they will go. . . .

. . . Yes, one of the brightest gems in the New England weather is the dazzling uncertainty of it. There is only one thing certain about it: you are certain there is going to be plenty of it. . . .

The lightning there is peculiar; it is so convincing, that when it strikes a thing it doesn't leave enough of that thing behind for you to tell whether— Well, you'd think it was something valuable, and a Congressman had been there. And the thunder. When the thunder begins to merely tune up and scrape and saw, and key up the instruments for the performance, strangers say, "Why, what awful thunder you have here!" But when the baton is raised and the real concert begins, you'll find that stranger down in the cellar with his head in the ash-barrel.

> "Speech on the Weather"
> *Mark Twain's Speeches* (1923), p. 53

. . . we were good Presbyterian boys when the weather was doubtful; when it was fair we did wander a little from the fold.

> "Sixty-Seventh Birthday"
> *Ibid.*, (1923), p. 251

. . . even the dead can't travel in such weather, without spoiling.

> *Mark Twain, Business Man*—Webster, p. 385

The rain is famous for falling on the just and unjust alike, but if I had the management of such affairs I would rain softly and sweetly on the just, but if I caught a sample of the unjust out doors I would drown him.

My Father • *Mark Twain*—Clara Clemens, p. 276

. . . it's been mighty nasty particler cold—a considerable sight colder'n coffee at the seckond table.

Adventures of Thomas Jefferson Snodgrass, p. 37

[In San Francisco]: When you want to go visiting, or attend church, or the theater, you never look up at the clouds to see whether it is likely to rain or not—you look at the almanac. If it is winter, it will *rain*—and if it is summer, it *won't* rain, and you cannot help it.

Roughing It, II, Chapt. XV, p. 151

WELSH *See* NAME

WEST, The *See* CALIFORNIA, INDIAN, MOUNTAIN, NEVADA, POETRY, PRIVILEGE, SPEED, STAGE-COACH, TRAVEL

WESTMINSTER ABBEY

The moonlight gave to the sacred place such an air of restfulness and peace that Westminster was no longer a grisly museum of moldering vanities, but her better and worthier self—the deathless mentor of a great nation, the guide and encourager of right ambitions, the preserver of just fame, and the home and refuge for the nation's best and bravest when their work is done.

"A Memorable Midnight Experience"
Europe and Elsewhere, p. 13

WEST POINT ACADEMY

Twain wrote his regret in not being able to attend a West Point Academy Festival:

Regret I can be with you only in spirit, not in body, but if I had my way, I'd prefer to be there in body with the spirit inside me—and plenty of it.

The Twainian, Feb. 1940, p. 1

WHALE *See* SMELL

WHEELER *See* EXAGGERATION

WIND *See* HAT

WINDOWS
There was no glass in the openings they believed to be windows. It is a little thing—glass is—until it is absent, then it becomes a big thing.
> *A Connecticut Yankee in King Arthur's Court,*
> Chapt. II, p. 56

WINE
Good wine needs no bush; a jug is the thing.
> *More Maxims of Mark,* p. 7

WINNING *See* WORK

WINTER *See* EYES

WISDOM *See also* BIBLE, CAT, EDUCATION, ERROR, EX-
  PERIENCE, HUMOR, KNOWLEDGE, LEARNING, MIND, NOISE,
  WANT, WIT
It is wiser to find out than to suppose.
> *More Maxims of Mark,* p. 8

[From a letter to Rev. Joseph Twichell]:
You taught me in my callow days, let me pay back the debt now in my old age out of a thesaurus with wisdom smelted from the golden ores of experience.
> *Mark Twain's Letters,* II, p. 767

We chase phantoms half the days of our lives. It is well if we learn wisdom even then, and save the other half.
> *Ibid.,* I, p. 150

A man never reaches that dizzy height of wisdom when he can no longer be led by the nose.
> *Mark Twain's Notebook,* p. 30

The Governor forgot that the wise man doesn't monkey with the buzz-saw.
> *Love Letters of Mark Twain,* p. 296

WIT *See also* HUMOR, JOKE, NIAGARA FALLS
Somebody has said "Wit is the sudden marriage of ideas

which before their union were not perceived to have any
relation."

Mark Twain's Notebook, p. 185

Wit and Humor—if any difference it is in duration—
lighting and electric light. Same material, apparently; but
one is vivid, brief, and can do damage—the other fools
along and enjoys elaboration.

Ibid., p. 187

Wit, by itself, is of little account. It becomes of moment
only when grounded on wisdom.

Abroad with Mark Twain and Eugene Field,
Fisher, p. 218

WITCH *See* BIBLE

WOMAN *See also* CIVILIZATION, FEAR, NEWSPAPER, RIVER,
SLANG

There is nothing comparable to the endurance of a
woman. In military life she would tire out an army of men,
either in camp or on the march.

Mark Twain's Autobiography, Paine, II, p. 116

So I loved her all the more, seeing she could be so cheerful when there wasn't anything to be cheerful about; for
I might soon need that kind of wife.

"The Million-Pound Bank-Note"
The American Claimant, Etc., p. 356

I am proud ... of being chosen to respond to this especial
toast to "The Ladies," or to woman, if you please, for that
is the preferable term, perhaps. It is certainly the older, and
therefore the more entitled to reverence.

I have noticed that the Bible, with that plain, blunt
honesty which is such a conspicuous characteristic of the
Scriptures, is always particular to never refer to even the
illustrious mother of all mankind as a "lady," but speaks of
her as a woman.

"The Ladies"
Mark Twain's Speeches (1923), p. 42

... women cannot receive even the most palpably judicious suggestion without arguing it; that is, married women.

> "Experience of the McWilliamses with
> Membraneous Croup"
> *Sketches New and Old,* p. 99

She sews on our buttons . . . gives us good advice, and plenty of it. . . . She bears our children—ours as a general thing.

> *Mark Twain to Mrs. Fairbanks,* p. 13

[The lecturer, Anna Dickinson]: She has got one defect, which you may notice in all women who make speeches: frequently, after she has got her audience wrought up ready to explode with enthusiasm, she does not spring her grand climax upon them at the precious instant, but drags toward it so slowly that by the time she reaches it they are nearly cooled down to a dignified self-possession again.

> "Miss Anna Dickinson"
> *Mark Twain's Travels with Mr. Brown,* p. 105

[He] skipped and dodged and scrambled around like a woman who has lost her mind on account of the arrival of a bat.

> *Personal Recollections of Joan of Arc,*
> II, Book II, Chapt. XXXVII, p. 81

[At Tiberias]: The young women wear their dower strung upon a strong wire that curves downward from the top of the head to the jaw—Turkish silver coins which they have raked together or inherited. Most of these maidens were wealthy, but some few had been very kindly dealt with by fortune. I saw heiresses there worth, in their own right —worth, well, I suppose I might venture to say, as much as nine dollars and a half. But such cases are rare. When you come across one of these, she naturally puts on airs. . . . Some people cannot stand prosperity.

> *The Innocents Abroad,* II, Chapt. XXI, p. 263

The women deserve a change of attitude . . . for they have wrought well. In forty-seven years they have swept an imposingly large number of unfair laws from the statute books of America. In that brief time these serfs have set them-

selves free—essentially. Men could not have done so much
for themselves in that time without bloodshed—at least they
never have; and that is argument that they didn't know
how. The women have accomplished a peaceful revolution,
and a very beneficent one; and yet that has not convinced
the average man that they are intelligent, and have courage
and energy and perseverance and fortitude.

It takes much to convince the average man of anything;
and perhaps nothing can ever make him realize that he is
the average woman's inferior—yet in several important details the evidence seems to show that that is what he is.
Man has ruled the human race from the beginning—but
he should remember that up to the middle of the present
century it was a dull world, and ignorant and stupid; but
it is not such a dull world now, and is growing less and
less dull all the time.

> *Following the Equator,* I, Chapt. XXXII, p. 315

I should like to see the time come when women shall
help to make the laws. I should like to see that whip-lash,
the ballot, in the hands of women. [1901]

> "Votes for Women"
> *Mark Twain's Speeches* (1923), p. 223

Our stay in Salt Lake City amounted to only two days,
and therefore we had no time to make the customary inquisition into the workings of polygamy and get up the
usual statistics and deductions preparatory to calling the
attention of the nation at large once more to the matter.
I had the will to do it. With the gushing self-sufficiency of
youth I was feverish to plunge in headlong and achieve a
great reform here—until I saw the Mormon women. Then
I was touched. My heart was wiser than my head. It
warmed toward these poor, ungainly, and pathetically
"homely" creatures, and as I turned to hide the generous
moisture in my eyes, I said, "No—the man that marries one
one of them has done an act of Christian charity which
entitles him to the kindly applause of mankind, not their
harsh censure—and the man that marries sixty of them has
done a deed of open-handed generosity so sublime that the

nations should stand uncovered in his presence and worship in silence." [1861]

Roughing It, I, Chapt. XIV, p. 121

WONDER

. . . when a thing is a wonder to us it is not because of what *we* see in it, but because of what *others* have seen in it. We get almost all our wonders at second hand. We are eager to see any celebrated thing—and we never fail of our reward; just the deep privilege of gazing upon an object which has stirred the enthusiasm or evoked the reverence or affection or admiration of multitudes of our race is a thing which we value . . . we would not part with the memory of that experience for a great price. And yet that very spectacle may be the *Taj*. You cannot keep your enthusiasms down, you cannot keep your emotions within bounds when that soaring bubble of marble breaks upon your view. But these are not *your* enthusiasms and emotions —they are the accumulated emotions and enthusiasms of a thousand fervid writers, who have been slowly and steadily storing them up in your heart day by day and year by year all your life; and now they burst out in a flood and overwhelm you; and you could not be a whit happier if they were your very own. By and by you sober down, and then you perceive that you have been drunk on the smell of somebody else's cork.

Following the Equator, II, Chapt. XVII, p. 203

WORDS *See also* DIPLOMAT, DRINK, GRAMMAR, LANGUAGE, SPELLING, TALK

Words realize nothing, vivify nothing to you, unless you have suffered in your own person the thing which the words try to describe.

A Connecticut Yankee in King Arthur's Court,
Chapt. XXVIII, p. 257

Gentle words and diplomacy—those are the tools to work with.

"Traveling with a Reformer"
Literary Essays, p. 99

I hurried off, boiling and surging with prodigious thoughts wombed in words of such majesty that each one of them was in itself a straggling procession of syllables that might be fifteen minutes passing a given point.

"Political Economy"
Sketches New and Old, p. 18

Gratitude? Lord, what do you want with words to express that? Words are only painted fire; a look is the fire itself.

A Connecticut Yankee in King Arthur's Court,
Chapt. XXXV, p. 329

Dyer can hunt quail or play seven-up as well as any man . . . but he can't *pronounce* worth a d—n; he used to worry along well enough, though, till he'd flush one of them rattlers with a clatter of syllables as long as a string of sluice-boxes, and then he'd lose his grip and throw up his hand. . . .

"An Unbiased Criticism"
Sketches of the Sixties, p. 159

I have been delighted to note your easy facility with your pen . . . [you have] style—good style—no barnacles on it in the way of unnecessary, retarding words. . . .

Mark Twain's Letters, II, p. 563

Ma says Axtele was above "suspition"—but I have searched through Webster's Unabridged, and can't find the word. However, it's of no consequence—I hope he got down safely.

Ibid., I, p. 68

He began to swell, and went on swelling . . . until he had reached the dimensions of a God of about the second or third degree. Then the fountains of his great deep were broken up, and for two or three minutes you couldn't see him for the rain. It was words, only words, but they fell so densely that they darkened the atmosphere.

Mark Twain in Eruption, p. 145

The right word may be effective, but no word was ever as effective as a rightly timed pause.

Introduction
Mark Twain's Speeches (1923), p. xv

A distinguished man should be as particular about his last words as he is about his last breath. . . . There is hardly a case on record where a man came to his last moment unprepared and said a good thing—hardly a case where a man trusted to that last moment and did not make a solemn botch of it and go out of the world feeling absurd.

. . .

I do wish our great men would quit saying these flat things just at the moment they die. Let us have their next-to-the-last words for a while, and see if we cannot patch up from them something that will be more satisfactory. . . .

. . .

What sort of tactics did Franklin pursue? He pondered over his last words for as much as two weeks, and then when the time came, he said, "None but the brave deserve the fair," and died happy. He could not have said a sweeter thing if he had lived till he was an idiot.

"Last Words of Great Men"
The Curious Republic of Gondour, p. 132

The German language . . . is a desperate language. . . . They hitch a cattle train of words together, and vestibule it, and because there isn't a break in it from one end to the other, they think that is concentration.

Mark Twain's Notebook, p. 219

The difference between the *almost right word* and the *right* word is really a large matter—'tis the difference between the lightning-bug and the lightning.

"The Art of Composition"
Life As I Find It, p. 228

You old scratch-gravel!

Mark Twain-Howells Letters, II, p. 768

Howells seems . . . almost always able to find that elusive and shifty grain of gold, the right word.

"William Dean Howells"
What is Man? and Other Essays, p. 229

An average English word is four letters and a half. By hard, honest labor I've dug all the large words out of my vocabulary and shaved it down till the average is three

669

letters and a half. . . . My page is worth eighty-four dollars to me. It takes exactly as long to fill your magazine pages with long words as it does with short ones . . . So I never write "metropolis" for seven cents, because I can get the same money for "city." I never write "policeman," because I can get the same price for "cop." . . . I never write "valetudinarian" at all, for not even hunger and wretchedness can humble me to the point where I will do a word like that for seven cents; I wouldn't do it for fifteen.

> "Spelling and Pictures"
> *Mark Twain's Speeches* (1923), p. 317

Things which are outside of our orbit—our own particular world—things which by our constitution and equipment we are unable to see, or feel, or otherwise experience—*cannot be made comprehensible to us in words.*

> "That Day in Eden"
> *Europe and Elsewhere,* p. 341

The unspoken word is capital. We can invest it or we can squander it.

> *Mark Twain's Notebook,* p. 345

The lowest form of embarrassed laugh is when you do it when soliloquizing; when you use it involuntarily—to cover a naked and poor remark made to a person who is present in your imagination only. (I wish the word *"only"* was in hell.)

> *Ibid.,* p. 365

. . . it is not the word that is the sin, it is the spirit back of the word.

> "Taxes and Morals"
> *Mark Twain's Speeches* (1923), p. 279

You have seen that kind of people who will never let on that they don't know the meaning of a new big word. The more ignorant they are, the more pitifully certain they are to pretend you haven't shot over their heads.

> *A Connecticut Yankee in King Arthur's Court,*
> Chapt. XVIII, p. 153

A powerful agent is the right word: it lights the reader's way and makes it plain; a close approximation to it will

answer, and much traveling is done in a well-enough fashion
by its help, but we do not welcome it and applaud it and
rejoice in it as we do when *the* right one blazes out on us.
Whenever we come upon one of those intensely right words
in a book or a newspaper the resulting effect is physical as
well as spiritual, and electrically prompt: it tingles exquisitely around through the walls of the mouth and tastes
as tart and crisp and good as the autumn-butter that creams
the sumac-berry.

> "William Dean Howells"
> *What Is Man?* and Other Essays, p. 229

. . . the words flowing in a continuous stream from his
mouth with inconceivable rapidity, and melting and ming-
ling together like bottle-glass and cinders after a conflagration.

> "Daniel in the Lion's Den—and Out Again All Right"
> *Sketches of the Sixties*, p. 147

It is always the way; words will answer as long as it is
only a person's neighbor who is in trouble, but when that
person gets into trouble himself, it is time that the King
rise up and *do* something.

> *Personal Recollections of Joan of Arc,*
> I, Book I, Chapt. V, p. 72

He would be eloquent, or perish. And he recognized only
one kind of eloquence—the lurid, the tempestuous, the volcanic. He liked words, fine words, grand words, rumbling,
thundering, reverberating words; with sense attaching if
it could be got in without marring the sound, but not otherwise. He loved to stand up before a dazed world, and pour
forth flame and smoke and lava and pumice stone into the
skies, and work his subterranean thunders, and shake himself with earthquakes, and stench himself with sulphur
fumes. If he consumed his own fields and vineyards, that
was a pity, yes; but he would have his eruption at all cost.

> "A Cure for the Blues"
> *The American Claimant, Etc.*, p. 389

The word flattened itself against my mind in trying to
get in, and disordered me a little, and before I could in-

quire into its pertinency, she was already throwing the needed light.

> *Christian Science*, Book I, Chapt. II, p. 21

[I] heard them say "cal'late" instead of "reckon" (which latter is a perfectly legitimate word, as the . . . readers may see by reference to the 18th verse of the 8th chapter of Romans.)

> "Notable Things in St. Louis"
> *Mark Twain's Travels with Mr. Brown*, p. 141

WORK *See also* ADAM, BED, COVETOUSNESS, DIRT, GOD, JOB,
     TIME

Work consists of whatever a body is *obliged* to do, and Play consists of whatever a body is not obliged to do. This is why constructing artificial flowers . . . is work, while rolling ten pins or climbing Mont Blanc is only amusement.

> *The Adventures of Tom Sawyer*, Chapt. II, p. 20

She says it is ordered that we work for our living hereafter. She will be useful. I will superintend.

> *Adam's Diary*, p. 49

Labor in loneliness is irksome.

> *The Innocents Abroad*, II, Chapt. XXI, p. 272

There's many a way to win in this world, but none of them is worth much, without good hard work back of it.

> *Personal Recollections of Joan of Arc*,
> I, Book II, Chapt. XXVII, p. 338

There are wise people who talk ever so knowingly and complacently about "the working classes," and satisfy themselves that a day's hard intellectual work is very much harder than a day's hard manual toil, and is righteously entitled to much bigger pay. Why, they really think that, you know, because they know all about the one, but haven't tried the other. But I know all about both; and so far as I am concerned, there isn't money enough in the universe to hire me to swing a pickax thirty days, but I will do the hardest kind of intellectual work for just as near nothing as you can cipher it down—and I will be satisfied, too.

Intellectual "work" is misnamed; it is a pleasure, a dissipation, and is its own highest reward. The poorest paid architect, engineer, general, author, sculptor, painter, lecturer, advocate, legislator, actor, preacher, singer is constructively in heaven when he is at work; and as for the musician with the fiddle-bow in his hand who sits in the midst of a great orchestra with the ebbing and flowing tides of divine sound washing over him—why, certainly, he is at work, if you wish to call it that, but lord, it's a sarcasm just the same. The law of work does seem utterly unfair—but there it is, and nothing can change it: the higher the pay in enjoyment the worker gets out of it, the higher shall be his pay in cash, also.

> *A Connecticut Yankee in King Arthur's Court,*
> Chapt. XXVIII, p. 257

Work and play are words used to describe the same thing under differing conditions.

> *More Maxims of Mark,* p. 14

[In little old Italian towns]: *They* have nothing to do but eat and sleep and sleep and eat, and toil a little when they can get a friend to stand by and keep them awake.

> *The Innocents Abroad,* I, Chapt. XXI, p. 268

I do not like work even when another person does it.

> "The Lost Napoleon"
> *Europe and Elsewhere,* p. 172

. . . work is the darlingest recreation in this world and whomsoever Nature has fitted to love it, is armed against care and sorrow.

> *My Father • Mark Twain,* Clara Clemens, p. 81

Let us save the to-morrows for work.

> *More Maxims of Mark,* p. 10

I love work. Why, sir, when I have a piece of work to perform, I go away to myself, sit down in the shade, and muse over the coming enjoyment. Sometimes I am so industrious that I muse too long.

> *Mark Twain, a Biography,* Paine, I, p. 156

WORLD *See also* ASTRONOMY, GOD

How insignificant we are—with our pigmy little world!—

an atom glinting with uncounted myriads of other atom worlds in a broad shaft of light streaming from God's countenance—and yet prating complacently of our speck as the Great World—

Do pismires (ants) . . . look abroad over the grand universe of an acre of ground and say "Great is God . . ."

Love Letters of Mark Twain, p. 133

It was a tranquil and dreamy picture, beautiful to the eye and restful to the spirit. If we could only make a change like that whenever we wanted to, the world would be easier to live in than it is, for change of scene shifts the mind's burdens to the other shoulder and banishes old, shop-worn wearinesses from mind and body both.

The Mysterious Stranger, Etc.,
Chapt. VII, p. 77

WORM

You can straighten a worm, but the crook is in him and only waiting.

More Maxims of Mark, p. 14

WORRY

Well, it was a thing which could not be helped, so I seldom fretted about it, and never many minutes at a time; it has never been my way to bother much about things which you can't cure.

A Connecticut Yankee in King Arthur's Court,
Chapt. XVIII, p. 142

But as soon as one is at rest, in this world, off he goes on something else to worry about.

Ibid., Chapt. V, p. 44

. . . it is curious how progressively little frets grow and multiply after they once get a start.

Ibid., Chapt. XII, p. 93

WORSHIP   *See also* BOYHOOD

. . . worship does not question or criticize, it obeys.

Christian Science, Book II, Chapt. XIII, p. 278

Some men worship rank, some worship heroes, some worship power, some worship God, and over these ideals they dispute,—but they all worship money.

Mark Twain's Notebook, p. 343

WRINKLE *See* SMILE

WRITING *See also* FACT, GRAMMAR, LECTURING, MIND, NARRATIVE, NOVEL

[From a letter to Edward Bok]:

Writing is my trade and I exercise it only when I am obliged to. You might make your request [for autograph and letter] of a doctor, builder or sculptor and there would be no impropriety in it, but if you asked either of those for a specimen of his trade, his handiwork, he would be justified in rising to a point of order. It would never be fair to ask a doctor for one of his corpses to remember him by.

The Americanization of Edward Bok, p. 204

Narrative *writing* is always disappointing. The moment you pick up a pen you begin to lose the spontaneity of the personal relation, which contains the very essence of interest. With shorthand dictation one can talk as if he were at his own dinner-table—always a most inspiring place. [1906]

Mark Twain, a Biography, Paine, III, p. 1268

Literature is an *art,* not an inspiration. It is a trade, so to speak, and must be *learned*—one cannot "pick it up" . . . And its capital is experience . . . the moment you venture outside your *own* experience, you are in peril—don't ever do it.

Love Letters of Mark Twain, p. 228

After writing for fifteen years it struck me I had no talent for writing. I couldn't give it up. By that time I was already famous!

The Twainian, May–June 1952, p. 4

To Watt Bowser, 12 years old: I notice that you use plain, simple language, short words, and brief sentences. That is the way to write English—it is the modern way, and the best way. Stick to it; don't let fluff and flowers and verbosity creep in. When you catch an adjective, kill it. No, I don't mean that utterly, but kill the most of them—then the rest will be valuable. They weaken when they are close together, they give strength when they are wide apart. An adjective-habit, or a wordy, diffuse, or flowery habit, once fastened upon a person, is as hard to get rid of as any other vice.

> Newly-found manuscript letter,
> *Saturday Review*, Feb. 27, 1960

When really learned men write books for other learned men to read, they are justified in using as many learned words as they please—their audience will understand them; but a man who writes a book for the general public to read is not justified in disfiguring his pages with untranslated foreign expressions. It is an insolence toward the majority of the purchasers, for it is a very frank and impudent way of saying, "Get the translations made yourself if you want them, this book is not written for the ignorant classes."

> *A Tramp Abroad*, II, Chapt. I, p. 20

It is perilous to revise a book while it is under way. All of us have injured our books in that foolish way.

. . . when you recollect something which belonged in an earlier chapter, do not go back, but jam it in *where you are*. Discursiveness does not hurt an autobiography in the least.

> *Mark Twain's Letters*, I, p. 379

I have entirely rewritten one book 3 (perhaps 4) times, changing the plan every time—1200 pages of ms. wasted and burned—and shall tackle it again, one of these years and maybe succeed at last.

> *Ibid.*, I, p. 324

I conceive that the right way to write a story for boys is to write so that it will not only interest boys but strongly interest any man *who has ever been a boy*. That immensely *enlarges the audience.*

Ibid., II, p. 566

I confine myself to life with which I am familiar when pretending to portray life.

Ibid., II, p. 541

When one writes a novel about grown people he knows exactly where to stop—that is, with a marriage; but when he writes of juveniles, he must stop where best he can.

The Adventures of Tom Sawyer, Conclusion, p. 321

One can't write a book unless he can banish perplexities and put his whole mind on it.

Mark Twain, Business Man, Webster, p. 152

For a forgotten fact *is* news when it comes again. Writers of books have the fashion of whizzing by vast and re-nowned historical events with the remark, "The details of this tremendous episode are too familiar to the reader to need repeating here." They know that that is not true. It is a low kind of flattery. They know that the reader has forgotten every detail of it, and that nothing of the tre-mendous event is left in his mind but a vague and formless luminous smudge. Aside from the desire to flatter the reader, they have another reason for making the remark. . . . They do not remember the details themselves, and do not want the trouble of hunting them up and copying them out. . . .

Following the Equator, II, Chapt. XXII, p. 259

It is easy for bookmakers to say "I thought so and so as I looked upon such and such a scene"—when the truth is, they thought all those fine things afterward. One's first thought is not likely to be strictly accurate, yet it is no crime to think it and none to write it down, subject to modification by later experience.

The Innocents Abroad, II, Chapt. XXVII, p. 380

There has never been a time in the past thirty-five years when my literary shipyard hadn't two or more half-finished ships on the ways, neglected and baking in the sun. . . . This has an unbusiness-like look but it was not purposeless, it was intentional. As long as a book would write itself I was a faithful and interested amanuensis and my industry did not flag, but the minute that the book tried to shift to *my* head the labor of contriving its situations, inventing its adventures and conducting its conversations, I put it away and dropped it out of my mind. . . .

It was by accident that I found out that a book is pretty sure to get tired, along about the middle, and refuse to go on with its work until its powers and its interest should have been refreshed by a rest and its depleted stock of raw materials reinforced by lapse of time. . . . When I had reached the middle of *Tom Sawyer* . . . I could not understand why I was not able to go on with it. The reason was very simple—my tank had run dry; it was empty; the stock of materials in it was exhausted; the story could not go on without materials; it could not be wrought out of nothing.

When the manuscript had lain in a pigeonhole two years I took it out one day and read the last chapter that I had written. It was then that I made the great discovery that when the tank runs dry you've only to leave it alone and it will fill up again in time, while you are asleep. . . .

Mark Twain in Eruption, p. 196

When your mind is racing along from subject to subject, and strikes an inspiring one, open your mouth and begin talking upon that matter,—or take your pen and use that. It will interest your mind and concentrate it, and it will pursue the subject with satisfaction. It will take full charge and furnish the words itself.

What Is Man? and Other Essays, Chapt. V, p. 71

People who write every week write themselves out, and tire the public, too, before very long.

Mark Twain to Mrs. Fairbanks, p. 128

The time to begin writing an article is when you have finished it to your satisfaction.

More Maxims of Mark, p. 13

The two greatest gifts of the writer, memory and imagination.

Mark Twain-Howells Letters, I, p. 55

I have suffered two months of literary gout; all pain and no getting on. [Dec. 2, 1882]

From a manuscript

WRINKLES *See* SMILES

WRONG *See also* BRUTALITY, FRIEND, MISERY

A letter written in a passion is a mistake . . . it usually wrongs two persons, and *always* wrongs *one*—yourself.

Mark Twain, a Biography, Paine, II, p. 860

We ought never to do wrong when people are looking.

"A Double-Barreled Detective Story"
The Man That Corrupted Hadleyburg, Etc., p. 292

. . . wrong cannot exist until the Moral Sense brings it into being.

"That Day in Eden"
Europe and Elsewhere, p. 344

. . . right is right, and wrong is wrong, and a body ain't got no business doing wrong when he ain't ignorant and knows better.

The Adventures of Huckleberry Finn,
Chapt. XXXVI, p. 318

The fact that man knows right from wrong proves his *intellectual* superiority to the other creatures; but the fact that he can *do* wrong proves his moral inferiority to any creature that *cannot*.

What Is Man? and Other Essays, Chapt. V, p. 89

No one can do wrong without knowing how to distinguish between right and wrong.

"That Day in Eden"
Europe and Elsewhere, p. 343

Y

YODELING

[In the Alps]: Presently we came upon half a dozen sheep nibbling grass in the spray of a stream of clear water that sprang from a rock wall a hundred feet high, and all at once our ears were startled with a melodious "Lul . . .l . . .l . . . lul-lul-*LA*hee-o-o-o!" pealing joyously from a near but invisible source, and recognized that we were hearing for the first time the famous Alpine *jodel* in its own native wilds. And we recognized, also, that it was that sort of quaint commingling of baritone and falsetto which at home we call "Tyrolese warbling."

The jodling (pronounced y*O*dling,—emphasis on the o), continued, and was very pleasant and inspiring to hear. Now the jodler appeared,—a shepherd boy of sixteen,—and in our gladness and gratitude we gave him a franc to jodle some more. So he jodled and we listened. We moved on, presently, and he generously jodled us out of sight. After about fifteen minutes we came across another shepherd boy who was jodling, and gave him half a franc to keep it up. He also jodled us out of sight. After that, we found a jodler every ten minutes; we gave the first one eight cents, the second one six cents, the third one four, the fourth one a penny, contributed nothing to Nos. 5, 6, and 7, and during the remainder of the day hired the rest of the jodlers, at a franc apiece, not to jodle any more. There is somewhat too much of this jodling in the Alps.

A Tramp Abroad, I, Chapt. XXVIII, p. 297

YOUTH   *See also* ADVICE, LUCK, MIND, WASHINGTON, GEORGE
Life should begin with age and its privilages and accumulations, and end with youth and its capacity to splendidly enjoy such advantages. As things are now, when in youth a dollar would bring a hundred pleasures, you can't have it. When you are old, you get it and there is nothing worth buying with it then.

Mark Twain's Letters, II, p. 709

It is good to obey all the rules when you're young, so you'll have the strength to break them when you're old.

"Mark Twain's Friendship Inspired a Little Girl
to a Successful Career", Dorothy Quick
Advance Magazine, Feb. 1940, p. 2

The tragedies of maturer life cannot surpass the first tragedies of youth.

My Husband • Gabrilowitsch, Clara Clemens, p. 8

[Remark of Dr. Baldwin's concerning upstarts]: We don't care to eat toadstools that think they are truffles.

"Pudd'nhead Wilson's Calendar"
Pudd'nhead Wilson, Chapt. V, p. 49

The heart is the real Fountain of Youth. While that remains young the Waterbury of Time must stand still.

Mark Twain's Notebook, p. 346

[Advice to Youth]:
Being told I would be expected to talk here, I inquired what sort of a talk I ought to make. They said it should be something suitable to youth—something didactic, instructive, or something in the nature of good advice. Very well. I have a few things in my mind which I have often longed to say for the instruction of the young; for it is in one's tender early years that such things will best take root and be most enduring and most valuable. First, then, I will

say to you, my young friends—and I say it beseechingly, urgingly—

Always obey your parents, when they are present. This is the best policy in the long run, because if you don't they will make you. Most parents think they know better than you do, and you can generally make more by humoring that superstition than you can by acting on your own better judgment.

Be respectful to your superiors, if you have any, also to strangers, and sometimes to others. If a person offend you, and you are in doubt as to whether it was intentional or not, do not resort to extreme measures; simply watch your chance and hit him with a brick. That will be sufficient. If you shall find that he had not intended any offense, come out frankly and confess yourself in the wrong when you struck him; acknowledge it like a man and say you didn't mean to. Yes, always avoid violence; in this age of charity and kindliness, the time has gone by for such things. Leave dynamite to the low and unrefined.

Go to bed early, get up early—this is wise. Some authorities say get up with the sun; some others say get up with one thing, some with another. But a lark is really the best thing to get up with. It gives you a splendid reputation with everybody to know that you get up with the lark; and if you get the right kind of a lark, and work at him right, you can easily train him to get up at half past nine, every time— it is no trick at all.

Now as to the matter of lying. You want to be very careful about lying; otherwise you are nearly sure to get caught. Once caught, you can never again be, in the eyes of the good and the pure, what you were before. Many a young person has injured himself permanently through a single clumsy and ill-finished lie, the result of carelessness born of incomplete training. Some authorities hold that the young ought not to lie at all. That, of course, is putting it rather stronger than necessary; still, while I cannot go quite so far as that, I do maintain, and I believe I am right, that the young ought to be temperate in the use of this great art until practice and experience shall give them that confidence, elegance, and precision which alone can make the accomplishment graceful and profitable. Patience, diligence, painstaking attention to detail—these are the requirements; these, in time, will make the student perfect; upon these, and upon these only, may he rely as the sure foundation for future eminence. Think what tedious years of study, thought, practice, experience, went to the equipment of that peerless old master who was able to impose upon the whole world the lofty and sounding maxim that "truth is mighty and will prevail"—the most majestic compound fracture of fact which any of woman born has yet achieved. For the history of our race, and each individual's experience, are sown thick with evidence that a truth is not hard to kill and that a lie told well is immortal. There in Boston is a monument of the man who discovered anæsthesia; many people are aware, in these latter days, that that man didn't discover it at all, but stole the discovery from another man. Is this truth mighty, and will it prevail? Ah, no my hearers, the monument is made of hardy material, but the lie it tells will outlast it a million years. An awkward, feeble, leaky lie is a thing which you ought to make it your unceasing study to avoid; such a lie as that has no more real permanence than an average truth. Why, you might as well tell the truth at once and be done with it. A feeble, stupid, preposterous lie will not live two years—except it be a slander upon somebody. It is indestructible, then, of course, but that is no merit of yours. A final word: begin your practice of this gracious and beautiful art early—begin now. If I had begun earlier, I could have learned how.

Never handle firearms carelessly. The sorrow and suffering that have been caused through the innocent but heedless handling of firearms by the young! Only four days ago, right in the next farmhouse to the one where I am spending the summer, a grandmother, old and gray and sweet, one of the lovliest spirits in the land, was sitting at her work, when her young grandson crept in and got down an old, battered, rusty gun which had not been touched for many years and was supposed not to be loaded, and pointed it at her, laughing and threatening to shoot. In her fright she ran screaming and pleading toward the door on the other side of the room; but as she passed him he placed the gun almost against her very breast and pulled the trigger! He had supposed it was not loaded. And he was right—it wasn't. So there wasn't any harm done. It is the only case of that kind I ever heard of. Therefore, just the same, don't you meddle with old unloaded firearms; they are the most deadly and unerring things that have ever been created by man. You don't have to take any pains at all with them; you don't have to have a rest, you don't have to have any sights on the gun, you don't have to take aim, even. No, you just pick out a relative and bang away, and you are sure to get him. A youth who can't hit a cathedral at thirty yards with a Gatling gun in three-quarters of an hour, can take up an old empty musket and bag his grandmother every time, at a hundred. Think what Waterloo would have been if one of the armies had been boys armed with old muskets supposed not to be loaded, and the other army had been composed of their female relations. The very thought of it makes one shudder.

There are many sorts of books; but good ones are the sort for the young to read. Remember that. They are a great, an inestimable, an unspeakable means of improvement. Therefore be careful in your selection, my young friends; be very careful; confine yourselves exclusively to Robertson's Sermons, Baxter's *Saint's Rest*, *The Innocents Abroad*, and works of that kind.

But I have said enough. I hope you will treasure up the instructions which I have given you, and make them a guide to your feet and a light to your understanding. Build your character thoughtfully and painstaking upon these precepts, and by and by, when you have got it built, you will be surprised and gratified to see how nicely and sharply it resembles everybody else's. [1882]

Mark Twain's Speeches (1923), p. 104

Z

ZEAL *See* RELIGION

Bibliography

Academy Notes and Monographs. *In Memory of Samuel Langhorne Clemens.* New York: The American Academy of Arts and Letters, 1922.

Ade. George. *One Afternoon with Mark Twain.* Chicago: The Mark Twain Society, 1939.

Allen, Jerry. *The Adventures of Mark Twain.* Boston: Little, Brown & Company, 1954.

Bok, Edward. *The Americanization of Edward Bok.* New York: Charles Scribner's Sons, 1912.

Clemens, Clara. *My Father • Mark Twain.* New York: Harper & Brothers, 1931.

———. *My Husband • Gabrilowitsch.* New York: Harper & Brothers, 1938.

Clemens, Samuel L. *The Curious Republic of Gondour.* New York: Boni and Liveright, 1919.

———. *S.L.C. to C.T.* New York: Private printing, 1925.

———. *A Suppressed Chapter of Following the Equator.* New York: Catalog #49, Philip C. Duschnes, 1928.

Clemens, Will. *Mark Twain, His Life and Work.* New York: F. Tennyson Neely, 1894.

Dane, G. Ezra., ed. *Letters from the Sandwich Islands.* Stanford, Calif.: Stanford University Press, 1938.

DeCasseres, Benjamin, ed. *When Huck Finn Went Highbrow.* New York: Thomas F. Madigan, 1934.

DeVoto, Bernard, ed. *Letters from the Earth.* New York: Harper & Row, 1962.

Fisher, Henry W. *Abroad with Mark Twain and Eugene Field.* New York: Nicholas L. Brown, 1922.

Harnsberger, Caroline Thomas. *Mark Twain, Family Man.* New York: The Citadel Press, 1960.

————. *Mark Twain's Views of Religion.* Evanston, Ill.: The Schori Press, 1961.

Henderson, Archibald. *Mark Twain.* London: Duckworth & Co., 1911.

Herzberg, Max J., ed. *The Mark Twain Omnibus.* New York: Harper & Brothers, 1935.

Hill, Hamlin, ed. *Mark Twain's Letters to His Publishers.* Berkeley: University of California Press, 1967.

Holbrook, Hal. *Mark Twain Tonight.* New York: Ives Washburn, Inc., 1959.

Honce, Charles. *The Adventures of Thomas Jefferson Snodgrass.* Chicago: P. Covici, Inc., 1928.

Hornberger, Theodore, ed. *Letters to Will Bowen.* Austin, Texas: The University of Texas Press, 1941.

Howell, John, ed. *Sketches of the Sixties.* San Francisco: John Howell, 1926.

Howells, William Dean. *My Mark Twain.* New York: Harper & Brothers, 1910.

Johnson, Merle, ed. *A Bibliography of Mark Twain.* New York: Harper & Brothers, 1935.

————, ed. *More Maxims of Mark.* New York: Private printing, 1927.

Johnson, Robert Underwood. *Remembered Yesterdays.* Boston: Little, Brown & Company, 1923.

Keller, Helen. *Midstream.* New York: Doubleday & Company, 1929.

————. *The Story of My Life.* New York: Doubleday, Page & Co., 1905.

Kipling, Rudyard. *From Sea to Sea.* New York: Doubleday & McClure Co., 1899.

Langdon, Jervis. *Samuel Langhorne Clemens*, Elmira, N. Y.: Private printing, 1935.

Larom, W. H. "Mark Twain in the Adirondacks," in *The Bookman*, January 1924, p. 536. New York.

Lawton, Mary. *A Lifetime with Mark Twain*. New York: Harcourt, Brace & Co., 1925.

Leary, Lewis, ed. *Letters to Mary*. New York: Columbia University Press, 1961.

Lorch, Fred. "Mark Twain in Iowa," in *Iowa Journal of History and Politics*, July and August 1929, p. 408. Iowa City, Iowa.

Lyman, George D. *The Saga of the Comstock Lode*. New York: Charles Scribner's Sons, 1934.

MacLaren, G. *Morally We Roll Along*. Boston: Little, Brown and Company, 1938.

Macy, John A. *The Spirit of American Literature*. New York: Doubleday, Page & Co., 1913.

Masson, Thomas L. *Best Stories in the World*. New York: Doubleday, Page & Co., 1913.

Meine, Franklin J. *American Humor*. Exhibit catalogue. Chicago: Private printing, 1939.

Merrill, W. H. "Mark Twain as a Lecturer," in *Harper's Weekly*, February 10, 1906. New York.

Neider, Charles, ed. *Life As I Find It*. Garden City, New York: Hanover House, 1961.

Orcutt, W. D. *Celebrities Off Parade*. Chicago: Willett, Clark, 1935.

Paine, Albert Bigelow. *Mark Twain, a Biography*, 3 vols. New York: Harper & Brothers, 1912.

———, ed. *Mark Twain's Autobiography*. New York: Harper & Brothers, 1924.

———, ed. *Mark Twain's Letters*. New York: Harper & Brothers, 1917.

———, ed. *Mark Twain's Notebook*. New York: Harper & Brothers, 1935.

———, ed. *Mark Twain's Speeches*. New York: Harper & Brothers, 1910, 1923.

———, ed. *Moments with Mark Twain*. New York: Harper & Brothers, 1920.

———. *Thomas Nast, His Period and His Pictures.* New York: The Macmillan Co., 1904.

Phelps, William Lyon. *Autobiography with Letters.* Oxford: Oxford University Press, 1939.

Pond, James B. *Eccentricities of Genius.* New York: G. W. Dillingham Company, 1900.

Quick, Dorothy. "Mark Twain's Friendship Inspired Little Girl to Successful Career," in *Advance,* February 1940. Chicago.

———. *Enchantment.* Norman, Okla.: University of Oklahoma Press, 1961.

———. "My Author's League with Mark Twain," *The North American Review,* Summer 1938. New York.

Read, Opie. *Mark Twain and I.* Chicago: Reilly & Lee, 1940.

Schulz, J. R. "New Letters of Mark Twain," *American Literature,* Mar. 1936. New York.

Smith, Henry Nash and Gibson, William M., eds. *Mark Twain-Howells Letters.* Cambridge: Harvard University Press, 1960.

Taylor, Coley B. *Mark Twain's Margins on Thackeray's "Swift."* New York: Gotham House, 1935.

Twain, Mark. *The Collected Works of Mark Twain,* 25 vols. Author's National Edition. New York: Harper & Brothers, 1899. (All titles from this set, here listed, will be designated *Collected.*)

———. *The Adentures of Huckleberry Finn. Collected.*

———. *The Adventures of Tom Sawyer. Collected.*

———. *The American Claimant, Etc. Collected.*

———. "From the Author's Sketch Book," Nov. 1870. Reprint in *The Twainian,* May 1940. Elkhorn, Wis.

———. "Chapters from My Autobiography," *North American Review,* Nov. 2, 1906; Jan. 4, 1907; Mar. 15, 1907; Apr. 5, 1907; May 3, 1907. New York.

———. "Unpublished Chapters from the Autobiography of Mark Twain. *Harper's Magazine,* Aug. 1922.

———. *Be Good, Be Good.* New York: Private printing, 1931.

———. *The Celebrated Jumping Frog of Calaveras County.* New York: Charles H. Webb, 1867.

———. *Christian Science. Collected.*

———. *A Connecticut Yankee in King Arthur's Court. Collected.*

————. "A Couple of Sad Experiences," *The Galaxy*, June 1870. New York.

————. *A Curious Dream*. London: G. Routledge & Sons, 1872.

————. *The Czar's Soliloquy*. *The North American Review*, Mar. 1905. New York.

————. "In Defense of General Funston," *The North American Review*, May 1902.

————. *A Double-Barreled Detective Story*. New York: Harper & Brothers, 1902.

————. *Europe and Elsewhere*. New York: Harper & Brothers, 1923.

————. *Eve's Diary*. New York: Harper & Brothers, 1906.

————. *Extracts from Adam's Diary*. New York: Harper & Brothers, 1904.

————. *Extract from Captain Stormfield's Visit to Heaven*. New York: Harper & Brothers, 1909.

————. *Following the Equator*, 2 vols. *Collected*.

————. *The Gilded Age*, 2 vols. *Collected*.

————. *The Innocents Abroad*, 2 vols. *Collected*.

————. *Is Shakespeare Dead?* New York: Harper & Brothers, 1909.

————. "From a Brooklyn Lecture," in *The Brooklyn Eagle*, Feb. 8, 1873. Reprint in *The Twainian*, Jan.–Feb. 1946. Elkhorn, Wis.

————. "A Letter to the Kansas City Jubilee Committee," in *The Hartford Courant*, July 24, 1901. Hartford, Conn.

————. "A Letter to the *Alta Californian*," Nov. 22, 1868. Reprint in *The Twainian*, Mar.–Apr. 1949. Elkhorn, Wis.

————. "A Letter from Mark Twain," in *The Youth's Companion*. Boston.

————. "A Quintus Curtius Snodgrass Letter," in *The New Orleans Crescent*, Mar. 1861. Reprint in *The Twainian*, June 1942. Elkhorn, Wis.

————. *Life on the Mississippi*. *Collected*.

————. *Literary Essays*. *Collected*.

————. *The Man that Corrupted Hadleyburg, Etc.* *Collected*.

————. Marginal Notes by Twain, in his own copy of *Views of Religion*, by Rufus K. Noyes. Boston: L. K. Washburn, 1906.

————. "The Centennial Edition of Mark Twain's Birth," *Hannibal Courier Post,* Mar. 6, 1935. Hannibal, Mo.

————. "About Mark Twain's Death," *Hannibal Morning Journal,* Apr. 23, 1910. Hannibal, Mo.

————. "Mark Twain at 70, Has No Regret," *New York American,* Dec. 1, 1905. New York.

————. "Mark Twain in Uncle Joe's Lair," *New York Herald,* Jan. 30, 1906. New York.

————. "Mark Twain's Seventieth Birthday Souvenir," *Harper's Weekly,* Dec. 23, 1905. New York.

————, ed. *Mark Twain's Library of Humor.* London: Chatto & Windus, 1899.

————. "Memoranda," *The Galaxy,* May, Aug., Dec. 1870.

————. *The Mysterious Stranger, Etc.* New York: Harper & Brothers, 1922.

————. "Official Physic," *The New York Sunday Mercury,* Apr. 21, 1867. New York.

————. *Personal Recollections of Joan of Arc,* 2 vols. *Collected.*

————. *The Prince and the Pauper. Collected.*

————. *Pudd'nhead Wilson. Collected.*

————. *Punch, Brothers, Punch!* New York: Slote, Woodman & Co., 1878.

————. *Roughing It.* 2 vols. *Collected.*

————. *Shotover Papers.* Oxford: Oxford University Press, 1874.

————. *Sketches New and Old. Collected.*

————. A squib by Mark Twain, *The Connecticut Courant,* Jan. 10, 1878. Hartford, Conn.

————. A story by Mark Twain, *East and West* magazine, Aug. 1911. Bombay, India.

————. *The $30,000 Bequest, Etc. Collected.*

————. *Tom Sawyer Abroad, Etc., Collected.*

————. *A Tramp Abroad,* 2 vols. *Collected.*

————. "Unburlesquable Things," *The Galaxy,* July 1870. New York.

————. *Twainian, The.* Bi-monthly magazine, ed. Chester Davis. Perry, Mo.

————. *What is Man? and Other Essays.* New York: Harper & Brothers, 1917.

BIBLIOGRAPHY

Wagenknecht, Edward G. *Mark Twain: The Man and His Work.* New Haven: Yale University Press, 1935.

Walker, Franklin, ed. and Dane, G. Ezra. *Mark Twain's Travels with Mr. Brown.* New York: Alfred A. Knopf, 1940.

Walker, Franklin, ed. *The Washoe Giant in San Francisco.* San Francisco: George Fields, 1938.

Wallace, Elizabeth. *Mark Twain and the Happy Island.* Chicago: A. C. McClurg, 1913.

Webster, Samuel Charles. *Mark Twain, Business Man.* Boston: Little, Brown and Company, 1946.

Wecter, Dixon, ed. *The Love Letters of Mark Twain.* New York: Harper & Brothers, 1949.

———, ed. *Mark Twain to Mrs. Fairbanks.* San Marino, Calif.: Huntington Library, 1949.

———, ed. *Sam Clemens of Hannibal.* Boston: Houghton Mifflin Company, 1952.

Wilson, Francis. *Francis Wilson's Life of Himself.* Boston: Houghton Mifflin Co., 1924.

Correlated Subjects Index

ANIMALS (Birds, Fish, Insects)

Ant	Congressman	Mosquito
Ass	Dog	Mouse
Bee	Fish	Mule
Bird	Flea	Nature
Brutality	Fly	Oyster
Camel	Horse	Rabbit
Cat	Locust	Sheep
Cayote	Man	Snake
Clam	Monkey	Worm

ARMS (Army, Guns, Killing, War, Weapons)

Armor, Suit of	Massacre	War
Army	Opportunity	Weapon
Gun	Peace	
Killing	Soldier	

ART (Talent)

Angel	Color	Music
Art	Masters, The Old	Painting
Beauty	Michelangelo	Picture

BEAUTY

Beauty	Color	Palestine
Browning	Flower	Perfection
California	Ice-Storm	Royalty
Change	Lake	Sphynx
Clothes	Mountain	

DEATH

Abroad	Funeral	Obituary
Cremation	Immortality	Tomb
Death	Life	Undertaker
Epitaph	Massacre	

DESTINY

Blunder	Predestination	Value
Luck	Providence	

EDUCATION

College	Punishment	Teacher
Learning	School	

FOOD

Banquet	Farm	Vegetable
Clam	Food	Water
Coffee	Fruit	Watermelon
Diet	Hunger	
Egg	Tea	

GAMES (Exercise, Sports)

Bicycle	Health	Swimming
Billiards	Racing	
Game	Skating	

GEOGRAPHY (History, Places, Scenery)

a) Countries

Abroad	Freedom	Mississippi River
Africa	Germany	Missouri
Alps	Glacier	Mountain
America	Government	Nation
Australia	History	New Zealand
Austria	Holy Land, The	Orient
Bermuda	Home	Palestine
Bounty	Hotel	Philippines
Country	House	Post-Office
Directions	Independence	Russia
Dirt	India	Sandwich Islands
Discovery	Ink	South, The
Eden, Garden of	Island	Spain
Egypt	Italy	Sphynx
England	Japan	Switzerland
Equator	Jubilee	Tibet
Europe	Lake	Water
Farm	Land	West, The
France	Measurement	

b) States

Arkansas	Missouri	New York
California	New England	Utah
Connecticut	Nevada	Virginia
Hawaii	New Jersey	

c) Cities

Berlin, Germany	Hannibal, Mo.	New Orleans, La.
Chicago, Ill.	Hartford, Conn.	New York City
Fire	Hotel	Niagara Falls

GEOGRAPHY (Cont'd)

Palestine	San Francisco, Cal.	Street
Paris, France	**Salt Lake City, Utah**	Washington, D. C.
Rome, Italy		

GOVERNMENT (Citizenship, Civilization, Municipal Government, Organizations, Patriotism, Politics)

Bounty	Liberty	President
Change	Man	Progress
Citizenship	Massacre	Public
Communism	Masses	Public Opinion
Congressman	Monarchy	Punishment
Country	Motto	Republic
Democracy	Nation	Revolution
Diplomat	Nationality	Right
Duty	New Deal	Rule
Fire	Nobility	Senator
Flag	Organization	Soap
Freedom	Party	Statesmanship
Government	Patent	Taxes
Grant, Gen. U. S.	Patriotism	Unions
Greatness	People	Voting
Hypocrite	Politics	War
Introduction	Population	Woman
Jury	Post-Office	
Killing	Power	

HEALTH

Bath	Head	Nature
Death	Health	Osteopathy
Dentistry	Illness	Pain
Disease	Indigestion	Sick
Doctor	Medicine	Talk
Exercise	Microbe	

HUMAN BEINGS (Man, People, Woman)

Accident	Conviction	Head
Achievement	Dirt	Hero
Acquirement	Disease	Heroine
Adam	Dream	Human Being
Adversity	Dress	Human Nature
Amazement	Duty	Human Race
Approval	Enemy	Hypocrite
Ark	Evidence	Idiot
Ass	Experience	Independence
Audience	Expression	Jews
Authority	Fame	Lady
Baby	Fool	Life
Blush	French People	Majority
Boyhood	Fright	Man
Castes	Genius	Manners
Change	Gentleman	Nature
Child	German People	Negro
Civilization	Girl	Obituary
Clothes	Guides	Opinion
Conscience	Habit	People

HUMAN BEINGS (Cont'd)

Prayer	Standard	Uncle
Royalty	Thanksgiving	Woman
Savage		

HUMAN RELATIONSHIPS (Ancestry, Character, Nationalities)

Advice	Information	Opinion
Ancestor	Inheritance	Pilgrims
Baby	Insanity	Population
Boyhood	Irishmen	Poverty
Brotherhood	Jews	Principle
Brutality	Joke	Progress
Castes	Jury	Public Opinion
Character	Life	Radical
Child	Liking	Romance
Circumstance	Love	Rumor
Experience	Man	Savage
Familiarity	Marriage	Self
Father	Masses	Selfishness
Friend	Mob	Self-Made
Funeral	Morals	Sex
Genius	Mother	Slave
Girl	Mark Twain's	Society
Greeks	Mummy	Stranger
Honor	Name	Titles
Humor	Nature	Traitor
Indelicacy	Negro	Trouble
Indian	Nobility	Uncle
Individual	Obligation	Woman
Influence	Obscurity	Youth

INVENTIONS (Conveyances, Gadgets, Household Articles)

Ark	Boat	Spectacles
Armor, Suit of	Bric-a-Brac	Stove
Ax	Elevator	Telephone
Balloon	Patent	Typewriter
Bed	Pen	Wall
Bicycle	Railroad	Watch

LAW

Jury	Policeman
Law	Politics

LIQUOR

Drink	Pledge	Water
Liquor	Prohibition	

LITERARY SUBJECTS (Books, Education, Knowledge, Languages, Learning, Speech-Making, Talk, Writing)

Alphabet	Browning	Editor
Audience	Change	Education
Author	Classic	English Language
Autobiography	Copyright	Fact
Beauty	Critic	Fiction
Biography	Diary	French Language
Book	Dictionary	German Language

LITERARY SUBJECTS (Cont'd)

Grammar
History
Humor
Ignorance
Information
Introduction
Italian Language
Journal
Judgment
Language
Learning
Lecturing
Letters
Library
Literary Criticism
Literary Hoax
Literature
Maxims
Memory
Motto
Narrative

Newspaper
Nonsense
Note-Book
Novel
Opinion
Page
Pause, The
Pen
Plagiarism
Play
Poetic Prose
Poetry
Preface
Profanity
Pronunciation
Publisher
Puns
Reader
Reform
Remark
Rumor

Satire
Scott, Walter
Shakespeare
Silence
Similes
Slang
Speech
Spelling
Story
Talent
Talk
Translation
Typewriter
Virtue
Vocabulary
Water
Wit
Words
Writing

MONEY

Capital
Gold
Money
Poverty

Riches
Speculation
Uncle
Value

Wages
Wall Street
Work
Worship

MUSIC

Critic
Hymn-Book
Jubilee
Minstrels

Music
Opera
Politics
Singing

Voice
Work
Yodeling

NATURAL PHENOMENA (Elements, Universe, Seasons, Weather)

Astronomy
Climate
Cold
Comet
Darkness
Earthquake
Echo
Environment

Fire
Glacier
Halley's Comet
Heat
Ice-Storm
Lightning
Miracle
Moon

Season
Storm
Sun
Universe
Volcano
Weather
Wind

NATURE

Compensation
Farm
Flower

Mountain
Nature
Sage-Brush

Tree
Watermelon

NEWSPAPERS

Editor
Interview
Irreverence
Journalism
Liberty

Lie
Name
Press
Printing

Public Opinion
Reporter
Reputation
Spelling

OCCUPATIONS (Abilities, Activities, Acts, Benevolences, Businesses, Habits, Pleasures, Pursuits)

Abroad	Fame	Pedestrian
Achievement	Farm	Philosophy
Advertising	Fault	Photograph
Army	Fool	Piloting
Art	Game	Plan
Astronomy	Gossip	Play
Author	Guides	Pleasure
Banquet	Gun	Plumber
Barber	Habit	Policeman
Bath	Hero	Politics
Beggar	History	Power
Behavior	Hobby	Praise
Benevolence	Holiday	President
Bicycle	Hotel	Printing
Billiards	Hurry	Progress
Biography	Insult	Prophecy
Birthday	Insurance	Prosperity
Boat	Interest	Publisher
Broker	Interruption	Racing
Capacity	Introduction	Radical
Change	Invention	Reform
Charity	Job	Robber
College	Jury	Royalty
Comfort	Killing	Rule
Congressman	Knight	Salesman
Conversation	Labor	School
Crime	Laundry	Science
Critic	Law	Skating
Custom	Lecturing	Slander
Deed	Leisure	Smoking
Delight	Liberty	Soldier
Dentistry	Lie	Speculation
Diplomat	Merit	Statesmanship
Dirt	Mining	Stealing
Discovery	Minister	Taster
Doctor	Minstrels	Teacher
Dueling	Missionary	Travel
Duty	Money	Tunnel
Early Rising	Moving	Turks
Editor	Murder	Undertaker
Education	Music	Unions
Elevator	Newspaper	Usefulness
Endeavor	Nobility	Vacation
Etiquette	Noise	Vice
Evidence	Notice	Virtue
Exercise	Novelty	Wages
Exit	Occupation	Work
Expedition	Page	
Experiment	Patent	

PERSONALITIES, Well-Known

Adam	Carnegie,	Clemens,
Browning,	Andrew	Samuel
Robert	Churchill,	Cleveland,
Cain	Winston	Grover

PERSONALITIES (Cont'd)

Columbus, Chris.
DeSoto
Eve
Grant, Gen. U. S.
Greeley, Horace
Harte, Bret
Hawley, Gen. Jos.
Joan of Arc
Keller, Helen

Kipling
Methuselah
Michelangelo
Noah
Rhodes, Cecil
Roosevelt, Theo.
Santa Claus
Satan
Scott, Sir Walter

Shakespeare
Smith
Snodgrass
Talk
Twain, Mark
Ward, Artemus
Washington, Geo.
Words
Writing

PHYSICAL CHARACTERISTICS (Senses)

Age
Death
Description
Dirt
Disease
Expression
Eyes
Face
Hair
Head
Health

Heart
Hunger
Illness
Impression
Itch
Measurement
Misery
Nose
Perspiration
Punishment
Size

Sleep
Smell
Smile
Sneeze
Snoring
Soap
Sock
Sound
Spectacles
Taster
Teeth

QUALITIES (Affections, Characteristics, Conditions, Emotions, Feelings, Moods, Tendencies)

Acquirement
Affection
Alarm
Amazement
Anger
Approval
Argument
Ass
Astonishment
Authority
Ax
Badness
Behavior
Belief
Blush
Bravery
Breeding
Brutality
Capacity
Censure
Character
Cheating
Cheerfulness
Circumstance
Clam
Comedy
Comfort
Compensation
Complaint
Compliment
Conceit

Conduct
Confidence
Conscience
Courage
Covetousness
Cowardice
Crook
Decency
Delicacy
Dignity
Disappointment
Disposition
Eccentricity
Ecstasy
Embarrassment
Emotion
Endeavor
Energy
Envy
Exaggeration
Example
Expectance
Experience
Failure
Fame
Familiarity
Fault
Fear
Feelings
Forbid
Forgetfulness

Formality
Frankness
Fright
Fun
Genius
Goodness
Gossip
Gratitude
Grief
Grudge
Habit
Happiness
Hardship
Hate
Heart
Honesty
Honor
Hope
Humor
Hurry
Ideal
Ignorance
Illusion
Imagination
Impulse
Indelicacy
Independence
Influence
Inheritance
Innocence
Insanity

QUALITIES (Cont'd)

Instinct
Intellect
Interest
Interruption
Intolerance
Irreverence
Joy
Judgment
Kindness
Laughter
Lazy
Liberty
Lie
Liking
Loneliness
Lost
Love
Loyalty
Luck
Madness
Malice
Martyrdom
Meanness
Memory
Merit
Misery
Misfortune
Modesty
Mistake
Monotony
Mood
Necessity
Nobility
Novelty
Obscurity
Opportunity

Optimism
Originality
Perseverence
Pessimism
Pity
Pleasure
Politeness
Popularity
Possession
Prejudice
Pride
Principle
Privilege
Procrastination
Profanity
Promise
Proportion
Prosperity
Punishment
Purpose
Recognition
Refinement
Reflection
Repentance
Reputation
Respect
Riches
Ridicule
Right
Romance
Sacrifice
Satisfaction
Serenity
Seriousness
Sham
Shame

Shudder
Shyness
Silence
Sinner
Sleep
Snobbery
Sorrow
Speculation
Spirit
Stupidity
Success
Superstition
Supremacy
Survival
Suspicion
Sympathy
Temper
Temperament
Temperance
Temptation
Timidity
Tolerance
Treachery
Truth
Understanding
Value
Vanity
Variety
Vengeance
Vice
Virtue
Vulgarity
Want
Weakness
Worry
Wrong

RELIGION

Angel
Bible
Christianity
Christian Science
Church
Clergyman
Conviction
Creeds
Doctrine
Eden, Garden of
Eternity
Faith
Fool
God
Heaven
Hell

Hymn-Book
Immortality
Irreverence
Land, The Holy
Martyrdom
Methuselah
Minister
Miracle
Missionary
Morals
Mormons
Prayer
Preacher
Predestination
Presbyterian

Priest
Providence
Religion
Repentance
Reverence
Rule
Sabbath
Saint
Sermon
Sin
Sinner
Soul
Survival
Worship
Wrong

SOCIAL MATTERS (Behavior, Conduct, Etiquette, Habits, Manners)

Advice	Conversation	Introduction
Behavior	Custom	Manners
Breeding	Diplomat	Marriage
Castes	Etiquette	Morals
Character	Example	Royalty
Child	Formality	Rule
Comedy	Freedom	Scandal
Complaint	Gentleman	Society
Compliment	Indelicacy	Training
Conduct	Influence	

THOUGHT (Beliefs, Ideas, Mind, Opinions)

Advice	Ideal	Opinion
Belief	Ignorance	Pessimism
Biography	Illusion	Philosophy
Brains	Imagination	Public Opinion
Christian Science	Impression	Reasoning
Civilization	Information	Reflection
Conscience	Inheritance	Remark
Controversy	Insanity	Repentance
Conversation	Insincerity	Size
Conviction	Inspiration	Stupidity
Convincing	Intellect	Superstition
Custom	Interest	Suspicion
Doctrine	Intolerance	Sympathy
Doubt	Joke	Talk
Dream	Knowledge	Theory
Evidence	Letters	Things
Fact	Learning	Thought
Feelings	Lie	Truth
Forgetfulness	Logic	Vacuum
Freedom	Madness	Value
Genius	Maxims	Wisdom
Happiness	Memory	Wit
Head	Mental Telepathy	Words
Humor	Mind	
Idea	Motto	

TIME (Calendar, Dates, Events, Happenings)

Age	Hurry	Speculation
Birthday	Jubilee	Speed
Change	Leisure	Sunday
Christmas	Moment	Thanksgiving
Climate	Month	Time
Clock	Night	Tomorrow
Early Rising	Past	Watch
Eternity	Santa Claus	Youth
Fourth of July	Slowness	

TRAVEL (Home, Hotels, Lakes, Rivers, Sea)

Abroad	Creation	Equator
Accident	Directions	Exaggeration
Bed	Discovery	Expedition
Boat	Distance	Food

TRAVEL (Cont'd)

Guides	Piloting	Stove
Hotel	Racing	Taj Mahal
House	Railroad	Travel
Lake	River	Turks
Measurement	Road	Twain, Mark
Mississippi River	Sea	Vacation
Monotony	South Seas	Voyage
Moving	Ship	Wall
Niagara Falls	Size	Water
Occupation	Sphynx	Wonder
Opinion	Stage-Coach	World

MARK TWAIN (Subjects pertaining to himself)

Advice	French Language	Mistake
Age	French People	Monarchy
Alphabet	Fun	Money
Ancestor	Funeral	Morals
Art	Gentleman	Mother,
Ass	God	Mark Twain's
Bath	Government	Moving
Billiards	Grant, Gen. U. S.	Mule
Birthday	Habit	Music
Boyhood	Happiness	Name
Charity	Hartford, Conn.	Noah
Child	Heaven	Occupation
Churchill,	Hotel	Poetry
Winston	Humor	Post-Office
Clergyman	Hymn-Book	Preacher
Clock	Ignorance	Printing
Clothes	Illness	Profanity
College	Information	Promise
College Degrees	Insanity	Punishment
Complaint	Introduction	Reflection
Compliment	Invention	Religion
Conscience	Jews	Repentance
Critic	Job	Royalty
Death	Keller, Helen	San Francisco
Debt	Kipling	Santa Claus
Description	Knowledge	Smoking
Disease	Language	Sock
Doctor	Lazy	Soldier
Dress	Lecturing	Spectacles
Exaggeration	Letters	Stealing
Experience	Lie	Talk
Fact	Literary Criticism	Telephone
Family,	Luck	Truth
Mark Twain's	Marriage	Twain, Mark
Father	Medicine	Typewriter
Feelings	Memory	Voting
Fire	Mind	Watch
Food	Minstrels	Watermelon
Fool	Mississippi River	Work
Forgetfulness	Missouri	Writing